Dissenting Voices in America's Rise to Power

This book offers a major rereading of US foreign policy from Thomas Jefferson's purchase of Louisiana expanse to the Korean War. This period of one hundred and fifty years saw the growth of the United States from fragile republic to transcontinental giant and David Mayers explores the dissenting voices which accompanied this dramatic ascent. He focuses on dissenters within the political and military establishment and on the recurrent patterns of dissent that have transcended particular policies and crises. The most stubborn of these sprang from anxiety over the material and political costs of empire while other strands of dissent have been rooted in ideas of exigent justice, realpolitik, and moral duties that exist beyond borders. Such dissent is evident again in the contemporary world when the US occupies the position of preeminent global power. Professor Mayers's study reminds us that America's path to power was not as straightforward as it might now seem.

DAVID MAYERS teaches at Boston University, where he holds a joint appointment in the History and Political Science departments. His previous publications include *George Kennan and the Dilemmas of US Foreign Policy* (1988); *The Ambassadors and America's Soviet Policy* (1995); *Wars and Peace: The Future Americans Envisioned, 1861–1991* (1998). His latest research deals with FDR's wartime diplomacy.

Dissenting Voices in America's Rise to Power

David Mayers

CAMBRIDGE
UNIVERSITY PRESS

CAMBRIDGE UNIVERSITY PRESS
Cambridge, New York, Melbourne, Madrid, Cape Town, Singapore, São Paulo

Cambridge University Press
The Edinburgh Building, Cambridge CB2 2RU, UK

Published in the United States of America by Cambridge University Press,
New York

www.cambridge.org
Information on this title: www.cambridge.org/9780521694186

First published 2007

Printed in the United Kingdom at the University Press, Cambridge

A catalogue record for this publication is available from the British Library

ISBN-13 978-0-521-87255-3 hardback
ISBN-13 978-0-521-69418-6 paperback

To my teachers,
to my students

Contents

Preface

This book traces the main debates and dissent in US foreign relations during a broad swath of history, from the early nineteenth century to the mid-twentieth. My theme is establishment dissenters. My orientation is catholic in that those of progressive and conservative bent are treated with equal seriousness. I aim to explain them in the context of their respective eras. Sometimes the dissenters and their lines were firm and clear, other times meandering or uncertain. In either case, I track the careers of prominent dissenters in the hope of better evaluating the nature of US international behavior at key junctures. Additionally, I try here to identify recurrent patterns of dissent – or strands – that have transcended particular questions and specific personalities. These strands are striking as they ran from the early days of the fragile American republic onward, still evident in one or another form in the twenty-first century, when the United States occupies the position of preeminent global power. The most stubborn line of dissent, with implications for today, has sprung from anxiety over the material and political costs of empire. Other dissents, not always compatible with the foregoing or with each other, have been rooted in ideas of exigent justice, realpolitik, and moral duty beyond borders.

My topic has particular bearing on our time when so much "triumphalist" literature has appeared on the US role as sole superpower. A good deal has been written about America as messianic democracy, peerless empire, hegemon, primary mover and designer of globalization. Much of this recent literature has been affirmative, celebrating an inexorableness in the US march toward glory. The point of my book is to remind readers that the story is not so straightforward or inevitable. Many possibilities and choices were open to Americans at significant moments in their history. At such times there were outspoken critics who questioned the direction the nation was taking, whether with regard to war or territorial expansion. The dissident voices examined in the following pages enriched the vocabulary of domestic political discourse and suggested alternative paths that the United States might have taken.

This book invites readers to consider the "what ifs" of history while paying tribute to many politicians and others who dared to debunk White House interpretations ("spin") or questioned policies that enjoyed majority support. There is richness, color, and texture in such a tale, which also gives weight to a side of history that has been understudied. An understanding of the dissenting past has not been well served by dominant paradigms of foreign policy scholarship – presumptions in favor of a rational state actor, formulaic assumptions about the national interest, or facile generalizations concerning White House orchestrated consensus.

In this writing I have benefited from generous institutions. Boston University and the Gilder Lehrman Institute of American History provided funds. They enabled me to conduct research at archives and allowed leaves of absence from teaching/administration.

Boston University's International History Institute, the International Studies Association, Mount Holyoke College, the Society for Historians of American Foreign Relations, and Jerusalem's Spinoza Institute gave me opportunities to present my work-in-progress to thoughtful audiences. My colleagues on the Board of Trustees of the Carnegie Council on Ethics and International Affairs have been an inspiration.

Scholars, relatives, and friends have helped, demonstrating again that all writing is collaborative. They have given constructive criticism. Several read chunks of this book as manuscript in rough shape. Many thanks to Susan Abel, John Archer, Andrew Bacevich, Silas Blodgett, Donald Brand, Walter Connor, Robert Dallek, Hermann Eilts, Stephanie Fawcett, Michael Field, David Fromkin, Anna Geifman, Erik Goldstein, Cathy Guyler, Gregg Herken, Robert Jackson, Elizabeth Kirkland Jones, Peter Kenez, William Keylor, Michael Kort, the late Murray Levin, Igor Lukes, Stephen Lyne, Peter Kirkland Mayers, Peter Michael Mayers, Carol McHale, Richard Melanson, Charles Neu, Cathal Nolan, Larry Plitch, Joel Rosenthal, Nina Silber, Michael Joseph Smith, William Tilchin, Jose Velasco, Peter Widdicombe, Fred Woerner.

I am also grateful to Michael Watson, the excellent and efficient History editor at Cambridge University Press. Working with him was a pleasure from start to finish. Additionally, the anonymous referees employed by Cambridge did much to improve the book. Its deficiencies are mine alone. They remain despite the best efforts of Michael and his conscientious reviewers.

This book is dedicated to my teachers of whom I will mention one. The late George Lanyi taught political history in the Government Department to generations of Oberlin College students. I was in this lucky multitude. He was a gifted teacher. His decency and intellect had a lasting impact on everyone who knew him. This book is also dedicated to my students.

One who has brightened my days was the late Commander Roger Lerseth, United States Navy. He was my Ph.D. student at Boston University. He wrote a first-rate dissertation on the concept and practice of unconditional surrender in World War II. He was not only a splendid scholar. He was also a Vietnam War hero, a man of compassion and courage.

D M
Newton, Massachusetts
March 1, 2006

Introduction

This book examines US foreign policy from Thomas Jefferson's purchase of Louisiana expanse to the Korean War. That period of one hundred and fifty years corresponded with the rise of US might from fledgling republic to transcontinental giant with overseas reach: empire. By mid-twentieth century, the US gross national product, exports as a percentage of world exports, and nuclear delivery systems dwarfed those of all competitors or other powers, including Great Britain, China, France, Germany, Japan, and the USSR.[1]

This study serves as a companion to my earlier *Wars and Peace: The Future Americans Envisioned, 1861–1991.* I reviewed in it how a broad range of Americans during security crises conceptualized future world orders. I did so with a conviction that political imagination is not an exclusive property of the policymaking elite: Americans of diverse political stripes have always flavored public discourse with their versions of truth and solutions to problems. Thus I scrutinized the views of nonconformists, civil rights activists, feminists, and scholars. I drew connections between this eclectic crowd and the ideas – plus decisions – of policymakers in Washington. In effect, I sought to reacquaint readers with prominent, often controversial, thinkers whose eloquence, passion, and even wrongheadedness gave texture to the debates of their times.[2]

My analytical concern here is more restricted than in *Wars and Peace.* The focus is on dissenters within the responsible class, coextensive with members of Congress, high-ranking soldiers, ambassadors, and cabinet officers. This category of humanity, carrying the stamp of official duty, is by definition not estranged from power.[3] Such people choose to live in this medium, divided between functions of policy conceptualizing (congressmen, cabinet ministers) and implementing (soldiers, diplomats). These persons derive pride, meaning, and occasionally comfort in manipulating types of power in public trust.

People intimately involved in the affairs of state have a perspective on events different from critics living outside the zone of authority. Failure in the responsible class can lead to national disaster. Hence the ethic of responsibility – Max Weber's terminology – supersedes its philosophical rivals: pure principle or the best solution. Their full expression is invariably inhibited by the logic of prudence and shifting contingency. Edmund Burke's observation on the distinction between scholars and statesmen is apt: "A statesman differs from a professor in a university; the latter has only the general view of society; the former, the statesman, has a number of circumstances to combine with those general ideas, and to take into his consideration ... A statesman, never losing sight of principles, is to be guided by circumstances; and judging contrary to the exigencies of the moment, he may ruin his country forever."[4] Such appreciation caused Immanuel Kant to admit that the governing class often sneers at advice given by schoolmen, who, unburdened by cares of consequential decision beyond classroom or study, can indulge varieties of fancy: "The practical politician tends to look down with great complacency upon the political theorist as a mere academic ... the state must be founded upon principles of experience; it thus seems safe to let him fire off his broadside, and the *worldly-wise* statesman need not turn a hair."[5] Philosophers, historians, and erudite pundits must content themselves in that faith consoling to economist John Maynard Keynes: the views of practitioners are derived from scribblers of previous generations.[6]

Properly exercised, power entails discipline in moderation and upholds pragmatic virtues. An outright dissenter in exalted office is by definition an "impossible thing," as A. J. P. Taylor shrewdly noted.[7] Yet insofar as the history of US foreign affairs can be framed as a series of debates, unorthodox viewpoints in lofty places are apparent. They have challenged the line emanating from the White House, the main expositor of official policy at any given time.[8] The spectrum of discontent has run from strenuous disagreement to mere skepticism. Implicit across gradations of contention has been the impulse to shape in contrary ways, sometimes to subvert, the prevailing policy.

Dissent within the US government has constituted a distinctive realm at odds with the mentality of "team spirit." Impatient, suspicious, frequently saturated in partisanship, dissent has tended toward the overthrow of existing policy by either pressing it toward greater energy or else reduced activity. Dissenters have often preferred that peculiar satisfaction enjoyed by contrarians opposed to majority wisdom and complacency. Such people, their pleasing attributes and foibles, have been examined by various writers – memorably by Taylor in his merry reading of British dissenters (*The Trouble Makers*) and by John F. Kennedy (*Profiles in Courage*).[9] My purpose here is not to add to or endorse this literature of intellectual–political heroism. Rather, I wish to explore the alternative history implied in those arguments waged at senior levels in Washington. This angle of approach does not lend itself to identifying heroes or villains, though they and ordinary mortals are treated here, but allows for better understanding of the choices made at turning points in US history. This approach yields another benefit – countering homogenizing brands of historiography that portray the emergence of US power as a succession of victories born of consensus about national purpose.[10] The record is neither bland nor compatible with claims to collective self-exoneration. American history has nothing to do with power produced in "immaculate conception."[11] Bitter controversies, unintended results, mishaps, and partial triumphs litter the chronicle.

Of the responsible class's four components, the legislative has always enjoyed most latitude in resisting the White House line. Constitutional provisions on Congress codify and dignify dissent as the republic's lifeblood. Politics in the absence of dissent would amount to ratification of the status quo or, phrased differently, sabotage of the US regime. Within Congress's province resides the authority to declare war, ratify treaties, fund operations abroad, and otherwise support or disrupt initiatives by the chief executive. Unsurprisingly, the majority of dissenters treated in this book have come from the Senate and House of Representatives.

Senator Timothy Pickering, examined in the first chapter, voted against the treaty transferring Louisiana territory from France to the United States. The next chapter includes Representative Josiah Quincy, one of the signers of the 1812 minority report that questioned the merits of James Madison's war against Great Britain.[12] Subsequent chapters feature the following: Representative Edward Everett brooded over the unwillingness of Washington officialdom to help Greek nationalists in the 1820s as they fought to wrest their homeland from Ottoman control. Senator Theodore Frelinghuysen opposed Andrew Jackson's expulsion of Native Americans to the Mississippi's western shore, authorized by the 1830 Indian Removal Act. Representative Joshua Giddings condemned the Mexican war of 1846–1848 as an odious venture to expand the slavery zone. Senator John C. Calhoun tried to curtail the nation's territorial appetite in the same war; he feared that new acquisitions would aggravate north–south friction. Neither did the 1867 transfer of Russian America (Alaska) to the United States in the Civil War's aftermath win universal support in Congress. Feisty objection came from such men as Representative Benjamin Butler. Senators Preston Plumb and Henry Moore Teller contested central parts of policy toward Native America in the 1870s–1880s. George Frisbie Hoar, a commanding figure in the Senate in the late nineteenth century, excoriated US policy in the Philippines. Senators William Borah, Robert La Follette, Henry Cabot

Lodge, and George Norris feared that the proposed League of Nations in 1919 would ensnare the United States in endless European imbroglios. Representative Jeanette Rankin voted against declarations of war in 1917 and 1941. Senator Robert Taft condemned the Nuremberg trial after World War II as an exercise in specious justice.

In most of these cases, what stood for congressional conscience was formed by varying parts of authentic conviction, self-interest, and party needs. Complicating this mix, congressmen had to resolve the dilemma created when the popular will, or what passes for it, conflicts with the legislator's own judgment.

The American military conscience subsumes the warrior and chivalric codes in solemn creed ("duty, honor, country" in West Point maxim). It gives the least margin for dissent and stresses obedience to civilian superiors. Yet discontent has percolated within the armed forces' upper echelons. The most spectacular instance occurred in 1951, when General Douglas MacArthur pressed Harry Truman to widen the war in Korea and thereby precipitated a constitutional crisis. Its resolution was decided in a race between the officer who contemplated resignation as a means of undermining a beleaguered president or his firing the soldier first. "The son of a bitch isn't going to resign on me," Truman vowed.[13] Less dramatic moments of military discontent have included General John Ellis Wool's unhappiness in the 1830s with removing the Cherokees from their ancestral homelands in the southeast. Later, Generals William Sherman and Philip Sheridan, who opposed President Grant's Peace Policy, urged alternative means of dealing with Native American tribes. General Nelson Miles became an object of President Theodore Roosevelt's scorn when he publicized the extent of army misdeeds in the Philippines during the early years of US occupation.

Between the extremes of military subordination to civilian authority and Congress's autonomy lies that area occupied by top diplomats and cabinet officers. Both groups serve at the pleasure of the president. They are creatures of the executive branch. Yet they are not circumscribed by imperatives of such strict obedience as apply to people serving in uniform. The ambassador as an instrument of policy is necessarily more subtle than the soldier and tries to advance national interests by measures short of violence. In times of war, diplomats concentrate their attention upon the post-hostilities era and tailor policy according to their understanding of future distributions of world power. The ambassadorial service has produced some of the scrappier dissenters in US history, even as diplomats have been disparaged in popular culture as effete or effeminate. Nicholas Philip Trist disobeyed direct orders from Washington in 1848 to end negotiations with Mexico. His persistence resulted in the treaty of

Guadalupe Hidalgo, ending hostilities and transferring vast territories to the United States. Ambassador Henry Morgenthau (senior), to cite another example, tried valiantly to stir Washington into meaningful action on behalf of Armenia in 1915, when by Ottoman decree it was vacated and murdered. Ambassadors Nelson Johnson in China and William Bullitt in France argued before Pearl Harbor for direct US involvement on the side of countries resisting Axis invasion.

Dissent within the cabinet has been infrequent. Heads of departments, notably those charged with diplomacy or security, have been among the primary architects of foreign policy. Usually, and rightly, they have been implicated with the achievements or failures of a given president. But even here striking instances have arisen of deviation from the main line, resulting in resignation or dismissal. Secretary of State William Jennings Bryan left Woodrow Wilson's cabinet in 1915 to protest the president's German policy. Truman fired Secretary of Commerce Henry Wallace in 1946 when he insisted that common ground could be established with Stalin's USSR and the Cold War impasse broken.

Not every disgruntled cabinet officer has lost the debate or felt obliged to depart. Secretary of the Treasury Albert Gallatin rued Congress's decision in 1812 to declare against Great Britain. But he stayed in the government; he worked doggedly to end a war damaging to the United States. Secretary of State William Seward in April 1861 sought de facto to replace Abraham Lincoln as chief executive in the crisis of disunion. Lincoln forgave his subordinate. He stayed on to become one of the more celebrated foreign ministers in US history. Secretary of the Treasury Henry Morgenthau (junior) brought about a crucial reversal in 1944. He galvanized FDR's policy of rescuing persecuted European Jewry, in which action the administration had hitherto been feckless.

Dissent as vocation has never been especially pleasant, despite safeguards to protect free expression. Even members of Congress, insulated from cruder types of executive retaliation by the status of elected office and rights accorded a loyal opposition, have been reluctant to defy presidents on major initiatives. Soldiers, diplomats, and cabinet officers out of step have risked forfeiting their commissions while living in discouragement or isolation.

* * *

Four strands of dissent are discernible amid the personalities, competing ideas, and rival interests that shaped debate on foreign affairs from Louisiana to Korea. These strands can be labeled as prophetic, republican, nationalist, and cosmopolitan. They interlaced even as they wove through the deeper fabrics of American society and polity: capitalist economy, technological change, population growth, racial-ethnic-religious diversity, class stratification, party competition, and regional tugging.

The prophetic is the most venerable of the four strands. It was nourished by the religious temper and puritan core of the colonial/early independence period. More precisely, this orientation originated in the outlook of seventeenth-century New England theocrats such as John Winthrop. Themselves dissenters – from Anglican ecclesiolatry – they feared God's wrath at creatures who strayed from His edicts or purpose.[14] Pronounced still in the nineteenth century, before the popular success of Charles Darwin's biology, the prophetic strand stemmed from belief in God (often depicted in anthropomorphic terms) who judges nations no less than individual souls. A number of dissenters, mainly reared in Protestant tradition, accepted in earnest this idea once expressed by the religiously unconventional Jefferson. This deist said (referring to slavery): "I tremble for my country when I reflect that God is just; that His justice cannot sleep forever."[15] From such anxiety, resolve could follow to put matters right, evident in voices opposed to enlarging the slave zone via the Louisiana acquisition, evicting Native Americans from their lands, or attacking Mexico in 1846. The idea that God reflexively enlisted on America's side constituted theological error – blasphemy – for the prophetically minded recusant.

The republican strand sprang from the country's democratic ethos and distrust of empire, inherited from the 1776 rebellion. This strand of dissent has manifested most frequently and vividly. It gained rhetorical power and influence from America's being a self-conscious republic – fed by the idea, as self-evident, that representative institutions and liberal values were superior to, also incompatible with, overweening power. In this case, the United States should not substitute the sham of imperium for estimable virtues. Possession of immense power was thought to be disorienting, even disabling. Americans must not lose their way in hubris or worship of imperial idols, against which the 1776 generation had properly mutinied. Republican-minded dissenters thus objected to Louisiana empire, the 1848 Mexican cession, the buying of Alaska, Filipino occupation after the Spanish–American war, and subsequent bids for hegemony. This preference did not recommend national introversion and eschewed sulky isolationism; republican dissenters emphasized instead the power of US example – accountable government, domestic tranquillity – as guarantor of Washington's influence abroad.

The nationalist strand, in tension with the first two, is related to the realpolitik school of thought and flows from colonial/pioneer anxieties about survival in a harsh environment, unforgiving of weakness and unrelieved by reliable allies. One should not explain or make excuses for the cultivation of power in this dangerous world. Therein feeble people perish. Energetic and fit ones survive in a ceaseless contest of all against all – Thomas Hobbes's state of nature writ large. By this standard, one should take confident steps to tame the Indian west. One should not surrender vital parts of sovereignty to a League of Nations or other internationally pretentious organizations. One should not be passive before adversaries, whether in Axis or Sino-Soviet garb, but act boldly to preserve security and economic well-being. This nationalist approach, properly understood, eschewed jingoism and chauvinism while insisting on the dignity of US interests defined in terms of power.[16] As realpolitik has dominated American practice, its adherents have only infrequently found themselves in a dissenting or minority position.

The cosmopolitan strand is connected to the extroverted and voluble quality of the citizenry, to the diversity of its religious–national origins, and to convictions (vaguely Kantian) about right international conduct. Moreover, this cosmopolitan strand – tending against the nationalist strand and sometimes reinforcing the prophetic and republican – arose from the notion that US power did not exist as an end in itself. Correctly conceived, American power in economic–military form should serve humanitarian aims on behalf, for instance, of persecuted minorities: Greeks and Armenians in the Ottoman empire, Polish subjects of czarist Russia in 1863, Jews in Nazi-controlled Europe. Such an attitude did not seek or justify eternal wars of intervention on behalf of humane causes. Yet the United States, Abraham Lincoln's "best hope of earth," was enjoined by ethical progress and universal principles to discharge duty whenever possible beyond political frontiers.[17] Embedded in this notion is a rejection of unvarnished empire in favor of that viewpoint which discerns states and peoples existing in a maturing society of norms, laws, and reciprocal obligations.[18]

The prophetic strand surfaces in chapters 4 (Removals) and 5 (Mexico) of this book. The republican is salient in chapters 1 (Louisiana) and 2 (1812). It shares space with the prophetic in chapter 5, reappears in chapter 6 (Russia), and occupies portions of chapters 8 (Philippines), 9 (Armageddon), 10 (Axis), and 11 (Containment). The nationalist strand twists through chapter 7 (Reservations) and controls bits of chapters 9, 10, and 11. The cosmopolitan strand runs through chapter 3 (Greece) and important parts of chapters 6, 9, and 10. All four strands of dissent, whether conspicuous in the substantive chapters or making only cameos, are treated as a bundle in chapter 12 (Dissenters) and refined upon individually.

Essentially, these strands are useful shorthand to distinguish among different individuals and philosophical positions. I am wary of getting too distracted by definitions, or applying them rigidly, and flagging every flash of one or other strand. When I have had to err between belaboring or gently touching upon, I have preferred the latter for stylistic reasons, even at the cost (slight, I hope) of analytical stringency. No schema can adequately account for the range of dissenting voices presented in this volume; the strands should be seen as kinds of leitmotivs.

* * *

This volume is divided into three sections. The first covers the period of continental expansion that began with the Louisiana acquisition and culminated in the eviction of Indians from the heart of US territory. The second section concerns land acquisition by primarily military means, beginning with the 1846 war against Mexico and ending with subjugation of the Philippines. By the early twentieth century, the United States constituted a sprawling empire built upon purchases, declarations of intent (e.g., the Monroe Doctrine), expulsion or containment of presumptive undesirables, invasions, and ocean routes that connected the mainland via the navy to Pacific provinces (Hawaii, Philippines). The book's third section considers those debates that flared as the United States emerged as the premier security state in the twentieth century, amid two world wars, totalitarianism, and Cold War conducted beneath the nuclear shadow.

Not every instance of dissent in high places has been treated in this book. I have been selective, not encyclopedic. I have chosen several cases (e.g., policy toward Native America, Armenia in World War One, Nuremberg) with an eye to how they intersect with current debates about US foreign policy (e.g., imperialism, genocide, status of international law). And I have approached familiar questions – say, on the Monroe Doctrine or the 1898 war – from an angle just off to the side of the conventional picture, thereby creating greater space for dissenters and their ideas than is found in standard narratives of diplomatic history. Together, I believe, my cases do illustrate the shape, feeling, and variety of dissent. My examples also promote this theme: the creation and maintenance of US power have taken place not only at the level of economic-military tectonics, but also upon the field of colliding ideas and uneasy conscience. Additionally, the requirements of national security have not always crushed other concerns that sustain an open society. The imperial republic, Raymond Aron's designation, has become more imperial than republican over the decades.[19] But as the history of dissent in high office demonstrates, the career of US power has benefited from the clash of interpretations. Policy has been improved, thought quickened. Neither has the democratic instinct been vanquished, albeit sorely tested.

* * *

The chapters in all three sections contain the following elements and adhere to this structure. First, I outline the main questions and give an exegesis of government policy. Then I switch focus to the response by establishment dissenters – their critiques, varying intensity of purpose, and preferred ideas (not always well-polished, especially when pegged to contradictory programs as in post-1865 policies toward the western tribes). An evaluation of consequences and implications concludes each chapter.

Only the book's final chapter departs from prototype. That chapter blends epilogue, synopsis of US foreign actions from Eisenhower's era to the second Iraq war, with rumination on dissenters and their vocation. One of their preoccupations since the Cold War has centered on the problem raised by America's possessing immense power – the resentments it arouses abroad, the temptation to use it casually. Such dissenters are in line with sentiments captured in Burke's 1793 injunction: "Among precautions against ambition, it may not be amiss to take one precaution against our *own*. I must fairly say, I dread our *own* power, and our *own* ambition; I dread our being too much dreaded."[20]

Part I

Expansion

1   Louisiana

One of the dramatic episodes in the building of American power occurred in 1803. France sold the immense territory of Louisiana to the United States. Roughly 828,000 square miles were ceded at a cost of $15 million (four cents an acre), thereby doubling the size of US holdings. Despite haziness in Washington and Paris about the precise placement of Louisiana's borders, they encompassed – according to US definition – most of the land between the Mississippi river and Rocky mountains.[1]

This acquisition accomplished several things simultaneously. It reconfirmed the expulsion of French power from North America, which even the audacity of Napoleon III's Mexican project would not later reverse (or Charles de Gaulle's verbal solidarity with Quebec vitiate).[2] Louisiana's transfer also eliminated the buffer zone between the United States and New Spain, imperiling Madrid's weak grip on such remote provinces as California, Texas, and Mexico. Additionally, this purchase smoothed the way for subsequent US expansion westward to the Pacific. The Empire of Liberty, Thomas Jefferson's construction of the US republic, thus achieved in a single stroke bloodless conquest and sturdy claim to future eminence.[3]

The overwhelming majority of Americans in 1803 was elated.[4] Pundits, Republican newspaper editors, and popular demonstrations greeted the annexation with praise. They called it noble, glorious, sublime.[5] Andrew Jackson, then a judge on the Tennessee superior court and major general in the state militia, reported to President Jefferson: "Every face wears a smile, and every heart leaps with joy."[6]

To this early approbation American historians have added their approval, dignifying with scholarly weight the endorsement of generations of their compatriots. The list of luminaries includes Henry Adams, Frederick Jackson Turner, Samuel Flagg Bemis, Samuel Eliot Morison. Their verdict has been loaded with superlatives. Hardly devoted to Jefferson, Adams nevertheless offered in 1889 that the Louisiana transaction had been "an event so portentous as to defy measurement . . . as a matter of diplomacy it was unparalleled." Turner sounded a triumphal note in 1903: "From this event [adding Louisiana] dates the rise of the

United States into the position of a world power." Bemis claimed in 1949 that the American acquisition was "the best buy of choice real estate that history can show." Similar sentiments were echoed by Morison. He labeled the sale "the greatest bargain in American history." Even William Appleman Williams, unsparing critic of the capitalist mainsprings of US foreign policy, allowed for the sale's significance.[7]

The mood in 1803 was not so exultant among Federalists, however. Their political fortunes continued to falter in the wake of Jefferson's Louisiana success. Alexander Hamilton – whose hunger for French Louisiana had earlier prompted him to favor military invasion – said that Jefferson's diplomacy was not shrewd but bumbling; it had succeeded only by dumb luck. Whereas future historians would credit Jefferson with adroitly exploiting European troubles to US advantage, Hamilton scoffed: "The acquisition has been solely owing to a fortuitous concurrence of unforeseen and unexpected circumstances, and not to any wise or vigorous measures on the part of the American government."[8] Still, despite this sulkiness, Hamilton was pleased: his republic, not a European imperium, absorbed the territory. Even as Jefferson amassed congratulations for adeptness, Hamilton consoled himself with the thought that his earlier bluster on Louisiana had impressed French officialdom with US seriousness, ensuring the glad outcome.[9] That most maverick of Federalists, Senator John Quincy Adams (Massachusetts), supported the Franco-US deal, despite misgivings about the legality of incorporating peoples and lands previously existing beyond American borders.

The only determined opposition to Louisiana came from a group of Federalist legislators, primarily New Englanders, who were a minority even within the ranks of their palsied party.[10] These resisters have not fared well in standard historiography. The likes of Senators James Hillhouse (Connecticut), Timothy Pickering (Massachusetts), and William Plumer (New Hampshire) have usually been depicted as perverse or narrowly partisan. One biographer of Jefferson, Merrill Peterson, hurled the epithet "witch-doctors" against these men. John Bach McMaster scolded in his popular account of the United States: "They ought to have been ashamed." Bemis remarked upon their supposed treachery. Stephen Ambrose, chronicler of the Lewis and Clark expedition, dismissed the Louisiana dissidents for putting themselves "on the wrong side of history."[11]

Such judgments are unhelpful. They show the subtle suspension of impartiality by scholars. They have too closely identified with their subjects, joining with them in the vitriol of early US debates, wherein Jeffersonians and Federalists resorted to extravagant language. This bias in scholarship, moreover, trivializes or overlooks the moral–political ambiguity of America's westward lunge in 1803, first glimpsed by the

company of discontents. Pickering's proposed remedy of northern disunion in 1804 may have been ill-advised, as Hamilton and other
Federalist sages argued. Yet the Pickering idea was not utterly irresponsible. It was based upon defensible concern for the Constitution, understandable anxiety about the shifting balance of power between north
and south, and premonitions of a stormy future centered on the slavery
question.[11]

Purchase

The wresting of France's North American empire by European rivals –
Canada by British arms in the Seven Years War, Louisiana by the 1762
transfer to Spain – infuriated governments in Paris. They regarded this
despoliation as the result of avoidable misadventure and criminal incompetence by Louis XV. Diverse administrations after him (monarchists,
Girondins, the Directory) looked hopefully to the day when French writ
returned to the lost territories. The assault on British power by General
Washington's insurgent army had been seen as advancing this end, thus
worthy of French aid. In the specific case of Louisiana, ownership of it by
enervated Spain was viewed by French diplomats, both of the *ancien régime*
and its successors, as a temporary condition. Spain by this logic should
function as custodian of Louisiana until such time as France recovered it.
This scheme was complicated by the success of the American rebellion,
however. The 1783 peace treaty sanctioned the movement of Americans
from beyond the Atlantic seaboard to the far side of the Appalachian
mountains toward the Mississippi, all of which land was subsumed in US
sovereignty. From this position the American population might spill farther
west into the sparsely populated and scantily garrisoned Spanish territory
coveted by Paris.[12]

America's westward drive was potentially hampered by Napoleon
Bonaparte in October 1800. The First Consul (not self-crowned emperor
until 1804) presided over negotiations that culminated in the secret treaty
of San Ildefonso. Its provisions included the retrocession of Louisiana in
exchange for an Italian kingdom for the duke of Parma, brother of the
Spanish queen. French possession of Louisiana would not actually take
place until after Bonaparte delivered the Italian properties (the specificity
of which fluctuated) to Parma, and France had gained international
recognition for the deal's legitimacy. A preponderance of evidence also
shows that Bonaparte made a verbal pledge to King Carlos of Spain that
France would not surrender Louisiana to any third party.[13]

To salvage France's Caribbean position, incidentally useful for
Louisiana's security and its logistical support, Bonaparte meanwhile

redoubled efforts in Saint Domingue (Haiti) to quell Toussaint L'Ouverture's slave rebellion (begun in 1791). Presumably, after restoring this profitable island colony to the imperium, France's army would proceed to Louisiana and police it for Paris. The able General C. V. E. Leclerc was chosen for the task, which in the event led to disaster. By spring 1803 several thousand French soldiers had died (plus Leclerc) on Saint Domingue from combat or tropical diseases, a sacrifice of manpower that ended prospects of this army's patrolling North American precincts.

Any French encroachment upon the New World mainland would have alarmed US officialdom. Jefferson's francophilia never confused calculations on the difficulties likely to arise from a French return to the continent. As early as 1785, while minister in Paris, Jefferson warned his hosts that a Franco-American collision would occur if Paris reestablished colonies near the United States or otherwise hindered its continental progress. Nor did he deviate from this wariness when serving as secretary of state (1789–1793) under George Washington or vice president (1797–1801) to John Adams. Despite the ardor of Jefferson for French revolutionary ideals, and worry that Washington–Adams policy tilted unwisely toward Britain (i.e. the 1794 Jay treaty, "quasi-war" with France), he never hesitated to reiterate his point: French power in the vicinity of the United States was antithetical to national safety. Spain in Louisiana was not a problem for him. Sooner or later Madrid's hold would fail altogether to US advantage – assuming, of course, that no European predator obtained the deed of property first. Soldiers of any great state concentrated in Louisiana, French included, would pose an unacceptable threat to the exposed western flank. As for the Federalists, their disquiet over France's geopolitical aim surpassed even Jefferson's – quickened by their antipathy to the 1789 upheaval. Indeed, throughout the Federalist ascendancy in the 1790s, the government had encouraged Spain to cling to its resolve – not always steady – to retain Louisiana against French importunities. To underscore Federalist determination, Pickering, as secretary of state (1795–1800), bluntly warned: Louisiana's retrocession would oblige the United States to eschew all pretensions of neutrality and place itself on the side of Britain in its contests against France.[14]

The Mississippi river and city of New Orleans were the foci of American preoccupation with Louisiana. The press of settlements and farms meant that the Mississippi by 1800 had become a major highway upon which much of the US citizenry depended for commerce. New Orleans functioned as the strategic port of entry into the American interior and the point of departure for agricultural products bound for shipment to the eastern seaboard or abroad. The city in friendly hands was an invaluable asset to the United States; under other authority the port held future prosperity hostage. When Spanish officials sought in the late 1790s (contrary to the 1795 Treaty of San Lorenzo) to tax or stall American goods from the northern Mississippi region before allowing their passage, the US government reviewed options for war. Sensitivity remained high afterwards, jangling nerves whenever rumors arose that Spain might try again to impose sundry tariffs. When in 1802 the terms of the treaty of San Ildefonso were broadcast, as the reality settled into the minds of Americans that Spain's mild rule in New Orleans would be replaced by French firmness, westerners clamored for decisive action. Federalist warhawks campaigned for an anti-French and/or anti-Spanish campaign in cooperation with Britain.[15] Jefferson managed to resist this stampede. Yet he did share this concern with his excitable countrymen, as he confided to his envoy in Paris, Robert Livingston: American growth would slow and Franco-US relations unravel were Bonaparte established in Louisiana. "There is on the globe one single spot," Jefferson said, "the possessor of which is our natural and habitual enemy. It is New Orleans, through which the produce of three-eighths of our territory must pass to market, and from its fertility it will ere long yield more than half of our whole produce and contain more than half our inhabitants. France placing herself in that door assumes to us the attitude of defiance ... The impetuosity of her temper, the energy and restlessness of her character placed in a point of eternal friction with us ... render it impossible that France and the US can continue long friends when they meet in so irritable a position." Upon Bonaparte's possession of New Orleans, the president predicted, the United States would have no alternative to cooperation with Britain: "From that moment we must marry ourselves to the British fleet and nation."[16]

Jefferson preferred to use diplomatic means before provoking France's wrath or resorting to the ignominy of alliance with Britain. In the first instance, America was unprepared for combat as indicated by the inadequacy of the navy. Its debilitation had been permitted by the administration, philosophically opposed to lavishness on defense, especially naval construction. As for cooperating with Britain: this expedient would hobble diplomatic maneuverability by fostering reliance on a perfidious nation. It might, in league with its Federalist friends, even try to shape an Anglo-US war against France into renewed political association, fatal to the 1776 decision.

Jefferson took measures to impede or otherwise discourage France in the New World, thus strengthening the hand of his emissaries (Livingston was joined by James Monroe) in Paris. Laying aside Republican scruples against a large military establishment, he ordered the building of gunboats for coastal defense and river districts. He hastened the drive of eastern Indians across the Mississippi to complicate matters for Frenchmen in Louisiana. Despite his dread of the spread of slave rebellion (Virginia had been rocked by a revolt in 1800 whose leaders were inspired by Toussaint's example), Jefferson ordered the supply of *matériel* to revolutionaries in Saint Domingue. Yet nothing was easy for the Americans in their Paris negotiations or obvious in advance about the outcome. Foreign Minister Talleyrand was not impressed by the diplomatic pretensions of a weak state situated on the geographical and cultural fringes of Western civilization. As for the actual selling of New Orleans and the adjoining territory, he shared with Bonaparte this sly conviction: the agreement would obtain briefly and be subject to reversal once France had liquidated the unfinished business of smiting Britain (delayed not canceled by the 1802 Treaty of Amiens). After that not only would Europe be secure for France. But the United States would also perforce yield to the logic of French power and its return to North America, where additionally the British position in Canada would have faded. Until then, French diplomacy had to adapt to stubborn facts: defeats in Saint Domingue; the impending renewal of hostilities against Britain, for which a contribution of several million dollars to Paris's treasury was welcome, as was an agreement that helped keep the Anglo-US powers apart; the irrelevance of faraway wilderness to the cause of victory in Europe.[17] As for the alleged promise to Madrid not to sell Louisiana to any third party, Talleyrand answered Spanish protests with sophistry: Madrid's persistent bad faith had obliged France to sell to avoid a snarl with the Yankees. Meanwhile, to Livingston, Talleyrand offered congratulations and these honeyed words: "You [Americans] have made a noble bargain for yourselves, and I suppose you will make the most of it."[18]

News of the French offer to sell more than New Orleans arrived in Washington on the eve of July 4th ceremonies to honor independence. Buying all of Louisiana far exceeded Jefferson's intentions or instructions to Livingston. Still, the president was eager that his countrymen seize Bonaparte's offer before the First Consul changed his mind, which evidence showed him ready to do. Jefferson managed quickly to overcome his own reservations concerning the legality of pushing the US boundary past the territorial limits that obtained at the moment of constitutional ratification. He had originally espoused this view: "The Constitution has made no provision for our holding foreign territory, still less for incorporating foreign nations into our Union." His conscience as advocate of small government also made him admit to Kentucky's Senator John Breckinridge: "The executive in seizing the fugitive occurrence ... ha[s] done an act beyond the Constitution."[19]

Jefferson toyed with the idea of sponsoring an amendment that would sanction expansion. But at the critical hour, to save time before opportunity passed, he permitted the arguments of cabinet officers to persuade him that such measure was unnecessary. The Constitution implicitly allowed the extension of national boundaries, reported Secretary of State Madison, Secretary of the Treasury Gallatin, and Attorney General Lincoln. Buoyed by this convenient interpretation, Jefferson then called Congress to convene in special session (October 1803) to ratify the sale treaty with France and pass other enabling legislation. The Republican-dominated Senate approved the transfer with more than the two-thirds of votes needed – only five against – after a debate lasting just two days.[20] The Republican-led House followed suit by approving necessary funds.

After dodges and delays, Spanish authorities in Louisiana delivered their territory to France in November. The French garrison in New Orleans surrendered its authority to the Americans weeks later (December 20). The United States did not assume possession of upper Louisiana in ceremony until March 1804 in St. Louis. Among the witnesses in what was then a scraggly town stood Meriwether Lewis. He was, with William Clark, captain of the Corps of Discovery which had earlier received Jefferson's commission and was already embarked on exploration. As for the president, he savored new visions of national destiny. Its embrace touched limitless horizons of land for yeomen farmers and honest democrats: "The world will here see such an extent of country under a free and moderate government as it has never yet [beheld]."[21]

Dissent

Jefferson's rapture was matched for intensity by the querulousness of Federalism, most pronounced in its New England redoubt. A Federalist newspaper in Boston railed that the new lands amounted to a desert, too desolate for cultivation, inhabited by savages, too expensive for the national treasury. Christopher Gore and George Cabot, party stalwarts in Massachusetts, hinted that fresh western tracts presaged the Union's disintegration along south–north and/or east–west political fault lines. The brilliant Fisher Ames fired from his farm in Dedham, Massachusetts: "Now, by adding an unmeasured world beyond that [Mississippi] river, we rush like a comet into infinite space. In our wild career, we may jostle some other world out of its orbit, but we shall, in every event, quench the light of our own." In less vivid language, Pickering marveled after Congress had voted treaty passage and funding: "The purchase of an immense territory which we did not want and at [steep] price."[22]

Federalism in New England was on the defensive at the time of the Louisiana debate, albeit not routed as elsewhere in the country. All the New England states, except Connecticut, would support Jefferson in his bid for a second presidential term in the 1804 election. Even so, Federalism in 1803 was not vanquished, bolstered still by resentment that could mount resistance to – if not block – Republican initiatives. Federalist grievances were legion. They included objection to the three-fifths clause. It gave added electoral value to the slave-owning southern states, notably Virginia over Massachusetts, and, in the procedurally tortured 1800 election, Jefferson over John Adams.[23] Bitterness over the three-fifths clause fostered Federalist opposition to slavery with con-comitant calls for its containment or abandonment. "Virginia people that preach about liberty and use their poor black devils like so many dogs" were routinely blasted in New England's refrain.[24] Federalism's prefer-ence for things British, borne by commercial connections to Atlantic trade, inclined the party to lump Jeffersonian Republicanism in the same infamy as French revolutionists. Curtailment of the Alien and Sedition Acts in 1801 seemed from this Federalist perspective to encour-age Jacobins in the United States as the broad population could not distinguish falsehood from truth. The uncouth would prove gullible enough to believe Republican demagogues as they bludgeoned – first verbally, then perhaps literally – the representatives of prudence and civility. "The ravages of demoralizing democracy," William Plumer's words, would obliterate the US system. In the end – feared Plumer, Ames, et al. – Jefferson would install himself as president for life while "the empire of principles" succumbed to "the assaults of popular pas-sions." He would from his proud perch wage ruthlessness against the urban-merchant-intellectual elite.[25]

Irredeemable flaws marked Jefferson, his adversaries charged, them-selves slow to adopt the techniques needed to win in electoral politics. Critics mocked him as a moonshine philosopher. His membership in, and presidency of, the American Philosophical Society tarnished that august body's luster. They circulated stories – then not fortified by DNA testing – of his liaison with the slave Sally Hemings. Ditties contained coarseness about Monticello's "luscious lass," thought libelous by Jefferson's champ-ions but gaily recited by the impertinent.[26]

Federalist congressmen, such as Representative Roger Griswold (Connecticut), actually blamed the unreliability of the mail service on Jefferson – "democracy deranges everything" – while nursing private slight as when he failed to invite them to dine at the executive mansion.[27] The depth of partisan enmity was never better conveyed than in this invective from Pickering to Rufus King (March 1804), leader of New

York's Federalism: "The cowardly wretch at [the Republican] head, while, like a Parisian revolutionary monster, prating about humanity, would feel an infernal pleasure in the utter destruction of his opponents. We have too long witnessed his general turpitude ... and the substitution of corruption and looseness for integrity and worth."[28]

Revulsion for Jefferson and his administration got ample airing in Congress during Louisiana deliberations. New lands available for slavery aroused ire among the high Federalists and set them against acquisition. Their objection was based partly on moral grounds. Hillhouse declared: "I consider slavery as a serious evil, and wish to check it wherever I have authority."[29] He therefore not only voted against Louisiana. He also introduced legislation that would have prohibited slavery's expansion into the territory, observing by the way: "These slaves are men – they have the passions and feelings of men. And I believe if we were slaves, we should not be more docile, more submissive, or virtuous than the negroes are."[30] Hillhouse also believed that the spreading of slavery would endanger national security. He opined that slaves in times of war would use such occasion to rebel. In tranquil times a standing army would be required to keep the peace in Louisiana. It would eventually teem with a species of desperate people. "If that country cannot be cultivated without slaves, it will instead of being a paradise prove a curse to this country," Hillhouse warned, in which connection he mentioned the gory example of Saint Domingue.[31] In advancing this line, he and other dissenters cited testimony by white refugees who had escaped to Louisiana with upsetting tales. Unruliness among radicalized black retainers spirited out of Saint Domingue added to the general unease in New Orleans, and was featured in the Federalist catalogue of objection. Yet these concerns did not delay the land purchase. Counter arguments overawed minority objection to pushing slavery westward: only Africans were capable of cultivating land in the steamy south (whites would suffocate from exertion in the heat); national commerce and prosperity, not just the southern economy, were entwined in the prospering of slavery; southern whites were within their rights to bring their chattels on the pioneer march. Rancorous talk from both sides of the Louisiana question made Plumer predict that slavery would one day split the nation.[32]

Dissenters opposed the buying of Louisiana and expansion of slavery not for humanitarian reasons alone. Indeed, fair to say, practical political reasons dominated the minority viewpoint. It read application of the three-fifths formula in the new territory as erecting an obnoxious national majority and repudiating the original regional balance of north–south. For years to come the number of white citizens in the north might remain greater than in the south (plus west). But northerners would labor under the liability of skewed apportionment as codified in the three-fifths provision. Nothing, then, could inhibit slave owning southern Republicans, abetted by western allies, from perpetuating the Jeffersonian legacy via their domination of Congress and the electoral college. The political influence of New England – other non-slave zones too – would be reduced and necessarily defer to a "Virginia dynasty." The Jeffersonian regime, combining francophile slavocracy and democratic fever, would finally transform the United States into a polity deadly to Federalism. Its philosophical precepts and economic-social links to the Anglo-Atlantic world would drop to minor status.[33] Few Federalists disagreed with Pickering's despairing words, uttered after Congress's Louisiana vote: "The Northern States have nothing to countervail the power and influence arising from the negro representation . . . we suffer all the mischiefs which flow from an unequal representation."[34]

Other legalistic questions riled the dissenters apart from the galling three-fifths matter. With the decline of their electoral fortunes came a new appreciation among Federalists for those constitutional provisions that circumscribed the chief executive's power. The Louisiana affair, in fact, provoked a subtle reversal of roles. While it helped Jefferson to shed qualms about strong central authority – to embrace it as an instrument for territorial expansion – his critics discovered virtue in constraints that they had previously denounced as inimical to competent government. According to their new reading, Jefferson's Louisiana involved usurpation and misuse of presidential power. The acquisition was manifestly unconstitutional.[35] At a minimum the Constitution required an amendment to permit the absorption of non-Americans (Spaniards, Frenchmen, Indians) and distant lands into the US body. That such was not forthcoming scandalized Fisher Ames. He sighed: "It seems the powers that be concern themselves little about the Constitution."[36]

The dissenters were also uncertain about France's professed ownership of Louisiana in 1803. They doubted Bonaparte's right to sell property that had long belonged to Spain and sought reassurance that the United States was not being hoodwinked out of $15 million. This sum, contributing to French military coffers, could not possibly secure a transaction that lacked definite legal basis. Support for this skepticism came from Spanish officials (including the minister to the United States, Carlos Martinez de Irujo), who maintained that France had not kept its side of the San Ildefonso agreement: Parma had not received his Italian estate; France had not yet paid Spain for the territory; France could not pass Louisiana to another country without the consent of the Spanish king. To determine whether Bonaparte had acted falsely, thereby voiding French rights of title, Federalists demanded that Congress inspect the texts of the 1800 Franco-Spanish treaty, deed of sale, and related documentation. Gaylord Griswold (Federalist, New York) was particularly diligent on this matter in the House of Representatives. If the administration failed to be cooperative, he exclaimed, he and his colleagues could not confidently identify the true owner of Louisiana or grant funding for its purchase. In the event, Jefferson could not disprove French fraud, let alone provide copies of confidential Paris–Madrid agreements. His government, though, managed to steer a House vote in which the request for authoritative documentation lost (just barely, 59 to 57).[37]

Other Federalist grumbling derived from an appreciation of Montesquieu's *The Spirit of Laws*. Therein the excellence of a compact republic is extolled (Book 8). A republic must not occupy too great a territory, lest it forfeit its soul, lest citizens lose touch with and sympathy for each other. The lesson of this teaching was plain: by extending US rule deep into the continent, the republic would debauch itself. Anarchy and dissolution might rend the ungainly country or, more likely, its sheer size would degrade the US experiment. Imperial habits and institutions required to coordinate life in immense territory would destroy the still tender shoots of representative government. Plumer wrote in his journal with Montesquieu in mind:

Our republican government derives its authority and momentum from the frequent meetings of the mass of the people in town and country assemblies. An extension of the body politic will enfeeble the circulation of its powers and energies in the extreme parts. A piece of our coin, an eagle, may be extended to the size of a coach wheel, but its beauty and use will be destroyed ... The testimony of history and the very nature of things unite in declaring that a republican government established over a large extensive country cannot long exist.[38]

From such anti-empire analysis arose more Federalist charges of bad faith against Jefferson. Perhaps, the writer of the Declaration of Independence had not only strayed from original republican principles. Perhaps, he had converted to Bonapartism and so wanted to donate $15 million to France. Such an exorbitant amount in exchange for worthless property could be given still more sinister interpretation: Jefferson had become a puppet – nay, the accomplice – of French policy. Paris dictated. He blithely executed his new sovereign's wishes.[39]

Northern confederacy

No Federalist in Congress held more dearly than Pickering to the charge of Jefferson's being a foreign vassal. The tenacity with which Pickering maintained this preposterousness is one reason why he has not fared better in US memory.[40] Even some contemporaries who shared his general outlook had reservations about him. His idol, Alexander Hamilton, felt that although Pickering was a "worthy man," he "has nevertheless something warm and angular in his temper and [requires] much a vigilant moderating eye."[41] Plumer pronounced Pickering as "honest, but passionate, and imprudent." His fierce partisanship prevented Plumer from inviting Republican acquaintances to dine at the Washington rooming house which he shared with Pickering. These people were invariably assailed by his choleric displays or rudeness.[42] Plumer had later to endure Pickering's fury after defecting from Federalist ranks. John Adams and his son, John Quincy, could not stand their Massachusetts compatriot, who despised them both for rejecting orthodox Federalism. Abigail Adams echoed her husband when she described Pickering as strident and implacable. As for his numerous Republican foes, they held him in sheer contempt. Jefferson thought him an unreconstructed monarchist.[43]

However reviled in certain quarters, however mixed his reputation in subsequent generations, achievements studded Pickering's career. This scion of a respectable Salem family had served with distinction during the War of Independence as the army's quartermaster general. After the war, he voiced disapproval of the confiscation, deportations, and other persecution meted to the Loyalists. At the behest of President Washington, he conducted delicate diplomacy in 1790, in what proved to be the first of several such missions, with the Senecas to dissuade them from making common cause with western tribes against white settlers. (Pickering developed an abiding respect for Native Americans as a result of his negotiation and sought to protect them against white depredations.) Washington then rewarded him with successive appointments of increasing responsibility: postmaster general, secretary of war, secretary of state. Pickering subsequently served as John Adams's secretary of state. The president dismissed him (May 1800) for intriguing with Hamilton against the administration and trying to thwart Adams's conciliatory policy toward France. Pickering was next chosen senator from Massachusetts, in which capacity he served from 1803 to 1811. Voters later elected him to the House of Representatives, where he thrived at the center of opposition to the 1812 war against Britain. Possessed of rugged good health, he lived into his eighties. Politics consumed him even in retirement, during which he spoke on behalf of favorite causes: abolition of slavery, humane treatment of Indians, friendly relations with Britain, Greek independence from Turkey.[44]

Pickering's public philosophy was nourished by Puritan forebears: elitist, pessimistic, stark. He cleaved to this unleavened outlook: life amounted to hard testing. Yet the upright few would receive solace and redemption for their earthly suffering: "We ever deem our thoughts in contemplating our present existence as a *probationary state* – a *school* of discipline and *instruction*, in which we are to be prepared for admission into the assembly of the saints and of angels, to spend in the presence and worship of the *Great source* of being."[45]

Quicker to see fault in other people than in himself, he applied harsh judgment with rigor. Case in point was his application of the Alien and Sedition laws, assigned to his portfolio while Adams's secretary of state. He joyfully prosecuted what he perceived to be the agents of Jacobin incubus: French diplomats, Republican newspapermen. His penchant for purging also made Pickering zealous in rooting out unreliable people in the cabinet. While Washington's secretary of war, he convinced himself that Secretary of State Edmund Randolph was a French collaborator. Pickering subsequently took steps that led to Randolph's resignation and his own promotion to the foreign affairs post.[46] The most loathsome creatures in his estimation were moderate Federalists, by his definition apostates. They had, in the flesh of the Adams family, flirted with France and had tried to smash his political career. The Adams–Pickering split in the Federalist party helped elect Jefferson in 1800 and otherwise contributed to the party's dismal fortunes. Pickering's hatred of the Adams clan never mellowed. Just before his death, Pickering had the pleasure of voting in 1828 for Andrew Jackson – the embodiment of plebeian democracy – and see him bury John Quincy Adams's bid for a second White House term. The trouncing vindicated ancient defiance.[47]

Pickering's preference for strong action to remedy injury surfaced in the 1804 design to create a northern confederacy. Pickering was the moving spirit for taking New England and other northern places – New York, New Jersey, eastern Pennsylvania – out of the Union. Jefferson's Louisiana purchase and the realities radiating from it, above all New England's political diminution, was the precipitating event. It threw Pickering into gloom, aggravated by other fast-moving events that had the effect of tightening Virginia's rule: Jefferson's decision to withhold full rights of citizenship to Louisiana's inhabitants until after they had passed an unspecified period of democratic apprenticeship; the inauguration of impeachment hearings by the House of Representatives aimed at Federalist judges Samuel Chase and the mentally unhinged John Pickering (no relation); the 1804 amendment to the Constitution (article twelve) that reformed the method for electing the vice president.[48]

This regime, propelled by narrowness and avarice, said Pickering, justified the measure of disunion. Henry Adams later succinctly captured the mood of the confederates: "Despair turned into conspiracy."[49]

Because the proposed confederacy miscarried, planning for it never advanced beyond the following rough outline. Pickering and his colleagues – Hillhouse, Plumer, Roger Griswold, Senator Uriah Tracy of Connecticut – conceived of a confederation that would associate itself with Lower Canada and the Maritimes. Cooperation might eventuate in political integration with these British territories. At the minimum, closer economic–political links would have resulted, leading to intensified diplomatic ties with Great Britain. Pickering held that his northern confederacy should not cease to have decent interactions with the remnant United States. Separation could be accomplished without bloodshed. A web of economic–social connections would ensure a peaceful and mutually beneficial relationship as before: "The Southern States would require the naval protection of the Northern Union, and the products of the former would be important to the navigation and commerce of the latter."[50] Nevertheless, by separating from the regime in Washington, New England and kindred regions would be spared further afflictions from the gathering tyranny centered on Jefferson.

Pickering's plotters hoped that Vice President Aaron Burr would lead the northern enterprise. They approached him cautiously. He treated them politely. He was solicitous. But he delayed and proved evasive on whether he would make himself available. Undaunted, they courted him anyway. Pickering meanwhile lobbied New York Federalists (notably Rufus King) to support Burr in his 1804 gubernatorial bid in their state. Burr as governor would enjoy enhanced stature; he could more easily assume the grander role intended for him. Pickering also tried to entice Hamilton into supporting the confederacy by offering him command of its future army.[51]

Prominent Federalists to whom Pickering was attached responded discouragingly to his scheme. Ames and Cabot thought that disunion might be desirable one day but was premature in 1804. They also worried that such a prescription would not necessarily cure the democratic contagion. Its growth and virulence were already infecting New England; the best antidote would be a Federalist party revival. Maybe in the future, following a crisis beyond the national government's solution, New England could revisit the secessionist idea. "I do not desire a separation at this moment," Cabot advised Pickering. "I add that *it is not practicable* without the intervention of some cause which should be very generally felt and distinctly understood as chargeable to the misconduct of our Southern masters: such, for example, as a war with Great Britain, manifestly provoked by our rulers ... Without some single event of this kind to rouse us, I am of opinion we must bear the evils which the delusion of democracy is bringing upon us." New York's Federalists were even more skeptical with Rufus King adamantly opposed. Hamilton too was against.

He explained in writing on the day before his death: "Dismemberment . . . will be a clear sacrifice of great positive advantage, without any counter-balancing good; administering no relief to our real disease, which is *Democracy*; the poison of which by a subdivision will only be the more concentrated in each part."[52]

Such planning as took place for a confederacy unraveled when Burr killed Hamilton in their July 1804 duel (Weehawken, New Jersey). It and Burr's swift flight into hiding disqualified the would-be leader. Hamilton's death stunned Pickering, who instantly decried the "foul murder." He called Burr a villain "destitute of every moral principle."[53] Moreover, the objection by Hamilton to disunion was impossible to refute in light of his martyrdom.[54] Federalism itself seemed beyond repair in New England or anywhere else after Jefferson's 1804 reelection. The Federalist slate (Charles Pinckney, Rufus King) received only 14 electoral votes versus Jefferson's 162.

An irrepressible core of New England Federalists was willing to wait. Pickering refloated his secessionist idea in 1808 – in response to Jefferson's embargo policy that damaged New England's sea-going commerce. Delegates to the 1814 Hartford Convention, as part of their resistance to James Madison's war on Britain and desire for a separate peace, examined the case for a regional divorce (before rejecting it).

* * *

The fragility of the US compact was apparent well before Pickering and company began to plot. Disgruntled westerners had talked in 1786 of severing cords to the government if it failed to press Madrid for reliable access to New Orleans and unimpeded navigation along Spanish stretches of the Mississippi. James Wilkinson, formerly a brigadier general in the Continental army (erstwhile associate of Burr), had conspired briefly in 1787 with Spanish officials to detach Kentucky from the United States and join it to Madrid's Louisiana.[55] Jefferson and Madison in 1798 had argued on behalf of nullification (*Kentucky Resolutions, Virginia Resolutions*) against the Alien and Sedition strictures. Quite apart from continuing agitation in New England, various Americans after 1804 thought that union was a temporary and not an obviously desirable condition. Jefferson himself concluded, after some hesitation, that the peoples of Louisiana might develop interests and habits incompatible with the larger nation. In that case the west might properly go its own way. The expansion in North America of a democratic zone mattered but it need not be subject to single government. At the core of the US experiment this principle controlled, hallowed by the 1776 rebellion: people have a right to break burdensome or unwanted political associations. "The future inhabitants of the Atlantic and Mississippi States will be our sons," Jefferson averred. "We leave them in distinct but bordering establishments. We think we see their happiness in their union, and we wish it. Events may prove otherwise ... God bless them ... and keep them in union, if it be for their good, but separate them, if it be better."[56]

Jefferson never thought to prosecute Pickering or his band. Their lives remained unmolested by police investigation or court trial. Plumer, who later repented of his secessionist impulse, was astonished that no stain of conspiracy ever spoilt his reputation or holding of public office. Jefferson's magnanimity did not, however, extend to Burr or his obscure plot in 1805–1806 to pull part of Louisiana from the United States. This Mephistopheles of US politics (Henry Adams's language) endured court trial for treason. Even so, he won acquittal.[57]

Disaffected southerners in 1861 rested their case on the right to secession in Pickering's idea: if one region's power or aggrandizement become too onerous for that of another, the aggrieved party ought to forge another path. After their failure in 1865, southerners hoped too for leniency in line with Jefferson's charity toward New England separatists. Jefferson Davis in his post-Civil War apologia for the South invoked Pickering as moral authority while paying him this tribute: "an undoubted patriot." Davis also argued: "Substituting South Carolina for Massachusetts; Virginia for New York; Georgia, Mississippi, and Alabama, for New Hampshire, Vermont, and Rhode Island; Kentucky for New Jersey, etc., etc., we find the suggestions of 1860–'61 only a reproduction of those ... outlined nearly sixty years earlier." Citing other unease in the northeast (i.e. 1808–1809, Hartford) with the restrictions of national life, Davis fired: "It is evident ... that the people of the South, in the crisis which confronted them in 1860, had no lack either of precept or of precedent for their instruction and guidance in the teaching and the example of our brethren of the North and East. The only practical difference was that the North threatened and the South acted."[58]

Dissolution of the Union was anticipated by foreign observers long before 1861. Bonaparte, for one, thought in 1803 that the United States would simply lose coherence as it bulged beyond the limits of feasible communication and transportation. American territorial integrity would prove a chimera. His successors during the Civil War – the British government too – openly favored the Confederate cause. Its success would have reduced the concentration of power in North America, leaving the New World susceptible to penetrations by Paris and London.[59] That such an outcome might have been realized in the 1860s, or even earlier, lurks behind the condemnation of Pickering's cabal by most historians. Thus

Morison held that only people devoid of ethics and out of touch with public opinion could have worked for disunion in 1804 or found fault with the Louisiana transfer.[60]

No doubt northern Federalists were out of touch with mainstream opinion in rejecting Louisiana. Their hyperbole about the new order in Louisiana did not help – "as despotic as that of Turkey in Asia." Their resistance was all the more suspect given Hamilton's hankering for Louisiana before Jefferson's sponsorship of it. Yet the skepticism of Pickering, Hillhouse, Plumer, Tracy, and the rest was not frivolously motivated. The Constitution was stretched beyond its original elasticity to accommodate the purchase, a fact recognized by Jefferson, who tried hastily to put matters right. Additionally, initial rule in Louisiana by Washington hardly constituted unsullied democracy. The inhabitants had not consented to – or even been consulted about – annexation, contra the first principle of US civic faith: governments derive "their just powers from the consent of the governed." Troops, not voting citizens, held sway in America's western acquisition, where Creoles and others were bereft of political rights. Not yet citizens, these subjects perforce complied with Jefferson's decrees and appointees.[61]

Jefferson's expectation that US reign in Louisiana would eventually add to the sum of human freedom, after a brief autocratic phase, also warranted Federalist reserve. The president's farmers, as agents and beneficiaries of the expanding zone of liberty, did indeed benefit in plausible ways. But this same realm did not entail promise of bright sunlit uplands for aboriginal Americans or African slaves. The former were soon expelled as Louisiana became a forbidden zone. Jefferson's own oft-quoted words on the wisdom of integrating the natives into republican society were ambiguous. Indian failure to convert to white ways, he confessed, would leave Washington no recourse but "to drive [Native America], with the beasts of the forests, into the Stony [Rocky] mountains."[62] Much of Louisiana, meanwhile, became a jailhouse for Africans, unchanged by occasional mutinies, as in the 1811 uprising near New Orleans led by the Haitian-born mulatto Charles Deslandes. The heads of the slain slaves, between sixty-five and one hundred victims, were displayed in the neighborhood as warning by local authorities against mischief-makers.[63] Thus did events vindicate that forecast by the Federalist newspaper *Litchfield Monitor*, when it editorialized in August 1803: "It may be added that Louisiana is to be a field of blood before it is a cultured field; and indeed a field of blood while it is cultivated. The natives of the soil, a numerous race, who have never injured us, and never will until encroached upon, must be driven out; and a still more numerous race from Africa must be violently brought in, to toil and bleed under the lath." The editors asked: "It is for such an extension of human liberty and of human happiness that we are called upon for such sacrifice?"[64]

Neither did post-purchase history support Jefferson's contention that regional chafing and strife would decline with US expansion (a proposition buttressed, incidentally, by Madison's *Federalist* No. 10 against Montesquieu). Jefferson had claimed hopefully in his second inaugural address: "The larger our association, the less will it be shaken by local passions."[65] Expansion manifestly had the opposite effect, as foretold by Ames in his prediction of an unsettled US world. Jefferson's acquisition compounded the testiness between north and south for years as both regions competed for domination in the west. The 1820 Missouri Compromise split Louisiana into northern free and southern slave areas, a formula that delayed but did not prevent denouement in 1861.

Federalist dissenters did not have a twenty-first-century sensibility regarding race. They were creatures of their time with corresponding vision.[66] Pickering never advocated black assimilation into white society. Such a proposition would have struck him as nonsense because of a presumed unbridgeable gulf between blacks and whites. His version of abolishing slavery was gradualist. His notions also included deporting African Americans, a solution he abandoned as unworkable only because of the large number of people involved. Nor did he deny to himself the benefits offered by servitude. He retained for his family's use a black bond servant, Anthony, for seven years.[67]

Although Pickering clung to the Federalist attitude toward politics – exercise in noblesse oblige – he did not idolize lofty authority. He evidenced this impulse early in his career by criticizing George Washington as mediocre in war and peace.[68] As for the Federalist allegiance of Pickering, it was not essentially philosophical. His mania was kin to that once found in his ancestral home, witch-hunting Salem, and he loathed careening frontier democracy.[69] Its embodiment, Andrew Jackson, entered the White House in 1829, the year of Pickering's death. Drunken revelers practically dismantled the executive mansion after inaugural ceremonies.[70] Pickering would have been aghast, his worst fears confirmed that mobocracy had scattered decorum to enthrone buffoonery.

What flexibility he did muster in life, such as his cranky vote for Jackson against Adams in 1828, was fleeting. The passions of Pickering (for social tranquillity and good order), his anxiety that US Jacobinism would produce mayhem, plus his pugnacity, made him immune to compromise. Rigidity of character and concept made this man one of the more resolute dissidents spawned by the responsible class. Soldier, diplomat, cabinet officer, congressman, his strength was his weakness. He could not stop, not even if his actions would undo national unity.

2   1812

Few moments in the history of Europe rival 1812 for drama. Emperor Napoleon turned on his erstwhile Russian ally, launching in June an invasion force of 500,000 soldiers. It captured Moscow in October. The Grande Armée was compelled to retreat before the year was out, however. Strangled logistics, frigid weather, and resistance by Czar Alexander's troops routed a seemingly invincible military machine led by a genius. The tattered remnants of the Grande Armée were then abandoned in December by Napoleon. He hastened home to a somber Paris. The sweep of Alexander's victory was abundantly clear to America's envoy in St. Petersburg, John Quincy Adams. He recorded in his diary in early December: "Within the compass of ten days the Russian armies have taken between forty and fifty thousand prisoners, with cannons, baggage, and ammunition in proportion. There is nothing like it in [saga] since the days of Xerxes."[1]

British–Spanish–Portuguese armies supervised by Sir Arthur Wellesley (later Duke of Wellington) meantime continued to fight French forces in the Iberian peninsula. They had entered in 1808. They were not expelled until 1813. Francisco de Goya etched the unforgiving Peninsular War that featured atrocities against civilians plus guerrilla tactics. His series, *The Disasters of War*, stood unmatched for more than a century as pictorial depiction of war's grotesqueness – until another Spaniard, Pablo Picasso, painted *Guernica*.

Military operations in 1812, stretching from Russia to Spain, culminated in French defeat at Leipzig, October 1813. Napoleon abdicated in April 1814. His final crushing at Waterloo, June 1815, followed his escape from exile on Elba, before which finale Jefferson in Monticello expressed this apprehension: "The establishment in our day of another Roman empire, spreading vassalage and depravity over the face of the globe, is not, I hope, within the purposes of Heaven." The restless spirit of Napoleon "leaves no hope of peace to the world; and his hatred of us is only a little less than that he bears to England, and England to us."[2]

The military–diplomatic events in 1812–1815 that ended Napoleon's career provoked an emergency for the young and tentative American republic. The War of 1812, however dwarfed by the struggle in Europe, also added to the store of US symbols and lore. The former included a nearly unsingable national anthem (as of 1931) with verses by an antiwar Federalist lawyer, Francis Scott Key. He gave this objection to President Madison's war and its northern strategy: "I shall not fight the poor, unoffending Canadians."[3] The most durable legend of the war, apart from that claiming it as a victory, virtually "a second war of independence," is that the conflict was forced upon Madison by British effrontery: impressment of roughly nine thousand US sailors (since 1793). Hence his repeated statements in 1812 that Parliament's suspension of such violations was prerequisite to terminating Anglo-US hostilities.[4]

No US president ever led a country less united into war, or less able to wage one, than Madison. The republic at the time of Congress's declaration against Britain possessed a paltry fleet, with no augment in sight. Congress had defeated Madison's proposed increased naval spending on the eve of combat. The US navy did not possess one ship of the line and consisted until the spring of 1813 of only six frigates, three war sloops, seven miscellaneous smaller craft, plus a collection of inadequate gunboats. The Royal Navy possessed three warships for every US cannon.[5] The US army was also puny. The treasury was hardly flush, burdened still by the cost of Louisiana and expenditures related to internal improvements. Divisions within elite and popular opinion on the wisdom of war were obvious too from the outset. They were evidenced by the viciousness of mob attacks in Baltimore on antiwar dissidents ("Light-Horse Harry" Lee left for dead), and the hounding in Boston of war advocates. Regional cracks were also serious, as shown in the 1812 presidential election. Every state north of the Potomac (except Pennsylvania and Vermont) supported the antiwar candidate, De Witt Clinton, in his losing bid against Madison. As for the president, he was an unlikely leader during emergency. He was diffident, contemplative, and philosophically disinclined to exercise brisk initiative even as commander in chief. He held as a theoretical principle and empirical truth that any government prone to wage war did so to establish tyranny at home. He abhorred violence. He penned his "Universal Peace" in 1792, three years before Immanuel Kant published his *Perpetual Peace*. Madison's treatise brimmed with Enlightenment faith in moral progress and the pacific predisposition of republics, premised in reason's objection to war's profligacy.[6]

Yet Madison did not shrink from violence when the time came two decades later. The hazards were worth running, he decided, if they extinguished British misbehavior and enlarged US territory.

Madison's war

Grievances against Great Britain in 1812 made for a lengthy recital. According to administration apologists, it had not been reduced by attempts to find a diplomatic solution, waged persistently but in vain to protect US independence and the dignity of neutral nations. Madison's June 1 war message to Congress elaborated upon outstanding problems summarized in the slogan: "Free Trade and Sailors' Rights." First, British cruisers had for years harried naval and merchant ships on the oceans by carrying off people – purportedly British subjects – sailing under the US flag. Behind the pretext of capturing deserters, British officers had seized innocent American citizens as well as refugees from the Royal Navy (its severity protested by the 1797 mutinies at Spithead and at the Nore). Second, British naval vessels had long disturbed the quiet of the Atlantic shoreline by harassing or intercepting maritime commerce as it entered and left US ports. Third, Britain's pretended blockade of ports on the European continent, enunciated in the Orders in Council, meant that US ships and cargoes ("millions of our property") were subject to British plunder on every ocean. This brazen practice threatened to prevent US commodities (mostly agricultural) reaching overseas markets. Madison also mentioned that hostile Indians in the northwest enjoyed sanctuary and other support in Canada.[7]

These complaints reflected the frustration of American diplomacy since the collapse of the Treaty of Amiens and resumption of Anglo-French fighting in 1803. The United States got sucked into the vortex despite maneuvers by Jefferson, then Madison, to avoid entanglement. Ideally, the government would have been content to see merchants conduct lucrative maritime business with the British empire and the French-organized European continent. The United States and its commerce were instead victimized – a type of collateral damage – by the economic warfare directed by France and Britain against one other. Roughly 950 US ships were seized by the French (558) or British (389) during 1807–1812.[8]

Napoleon proclaimed in November 1806 the British Isles to be in a state of land and sea blockade (Berlin Decree), a retaliation for the British blockade of Europe's coast from Brest to the Elbe river. His prohibition on continental trade with Great Britain meant that all goods from it, or British colonial ports, were subject to seizure. Thus despite Admiral Nelson's victory at Trafalgar (October 21, 1805), Napoleon hoped to humble the mistress of the seas by denying it access to Europe and making British maritime commerce everywhere risky and unprofitable. The British government responded with its Orders in Council in January 1807 (made stricter in November, reiterated in 1809 and 1811) that proscribed trade with French controlled ports on pain of capture and confiscation. Neutral vessels were also obliged to report to British ports or submit to search by British authorities looking for contraband. Every neutral vessel had to pay duties too and obtain licenses for trade with France. Napoleon's Milan Decrees (November and December 1807) allowed, in turn, for the capture of any neutral ship as British that submitted to London's regulations. The emperor's Bayonne Decree (April 1808) permitted authorities to impound any US ship in a French-controlled port on the assumption that such a vessel was British but in disguise.[9] This system, then, of French and British decrees and counter-decrees jeopardized, at least in theory, US seaborne commerce while obliterating any concept of neutral rights.

Evasions, special licenses, and other improvisations, however, permitted US shipping to continue. The continuance of Anglo-French molesting nevertheless justified to Jefferson his short-lived Non-Importation Act (April 1806) and ambitious Embargo Act (December 1807). The latter suspended American trade with Europe and banned some British products from the United States as a means of pressuring the offending nations. But instead of causing France or Britain to abandon disruptive practices, the Embargo crippled US shipping and exports. Consequently, Jefferson repealed the law just before leaving office, but not before sparking a Federalist resurgence that rode the crest of anti-Embargo rage in New England (and elsewhere). Although the Embargo actually spurred New England's manufacturing economy, to the generation living through this crisis the Embargo amounted to a wrecking action. Boston's Christopher Gore testified: "The people of our Country are suffering extremely and must soon be reduced to absolute wretchedness; I mean that portion of them, who have hitherto subsisted by navigation ... They are obliged to depend on charity for food & fuel."[10] New Englanders might respond with organized violence against the existing laws, he intimated in 1808, unless relief arrived.

Subversion of the laws did in fact follow the Embargo's enactment. Smuggling exploded along the New England–Canadian frontier and between the ports of Boston and Halifax. A majority of the illegal traders eluded capture by federal enforcement. Congress replaced the Embargo Act with the Non-Intercourse Act in March 1809. It provided for the restoration of trade with all countries except Britain and France. Once again neither belligerent made concessions. As before, the resultant damage to US commerce was great, so much so that Congress renounced Non-Intercourse (May 1810). Washington thenceforth allowed merchants and ship masters to resume business with all sides (Macon's Bill No. 2). Finally, Napoleon offered in May 1810 to suspend the French blockade of the United States in exchange for Britain's revoking the Orders in Council. Madison afterwards (November 1810) accepted the French claim – false in the event – that Napoleon had revoked his edicts against US shipping. Congress, thereafter, declared that Non-Intercourse with Britain would recommence unless Prime Minster Spencer Perceval discarded the Orders in Council by February 1811. The British did comply in June 1812, after the murder of Perceval and under pressure from Whigs and squeezed manufacturers. This action, though, came too late to influence either Madison's renewal of trade restrictions against Britain (March 1811) or Congress's deliberations on the merits of war.

Congressional hotheads, such as Representative John C. Calhoun (Republican, South Carolina), thought in June 1812 that justice required a declaration of war jointly on France and Great Britain: both nations had sorely tried US patience. "The Devil himself could not tell [whether] England or France is the most wicked," said an exasperated Representative Nathaniel Macon (Republican, North Carolina). Secretary of the Treasury Albert Gallatin, albeit against making war, vented disgust for the Anglo-French assaults on US honor and judged them equally intolerable.[11] A motion to declare war on both powers was barely defeated in the Senate, 18 to 14. Triangular war, its proponents argued, would have caused Paris and London – soon rather than later – to desist from their preying upon US shipping.

Irrespective of the absurdity of fighting Europe's preeminent powers simultaneously, the apparent symmetry between French and British practices was misleading, Madison taught. France was hardly blameless, he admitted in his war message, emphasized by the arrival of word (March 1812) that a French frigate had destroyed two US merchantmen bound for Spain.[12] But France still enjoyed the sentimental affection of many citizens for its aid during the War of Independence and 1789 republican revolution, while Britain defended Europe's monarchical status quo. The greater weight of horrid play, in any case, lay upon the British, according to Madison. They alone inflicted the singular insult to national sovereignty: kidnapping of American sailors. Only British warships cruised imperiously along the coast. They had, as in the *Chesapeake–Leopard* engagement (June 1807), spilt American blood and removed crewmen near the US shoreline. Subsequent British diplomacy, aimed at amends and placing Anglo-US trade on a normal basis, struck Madison as done in bad faith, illustrated when Foreign Minister Canning repudiated (1809) agreements concluded by his conciliatory envoy to Washington, David Erskine. Secret British agents meanwhile scrutinized the extent of separatist feeling among New England Federalists and allegedly encouraged it. That was the logical reading of the sensational John Henry reports – of murky authenticity – obtained by Madison for $50,000 and submitted to Congress (March 1812) to embarrass his foes.[13] Finally, said the petitions of northwestern pioneers, the British stirred unrest among the Shawnees and other tribes, led by the Prophet and his brother Tecumseh. Their rampages were only temporally halted by William Henry Harrison's victory at Tippecanoe (November 7, 1811). None other than Jefferson, downplaying the idea that volatility along the frontier stemmed from spreading westward settlement, charged the British with corrupting the otherwise contented Indians, then turning them against the United States.[14]

The following opinions broached by military advisors and militants in his party also swayed Madison. Calhoun, Speaker of the House Henry Clay (Kentucky), and Representative Felix Grundy (Tennessee) allowed that even if a similarity existed between French and British disdain for US strength, only one country lay within striking distance. In the absence of a potent naval force neither the French nor British mainlands could be touched. Yet sparsely populated Canada (half a million widely dispersed souls) sat within marching range of American armies, obtainable from a population of 7.2 million people. Canada's capture could be used as leverage against Great Britain to respect US maritime rights. Conquest would help eliminate the Indian nuisance. If warranted by events, Canada – blessed by its fur trade, timber resources, fisheries – could be incorporated into the United States. The Americans could also strike south against Britain's ally Spain, vulnerable in eastern Florida (the western chunk already occupied by the United States in 1810). No comparable French prizes were reachable by US arms. Distracted by the contest against France, Great Britain presumably could not spare many soldiers, ships, or *matériel* to protect Canada or buttress Spanish Florida. The prospect for satisfactory outcome, then, seemed obvious: overextended Britain, spread from the West Indies to India, could not mobilize decisive force against the Americans.[15]

Madison proclaimed war on June 18 following secret congressional debates (which satisfied Napoleon's pet hope that the United States would involve itself in open conflict with Britain). The House vote on June 4 in favor of war counted 79 to 49. The Senate vote two weeks later was closer, 19 in support of war to 13 opposed. The regional and party divide was glaring. Only two of ten New England senators voted affirmatively. Just a handful of men from New York voted in favor. Overall, 49 of the House's negative votes came from the northeast while a majority of southerners and westerners endorsed the war resolution. Not one Federalist of the 40 that cast ballots voted for it. Only a smattering of

Republicans voted against war, although a quarter of them abstained. A generational shading also marked the vote. Younger men, under forty years, craved action and derided what they saw as plodding diplomacy. The 24-year-old Representative William King (Republican, North Carolina) exclaimed in youthful bravado: "Forbearance has ceased to be a virtue . . . We shall take Canada. Yes, sir, by force; by valor."[16]

To summarize, Canada was neither the cause nor the aim of Congress's declaring war. The cause lay with tangible British injuries to the United States. The aim was to compel the hereditary enemy to treat the Americans on the basis of equality, from which lesson other European nations – especially France – should also draw useful lesson. Yet Canada riveted US attention. Successful northern campaigns would amount to defensive expansion, a prospect that prompted pro-war congressmen to devise plans for creating new states out of Canadian provinces. Their conquest could also be used to make Britain end the war on satisfactory terms, as warhawks tirelessly reiterated. Madison, himself, was lucid on the subject of Canada's value to Great Britain as producer of lumber (vital to the Royal Navy, denied access to traditional sources in Europe), furs, and foodstuffs harvested on land and at sea. Security in the northwest, moreover, would be advanced by eliminating the Canadian sanctuaries of Indians and breaking the Anglo-aboriginal alliance. "We shall drive the British from our Continent," predicted Grundy. "They will no longer have an opportunity of intriguing with our Indian neighbors, and setting on the ruthless savage to tomahawk our women and children."[17] A final dividend, said war enthusiasts, would be a halt to illegal trade along the Canadian–American frontier, a depressing habit deleterious to federal authority.

Few people were more avid than Jefferson for invading Canada. He maintained that Anglo-US peace required Britain's surrender of the northland: "The infamous intrigues of Great Britain to destroy our government . . . and with the Indians to [endanger US lives and property], prove that the cession of Canada, their fulcrum for these Machiavellian levers, must be a *sine qua non* at a treaty of peace." Even after the struggle ended, with Canada firmly in Britain's protective grip, Jefferson hoped for a future when Americans would gain the provinces. He had previously made this confident wager: "The acquisition of Canada this year [1812], as far as the neighborhood of Quebec, will be a mere matter of marching." Clay too had boasted; Kentucky's militia alone could seize Montreal and Upper Canada. And Calhoun foresaw this certainty: Canada would be a US possession within four weeks of war's commencement. This path of conquest would be eased, Hezekiah Niles editorialized in his *Weekly Register*, by the presence of disaffected US emigrants and Frenchmen.

They would surely cooperate against their British overlords in a US-led war of liberation. Secretary of War William Eustis held that the unfortunate Americans and Frenchmen in Canada would rise as a single body to topple British tyranny.[18]

Unluckily for US arms nothing like a fifth column emerged in Canada to assist the three attempted invasions. Loyalist refugees from the 1776 revolution and the descendants of original French settlers were oblivious to the siren call of American democracy. Case in point was the legendary heroine and Canadian patriot Laura Ingersoll Secord (1775–1868), who hailed from Massachusetts. She is credited in tradition with delivering warning – after trekking twenty miles across forbidding terrain – to British Lieutenant James FitzGibbon, a feat that led to the repulse of US forces at Beaver Dams (June 1813). Secord's soldier-husband, whom she saved from US execution after his capture at the battle of Queenston Heights (October 1812), came from Loyalist stock.[19] Britain's Indian allies also proved steadfast. Tecumseh served with the rank of brigadier in the British army.[20] He fought bravely against the Americans – some admired him – before his death in battle at the Thames (October 1813).

Not only did Canada withstand all assaults but US defeats elsewhere were depressing. They raised questions about the absence of skilled generalship and soldiery.[21] The surprised garrison at Fort Michilimackinac in Michigan surrendered in mid-July 1812. General William Hull surrendered the entire Detroit garrison (August 1812) to a British–Indian force inferior to his own in numbers and supplies. Fort Dearborn (Chicago) was abandoned at roughly the same time by US forces. The retreating column, with women and children in train, was mauled by Potawatomi warriors allied to the British. Dazed survivors were later ransomed. Horrors were visited on American prisoners after the River Raisin battle (January 1813). The British officer in charge, Colonel Henry Procter, watched passively as drunken braves killed defenseless captives. At least 350 Americans at Fort Mims near Mobile were killed or injured in an attack (August 1813) by Upper Creek (Red Stick) warriors, aligned with Spain and Britain.[22] British soldiers late in 1813, led by Major General Phineas Riall, burned the village of Buffalo in New York. His Indian allies scalped a dozen civilians.

His Majesty's forces redoubled efforts against the United States after Napoleon collapsed in Europe. The idea was to render such a thrashing that Washington would never again think that it could side against London with impunity. John Wilson Croker, secretary to the Admiralty, wrote darkly: "Let [America] beware how she raises her parricidal hand against the parent country." Sir Walter Scott echoed the sentiment, when he advised that it was Britain's "business to give them [the Americans] a fearful momento that the babe unborn should have remembered."[23] Ministers entertained the idea of dispatching Wellington to wage punitive campaigns against the upstart republic. Thousands of veterans of the Peninsular War were sent to North America, where they saw action, but Wellington managed to avoid New World assignment. He thought it a diversion from the main business in Europe. The pace of British sea-borne marauding along the coast, meanwhile, did increase, including against New England (previously spared London's wrath). Parts of eastern Maine were occupied. Adult males had to take an oath of allegiance to King George. The British naval blockade against Atlantic and Gulf ports – extending all the way to the Mississippi – became more stringent, despite the US navy's plucky skirmishing. The national economy approached ruin while illicit trade with the enemy intensified along the New England–Canadian frontier. American morale was devastated when in August 1814 British forces operating in the Chesapeake region, commanded by General Robert Ross and Admiral Alexander Cochrane, captured Washington after scattering feeble resistance by local militias. The executive mansion was desecrated. Government buildings throughout the capital were torched, supposedly to answer similar indignities perpetrated by Americans in Canada at Newark (Niagara-on-the-Lake) and York (Toronto). To Madison and his party, this Washington fiasco confirmed British barbarism. "It was reserved for England," Jefferson fumed, "to show that Bonaparte, in atrocity, was an infant to their ministers and their generals."[24] Even New York's Senator Rufus King – his wont was to call Madison an imbecile – denounced the destruction of public property. Britain's depraved action, "contrary to the usage of modern war," obliged him to support a military policy.[25]

Madison fled with his entourage just before the capital fell. He sought refuge in the Maryland–Virginia neighborhood, lest his capture by roaming redcoats add to disaster. Federalists called this flight ignominious. Representative Daniel Webster labeled Madison a "faint-hearted, lily-livered runaway." Senator King noted laconically: "The General Government has deserted its duties."[26]

The British in their southern operations also detached slaves from their masters. Of the freed – numbering around 3,600 – some took up arms against the United States and were drilled by British officers. They provided weapons and ammunition along with asylum.[27] This with other setbacks dampened, if briefly, Jefferson's ardor for Canada. He suggested in October 1814: "We must prepare for interminable war."[28]

The explanation for American mishaps is twofold, centered on British assets and US military–political deficiencies. Concerning the former, despite commitments borne by the British navy and army against

France, plus soaring treasury costs, Lord Liverpool's government mobilized enough force against the pesky Americans to protect Canada in the war's first phase while mounting harassing operations along the seaboard. After Napoleon's defeat gave London a freer hand, it drew deeply from the regular army and militia. They totaled 370,000 men in 1812. British land forces in Canada on the eve of war had numbered merely 8,100 (excluding their Indian supplement). But their naval bridge to Britain, carrying a reliable supply of reinforcements and *matériel*, was never in jeopardy. Finally, although London kept better generals in Europe for fighting Napoleon, those sent to North America were a good match for – usually better than – their US counterparts (exceptions being Generals Jacob Brown and Andrew Jackson). As for the US army, not only was the quality of leadership wildly uneven. But also the lower ranks were not properly filled. Madison's government commanded only 6,000 regular troops when war was declared and never fielded an army of the size stipulated by Congress. Rather, the gap remained substantial between authorized men under arms and actual numbers. In early 1814, as the war showed no sign of abating or taking a favorable turn, the regular army's enrollment (30,000) stood at practically half its authorized strength (58,250). Bounties for enlistment and promises of public land to each soldier (320 acres in 1814) proved poor incentive to fill army rosters.[29] As for state militias, they were typically less well trained than regular army units. Militia officers were often reluctant to relinquish command to regular officers or obey their orders. These problems were compounded by the unwillingness of various militias to cross into Canada for offensive action. The governors of Connecticut and Massachusetts refused in 1812 to put their militias under federal authority or to furnish troops for even defensive operations along the Canadian frontier.

The chronic shortage of dependable US soldiers was evident at New Orleans. General Jackson gratefully received the aid of free blacks, black slaves, and Jean Laffite's buccaneers to complement his thin ranks. Jackson later publicly acknowledged this exotic muster, implying that without it the battle might have gone quite differently. The buccaneers, incidentally, were granted pardon for their previous misdeeds by Madison in recognition of their timely assistance at New Orleans. Black survivors were less celebrated; they were forbidden from marching in victory parades.[30]

The administration's wobbly leadership also hurt the war effort. Madison, never robust, was frail by the time he became president at fifty-eight and thereafter subject to bouts of serious illness. Worse still, he was, in one scholar's understatement, "an inept manager of men."[31] His divided cabinet was infested with marplots, some of whom detested the president (and he reciprocated). Resignations plagued it. The cabinet deserved the scorn heaped upon it by historians. Henry Adams rated Madison's cabinet "the least satisfactory." Its principal secretaries – Robert Smith (State), William Eustis (War), and Paul Hamilton (Navy) – were at one time arrayed against the only competent minister in their company, Gallatin of Treasury.[32] James Monroe replaced Smith in April 1811, but too late to cleanse what had become a noxious cabinet culture (emphasized by Monroe's clashes with John Armstrong, appointed secretary of war in 1813). Gallatin, an object of unmitigated animosity, gladly relinquished his portfolio in 1813 to begin a career as diplomat in the less treacherous environment of European courts.[33]

This shambles at the nerve center of government radiated throughout the country. Republican mavericks and Federalists in Congress attacked Madison's unsteady prosecution of the war. They exhibited even less sympathy for the president after Washington was torched. New Englanders seethed as their trade with British territories (Canada, the West Indies) became outlawed, but still conducted profitable clandestine business with the enemy. Sir George Prevost estimated in August 1814, while preparing his army in Canada for offensive against Plattsburg, that two-thirds of his forces subsisted on beef provided by US contractors. Tidy sums of New England specie also made their way northward.[34]

New England banks manifested slight confidence in Washington's authority. They denied specie payments to the hard up administration whose treasury admitted bankruptcy in late summer 1814. Discontent in New England peaked after the region, virtually unprotected by federal troops, was targeted by British warships and armies. Talk of disunion flared as the local economy tumbled; people like Timothy Pickering again played a part. At the behest of the Massachusett legislature, the Hartford Convention convened (December 15, 1814–January 5, 1815), where representatives from every New England state examined anew the region's relations to Washington. Conferees remarked lengthily upon the continuing baleful effects of the "Virginia dynasty." Amendments to the Constitution were recommended to reduce southern preponderance, break Virginia's lock on the presidency, and raise the bar against both war and the admission of new states. These proposed measures could not satisfy secessionist sentiment and were meant by the convention's twenty-six delegates to defuse it.[35] Yet the very holding of such a meeting in the midst of war, and in secret sessions, abetted the spread of rumor. Madison viewed the commissioning by Massachusetts Governor Caleb Strong of three emissaries, most prominently Harrison Gray Otis, to Washington to plead the Hartford cause as proof of New England's rebelliousness. Madison prepared to squelch attempts by New England to make a separate peace with Britain – if necessary via a campaign by US regulars against a coalition of New England militias and redcoats. To the president, who had earlier bewailed "the seditious opposition" emanating from Massachusetts and Connecticut, New England's misconduct by late 1814 constituted "our greatest difficult[y] in carrying on the war, as it certainly is the greatest . . . inducement with the enemy to persevere."[36]

The US war was not a total calamity, despite multiple handicaps that plagued national policy. American land forces occasionally performed well. General James Wilkinson, for example, made the Spanish garrison at Mobile surrender and evacuate (April 1813). Harrison routed an Anglo-Indian force at the Thames in Canada. Andrew Jackson's Georgia and Tennessee volunteers, with the 39th US Infantry, annihilated a Red Stick force at the appalling battle of Horseshoe Bend (March 1814). It permitted the cession of twenty-three million acres of Creek territory in southern Georgia and future Alabama to the United States (Treaty of Fort Jackson, August 1814). Jacob Brown's army of 2,100 inflicted high casualties in its tangle with a larger British army at Lundy's Lane (July 1814). The British assault against Baltimore was confounded (September 1814). The navy also showed to advantage in single-ship engagements, as with USS *Constitution* versus HMS *Guerriere* (August 1812). Such encounters did not alter the naval imbalance or dent the British blockade of ports. But these occasional triumphs boosted US spirits. Victories at sea had the effect, too, of turning the Republican party away from its accustomed antipathy to a position that favored naval building. American fortunes were advanced too in fresh water fighting, when Captain Oliver Hazard Perry's ships prevailed in Lake Erie (September 1813), as did Thomas Macdonough's on Lake Champlain (September 1814). This second victory helped abort the British invasion of New York and forced Prevost's army back to Canada. Two months after the peace treaty at Ghent was signed (December 24, 1814), unbeknownst to crews at sea, *Constitution* defeated and captured two British vessels (*Cyane* and *Levant*) off the African coast.

The most spectacular defeat of British arms, at New Orleans (January 8, 1815), also occurred after American and British signatures were affixed to the Ghent documents. Naturally, the battle's outcome had no impact on the treaty's provisions, which upheld the *status quo ante bellum*. Jackson's victory, though, fueled the myth that the war had not been futile. The battle also made the Hartford exercise irrelevant and placed its envoys to Washington in an untenable situation. They suddenly seemed reprehensible or downright silly. News of the battle arrived simultaneously in Washington with the documents and reports from Ghent. They announced that the peace commissioners – Adams, Gallatin,

Clay, seasoned diplomat Jonathan Russell, Senator James Bayard of Maryland – had struck a deal with their British counterparts. It culminated negotiations traceable to Czar Alexander's offer of mediation in September 1812 (spurned by London) and running hard from August 1814 to Yuletide. The Senate immediately approved the treaty. Hostilities officially ended with the Anglo-US exchange of ratifications in mid-February 1815.

Little in the treaty cheered the original warhawks. It did not contain a renunciation of impressment or uphold neutral rights. The treaty did not satisfy US demands for losses of seaborne property or ships seized by the Royal Navy. British power in Canada remained intact. Provisions to evacuate elements of the British army policing territory in Maine and pledges to restore slaves to their owners were unexceptional, as were the terms on sharing fisheries and settling future boundary disputes. Still, the treaty contained nothing overtly damaging to US interests. It was in this sense better than America's military performance warranted. The thorny question of impressment anyway became moot with the end of Napoleonic fighting. Those people in Liverpool's cabinet who had wanted to punish US impudence for striking Britain, when grappling with France in mortal combat, also acknowledged the benefits of peace. The financial burden involved in fighting Napoleon for long years also argued for calm with the Americans; the public debt exceeded £840 million in 1815. Naval combat, yielding a higher loss of British merchant ships to US privateers than anticipated, additionally favored peace, no matter how disappointing to the spirit of retribution. Jefferson could exult if he wanted, as in June 1815: "[Britain] has found that we can do her more injury than any other country on earth, and henceforward will better estimate the value of our peace." In truth, however, the United States had narrowly escaped severe chastisement. British preoccupation with Europe – obvious in Castlereagh's Viennese chores – had bought the Yankees a reprieve. It did not deliver them from London's reach, palpable in the postwar renovation of forts and harbors in Canada.[37]

Against war

Varieties of discontent within the responsible class were exemplified by the wartime careers of four men: the cabinet's Gallatin and Congress's Josiah Quincy, John Randolph, and Daniel Webster. Two were Republicans: Gallatin, Randolph. Two were Federalists: Quincy, Webster. One was a southerner: Randolph. Two were New Englanders: Quincy, Webster. One was European-born (Switzerland) whose American life was tied to Pennsylvania: Gallatin. None of these men was old in 1812. They belonged to the same cohort – except Gallatin – as the warhawks. Gallatin, senior in this context, was born in 1761. Quincy and Randolph were in early middle age in 1812 – born 1772 and 1773, respectively. Webster was a youngster, born 1782. All four men were ambitious for themselves and their nation.

Republicans

A review of Gallatin and Randolph helps underscore the scope of Republican opposition to Madison's war policy while also showing the range of strategies available to dissenters. Subtlety was indicated in the cabinet. The House, then the more dynamic congressional chamber, permitted flamboyance.

Gallatin breathed circumspection. Party fealty, loyalty to Madison, and cabinet office muted his objection to such extent that he is seldom counted by historians among the 1812 dissenters. Yet he was hugely skeptical. He foresaw well before hostilities that war would wound the United States.[38] He proved subsequently to be more effective in ending the violence than were the overtly critical Randolph, Quincy, or Webster.

Gallatin was aristocratic by comportment. His aesthetic outlook was refined. He harbored some attachment for the House of Bourbon. Born, reared, and educated in Geneva, this patrician enjoyed few points of cultural contact with his homespun neighbors in western Pennsylvania. He flinched from unctuous lawyers and grasping businessmen. The latter he feared might overrun the United States. He enjoined his son not to sully the family name that for centuries had avoided stain by corruption or greed.[39]

Despite this bundle of privilege and prejudice, Gallatin was philosophically a democrat. His commitments drove him to America in 1780. They fed his dislike of slavery. They quickened his support of educational reform. They caused him in 1823 to advocate naval intervention on Greece's behalf against Ottoman rule. They excited his friendly interest in Indian cultures and inspired his ethnological study.[40]

Gallatin pegged his career to the fortunes of Jefferson's party. The Pennsylvania legislature, where he represented Fayette County, elected him to the Senate in 1793 after he helped defuse the Whiskey Rebellion. Voters then sent him to the House of Representatives, serving from 1795–1801. He was acclaimed there for his knowledge of finance and opposition to the "quasi-war" with France. Republicans also lauded his hostility to the Alien and Sedition laws. Furthermore, Jefferson appreciated him for endorsing his candidacy against Burr in 1800 and subsequently selected Gallatin for the Treasury post. He sought in that capacity (1801–1814) to reduce the public debt – $80 million – by strict economy and curbing defense expenditure.

Gallatin early revealed independence of mind as Treasury secretary. He deviated from Republican orthodoxy and shared with his predecessor, Alexander Hamilton, an affinity for manufactures, federal sponsorship of domestic improvements (the Cumberland Road), and establishment of a strong banking system.[41] This last item clinched Gallatin's support for the Bank of the United States, excoriated by most Jeffersonians as the repository of evil. One conservative admirer of Gallatin, Henry Cabot Lodge, later judged that the secretary had been a Federalist in all but name.[42]

Gallatin disliked the 1807 Embargo Act. He enforced it reluctantly. He felt that the alternative was war for which the United States was woefully unprepared. In this spirit, he persuaded Jefferson (1807) and Madison (1811) to modify bellicose language in their statements to Congress on British depredations on the high seas. Gallatin guessed, not inaccurately, that about fifty percent of sailors on US merchant ships were British subjects, deserted from His Majesty's service.[43] He told Congress and cabinet ministers in late 1811, as the drift toward war accelerated, that revenues to meet the costs of military preparation would have to be gotten by unpopular means: raising import duties, levying internal taxes ($5 million), and securing hefty loans (initially for $1.2 million at 8 percent, two points above the legal rate). Otherwise, he claimed, the Treasury's patiently tended surplus of $5.5 million would turn to deficit. This candor caused Senator William Branch Giles (Republican, Virginia) to retort that a clever financier, possessing patriotic grit, could devise ways to safeguard US security without imposing undue hardship. Did Gallatin want to scuttle manly policy by inciting fear of bankruptcy? The Republican press assailed him when he later delivered a detailed report to the House Ways and Means Committee on the discipline needed to pay for army enlistments and supplies. "The rat in the treasury" evidently put reduction of public debt above national honor. William Duane, editor of Philadelphia's *Aurora General Advertiser*, suggested that Gallatin had – in cahoots with British agents in Washington – miscalculated and inflated the projected cost of war.[44]

Gallatin, against his better judgment, labeled the war "unavoidable." This cautious language soothed his conscience on the wisdom of war and justified his decision to stay in the cabinet.[45] He devoutly hoped that the fighting would be brief. Yet he was shocked in the event by that administrative sluggishness, army blundering, and sectional bickering that hindered the war. He confided to Jefferson in late 1812: "The series of misfortunes experienced this year in our military land operations exceeds all anticipation made even by those who had least confidence in our inexperienced officers and undisciplined men."[46]

Gallatin never gave up, though, and surmounted his worst doubts. He retained a touching faith in the ability of his compatriots to weather their many defeats. He labored during the remainder of his Treasury tenure to fund the war and position the United States for a rapid recovery. He secured loans of $16 million for the government – from John Jacob Astor, Stephen Girard, David Parish – that allowed it to continue the war at a time when federal reserves were depleted. Nor did Gallatin hesitate to overstep departmental lines to invigorate the war effort. He offered advice on military strategy. He suggested reforms to rescue the army's general staff and tried to improve naval management.[47]

His most important contribution sprang from this unblinking clarity: war was a bad bet. Hostilities could not end too quickly. He successfully lobbied Madison for assignment to Russia in response to Alexander's mediation offer. Before this initiative finally withered, Gallatin had spent idle months waiting at St. Petersburg. He then accepted with alacrity appointment (1814) to the peace commission to negotiate with British envoys. He established himself as the leading figure on the five-man team, no mean feat in the company of Clay and John Quincy Adams. Gallatin calmed the storms stirred by the two luminaries, who represented regional interests with little in common (New England in fisheries, the west in Indians and the Mississippi). He never lost his compusure in the midst of excruciating negotiations. He rallied the commission as London's delegates, an unprepossessing lot, pressed the advantage won by British arms.[48] At their zenith in August 1814, they gave London's diplomats this latitude: to refrain from discussing impressment; to push for revision of the Canadian–US border to Washington's detriment; to demand that the Old Northwest (Ohio, Indiana, Illinois, Wisconsin, Michigan) be returned to Indian ownership, thereby securing a buffer zone and fur rich territory; to insist that all military installations on the Great Lakes be placed under London's control and British ships allowed to navigate the Mississippi river; to acquire parts of Maine to secure a Halifax–Quebec land bridge.[49] Gallatin inspirited the American commission against this punitiveness. If realized, it would have reduced the United States to semi-colonial status.

His perseverance was rewarded by the Christmas Eve agreement which affirmed the prewar status quo. Henry Adams's verdict still stands as apt recognition of Gallatin's salvaging operation: "The treaty of Ghent was the . . . work and peculiar triumph of Mr. Gallatin."[50]

No Republican dissenter contrasted more sharply with Gallatin than Randolph of Virginia. The former was meticulous, modest, self-contained. The latter was loquacious and extravagant. A fabled eccentric, he ended his years emotionally disordered. Gallatin was broad in outlook and cosmopolitan by experience, Randolph militantly provincial. Gallatin adjusted his Republican preferences to evolving security desiderata and came to realize that the United States required a robust navy. Randolph clung to what he cherished as Republican principles of agrarian democracy, from which Jefferson and Madison had shamefully departed. Gallatin was tactful in opposition and tenacious in achieving an acceptable peace. Randolph breezily challenged party pilots, but was useless in acquiring US respite from war. He satisfied only his romantic attachment to stances of lonely opposition.[51]

Randolph as leader of the "Quids," disillusioned southern Republicans, charged well before 1812 that party leaders had betrayed their first principles: a commitment to unobtrusive federal authority; to limited presidential power and patronage; to treasury surplus without taxation; to the primacy of agricultural economy; to individual prerogative and taste unencumbered by onerous military obligation. Jefferson et al., according to this indictment, had been knocked dizzy by the pomposity of empire. They had renounced the intimacy and dignity of authentic republicanism. Randolph on this last point rued the day, when, as a Jefferson-idolizing congressman, he had worked to obtain France's Louisiana. Jeffersonian chicanery manifest in the Yazoo land fraud in 1805 was one early bit of damning evidence to Randolph. He was later incensed by the administration's attempt to buy Florida and then by the non-importation law as it could lead the nation to war. He was in open revolt by the time Jefferson bequeathed power to Madison. Against them both, Randolph used oratory dripping with venom. Of the purported wisdom of war in 1812, he saw none.

He made numerous points during Congress's deliberations, beginning with an amplification of Gallatin's concern that the country was unready. Randolph expressed this amazement: "Go to war without money, without men, without a navy! ... The people will not believe it!"[52] Speculators, contractors, and a handful of wily merchants might profit from an anti-British show, he said. The majority of Americans, however, would suffer by the flow of their blood and taxes. The owner of nearly four hundred slaves, he added that a commencement of hostilities posed special problems to the south. The spread of "infernal" French ideas loosed by the 1789 deluge had disturbed the once contented slaves. They had become restive and could be manipulated by foreign armies: "God forbid ... that the southern States should ever see an enemy on their shores, with these [wicked] principles of French fraternity in the van. While talking of taking Canada, some of us are shuddering for our own safety at home ... [The] night-bell never tolls for fire in Richmond, that the mother does not hug the infant more closely to her bosom."[53]

On the subject of Canada, Randolph condemned invasion as ignoble. It shifted the United States to the side of aggression: "In the eye of heaven, we [Americans] must appear like so many descendants of Cain, seeking to imbrue our hands in our brothers' blood!"[54] The Constitution forbade wars of conquest, Randolph asserted, and if so abused would shred the fine weave of republicanism. As the first march on Canada was being planned, he predicted that the campaign would fail because it rested on injustice and the unwarranted assumption that Canadians looked southward for deliverance. He reasoned too that if Canada fell to US armies, British power would not be reduced an iota, having forfeited only the "frozen deserts of Labrador." Britain from indignation would besiege the Atlantic seaboard, however. He mentioned in prescient warning the exposed recesses of the Chesapeake.[55]

Randolph also argued that Madison's war had put the United States on the wrong side of history. He used apocalyptic language: on the outcome of Napoleon versus Britain hung humanity's hopes. Previously they had barely survived hard battles against savagery. If unchecked, Madisonian miscreants would unsettle the balance of good versus evil to despotism's everlasting satisfaction. British actions against US shipping, however bad, simply did not match France for despicableness. This central reality dwarfed all others: London's war against Napoleon was synonymous with a hopeful future. Reason opposed the creating of extra difficulties for liberty's champion. A disconsolate Randolph exclaimed during the final phase of congressional debate:

And shall republicans become the instruments of him who has effaced the title of Attila to the 'scourge of God!' Yet, even Attila, in the falling fortunes of civilization, had, no doubt, his advocates, his tools, his minions, his parasites, in the very countries that he overran – sons of that soil whereon his horses had trod, where grass could never after grow. If perfectly fresh instead of being as I am – my memory clouded, my intellect stupefied, my strength and spirits exhausted – I could not give utterance to that strong detestation which I feel toward (above all other works of the creation) such characters as Zingis, Tamerlane, Kouli Khan, or Bonaparte. My instincts involuntarily revolt at their bare idea – malefactors of the human race, who ground down man to a mere machine of their impious and bloody ambition. Yet, under all the accumulated wrongs, and insults, and robberies of the last of these chieftains, are we not, in point of fact, about to become a party to his views, a partner in his wars?[56]

Randolph also urged restraint toward Britain as that country was the source of American civilization. The tongue spoken in the United States, the Protestant versions of Christianity observed by citizens, the laws, political institutions, and philosophical orientation of Americans were all heir to British legacy. France was quite another matter: Latin, historically

Catholic, now tyrannical. War against Britain amounted not only to alliance with France, he charged, but constituted a type of US suicide.[57]

Opposition to the 1812 war cost Randolph dearly. He lost reelection to the House in 1813 (but recovered it in 1815). Republicans damned him as pro-British sympathizer, defeatist, and spy. The *Richmond Enquirer* designated him a dangerous "nuisance."[58]

He repaired to his plantation at Roanoke during his time out of office. There he monitored the war's unfolding, suffered personal tragedy (a beloved nephew succumbed to dementia, another to consumption), and coped with near destitution related to crop failures. These misfortunes drove him into intense religiosity.[59] Still, he continued to track the war. Only after the capture of Washington did he cool his criticism of the administration. He served briefly too in the Virginia militia, when a British invasion of the state seemed likely. When that threat faded, as the British switched their attention to Baltimore, Randolph returned to Roanoke to await the war's climax. He did fret also on learning of the Hartford Convention, praying that New England Federalism ("the school of Arnold") would not disunite the republic: "It belongs to New England to say . . . whether she will dwindle into that state of insignificant, nominal independence, which is the precarious curse of the minor kingdoms of Europe."[60]

Federalists

Randolph possessed few friends, cut off as he was from humankind by doleful humor and imposing oddity. Yet he did forge a bond with Josiah Quincy, representative from Massachusetts during 1805–1813. Outwardly, the two men had little in common. They normally would not have met. They became acquainted only by virtue of their overlapping terms in Congress. Quincy once confessed: "I had no predilection for John Randolph."[61]

In contrast with Randolph's brand of democracy, Quincy adhered to "the good cause" (Federalism).[62] He had defended the Alien and Sedition Acts. He had opposed the Louisiana Purchase. He later worked against the creating of new states therein, predicting that they would invite national dissolution.[63] He harbored abiding suspicion of the Virginia clique. He resented the diminution of New England's standing. He despaired in 1814 of the Hartford Convention as deficient in daring. His flirtation with secessionism pivoted on what he saw as the south's lockhold on political life.[64]

The profoundest difference between Quincy and Randolph related to the slavery question. Roanoke plantation depended on the unceasing toil of slaves, a plain evil to the mind of Randolph but necessary. His much-disputed will allowed for the manumission of his slaves, from whose number he counted several of his rare human attachments. But he never thought to part from slave services during his lifetime. Such equivocation on slavery staggered Quincy. He detested it. The institution degraded white owners, he alleged, tangible in the south's mulatto population. It contributed additional slaves and instances of manacled offspring serving their white sires, as at Montecello. Quincy's concept of a divinely mandated moral order left no room for bondage: "The African is as much entitled to be protected in the rights of humanity as any other portion of the human race."[65]

Despite these obstacles to sympathetic understanding, Quincy and Randolph became close. They were foremost in the Federalist–Quid alliance, founded in opposition to the Jefferson–Madison combination. This "cabal" employed suspect foreigners (i.e. Gallatin). It bore responsibility for delivering the United States from tranquillity to heedless war in 1812 and deserved removal from office. Like Randolph, Quincy deemed the attempted capture of Canada for British ransom a piratical action. Like Randolph, he objected to a war that objectively aided Napoleon, the modern "Genghis Khan."[66]

Quincy also believed that the Virginia "dynasty," built upon human chattel and nourished by Napoleon's aid, might erect a military despotism. Overthrow of the US regime would presumably be led by Monroe, pretender to the Jefferson–Madison line. He possessed in early 1813 the portfolios for State and War. This crafty cabinet officer, whose army was waging a criminal northern campaign, had supposedly positioned himself to become president for life. "Whoever plants the American standard on the walls of Quebec conquers it for himself, and not for the people of these United States," Quincy told House colleagues. At the least, a US empire in Canada would leach its corrosive influence southward. This phenomenon would give rise to a domineering mentality antipathetic to republicanism. Apart from disruption to New England's commerce caused by the war, then, the region stood in a path of mortal danger:

Whoever lives to see [US conquest of Canada] will witness a dynasty established in that country by the sword. He will see a king or an emperor, dukedoms and earldoms and baronies distributed to the officers, and knights' fees bestowed on the soldiery. And such an army will not trouble itself about geographical lines in apportioning out the division of its new empire, and will run the parallels of its power by other steel than that of the compass. When that event happens, the people of New England, if they mean to be free, must have a force equal to defend themselves against such an army. And a military force equal to this object will itself be able to enslave the country.[67]

Quincy perceived the enlistment of minors in the regular army and subordination of state militias to Washington authority as first indications of trampling empire and militarism. "Corrupt not our youth," he pleaded. "Have compassion for the tears of parents."[68]

Unable to divert or reverse the course of war, Quincy quit Congress. He returned to Boston for the duration. Promptly elected to the Massachusetts Senate, he introduced a resolution that condemned the war as unjust and blasted Madison's bumbling. Because he had in contrived militancy previously supported defense appropriations – to taunt the administration, which he felt would only bluff at war – he was largely immune to charges of having neglected national security.[69] His claims to patriotism were also boosted by his taking a commission in the Boston Hussars, a sartorially splendid militia that bivouacked and paraded on the Boston Common (but participated in no fighting).[70] His running correspondence with Randolph on the war's miseries was gratifying to both men in their rustication. But Quincy, like his Virginia comrade, had to adjust to an uncomfortable position: life outside the main events.

Not so Daniel Webster. He continued the Quincy–Randolph resistance to the war as a freshman congressman (seated 1813) from New Hampshire.

His vocation as outspoken critic had its paradoxical side. He had no taste for dissent. Quincy was acerbic, resentful, prone to look for conspiracy. Randolph by his own admission was an idiosyncrasy. But Webster never viewed himself as belonging to that "school in which insurrection is taught as a virtue." He prized compromise over defiance.[71]

Still, he reviled the war from its start. This view arose from his legal–business involvements with New England's maritime economy and was reinforced by his attraction – vintage Federalism – to British culture. He also harbored a dislike of the Republican ascendancy. A lawyer-orator of New Hampshire renown, he first spoke against the war in a July 4th address to Portsmouth's Washington Benevolent Society in 1812. He soon afterward penned the Rockingham Memorial (signed by 1,500 citizens), the most definitive brief by New England Federalists against the war and laden with implicit disunion. Both statements contained familiar themes: the lack of commonality between New England Protestantism and republican institutions versus France of the pope, infidels, "and the most merciless tyranny that ever Heaven suffered to afflict mankind." Also elaborated upon were New England's distress since the 1807 Embargo, British impressment policy as insufficient reason for war and no fouler than French trespass upon US shipping, the absence of military preparedness, and southern domination of national politics and cavalier attitude toward northern needs. Regarding the risk of future fracture, Webster wrote in the Rockingham Memorial:

We shrink from the separation of the states, as an event fraught with incalculable evils, and it is among our strongest objections to the present course of measures, that they have, in our opinion, a very dangerous and alarming bearing on such an event. If a separation of the states ever should take place, it will be, on some occasion, when one portion of the country undertakes to control, to regulate, and to sacrifice the interest of another; when a small and heated majority in the Government, taking counsel of their passions, and not of their reason, contemptuously disregarding the interests, and perhaps stopping the mouths of a large and respectable minority, shall by ... ruinous measures, threaten to destroy essential rights; and lay waste the most important interests.[72]

Madison did not respond to the Rockingham Memorial, though New Hampshire's Governor William Plumer found disparaging words for it. In any case, it so caught the fancy of local Federalists that they nominated Webster at their October convention to run for the House of Representatives. He won as part of the Federalist sweep of New Hampshire's congressional delegation. Once in Washington, Webster made himself felt, and did so despite the Federalist–Republican imbalance (House: 68 versus 114, Senate: 10 versus 26). He ingratiated himself with the Federalist leadership, above all with Senator King whom he thought supremely eloquent. And Webster beset the administration.[73]

His first action was to introduce in June 1813 five resolutions of inquiry that he composed with Pickering (recently elected by Massachusetts voters to the House). They aimed ostensibly at determining how much – and when – Madison knew of Napoleon's supposed intention of lifting the Berlin and Milan decrees. The real aim of the resolutions was to embarrass Madison by suggesting that he had withheld crucial information from the British, lest they revoked the Orders in Council, thus eliminating Congress's pretext for declaring war. In other words, the public had been duped into waging gratuitous hostilities. The resolutions passed. Webster was chosen with Representative John Rhea (Republican, Tennessee) to present them in person to Madison, at the time stricken by fever. Unaware of the gravity of Madison's condition, and anyway gloating at what he imagined to be a telling blow on him, Webster crowed: "The President was in his bed, sick of a fever. His night cap on his head – his wife attending him &c &c. I think he will find *no relief* from my prescription." The government's July response (written by Monroe) to the inquiries amounted to evasion, dismissed by critics as Jesuitical.[74]

Subsequent speeches by Webster piled one attack after another on what he dubbed "poor Madison." Webster took him to task for stupidity on all fronts as the administration miscarried against Canada, neglected coastal defense, experimented with hasty tax schemes, and considered implementing conscription. On this last point, in the manner of Quincy, Webster asked rhetorically: "Where is it written in the Constitution, in what article or section is it contained, that you may take children from their parents ... and compel them to fight the battles of any war in which the folly or the wickedness of government may engage it?"[75] Conscription eventually failed as law in the Senate.

New Hampshire Federalists chose Webster in 1814 to head their American Peace Ticket, which again swept the state's congressional slate. On leave during Congress's summer break that year, Webster, as chairman of the Portsmouth safety committee, had time to coordinate municipal defenses against impending British assault. Under his authority, men were summoned to drill on the parade grounds. His appeal to the New Hampshire government resulted in its timely dispatch of troops to the port city to protect property and ships at berth. Persuaded that Madison had no interest in easing New England's plight and would not help local authorities repel British attacks, Webster took a keen interest in the Hartford Convention. He concluded that the federal government was so infirm that it would sink under the war's final blows. New England would necessarily have to look to its own devices for safety. In the meantime British forces were converging on New Orleans. "I have no doubt [they] will take it," Webster wrote to his brother in early January 1815. "If so, we get no peace."[76]

* * *

Unexpected results at New Orleans and the mildness of Ghent obscured America's near brush with major defeat. The so-called era of good feelings that followed softened domestic divisions. Recriminations dissolved into a comforting haze. It allowed even wartime dissenters to give a distorting gloss to events that had produced 2,000 US battlefield fatalities (many more maimed or dead from illness and overexposure), pushed the economy out of joint, and bared the depth of sectional jealousies while aggravating them.[77] Buoyed by assurances from his German friend, Alexander von Humboldt, that America would become a dynamic civilization, Gallatin in 1816 averred that the war had improved collective character: selfishness and regional pride had receded. Quincy, who had frequently called Monroe a dictator-in-the-making, entertained him at home in 1817, as the newly inaugurated president visited New England. Quincy and Madison also became reconciled.[78]

The war, though, had offered a spectacle of US statecraft gone wrong. Madison, the talented political theorist, proved wholly inadequate in emergency. His cabinet had almost disintegrated. European conservatives interpreted the US crisis as added proof of the common man's inability to discharge public affairs responsibly. The czar's envoy in Washington, Andre Dashkov, reported to his liege after the city's capture in 1814:

> Artisans, innkeepers, and even butchers demand to be deputies, generals, colonels, and so on, and their wishes are more or less granted, depending on their influence upon the votes of their neighbors. In the hands of people of this kind, who account for the indisputable majority of the votes of American citizens, are the foundations upon which the President is raised. He must constantly flatter them and blind their judgment with strategies of every kind . . . He will be the first victim of the inconstancy innate in every band of rabble.[79]

The war helped fix a disturbing pattern in US history: the felt needs of security have recurrently endangered democratic forbearance and eroded civility. The Federalist party, already much diminished since its halcyon days in the 1790s, was fatally victimized. Republican leaders effectively linked it in the public mind to dishonor, deceit, disunion. Propagandists charged Federalism with groveling before Great Britain. They misportrayed the Hartford Convention as secessionist plotting. Jefferson cursed the New England "incendiaries" and wished them to Hell.[80] Federalism did manage to linger as a political force in some northeastern locales until 1828. But it ceased to exist as a national party in 1816. It ran its last presidential candidate that year, Rufus King. He carried only Connecticut, Delaware, and Massachusetts.

Individual dissidents also fared badly. Madison hated their criticism and was censorious. Grundy lashed out against their "moral treason." Republican party bloods faulted Gallatin for want of patriotism. The same people plastered Randolph with epithets. Republicans called Webster a tool of the enemy. They wondered aloud whether he was on Britain's secret payroll. Bits of the smear stuck. He never entirely escaped in later years the suspicion that he had schemed with New England secessionists. His adversaries implied that the champion of "Liberty and Union, now and forever" lacked the bona fides to admonish southern nullifiers and regional loyalists. Even Quincy astride his white stallion, Bayard, and suited for maneuver with the Boston Hussars did not duck all charges of accepting "British gold."[81]

With allowances made for Gallatin, the dissenting band gave as good as it got. It talked loosely of Jacobins, whispering conspiracies, despots, and Madison as Jefferson's "political pimp." It celebrated Anglo-Russian victories over Napoleon and relished his demise, expecting that it would signal Madison's political extinction. Quincy and Webster also shared some positions held by crustier Federalists (Pickering, John Lowell), who saw the war as opportunity: defeat by Britain would so drain public confidence in the Republican party that Federalism would be catapulted to its rightful place as the governing party. Pickering relied on nautical metaphor in 1814: "Let the ship run aground. The shock will throw the present pilots overboard, and then competent navigators will get her once more afloat, and conduct her safely into port."[82]

None of the 1812 dissenters suffered permanent injury to their careers. Gallatin went from strength to strength as diplomat and financier. Randolph returned to the House where he emphatically defended southern interests. He also briefly served as minister to Russia in 1830. Quincy became a municipal court judge in Boston. He later won mayoral election. He then obtained the presidency of Harvard (1829–1845), itself a hotbed of antiwar sentiment in 1812. The postwar career of Webster as senator, Whig leader, defender of the Union, and secretary of state ensured his place in US annals.

Randolph, Quincy, and Webster were part of a larger function of which they were unaware. Their dissent became precedent for the unformed and raw country: the right even in wartime to challenge national policy – to oppose, accuse, question, and annoy. As for Gallatin, his distance from Republican war passion and attempt to tame it illustrates the dilemma of persons in high office at odds with prevailing policy. He promoted prudence against majority feeling: the United States surely had cause to make war in 1812, but lacked the extra disposable power to fight Britain and, therefore, should have abstained. When hostilities nevertheless began, he dutifully did what he could at Treasury to ensure US well-being. As dissident, he did not, contra shrill critics, try to sabotage the US war effort. Still, his major contribution to it sprang from his original skepticism, painfully validated by US reverses in 1812–1814. This blend of attitude and events defined the purpose of Gallatin's Ghent diplomacy and gave it zest. Edmund Burke once observed in another context but applicable to the wartime career of Gallatin: "The speculative line of demarcation where obedience ought to end and resistance must begin is faint, obscure, and not easily definable."[83] The speculative line on the appropriate means and instruments with which to resist is comparably fuzzy. Gallatin chose to retain his insider's position. He used it to end a policy whose risk and ruin he had foretold.

3   Greece

The 1789 French political earthquake produced aftershocks long after the 1812 War and Napoleon's later banishment to St. Helena. These included the continent-wide revolt in Latin America against Madrid's authority, triggered by French invasion of Spain in 1808. Washington fully acknowledged the success of this liberation, led by Simon Bolivar and Jose de San Martin, in a presidential statement on December 2, 1823 (subsequently christened the Monroe Doctrine).[1] Emperor Pedro I of Brazil had earlier declared independence from Portugal (1822), itself ruled since 1820 by a liberal constitution.

Moments of democratic-national intensity also flared during the twenties in Naples and Piedmont (1820–1821), Spain (1820–1823), and among Russian military officers imbued with French convictions, the Decembrists of 1825. Countervailing legitimacy – solemnized by the Treaty of Vienna, embodied in the Holy Alliance, powered by oppressive military engines – buried these projects in reaction.

The turbulent character of the 1820s was nowhere more apparent than in the ramshackle, polyglot, multireligious, ethnically diverse Ottoman empire. Its Egyptian and Syrian provinces were jolted by the Napoleonic commotion. French notions of liberty also reinforced impatience with Ottoman overlordship in the empire's European intelligentsia, particularly the Greek component.[2] The eminent Rigas Velestinlis composed a constitution, among other radical documents, suffused with French ideas for a future Hellenic republic. He translated the *Rights of Man* into Greek. He had hoped before his martyrdom in 1798 by agents of the Sublime Porte to consult with Napoleon.[3]

Eruption of the 1821 Greek independence war in the Danubian provinces (Wallachia, Moldavia) and the Peloponnesus (Morea) began a religious-ethnic conflict of exterminating fury. When it ended and a portion of Greece attained independence, confirmed in the 1830 London conference and protocols, the Peloponnesus had been purged of its Turkish inhabitants. Upwards of 20,000 Turks, to whom the Peloponnesus had been home for centuries, were killed by their Greek neighbors in the spring of 1821 following a declaration of holy war by Archbishop Germanos. All mosques were razed.[4] This uprsising provoked Turkish reprisal. It amounted to mass punishment by Sultan Mahmud II for what he saw as collective guilt. Ottoman authorities executed Patriarch Gregorios and other prominent Greek Orthodox clergy. Turkish armies in April 1822 overran the island of Chios, mythical birthplace of Homer and populated by 67,000 Greeks. Persons not murdered were sold into slavery. The Turkish–Egyptian siege of Missolonghi in Roumeli ended in April 1826 with the city's fall and slaying or enslavement of the residents. This war without clemency, punctuated by sadism and massacring on both sides, shaped Greek imagination for generations. Visions haunted Nikos Kazantzakis, who lived deep into the twentieth century: "All my grandfathers that had been murdered by the Turks, all my grandmothers whom the Turks had tortured by ripping off their breasts."[5] Famine worsened the effects of fighting in 1826–1827 and threatened to depopulate Greece by starvation.

Steeped in classical history, the public mind in western Europe pronounced Greece's rebellion magnificent. It melded the romance and exoticism of the Orient with promises of justice for the sons and daughters of legendary statesmen, poets, and philosophers. The war was additionally compelling as it pitted Christian Europeans against Islam – the cross versus the crescent, to use that locution of Professor Edward Everett, America's foremost philhellene.[6] Achilles, Pericles, Sophocles, Aristotle, Christ's disciples, and St. Paul were thus bundled into a cause that transcended backwater Greece of the 1820s. At stake was the vindication of western civilization. Percy Bysshe Shelley taught in 1821: "We are all Greeks. Our laws, our literature, our religion, our arts have their roots in Greece ... The modern Greek is the descendant of those glorious beings whom the imagination almost refuses to figure to itself as belonging to our kind."[7] Professors in Germany amid the Hellenic fervor focused lectures on the nursery of European culture. Eugène Delacroix portrayed the Greek passion in paintings, above all in his gripping *Massacre of Chios* and *Greece Expiring on the Ruins of Missolonghi*. The Marquis de Lafayette spoke eloquently in the Chamber of Deputies on the aims of Greek patriots, striving "to reconstruct their ancient country."[8]

Even as their governments temporized or maneuvered diplomatically, nearly a thousand young Europeans went to Greece to fight. They did so for a mix of motives: adventure, escape, the chance to merge one's little self with a good cause. The philhellene bunch also contained knockabout types: womanizers, duelists, reprobates. An American observer, otherwise sympathetic to Greece, termed the lot "crack-brained."[9] Germans, particularly university students, composed the largest contingent of phil-hellenes at more than 340. They were followed by French, then Italians, British, miscellaneous others. Many of these people became disillusioned when Greek reality contradicted their preconceptions. Poverty, vengeful-ness, and squabbling among rival chiefs, culminating in two internecine wars (1824–1825), made a hash of idealism centered on the claim: "We are all Greeks." Even their brand of Christianity bothered Protestants whose views were influenced by the small colony of Anglo-American missionaries in Greece. They tended to lump Orthodoxy with Roman Catholicism in the category of superstition and anathema. An American divine, Reverend Eli Smith, concluded after a Greek tour in the 1820s: "One characteristic of the clergy is ignorance ... The common clergy generally have their origin in the lowest classes of society, in such slight estimation is the sacred profession held."[10]

Disappointment fueled this suspicion. The lionized race of antiquity, endowed with golden limbs and elevated thoughts, seemed unrelated to the "poor curs" – an admixture of Slavs, Albanians, and sundry "lesser breeds" – who occupied Greece's landscape in the 1820s. Had rogues deserving Newgate detention displaced Plutarch's heroes?[11] The Greek kaleidoscope of political-military alliances that formed, dissolved, and pro-duced new ephemeral combinations equally disconcerted the philhellenes.

Most did not scurry home, however. A few made sizable military con-tributions to the Greek cause: Britain's Sir Richard Church and Admiral Thomas Cochrane, and the Bonapartist Colonel Charles Fabvier. A third of the philhellenes died in combat or, more often, from illness. The battle of Peta (July 1822) wiped out most of the Philhellene Battalion. Lord Byron died in April 1824 from fever at Missolonghi, where earlier he had established contact with Prince Alexandros Mavrokordatos, leader of local resistance and author of the independence proclamation. Byron's poetry, sprinkled with Greek imagery, became all the more dear to European audiences as in *Don Juan*: "I dreamed that Greece might still be free."[12]

The example of Byron in Greece appealed to literary minded American youths looking for worthy vocation. Upon finishing his printer's appren-ticeship, William Lloyd Garrison (b. 1805) hoped to take Byron's path to Greece. He composed some juvenile verse in Byronic rhythm. He never-theless decided to avoid the perils of sea travel and stayed in Massachusetts. Equally infatuated with Byron was Edgar Allan Poe (b. 1809). He invented a tale of his going to Greece to fight but getting waylaid in Russia, pure fiction that sneaked its way into various accounts of Poe's life. As a university student, Professor Everett (b. 1794) had met with Byron in London before the Balkans war began. From him Everett received not only doses of inspiration but also letters of introduction that he used in his 1818 Greek sojourn. The handful of Americans (between fifteen and twenty) who actually saw military action in Greece were also influenced by Byron. Dr. Samuel Gridley Howe and George Jarvis were cases in point. The verse, life, and legend of Byron intoxicated Howe, whose humanitarian career began as a soldier–doctor in Greece. Devotion to Byron helped him surmount bitterness on realizing that modern Greeks bore faint relation to his expectations: "one of the most disagreeable of all people in the world." Howe later softened this judgment by attributing Greek debasement to four centuries of Ottoman misrule. Byron's sacrifice, in any case, helped sustain him for years in dedicated service to Greece's revolution. He impoverished himself for it. He barely escaped violent death. The stalwart Jarvis – only thirty-one when he died from disease in Greece – cooperated closely with Byron at Missolonghi. Like Byron, Jarvis donned Greek garb. He served as Adjutant General of Byron's Brigade. He trained the troops.[13]

The cult of Byron reinforced US feeling for Greece, as ardent as in western Europe. Geographical distance did not obviate cultural allegiance, earlier evidenced when the constitutional convention had debated whether to adopt Greek as the official US language. American attitude was expressed too in the naming of towns after Greek places, not to mention the privileging of classical literature and languages in school curricula. As in Europe, charitable societies to support Greece's struggle proliferated in America of the 1820s: Charleston, Natchez, Albany, Cincinnati, Philadelphia, Baltimore, Boston, New York, Washington. They sent grants raised through subscriptions, celebrity lectures, concerts, and balls – $40,000 by late 1824 – to purported Greek leaders (too often jobbers who did not distribute the aid fairly). Non-perishable food items, medical supplies, and light weapons were also sent by these organizations. Money raised by college students came from Columbia, Brown, Yale, and elsewhere. Cadets at West Point collected $700 for Greek donation. Demonstrations and candlelight vigils were undertaken on behalf of Greek freedom. Women in New York erected an enormous cross on Brooklyn Heights in September 1823 with an inscription: "Sacred to the Cause of Greece." The frontier town of Ypsilanti in Michigan was named for Prince Alexandros Ypsilanti, who gained fame in the liberation war by organizing the luckless Wallachia–Moldavia expedition. Newspaper editors, clergymen, and professors also endorsed the Hellenic cause. They were often misled by the superficial resemblance between the 1776 insurrection and the Greek–Turkish war, seeing essential similarities where none existed. (The first was a republican revolt/ taxpayers' protest, the second a series of mutual slaughters prompted by rival holy writ and exclusive claims.) The historian George Bancroft wrote in his diary on July 4, 1821: "The contest of the Greeks at present is too interesting a subject to be talked of lightly, or to be regarded as a commonplace war of ambition or interest. It is a nation rising against tyranny and vindicating the rights of man."[14]

Sympathy for Greece in 1823 generated citizens' petitions, resolutions by state legislatures, and pronouncements by governors to one effect: President Monroe should aid the Greeks and confer recognition upon them. They had severed their bonds of servitude as sharply as the generation of 1776 had broken with George III. Typical of this idea was a declaration by the South Carolina legislature that praised "the noble and patriotic struggle of the modern Greeks to rescue from the foot of the infidel and barbarian the hallowed land of ... Socrates." South Carolina lawmakers were set to "hail with pleasure the recognition, by the American government, of the independence of Greece." Pundits testified that direct US military force should be deployed to ensure the new day. "Humanity, policy, religion – all demand it. The Star-Spangled Banner must wave in the Aegean," urged the hero of Tippecanoe in January 1824, William Henry Harrison. Earlier, after details of the Chios disaster hit the United States, journalists had suggested that Monroe dispatch warships and soldiers to the Aegean. In alliance with native resistance they would "bring the haughty and supercilious musselmans and their tyrannical masters to terms."[15]

Reports of Ottoman severity against Greek subjects stirred Secretary of State John Quincy Adams. The case for humanitarian intervention, though, did not persuade him. Dr. William Thornton of the Washington philhellenes asked him in May 1824 to make a cash donation (one day's pay) to alleviate Greek suffering. Adams curtly refused: "We had objects of distress to relieve at home more than sufficient to absorb all my capacities of contribution."[16] Any such subscription, Adams also felt, would violate that neutralist course upon which he had painstakingly set the administration. This course was premised on the idea of two distinctive spheres (the Old World, the New), each of whose integrity required scrupulous observance by the other. Overtly pro-Greek exercises would confound the plausibility of this schema. Also Adams's ongoing effort, discreetly pursued beyond public gaze by an agent, George Bethune English, to obtain a Turkish–US commercial treaty would miscarry. Failure would jeopardize profitable bilateral trade, valued at nearly $800,000 in 1822.[17]

Neutrality

Adams was not just America's senior diplomat during his State Department tenure, 1817–1825. He was also the "master spirit" of foreign policy (Carl Schurz's phrase), to whom Monroe deferred.[18] Adams oversaw demilitarization of the Great Lakes via the Rush–Bagot pact. He won in 1818 the right for US fishermen to ply Canadian waters and secured the forty-ninth parallel as the US–Canadian boundary. He acquired eastern Florida from Spain. He prevented desultory talks with France on claims (valued at $23 million), dating to Napoleonic interference with US shipping, from degenerating into sterile recriminations. He got the British crown to agree to czarist mediation on indemnity for slave owners despoiled by His Majesty's forces in the 1812 war. (Alexander judged for the United States.) Adams settled Russian claims in the Oregon territory in 1824 to US favor. He shaped and worded what became the chief legacy of Monroe, the doctrine bearing his name.

Adams's career before these achievements entailed long training. Apart from peacemaking at Ghent, he had been US envoy to the Netherlands, Prussia, Russia, and Great Britain. Despite a paucity of charm, but because of his diligence and versatile mind, he distinguished himself in these assignments. His education also included the devising of a coherent outlook. It was conceptually tied to themes enunciated by George Washington. First, the United States should pursue trade with Europe but forgo involvement in its wars, shifting coalitions, and knotty diplomacy. Second, European entanglement would inevitably undermine the republic's security by sweeping Americans into disputes beyond their ken or ability to resolve. Adams in 1794, only in his twenties, affirmed the wisdom of a New World system isolated from the monarchical: "It is our duty to remain, the peaceful and silent, though sorrowful spectators of the European scene." Years later when, as secretary of state, he declined Czar Alexander's invitation (1820) to enlist in the Holy Alliance, he explained: "It may be observed that for the repose of Europe as well as of America . . . the European and American political systems should be kept as separate and distinct from each other as possible."[19]

Adams's most comprehensive statement on the merits of US separateness appeared in his speech of July 4, 1821, delivered to Washington residents in House chambers. This meditation on prudence constituted a rebuttal to critics who had recently advocated a policy to support fledgling republican regimes wherever they formed. Vexatious Henry Clay, and the *Edinburgh Review*, which had charged Americans with doing little to advance humanity, were Adams's specific targets. On the very day that Bancroft remarked the purity of Greece's cause in his diary, Adams warned against moralistic diplomacy and crusades on behalf of faraway peoples. Such ventures would sap US power. They would crack republican institutions and democratic habits of mind. America's posture during the eternal combat between "oppressions of power and the claims of right" should be of a justly ordered society, an upright pacific polity. By definition it eschewed temptations to use coercion. Adams famously stated for the United States:

Wherever the standard of freedom and independence has been or shall be unfurled, there will her heart, her benedictions and her prayers be. But she goes not abroad in search of monsters to destroy. She is the well-wisher to the freedom and independence of all. She is the champion and vindicator only of her own. She will recommend the general cause, by the countenance of her voice, and the benignant sympathy of her example. She well knows that by once enlisting under other banners than her own, were they even the banners of foreign independence, she would involve herself, beyond the power of extrication, in all the wars of interest and intrigue, of individual avarice, envy, and ambition, which assume the colors and usurp the standard of freedom ... She might become the dictatress of the world: she would be no longer the ruler of her spirit.[20]

Adams's plea that the US keep aloof from Old World politics applied also to South America for however long it remained attached to Europe by Spanish and Portuguese tendrils. Even as the hold of the Iberian powers on their colonies weakened, he counseled caution, lest sympathy for the southern revolutions ensnare the United States in uneconomical wars. They would not necessarily prove as bleak as the recent one against Britain; Spain and Portugal were demonstrably feeble. But any war, he thought, with the lessons of 1812 in mind, would subvert the loosely bound United States and discombobulate its jealous regions.[21] The 1819 depression reinforced his desire for a calm period.

Adams's commitment to preserving peace and domestic tranquillity became inalterable as Monroe's second term lengthened, as the secretary's presidential ambitions ripened. Adams managed to check the recommendations of Speaker Clay and Secretary of War Calhoun for measures – barely short of war – to support South American revolutionaries. These two men, as intent on the White House as Adams, were unable to dislodge his mastery over diplomacy or refute his warnings against external adventures. He eventually did send a commission of inquiry to evaluate conditions in the rebelling Latin lands and determine prospects for increased trade with them. The administration also permitted private construction of frigates for South American purchase. But direct US assistance was not forthcoming. Adams did not allow Monroe to recognize South American independence until 1823, after it had been plainly won by local armies.

Composed in response to British Foreign Secretary George Canning, the Monroe Doctrine constituted in its original interpretation a statement of preference, not an enforceable set of principles. The doctrine's first point on non-intervention – that the Americas were unavailable to

European colonization – had viability insofar as the United States acqui-
esced to the Royal Navy's patrolling the south Atlantic. The reciprocal
point – that the United States would stay out of Europe's affairs – was
not just a matter of American self-restraint but an implicit recognition
of limits: US power could not be projected far. Unsurprisingly, then,
Monroe's statement aroused more ridicule in European chancelleries
than it did respect. The czar's foreign minister, defending Russian prerogatives along the Pacific northwest, opined that the president's words
deserved "contempt." Austria's Clemens von Metternich called them an
"indecent declaration."[22]

However impudent foreign critics viewed Monroe's communication, it
had the virtue of consistency. The passages on Greece did not deviate from
the logic of those on Latin America. The United States would not meddle
in the internal affairs of any European sovereign state, not even for gallant
Greeks resisting Turkey. The president declared in December 1823 in
favor of their liberty but pledged neither aid nor recognition: "A strong
hope has been long entertained [that] the Greeks [will] succeed in their
contest and resume their equal station among the nations of the earth."[23]

This Greek section of Monroe's message implicitly buttressed the idea
of mutual non-intervention, as specified by Adams, and signaled his
victory in cabinet debates on Greece. He had during the previous year
countered advice by Calhoun and Secretary of the Treasury William
Crawford (also a likely contender for the presidency) that the United
States not stand by idly as brave people fought for liberation. Calhoun
and Crawford hoped that the small US naval force in the Mediterranean,
on detail to suppress Barbary rascals, could sail eastward to assist the
Greeks. Just how the ships – a frigate, one corvette, and a schooner –
would fare and to what practical end was ignored by these advocates.
They won only Adams's scorn: "Their enthusiasm for the Greeks is all
sentiment, and the standard of this is the prevailing popular feeling."[24]

Calhoun and Crawford had allies. They included Gallatin, then US
minister to France. He was susceptible to tales from Greece and open to
entreaties by Lafayette and Greek diplomats in Paris. They requested
warships (number and type varied), funds ($2 million), and *matériel* to aid
Christianity's eastern outpost.[25] While on Washington furlough, Gallatin
appealed directly to Monroe (November 1823) for a Greek subsidy and
the sending of ships. Adams charged that Gallatin persisted in striking
this pro-Greek pose from political calculation, no different from Calhoun
or Crawford: "Mr. Gallatin ... builds castles in the air [and] patronizes
the Greek cause for the sake of raising his own reputation."[26] Richard
Rush, US minister at the Court of St. James, also waxed eloquent on
Greece, until brought into line by Adams.[27]

The Russians too hoped to inveigle Monroe into using naval power to demonstrate against Turkey. To them and other Europeans who urged US intervention, but bore no responsibility for any costs, Adams let fly: "Erroneous moral principal is the most fruitful of all the sources of human calamity and vice." He placed prancing Byron in the category of "corrupters of both taste and morals."[28]

Less easy to brush aside were the views of former presidents Jefferson and Madison, and their influence on Monroe. Luckily for Adams, Jefferson's eagerness for Greece, and correspondence with the intellectual–patriot Adamantios Koraes, did not translate into calls for US action. Jefferson was circumspect on this score, sobered no doubt by the spectacle of US disarray in 1812–1814. Jefferson's Hellenic advocacy did however make an impression on Monroe and quickened his sense that justice upheld Greek claims. As for Madison, he advised his successor that the United States combine somehow with Britain – the modalities left vague – to help Greece.[29] Monroe's penchant for speaking supportively of Greece was thereby reinforced. He also occasionally considered plans, when outside Adams's supervision, of organizing a version of assistance for the revolutionaries.[30]

However delighted Greek leaders were by Monroe's warm words, however much they encouraged Greek hopes of getting aid, Adams would not budge. His constant warnings (in cabinet meetings or in private conferences with the president) against enterprises that might damage the nation dissuaded Monroe from matching rhetoric with deeds. Adams, for his part, could tolerate highfalutin words as long as they did not incite action contrary to core interests: safety, peace, prosperity. This situation allowed Monroe, even as he chafed at being hemmed in, to hymn harmless praises of the beacon light cast by America to freedom-loving peoples abiding abroad.[31]

The only US warships on patrol near Greek and Turkish territories in late 1823 were on strict assignment, to protect US maritime commerce from assault by either belligerent or by neighborhood pirates. Monroe in 1824 said only a few words about Greece in his annual statement to Congress. This reticence testified to Adams's command of foreign policy. The secretary had defined it and driven it against deep currents of popular feeling.[32]

Freedom

The line laid down by Adams was challenged in the House of Representatives. Daniel Webster, returned to Congress after an absence of nearly seven years, led the dissent. He introduced a resolution, six days after Monroe's December 1823 speech, that ran counter to the policy of verbal aid only. The resolution on its surface was innocuous: the president ought to appoint and Congress should underwrite a commissioner to investigate conditions in Greece, as done earlier in South America.[33] The resolution's logic, however, raced in the direction of recognizing Greek freedom and providing something besides moral support. Representative George Cary of Georgia correctly called Webster's proposal "an entering wedge to more." Not debated until late January 1824, the resolution became the subject of one of Webster's dazzling forensic displays.[34]

Webster's motive was not to make life difficult for Adams or Monroe. Webster agreed with the idea of two separate realms: the European, the American. Until disabused by Adams, he had actually assumed that his pro-Greek outlook harmonized with the administration's – for which evidence he could cite Monroe's oft expressed sympathy for the Greeks. As scholars have shown, Webster's Greek concern was intimately connected to his desire for national attention and advancement. He was eager upon resuming his House career, this time representing Massachusetts, to show that he was not just a New England Federalist (the party was moribund) whose concern extended only to the frontiers of his region. He also wanted to demonstrate that he was more than a deft lawyer with opinions restricted by a client's purse. Webster had generous thoughts; people needed to know their contours. Determined, then, on a splashy reentry into House life, he settled on the day's momentous question: Greece. He would make its cause his own. Encouraged by recent intelligence of Greek victories – at St. Luca and Levadia – he felt too that the overthrow of Ottoman rule was not a fantasy but impending reality. The Greeks, he held, "have character enough to carry them through." People of good faith should rally to them. He told Everett: "These are interesting times – let us improve them." As for violating the sanctity of two distinct spheres, Webster admitted the inconsistency. He also made allowances of cosmopolitan hue: "I think we have as much Community with the Greeks, as with the inhabitants of the Andes, and the dwellers on the borders of the Vermilion Sea."[35]

Adams signaled his opposition to Webster's resolution during the interval between its introduction to the House and January's debate. Through Representative Joel Poinsett (South Carolina), Adams alerted Congress that a sensitive commercial errand under way in Constantinople – English's name remained undisclosed – would fail were Webster's proposal adopted. Adams's House friends, to underscore the importance of Turkish–US commerce (centered on the purchase of fruits and opium, the latter for resale to China), moved in late December that the Treasury secretary report on the volume of bilateral trade. Adams also complained that Webster's initiative encroached upon executive turf and discretion. This point, bearing directly on the locus of responsibility for foreign policy, was relayed personally to Webster by Poinsett, himself skeptical of making Greece into a US project. Later on, in private conversation with Webster, Adams traced the lines of his objection. Webster countered that two Cabinet officers supported him, Calhoun and Navy secretary Samuel Southard, and intimated that Monroe did not mind.[36]

That Calhoun and Southard were trying to scuttle concepts recently enunciated by Adams did not startle him. But the notion that Monroe wanted already to bend policy surely made Adams pause. Whether he actually believed Webster or thought him disingenuous is unclear from archival documents. Adams's position meanwhile was potentially compromised by revelations from a House inquiry showing that the secretary of state had been corresponding with Andreas Luriottis, a Greek agent in London. Although Adams's letters maintained neutralism, they also saluted the Greek cause as fine. Thus Adams could be interpreted by critics, including rival presidential aspirants, as unfeeling toward Greece or else – contrary to his ballyhooed principles – meddling in European affairs. Webster enjoyed what he imagined to be the secretary's discomfort. He thought the Greek resolution sure to win quick congressional approval.[37]

This optimism proved unfounded. Adams's displeasure registered with the House majority. It shelved the resolution after a week of debate, along with a diluted version presented by Poinsett. Webster pronounced that Adams constituted "the most formidable obstacle."[38]

Webster before this anticlimax had held the House and visitors' gallery spellbound when (January 19) he thundered that the main contest of the age featured absolutism versus democratically regulated regimes. The United States was neither a passive observer nor a neutral in this struggle. America's own political institutions and conscience placed the nation on the side of free institutions everywhere: "What do *we* not owe to the cause of civil and religious liberty? To the principle of lawful resistance? To the principle that society has a right to partake in its own government? As the leading republic of the world, living and breathing in these principles, and advanced, by their operation, with unequaled rapidity in our career, shall we give *our* consent to bring them into disrepute and disgrace? . . . Does it not become us . . . is it not a duty imposed on us, to give our weight to the side of liberty and justice, to let mankind know that we are not tired of our own institutions, and to protest against the asserted power of altering at pleasure the law of the civilized world?" Dereliction of duty to creed would entail shabbiness greater than transgression against the idea that

Europe and America must live sealed apart. Such literalness of mind and pinched imagination overlooked Ottoman atrocities: "The world has no such misery to show."[39]

The resolution embodied popular indignation, cried Webster. This high feeling carried the promise of a better future for all nations, when the people's voice would thrive. Until then democratic opinion, already a factor in the calculations of governments, could help sustain the most forlorn victims of despotism. The choice of the United States in these circumstances was inescapable:

[The Greeks] stretch out their arms to the Christian communities of the earth, beseeching them, by a generous recollection of their ancestors, by the consideration of their desolated and ruined cities and villages, by their wives and children sold into an accursed slavery, by their blood, which they seem willing to pour out like water, by the common faith, and in the name, which unites all Christians, that they would extend to them at least some token of compassionate regard.[40]

Webster's keenest ally in House debate was Clay. He chose to ignore past and partisan differences with Webster. The Speaker reasoned that the resolution's passage would help him against Adams in the upcoming presidential race, showing the former a friend of humanity, the latter a troglodyte. Clay chastised fellow Republicans who opposed the proposal. He made a target of New Hampshire's Ichabod Bartlett after he opined that Americans had no more right to intervene in Turkish affairs than Haitians would have in assisting a black uprising in the south (an arresting image in the wake of Denmark Vesey's proposed 1822 revolt around Charleston which had envisioned Anglo-Haitian aid). Clay gleefully denounced those merchants, primarily Boston chums of Adams, who worried that Turkish–US trade would languish were Congress to take a position friendly to Greece: "A wretched invoice of figs and opium has been spread before us to repress our sensibilities and to eradicate our humanity."[41]

Other supporters of Webster, connected to diverse presidential aspirants, included Sam Houston of Tennessee (an Andrew Jackson partisan). He made his maiden speech on the House floor with this comparison between the Greek war and 1776: "The people of Greece had expressed a wish to alter their Government, and according to the fundamental principles of our institutions, they have a right to do it."[42] Francis Baylies (a Crawford man) and Henry Dwight (an Adams man), both of Massachusetts, had to face the same disapproving Boston businessmen as did Webster but still backed the resolution as an inspired gesture. Dwight also argued that the entrepreneurial Greeks, endowed with an impressive merchant marine, were certain to be fit partners for the United States.

They would fill any gap created by the Turks should they retreat into sullenness after Congress acted. Baylies predicted that the Greeks in a short time would acquire a formidable navy: "The wooden walls of Athens may be seen, ere long, floating upon every sea." Patrick Farrelly of Pennsylvania (supporting Calhoun) and Daniel Pope Cook of Illinois (favoring Clay) praised the rich Greek past plus America's solidarity with oppressed peoples. Cook asked in the wake of fresh enactments against trans-Atlantic slave trade and piracy: "We pity the captive African, and call the man that stole him a pirate; shall we not pity the suffering Greek, stolen, sold, and then butchered by the most ruthless of all oppressors? Shall he have no share … in our expressions of compassion? In like manner, the bold spirit of this Government has set its face against the practice of privateering … Why shall we be backward in this one cause of humanity while so prompt in every other?"[43]

Against Webster's coalition stood Adams men and Crawford supporters. Their answer to Cook's question rested on several concerns. These included a regard for executive leadership in foreign affairs, best evidenced when Virginia's Alexander Smyth frothily disputed the constitutionality of Webster's resolution, calling it an arrogation to Congress of presidential prerogative. Opponents also wondered about the Holy Alliance's commitment to legitimacy that encompassed even infidel Turkey. They warned that the alliance, then reviewing the desirability of reestablishing order in South America, might enact punitive policies against the United States. The Holy Allies at minimum would not feel inhibited in their New World sports if Washington interfered in a European matter. Smyth objected as rumors – in the event groundless – circulated about a French force of 12,000 troops headed for Latin American deployment on Holy Alliance bidding: "We say to the Allies, that any attempt on their part to extend their system to any portion of this hemisphere, we shall consider as dangerous to our peace and safety. And is not the extension of our system to their hemisphere equally dangerous to their peace and safety? We say that, with the existing colonies or dependencies of any European Power we have not interfered, and shall not interfere. How can we then interfere with the Morea, a province of Turkey, without a violation of our … declaration?" Adoption of the resolution might even lead via a chain of complications to another war for which Americans were as unprepared as in 1812. "We ought not to refuse instruction from the experience of the late war," Bartlett urged. Randolph of Roanoke, fulminating still against the outside world's intrusions, worried that the United States might blunder into a war against both Turkey *and* the Holy Alliance. "Recollect the embarrassments of the year 1814 for men and money," he advised. "Let every man lay his hand on his heart, and ask himself, if such was our distress, when engaged only with a single Power, what would have been our condition, against the world in arms?" Mississippi's Christopher Rankin warned against an infinity of US wars of interference against the world's many abominable regimes; such a career would dishearten the American public and empty the treasury. As corollary to this point, added Smyth, the identifying of wicked regimes was never a simple theoretical task. Attributing right-eousness only to the Greeks and evil to the Turks was ludicrous. The latter by virtue of their tolerance, codified in the *millet* system, were notably more decent than Christians with their string of inquisitions, crusades, and other persecutions of non-believers. Besides, he added for good measure, the Greeks were manifestly unfit for self-government. But, Randolph interjected, if they were as splendid as their defenders claimed then there was little the Americans ought to do. Inflating Greek numbers and lapsing into Anglophobia, he suggested: "Let us say to those seven millions of Greeks: We defended ourselves when we were but three millions, against a Power, in comparison to which the Turk is but as a lamb. Go and do thou likewise."[44]

The House never revisited Webster's resolution after the January deci-sion to shelve. Even had the House adopted the measure, preponderant feeling among Senators was unpromising and would have prevented Webster's idea from going forward. Congress's attention during the remainder of 1824 shifted to other business (tariff bill, road and canal construction, navy appropriation) and then fixed on the presidential election. It resulted in an electoral college stalemate: 99 votes for Jackson, 84 for Adams, 41 for Crawford, 37 for Clay. The House was obliged to decide. It chose Adams after much wrangling.[45]

The 1824 election season likewise distracted popular attention from Greece. The pro-Greek *Statesman* of New York groused in spring of that year: "The Greek fever, which raged with such violence during the last winter, has so completely subsided, and been followed by such a state of total apathy to the good cause, that our readers will hardly condescend to read a paragraph relating to the subject."[46] That popular interest in Greece was waning in 1824 is indisputable, but the *Statesman* exagger-ated the fickleness of opinion. It remained friendly to Greece, albeit less demonstrative. Special lectures and charity balls still drew celebrities and subscribers. State legislatures continued to issue pronouncements along with recommendations to Washington favorable to Greece. Webster's January speech was widely published in newspapers. It was praised throughout America and the British Isles. Translated copies of it were said to have reached readers in distant Greece who gratefully devoured the text and US news. Doubtless Greek audiences, too, had they the means of reception, would have applauded Webster's additional public comments. He contrasted for the sake of rapt listeners in June 1825 the "Christian and civilized Greek" with "the barbarian Turk."[47]

The war against Ottoman rule meanwhile began to go awry for the Greek insurgents. Turkish force was augmented by Egyptian soldiers and sailors under the command of Pasha Ibrahim. They captured Crete in March 1824. They next subdued resistance on the islands of Kasos and Psara. Civil strife also afflicted the Greeks at this time and lowered US confidence in them. Nor did they make headway on the diplomatic front. In summer 1824 Greek deputies based in London asked the Monroe–Adams administration to place Greece under its protection in exchange for commercial preference and the transfer of an Aegean island to US possession. The government refused. The British declined a similar offer (the Act of Submission) in 1825, during which year Egyptian troops invaded the Peloponnesus. Ottoman forces took Athens in August 1826.[48]

The steadiest support in Washington of the Greeks during this grim period came from Everett, about whom some general comments are here necessary. He was fated to be remembered by future generations for delivering the tedious and endless speech in November 1863 at Gettysburg just before Lincoln gave his address. Biographers of Webster still politely mention Everett as compiler of their hero's papers and loyal protégé. In short, he has been relegated by History (capital H) to being the eternal ancillary.

A fairer reading of his biography must include the following. He was an esteemed orator. His speeches, if florid by the standard of latter-day critics, were prized by audiences for erudition and mellifluousness. Jefferson congratulated Everett after reading the text of his speech in honor of Lafayette, calling it unsurpassed. John Quincy Adams pronounced on first hearing Everett (February 1820) that his performance was exquisite. Ralph Waldo Emerson as a young man was mesmerized by the electrifying language of Everett. When an old man, his voice still retained a fine timbre. He was much sought as the nation's top speaker, hence his star billing at Gettysburg.[49]

Everett was also a clergyman, ordained a Unitarian minister in 1814. He was among the first Americans to earn a doctorate (at Germany's University of Göttingen in 1817). He was the first occupant of the Samuel Eliot Chair of Greek at Harvard. He commanded international recognition as a discriminating scholar. In 1819–1823 he edited the nation's premier journal of commentary and thought, the *North American Review*. He participated in the early phase of the most far-reaching philosophical movement of his day, Transcendentalism.

Everett was also exceptionally well traveled, which gave a cosmopolitan fillip to his nationalism. During his first trip abroad, 1815–1819, he made himself at home in Germany, France, and Britain. His wanderings took him as far as the Ottoman empire, where he explored both Constantinople and Athens. While a young man in Europe he become personally acquainted with Sir Walter Scott, Johann Wolfgang von Goethe, French philhellene Viscount de Chateaubriand, and the anti-slavery activist William Wilberforce. Everett met too in Turkey with Ali Pasha of Jannina whose 1820 revolt against the sultan ignited the Greek revolution.[50]

Finally, Everett remains the archetype of the scholar in politics. The life of the mind did not satisfy his hunger for engagement. He swapped his Harvard professorship in 1825 for a place in Congress, where he represented the Middlesex district of his native Massachusetts for the next decade. He subsequently served as governor of Massachusetts (1836–1839), minister to Great Britain (1841–1845), president of Harvard (1846–1849), secretary of state (1852–1853), and senator from Massachusetts (1853–1854). He accepted the Constitutional Union Party's nomination for vice president in 1860. During the Civil War, he stumped the North – attracting throngs – to muster support for defeating the Confederacy.

Throughout this varied career Everett remained fascinated by contemporaneous Greek matters. He had, more than anyone, galvanized interest in the United States for revolutionary Greece.[51] His *North American Review* in October 1823 published a translation of Greece's provisional constitution, promulgated in January 1822 on US and French models. He placed in the same volume an appeal for aid by the Messenian Senate of Kalamata (May 1821) directed to US citizens.[52] Accompanying these documents in the *North American Review* was Everett's endorsement of Aristotle's *Ethics* with introduction and annotation by Koraes. Dedicated to Greece's newly founded government, Koraes's work combined learned treatise with manifesto-like call to arms.

The moral weight of Greece – apparent in the provisional constitution, the Messenian appeal, Koraes – argued overwhelmingly to Everett against "the merciless domination of mahometanism." He told his readers that the United States, appointed by providence to regenerate the world, should help with Greek rescue. Americans in their private capacity should send funds and supplies to Greece. The government ought to recognize it as a free state. Monroe might send friendly representation. On this last point, Everett wrote: "There is an animation produced in [such] perilous [struggle] of a resolute few against a barbarous host, at feeling that their efforts are observed with sympathy by others; that they are not toiling and bleeding without an eye to witness or a heart to feel for them." Not to his readers but in earnest to Secretary Adams, Everett put himself forward to play the role of agent to Greece.[53]

Webster numbered among those *North American Review* readers who followed Everett's depiction of Greece's fight for liberty. He turned to the scholar, with whom he was already on cordial terms, for fresh information on events. Everett obliged with celerity. He showered Webster with maps, statistics, an advance copy of a *North American Review* article on Ali Pasha's life, and assurances that Greece would overcome. These materials formed the empirical basis to Webster's speech in January 1824. He was otherwise ignorant of Greek matters. Webster, for his part, lobbied for Everett's appointment as special agent. He acknowledged the professor's key role. It had been to "keep up" Webster's "temperature," in danger of dropping as Adams mobilized Congress against the Greek resolution.[54]

Everett was comparably bent on keeping America's "temperature" high for Greece during his House tenure. But direct assault on the neutralist policy was even less an option during Adams's presidency (1825–1829) than before. The president vehemently opposed any move that might be construed as tilting toward Greece or deviating from the two-spheres idea. Complicating matters, Everett enjoyed pleasant relations with Adams and family, and hoped not to disarrange the connection. Everett elected to push the Greek cause with utmost discretion.

The nearest he came to launching a frontal challenge occurred in early January 1827. Representative Edward Livingston of Louisiana, a senior figure whose standing far outstripped Everett's, introduced legislation to ease Greek distress. Humanitarian assistance was urgently required, Everett had emphasized to Livingston, as hunger and famine stalked the Peloponnesus. Citing evidence from reputable observers, Everett charged that this new problem of starvation superseded even that desolation visited by Ottoman armies. So prevailed upon, Livingston (a Jackson associate, somewhat reserved toward Adams) proposed that $50,000 be made available to purchase provisions for the Greeks with specific attention to the plight of non-combatants. Clothes, foodstuffs, and medicines – like that granted Venezuela in 1812 after destruction by earthquake – should lighten Greek burdens but not irritate Turkish sensitivity. None of the instruments of war would be sent, said Livingston. Moreover, the proposed distribution of aid would bypass Greek officials, thereby withholding from them claims to state status. American suppliers would deal only with ordinary people.[55]

The Everett–Livingston initiative fared no better than Webster's 1824 resolution. Representative George McDuffie (South Carolina) argued

that the envisioned aid patently violated US neutrality – if adopted would
amount to an act of war. James Hamilton (South Carolina) chimed that
the assistance package however shaped to exclude *matériel* would
nevertheless add to Greek military advantage. Food needs would slacken
with the arrival of US help. The competing claims of soldiers and civilians
to scarce resources would melt away, leaving Greek armies stronger than
before. Hamilton explained, in the logic of total war, that "there were
circumstances under which an aid by provisions might be the most
efficient [relief] a belligerent could receive ... that food is one of the
most material of [war's] sinews." Food aid would inevitably make an
impact on the war's course and "invigorate the nerves of the Grecian
warrior." American protestations of non-alignment would ring hollow,
indeed. The House voted 109 to 54 against Livingston's proposal.[56]

Unwilling to wage a full-fledged campaign in House chambers, Everett
resorted to another tack. He used his public standing to benefit Greece
and drew strength from his positions as congressman, orator, student of
classics. His admirers gushed praise. They fortified his determination to
work simultaneously on several fronts.[57] He stayed in close touch – as
long distance and irregular mail permitted – with Greek leaders, particularly with Mavrokordatos. Everett monitored Greek events through
him, offered advice, and kept him abreast of US thinking.[58] Everett also
maintained a presence in the Boston Greek committee and was its principal liaison to like-minded associations. The Boston committee along
with those of New York and Philadelphia sent eight shiploads of relief
supplies in 1827–1828. The food and clothing, valued at roughly
$140,000, were distributed in Greece by Jarvis, Howe, and US army
veteran Jonathan Miller. Everett also raised moneys through the Boston
committee to sponsor volunteers, most notably Howe and Miller. Everett
also did what he could to boost morale among the American volunteers.
He assured Howe, whose spirits sometimes faltered, that in Greece he
was rendering important services to deserving people "and promoting the
cause of liberty." By so doing, he was sure to acquire "enviable personal
distinction and influence."[59]

Everett secured publication in the popular press for letters from philhellenes in Greece. He lavished attention on them during their home
leaves. He helped organize lecture tours so that US audiences could learn
directly from witnesses. Their tales were heartbreaking and aimed at one
purpose: more aid for blameless victims. Howe told one audience:
"[Greece] has tasted your bounty and expects a continuance of it, and
I will venture to say that of those encamped on her sea shore, thousands of
women and children are watching every sail that comes from the west ...
[hoping] that it may be an American ship with provisions for them."

Howe's own hospital in Poros and public works project among the refugees of Aegina (building a mole in the harbor) depended on Everett's rolling public relations campaigns and fund drives. Howe dedicated his engrossing *Historical Sketch of the Greek Revolution* to Everett.[60]

He also joined with Webster on the side of Greek buyers of two privately built frigates by New York naval contractors (Le Roy, Bayard and Company; Gardiner and Samuel Howland). Construction of these ships pressed to the limits of US neutrality laws. Purchase was nevertheless allowed, consistent with the precedent set when South American republicans had commissioned privately assembled ships for use against Spain. Unhappily, the Greek ships became the object of cost overruns, litigation, building delays, and public embarrassment. The Greek purchasing agent in New York, Alexandros Contostavlos, complained that the arbitrators detailed to cut through the legal-commercial tangle acted "more as Turks than as Christians." In the event, just one of the ships made its way to Greece. The *Hope* – renamed *Hellas* – arrived late in 1826 but made only marginal contribution to Greek naval operations. Still, in the absence of Everett's interventions with congressional colleagues and cabinet officers, and without his perseverance behind the scenes, even the *Hope* would not have sailed. (The ship's career ended in 1831 when destroyed by its commander, Admiral Andreas Miaoules, during the first violence that unsettled post-independence Greece.)[61]

Overall, Everett's activities had an effect. They nudged America's Greek policy from strict neutrality to something less rigid, a species of "benevolent neutrality."[62] This assessment does not mean, of course, that Everett bore sole responsibility for the shift in diplomatic tone and substance. He certainly did not raise all of the private funds for Greek relief. Other people were closely connected to that task, such as the indefatigable Matthew Carey of Philadelphia's Greek committee.[63] Neither was Everett the only publicist directing attention to Greek woe and needs. Lafayette bombarded American officials with missives on the need for aid. He spoke tirelessly about the emergency to crowds during his triumphal tour of the United States in 1824–1825. This procession was joined at times by Gallatin, who was equally impassioned about Greece in front of approving audiences.[64] As for the New York-built frigates, the decision permitting their construction and making one of them financially feasible for Greek purchase rested ultimately on Adams, with Congress playing an obliging role. Yet Everett was in some sense everywhere and always involved in the Greek question. He even tried to reassure Lafayette, who had followed the frigate misadventure, that the bungle did not indicate American callousness but reflected merely the eccentricity of New York business practice.[65]

Everett's pervasive involvement touched upon Adams's willingness to deploy confidential agents in Greece. Such operatives aimed at gathering intelligence without pricking the Porte's resentment, inflamed in the first place by displays of pro-Greek feeling in Congress. As early as May 1824, while still secretary of state, Adams had approached Poinsett with a suggestion that he visit Greece as an extension of his scheduled travel to Europe. Poinsett did not go. But he was encouraged to by Everett, who disallowed whatever personal feelings he had on not being selected. Everett also lent himself to the cause of Estwick Evans with letters of introduction to Greek personages, when he set off for the eastern Mediterranean to make unofficial observations (which he submitted after a hurried visit). Later, after a third agent died on his way to Greece (William Clarke Somerville), Everett suggested to President Adams that he take advantage of Jonathan Miller's presence in Greece. From the soldier, Adams might get sound intelligence; if circumstances warranted, Miller could be used as a point of contact between the administration and emergent Greek authority.[66]

Adams's confidence in the efficacy of covert agents is hard to gauge. He went on written record as doubting their ability to accomplish much: "Our agents never will be secret."[67] Yet he sent a few to Greece and implicated Everett in the presumed efficacy of such practice. Adams was inventive too in conducting trade negotiations with Turkish officialdom via shadowy people. Their talks, just as he anticipated, also drew criticism once their existence was discovered. In the name of insulted cosmopolitanism, Howe wrote to a friend (January 1829):

It is all in vain to talk of right, of principle, of honor, or even of religion in this age … no government on earth is actuated by any higher or more liberal principle than the narrow one of self-interest. Is not that of the United States the freest, purest, and most supportable in the world; and is not that Government at this moment using every exertion to conclude a treaty with the Bloody Butcher of Constantinople?[68]

Trade accords assiduously pursued by Adams eluded his grasp. He was morose in his last message to Congress about the suspicions that plagued Turkish–US relations. Not until May 1830, during Andrew Jackson's first administration, did the two countries finally sign a commercial agreement.[69]

That same year the London conference confirmed Greek independence guaranteed by Russian, French, and British power. Greece's emergence, territorially slighter than would be the case in future decades, owed practically nothing to the United States. Contributions of humanitarian aid had helped people to survive, but added little to their fight against the Ottomans. The sources of victory lay elsewhere. Turkish efforts had been hampered in the early stages of 1821–1823 by scattered rebellions in the empire: Persia and Druse-rocked Syria. Squelching them diverted men and *matériel* whose concentration could have contained the exploding Greek provinces. Contagion and fires in Constantinople in 1826, plus a mutiny by the janissaries, helped to scramble Ottoman operations against Greece. Casualty rates climbed among the forces. Pasha Ibrahim's Egyptian army, originally hurled against the Peloponnesus, had been reduced (24,000 to 8,000 effectives) by combat, diseases, food short-ages.[70] Ultimately, Greek success derived from the intervention, albeit belated, of the three main European powers following their diplomatic realignment in 1826. It allowed that impetuous sailor, Admiral Edward Codrington, in October 1827 to lead an international squadron – composed of British, French, Russian warships – into Navarino bay. Misunderstanding and the opening of fire by flustered Turks allowed his ships to respond. They annihilated the Ottoman fleet. Czar Nicholas declared war on Turkey in April 1828. The lopsided combat thereafter culminated in the peace of Adrianople (September 1829) that exacted Ottoman concessions in favor of Russia, Serbia, and Greece. That Turkey was not dismembered but allowed to live as a sclerotic entity suited the British government (i.e. the Duke of Wellington), otherwise faced with a Russian surge through the Straits and into the Balkans. To Greek patriots, the Russian war equaled their certain victory.

American philhellenes began to wonder at this time about the ability of Greeks to create national unity or an authentic republic. Dr. Thornton summarized this worry first (October 1827) after news arrived that vying captains had resumed their brawling:

I lament that the Greeks are in such a state of internal confusion; they appear to be composed of the same turbulent materials as the Greeks of old; and though we ought to make many allowances for those who are but just rising again into national Existence from a state of the abjectest thralldom, we cannot but lament that the personal Jealousies of contending chiefs has much retarded their complete deliverance.[71]

The president of new Greece, Ioannis Antonios Kapodistrias, was assassi-nated in 1831. The country was knocked off kilter and plummeted into civil war. Three decades later Everett told Ottoman naval officials touring ship yards in Boston that Greece – battered by social turmoil and political unrest under King Otho – was in worse shape than under the Porte. In the absence of stability and commercial opportunity, the United States did not bother to send an accredited minister (Charles Tuckerman) to Athens until 1868.[72]

***

The Monroe–Adams policy of neutrality benefited the United States in substantial ways. The Ottoman empire after Navarino sought US ship-builders. It spurned offers from British, French and other constructors. Americans played the crucial role (Henry Eckford and Foster Rhodes of New York) in resuscitating Turkish naval power; they profited hand-somely by the demand for new capital ships. Mahmud's navy by 1838 included eleven ships of the line and a dozen frigates, putting Turkey on par with the Russian Black Sea fleet. Turkish–US trade also grew after 1830. Trade became brisk in US exports of distilled spirits and cotton manufactures versus imports of fruits, wool, silver, and China-bound opium. The annual value of exchange exceeded $1 million by 1850. A decade later the value had jumped to more than $2 million. This mix of naval assistance (including Ottoman recruitment of US officers and sailors) and improving business stiffened the Porte's pro-Union stance during the Civil War. Northern ships were allowed in Smyrna and other harbors to transact trade, seek shelter and repair, lay on fresh provisions. Confederate cruisers were denied use of the empire's facilities.[73]

Regarding Greece and the Monroe Doctrine: had Webster–Everett succeeded circa 1824–1827, the Monroe Doctrine ideas would have been compromised, perhaps overthrown, before they had time to coa-lesce into a body of principles. Future US policymakers would have been deprived of a design that aimed at foreign exclusion from the Americas while deflecting intimacy with Europe.

Doubtless South American critics of US policy would have approved had this so-called doctrine been disabled. To them, Monroe's statement, along with emendations by subsequent US leaders, was meant to conceal the face of northern domination. The respected Argentine lawyer Dr. Lucio M. Moreno Quintana gave this opinion in 1920: "The doctrine is dangerous because it is North American imperialism hidden under a principle of international law."[74]

American policy absent Monroe's principles might have been more easily embarrassed and, therefore, circumspect from the outset. But probably not. Simon Bolivar once observed, well before the Monroe Doctrine obtained vitality, that the resourceful North Americans had a peculiar genius to devise clever rationalizations to soothe themselves as they trespassed. "The United States seems destined by providence," he mused, "to [beset] Latin America with misery in the name of liberty."[75]

To US imagination in the early nineteenth century, Greece occupied a central place in moral history. This position eclipsed that of Ireland, Poland, and Hungary. The plight of these three captive nations did call forth popular and official indignation. The Hungarian instance occasioned another Everett–Webster collaboration: the 1850 Hulsemann letter, which reproved Habsburg arrogance.[76] But none of these cases provoked a serious debate on intervention. Only Greece, burdened and mythologized by US imagining, could have sparked the brilliant duel of Webster versus Adams.[77]

To Webster and Everett, the United States was not just another self-aggrandizing power. Rather, the country stood for universal humane values. This understanding required the shouldering of risks and obligations alien to practitioners of traditional diplomacy. Everett to this cosmopolitan end invoked Edmund Burke (in the *North American Review*): "Wheresoever the chosen race, the sons of liberty, shall worship freedom, they will turn their faces to us."[78] To betray these expectations with inaction or indifference would subvert freedom's cause and, by extension, hurt the US experiment.

Flaws abounded in this Webster–Everett approach to policy, said skeptics. The power of self-deception was an aspect of the question and obscured the part played by personal motive. Reluctant to second-guess himself, Adams was nevertheless quick to detect impurity in other people. Competitors such as Clay had, indeed, aligned themselves with Webster for their own sake and used the Greek question to embarrass Adams in the election season. And certainly Webster had wanted to draw attention to himself in 1824, for which purpose Athens was handy. On these points Adams was tart, ungracious, and accurate.

Of paramount importance to Adams, as he reminded his audiences (Thornton, Monroe, fourth of July votaries), good intentions were not enough. The United States confronted irksome problems near to home. Their resolution would not be advanced by going "abroad in search of monsters to destroy." The republic as humanity's knight errant would only aggravate existing difficulties while creating new ones. In this respect, said he, the 1812 war stood as cautionary tale.

Not only did the United States lack the technical wherewithal to rescue Greece, chided critics of Webster–Everett. But also it was so weighted with moral failings that it should not seek to instruct other nations or censure them for inadequacies. The cataract of ills associated with slavery constituted a far worse offense to justice than did the condition of Greeks under the sultan, declared one Acacius in 1825. (This pseudonym probably belonged to a Reverend Barnabus Bates of Rhode Island.) He had in mind the following facts of pre-1821 Greek life: although a subordinate class in the Ottoman empire, Greeks were not persecuted and enjoyed privileges – exemption from military service and tolerance of their faith, language, customs, and culture. Seldom molested, Greeks also occupied civil posts and participated in the empire's commercial life. They dominated its maritime trade. African slaves in the United States by contrast with this mild regime were severely mistreated: "Prior to a resort to arms, the condition of the Greeks was far less deplorable and degraded than that of the slaves of our country; and the Negroes have far more cause of complaint against our government, than the Greeks had against the Turkish despotism." Acacius asked: "Why, then, should we feel more for the Greeks of Europe, than for the Negroes of America? Are we bound to feel *less* for the oppressed in proportion as they are *more* insulted and injured? Or should we feel more for them in proportion as their distance from us is greater? Who does not know that our Negroes have a thousand fold more reasons to rise against their oppressors, than their Masters had to rise against the government of Britain?"[79] In 1831, just a year after Greeks won international recognition of their independence, Nat Turner unleashed his Virginia rampage.

Not for the last time, many Americans in the 1820s were excited by overseas drama, seemingly more susceptible of remedy than domestic perplexities. Congressional dissenters from Adams's line were sustained by the prevalent feeling that Greece should be sprung from Ottoman bondage. Everett's guerrilla operation against the White House's preferred policy capitalized on this emotion and enabled Everett to push a policy of officially sanctioned private philanthropy. Albeit modest, it helped succor the dispossessed.

4   Removals

Congressional debate over Greece in the 1820s rehearsed questions that agitated future American generations. Under what circumstances should the nation intervene abroad to promote humanitarian purposes? By what means?[1] Cases in point were Cuba in 1898, former Yugoslavia in the 1990s. In the Bosnia-Herzegovina and Kosovo cases, a new term was coined to convey the essence of unconscionable violation: ethnic cleansing.

The Bureau of Indian Affairs (BIA) used this same vocabulary in its September 2000 confession: "This agency participated in the ethnic cleansing that befell the ... tribes."[2] Founded as an office in the War Department in 1824, when Webster and Everett were declaiming for Greece, the BIA had long been reviled by critics. They blamed it for causing the deaths of tens of thousands of Native Americans and the degradation of countless others. Coercion, devastation of bison herds, widespread abuse of liquor plus the banning of traditional customs and religious practices constituted a tragedy. The BIA apologized for abetting it. The scale, said BIA head Kevin Gover, himself a Pawnee, had been "so ghastly that it cannot be dismissed as merely the inevitable consequence of the clash of competing ways of life."[3]

Six years after the BIA's establishment Congress passed the Indian Removal Act in compliance with President Jackson's wishes. It enabled Washington to intensify and systematize what had been under way since Jefferson's presidency: to exile by legal means the weak and few. James Fenimore Cooper's Tamenund in *The Last of the Mohicans* (1826) captured the situation's crux: "The pale-faces are masters of the earth, and the time of the redmen has not yet come again."[4]

The removal legislation nullified the Indian Trade and Intercourse Acts. Their promulgation in the 1790s held that the tribes were sovereign entities with which Washington appropriately dealt via its foreign policy apparatus. Removal presumed no such claims of Indian sovereignty. Removal maintained that individual tribesmen had to submit to the laws of the states in which they resided. Tribal forms of governance therein no longer obtained. Indians who found this regime obnoxious were free to go west to continue their preferred corporate life. Specifically, the Removal Act allowed the president to exchange territory west of the Mississippi river for lands owned by tribes in the east. Congress appropriated $500,000 to buy these Indian tracts. This sum was also to cover other costs: compensation to owners for improvements they had made on the relinquished land, transportation of the emigrants to their designated new allotment, subsistence during the first year after their removal. The Act provided too for federal protection of the newcomers against tribes already resident or other people coveting the arrivals' land. It would belong to the emigrants in perpetuity unless, in the Act's ominous language, "the Indians become extinct, or abandon the same." In that event the land reverted to US ownership.[5]

Within the Act's framework the government negotiated removal agreements with numerous tribes. Nearly seventy-five treaties were signed during Jackson's presidency (1829–1837), a number unequaled by any other administration. Thus the expulsion quickened of those Indians remaining on the eastern side of the Mississippi. The United States during these years added roughly 100 million acres of Indian lands to the national holding in exchange for 30 million acres west of the Mississippi at a cost far exceeding that originally envisioned: $68 million. Roughly 46,000 Indians migrated during Jackson's presidency. Many went to territory later encompassed by the state of Oklahoma. They were followed by thousands more in the decade that followed Jackson.[6] Northern tribes that agreed to extinguish their land claims in the 1830s and 1840s included the Shawnees, Sac and Fox, Senecas, Osages, Miamis, Ottawas, Sagninwas, Iowas, Peorias, Potawatomis, Chippewas, Wyandots, Menominis, and Winnebagos. The "five civilized tribes" of the south also agreed to leave: Choctaws, Creeks, Chickasaws, Seminoles (after the violence of 1835–1842), and Cherokees. Seventy thousand southern Indians were ultimately removed. Only a few thousand by 1844 kept to mountain hideaways in western North Carolina (Cherokees) or hid in Florida's Everglades (Seminole resistors).[7]

The uprooting of Indians from their homes created a spectacle. It featured deceitfulness in the form of flimsy treaties, some so transparently false that Congress refused to act until they were recast to resemble normal legality. Bribery, purveying of alcohol, and instances of bad faith by private contractors – on federal detail to help the tribes on their treks – aggravated matters. The contractors, as men of profit, sought to keep overheads low. This concern frequently produced food rations, equipment, and vehicles of shoddy quality or inadequate quantity. Unfailingly, too, the contractors were in a hurry to get their Indian charges to their appointed destinations, a goal not easily harmonized

with the emigrants' welfare. Even without white chicanery or other difficulties, the passages westward were rough. Many took place in inclement
weather. They yielded high rates of morbidity and mortality among
women, children, and elders. Hale and frail alike traversed rugged terrain,
bound for uncertain lives in unfamiliar settings. War and removal
reduced the Seminole population by 40 percent. Nearly half of the
Winnebagos died.[8]

The removals triggered protest by some northeastern observers. It
recalled Father Francisco de Vitorio's response in the sixteenth century
to Spain's Indian policy in South America: shock and stupefaction.[9] Ralph
Waldo Emerson emerged briefly in 1836 from his Transcendentalist rev-
erie to warn Martin Van Buren, Jackson's hand-picked successor, of the
stench of sin should he approve the treaty of New Echota foisted upon the
Cherokees. Emerson predicted to the newly elected chief executive: "You,
sir, will bring down that renowned chair in which you sit into infamy if your
seal is set to this instrument of perfidy; and the name of this nation, hitherto
the sweet omen of religion and liberty, will stink to the world."[10]

The republic's Indian policy also dismayed such visitors to the United
States as Britain's Frances Trollope, who wrote in 1832 of US pretensions to rectitude. Sham lurked behind the prattle about freedom and
equality, she charged: "It is ... from [Americans] themselves, that I have
heard statements which represent them as treacherous and false almost
beyond belief in their intercourse with the unhappy Indians."[11]

France's Alexis de Tocqueville asserted that the conquistadors had
been less thorough and efficient than the United States in eliminating
Indian life. He wrote in *Democracy in America* (1835): "The Spaniards, by
unparalleled atrocities which brand them with indelible shame, did not
succeed in exterminating the Indian race and could not even prevent
them from sharing their rights; the United States Americans have
attained both these results with wonderful ease, quietly, legally, and
philanthropically, without spilling blood and without violating a single
one of the great principles of morality in the eyes of the world. It is
impossible to destroy men with more respect to the laws of humanity."
Tocqueville had been in Memphis in December 1831, when a band of
Choctaws forded the ice-choked Mississippi. He left this account:

That year the cold was exceptionally severe; the snow was hard on the ground ...
The Indians brought their families with them; there were among them the
wounded, the sick, newborn babies, and old men on the point of death. They
had neither tents nor wagons ... I saw them embark to cross the great river, and
the sight will never fade from my memory. Neither sob nor complaint rose from
that silent assembly. Their afflictions were of long standing, and they felt them to
be irremediable.[12]

Tocqueville concluded that extinction awaited every North American tribe.

Champions of removal countered that the critics exaggerated wildly. Cooper argued that removal, despite procedural defects, was the only plausible remedy to Indian demise, manifest in declining numbers and proliferating social pathologies. Continued exposure to and interaction with white civilization would overwhelm what remained of Indian life. It would, he taught, collapse into a putrefaction of tribal practices while fostering pathetic mimicry of a culture too alien to be assimilated. The humane alternative was to place the Indians beyond harm's reach. In the unincorporated western lands they could revivify their ancient habits unencumbered by trespassers or white agents of temptation. Cooper clung to this hope: "If the [removal] plan can be effected, there is reason to think that the constant diminution in the numbers of the Indians will be checked, and that a race, about whom there is so much that is poetic and fine in recollection, will be preserved."[13]

Indian Removal Act

Concern for tribal welfare akin to Cooper's was an element in the contradictory outlook of Jackson. Nobody indulged a friendlier feeling than he toward America's aborigines, so he claimed.[14] This disposition led to his adopting a Creek baby boy, Lyncoya, orphaned by the 1813 battle of Tallushatchee. Jackson lavished attention on his son, later hoping to enroll him as a cadet at West Point. Lyncoya died when sixteen from "pulmonary complaints" in 1828, just months before Jackson's inauguration as the seventh president.[15] From this office Jackson routinely preached the value of removal – the best method of protecting Indian tribes. Otherwise, inexorable US civilization doomed them. "Humanity and national honor demand that every effort should be made to avert so great a calamity," he told Congress in his first annual message (1829). Only in the west, he reiterated to acquaintances, could the Indians live unmolested by mercenary white men and escape decay.[16]

This protective paternalism toward Native America conflicted with the other side of Jackson's character: stern, obsessive, unyielding. These traits surfaced repeatedly in his career as Indian fighter along the frontier and as land agent for southern buyers. He ignored provisions in the Treaty of Ghent (article IX) that provided for the return of territories surrendered by Britain's Indian allies to the United States – 23 million acres ceded by the Creeks in 1814. Jackson worked instead to accelerate Creek emigration and dared anyone, Briton or Washington functionary, to stop him as he pushed the cause of land-hungry cotton planters.[17] He also obtained outlandish deals to despoil Cherokees, Choctaws, and Chickasaws of properties in 1814–1820. He led an invading army against Spanish Florida in the First Seminole War (1817–1818). In a precursor to full-scale hostilities, Jackson had ordered General E. P. Gaines to raze Negro Fort in northern Florida – accomplished in July 1816 along with the destruction of 270 persons who sheltered within, Indians and escaped slaves from US plantations.[18]

This Indian experience inclined Jackson away from the idea entertained by earlier presidents. George Washington and Jefferson believed that North American tribes might blend into mainstream US society as yeomen farmers; genuine concord could mark relations between white and red peoples. Jefferson had meant to reassure the western tribes during his second administration with these words: "The day will soon come when you will unite yourselves with us, join in our great councils, and form a people with us, and we shall all be Americans."[19]

Jackson rejected such sentimentality. He held as self-evident truth that the Indian and white worlds could not meld, from which this followed: Indians faced either eviction or cultural and physical annihilation as the US edged westward. By and large, he viewed the prospect of Indian disappearance with equanimity, as long as the United States prospered. Besides, he reflected, since ancient times lesser cultures had made way for superior ones. He liked to cite in this connection the archeological evidence concerning North America's "mound builders," exterminated he supposed by the ancestors of modern Indians. Fate in the nineteenth century, he held, had ordained the commencing of their supreme trial.[20]

Necessity, then, not only frontier vindictiveness, shaped Jackson's thinking on Indian destiny. He asked rhetorically in 1830 in the language of Manifest Destiny: "What good man would prefer a country covered with forests and ranged by a few thousand savages to our extensive Republic, studded with cities, towns, and prosperous farms, embellished with the improvements which art can devise or industry execute, occupied by more than 12,000,000 happy people, and filled with all the blessings of liberty, civilization, and religion?" Philanthropy, he answered, would never want the continent restored to its primeval condition.[21]

Jackson had two additional concerns. First, he was anxious about the reliability of Indians, especially in the south. He worried that they were susceptible to the blandishments of foreign powers, as had been the case in 1812, and might one day make common cause with them against the United States. Security, in other words, argued for the removal of tribes from the nation's soft underbelly. Second, the state government of Georgia wanted the federal authority to make good on its side of an agreement struck in 1802: Georgia in exchange for surrendering colonial charter claims in the west (in what became Alabama and Mississippi) would receive not only cash compensation ($1.25 million); Georgia would also be unburdened of its Indian population. Accordingly, the federal government was to purchase the land title from tribes (Creeks, Cherokees) in Georgia and make the vacated area available to white planters, farmers, and settlements. By the mid-1820s most of the Creeks had moved out of their zone (in the Chattahooche river valley) because the violence and other pressure brought to bear by Governor George Troup had become intolerable. The Cherokees stayed on, however. Their presence, complained such notables as Wilson Lumpkin, prevented Georgia from realizing its full economic-social potential. The 1829 discovery of gold in northwestern Georgia on Cherokee land heightened the irritability of state officials with federal dawdling on expulsion. If left permanently unsatisfied, the victim as it were of Washington's neglect, Georgia might take matters into its own hands, thereby strengthening nullification impulses in the south. Nullification at the time was corroding confidence between South Carolina and the federal government, high tariffs being the point of contention. A prospective Georgia–South Carolina alliance against Washington, Jackson thought, could lead to a disunion crisis. For the good of the republic, therefore, forced evacuation should not be further delayed. Upon leaving office in 1837, Jackson judged his removal policy a success from all standpoints: righteousness, security, national cohesion.[22]

His Indian initiative benefited from key support. It included Lewis Cass, governor of Michigan Territory during 1813–1831. He praised Jackson's policy as welcome boldness.[23] He subsequently served as Jackson's secretary of war (1831–1836), in which office he presided over the removal program. A member of the American Philosophical Society, plus a student of Indian languages, Cass gave scholarly cover to Jackson's action per a well-regarded article in the *North American Review* (January 1830). He elaborated upon the incompatibility of white Americans with the Indian race, its numbers tumbling: "A barbarous people, depending for subsistence upon the scanty and precarious supplies furnished by the chase, cannot live in contact with a civilized community." He regretted that all efforts to date to improve the Indians – by instruction in agriculture, Christianity, letters – had failed. Improvidence, indolence, and linguistic disability accounted for the Indians' chronic ignorance. To halt the further demoralization of eastern tribes, an inspired government had devised removal as vehicle of deliverance: "A region is open to them, where they and their descendants can be secured in the enjoyment of every privilege [of] which they may be capable."[24] Even the words of Jackson's nemesis, John Quincy Adams, were replayed to support administration policy. He had framed these questions in 1802 (which later embarrassed him):

What is the right of the huntsman to the forest of a thousand miles over which he has accidentally ranged in quest of prey? . . . Shall the fields and valleys, which a beneficent God has formed to teem with the life of innumerable multitudes, be condemned to everlasting barrenness?[25]

Neither were Protestant leaders ignored by Jackson's government. It had to contend with those divines who thought that Native Americans were descended from the lost tribes of Israel, thus peculiarly deserving of helpful attention. Socially engaged Christianity, moreover, stoked by Charles Finney in the Second Great Awakening, made justice for Indians a goal (along with abolition, temperance, women's rights). Thomas McKenney, first BIA director and of genuinely humanitarian impulses, helped in 1829–1830 to organize Episcopalian and Dutch Reform endorsement of removal. He thereby denied to removal's opponents a monopoly on Christian–moral language. Faith-based support was institutionalized in his New York Board for the Emigration, Preservation, and Improvement of the Aborigines of America.[26] It elected the influential Stephen Van Rensselaer as president. This association eventually drew aid from other denominations and counted Methodist, Baptist, and Presbyterian clergymen in its membership. They sermonized that only in exodus did the Indians have a realistic chance at survival.

Jackson's removal allies in Congress came primarily from the south and west. They included fellow Democratic Tennesseans, John Bell in the House of Representatives and Senator Hugh Lawson White. Both men chaired their respective chamber's committee on Indian matters and defended the Removal Act against attempts to amend it in lenient directions. Active too in this cause were Senators John Forsyth (Georgia) and Robert Adams (Mississippi), and Representatives Wilson Lumpkin (Georgia), James Wayne (Georgia), and Dixon Lewis (Alabama). The tone and substance of this group's language were exemplified by Wayne, who made bare mention in his House speech (May 24, 1830) that removal might protect Native America by placing the tribes in safe havens. Rather, he spoke directly to the white right to Indian-occupied land. He mentioned the precedent set by New England colonists as they acquired territory at the expense of original inhabitants. He summoned the authority of philosopher Emerich de Vattel to show that possession by people able to cultivate land and establish settlements trumped claims by nomads.[27]

To Wayne's arguments, Lumpkin added this determination. The Cherokees and other tribes would head west, come what may: "Pages may be filled with a sublimated cant of the day, and in wailing over the departure of the Cherokees from the bones of their forefathers. But if the heads of these pretended mourners were waters, and their eyes were a fountain of tears, and they were to spend days and years in weeping over the departure of the Cherokees from Georgia, yet they will go."[28]

Acid-tongued Forsyth ridiculed removal's critics for their tenderness toward Indians. He asked whether their white champions would shed the blood of US citizens to protect the territorial claims of vengeful heathens.[29] Besides, he wondered, who were the northerners to scold? They had directed so much violence in earlier years against Indians (in New England, New York, and elsewhere) that they had mostly vanished. Once proud red men were indigent. Only the vagaries of white charity kept doleful survivors alive.[30]

Opposition to the Removal Act ran deep among northeastern congressmen of the incipient Whig party. They combined antipathy for Jackson, whom they regarded as a demagogue, with coolness toward the south's plantation economy. Impetus for their opposition came from such constituents as Pennsylvania Quakers and New England churchmen (Congregationalists, Presbyterians). They expressed this dual concern: southeastern Indians were entitled to their properties because of ancient right; dispossession served the interests of slaveholders driven by land greed. The Boston-based American Board of Commissioners for Foreign Missions, preeminent Protestant missionary association of its day, was a bastion of anti-removal attitude.[31] The Board's corresponding secretary, Jeremiah Evarts, using the pseudonym William Penn, composed a series of anti-removal essays in 1829 for Washington's *National Intelligencer*. They were reprinted in other newspapers, served as texts for sermons and congressional speeches, and energized petition drives.[32]

Evarts's thesis was that the United States, God's instrument for spreading Christ's word, would betray vocation by expelling the blameless. Persecution of innocent people defied the moral laws, as applicable to countries as to individuals. Divine retribution, Evarts warned, would smack a guilty United States. "May a gracious Providence," he wrote, "avert from this country the awful calamity of exposing ourselves to the wrath of heaven, as a consequence of disregarding the cries of the poor and defenseless, and perverting to purposes of cruelty and oppression, that power which was given to us to promote the happiness of our fellow-men."[33] Evarts repeated similar points in the *North American Review* in a rebuttal (October 1830) of Cass's earlier pro-removal essay: Jackson's proposal would bring ruin to the tribes "and upon ourselves the deep and lasting infamy of a break of faith."[34]

The most important conduit of Evarts's ideas to official Washington was his friend Senator Theodore Frelinghuysen of New Jersey. In a varied career he practiced law, served as New Jersey's attorney general, took a turn in the US senate (1829–1835), presided in Newark as mayor (1836–1839), sought the vice presidency in 1844 on Henry Clay's unsuccessful Whig ticket, and held two college presidencies (New York University 1839–1849, Rutgers 1850–1862). Quick and articulate, he was above all devoutly religious in the Dutch Reform tradition of his forebears.[35] He never entered the ministry, despite tugs in that direction, but involved himself with a number of benevolent organizations. He served at one time or another as president of the American Board of Commissioners for Foreign Missions (1841–1857), the American Tract Society (1842–1848), and the American Bible Society (1846–1862). He also held offices in the American Colonization Society, the American Temperance Union, and the American Sunday School Union. He used all these positions to boost social reform within the context of evangelical witness – including support of Dorothea Dix's efforts to humanize care of the mentally ill.[36] Not a militant abolitionist, by inheritance a one-time slaveholder, he did count Wilberfore a hero and loathed slavery.[37]

Frelinghuysen campaigned for recognition of Indians as fully evolved human beings with souls worthy of respect and salvation. For their welfare a benignant Providence cared as much as for the lives of white people. The senator viewed with consternation and prophetic conviction the prospect of another round to exploit Native America.[38]

He overcame the diffidence normally shown by freshmen lawmakers to address his Senate colleagues in April 1830. He delivered a speech in two-hour installments over three days, which earned him the appellation "Christian statesman" from William Lloyd Garrison.[39] Frelinghuysen explained in imagery, borrowed from Evarts, that removal would cancel America's divine mission: "*We*, whom God has exalted to the very summit of prosperity – whose brief career forms the brightest page in history; the wonder and praise of the world; Freedom's hope, and her consolation: *We* [are] about to turn traitors to our principles and our fame – about to become the oppressors of the feeble, and to cast away our birth-right!" Such betrayal, Frelinghuysen predicted, would draw censure by generations yet unborn and justify God's punishing His wayward US children.[40]

He emphasized that the republic was already rich in territory. More was not needed. The Indians should be left alone to enjoy vestiges of their patrimony: "Millions after millions [of acres] he [the Indian] has yielded to our importunity, until we have acquired more than can be cultivated in centuries – and yet we crave more. We have crowded the tribes upon a few miserable acres on our southern frontier – it is all that is left to them of their once boundless forests – and still, like the horseleech, our insatiate cupidity cries, *Give, Give*." He lamented that the tide of white settlement would erase Native America unless self-restraint were exercised. Its main-springs lay in conscience, in a regard for justice that placed Christian ethics above swaggering power. The obligation to practice right conduct, Frelinghuysen insisted, did not vary with the different racial groups with whom one dealt. He asked: "How shall we justify this trespass to ourselves? ... Let us beware how, by oppressive encroachment upon the sacred privileges of our Indian neighbors, we minister to the agonies of future remorse."[41]

Umbrage approaching Frelinghuysen's came from the lips of Senators Peleg Sprague (Maine) and Ascher Robbins (Rhode Island). Representatives Henry Storrs (New York), George Evans (Maine), Joseph Hemphill (Pennsylvania), Kensey Johns (Delaware), Jabez Huntington (Connecticut), William Ellsworth (Connecticut), Isaac Bates (Massachusetts), and Edward Everett (Massachusetts) were outspoken in House hearings. Everett came second only to Frelinghuysen in disparaging the removal plan. To effect it would surpass the projected cost of $500,000, Everett argued. The price he estimated would come to about $24 million. The moral cost would be incalculable in any event: an eviction of tens of thousands of people against their wishes constituted criminality. The Classics professor told his House comrades:

It was the practice – the barbarous and truly savage practice – of the polished nations of antiquity, to bring home a part of the population of conquered countries as slaves. It was a cruel exercise of the rights of the conqueror, as then understood, and, in turn, practiced by all nations. But in time of peace, toward unoffending communities, subject to our sovereignty indeed, but possessing rights guaranteed to them by more than one hundred treaties, to remove them against their will, by thousands, to a distant and different country, where they must lead a new life, and form other habits, and encounter the perils and hardships of the wilderness: Sir, I never heard of such a thing; it is an experiment on human life and human happiness of perilous novelty![42]

Not all westerners cared for the Removal Act. Some voted against it, among whom were John Test (Indiana) and Davy Crockett (Tennessee). A veteran of Indian campaigns, Crockett had fought under Jackson in the Creek War. But by 1830 the Jackson–Crockett friendship had begun to fray. (Crockett eventually defected to the Whig party, where party leaders congratulated him for enlisting against "King Andrew.") Unlettered Crockett spoke from a text prepared by another westerner opposed to removal, Representative Thomas Chilton (Kentucky). Crockett later reminisced: "I voted against [the] Indian bill, and my conscience yet tells me that I gave a good honest vote, and one that I believe will not make me ashamed in the day of judgment."[43]

Congress's debate culminated in this result. The House carried the legislation by 102 to 97, close enough to gratify anti-Jacksonians eager to discomfit the president. The Senate margin of victory was better for him, 28 to 19. He signed the Indian Removal Act on May 28, 1830.

Resistance

The eastern tribes employed varied means against removal. A few resorted to violence. The Black Hawk War in Illinois and Wisconsin lasted fifteen weeks in 1832. Army regulars and state militias devastated the Sac and Fox. Their women and children figured conspicuously among the dead. People who survived the conflict and retreated to the western bank of the Mississippi were preyed upon by Sioux raiders. Captured by US soldiers, Chief Black Hawk was imprisoned for a year in Fortress Monroe (Virginia) before rejoining what remained of his tribe in Iowa territory.

Sporadic violence by the Creeks in 1836 constituted a war of sorts. It climaxed in the expulsion of 15,000 Creeks from Alabama, without the cosmetic of treaty, with many warriors shackled in chains.[44] The small Seneca nation of 2,500 people in western New York managed to prevail via non-violent method. They were allowed to remain thanks to deft legal maneuvering and intervention by the Society of Friends.

In the estimation of one first-hand observer, Ethan Allen Hitchcock of the US army, the people most "grossly defrauded" were the Seminoles and Cherokees.[45] They also offered the most stubborn resistance to removal. The Seminoles made war. The Cherokees appealed to the Supreme Court. Neither tribe won. Yet each provoked political firestorms before succumbing.

Seminoles

The Second Seminole War of 1835–1842 cost the United States much. Eleven thousand regular troops saw combat, recruited typically from the poor and/or recently arrived from Europe (Irish, Scottish, English, German). Fifteen hundred died, mainly felled by tropical diseases such as malaria. Perhaps one hundred Florida civilians were killed. Dollar estimates of wartime expenditures vary. The amount commonly given, on the conservative side, places them at $25 million. A total of 30,000 men drawn from state militias was involved in the Florida action. Their performance was indifferent, their casualties light. Overall, the Seminole episode was the most expensive and upsetting Indian war in US annals.

The violence did not end in clear victory but petered out. Some scholars have likened the Seminole campaign to America's later discouragement in Vietnam. In each case, overwhelming material advantage was frustrated by inhospitable terrain and an enemy ingenious in the art of concealment. As for the Seminoles, their fatalities are nowhere reliably given. Estimates put them between one and two thousand – from a tribe numbering fewer than six thousand people. Most of the survivors were relocated to Oklahoma on a land parcel north of the Creek zone. Roughly five hundred fugitives melted into the Florida swamps (to reappear in the Third Seminole War, 1855–1858).[46]

The war's immediate cause sprang from rejection by a tribal majority of the treaties signed at Payne's Landing (May 1832) and Fort Gibson (March 1833). They called for removal to western lands, supposedly suitable for Seminole use. Before these treaties were signed by tribal delegations, acting under duress of intimidation and poverty, the Seminoles had resided on a reservation in central Florida per the 1823 Treaty of Camp Moultrie. The tribe had also received a government annuity of $5,000 and livestock. Seminole delay in complying with the new treaties led to the dispatch of US army forces in 1835 to assemble the tribe and arrange its transportation by ships for western ports. On December 28 a group of warriors led by Osceola killed Wiley Thompson, the government's Indian agent in Florida. That same day a party of braves and blacks ambushed a column of troops under Major Francis Dade. All but three men of his unit (of 110) were killed. A few days later a battle was fought at the Withlacooche river in which most of the Florida volunteers, to the disgust of the 200 regulars, avoided combat. The Seminoles, led by Osceola, and their black allies carried the day.[47]

American slavery was a contributing cause of the war. Between one fourth and one third of the Seminole nation (a Creek offshoot) was composed of people who were wholly or in part black. They were escaped slaves from Georgia or Alabama plantations or descended from earlier runaways. The mild servitude these people experienced as Seminole vassals was far preferable to plantation rigors. It shaded into amalgamation. The wife of Osceola was black. Her capture by slave catchers led to his starting the war. Slave catchers for years prior had intruded upon Seminole lands, in defiance of the Camp Moultrie treaty, in pursuit of escapees. The aim was to restore them to their legal owners or, failing that, to sell the slaves to third parties. Seminole-born free blacks were also sought by hunters who could realize additional profit for their exertions. In sum, Seminole lands had little value for white settlers or agriculture but the tribe's blacks were of theoretically great monetary reward. A southern demand was that Seminole removal not involve the transport westward of former (or potential) slaves. Still, slaveholders yearned for Seminole expulsion as it would eliminate the runaways' sanctuary.

Northern war critics perceived the following. The desperation of former slaves to avoid repatriation and the reluctance of Indians to part from their blacks (servants, allies, and kin) explained the Seminoles' persistence against vast odds. Some northern congressmen, otherwise agnostic about removal, were attracted to the Seminoles precisely because they harbored black escapees. Representative Joshua Giddings of Ohio, a Whig abolitionist, personified this mentality.

He used the war to test the limits of the "gag rule," that body of resolutions from 1836 which forbade House debate on antislavery petitions. He took the introduction of a bill by South Carolina's Waddy Thompson in February 1841 – which appropriated $100,000 to ship Seminole warriors westward – as occasion to criticize the war and, by extension, slavery. Giddings charged that the war was a slave-trapping operation and existed to benefit southern planters in danger of losing their work force to Florida freedom. Amid booing by southern colleagues, he declared that the war sullied the flag and name of the US army, as when Major General Thomas Jesup decreed (August 1837) that troops could dispose of Seminole property as they chose. The property mentioned "Negroes," as well as cattle and horses. Soldiers could win a bounty of $20 for each black person restored to white authority. Giddings fired:

Our national flag, which floated in proud triumph at Saratoga, which was enveloped in a blaze of glory at Monmouth and Yorktown, seems to have been prostituted in Florida to the base purpose of leading on an organized company of "Negro-catchers." No longer is "our country" the battle-cry of our army in their advance to victory, but "slaves" has become the watchword to inspire them to effort. No longer does the war-worn veteran amid the battle's rage think of his country's glory and nerve his arm in behalf of freedom, but with eagle eye he watches the wavering ranks of the enemy, and as they flee before our advancing columns, he plunges among them to seize the sable foe, and make him his future slave.[48]

Among southern legislators, Georgia's Edward Black stood out. He told the House that Giddings would be lynched should he ever set foot on sacred Georgia soil. (Black used his cane in 1845 to take a swing at Giddings on the House floor.)[49]

Despite threats, Giddings pressed on. The use of Cuban-bred bloodhounds to track Seminoles and runaway slaves in Florida particularly riled him. He later published (in 1858) an indictment of the war, *The Exiles of Florida*. Abolitionists hailed this book. Dixie reviewers called it a rant. "At a time of profound peace," Giddings had written, "our army, acting under the direction of the Executive, invaded Florida, murdered many ... free men, and brought others to the United States and consigned them to slavery."[50]

Representative John Quincy Adams agreed with Giddings on the nature of the Florida war. The former president and abolitionist convert also gave publicity to the bloodhounds. He once submitted a resolution that included this language:

> That the Secretary of War be directed to report to this House, the natural, political, and martial history of the bloodhounds, showing the peculiar fitness of that class of warriors to be the associates of the gallant army of the United States, specifying the nice discrimination of his scent between the blood of the freeman and the blood of the slave ... between the blood of savage Seminoles and that of the Anglo-Saxon pious Christian.[51]

Discussions in Congress became even testier as the war dragged on and as millions of dollars were spent. The war's inconclusiveness, along with the Panic of 1837 and economic turmoil, had already defeated Van Buren's reelection bid in 1840. In the meantime Van Buren's secretary of war, Joel Poinsett, had been accused by Whigs of lethargy. Generals were criticized too – particularly Jesup and his predecessor in Florida, Winfield Scott – for their purported lack of competence. Exasperation with the war was never more clearly evidenced than when South Carolina's Senator William Preston uttered these words: "Here has been a war ... of fifteen million prosperous people against a miserable band of naked savages; a war of the whole territory, army, and military of the Union, against a few bandits in Florida, and with all this the war is disastrous."[52]

Perhaps the most discouraged Americans of all, outside pacifist denominations or the small peace movement, were those soldiers charged with fighting the war. A number of officers sympathized with the Seminoles. Lieutenant John Sprague confided in his diary that they were true patriots defending their homeland. Hitchcock, then a major, detested his assignment in Florida. He thought the treaty of Payne's Landing a swindle inflicted on people who naturally disavowed it; he regretted that his army had become a tool of iniquity. Senior grade officers also found the war dismal. One general after another failed to win anything but criticism from pundits and civilian supervisors. None of the commanders – Gaines, Duncan Lamont Church, Zachary Taylor, Alexander Macomb, Walker Armistead, William Worth – could interdict or destroy the foe's main force but resorted to unsatisfactory stratagems of attrition. General Scott ("Old Fuss and Feathers") rued that neither glory nor professional advancement could be achieved in the sweltering swamps. The most outspoken officer was Jesup. He quarreled with superiors about operational matters. He doubted in public forum, a letter to the *Army and Navy Chronicle*, the logic of expelling the Seminoles: "We have committed the error of attempting to remove them when their lands were not required for agricultural purposes; when they were not in the way of white inhabitants; and when the greater part of their country was an unexplored wilderness."[53] Despite reservations, Jesup did what he could as dutiful soldier to end the war on terms favoring the United States. He is best remembered for capturing Osceola in October 1837 under a flag of truce, then sending him to captivity at Fort Moultrie in South Carolina (where he died in 1838).[54]

Disquiet among army officers with removal was not confined only to the Seminole war where, on balance, their misgivings had negligible influence on the outcome. In the Cherokee removal a couple of officers did modestly affect policy.

Cherokees

The once expansive Cherokees domain had been reduced by 1830 to bits of North Carolina, Alabama, and southeastern Tennessee. Northwestern Georgia contained the largest concentration plus the capital of New Echota. Even as the tribal realm shrank with treaties and land sales, the Cherokees had tried to acculturate to US life.

The Cherokees at the moment of Jackson's Removal Act possessed a written language, the product of a genius: Sequoyah. He introduced his syllabary in 1821, which was quickly adopted. Clan-based law enforcement and blood vengeance in accidental deaths meanwhile yielded to a new order. This established a supreme court, fielded a national police force, and emplaced written codes. Legal protections were extended to such things as private property. Provisions were made for the welfare of widows and orphans. The Cherokees adopted a constitution in 1827 – based on the US model with corresponding legislative, executive, and judicial branches – that asserted national sovereignty. A bilingual newspaper (English/Cherokee) began publication in 1828, the *Cherokee Phoenix*. It operated under the editorship of another talented tribesman, Elias Boudinot.[55] Portions of the Bible were also translated from English. By 1835, 10 percent of the 16,000-strong Cherokee nation professed Protestant versions of Christianity: Baptist, Congregationalist, Methodist, Presbyterian. Belief in witchcraft and magical arts declined. The flourishing of tribal schools, lending libraries, benevolence societies, and the like (plus plans for a national academy and museum) were other expressions of Cherokee desire: to create an unassailable niche within US society.[56]

The Cherokee elite was economically and racially entwined with the southern white world, in Georgia above all. Affluent chiefs such as John

Ross claimed substantial portions of European ancestry (Scottish in his case). They owned productive plantations worked by black slaves and lived in fine houses. Major Ridge, who had served under Jackson in the 1814 Creek War, and Joseph Vann were also prominent Cherokees integrated into the planter-economy life. A census in 1835 indicated that nearly sixteen hundred black slaves were owned in the Cherokee nation.[57] Ridge's son, John, and nephew, Elias Boudinot, were educated in Connecticut. They married white women and dealt as equals with Gallatin and other ethnologists fascinated by Cherokee customs. This version of assimilation equaled civilization in the minds of the Cherokee elite, an idea glowingly refrained by the tribe's white defenders. Everett, for one, impressed that the Cherokees had acquired habits of mind and outward trappings of white America, said that nature's formerly wild children had become irreversibly elevated: "They are planters and farmers, trades-people and mechanics. They have cornfields and orchards, looms and workshops, schools and churches, and orderly institutions. The political communities of a large portion of civilized and Christian Europe might well be proud to exhibit such a table of [accomplishment]."[58] These advances into the white world, though, did not equal safety.

Georgia proponents of expulsion were heartened by Congress's passing the Removal Act. State officials, long intent on this goal, could not tolerate an autonomous nation – presumed by the 1827 Cherokee constitution – within their borders (*imperium in imperio*). This feeling was quickened in the summer of 1830 as thousands of prospectors invaded the Cherokee gold fields. State legislators in Milledgeville that year enacted a land lottery to provide for the distributing of Cherokee land to white Georgians. The legislature also disallowed any laws approved by the Cherokee National Council, holding that the state's writ applied everywhere, thus demolishing any claim of rival sovereignty. Subsequent Georgia legislation (December 1830) banned the Cherokee government from convening or acting. White people living in Cherokee territory were obliged to take an oath of allegiance to Georgia, a stringency pointed at the dozen missionaries who resided in the Cherokee nation. (These busybodies shielded their charges against state authority and championed them as newcomers to society with commensurate rights.[59])

A police force, the Georgia Guard, was established to enforce Milledgeville's rule among the Indians. This Guard contained ruffians who harassed Cherokees (including Major Ridge, Ross, Boudinot), stole from them, and seldom defended them against theft or flogging by white intruders. Several missionaries were manhandled by the Guard. This attack upon the Cherokee regime was aided by a law that forbade

Indians from testifying against white citizens in Georgia courts. Cherokees were additionally forbidden from employing any white man (or slaves owned by whites), could not mine gold, and could not cultivate more than 160 acres of land. Georgia's assault on the Cherokees, which enjoyed Jackson's personal blessing, had one purpose: to quicken the Indians' exodus. Frelinghuysen remarked: "Here we find a whole people outlawed – laws, customs, rules, government, all ... abrogated, and declared to be void, as if they never had been." Referring to nationalist revival in Poland, an object of American sympathy at the time, he commented: "The dismemberment and partition of Poland was a deed of humane legislation, compared with this."[60] Meanwhile Indians who spoke against removal or advised their neighbors against emigration were subject to arrest.

Cherokee leaders countered Georgia's oppression. They publicized their position in the *Cherokee Phoenix* and via northern newspapers: "We wish to remain on the land of our fathers."[61] Chiefs petitioned Congress for protection against Georgia. They wrote letters to friendly congressmen, thanking them for previous support and urging them not to relent because ultimately, as Ross told Crockett: "Integrity and moral worth will predominate and make the shameless monster hide its head."[62] The Cherokees invoked the sanctity of previous treaties that guaranteed the inviolability of tribal holdings. Delegations led by Ross in 1832–1833 went to Washington and pestered officials (primarily Cass of the War Department) for fair play. Missionaries on Cherokee assignment wrote for the popular press – also to their denominations – on behalf of the embattled people. Sam Houston, who since boyhood had been on intimate terms with Cherokees, tried to coax Jackson into taking a more generous position. Abolitionists Arthur Tappan and Garrison, ignoring slavery among the Cherokees, convened mass meetings to protest Georgia's displacement (joined by Alabama) of the Indians.

The Cherokees also hired legal aid in the person of William Wirt. Former attorney general of the United States, and antimasonic presidential aspirant in 1832, he argued their case before the Supreme Court. The court issued two crucial judgments in response. The first, *Cherokee Nation v. Georgia*, ruled that the tribe contra Wirt's contention was not a sovereign entity but instead a domestic dependent nation – a ward in effect to the United States guardian. In the words of Chief Justice John Marshall in March 1831: "They [Cherokees] are in a state of pupilage." Although he rejected Cherokee claims of sovereignty, he did declare as anathema Georgia's attempt to place the nation under Milledgeville's authority.[63] The tribe chose to interpret Marshall's ruling as in its favor, making the federal government responsible for Cherokee safety against Georgia's multiple harassments. The second court decision,

Worcester v. Georgia, unequivocally supported the Cherokees. Marshall delivered the court's majority view in March 1832, when he pronounced that all the laws passed by Georgia pertaining to the Cherokee nation were unconstitutional.[64] The onus, then, for Cherokee safety fell upon the federal authority. Palpable relief swept through Cherokee lands.

Jackson made clear that he would not pit the power or prestige of the federal government against Georgia. Of Marshall, whom he anyway disliked, he apparently said: "John Marshall has made his decision. Now let him enforce it!" Jackson ostentatiously withheld protection from the Cherokees. His reelection in 1832 made obvious to several of their leading men, comprising the Treaty party, that nothing existed to buffer the tribe against Georgian designs. Boudinot, previously dedicated to the proposition that Cherokee–white harmony was feasible, endorsed this sad realism: "Instead of contending uselessly against superior power, the only course left [to Cherokee leaders] was to yield to circumstances over which they had no control." Crusty Major Ridge confessed that he would willingly fight to preserve the Cherokee homes, "but any forcible effort to keep them will cost us our lands, our lives and the lives of our children." Frelinghuysen concurred in these views. He reluctantly advised that no alternative existed to removal.[65]

The denouement occurred in December 1835 with the signing of the treaty of New Echota (coinciding by chance with Major Dade's Florida disaster). By its provisions the Cherokees relinquished all of their holdings, eight million acres, east of the Mississippi to the United States for $5 million. The nation would move at federal expense to Oklahoma territory within two years of the Senate's ratification of New Echota. Subsistence for the first year would be provided by the US government to the arrivals (who would, incidentally, be joining a previously settled Cherokee colony in Oklahoma). Reverend John Schermerhorn and William Carroll represented the United States at New Echota. Figures in the Treaty party, most importantly Major Ridge and Boudinot, signed for the whole Cherokee nation.

The difficulty in this arrangement arose from the fact that most Cherokees still opposed removal. They backed Ross and his National party. He would not turn, no matter the copious slurs that Jackson proceeded to rain upon the chief's character and motives. Ross rejected the New Echota treaty, signed by dishonorable negotiators, he alleged, who were too eager to placate white aggression and retain whatever possessions possible. Majority thinking had been misportrayed; the tribe had been surrendered. Ross organized a petition drive among the people. Twelve thousand signatures were gathered and sent to Washington. Another three thousand Cherokees in North Carolina signed a resolution of protest that was also delivered to Congress. Ross in a 1837 interview with newly installed President Van Buren asked that the treaty be abrogated, but in vain. The commander in chief stood on these facts: Congress had already acted in May 1836 – the Senate had ratified New Echota, the House had appropriated necessary funds.

Senate ratification of New Echota in 1836 had not been an easy matter in that political season. The Whig opposition used the treaty question for partisan purpose: to illustrate the depth of Jackson's callousness and the unfitness of Vice President Van Buren to follow him into the White House. The Whig press touted Chief Ross as the heroic leader of an upright people snared by trickery. Senators Webster and Clay spoke against the treaty. The former, anxious that his name not be attached by the public to New Echota, jeered at its fraudulence. The latter held the standard prejudice of his day and region against Indians. But Clay begged his legislative colleagues – even before they read the treaty text – "to treat with ... kindness, and the most perfect justice, the aborigines whom Providence has committed to our guardianship."[66] This appeal almost succeeded. The upper house barely approved the treaty by the required two-thirds vote, 31 to 15. Neither did Jackson win House appropriations without a struggle. Adams called the treaty a blot on the US record. Yet the House went along in the end, carrying such unlikely men as Everett. Georgia's treatment of the Cherokees scandalized him as did Jackson's unwillingness to protect them. The Treaty party's reasoning, though, persuaded him: "They are reduced to the alternative of [going west], or of sinking into a condition but little ... better than slavery."[67]

Members of the Treaty party were the first to leave Georgia and other Cherokee states. This migration took place in 1837. It was effected smoothly and in relative ease – also speedily, to escape retribution by Nationalists. The extended Ridge family with black retainers rode west in fit carriages drawn by teams of fresh horses. The Ridges and fellow emigrants had adequate stocks of food, camping accouterments, and appropriate clothing. Government employed private contractors proved satisfactory as guides and provisioners. This Cherokee band established itself in Oklahoma in autumn 1837 and was reasonably organized when new waves of immigrants arrived, 1838–1839.[68]

The post-1837 Cherokees traveled the "trail of tears." Seven thousand soldiers uprooted families from their homes and villages at bayonet point in the sizzling summer of 1838. Collected thus, the Indians were then confined under military guard in crowded stockades and departure depots, where unhygienic conditions bred cholera, dysentery, typhoid. The people were next formed into sections that marched west in varieties of weather. Infirm elders, infants, and youngsters were exposed to the elements without benefit of nutritious food, proper clothing, or suitable conveyance. Parents and children were sometimes separated in clumsy handling at river crossings or husbands and wives divided. Throughout this ordeal troops, not always well disciplined, loosely herded the dejected civilians. Western settlers along the way occasionally taunted the Indians, tempted them with vice, charged exorbitant prices for goods and services, or were otherwise uncharitable. More than four thousand Cherokees died in these circumstances. The survivors once arrived in Oklahoma took revenge. The National party denounced Major Ridge, John Ridge, and Boudinot. Its agents killed them in June 1839. A low level civil war ensued until Chief Ross reached a modus vivendi (1846) with Stand Watie of the Treaty group.

Not all Georgians were indifferent to Cherokee suffering. Onlookers from the university town of Athens signed a protest handed to the army officer in charge of Cherokee roundup in 1838. Citizens of Monroe and Blount counties also formally registered their disapproval. A number of ordinary soldiers disliked the expulsion policy. A Georgia volunteer, who afterward served in the Confederate army, recollected: "I fought through the Civil War and have seen men shot to pieces and slaughtered by thousands, but the Cherokee removal was the cruelest work I ever knew."[69] East Tennessee militiamen assigned to Georgia became so disillusioned that they withdrew in September 1836. Their commander, Brigadier General R. D. Dunlap, called the New Echota treaty spurious; he was unwilling to implicate Tennessee arms in "a servile service."[70] Even Lumpkin, employed from mid-1836 as federal commissioner to execute New Echota, enjoined the army to deal humanely with the Cherokees, if only to expedite removal with minimal friction.[71]

Detachments of Cherokee families moving west did at times meet decent churchmen and townsfolk. They donated palatable food and clean clothing. White volunteers were also known to intervene with needed medical help. Missionaries who accompanied the nation, such as Baptist preacher Evan Jones, did what they could to help and bolstered morale. The missionaries also interceded when possible with military authorities. Jones confronted Brigadier General John Wool, the senior officer detailed in 1836–1837 to effect Cherokee removal. Jones tried to persuade him of their physical distress and anguish at leaving the southeast.[72]

Wool was a stolid soldier. His army career dated to the War of 1812 wherein he won renown for bravery at the battles of Queenston and Plattsburg. Standing slightly above five feet, he was lissome, nimble, and strict (disinclined to suspend the military's reliance on corporal punishment). He was the army's inspector general from 1816 to 1841.

During those years he helped professionalize the small peacetime force. He traveled in his inspectorial capacity to France and Britain in 1832; he familiarized himself with European standards and ordnance. He was a close friend of Lewis Cass. Wool was also a politically engaged soldier. A Democrat, he openly supported Old Hickory in the 1828 presidential election.[73]

Nothing in his background suggested that Wool would object to an important national policy of Democratic origin. The only hint of dissident temper surfaced in 1819, when he urged that the curriculum of mathematics and engineering at West Point be leavened by attention to the humanities. He had ethics foremost in mind (plus history, foreign languages, geography). Mathematical study, he admitted, enhanced clarity of mind, but "like the blasts from the polar regions" froze imagination and "the heart [against] those generous qualities, which are always the result of energy and liberal investigation." Wool also possessed a streak of piety (Presbyterian) deeper than that found in contemporaneous officers.[74]

Released temporarily from inspector general duties and invigorated by field assignment, he at first relished his posting to Cherokee country. He luxuriated in the idea that his new assignment enjoyed approval among grateful citizens in Tennessee, Georgia, North Carolina, and Alabama (while Floridians skewered the army for not pacifying the Seminoles). Wary of Ross, Wool moved deftly to gather the Cherokees' firearms, mainly antique muskets used for hunting game but seen by him as hazardous to his men. He confiscated stores of spirits secreted on or near Cherokee land. He got white missionaries to cooperate with him, against their scruple but with threats of incarceration or banishment. He welcomed the aid of southern militias as his soldiers policed the peace between Indians and civilians. He had his men track Creek refugees in the Cherokee nation for delivery west.[75]

The removal job unnerved Wool after only three months. Unwholesome displays by eager whites offended his sense of fairness. They too obviously coveted Cherokee land upon which they trespassed with abandon. They sought profits at the expense of forlorn people and sold goods at inflated prices. Wool likened the swarming land speculators and merchants to vultures. He feared that their victims would arrive penniless in the west. He thought Lumpkin uncommonly ambitious, a mix of vulgarian and Jesuit.[76] Random violence by white civilians against Cherokees also alarmed Wool. It made his assignment complicated and personally objectionable. He wrote to the secretary of war: "With these people it really seems to be no crime to kill an Indian . . . [as when a man at home was] shot down and basely murdered by a party of white men, who had not the semblance of provocation."[77] Wool came to hate the situation, which he labeled heart-wrenching. He intimated to War Department superiors that the New Echota treaty lacked legitimacy. He reported that the Cherokee majority thought it derisory; many preferred death to removal. He asked Washington to be recalled.

Recall was slow in coming. Wool did what he could in the interim to ameliorate Cherokee hardship. He sent to Washington petitions by Ross that asked for clemency: "How have we offended?"[78] Wool upbraided officers who failed to control their men in interactions with Cherokees. He disciplined soldiers who behaved lewdly toward Cherokee women.[79] He ordered all ranks to treat the Indians with courtesy. He made blankets, food rations, shoes, and sundry other items available to the nation's neediest upon application. He prosecuted white gamblers and purveyors of whiskey who plundered Cherokee wealth. He tried to administer impartial justice among the Cherokees, their own tribunals having been emasculated by southern legislatures. In Alabama, where white claimants had seized Cherokee farms and livestock, Wool had the properties restored to their rightful owners.[80]

The general's actions angered Washington officialdom while they incensed authorities in Alabama and Georgia. President Jackson rebuked him for forwarding petitions by Ross and other Cherokee chiefs. Lumpkin charged that Wool disobeyed Washington's orders. He was "a Ross man at heart."[81] Alabama's governor, C. C. Clay, charged that Wool exceeded his authority, usurped the supremacy of local courts, disturbed the domestic tranquillity, and violated citizens' rights. This cumulative criticism led a military court of inquiry to investigate Wool's behavior in Alabama's Cherokee country. The court met in September 1837 with General Scott presiding.

Military and civilian witnesses testified, the bulk in defense of Wool. He explained in his own statement to the court that persecution of the innocent was not his business. Protection of the defenseless was his duty: "If I had acted otherwise than I did, I should have considered myself recreant to the sacred trust reposed in me." He invited the court to consider his dilemma in Alabama:

An Indian presents himself before me, and ... details his complaint. He says: I have been dispossessed by the white man of the house which I built, and the fields which I have cultivated for years; my property has been taken from me, and my family turned out to the shelter of the forest; your government is pledged to protect me ... I ask justice at your hands. I say to him, go to the civil tribunals of the States, they will redress your wrongs. What would be his answer, what would be your answer, or that of any other man in the community? It would be the voice of nature, universal as the human family. He would say, you insult me with such protection; it is a miserable mockery. Is this your justice? This your faith, so often, so solemnly pledged to us? In the language of Scripture he might exclaim, I have asked you for bread, and you have given me a stone.[82]

Wool next confessed that during his Alabama errand he had not always been diligent in cooperating with municipal authorities. He also expressed a general gripe to brother officers against people in elected office. He accused those in Alabama of mixing sophistry with arrogance:

My crime has been . . . in listening to [the Indian's] complaints and redressing his wrongs. I have endeavored to do him justice without inquiry into the particular provision of this or that State law. I have not perplexed myself with the subtle arguments of politicians about the indivisibility of sovereignty, or such like cobwebs of the brain.[83]

Justice alone was the sovereign to which Wool felt obedient. Self-seeking Alabamans were another story: "The path of justice being clear, I but obeyed the still small voice of conscience which frequently, in the advance of reasoning, overleaps those barriers with which subtlety and ingenuity sometimes successfully oppose its progress." Finally, with an eye to other dealings between the federal government and Native America, Wool told the court that fair practice was the only way to ensure peace. He had avoided the snare in Alabama of begetting violence by despotism:

The course of justice and humanity are but the dictates of an enlarged and liberal policy. By such a course the Indians were taught that some remains of justice, some touches of feeling yet existed in the bosoms of white men for their unfortunate and peculiar situation. I trust that it softened in some degree the asperities of their feelings, and caused them to look with some confidence to the future. Suppose a different course had been pursued – that every . . . oppression and cruelty was practiced towards them, and they could find no redress. Might they not justly say: We can but die, let us first be revenged?[84]

History was replete with bloody-minded resolution rooted in despair, he concluded.

The court of inquiry exonerated Wool following his testimony. The impact of his words on General Scott's thinking cannot exactly be determined. Scott's decision to drop all charges rested on an evaluation of the evidence, not only Wool's apologia. Still, as the next officer placed in charge (April 1838) of Cherokee removal, Scott had reason to heed Wool's analysis. His decision to proceed with regard for the emigrants, in any case, dovetailed with Wool's admonition to treat humanely with them. Scott was also buttressed in this thinking by his dealings with Chief Ross. The articulate Cherokee and the soldier met in Washington just before Scott left for New Echota. They discussed the tribe's grievances and prospects in Oklahoma. Scott spoke reassuringly of his determinations to avoid bloodshed while alleviating Cherokee hardships.[85]

On arrival in the southeast, Scott ordered his command to behave with civility. He set this standard: "Every possible kindness, compatible with the necessity of removal, must . . . be shown by the troops; and if, in the ranks, a despicable individual should be found capable of inflicting a wanton injury or insult on any Cherokee man, woman, or child, it is hereby made the special duty of the nearest good officer or man instantly to interpose, and to seize the guilty wretch to the severest penalty of the laws."[86]

Years after the removals, Scott recorded unabashed admiration of the Cherokees. He also expressed this opinion: "The Georgians [seemed] to forget, or, at least, to deny that a Cherokee was a human being." Most remarkably, given his life-long quest for glory and self-vindication, Scott revealed regret for his role in the Cherokees' exile.[87]

Well he might. Contra his intentions, the removal program went wrong during his supervision. Under the best of circumstances having to evict people from their homes, to place families under guard, and escort them abroad cut against his conception of chivalry. Scott's troops in the event proved overly tough in dealing with an unarmed people. Threats, curses, and rifle butts were frequently employed. Shootings took place. One soldier recounted late in life: "Men working in the fields were arrested and driven to the stockade. Women were dragged from their homes by soldiers whose language they could not understand. Children were often separated from their parents and driven into the stockades with the sky for a blanket and the earth for a pillow."[88] Squalor in the camps and drought along the westward trails in summer 1838 intensified Cherokee misery. Scott became so startled by the high number of deaths that he agreed, without consulting President Van Buren, to Ross's suggestions: the remaining Cherokees should be allowed to postpone emigration until salubrious weather returned in early autumn; they could go west under their own responsibility relieved of military escort. Scott also approved the travel and cost schedules submitted by Ross for Cherokee removal, $65 per person. The budgets made provision for soap, originally not itemized in federal inventories. Removal from the southeast resumed in early October. Twelve thousand people divided into a dozen detachments decamped. Ross's wife, Quatie, numbered among the refugees who died during the thousand-mile tramp.

* * *

Chief Ross philosophized as the Cherokee crisis of dispossession reached its finale: "The perpetrator of a wrong never forgives his victim."[89] He meant by this that a victimizer denies pardon because of this self-awareness: villainy has diminished him as a human being, a creature whose identity involves morality. The victim, in this case the Indian, was a reproach whose presence reminded white Americans of their transgression. Hence the appeal of banishment. Of prominent people who supported Jackson's policy, only McKenney repented of it. Not until 1962 did the Georgia legislature repeal its 1830 laws, saying that they "must now be read with humility and sadness."[90]

Robert Remini, biographer of Andrew Jackson, has offered a partial defense. While deploring the eastern tribes' fate, Remini has argued that, however much the Five Civilized Nations lost, they did survive as entities in contrast to tribes that stayed behind or never had the chance to migrate. Yamasees, Mohegans, Narragansetts, Pequots, and Delawares simply vanished.[91]

Anthony Wallace, one of the doyens of Native American history, has placed Jackson's expulsion program in useful comparative context. He wrote in 1993: "The removal of inconveniently located ethnic groups and their resettlement in out-of-the-way places is, and has been for thousands of years, a common phenomenon in the history of states and empires."[92] Wallace could have added that the English-speaking world outside Jackson's America was well-acquainted with such practice. It touched not only undesirable ethnic groups but also the lower classes. Clearances in Scotland, deportations of French-speaking Acadians from Atlantic Canada, and enclosures in England disrupted the lives of countless people in the eighteenth and nineteenth centuries (never mind refugees from famine-stricken Ireland). Rural districts were left as empty as any in Cherokee land. Enactment of such sorrow produced protests in Great Britain. So too in America, where dissenters mocked paeans to the US system as acme of human achievement. Iconoclasts instead focused public attention on evictions and slavery. Garrison censured the Seminole war in verse:

> Our land, once green as Paradise, is hoary,
> E'en in its youth, with tyranny and crime;
> Its soil with blood of Afric's sons is gory,
> Whose wrongs eternity can tell, not time.
> The red man's woes shall swell the damning story,
> To be rehearsed in every age and clime.[93]

Everett gulped at how easily the responsible class could lay sanctions upon the vulnerable or voiceless. He asked House members in 1830, enjoying their comfort and status, to ponder the effects of removal: "Will the contractor stop for the old men to rest, for the sick to get well, for the fainting women and children to revive? He will not; he cannot afford to. And this process is to be extended to every family ... It is very easy to talk of this subject, reposing on these luxurious chairs, and protected by these massy walls, and this gorgeous canopy, from the power of the elements. *Removal* is a soft word, and words are delusive." Aggravating this failure of imagination, said Everett, Congress embraced false standards of justice based on unequal power. He wondered: "Are there two kinds of rights, rights of the strong, which you respect because you must, and rights of the weak, on which you trample, because you dare?"[94]

In similar heat Whig leader Senator Clay attacked the New Echota travesty. He charged that enforcement of its provisions would besmirch US reputation. Alas, once Whigs won the White House, they deviated not at all from Indian policy promoted by Jacksonians. Their cruelty was mainly cited by opponents to discredit them. The unfeigned indignation and prophetic voice of Frelinghuysen gave added value. But once in power the Whigs lacked compelling reason to belabor the subject or shield people unwanted in white America. Whig presidents (William Henry Harrison, John Tyler, Zachary Taylor, Millard Fillmore) did nothing to redress earlier unfairness. They stuck to paths taken by Democratic incumbents.[95]

The army officer corps was not a school for dissent in the 1830s. Generals Wool and Scott were nevertheless shaken by witnessing the Cherokees' predicament and implementing dubious mandates. Whereas opposition to removal by partisans could raise questions about sincerity, discontent among officers sprang from plainer source. The party preferences of Scott (a Virginia Whig) and Wool (a New York Democrat) had no connection to their distaste for mission: dislodging a peaceable population to make way for another whose virtues were not obvious to the soldiers.

Wool risked his career by trying to cushion removal's harshness. Alabama's charges could have led to court martial proceedings. Scott took two decisions without consulting higher authority: to delay further Cherokee departures until fall 1838; to allow the nation thenceforth to conduct its own transfer. Scott's directives made Jackson (in retirement) livid. Still, they did not lead to untoward consequences for the officer. Like Wool, Scott continued in a military career that boasted successes. Both men remained in service until the early 1860s.

Any lingering doubts over the generals' Cherokee performance were dispelled during the 1846 Mexican war. Each officer earned accolades. General Zachary Taylor admired Wool as the "little great man."[96] Citizens praised his and Scott's several victories. Scott became a plausible, albeit losing, presidential candidate in 1852.

Part II

Conquests

5   Mexico

The United States acquired an immense territorial tract during James Polk's presidency, 1845–1849. A determined expansionist, Polk attached 1.2 million square miles to the US domain, a feat effected in three phases.

First, the Texas republic, independent of Mexico since 1836, became the Union's twenty-eighth state in 1845. This event, aided by Polk's predecessor, President Tyler, caused the government in Mexico City to sever diplomatic ties with the United States. Texas in the mind of Mexican officialdom was a province in rebellion, belonging to the state of Coahuila, and unavailable to any foreign power. Yet the Mexican minister to Washington, Juan N. Almonte, could only protest the US annexation of Texas. His country's political fragility prevented decisive counter-action.[1]

Second, the simmering dispute between London and Washington over the Oregon country, provoking Polk's bluster and threats of another British–US–Canadian clash ("54–40 or fight"), was resolved peacefully in June 1846. Settlement via the Buchanan–Parkenham treaty spared the administration from strife in the northwest while contemplating a Mexican adventure. Agreement with Britain also entailed US frontage on the Pacific and secured lands that later encompassed three states: Oregon, Washington, Idaho (bits of Montana).

Most dramatic, by right of conquest in 1846–1848, Polk presided over the addition of Mexican holdings to the United States. This cession exceeded 40 percent of the Mexican republic. From the spoils, dignified by the Guadalupe Hidalgo treaty and purchase price of $15 million, arose several states: California (with gold discovered in 1848); Nevada, Utah; Arizona and New Mexico (augmented by the 1853 Gadsden deal); parts of Wyoming, Colorado, Oklahoma, Kansas, Texas.[2] Roughly 100,000 Mexicans were also transferred to US authority.

Enthralled by visions of dynamic America, Walt Whitman wrote before the final success of US arms: "We love to indulge in thoughts of the future extent and power of this Republic – because with its increase is the increase of human happiness and liberty ... What has miserable, inefficient Mexico ... to do with the great mission of peopling the New World with a noble race?"[3] He added that the torpid nation would benefit by applications of US tonic – upright government, profitable commerce, liberal education. James Fenimore Cooper also perceived exertions against Mexico as confirming the regenerative impact of US power on the western hemisphere. As for Polk, he not only congratulated lawmakers in his last message to Congress (December 1848) for having supported military operations and then approving the peace treaty that yielded new holdings. He also allowed that plenty and contentment reigned in the land. He flattered collective vanity: "Our beloved country presents a sublime moral spectacle to the world."[4]

Surging US power celebrated by Polk and devotees of Manifest Destiny was not lauded by Mexicans. Memory of northern aggression (la invasión norteamericana) festered as a wound for generations. Resentment joined anticlerical republicans with their antagonists, army conservatives and Church traditionalists, in a solidarity of the dispossessed. Antonio Lopez de Santa Anna damned the United States in his memoirs for starting the war, then imposing an extreme peace. Nobel laureate Octavio Paz stated more than a century later that the United States had conducted "one of the most unjust wars in the history of imperialist expansion."[5] Subsequent Mexican scholarship has argued that the lopping off of valuable territories hobbled national modernization. The ache of defeat was eased in the popular mind only by the legend of brave boy cadets (niños héroes) who fought American "vandals" in the climactic battle of Chapultepec, September 1847.[6]

Conquest

Mexico in 1846 was only twenty-five years removed from colonial rule. The liberation war against Spain had been grueling, briefly replayed in the ill-advised reconquista of 1829 (foiled by Santa Anna's battlefield successes). During free Mexico's first quarter-century political crises plagued the nation. They sprang from economic weakness, class antagonisms, and racial enmities.

Government and private indebtedness soared. Ownership of the country's mines, the most productive element in Mexico's economy, slipped into foreign hands.[7] Indemnities claimed by French, British, and US nationals for damage to their property during Mexican disorders reached awful proportions (more than $2 million in the American case). Rivalry between federal versus state authorities compounded the polity's weakness. Palace revolutions and disputed elections drove the high rate of government turnover. Between the aborted reconquista and the 1844

US election won by Polk, the Mexican presidency had changed hands twenty times; fourteen different men held the executive post.[8] The army, the most influential player in national politics, was officered by privileged men of pure Spanish ancestry (*criollos*). They commanded poorly drilled Indian troops, who possessed little of national identity or allegiance. Symptomatic of this malaise was the relative absence of public support for the government's war against American invaders, particularly evident in provinces far from the center, such as California.[9] Mexico at the moment of profoundest insecurity since Cortes qualified, in contemporary parlance, as a failed state.

The 1846 Mexican–US collision capped a melancholy history. Washington had readily acknowledged Mexican independence in 1821. But no US envoy presented credentials until 1825. The first minister, Joel Poinsett, became unpopular with his hosts. They reproved his elephantine clumsiness as he tried to promote US-style political institutions. Washington was obliged to recall him. Presidents John Quincy Adams and Jackson meantime sought to obtain all – or substantial chunks – of Texas, which met with Mexican rebuff. This Adams–Jackson policy also fed suspicions of long-term US aims. Consequently, Mexican officials took steps to curtail US immigration to Texas and to assimilate the English-speaking Protestants already resident. They were expected to convert to Roman Catholicism, abide by President Vicente Guerrero's 1829 prohibition on slavery (reconfirmed by parliament in 1831), and otherwise align themselves with local customs and law.

The number of Anglo-American settlers, originally led by Stephen Austin in the 1820s, exceeded 20,000 by the start of the 1835 Texas revolution. They outnumbered local Mexicans, per varying estimates, by a ratio between seven to one and ten to one.[10] Slave-owning gringos kept their African property: 2,000 souls. Most of the immigrants also kept faith with their Protestant denominations. Santa Anna's determination to enforce the writ of Mexico City in Texas, while discarding the national constitution, precipitated the Anglo uprising. It enjoyed wide support in the United States. Private contributions of men and *matériel* poured into Texas. American horror for Mexican ruthlessness at the Alamo and Goliad (where 445 captives were ordered slain by Santa Anna) was palpably strong. Delight in the capture of Santa Anna at San Jacinto by Sam Houston's troops, April 1836, was unreserved among pundits. These demonstrations of public feeling were resented in Mexico City, despite Jackson's assurances of US disinterest and decision to bar Texas from the Union.

Subsequent delays in admission derived from this northern anxiety. Allowing another slave state would unbalance the US regional-political equipoise. When Congress finally relented and admitted Texas – partly to check British meddling and forestall London's potential suzerainty – the federal government adopted as it own this longstanding Texas claim: namely, the southern border of Texas ran along the Rio Grande river, 150 miles below that line asserted by Mexicans and corresponding with the Nueces river.[11] The Texas psychology of grievance against Mexico also gradually passed into US officialdom – related to border skirmishes during the life of the Lone Star republic.

Yankeephobia meanwhile became entrenched below the border, born of Washington's presumed role in Texas's continuing independence, 1836–1845. Concern also grew over the fate of sparsely populated borderlands lying near the restless Americans. Under the misimpression that Mexico and the United States had actually gone to war, Commodore Thomas Jones used his warships and marines to seize the provincial capital of California (Monterey) in October 1842. However embarrassing this mistake, his action illustrated the vulnerability of remote provinces. This episode also seemed to confirm the US proclivity for violence. Aggravating matters, Mexican luminaries called the United States an unevolved culture, incurably uncouth. It permitted slavery, polygamy (the Mormons), and atheism.[12]

Such notions paralleled US scorn of Mexico as racially inferior, politically inadequate, priest-ridden, and wallowing in superstition. In this guise, then, the historic antagonism between English-speaking Protestantism and Latin Catholicism fueled the Mexican–US war. South Carolina's John Calhoun remarked that its frenzy sprang from antipathy between incompatible races and creeds whose rivalry preceded the Armada.[13]

The failure in March 1846 of John Slidell's diplomacy in Mexico City to treat with Jose Herrera was the immediate cause of hostilities. Slidell's mission was threefold: to settle US damage claims, buy New Mexico and California, win recognition of the Rio Grande boundary for Texas. Sent in November 1845, Slidell lacked much chance of success. The wobbly Herrera administration could not have easily survived criticisms sure to follow from any appeasing of the Americans. Indeed, despite Herrera's refusal to meet with Slidell, the government fell in a coup (December 1845) led by General Mariano Paredes; he charged Herrera with treasonous intentions of surrendering northern Mexico. Paredes was both less inclined than his predecessor to negotiate with Slidell and harbored delusions of Mexican military prowess. Paredes predicted that his army would trounce the Americans; their showings against Britain in 1812 and against the Seminoles were, at best, mediocre. And Mexico had done well in recent memory: against Spain, against France in 1838 (*Guerra de los pasteles*).[14] Furthermore, Mexico could expect friendly mediation by the

British, perhaps even their naval/military cooperation against the United States. Most evidence, in any case, suggests that Polk anticipated the collapse of Slidell's mission, a ready pretext to commence hostilities. He presumed they would be of brief duration.[15]

Polk felt that Mexico's political instability, economic liabilities, and military deficiencies (under-equipped army of divided loyalties) would dissuade Herrera, Paredes, or anyone else from tangling with the United States. Coincidental with Slidell in Mexico, Polk had assigned (January 1846) General Zachary Taylor's Army of Occupation of Texas – 4,000 soldiers – to assume control of the disputed territory above the Rio Grande. This army marched from Corpus Christi to the left bank of the river and established Fort Texas, opposite the town of Matamoros, protected by General Francisco Mejia's garrison.

Taylor's move was read in Mexico City as bald aggression. It justified a war of defense. The ambush of Captain Seth Thorton's patrol, April 1846, by Mexican cavalry that had previously crossed to the left bank marked the first violence. Taylor subsequently informed Washington that open hostilities had begun at Mexican initiative. Pitched battles were fought in early May between his army and numerically superior Mexican forces. The latter were defeated at Palo Alto and Resaca de la Palma.

Polk seized the moral high ground upon learning of Thorton's ambuscade. He reported to Congress (May 11, 1846) that American blood had been shed on US territory by intruders. "The cup of forbearance," he exclaimed, "has been exhausted ... After repeated menaces, Mexico has passed the boundary of the United States, has invaded our territory."[16]

Polk did not ask Congress for a formal war declaration. He wanted the legislators instead to recognize that a state of belligerency already existed. Congress's duty was to aid Taylor's troops, purportedly under threat of withering Mexican attack, by permitting the executive to enlist volunteers (50,000 men) and buy $10 million worth of munitions plus other supplies.

Both congressional chambers held brief debates. Polk's men controlled them. In the Senate just two Whigs voted against the president: John Davis of Massachusetts, John Clayton of Delaware. Democratic party loyalty prevented Calhoun from voting against Polk's war bills. He abstained. Still, he felt that the Senate's deliberations were rushed and constituted a Polk-driven stampede. He worried aloud that the president had usurped Congress's war making authority; war should commence only after Congress committed the nation by solemn declaration. Michigan's Lewis Cass countered that sanguinary events produce war and do not wait upon approval by legislators: "I, for one, shall consider public hostilities as war, giving us all the rights which that condition brings with it – the right to drive our enemy from our soil, and to follow him wherever he may go, till we conquer him into a state of peace."[17]

Only fourteen members of the House (all Whigs), led by John Quincy Adams, voted against Polk's obtaining men and equipment. The bipartisan majority chose not to scrutinize Polk's contention that Mexico had mounted an invasion of US territory. This reasoning of Ohio's Jacob Brinkerhoff carried: "I am in favor of prosecuting this war in such a manner that our enemy shall be at once crushed."[18]

The war yielded a string of US victories, notwithstanding a high rate of deaths, attributable primarily to diseases: cholera, dysentery, yellow fever. (Altogether 13,768 men died from a regular-volunteer army of 104,566.) At sea the navy dominated. Mexico did not possess a blue-water force and the US navy blockaded the ports. Additionally, the navy ran competent logistical-combat operations in the Gulf, most conspicuously in cooperation with Winfield Scott's amphibious assault on Veracruz, March 1847. The navy also played a harassing role along the Pacific coast that contributed to California's capture. Land operations were comparably effective. Beginning in the north, Taylor's army fought its way through various Mexican states: Tamaulipas, Nuevo Leon, Coahuila. This army's success at the battle of Buena Vista, February 1847, assured Taylor's fame and propelled the politically neutral soldier (nominally a Whig) toward the White House. General Stephen Kearny's Army of the West (1,700 men) in August 1846 captured the capital of New Mexico, Santa Fe, with minimal bloodshed. A portion of that army reached San Diego in December 1846. Kearny subsequently became stymied in the *opéra bouffe* intrigues of occupied California (which culminated in Captain John Fremont's court martial and an imbroglio that concerned Fremont's father-in-law, Senator Thomas Hart Benton). As for General Scott's campaign in the Mexican heartland: his maneuvers followed the path of Cortes's sixteenth-century invasion. They ended with the capital's capture in September 1847. American imaginations were thrilled by the exploits of the latter-day adventurers whose triumphs seemed foretold in William Hickling Prescott's lively 1843 account of Cortes, *History of the Conquest of Mexico*. The Duke of Wellington was among the foreign observers who praised Scott as the era's foremost soldier.[19]

This US triumph was not preordained but had surmounted many obstacles. They involved graft plus waste in wartime production and procurements. Instances of indiscipline among volunteer units also hampered the military effort. The unruly Texas Rangers committed a disproportionate number of reported atrocities against Mexican civilians: pillaging, raping, shooting, scalping. Generals Taylor and Scott periodically reprimanded the Rangers. They were retained, however, because of their scouting skills and success against guerrilla bands. Potentially the biggest hurdle to victory came from civil-military knottiness. Jealousy arose between field commanders (Taylor versus Scott, William Worth versus Scott). And Polk nursed a morbid suspicion of Taylor and Scott, both Whigs. The president hoped to blunt the appeal of his two top generals by appointing Benton to a lieutenant generalship (thereby outranking Taylor and Scott, each only a major general). Polk hoped also to contain Scott via the beetley ambitious General Gideon Pillow, an incapable amateur who owed his rank to political favor. He became the focal point of an anti-Scott cabal of officers. Their plotting resulted in a muddle of official inquiries and courts martial. They ultimately led to Scott's being relieved of command in January 1848. General William Orlando Butler replaced Scott with orders to supervise the unfinished business of treaty negotiations. The future general, George Meade, who served as a lieutenant in 1846–1848, concluded that the United States had been blessed with Mexico as an enemy: "Were it any other power, our gross follies would have been punished severely."[20]

Santa Anna could not mount vital offensive operations. But he was shrewd, evident when he snookered the Polk administration. It allowed him, on receiving bona fides during his Havana exile, to return to Mexico without interference by blockading US ships. Once home, he would organize a new government. It would presumably cease hostilities and offer good terms to Polk. Instead, Santa Anna raised an army upon reaching Mexico City in August 1846. He immediately marched northward to accost Taylor's forces at Buena Vista. Thereafter, he tried to slow Scott's onslaught. He gave up this futility only after the Americans captured Mexico City, which caused him to relinquish the presidency in favor of Pedro Maria de Anaya and flee again into exile (Jamaica).

An effect of Santa Anna's obstinacy was the emergence in the US of the "All Mexico" campaign.[21] It combined punitiveness with land lust. This movement, in which prominent Democrats played parts, aimed at annexation of the entire southern country. The "All Mexico" collection included Secretary of the Treasury Robert Walker, Vice President George Dallas, Secretary of State James Buchanan, Cass, and Illinois's Senator Stephen Douglas. Commodore Robert Stockton shared their viewpoint. This veteran of California combat told Philadelphians in January 1848: "If I were now the sovereign authority ... I would prosecute this war for the express purpose of redeeming Mexico from misrule and civil strife ... I would with a magnanimous and kindly hand gather these wretched people within the fold of republicanism."[22]

The war's opponents could not comprehend such reasoning. They replied that any projected cost of reshaping millions of Mexicans into US form beggared imagination.

Protest

Nothing like a consensus ever sustained Polk's war. As it wore on deeply into 1847, with no definite end in sight, dissenters grumbled about rising costs and the moral–political implications.[23] No foreign war would so roil Congress and divide public opinion until Vietnam in the 1960s.

Broadly speaking, the Mexican war enjoyed support in the west and new south (Texas plus those states connected to the Mississippi river). This area provided the bulk of militias and volunteers. The first allotment of 50,000 men greatly bolstered the regular army (7,500 soldiers in 1846). The northeast and old south, in contrast, were unenthusiastic. The muster from the original thirteen states numbered a scant 13,000. New England dissented outright. The Massachusetts legislature denounced the war as unconstitutional and insupportable.[24]

Henry David Thoreau justified civil disobedience in defense of his not paying a wartime poll tax. He consequently suffered a night away from his Walden hut – detained in the Concord jail. He labeled the war an abomination, pursued solely at the behest of slave-owners to enlarge their plantation realm. This situation required that a conscientious person deny approval to established authority. Better yet one should subvert it:

When a sixth of the population of a nation which has undertaken to be the refuge of liberty are slaves, and a whole country is unjustly overrun and conquered by a foreign army, and subjected to military rule, I think that it is not too soon for honest men to rebel and revolutionize. What makes this duty the more urgent is the fact, that the country so overrun is not our own, but ours is the invading army.[25]

William Lloyd Garrison in nearby Boston also opposed the war. He thought that Massachusetts would be well served by leaving the Union, for which purpose he petitioned (2,800 signatures) the state legislature. He also declared in favor of Mexico's winning. The abolitionist Theodore Parker condemned the fighting from his pulpit (housed in Boston's 28th Congregational Church). He tempered his remarks only by recognizing Anglo-Saxon culture as superior to that of decadent Mexico. War in general, he taught, violated Christian precepts on mercy and brotherhood. War also glorified men of coarseness while it squandered national wealth. The Mexican war was especially iniquitous as its object was to extend the slave zone, thus depleting whatever goodwill distant nations reserved for the United States.[26]

The Boston-based American Peace Society too identified slavery as the war's engine and warned against a conquering American Napoleon. He might turn his legions on the United States after Mexico, then enthrone himself as president for life.[27]

Less lugubrious than the Thoreau–Garrison–Parker line, but equally passionate, were those protests made by James Russell Lowell. He wrote satiric verse in his *Biglow Papers*, which featured the New England rube Hosea Biglow. He saw through every grandiloquence. Patriotic talk did not blind him to the reality of Polk's Mexican operation, to create "bigger pens to cram with slaves."[28]

Other northeastern literati against the war included Ralph Waldo Emerson, Horace Greeley, Herman Melville, Quaker-poet John Greenleaf Whittier, and the mordant writer-editor Seba Smith. His *My Thirty Years Out of the Senate* centered on fictional Major Jack Downing. A caricature of the Manifest Destiny crowd, he advised Polk to rid Mexico of its obnoxious inhabitants and replace them with "plenty of our folks." Downing dreamed too of other conquests. They would girdle the planet in US idealism:

We had got through annexin' all North and South America; and then I thought our whole country was turned into a monstrous great ship of war, and Cape Horn was the bowsprit, and Mr. Polk the captain. And the captain was walking the deck with his mouth shet, and everybody was looking at him and wondering what he was goin' to do next. At last he sung out, "Put her about; we'll sail across now and take Europe, and Asha, and Africa in tow."[29]

To turn such aim into reality required more money and men than Polk could find. Yet Downing saw no reason to confine the spread of America's bracing influence to Mexico. He allowed: "I can't help thinking a good deal of Cape Horn, and naterally feel anxious to get along down that way."[30]

Abolitionists, liberal churchmen, and other sensitive types did not monopolize the objection. Discontent also seeped into the army. Ulysses S. Grant, who served as a junior officer in the war, later referred to it as an indefensible cause: "one of the most unjust [wars] ever waged by a stronger against a weaker nation." More than 9,200 uniformed Americans deserted their units. A number of deserters actually defected to enemy ranks. Santa Anna's ill-fated San Patricio battalion was composed of disgruntled men who fled US service to join Mexico's – some Irish, many Catholic, led by Galway-born John Riley.[31]

Retired members of the responsible class were also displeased. Poinsett, one-time secretary of war (1837–1841) as well former minister to Mexico, thought the conflict regrettable as it pit two republican regimes against each other. It would materially help Mexico's reactionaries, he predicted; they had sought to uproot the tender shoots of democracy ever since their 1824 appearance. Waddy Thompson, envoy to Mexico (1842–1844), argued for diplomacy and felt the war inadvisable as it would surely deny to Washington a future Mexican ally against Europe's New World schemes.[32] Elderly Albert Gallatin, possessed still of a clear mind, warned against the damages to republican virtue entailed in imperialist enterprises. His compatriots were in danger of forsaking their better angels, he wrote in 1847 in two pamphlets: *Peace with Mexico* and *War Expenses*. The unredeemed world, focused hopefully on the United States, would lose if the country yielded to atavistic ambitions.[33]

Your mission was to be a model for all other governments and for all other less-favored nations, to adhere to the most elevated principles of political morality, to apply all your faculties to the gradual improvement of your own institutions and social state, and by your example to exert a moral influence most beneficial to mankind at large. Instead of this, an appeal has been made to your worst passions; to cupidity; to the thirst of unjust aggrandizement by brutal force; to the love of military fame and of false glory . . . The attempt is made to make you abandon the lofty position which your fathers occupied, to substitute for it the political morality and heathen patriotism of the heroes and statesmen of antiquity.[34]

Polk Democrats and supporters in the press rebuked this dissent. They called Gallatin an old fogy who harbored queer sympathies. His tastes were quaint, not truly American. Poinsett and Thompson were equally out of touch. The Massachusetts extremists represented only themselves. Despite their fringe status, all the dissenters came dangerously near to treason, Polk charged. They buttressed the enemy with "aid and comfort," different in degree from the San Patricio bunch but not in kind.[35]

Congressional objection

Congress served as cockpit of the Mexican debate. Disputes within chambers on the war's merits not only separated the two parties. Disagreement also drove wedges into each one. Whigs divided amongst themselves. So did Democrats. Bipartisan alliances formed according to varied preferences among individuals. Regions were conflicted too. Not all northerners opposed Polk's policy. Not all westerners approved it. Dissent simply leapt partisan and sectional fault lines.

Of the legislators who assailed Polk's policy, two stood out. They were Ohio's Representative Joshua Giddings and the south's foremost proponent, Senator Calhoun. Polk contrasted dimly with the intellectual vigor of both men, never more so than when he averred that the question of slavery's extension into Mexican holdings should not distract Americans.

This "abstract" question did not warrant "practical" concern: "Slavery has no possible connection with the Mexican War."[36]

Polk was an accidental president. His 1844 defeat of Henry Clay had been by slender margin. Before then, Polk's political career had nearly flickered out. Polk had served in Congress for seven terms beginning in 1825. He became speaker of the House in 1835, where he earned a reputation for plodding diligence. He next won the governorship of Tennessee in 1839. But he lost reelection in 1841. He was defeated again in the 1843 gubernatorial race. He became the prototypical dark horse candidate in 1844. His only sure virtue was loyalty to Andrew Jackson and his philosophy, earning Polk the nickname Young Hickory. His dearth of charm and penchant for secrecy did not endear him to members of his own party. Calhoun could not abide his mental shallowness – or forgive his occupying the executive mansion in lieu of the South Carolinian. Northern Democrats, such as Martin Van Buren ("barnburners"), disliked Polk as slave-owner and apologist. The loss by Democrats of their House majority in the 1846 midterm elections flowed from Polk's inability to end party discord – aggravated by western resentment of his vetoing the rivers-harbors bill, passage of the Walker Tariff which offended protectionists, and establishment of an independent Treasury that irked financial conservatives. Continuance of an apparently open-ended war also hurt. It had originally promised much gain for minimal exertion, not the millions of dollars and tens of thousands of men that Polk requested.[37]

Whigs and Joshua Giddings

Illinois's Abraham Lincoln was among the Whigs elected to Congress in 1846. Upon taking his House seat, he launched scorching attacks on the president. Lincoln hoped by them to advertise Polk's deficiencies and the incapacity of Democrats to govern.[38] He never went as far as Senator Daniel Webster, when he suggested that Polk be impeached. But Lincoln did mean by his "spot" resolutions (December 1847) to humiliate the president. Where was the pristine US soil, demanded the freshman congressman, violated by dastardly Mexican invaders whereon the blood of American innocents had been shed? In fact, he volunteered, the spot where the violence occurred belonged to the category of contesting claims, not legal certainty. The land's inhabitants, moreover, had never been subject to US laws or protection. And the violence done had been committed against armed soldiers; naturally the Mexicans perceived their presence along the Rio Grande as provocation. Lincoln later added (January 1848) that Polk had lied to bring about an avoidable war: "He feels the blood of this war, like the blood of Abel, is crying to Heaven against him."[39] Only unwillingness to see soldiers in the field injured made Lincoln vote repeatedly to stock them with *matériel*. Most dissenting Whigs adopted this same stance of supporting the army. They feared to do other would invite comparison with Federalism in 1812 and saddle them with defeatism or disloyalty, leading perhaps to Whiggery's extinction.

Lincoln's criticisms did not cut deeply. Polk never answered the prosecutorial questions. He ignored Lincoln's brashness in his diary, a revealing omission as Polk's memoir brimmed with venom for people that perturbed him. Nor did Polk deign to respond to other pesky Whigs such as Georgia's Robert Toombs, when he accused the president of sending an army into Mexico without authority of law. Toombs sounded themes hardly different from those New Englanders who attacked Polk. "War in a just cause is a great calamity to any people," the Georgian asserted, "and can only be justified by the highest necessity. A people who go to war without just and sufficient cause, with no other motive than pride and love of glory, are enemies to the human race and deserve the execration of all mankind."[40] Another Georgia Whig of rising fame, Alexander Stephens, called the war an affront to republican honor.[41]

Less easy for Polk to overlook than Lincoln or Toombs or Stephens were Whig eminencies, Webster above all. He had his mind fixed on a presidential run in 1848. This ambition – his burning condition – inhibited him from saying things obnoxious to southern Whigs, essential to obtaining the party's nomination. They were already stirred thanks to charges of war conspiracy made by John Quincy Adams and Theodore Parker and their traducing of southern integrity. Consequently, Webster's public remarks were somewhat muted. A "cotton Whig" who appreciated the centrality of southern production for northern textile industry, Webster never characterized the war as one to expand the slave zone. Still, despite this caution, he was formidable. He taught that the war relied on Polk's frauds and fiction that justified naked aggression to the gullible. He favored the proposal by Georgia's Senator John Berrien to bar the annexation of any new territory. Webster ultimately voted against the 1848 peace treaty on two grounds: it was absurdly harsh; the last thing Americans needed was indigestible lands ripped from Mexico's body.[42]

Unbending abolitionists in Whiggery were driven by feelings deeper than ordinary partisanship à la Lincoln or Webster. The "ultras" used every device to stall or quell Polk's war. The major figures were querulous Adams and the embodiment of crusader ardor, Giddings. Adams by his standing as *éminence grise* gave this noisy faction an aura of credibility.

Poor health and the effects of stroke, though, meant that he could not provide daily leadership. That fell to Giddings. Adams in effect was titular head, Giddings the animus.[43]

To them the sin of Polk's aggression was compounded by worse crime: enlargement of the slave belt. Adams hoped that soldiers would desert rather than lend themselves to this aim. Of Polk, he once blurted that he was a "slave-holding exterminator of Indians," barely qualified to be a county court lawyer. Yet this second-rater doggedly advanced the plantation power, which had killed Adams's proposed 1839 constitutional amendment to end slavery.[44]

Giddings acted on behalf of New England sensibility in Ohio's Western Reserve, originally settled by emigrants from Connecticut. He represented this distinctive region for two decades in Congress, 1838–1859. Like many within his constituency, he was a Congregationalist and affected by the Second Great Awakening. He accepted as commandment the imperative of working for society's improvement. None of the evils afflicting America surpassed that of slavery, he maintained. His home was not far from the abolitionist-Congregationalist center at Oberlin. It sustained his sense of mission during trying times. They included his being censured by the House in 1842 for insulting the institution of slavery. He had, noted the sponsoring motion, betrayed public trust by creating "excitement, dissatisfaction and division." Planters described him as their "rabid" foe, no less vile than old Adams. Justin Smith, respected historian in the early twentieth century of the Mexican War, thought Giddings "a calculating fanatic."[45]

To his friends he was a splendid figure. Giddings's athletic nature and large frame – six feet and two inches, two hundred pounds, topped by blond mane – helped him withstand taunts and threats from southern hotheads. He had survived military service in the War of 1812. He had overcome bouts of depression to establish a prosperous law practice. He believed that all people were capable of seeing the truth, especially as he saw it, in which case the ethically impoverished plantation caste might eventually improve. His craving for activity made him incessant in anti-slavery. He remonstrated against the "gag rule." He challenged the legality of slave markets in the District of Columbia. He called for investigations of suicide rates among slaves awaiting auction in the capital. He rejected as repellent that "evidence" marshaled by Calhoun to show that slavery benefited the intellectual-social development of Africans. This southern brief depended on politicized biology and misconstrued Bible scriptures, rejoined Giddings.[46]

He declared in May 1846 that Polk's resort to violence betrayed the American founders – the Gallatin line – as they had never dreamed that their descendants would become intoxicated with love of military life or mobilize to devastate innocent neighbors: "This war is waged . . . with the design to extend slavery; in violation of the Constitution, against the dictates of justice, of humanity, the sentiments of the age in which we live, and the precepts of the religion we profess."[47] He did not trifle when he promised to oppose the war unstintingly or called Polk mendacious. He could not conceal true facts, said Giddings. The administration had unleashed a tide of crime in Mexico that produced misery for Mexican children, women, and families, a misdeed that promised dreadful reckoning for the United States. God in history was watching, weighing, His ineluctable will to be felt: "The history of the world shows that national crimes have ever been followed by national judgments . . . And can we hope to escape the penalty so manifestly due for our national crimes? Do we expect that the immutable law of justice will be suspended or repealed, in order that our nation may pass unpunished?"[48] Giddings responded to the president's December 1846 annual message, which recited a sanitized version of the war's origins, with this confidence in Americans. They would inevitably turn against the war:

It is impossible that a Christian people – a people who worship a God of justice – can uphold a rapacious war of conquest like this, and spend their money in spreading distress, devastation, and death . . . It is impossible that a Christian people shall lend their sanction, their encouragement, to a war waged with the openly avowed purpose of extending slavery, of perpetuating oppression, of opening up new slave-markets for the sale of mankind . . . [Americans] are conscious that this vast expenditure of treasure and blood is made to sustain the most revolting system of oppression that has ever cursed the human family.[49]

Giddings called for an immediate withdrawal of all US soldiers from Mexico and a unilateral cessation of hostilities. An agreement genuinely fair to Mexico, which he called a deserving "sister republic," should follow.[50] He was an avid supporter of the 1846 legislation sponsored by Representative David Wilmot (Democrat, Pennsylvania) that forbade slavery in any territory acquired from Mexico. Framed as an amendment to an appropriations bill, the Wilmot Proviso passed the House (with endorsements by ten northern state legislatures), but repeatedly failed Senate tests. Whereas Lincoln and Webster tried to calm the acrimonious debates on Wilmot or ducked them, Giddings steamed: "There can be no compromise between right and wrong, between virtue and crime." Enactment of Wilmot would deprive the south of its war aims and, maybe, lessen the severity of divine chastisement.[51]

To the dismay of mainstream Whigs, Giddings voted against measures to supply the army. He claimed that his method would hasten retreat from Mexico. He chided moderate Whig leaders in the House – notably

Massachusetts's Robert Winthrop – for timidity, manifest in their opposing the war but voting for appropriations. Giddings's stridency on this
score provoked retaliation. Winthrop compared Giddings to Timothy
Pickering and other Federalists of questionable patriotism. Hoping to
preserve party integrity, Winthrop attacked Giddings and fellow renegades: their antics encouraged Mexicans to fight on. This charge invited
tart response by Giddings and his journalist friend, Horace Greeley of
the *New York Tribune*. The resulting escalation threatened to break
Whig discipline beyond repair. Giddings hoped that Ohio's Senator
Thomas Corwin would lead the party to respectability after he made
brave against the war in February 1847, referring to it as larceny. But
Giddings's infatuation with the senator died when he disavowed the
radical Whigs and rejected the Wilmot idea. Political isolation within
Whiggery also had a personal side for Giddings. He and Lincoln got
into a name-calling spat based on their differing approaches to Mexico.
Their friendship chilled.[52]

   Giddings cast the only vote in 1848 against House resolutions to honor
Generals Taylor and Scott for their part in defeating Mexico. He called
instead for a vote of thanks to Gallatin for publishing his pacifist essays.
The war, in any case, had essentially dissolved the Union, Giddings felt.
Something tawdry stood in its place.[53]

Calhoun

Adams, Giddings, and New England polemicists were not alone in
ascribing the war to southern conspiracy. This line subsequently established itself in historiography, associated with such writers as James Ford
Rhodes: Mexico had been goaded into attacking to provide an excuse for
war at the slavocracy's behest. Objections to this interpretation have been
many and varied. Some analysts have stressed the importance of Manifest
Destiny notions to explain the war. No conspiracy hatched it. But a
doctrine of US chauvinism created a permissive environment that
allowed aggression. Other historians have emphasized the role of key
actors, especially that of Polk. Still other scholars have underscored
Mexico's vulnerability in 1846 to predators – including Britain and
France – of whom the United States was nearest. In this spirit strongman
Porfirio Diaz apparently remarked: "Poor Mexico! So far from God and
so close to the United States!" Friedrich Engels located the war in the
larger play of history's underlying forces; he was delighted that "magnificent California" had been "snatched from the lazy Mexicans" to be used
henceforth by "energetic Yankees" in compliance with world progress.
The strongest counter to the Adams–Giddings–Rhodes view stems from

this evidence. Calhoun, devoted to southern prerogatives, opposed the war. He called it unexampled "wantonness."[54]

Planter, slave-owner, Democrat, he had by the Mexican war held elevated offices, except the one he most coveted: the presidency. Calhoun had served in the House (1811–1817), where he had been a firebrand for war in 1812 and a nationalist committed to efficient armed forces, internal improvements, modern manufacturing, and the second US Bank. He had worked well as Monroe's secretary of war, 1817–1825. His terms as vice president under John Quincy Adams (1825–1829) and Andrew Jackson (1829–1832) had been marked by controversy that alienated him from his chiefs. Calhoun began his Senate career in late 1832. He interrupted it briefly to serve as Tyler's secretary of state (1844–1845) in which role he ensured Texas's admission as a slave state. Calhoun's sectionalism by 1846 had eclipsed his earlier nationalist outlook. He defended minority rights and nullification within the framework of equal states in compact. He wrote two learned essays in this field toward the end of his life: *Disquisition on Government* and *Discourse on the Constitution*. As his earlier sympathy for strong federal authority had ebbed, so also his thirst for dramatic action – circa 1812 – had dropped. Frail and in his mid-sixties, he compared US war zeal in 1846 with youthful enthusiasm, "full of health ... and disposed for adventure of any description but without wisdom or experience to guide."[55]

This laxity disclosed itself, Calhoun believed, in the way Americans went to war: without congressional mandate or careful deliberation. He feared, too, that the violence would be protracted with Mexico no more a pushover than the Seminoles. A long war could cause Mexico to seek safety in British protection and becoming London's dependency. An Anglo-Mexican combination would constitute a powerful free zone perilously near the slave south.

Calhoun kept a discreet silence after the May 1846 war debates, despite his worries. Other men could cavil but he did not want to break with his president or party. Yet as the scope of military operations widened, as "All Mexico" gained momentum, Calhoun felt obliged to object publicly. He asked whether the government knew what it was doing, its incompetence shown by abetting Santa Anna's return from Havana and then Polk's trying to assign Benton to senior command. (Calhoun disliked the Missouri senator, seeing in him a rival for the 1848 Democratic presidential nomination, and helped block his generalship.) The South Carolinian also blamed Polk for party mismanagement and 1846 Democratic losses.[56]

Another disquieting aspect of the war for Calhoun was that it threatened to corrode republican rectitude. He marveled whenever Americans extolled military heroes, too happy to substitute their wisdom for that of the accountable political class. General Taylor in particular disconcerted Calhoun, not just because the soldier's popularity among voters seemed likely to dash Calhoun's presidential bid, but as a matter of principle: military careers were not appropriate apprenticeships for high office. Martial mentality and reflexes ran against the grain of representative democracy. He ruminated in July 1847:

> It does really seem extraordinary, that mere soldiership should be regarded by the great body of the American people, as furnishing the best proof of statesmanship – and it is certainly a very unfavorable omen, as to the duration of our institutions. I go farther and admit, that the election of the successful General is calculated to impress more deeply on the public mind the idea that soldiership is the only certain road to the highest civil honors, and to increase, in the same degree, the military spirit of the country, which is already too high for its institutions and liberty.[57]

Calhoun hoped that future presidents would be more circumspect than Polk and not allow situations to arise in which soldiers gained political stature. Indeed, said Calhoun, had Polk known that war would make an unknown soldier into presidential timber for the opposition party, the administration would have abandoned its Mexican folly. Only in cases of absolute necessity, Calhoun taught, should the government lead the nation away from peace. All other causes were irrelevant or frivolous. The cost of even a good war entailed the acclaiming of soldiers to unwholesome degree.[58]

Calhoun abhorred the idea of absorbing all or most of Mexico and held that the effect on US political institutions would be ruinous. If Washington decided that Mexican territories were unsuited for state-hood, and Mexicans were unfit for citizenship, then Americans would have to rule them as a colony. This arrangement would resemble Spain in Mexico or Great Britain over the thirteen. He doubted that the United States could retain a republican essence while pursuing an imperial career. Empire would extinguish the US experiment by concentrating excessive power in the executive branch and producing proconsuls, legions of occupation troops, and ukases. The executive branch would inevitably become a despotism of overwhelming "splendor." Neither Congress nor the state legislatures and governors could then resist federal pretensions. In short, US liberties would be expunged simultaneously with those of Mexico.[59]

If, instead, federal authority granted rights of citizenship to Mexicans and recast their territories into new states then dicey problems would arise, Calhoun warned. White rule in the United States would unravel. Mexico was a hybrid nation in which the blood of whites had been diluted through intermarriage with non-Europeans. Only a small minority of Mexicans were of full Spanish origin. Many were Indians or an admixture. Some were African. Such a hodge-podge people lacked the temperament and mental equipment for sturdy citizenship. He advised that the recent history of Latin America be read as cautionary tale. Racial impurity and the placement of "colored races on an equality with the white race [had] destroyed the social basis of society," spawning gore and anarchy. At a minimum, even if Latin America's sorry fate were not duplicated, the genius of the white race in the US would drown in alien mediocrity, too dull to understand or master republican protocols. Dark-skinned peoples could not learn, he insisted: "It is a remarkable fact, that in the whole history of man . . . there is no instance whatever of any . . . colored races being found equal to the establishment of free popular government."[60]

The inclusion of millions of Catholics also constituted an unappealing prospect. Their coreligionists from Irish famine were already making their way in unwanted numbers to what was, in the nativist refrain of Know Nothings, a defiantly Protestant country. Calhoun spoke in deep earnest when he asked in February 1847: "Can we bring into our Union eight millions of people all professing one religion – and all concentrated under a powerful and wealthy priesthood, without subjecting the country to the most violent religious conflict, and bringing the government in the end under control of a single sect?" A year later he wondered in disbelief: "Are we to associate with ourselves as equals, companions, and fellow-citizens, the Indians and mixed race of Mexico?" If so, the United States would disintegrate.[61]

As for the Wilmot Proviso: Calhoun agreed with those many observers, Polk being one, who felt that most Mexican territories were too arid to sustain cotton economy; it probably would not be introduced by American growers. But, Calhoun contended, this practical reality should not obviate a transcendent point: the right of citizens to bring their property and preferred ways of living into new lands obtained by the United States. Phrased bluntly, southerners should not be expected to bear war costs and be denied access to areas per Wilmot. (South Carolina's Palmetto Regiment suffered 43 percent fatalities.) Automatic exclusion of an entire category of law-abiding citizens galled Calhoun. As he also appreciated, Wilmot meant that all areas lifted from Mexico would one day constitute a swath of new free states. They would operate with those north of Mason–Dixon like a noose around the south. Dixie would be outnumbered in Congress, outvoted in national elections. Its fate would rely upon scraps of sympathy from indifferent northerners, obsessed with machine-generated wealth. The south would finally surrender to a conglomeration of swarming cities and smoke-belching factories run by ghoulish proletarians. Were Wilmot's proposal made law, Calhoun persisted, then the south by rights of self-protection – to preserve its refined culture based on nature's growing seasons – could leave the Union: "The south will be united in opposition to the scheme. If [southerners] regard their safety they must defeat it, even should the Union be rent asunder." Calhoun explained in private interview with Polk that he would fight ratification of any Mexican treaty that restricted slavery.[62]

Moderate Whigs, to avoid a sectional showdown, the Websters and Winthrops, proposed to end the war without annexations. By refusing the forbidden Mexican fruit (Calhoun's imagery), the United States would avoid exile from the Eden of domestic tranquillity. Such a resolution to the Wilmot dilemma vexed Calhoun, however. A prize of territorial indemnity had to be wrested from Mexico to validate arduous exertion – and buoy his standing among voters for whom the war was agreeable. He advised that the United States erect a series of forts along the Rio Grande and west along New Mexico's southern border (32nd parallel) to the Pacific. This territory did not include the Mexican heartland with its millions of undesirables but corresponded to the country's under-populated area. It should be held until such time as a final settlement could be struck. This military cordon, Calhoun told senators, would secure conditions favorable to negotiations and set foundations for future Mexican–US reconciliation: "Our true policy ... is not to weaken or humble [Mexico]; on the contrary, it is our interest to see her strong, and respectable ... there is a mysterious connection between the fate of this country and that of Mexico, so much so, that her independence and capability of sustaining herself are almost as essential to our prosperity, and the maintenance of our institutions as they are to hers."[63] Americans by ensuring Mexico's preservation would be spared bitter new confrontations among themselves. The republic of mechanized north and agrarian south might yet endure.[64]

Treaty of Guadalupe Hidalgo

Polk faced problems by spring 1847 unforeseen when Congress authorized his war. The House of Representatives after the 1846 midterm elections, with thirty-five fewer Democrats returned, passed a resolution that declared the Mexican war to be unconstitutional and the reckless creation of Polk.[65] Moreover, General Taylor had emerged as a potential and potent rival to any Democratic nominee in the approaching electoral season. Polk had earlier pledged that he would serve a single term (a stance that he came to regret). Nevertheless, as party leader, he wanted one of his own to succeed to the White House. The Wilmot Proviso in the meantime had fractured Democratic unity, laying bare the party's sectional schism. Polk's attempts to mend it had somehow to reconcile the likes of Calhoun with such antislavery men as New Hampshire's Senator John Hale. He believed "beyond a doubt" that the war sprang from the "policy of the American Government . . . to make the extension of human slavery its primary [goal]."[66] The sole point of sympathetic understanding between Hale and Calhoun gave cold comfort to Polk: inalterable opposition to him and the war. Hoopla for "All Mexico" was also growing. The president inadvertently stoked it by his rash talk but actually hoped the movement would fizzle. He hoped to slice off generous parts of Mexico. Yet he doubted with Calhoun that the whole population should be integrated into the United States. As for military operations, from Polk's standpoint, the Mexicans were perverse in defeat. They lacked sense enough to surrender, even as Scott marched on their capital. Unless something were done, the war could continue for years or sputter in stalemate. Weary voters would surely punish the reigning political party. Wily Santa Anna might actually win by tenacity in a war of military-political attrition.

Polk needed deliverance from these accumulating dilemmas. His *deus ex machina* was Nicholas Philip Trist, chief clerk of the State Department. He had lived unnoticed in the shadows of power until his selection as peacemaker in April 1847. He then achieved fame for flagrant disobedience and diplomatic virtuosity.

Nothing in his background suggested future notoriety. He was a Virginian whose family had fallen into genteel poverty. This condition was not improved by his going to West Point, from which he resigned (1821) before earning a commission. Illness and dislike of military regimen got in his way. He later studied law. Although admitted to the Virginia bar, legal practice bored him. He gave it up. He did become intrigued by journalism, at least for a while. He acquired ownership of the pro-Democratic *Virginia Advocate*. This enterprise failed to flourish under him.

However lackluster his early career, Trist did succeed in his personal attachments. They became vehicles for vocational advance. He became close to aged Thomas Jefferson, who blessed Trist's marriage to his granddaughter, Virginia Jefferson Randolph. She entertained ambitions for her husband and expected that one day he would sit on the Supreme Court bench. Trist meanwhile developed prodigious powers of literary verbosity while serving as Jefferson's amanuensis. He managed Monticello. He became acquainted with Jefferson's neighbor, James Madison. Trist was at Jefferson's deathbed on July 4, 1826. One effect on Trist of living in this circle, with glimpses of Lafayette and Gallatin, was his exaggerating the Old Dominion's virtues. This inclination was common enough to patricians and would-be patricians in the state that provided four of the republic's first five presidents. They were best evidence to Trist of a race of superior political beings whose residue he thought clung to himself via exposure at Monticello.[67]

He received his first assignment to the State Department in 1828 as a factotum, thanks to Secretary Henry Clay. Trist remained at this post after the 1828 election, surviving Andrew Jackson's purge of the Adams–Clay bureaucracies. He become a favorite of Old Hickory and frequent guest at White House dinners. Trist served sporadically as private secretary to Jackson, including during the Peggy Eaton affair, when the president faced mutiny in his official family. Trist's loyalty during this unpleasantness, plus taking the president's side on nullification and tariff, cemented the friendship.[68] Trist thus became a living bridge between the Virginia sage and Jackson, through whom the Democratic party took shape. From them Trist acquired stature and self-assurance otherwise undeserved by his modest achievements.

Jackson rewarded Trist's fealty with the lucrative consularship in Havana in 1834. Trist held this post for seven years, until he became the object of a congressional probe into charges of malfeasance. They ranged from accusations by sea captains who complained that he truckled to Spanish authorities, and failed to uphold US interests, to allegations that he aided the illegal slave trade.[69] He was not convicted. But he was sufficiently compromised not to fuss when Secretary of State Daniel Webster replaced him in 1841 with a Whig loyalist.

Trist counted James Buchanan an ally, dating to Jackson's presidency. Upon succeeding to the State Department in 1845, he picked Trist to be its chief clerk. This position was second highest in the department, equivalent to the latter-day rank of deputy secretary of state. Trist oversaw in this capacity the State Department's daily routine. Composed of three bureaus – diplomatic, consular, home – the department employed about a dozen clerks to handle all correspondence between Washington and its scattered ministers and 150 consuls. Trist substituted for Buchanan during his absences from Washington. Poise, courtesy, and intelligence kept Trist comfortable among the capital's elite. Personages and foreign dignitaries rarely faulted him.[70]

Polk selected Trist for the Mexican errand for three reasons: his diplomatic polish, his fluent command of Spanish, his obscurity. In the last case, should his mission miscarry, US prestige would suffer little. Also his low public visibility and apparent lack of interest in lofty office indicated that he would conduct himself wholly with a view to advancing

US interests defined by Polk. In short, Trist seemed an able person free of that vaulting ambition which could complicate matters, unlike Buchanan or other contenders for the White House. Polk recorded: "Such is the jealousy of the different factions of the Democratic party in reference to the next Presidential Election towards each other that it is impossible to appoint any prominent man or men without giving extensive dissatisfaction to others, and thus jeopardizing the ratification of any treaty that they might make."[71]

These considerations, albeit sound, omitted certain qualities of Trist that soon expressed themselves: high-strung pride, stubbornness, proclivity for the histrionic. Polk may not have been entirely oblivious to these traits. He suggested to Trist that handsome Democratic preferment would come his way if he handled the Mexicans and General Scott with aplomb.[72]

After haggling in the cabinet on means and aims – Buchanan took a minority position in favor of parsimony in dealing with Mexico – instructions were delivered to Trist. He was to rendezvous with Scott's command, elated by the capture of Veracruz and headed toward Mexico City. At the opportune time he was to offer payment, as much as $30 million, to whatever passed for Mexican government to buy new territories. He might get New Mexico, Alta and Baja California, and the right of transit across the isthmus of Tehuantepec (separating the Gulf of Mexico from the Pacific). Purchase of New Mexico and Alta California, with estimable harbors at San Francisco and San Diego, was "a *sine qua non* of any Treaty." Trist could spend $20 million for them. Tehuantepec and Baja California were less important. He was not to exert himself unduly in face of Mexican reluctance or pay more than $5 million for either property. Washington would also assume responsibility in any forthcoming treaty for the financial claims of US citizens against the Mexican government. The Rio Grande, of course, marked the boundary between the two republics.[73]

Polk instructed Trist to proceed with secrecy, lest administration enemies learn of another approach to Mexico that involved land indemnity. Its like had been routinely disavowed by Polk, who stated that his sole object was a restoration of peace. Only if Trist's mission succeeded would Polk acknowledge its existence. With this steeliness in mind, the envoy began his trip to Mexico – rough passage in crude conveyance and inclement weather. The cloak of secrecy was almost instantly pierced by the opposition press, however. By mid-June the *New York Herald* had obtained Polk's proposals for a huge Mexican cession.[74]

Matters that June became further tangled as the two US principals in Mexico became violently opposed to one another. Trist and Scott exchanged menacing charges. Both sent petulant outpourings to superiors in Washington. The tempest at one point so shook Polk that he despaired of diplomatic success and was tempted to withdraw the brawling egoists. The main question between them pivoted on who properly bore authority to negotiate a treaty. Secondary matters hinged on Scott's suspicion of Trist as an agent of the general's destruction, sent by crafty Polk. Scott also needled Trist as a menial clerk, unworthy company for one at the head of a conquering army.

Buchanan and Secretary of War William Marcy, at Polk's behest, ordered their feuding subordinates to reconcile. They obliged with steps – tentative – toward rapprochement. The breakthrough occurred only when the diplomat was overcome by fever at Puebla. Scott declared "*pax.*" He sent Trist a jar of guava jelly plus folksy encouragement. The men thereafter became friends and collaborated. (They also became, in Polk's gloomy view, conspirators intent on humiliating the government.) Scott later reported of their months in Mexico: "I never had a more amiable, quiet, or gentlemanly companion." Trist for his part asked the State Department in July to remove from its files reports by him that cast aspersions on the "noble" soldier.[75]

The Scott–Trist team tried to induce Mexican officials to sue for peace while military operations against their forces proceeded at Contreras, Churubusco, and Molino del Rey. By the time Scott's army occupied Mexico City (September 14, 1847), Trist had established working relations with Britain's diplomats: Minister Charles Bankhead and legation secretary Edward Thornton. They hoped to salvage something of Mexico. The imperative for Prime Minister John Russell was to check the expanding New World titan. For this purpose Mexico had earlier been assigned a role by the Foreign Office and been recipient of sizable loans. (Should Mexico default on the loans or Britain cancel them, then perhaps Queen Victoria's government could accept California as compensation.) In this spirit Bankhead encouraged Mexican authorities in summer 1847 to come to terms with Trist and prayed that he would be lenient. Thornton, meanwhile, urged the expediency of bribery upon Scott and Trist, alleging that moneys shrewdly dispersed among Mexican leaders would persuade them to surrender. After consulting with Scott's senior staff and overcoming qualms of their own, Trist and Scott decided to make $10,000 immediately available to Santa Anna. He and other worthies would be paid a million dollars from Scott's contingency funds upon the signing of a peace agreement. Alas, the lubricant did not work. The Mexican Congress deliberated in mid-July on the wisdom of opening formal talks with the Americans. The idea was rejected. Santa Anna kept the gratuity, whether for personal use or national defense is still unclear. Trist later judged that Santa Anna was "no patriot, just the reverse." Fighting resumed.[76]

Administration officials were at first incredulous, then irate. Buchanan wrote to Trist as rumors of the attempted bribery surfaced in Washington: "The president ... hopes that you have not been engaged in a transaction which would cover with ... disgrace all those who may have participated in it, and fix an indelible stain upon the character of our country."[77]

Quite apart from the bribery fiasco, Polk lost confidence in the efficacy of negotiations. Since mid-September the Mexican capital had resided in American hands. Yet a state of war existed with no conclusion near. Consequently, Polk told Buchanan in October to recall Trist from Mexico City and suspend negotiations. Future initiatives for peace would have to come from the Mexicans. Scott should impose levies on the local population to defray the expenses of his army until parleys resumed. As for Trist, Polk had increasingly little regard. The envoy had implied to Mexican interlocutors that their proposal to create a buffer zone from territory between the Nueces and Rio Grande rivers had possible merit; he never directly rejected this idea at Texas's expense. And he said too much when he volunteered that the US was not fully intent upon Baja California. On learning of this unauthorized flexibility, Polk fumed:

Mr. Trist has managed the negotiation very bunglingly and with no ability ... [He has] greatly embarrassed any further negotiations with Mexico. Mexico will hereafter claim terms equally as favorable as those he has suggested, and these terms I can never approve, and if a Treaty were signed, and ratified by Mexico, I would not submit it to the Senate ... I thought he had more sagacity.[78]

Buchanan's letter of recall (October 6, 1847) reached Trist in Mexico City in mid-November. A scolding one followed shortly after that spoke to the inviolability of the Rio Grande border.[79]

Trist was taken aback. Until these communications arrived he had thought his conduct conformed to orders. Negotiations with the Mexicans, he also believed, would soon result in Polk's satisfaction. He nevertheless notified Scott, the Mexican government, under Manuel de la Pena y Pena, and the British legation of the recall notice. Trist prepared to return to Washington. Under the prompting of these people, however, and because of his own certainty that peace was at hand, he hesitated. Then in early December he decided to stay on. He would complete the negotiations despite Buchanan's instruction to end them. He advised the secretary of state in a 65-page letter that peace as sought by Polk was obtainable. But unless the opportunity was seized it would vanish, "probably forever." The position of the Mexican peace party was awkward.

It would collapse unless hostilities ceased: "Go down it must and will, unless that Peace be ... made." The United States would then be involved in an occupation of endless duration and infinite cost. Woven in this epistle were additional themes: Mexican backwardness, Scott's probity, Pillow's flaws. Trist's most telling point came from opposition to "All Mexico" sentiment to which he thought, erroneously, Polk was committed. Trist's logic was straight Calhoun:

I have been bro[ught] to look upon this terrible calamity [dissolution of the Union] as a great good, when compared with the annexation ... of this country [Mexico] to ours, be it by conquest or "occupation", or be it by compact ... This incorporation [cannot] happen without incalculable danger to every good principle, moral as well as political, which is cherished among us; without almost certain destruction to every thing, on the preservation of which depends the continued success of our great experiment for the happiness of our race.[80]

This anxiety for future American happiness sprang from Trist's anti-Catholicism as much as from race prejudice. Whereas Polk countenanced Catholic chaplains in the US army, and turned to propaganda advantage the Mexican government's confiscation of Church properties to finance the war, Trist recoiled from the Papacy and its works. Few versions of them could be assimilated into American society, certainly none of the low Mexican variant. In one dispatch to Buchanan, he described "the lazy, ignorant and stupid monks, whose views do not extend beyond the round of purely animal enjoyments, of which their lives are made up, and who have in their characters no element whatever for an *esprit de corps*, save the common love of and greed after, money and property, mixed up with an idol-worship fanaticism (for them, religion is sheer idolatry and burning of candles) no less gross and base than their gluttony and lasciviousness."[81] Trist felt honor bound to preserve his Anglo-Protestant country from silent takeover by dusky Spanish-speaking Catholics. The social coherence of the United States was at stake; national well-being trumped directives from superiors, even those issued by the White House.[82]

Beyond the reach of Polk's fury and in the company of backers, Trist resumed his side of negotiations. They culminated in treaty on February 2, 1848, signed at a place sacred to Mexicans: Guadalupe Hidalgo, where the Virgin Mary supposedly appeared in 1531. The Mexican signatories included Luis Gonzago Cuevas (former foreign minister) and Jose Bernardo Couto (prominent lawyer), both ready to settle lest Trist's successor, or events, demanded greater forfeiture. The treaty did not transfer passage rights across Tehuantepec as the British had earlier acquired them. Nor did the treaty cede Baja California to the United States. Everything else, though, Polk specified to Trist in 1847 was gotten and at half the amount he was stipulated to pay.[83]

Arrival of the treaty text in Washington on February 19, 1848, conveyed by James Freaner – journalist and fan of Trist – created a dilemma for Washington. The treaty could be rejected because it was negotiated by an agent without standing and repellent to Polk: "He has acted worse than any man in the public employ whom I have ever known."[84]

Yet the treaty's content, if not containing all that was sought, was eminently defensible. It did not deserve automatic refusal. Also peace with Mexico was entirely worthwhile. Polk decided, therefore, to recommend the treaty for Senate ratification. Secretaries Buchanan and Walker dissented. The former argued for more Mexican territory to the south, extending to the Sierra Madre mountains.[85]

Senate debate was sharp. Calhoun lobbied for the treaty. But proponents of no territory (Webster) and advocates of more spoils (Sam Houston) protested various provisions. Nobody had a kind word for Trist. The Senate finally ratified his treaty, with minor modifications, in March 1848 by a margin of 38 to 14. (The US government also assumed $3.25 million claimed by citizens against Mexico.) Justice had been done, Stephen Douglas proclaimed, and US safety ensured: "Mexico made the attack; we repelled that attack, and carried the war into the enemy's country, with a view of getting indemnity for the past, and, if you please, security for the future."[86]

The droll Philip Hone passed this verdict on Trist's treaty. It had been "negotiated by an unauthorized agent, with an unacknowledged government, submitted by an accidental president to a dissatisfied Senate."[87] A disconsolate Mexican parliament accepted the treaty in May after debates. The Chamber of Deputies approved by a vote of 51 to 35, the Senate by 33 to 4.[88] American troops in Mexico City decamped in June.

* * *

Thoreau was audacious in words: "It is not too soon for honest men to rebel and revolutionize." Trist was audacious in deed. The wages of their dissent fell unevenly. Thoreau had a night's incarceration, which spurred his meditation on disobedience. It has touched a tribe of inspired troublemakers among whom are Leo Tolstoy, Emma Goldman, Mahatma Gandhi, and Martin Luther King. Thoreau's essay occupies to this day an honorable place in the American canon.[89]

Trist became a pariah. He was arrested in Mexico City by General Butler in March 1848 for not leaving the capital per Buchanan's orders. He sent Trist packing to Washington, where an icy reception awaited. Polk decreed that he should not receive any salary past the date when he learned of his recall (November 16, 1847). Neither should Trist be reimbursed for his expenses in Mexico. The chief clerkship, meanwhile, had been occupied since Trist's departure from Washington (by William Derrick of Maine). No other State Department niche could be found. Senators also had no use for him. Neither Calhoun nor other supporters of the treaty stirred on behalf of Trist. They ignored his suggestion to Whig leaders that Polk be impeached. Trist never gained readmission to high public service. He was instead rusticated to West Chester, Pennsylvania. He landed a job there as minor clerk for the Wilmington and Baltimore Railroad. He finally worked his way up to paymaster. His wife helped run a girls' school. It foundered. Through this bleakness, punctuated by impecuniosity and bad health, only a few people bothered to think about him or seconded his petitions of Congress for Mexican compensation.[90] General Scott was one whose appreciation did not falter. He regretted Trist's travails in 1864: "Poor and retaining all his good habits and talents, [Trist] has been strangely neglected by his Government."[91] Not until after the Civil War, during President Grant's first term, did matters improve. Senator Charles Sumner, alert to Trist's usefulness in scuttling "All Mexico," persuaded Congress to make good on the government's arrears. Trist's unpaid salary and expenses, along with twenty-three years of interest, were paid in 1871: $14,600. At the suggestion of Senator Simon Cameron, Grant also appointed Trist to postmaster general of Alexandria, Virginia. He was then past seventy. His death in 1874 was little remarked upon.[92]

Penalties varied for the war's objectors between the extremes of Thoreau and Trist. All the dissenters had to weather accusations of disloyalty. Warhawks in Illinois were disenchanted with Lincoln. Questions about his patriotism hounded him for years after the war. Douglas charged him in the 1858 senate race with not supporting the country during emergency. Polk became convinced that Calhoun was unpatriotic and ostracized him from the Democratic party. This ejection ended for good his presidential chances. It also fed his romantic idea of founding a southern political party capable of defending its own and putting him in the White House. As for the likes of Gallatin, Giddings, and Webster: critics ceaselessly lambasted them for having prolonged the war and encouraging Mexican resistance premised on weak US resolve.[93]

This last charge did not stick. It was easy to level but hard to prove. Evidence from Mexican sources never corroborated it. Senator Mariano Otero did cite Whig and New England dissent in 1848 as reason to persevere. He expected that US weariness, combined with guerrilla operations, would produce better terms for Mexico. This view was not shared by many comrades, however. He was one of four senators to vote in favor of Mexico's continuing the war. Manuel Crescencio Rejon of the Chamber of Deputies mentioned the irregularity of Trist's status as reason to refuse the Guadalupe Hidalgo treaty. But this concern was technical. The main basis for his rejecting the treaty had to do with Mexico's cloudy economic future after losing its northern tier of provinces. Rejon also worried over the fate of citizens marooned among a racially fixated people: "The North Americans hate us."[94]

Defeat subjected Mexico's political elite to a crisis of confidence. Symptomatic of it was an offer (1848) to anoint Scott the national leader.[95] Instability marred the social-political landscape for decades. An Indian peasant uprising swept the Yucatan peninsula immediately after the war. Liberals and traditionalists traded recriminations. Each side blamed the other for the nation's want of military preparedness in 1846. Vainglorious Santa Anna returned to power as "perpetual dictator" in 1853. He was deposed in 1855. Benito Juarez and associates composed a new constitution in 1857 that reduced Church and army privileges. Conservative action followed. It precipitated a civil war in 1858–1861. Juarez triumphed. But further attempts at reform misfired. Diaz established a period of iron rule. The inequalities it fostered gave rise to a fresh round of violence, the 1910 revolution. Meanwhile Britain's flop as a distant protector prompted Mexican governments to look elsewhere for guarantee against the United States. Napoleon III put France's case forward in 1864 in the person of Ferdinand Maximilian. Germany in 1917 went trawling in Mexican resentments, the Zimmerman mischief.

As for Americans, the war sealed their Union into two solitudes of north and south. Calhoun stated in 1847 that he could not, for the first time since entering public life, imagine better days ahead: "[The war] has dropped a curtain between the present and the future, which to me is impenetrable." He knew only that US armies were winning portentous victory.[96] One year later antislavery Whigs and Democrats founded the Free Soil party that soon led to the northern-based Republican party. The south remained predominately Democratic.

Calhoun died just as Henry Clay was conjuring the Compromise of 1850. It allowed for stricter fugitive slave laws and admitted California as a free state, but delayed decisions on slavery elsewhere in the Mexican cession. Later, the 1854 Kansas–Nebraska Act let settlers decide for themselves (popular sovereignty) whether to permit slavery north of the line established by the 1820 Missouri Compromise. Violence engulfed Kansas. Proslavery "Border Ruffians" raided Lawrence in May 1856. John Brown's gang retaliated against slaveholding settlers along Pottawatomie Creek. The disorders worsened. "Bleeding Kansas" did not enter the Union until January 1861. A few months later Fort Sumter in Charleston harbor was shelled by southern secessionists. Paralleling Giddings's dread of US belligerency in 1846, Grant wrote in prophetic mood after the fratricide of 1861–65: "The Southern rebellion was largely the outgrowth of the Mexican war. Nations, like individuals, are punished for their transgressions."[97]

Guilt and remorse have occasionally arisen in modern America, as when Senator Robert Kennedy in the 1960s called the Mexican war deplorable. Such feelings, however, have not translated into calls for retrocession of that property taken in 1848.[98] The tenacity meanwhile in thought of racial categories laced with condescension has been striking. Calhoun and Trist, each in his way eager to preserve Mexico, would have understood the musings of George Kennan in 1950. He attributed Mexico's misfortunes to its racial mixture, a blend of domineering Spaniards and traumatized natives: "Here is the true illustration of the crimes of the fathers being visited on their progeny; for, as the Spaniards intermarried with these native peoples the course of whose history had so ruthlessly been interrupted, they had to share the scars and weaknesses which they had themselves inflicted."[99] To Kennan the resultant neuroses and foibles dictated Mexico's political defects. They, in turn, diminished the likelihood of Anglo-American intimacy with Mexico. Still, a modus vivendi did take hold by the late twentieth century, illustrated by a regime of economic utility (NAFTA) and immigrants seeking better life in the United States.

6   Russia

Internal strife undid the Union thirteen years after Trist obtained his Mexican treaty. Secretary of State William Seward tried to avert disaster by drastic expedient. Had Trist known of it, even he would have blanched at Seward's impudence.

Seven slave states had left the Union by late March 1861: Alabama, Florida, Georgia, Louisiana, Mississippi, South Carolina, Texas. Their delegates, gathered in Montgomery, had declared a new nation in February. They selected Jefferson Davis to lead the Confederate States of America. Federal territory in the south meanwhile had either capitulated to secessionists or lay under siege. Fort Sumter lived under mounting pressure of isolation in bristling Charleston.

This unprecedented crisis paralyzed the federal will, Seward concluded, and overwhelmed newly inaugurated Abraham Lincoln, himself no more than a prairie bumpkin, an unlikely president. He had won the White House by a series of flukes. Their cumulative effect had prevented the best man – suited by experience, sterling character – from exercising executive command, namely Seward himself. Presentable and cultured, he had twice been elected governor of New York, twice senator.[1] He was in his own mind the preeminent Republican with a solid record of opposition to slavery. His duty in the 1861 emergency was to take the initiative. Otherwise, he thought, events would spin out of control. The republic would split, then sink into oblivion.

Seward suggested in a memorandum to Lincoln (penned April 1, 1861) that he yield pride of place to the secretary of state. Seward had recently determined a course of action: "It must be somebody's business to pursue and direct it, incessantly."[2] He evidently had not consulted with anyone in advance of giving this advice. But it confirmed the expectations of pundits and politicos: by force of personality he should exercise main power in the administration, allowing Lincoln to be ceremonial head of state.[3] Cabinet rivals of Seward's, including Salmon Chase of Treasury, had earlier resigned themselves to the primacy of the ambitious New Yorker.

Seward's plan entailed additional measures to the supplanting of Lincoln. They aimed at retaining federal forts in the south (except Sumter) and preparing the navy for blockade operations. Seward also recommended demonstration against European powers as a device to mend the north–south breach and revive national unity. Spain and France should be notified that their proposed interventions in unstable Santo Domingo and Mexico were intolerable to the United States: "If satisfactory explanations are not received from Spain and France, [I] would convene Congress, and declare war against them."[4] The British government too should understand that its meddling in North American affairs, in which Mexico again figured, was no more allowable in stirred times than in placid ones. Czar Alexander II should also strictly mind his affairs. He ought not, as rumors held he might, to recognize the Confederacy. Nor should St. Petersburg's envoy in Washington, Edouard de Stoeckl, overreach by repeating his earlier offers to mediate between Lincoln and Davis.[5]

Lincoln rejected Seward's brassy counsel.[6] Acceptance would have meant usurpation of power by the secretary. And foreign war during a moment of incapacity struck Lincoln as mad. He taught: "one war at a time."[7] Seward subsequently adjusted himself to presidential authority and never again challenged it. He disciplined his vanity to become one of the more reputable State Department heads.

His chief successes were two. First, he discouraged European powers from either intervening in the war of disunion or taking advantage of it. Not one foreign government recognized the Confederacy.[8] Second, after the crisis, he added the Alaskan realm – more than twice Texas's size – to the United States. The first achievement constituted adroit diplomacy amid peril. The second in 1867 confirmed the republic's abiding vitality.

France and Great Britain were the countries likeliest to reap benefit from US dissolution. A disintegration of power – yielding a rump United States plus a southern Confederacy, both viewing each other with suspicion – would foster a North American order susceptible to outsiders' manipulation. Not only would the overthrow of US supremacy produce two rivals in the place of a single sovereignty. Such an overthrow would also cast doubt upon the viability of the surviving entities. For them the question of future secessionist movements would surely arise, presaging shrinking power and diminished prestige. Mexico and Canada would gain relatively even in the absence of further unravelings. In short, a reconfiguration of power at the expense of US hegemony would mean a more politically fluid system; its weak component parts and shifting enmities and alliances would multiply the opportunities of interested Europeans. Britain's Benjamin Disraeli forecast in 1863 that North

America would henceforth be a captive "of armies, of diplomacy, of Rival States and maneuvering Cabinets, of frequent turbulence and probably of frequent wars."[9]

Temptation manifested first in Napoleon III's Mexican adventure, roundly condemned by North and South.[10] This enterprise along the southern flank was feasible only because of Civil War distractions. Otherwise, even Napoleon's imagination, driven by ambition to restore grandeur to France, and France to North America, would have hesitated.[11] His effort to enthrone Austria's Archduke Maximilian with 30,000 French troops, and establish a puppet regime in Mexico, melded opportunism with an appreciation of changing power realities. Understandably, his minister in Washington, Henri Mercier, wanted quickly to confer recognition upon the Confederacy. He and Napoleon also expected to boost its claims of independence by mediating the war's end on Southern terms.

Queen Victoria's government, under Prime Minister Palmerston and Foreign Minister Russell, also sought advantage from US troubles. Action on behalf of the Confederacy, diplomatic or other, should secure the steady and economical importing of cotton, critical to British textile manufacturers. This point of "King Cotton" was actually overplayed by Southern publicists; they overlooked both the abundance of stockpiles in Britain on the eve of war and Britain's ability to get cotton elsewhere (Egypt, India).[12] Less open to exaggeration was this reasoning: a splintering of Yankee power would help safeguard Canada, still an object of expansionist appetites in Washington, notably Seward's.

Before Union victories in July 1863 (Gettysburg, Vicksburg), the French and British governments tilted heavily toward that of Jefferson Davis. They toyed with granting recognition to the Confederacy and exchanging ministers. The Anglo-French foreign offices cheerfully proffered their service to end the fighting. They also early recognized the South as a legitimate belligerent (with London and Paris protected under the code of neutral rights). At cost the Confederacy acquired British built ships. They included the *Alabama* that caused damage to Northern maritime commerce valued in millions of dollars.

Seward had trusty instruments of his own to blunt European interference. He fielded in London, the capital most diligently wooed by North and South, an unusually capable diplomat, Charles Francis Adams. His lucidity and candor helped stifle the appeal of the South's commissioner, James Mason, to wavering British parliamentarians. They and War Ministry experts were anyway mindful that Canada stood hostage to London's good behavior as defined in Washington, a reality felt during the *Trent* crisis (November–December 1861) and in Seward's sharp warnings against recognizing the Confederacy.[13] The prestige of US diplomacy also improved as the war continued, indicating neither immediate Confederate victory nor Union irresolution. The effects of Northern defeats in 1861 and 1862 were first offset by the thwarting of General Robert E. Lee's northern invasion: Antietam, September 1862. This battle sobered French and British officials, especially Palmerston, about Southern prospects.[14] Disparities in Northern and Southern war resources – men under arms, financing, industrial production, ships, food supply – thenceforth became more telling as casualty rates skyrocketed and campaigns consumed stores of *matériel*.

Moral questions involved in the war also aided the Union diplomatically. Lincoln fell in line with Europe when he placed his administration on the side of antislavery. Britain had abandoned slavery in 1833, France in 1848. Serfdom had been abolished by Austria in 1848, by Russia in 1861. An effect of the Emancipation Proclamation (January 1, 1863) on European feeling was to shift it away from the underdog South to the Union, manifestly fighting for more than national preservation. The rights of African men, women, and children in America were at stake. Britain's liberal activist Richard Cobden told Senator Sumner in February 1863: "The President's emancipation policy ... has closed the mouths of those who have been advocating the side of the South."[15]

Finally, among his diplomatic assets, Seward listed Russian interest and sentiment. Officials in St. Petersburg still harbored grievances against the Anglo-French powers dating to the Crimean War, 1853–1856. American feeling for Russia during that conflict, based on proverbial Anglophobia, had been noted in St. Petersburg, where officials perceived the United States as a possible ally. Neither Alexander II nor his ministers wanted a diminution of US power in 1861; they valued it as a naval-commercial counterpoise to Britain, an element to ensure a stable European balance of power.[16]

This Russian viewpoint allowed society in St. Petersburg to suffer Lincoln's envoy, the miscast Cassius M. Clay – pugilist, womanizer, braggart – whose antics and flaws of judgment became lore.[17] Both sides concentrated instead on promoting mutual understanding. It blossomed. Amity benefited each country in the 1860s and culminated in the transfer of Russian America (Alaska) to the United States.

Amity

Seward and Lincoln before 1861 shared the standard view of their generation on things Russian. Despots ruled the empire. Thieving priests infested it. Superstitions enthralled it. This repository of reaction also threatened its neighbors. Both men had joined the celebrations of Louis Kossuth, when in 1851–1852 the fighter against Russo-Austrian oppression toured America and basked in the glow of Hungary's 1848 martyrdom. He preached the gospel of Russian containment to cheering crowds. Seward, for his part, in Senate chambers decried Russia's crushing of Hungary. He declared that the United States stood as eternal reproach to Russian tyranny. Lincoln, a private lawyer in Illinois, was appointed to a specially convened panel of leading Springfield citizens. To it he submitted pro-Hungarian resolutions. They affirmed the right of mistreated peoples to snap their bonds of submission and establish independent self-governments consistent with the colonists of 1776. He called Russia a land "where despotism can be taken pure, without the base alloy of hypocrisy."[18]

Poland's plight during the Russian trampling of 1830–1831 had likewise won the sympathies of Seward. He contributed to a subscription to relieve civilian suffering and participated in the activities of the Polish–Slavonian Literary Society.[19] How much young Lincoln (b. 1809) in rural Illinois knew of the Polish uprising at the time is uncertain. His feelings, in any case, would surely have gravitated toward the liberation side.

Alexander's reforms (after Crimea) in educational, legal, social, and administrative matters did not much alter the views of Seward or Lincoln. Russia remained freedom's intractable enemy, superseded only by southern slaveowners. Lincoln said in 1855, the year of Alexander's ascension to the throne: "The Autocrat of all the Russias will resign his crown, and proclaim his subjects free republicans sooner than will our American masters voluntarily give up their slaves."[20]

The Civil War caused Lincoln to dispense with his oft stated distaste for Russian coerciveness. To suppress rebellion he waged not only relentless war upon the Confederacy. He also suspended the writ of habeas corpus. He permitted military arrests and evacuations of civilians, imposition of martial law, mail tampering, press censorship, seizure of private property.[21] This scrapping of constitutional provisions on civil liberties made comparable Russian practice seem less odious. Besides, he was grateful to the czar for Russia's benign neutrality which shone brightly in contrast with the other great powers. Thus Lincoln's realism trumped democratic fastidiousness at home and abroad.

The Russian connection served the Union in practical ways. Foreign Minister Alexander Gorchakov declined to join his Anglo-French counterparts in a *démarche* to the belligerents, aimed at producing a North–South armistice. This initiative came from Napoleon in October 1862, after months of his trying to persuade Palmerston and Russell. They did want to pursue it, although they distrusted France. But this undecided pair,

juggling eagerness with prudence, balked at Napoleon's idea in the wake of
Antietam. London felt further restrained upon receiving word of
Gorchakov's unwillingness. Only if North and South expressed a willingness on their own in European mediation would St. Petersburg cooperate,
said Gorchakov. Otherwise, he hoped the Union would prevail and before
the United States endured irreparable harm. After citing Anglo-French
desires for US demolition, he told Bayard Taylor, the US chargé d'affaires
in St. Petersburg (October 1862): "We desire, above all things, the maintenance of the American Union as one indivisible nation ... There will be
no proposals for intervention."[22]

The Russians, unlike the Anglo-French, did not recognize the
Confederacy as a proper belligerent and its pretensions to independence
met with frosty indifference. Alexander's court declined to receive L. Q. C.
Lamar. This would be Southern commissioner never set foot on Imperial
territory. Confederate Secretary of State Judah Benjamin recalled him
from Europe before he was actually exposed to formal rebuff.[23] Officials in
St. Petersburg meanwhile patiently tolerated Clay's eccentricities, briefly
interrupted when Simon Cameron served as minister, June–September
1862 (after his mishandling of the War Department).

A squadron of Russian warships unexpectedly entered New York
harbor in September 1863, commanded by Admiral Stepan Lesovskii.
Weeks later a similar Russian contingent, under Admiral Andrei Popov,
arrived in San Francisco. Altogether the ships in both Union ports
numbered ten, their combined crews more than 4,000 men and officers.
St. Petersburg authorities had ordered the ships to North America so that
the crews might acquire training on long-range cruises in what were relatively modern vessels for the Russian navy. Tantalizing evidence suggests
that the Russians were also on a buying errand. Lesovskii's ships carried
double crews that could have been halved to sail the original ships and
whatever new ones were gotten from US builders.[24] Behind the naval
exercise and possible purchases was this Admiralty concern: war might
erupt between Russia and the Crimean coalition of Britain and France.
The question in 1863 turned on the czar's ongoing suppression of rebellion in the Russian zone of partitioned Poland, and the Anglo-French
desire to limit the violence while favoring the insurgents. (Napoleon
hoped for Polish success as it would have eroded Russian power in central
Europe, also desirable from a British standpoint despite unease over
France's expansionist aims.[25]) The czarist ministry of marine wanted its
ships dispersed, and, where possible, placed beyond the reach of Anglo-
French flotillas that could dominate the Baltic or besiege Russian ports.
The quality of Russian seamanship was inadequate for directly confront-
ing Anglo-French naval supremacy. (One of the Russian ships bound for

San Francisco missed its destination by thirty miles and wrecked on the pounding Point Reyes coast.) Yet from US sanctuaries the czar's ships could sally forth against Anglo-French merchantmen – in the Atlantic, Caribbean, Pacific – to inflict hefty cost. Also, depending on circumstances, these warships could harass Napoleon's Mexican venture.

War weary Northerners welcomed the Russian ships. Secretary of the Navy Gideon Welles entered in his diary: "God bless the Russians!"[26] Politicians and newsmen interpreted their appearance in Yankee ports as betokening Alexander's support and implying that Anglo-French interference in the Civil War would have far-reaching consequences. At the time of the naval visits, the North had just been jolted by another defeat: Chickamauga with 16,000 casualties (September 19–20, 1863). Deadly race and anti-draft riots in July in New York had earlier sapped public commitment to continuing the fight. Spreading doubts about the quality of Lincoln's leadership meantime indicated that he might be a one-term president. He had neither prevented the destruction of war nor produced victory.

Banquets, parades, and balls were held in New York and San Francisco (later Boston plus Washington) for the Russian visitors. Receptions on the eastern seaboard were elaborate. They included a sumptuous affair at the White House. Congressmen, cabinet officers, Supreme Court justices, and the First Lady met the ships' officers. Diarist Benjamin Brown French described his feeling after attending one gala event: "The Russians were exceedingly polite ... I have always regarded the Russians as a noble people."[27]

Russian officers as guests of the New York Central Railroad were conveyed to view Niagara Falls. When in San Francisco a fire threatened to engulf whole neighborhoods, two hundred Russian sailors volunteered to extinguish it. They received gold medals from a grateful citizenry. Admiral Popov, in reply to rumors in early 1864, prepared his crews and ships to intercept Confederate raiders should they attack San Francisco. No rebel warships materialized. Officials in St. Petersburg promptly registered with Popov via telegram their dim view of his tangling with Southern forces. Still, Californians welcomed his willingness and were delighted by the valliant fire-fighting sailors, all of which fit this thesis: the Union had true friends in Russia.[28]

Ministers in St. Petersburg were glad of the warm reception given their ships, coinciding as it did with denunciations in Paris and London of Alexander's Polish policy. Neither did Russian and Northern spokesmen dispel concurrent rumors that a formal alliance between the two powers was in the offing. In fact, neither side seriously contemplated such a move. But both benefited from the anxiety such chat produced in their enemies. Southern satirists and British cartoonists in *Punch* retaliated by depicting Lincoln and Alexander in an unholy marriage. Both ignored civil liberties respected in western Europe, mounted violence against weaker peoples, and were oblivious to outraged humanity. Lincoln, democrat in name only, matched the autocrat of all the Russias as brute.[29]

Lincoln tried to shore up Russian confidence in the Union. He was most solicitous of Stoeckl, a difficult chore given his skepticism. It stemmed from several sources: disdain for Lincoln as yokel; doubts about the quality of Seward's judgment on international affairs; a tendency to blame abolitionists for the war; admiration for Jefferson Davis; scorn for the ability of common men to conduct public affairs responsibly.[30] On this last point, a fixed idea in Russian conservative thought, Stoeckl wrote to Gorchakov after the New York riots:

> The republican form of government so much talked about by the Europeans and so much praised by the Americans is breaking down. Democracy in the United States has become irresponsible [and chaotic]. This is democracy in practice, the democracy that the European theorists rave about.[31]

Stoeckl nevertheless did not deviate from his government's line. An intact United States upheld a balance of power conducive to Russian security and tipped against Anglo-French preponderance. He always lent himself to Union overtures. They included his joining Seward (plus other foreign dignitaries) on a tour in 1863 of Northern cities and industrial centers, the aim being to underscore the Union's boundless material resources. Stoeckl enjoyed cabinet confidences and courtesies that outstripped those shown to other diplomats in Washington. He received blueprints for the ironclad *Monitor*. His agents were allowed to track Polish agitators in New York hoping to elicit popular support for their cause. The administration's decision to arrest and extradite a Polish sailor, Aleksander Milewski, who had deserted his Russian warship, also gratified Stoeckl. Milewski, who had enlisted in the US army, was subsequently brought before a Russian court martial, then hanged. (Other Polish sailors who jumped ship eluded capture.)[32]

Seward's refusal to join an Anglo-French attempt to effect a Polish truce at the expense of Russian authority particularly pleased Stoeckl. Napoleon had in early April 1863 informed the Union envoy in Paris, William Lewis Dayton, that the governments of France, Britain, and Austria were conferring on the text of a document to submit to Alexander. It would emphasize the desirability of peace in Poland and plead for justice tempered by mercy. Dayton demurred. He asserted that Poland was strictly a European matter. The United States, preoccupied with problems of its own, could not possibly involve itself. Unfazed, the

French foreign ministry next had Mercier appeal directly to Seward.[33] He responded by professing faith in the humane Alexander; he would enact fair measures to restore Polish tranquillity. The good offices of third parties were not needed. Seward also invoked the US tradition of restraint in European matters to explain his abstaining.

Russia's government-controlled press gave wide coverage of Seward's non-compliance with Napoleon. Gorchakov, otherwise anxious about an open clash with the Anglo-French, wrote to Seward in June: "His Majesty has greatly appreciated the firmness with which the government of the United States maintains the principle of non-intervention, the meaning of which in these days is too often perverted."[34]

To add weight to Seward's support of Russia in Poland, Minister Clay unburdened himself of anti-Catholic and anti-Polish diatribes. Priests and reactionary aristocrats had brought sorrow to their land while discombobulating the reign of a sagacious emperor. Bayard Taylor opined that history teaches that a nation once dead cannot be resurrected. Protestant divines – Charles Boynton, Joshua Leavitt – sermonized that in suppressing the Poles the czar was also striking against Vatican intrigues. Their nefariousness threatened liberty-loving people everywhere.[35]

Russian–US goodwill continued after Appomattox. This career rested upon similarities of national experience, cheered essayists. The liberator czar had acted courageously against serfdom, the emancipator president equally against slavery. Both captains had defeated regional insurrections of bogus merit. Both shared an antipathy for the Anglo-French empires and barely escaped their sting. The popular New England poet Oliver Wendell Holmes acknowledged that Alexander had been "our friend when the world was our foe."

The unease of foreign observers – Napoleon, Russell, Palmerston – over a possible Russian–US entente quickened in 1866. Congress congratulated Alexander on his narrow escape from assassination in St. Petersburg. Congress also commended him on enacting a peaceful social transformation that contrasted with the nightmares of Civil War and Lincoln's murder. A written proclamation to these ends was delivered to Alexander's court by Assistant Secretary of Navy Gustavus Fox. He and his entourage were carried to St. Petersburg by US warships led by the modern ironclad *Miantonomoh*. Like their Russian counterparts in 1863, this naval party was feted. It toured parts of the empire (Moscow, Nizhni Novgorod), was introduced to celebrities, and hosted by personages. This love feast helped prepare the next step in America's rise to power: acquisition of Alaska.[36]

Not every Russian official welcomed the selling of czarist holdings in North America. They belonged to the eighteenth-century patrimony.

Daring explorers (Vitus Bering, Aleksey Chirikov) and entrepreneurs (Alexander Baranov) had established Russia's New World colony. Its alienation should not be lightly tendered, Gorchakov argued in 1867. Decades later Soviet historians belatedly backed him. They sourly noted that Alaska had been sold for a "pittance" and constituted a sorry chapter in czarist diplomacy.[37]

Gorchakov's view ran counter to the main thrust of thinking in St. Petersburg, where interest in Russian America had gradually declined. Czarist and US diplomats conducted desultory talks during and after the Crimean War on the feasibility of Washington's buying the land, perhaps as supplemental sanctuary for Utah's Mormons. Negotiations languished as disunion overcame the United States. Even so, it did not cancel these stubborn facts. The province lay beyond Russia's ability to protect, lying close to British power in Canada and was vulnerable to naval assault. The Russian-American Company centered on fur trade no longer turned profits. The St. Petersburg government would shortly have to act as receiver. Animated still by notions of Manifest Destiny and drawn to the area's fisheries, Americans were becoming ubiquitous. They would no doubt establish themselves as the economically dominant element. Russian America would become theirs by silent invasion. Dignity and economy argued for selling the territory. Moreover, as the persuasive Grand Duke Constantine reasoned, life for Britain in the north Pacific would become complicated by US possession of Alaska. Americans located in Washington state and in Alaska would inevitably exert pincer pressure on British Columbia (an idea consonant with the apprehensions of London's envoy in Washington, Sir Frederick Bruce). Very likely these circumstances would lead to British Columbia's becoming US territory, thus driving England from the North American edge of the Pacific. Russia's own position in the Pacific basin had been importantly augmented by the founding in 1860 of a military post at Vladivostok. It made Russia's American settlement strategically superfluous. Why not, then, sell the property, taking profit where possible while creating trouble for London? The czar agreed. He authorized Stoeckl to make a sale, suggesting that $5 million would be fair compensation.[38]

Seward seized the main chance on March 30, 1867. He and Stoeckl agreed in nocturnal secrecy to a treaty sale at $7.2 million (two cents an acre). A week later the Senate upheld the treaty by a vote of 37 to 2. President Andrew Johnson detailed soldiers to Alaska to receive the transfer to US ownership before the House appropriated necessary funding. Delayed by impeachment proceedings against him, the House did not allocate moneys for buying until July 1868.

Proponents of purchase argued along several lines. Lodgment in Alaska would hasten the day when the Union absorbed British America (never mind the 1867 British North American Act which certified self-governing Canada). Additionally, Alaska and the Aleutian islands were admirably located for supply stations and shelters on the way to East Asia's emporium: Japan, China. Lumber, pelts, fisheries, and precious minerals were also available in Alaska. They only needed Yankee ingenuity to extract their true market potential. The puzzle for future generations, according to Clay, would be that Americans had bought a rich province – worth at least $50 million – at bargain rates. Crucially, Russian support during the recent war deserved reciprocal favor. Friendship in this case meant relieving Russia of a liability and contributing something to Imperial coffers.

Only Senator Sumner (Republican, Massachusetts) among treaty supporters struck a dissonant note on the ballyhooed theme of Russian–US harmony. While thankful for Russia's benign neutrality in 1861–1865, he reveled in the continuing expulsion of all monarchical influence from the Americas. He said in his speech supporting ratification: "The present treaty is a visible step in the occupation of the whole North American continent. As such it will be recognized by the world and accepted by the American people. But the treaty involves something more." Lest the point be mentioned but not noticed, he exulted: "We dismiss one monarch from the continent. One by one they have retired – first France, then Spain, then France again, and now Russia."[39]

Doubts

Against the main current of good feeling for Russia raced another in 1861–1867, fed by two streams of skepticism: one based on sympathy for Poland, the second on misgivings about Alaska and the people responsible for buying.

Poland

Smoldering Polish nationalism – not spent by failed uprisings in 1830, 1846, or 1848 – flared in January 1863. Provoked by the laying of conscription on urban youths, the insurrection was not easily smothered. Hundreds of thousands of people responded to the Manifesto of January 22 issued by the underground National Government of Poland: "All sons of Poland without regard to religious belief or birth, status or origin" would henceforth be "free citizens of the nation." They would be liberated from the shackle of feudal obligation, Alexander's 1861 emancipation edict not applying to Poland's serfs. They could acquire land in their own name. Poles to this end staged a guerrilla campaign against Russian occupation. Like the Confederacy, they scored early victories against larger forces, as in General Marian Langiewicz's success at Wachock. Polish soldiers in Russian formations bolted from units or took up arms against them. The National Government sent Wladyslaw Czartoryski on diplomatic missions to London and Paris to obtain Western aid. He found the reception fine at first, the rhetoric right. But closer inspection revealed bluff not iron. The Anglo-French powers were disobliging, albeit desirous of a reduction in Russian power. They were even less forthcoming than to the Confederacy. The end arrived in August 1864 when rebel leaders were executed by hanging in Warsaw's Citadel. Victims included the inspiring Romuald Traugutt. A combination of reprisals against the families of insurgents, torture, mass deportations, and the absolute bulk of Russian military force ultimately restored czarist control. Two unblinking disciplinarians imposed it: "Hangman" Mikhail Muraviev, Count Theodore Berg. A draconian order subsequently engulfed the mutinous Polish districts. Their vestigial autonomy was crushed in Russification, lightened slightly by agrarian reforms favoring the peasantry.[40] Poles at the time might have pondered questions that earlier anguished Frédéric Chopin. The composer asked an unmoved God in 1831 as freedom fighters died: "Moscow rules the world! Oh God, do You exist? You're there, and You don't avenge it – How many more Russian crimes do you want [or] are You a Russian too!!?"[41]

Polish resistors before defeat in 1864 appealed not only for European relief. They also sought US assistance in funds, recognition, mediation. Thus the Central Polish Committee in the United States published an address in New York's *Herald* in April 1863. Drawn from émigrés and veterans of Polish liberation wars (three men were also serving officers in the Union army), the Committee invoked the spirits of 1776 heroes, "laurel-crowned" General Thaddeus Kosciusko and Casimir Pulaski: "Are they not household words among Americans?" In memory of their service to US freedom, in acknowledgment of justice in 1863, the Union should take a stand on behalf of "crucified" Poland. The Union would thereby gain for its future an ally in the ancient contest against despotism: "Rally in [Poland's] cause, and her millions shall greet you from across the sea; the warm tide of gratitude shall surge your souls with the bliss of well-doing; and the Brotherhood of the world shall have made its first great step in the new path now opening for fraternal advance of ever-progressive humanity!"[42] Polish publicists asked in like tone in December 1863: "Why should not a free nation aid another struggling for liberty?" They answered with this prediction: "If you permit freedom to be crushed *abroad*, your own will share the same fate *at home*. Therefore, *aid the struggling Poles!*"[43]

These appeals received some sympathetic notice in the Union, primarily in the Roman Catholic and immigrant communities: Polish, German, Irish. Compared with the mainstream press, ethnic journals reported extensively on the suppression. This same press, and a few Democratic papers, protested Milewski's extradition and execution. Meetings were also held. Resolutions passed. Relief supplies were collected by private charity. But none of these events took place on a grand scale. They were dwarfed by previous public displays on behalf of Poland (notably in 1830–1831), never touched the level of pro-Greek agitation in the 1820s, and were overshadowed by lavish receptions given to Alexander's visiting warships. The most prominent immigrant American to speak publicly for Poland was Major General Franz Sigel. This German-born Union officer was, like his better known compatriot Carl Schurz, a veteran of 1848. Sigel had during that "springtime of the peoples" fought at the side of General Louis Mieroslawski, conspicuous among insurgent leaders in 1863. The attention showered on the Russian ships in New York and San Francisco made Sigel doubt the soundness of US thinking. He told audiences in graphic language of Polish predicament under Russian boots. He cautioned against anything that might lead to Russian–US alliance.[44]

The most eminent Polish-American in 1863 was Adam Gurowski. He had fought for his homeland in 1830. As an exile in the United States, he worked in the State Department, aligned himself with militant abolitionism, and became a man of letters. One time confident of Seward, Gurowski had converted by 1863 to pan-Slavism. It subsumed Polish aspirations within Russian preeminence and fraternal guidance. He uttered not a word for Poland. He endorsed Seward's Russian policy, thereby denying to Poles a potentially important advocacy in Washington.[45]

Gurowski counted Sumner among his acquaintances. By 1863 chairman of the Senate Foreign Relations Committee, Sumner had long been antislavery's chief standard bearer. He bore the scars of Preston Brooks's 1856 cane assault that bloodied the Senate floor and gave to abolitionists a living martyr. He inspired his disciples by erudition and eloquence.[46]

Sumner had been disappointed when no post was found for him in Lincoln's cabinet. He certainly thought himself better equipped to lead the State Department than Seward. The senator castigated him as a "warmonger," itching to involve the Union in conflict with one or another European power.[47] Russian Poland figured among the many areas of Seward–Sumner disagreement.

Only a handful of Republican newspaper editors, like Horace Greeley, examined the czar's Polish policies. But the party leadership made no criticism. Lincoln kept fully silent in 1863, riveted as he was by American events that terrible year and grateful for Alexander's indulgent attitude. Seward merely hinted that Alexander would do right by his Polish subjects.[48]

Sumner stood utterly alone when in September 1863, in a well-advertised speech in New York (at Cooper Union), he commended the Anglo-French for taking the liberal side in Poland against czardom. He spoke with unmistakable cosmopolitan inflection: Poland's original partition, and Russia's participation in it, were "inexcusable, illegal, and scandalous." Vindication of such behavior, he charged, existed "only in the effrontery that might makes right." On the very eve of festivities for the Russian warships, Sumner posited that a republic conceived like the United States could not bet "upon the certain friendship of any European power." In correspondence with British reformer John Bright, Sumner also sneered at those Northerners who hobnobbed with czarist naval officers. He professed his attachment to Western civilization, to which France and Britain were vital but Russia unconnected.[49]

Sumner's voice drowned in the gathering din of Russian–US celebration. And Clay, who anyway detested Sumner (for opposing his appointment to St. Petersburg), belittled the senator's New York speech in dispatches to Seward. Clay also assured Russian interlocutors that Sumner's words represented a motley minority in Northern opinion (treasonous "Copperheads," disloyal Democratic newspapers, outcasts). To help put things right, he purged his legation of one of its secretaries, Henry Bergh. He had the temerity to raise indelicate questions about repression in Poland.[50]

Alaska

Without influence on Lincoln's Russian policy, Sumner did play a large role in the Alaskan matter. Here too he did not champion Russian–US intimacy, albeit he once spoke glibly about an emergent *entente cordiale* and twittered about the obligations owed Russia for its Civil War stance.

His first response inclined strongly against Alaska. He cared no more for Seward in 1867 than in earlier years. Sumner also disliked President Johnson, opposed his brand of Reconstruction as too lenient, and wanted him impeached. Sumner hardly savored the idea of a Seward–Johnson diplomatic coup and the administration's getting an undeserved respite or bump in popularity. He expected, moreover, that Alaska would eventually plop into the US domain. The north land, in any case, did not warrant expenditure in the aftermath of expensive civil war. Additionally, he objected to the prospect of abruptly shifting native peoples and Russian subjects in Alaska to US sovereignty. They, however small in number, had not given their consent to regime change.[51]

Sumner polled his colleagues on the foreign relations committee concerning their attitude toward the Seward–Stoeckl treaty. The findings reinforced his own coolness. He then advised the Russians that Senate ratification would fail. To avoid embarrassment, therefore, they should withdraw their offer. Stoeckl replied with an emphatic no. The Imperial gift could not be returned. The Americans would have to find a graceful way of accepting.[52]

Sumner changed course, essentially from geopolitical logic. As mentioned above, he welcomed the expulsion of every European trace from the New World, Russian no less than Spanish or French. He also hoped in 1867 that London would award Canada to the United States in compensation for injury done by the *Alabama* and other British-built Southern ships. Washington's ownership of Alaska made sense, then, as it added to the logic of Britain's abandoning all North American claims. New England commercial and mercantile constituents meanwhile pressed Sumner in favor of Alaskan annexation as did Republicans in the western United States, where pro-treaty feeling ran high.[53]

Sumner lent himself to Seward's campaign to persuade skeptics and proved critical in obtaining Senate approval, where he lobbied averse colleagues. He delivered in chambers a scholarly treatise (April 9, 1867) on natural riches stored in the northern entrepot. Sumner actually gave Russian-America its new name of Alaska (derived from Aleut usage for "mainland"). Yet at the fateful moment he issued a caveat. It reflected his longstanding squeamishness about the Alaskan deal. It smacked of diversion from the pressing business of Reconstruction. Empire building in the far north simply bore no relation to the conceptual or practical problems that beset freed slaves and southern occupation. Resolution of these matters would shape US destiny and determine whether the nation achieved genuine greatness. Alert to Seward's appetite for acquiring more (Central American isthmus, Denmark's West Indies, Hawaiian islands) and angry with southern roadblocks to African–American progress, Sumner warned:

This [Alaskan] treaty must not be a precedent for a system of indiscriminate and costly annexation ... I cannot disguise my anxiety that every stage in our predestined future shall be by natural processes, without war, and I would add even without purchase. There is no territorial aggrandizement worth the price of blood. Only under peculiar circumstances can it become the subject of pecuniary contract ... Our first care should be to improve and elevate the Republic, whose sway will be so comprehensive. Plant it with schools; cover it with churches; fill it with libraries; make it abundant with comfort, so that poverty shall disappear; keep it constant in the assertion of Human Rights.[54]

Only Senators Justin Morrill (Republican, Vermont) and William Fessenden (Republican, Maine) voted against the treaty. They were unhappy with Johnson's southern policy. Even more than did Sumner, they disliked Seward. They thought him a party deserter and guilty of fawning over Democratic Johnson. These dissenters also thought the moneys required for purchase ill-spent in a time of stringency. Fessenden suggested that Seward be forced to live permanently in Alaska for his sinful pride of buying.[55] Other Senate skeptics, of whom there were at least ten, ignored their doubts to vote for treaty ratification.

The House of Representatives contained a feisty minority that wanted to scuttle Alaskan transfer and opposed payments to Russia. The hold-outs finally mustered 43 votes against appropriations with 44 abstaining (versus a majority of 113). On the general topic of territorial expansion, the House was less than lukewarm. Members passed a resolution in late 1867 – before the vote on Alaskan funding – that put them on record against new land purchases. They could only aggravate the nation's financial precariousness while weakening republican institutions.[56]

House dissenters with their press supporters, Greeley most memora-bly, advanced several points against Alaska. It occupied a frozen region – "Icebergia," "Walrussia" – unsuited for refined people or civilization. To date it had attracted primitives who dined on whale blubber and seal flesh. Neither the higher arts nor modern agriculture could be practiced in this inhospitable setting. The land's ice-jammed harbors did not con-stitute usable way stations to Asia's trade depots. And the proposed price ran exceeding steep. Yet if securing Russian friendship were really impor-tant, advised Benjamin Butler (Republican, Massachusetts), then the Treasury Department should make a cash gift of $7.2 million to Alexander. The United States, though, should not be saddled with inef-fable wastes of snow and numbing temperatures. Opponents to the Alaska transaction also revived the dormant Perkins claim. This matter, involving hundreds of thousands of dollars in alleged damages that dated to the Crimean War, centered on costs not recovered by the heirs of Benjamin Perkins. He had supposedly secured munitions for St. Petersburg (not delivered in the event) but never received payment. Until or unless this matter were resolved, said sticklers, there should be no truck with the Russian government, a demonstrably bad business partner. Much of the House's recalcitrance stemmed from frustration over the failure to remove Johnson from office by Senate impeachment trial (March–May 1868). Most men who voted against Alaska had earlier opposed Johnson's continuing in office, ostensibly for his violating the Tenure of Office Act but in reality for his Reconstruction at odds with Radical Republican design.[57]

Butler embodied Radical Republican feeling against Alaska. His polit-ical evolution had begun with Democratic allegiance. It changed to his becoming a Lincoln partisan. A political general during the Civil War, he helped form African-American regiments in 1863. He won notoriety for his administration of wartime New Orleans, where he antagonized the better classes. Butler befriended the city's poor whites and acted charitably toward common laborers. He organized protections for freedmen against white supremacists (and in later years worked against terrorist groups, such as the Ku Klux Klan). High-handed, deliberately provocative, and not immune to varieties of venality, he was dubbed "Beast" by the insulted ladies and gentlemen of occupied New Orleans.[58]

Butler ran for Congress in 1866 on a pledge that he would ensure Johnson's dethronement. He pursued this aim as one of the seven House managers – their de facto chairman – during the impeachment trial. His vituperation caused him to charge that Johnson had a part in the conspiracy to assassinate Lincoln. Butler's enemies gave as good as they got. One newspaper wrote in 1868 that Butler was "the incarnation of Hell itself . . . John Wilkes Booth is an angel compared to him."[59]

Ambition for America and practiced Anglophobia once led Butler to recommend that London cede Canada to Washington, "recompense" for Britain's misbehavior in 1861–1865. Alaska should, then, have been attractive to him as part of that drive to establish US power everywhere in North America. Anything that might redound to Johnson's advantage alarmed Butler, however. He feigned horror at the idea of granting citizenship to Alaska's "fat-sucking inhabitants" and Russian cast-offs. Before voting against funding, he said that if the administration wanted distant territory, it should buy Crete, thereby saving that miserable island from Ottoman grip.[60]

Milder types than Butler also opposed Alaska. Cadwallader Washburn (Republican, Wisconsin) compiled a careful study in 1868 based on government commissioned reports. He concluded that Alaska lacked all interest. Seward and Sumner were gravely mistaken to think other. The place was a void. The jagged coasts were dark, fog-bound, drenched in sheeting rain, irrelevant to maritime commerce with East Asia. Washburn told colleagues that Alaska's frozen ground contained nothing: "No coal of any value has been discovered in that region. No gold has ever been discovered in Russian America . . . No silver has been discovered there. No lead has been discovered there. There is no proof that any copper has been discovered . . . There is no proof that any metal, precious or base, has yet been discovered there."[61] He offered as late as 1871, in congressional hearings on Alaskan governance, to pay the original purchase price to any country willing to relieve Washington of its godforsaken barrenness.

Washburn also argued in 1868 that obligation did not automatically devolve upon the House to bankroll a treaty secretly negotiated by the executive branch. Johnson had acted in defiance of constitutionally ordained protocol and republican principle by taking hold of Alaska before the House voted funds. The fundamental problem, Washburn claimed, resided with a presumptuous president, not with the people's thrifty representatives in Congress.[62]

Stoeckl feared in 1868 that further House delay on the Alaska transaction would unmake the deal. He suggested in exasperation to Gorchakov that Russia simply give Alaska to the fickle Americans. They would then have to live with the mortification of reneging and of shabbily treating their friend, Alexander. In fact, Stoeckl was not pure injured innocence. He had a personal interest in Alaska, namely an Imperial fee (25,000 roubles) would be his on completing the sale. He evidently suggested freely handing Alaska to Washington as a way of shaming the House to provide funding pronto. He was, himself, without compunction about employing Americans as propagandists for handsome salary: Robert Walker, Frederick P. Stanton, John Forney. Their assignment was to awaken the House to the purported public clamor for buying Alaska. Stoeckl also greased the palms of congressmen to garner support for Alaska. A dozen representatives may have been paid tens of thousands of dollars. The miscreants probably included – nothing conclusively proven – Nathaniel Banks, chairman of the House Committee on Foreign Affairs and ailing Thaddeus Stevens, one of Johnson's more implacable enemies.[63]

Stoeckl's shenanigans were not decisive. At most they accelerated the House's enabling legislation, basically assured by the Senate's confirming the treaty.[64] The House provided the needed funds by a margin of more than two affirmative votes to every nay. Seward had tirelessly promoted the cause, not letting up even during the direst days of impeachment trial. He considered Alaska as his legacy to the nation. He told a Sitka audience during his 1869 tour of the territory that it possessed a brilliant future. Nearly seventy years old, he exclaimed:

Within the period of my own recollection, I have seen twenty new states added to the eighteen which before that time constituted the American Union ... I have seen in my own time not only the first electric telegraph, but even the first railroad and the first steamboat invented by man ... These are the guarantees, not only that Alaska has a future, but that future has already begun ... Nor do I doubt that the political society to be constituted here, first as a territory, and ultimately as a state or many states, will prove a worthy constituency to the Republic.[65]

* * *

The years just before Seward's Sitka appearance were among the most harrowing in US history. His vaunted republic barely escaped dismemberment. At the cost of copious blood and wealth Americans rid themselves of an inherited evil, slavery. Combined US fatalities in all conflicts between 1776 and 1953 did not equal that of soldiers who died in the Civil War: 620,000 (360,000 Northern, 260,000 Southern).[66]

Intensity of Union purpose in 1863 caused most people in Washington to become more inward-looking, to narrow their cosmopolitan outlook, such as it was. Lincoln and Seward judged Poland's cause as patently at odds with decent relations with Russia. The Polish matter did, however, distract the Anglo-French governments from their scrutiny of American discord to the distinct relief of Union diplomacy. Minister Adams in London observed in March 1863: "There is no denying that the Polish troubles have done something to take off continental pressure from us."[67] Only Sumner among senior Republicans expressed qualms about Alexander's Polish policy. He did not want the United States, in principle commited to self-determination everywhere, to be implicated in the czarist oppression of Poland.

Hoping to be remembered, Polish exiles in Switzerland (under the aegis of the Polish Mutual Aid Society of Geneva) sent Congress a reminder in April 1865. Following condolences for the death of Lincoln, they declared: "After a fatal struggle of twenty months for the independence and liberty of our country, after countless losses, we … contemplate with hearts palpitating with emotion your gigantic struggle, supported by rights the most sacred to humanity. The news of your heroic and glorious exploits filled us with admiration, and your triumph made us poor Poles forget our own misfortunes on beholding the great champion of liberty."[68]

As for the building of US power, it could be read by the late 1860s as a dismal chronicle about the emptying of lands belonging to native peoples and filling southern vacancies with African slaves. This rising US power shooed non-hemispheric states away from New World affairs, threatened Canada, and robbed Mexico. And the Alaska episode introduced unsavoriness: empire by financial lubricant. Congress investigated the matter in late 1868, heralding the sleaziness of the dawning Gilded Age.

Accumulating American power could also be read as testifying to the dangers of expansion, manifest in 1861–1865 when jealous local allegiances almost sundered the republic. Even so during those years the United States attracted people from abroad. Roughly 800,000 immigrants arrived during the Civil War on the optimistic assumption of better lives in a country of positive purpose.[69] It seemed confirmed in 1867 not only by the Seward–Stoeckl treaty, but also by the climax of Napoleon's adventure and Maximilian's death by Mexican firing squad.

The United States reached a conclusion of sorts in 1867. Alaska constituted the last great land acquisition in a line of treaty sales: Louisiana

(1803), Florida (1819), Mexican cession (1848), southern Arizona and New Mexico (1853). Three decades then elapsed before the republic thrust outward again – against Spain, into the Pacific and Caribbean.

The House's mixed response to Alaska in 1867–1868 anticipated Congress's future ambivalence. Arguments premised on imperatives for more and distant land were underwhelming. Voters never punished Butler or Washburn for opposing Alaska; each man later served as governor of his respective state. Indeed, problems closer to home concentrated the public mind, not faraway places accessible by sea routes. National mending, the south's role in a reunited country, unsettled race relations, taming the west, and social turmoil amidst economic uncertainty (1869 stock market crash, depression in 1873) crowded the US agenda.

Sumner's initial objection to Alaska and then conversion exemplified the public's ambivalence toward expansion. His opposition to expansion for its own sake later made him collide with President Grant over his attempt (1870–1871) to annex Santo Domingo. Sumner opposed the United States "warring down the humble."[70] He won against Grant, but at cost. He had Sumner removed from his cherished chairmanship of Senate Foreign Relations.[71]

Sumner stood in the humanitarian succession of Everett, Frelinghuysen and Giddings. Sumner meant, as in his words on Alaska, to stay "constant in the assertion of Human Rights." He waged war on slavery. He paused over the rights of little Poland against crushing power.[72] He glimpsed the limits of Russian–US cordiality which could not long be sustained by profoundly different political regimes.

The Alaska treaty that delivered to Washington what turned out to be a plenitude packed with gold, oil, and other treasures marked the apex of czarist–US cooperation. Instead of entering into alliance, as some political commentators presumed, the eastern autocracy and western republic grew estranged. American impatience with Russia's anti-Jewish pogroms helped drive this decline in mutual confidence. They obliged hundreds of thousands of Jews to seek refuge in America during the late nineteenth century. Their impecuniousness on arrival alternately provoked anxiety and contempt among nativists, who worried that charitable organizations would be swamped by a flood of unassimilable people. Washington's protests over Jewish mistreatment were dismissed by Russian officials as unwarranted interference in a sovereign power's affairs. Heightened awareness, meanwhile, in America of the scale of political repression in Russia, and the grimness of its penal system, led to pro-revolutionist feeling during the reigns of Alexander III and Nicholas II. Mark Twain expressed this disenchantment when he said that czardom deserved strong remedy: dynamite.[73]

Incipient Russian–US rivalry for commercial–diplomatic advantage in East Asia produced further complications. Concern over them in Washington dissipated somewhat with Japan's victory against czarist forces in 1904–1905. Russian defeat also strengthened the disdain felt by Americans, among whom Theodore Roosevelt, for backward czarist institutions. He had been thrilled as a youngster with the color and reception of Russian sailors in New York. As president, he referred to Nicholas II as a "preposterous little creature," no more worthy of confidence than his predecessors whose departing influence in North America Sumner had hastened.[74]

7   Reservations

The Civil War delayed US consolidation of North American territory. This postponement constituted a reprieve for western Indians that lived free of Washington. Their independence became quickly circumscribed after 1865, however. It vanished in the culminating Sioux-army melee at Wounded Knee in 1890.

Superior military technology, embodied by Hotchkiss mountain howitzers, played a role against those tribes living between the Pacific and Mississippi: Apache, Arapaho, Blackfeet, Cheyenne, Comanche, Crow, Kiowa, Modoc, Navajo, Nez Perce, Paiute, Pawnee, Ponca, Shoshoni, Sioux, and Ute among others.[1] Diseases afflicted these peoples with catastrophic rates of mortality.[2] Changes to the environment disconcerted the tribes: installation of railroad and telegraph lines, liquidation of buffalo herds. The hammering of the golden spike in Promontory, Utah (May 10, 1869) symbolized a new order. It left scant space for customary Native American life. The tribes' inability to make common cause against the United States, logistical vulnerabilities, and casualness in planning longterm campaigns also reduced Indian chances.

The vise of white advance from the eastern edge of settlement, along the Mississippi, and the west coast crushed indigenous populations. Their dwindling numbers in the US hovered around 250,000 by 1890.[3]

California highlighted the rapidity of native decline. The population stood at 150,000 before the forty-niners arrived. Indian count in the Golden State dipped below 30,000 by 1870. The California-born philosopher Josiah Royce recounted in his 1886 study of the state: "We reserved [abuse] for the defenseless Digger Indians whose villages certain among our miners used on occasion to regard as targets for rifle-practice, or to destroy wholesale with fire, outrage, and murder, as if . . . wasps' nests in our gardens at home."[4]

The burgeoning US population totaled 40 million in 1870, 50 million in 1880, 63 million in 1890. The Director of the Census reported in 1890 that an unbroken frontier line no longer existed, prompting Frederick Jackson Turner's meditation on Americans having vanquished the wilderness.[5] The Ghost Dance, meanwhile, that had swept the western tribes collapsed. It had thrived on mystical hopes of banishing white people from the west, restoring buffalo herds to their abundance, and returning dead Indians to their previous integrity and lives. A Cheyenne elder taught in 1890: "My children, today I tell you to travel a new trail, the only trail now open – the White Man's Road." The Chiricahua Apache, Cochise, had earlier mourned the southwest's subjugation:

When I was young I walked all over this country . . . and saw no other people than the Apaches. After many summers I walked again and found another race of people had come to take it . . . The Apaches were once a great nation; they are now but few, and because of this they want to die.[6]

Federal officials, spurred by social reformers and self-appointed friends of the Indians, evolved a policy to save aborigines from extinction, the so-called Peace Policy, based on "endeavoring to conquer by kindness."[7] This program was fitfully planned, unevenly applied, and conceptually muddled. Party bickering hurt it. This policy, more accurately a series of directives, was also exposed to hazards of administration by an enfeebled central authority. Johnson's impeachment and the scandals that marked Grant's presidency were emblematic of overall deficiency. The Peace Policy at times seemed merely a state of mind or pose amid the shambles of "Grantism" – Credit Mobilier fiasco, malfeasant War chief William Belknap, shifty presidential secretary Orville Babcock.[8] Still, the aim, despite slippage and vacillation, rested on the idea that worthwhile things could be salvaged from aboriginal societies. Like any human creature of God, ran the argument, Indians could be saved, indelibly stamped in the image of Euro-America. They might eventually qualify for citizenship. From this honorable estate they would simultaneously add to and benefit from life in the world's premier republic.[9] Grant in his first inaugural address declared (March 4, 1869): "The proper treatment of the original occupants of the land, the Indian, is one deserving of careful study." He intoned: "I will favor any course towards them which tends to civilization, christianization and ultimate citizenship."[10]

This line of thought held that Indians during transition from barbarism to civilization should live on land reserves away from mainstream America. Ideally, Indian removal to these reservations would be achieved by moral persuasion, by armed force only as second resort. They were, in any case, to be off limits to white people, thus allowing inhabitants to live unmolested. American settlers, in turn, could prosper in this confidence: neither their families nor enterprises, from homesteads and mines to churches and schools, would be threatened by Indian marauders. The reservations would in time cease to exist as Indians shed obsolete identities and ways of life in preference for the US world. All people therein would be joined as social–legal equals, fully equipped to face "the battle of life."[11]

This assimilationist policy met with objections. Tribal leaders and their followers disapproved of a future that tolerated their physical existence but scheduled their cultural disappearance. Resistance took many forms: litigation, entreaty, meetings in Washington between chiefs and personages, and violence. Regarding this last category, roughly a thousand combat actions occurred between army regulars and Indians in 1866–1890. These episodes, from rare pitched battles to hit and run operations involving few combatants, produced 2,000 military casualties. Indian casualties were three times higher.[12]

Some ethnologists questioned the idea that Native Americans could be molded into red versions of white people. Content to cultivate farms? Attend Christian worship? Submit to the habits and regulations of an alien society? If such a transformation were possible at all, these critics advised, it should not be rushed.[13] Guidance to be effective should be subtle, attuned to Indian norms and traditions. George Bird Grinnell, a perceptive student of Native America, attributed the failure to recast Indian life to ignorance. He penned this critique of social engineering in 1899:

In all their reasoning about Indians there has been one point of weakness [among philanthropists and policymakers]: they had no personal knowledge of the inner life of the people they were trying to help. Their theories appear to have assumed that Indians are precisely like white men, except that their minds are blank and plastic, ready to receive any impression that may be inscribed on them. These friends of the Indian had little acquaintance with Indian character; they did not appreciate the human nature of the people. They did not know that their minds were already occupied by a multitude of notions and beliefs that were firmly fixed there – rooted and grounded by an inheritance of a thousand years. Still less did they comprehend ... the tenacity with which [the Indian] clings to his beliefs which have been handed down to him by uncounted generations.[14]

Additionally, few pioneers were persuaded by the federal government's assimilationist goal. Contra it (and contra Grinnell), they had little use for Indians. They were appalling when left to their own devices. Paternal guidance, went the protest, could not alter this base condition. A patina of civilization would not cause Indians to become upright citizens. It would not offset Indian hostility or justify white lives and property stolen over decades. Heathens deserved chastisement. Colonel Thomas Moonlight of the Colorado militia reasoned in this spirit in 1866: "Nits make lice." One is right to eradicate them. Americans should dispense with Indian nuisances. Spare none, he urged: "Kill all ages and sexes." The editor of the *Kansas Daily Tribune* wrote that same year in response to warfare on the plains: "There can be no permanent, lasting peace on our frontiers till these devils are exterminated."[15] A newspaper in Omaha, after the 1873 murder of General Edward Canby during peace parleys with Modoc tribesmen, recommended a similar line toward a species not fully human:

> Death these fiends have broadcast sown.
> Let them pay each gory crown.
> Hunt them down![16]

The army in these circumstances had a clear mission. Either exterminate the savages or, at the very least, thrash them. Thankfully tough-minded veterans of Union victory, Generals William Sherman and Philip Sheridan, were willing to serve this western cause. (Sherman was commanding general in 1869–1883, during which time Sheridan headed the Division of the Missouri. Its borders ran from Minnesota to Texas, from Utah to Illinois and contained roughly 175,000 Indians. Sheridan served as commanding general in 1883–1888.[17]) Mercifully, from this perspective, the west also had its guardians in Congress, preeminently Colorado's Senator Henry Moore Teller and Kansas's Senator Preston Plumb. They were no more susceptible than Sherman or Sheridan to fiction about reputable savages or cowed by snooty pedants happy to correct hardscrabble pioneers. The frontier to them was not romantic exotica visited in leisure reading but an experience strewn with dangers: devouring insects, body-snapping toil, remoteness from ordered society. Indians in this context and on inspection were frightening to behold. They scalped. They stood in the way of national progress.[18] Sheridan had gotten the facts right: "The only good Indian is a dead Indian."[19]

Peace Policy

Even as Union and Confederate armies slammed into each other, white–Indian violence rocked the west. Two episodes signaled to reformers the need for change in Washington's policy: the 1862 Santee Sioux uprising in Minnesota, the 1864 Sand Creek massacre of Southern Cheyennes in Colorado.

The Minnesota violence began during a bleak moment for the Union, August 18, just days after the rout at Cedar Mountain and two weeks before thumping defeat at second Bull Run. Sioux warriors killed hundreds of Minnesota settlers. They were people of modest means. Many had recently immigrated from Scandinavia or Germany. Estimates of fatalities range from 450 to 800. New Ulm was besieged, Fort Ridgely attacked. Refugees poured into Minneapolis. Terror gripped the countryside. One immigrant, Sophie Bost of Switzerland, wrote from her farm to relatives in Europe: "This Indian business troubles me terribly. I've always loved Minnesota and have cheerfully put up with the drawbacks of our existence here, but the idea of seeing our babies tortured by savages is quite enough to make a person disgusted."[20]

The scale of Sioux attacks suggested to officialdom that Confederate and/or British instigators, based in Canada, had played a foul role. These suspicions, briefly entertained by President Lincoln, did not withstand examination, however. The cause of violence lay in Sioux grievances, aggravated by hunger. It debilitated children, women, and elders. The Santee reserve, hugging the Minnesota river (remains of an expansive domain), was penetrated by white settlers in 1861, who sought Federal protection. Fraudulent land claims, shady trading by merchants, tardy delivery of annuity payments, poor harvests, the withholding of food supplies by agents, and elimination of game endangered Santee survival.[21] Sophie Bost's husband, Theodore, unsettled by the Minnesota carnage, nevertheless allowed: "I don't forget that these Indians have been deceived and cheated by government agents." He compared the Sioux war to the Sepoy insurrection in British India (1857–1858): the downtrodden in each instance were striking for liberty.[22]

The War Department to quash the Sioux dispatched General John Pope, lately humbled at second Bull Run. He cooperated with Minnesota volunteers, led by Colonel Henry Sibley. They contained the uprising that at one time threatened to drain men and resources from Civil War theaters. The battle of Wood Lake (September 23) marked the end of Minnesota hostilities. Some Santee fled west to join Yankton Sioux bands in the Dakotas. Other Santee sheltered in Canada. They included war leader Little Crow. Those Santee who fell into the hands of white authority, 1,500 prisoners according to Pope, were subject to prosecution. Of these, 303 warriors were convicted, then sentenced to hang for crimes: theft, rape, murder. Appeal to the federal government by Henry Whipple, Indian rights advocate and Episcopal bishop of Minnesota, resulted in Lincoln's review of the cases. He commuted all but 38 death sentences. The condemned were executed in late December 1862 in Mankato. Thirteen hundred Santee survivors were subsequently deported from Minnesota to the west.[23]

Called Straight Tongue by Indians, Whipple had warned Washington officials as early as 1860 that violence would occur unless shabby practices ceased. He blamed the 1862 horror on pushy settlers, mercenary politicians in charge of local Indian affairs, and lunacy stirred by liquor sales. He wrote to military and civilian officials in quest of clemency. He managed to meet with Lincoln in the White House. Convinced by

Whipple's account, he resolved to improve the Indian administration: "If we get through this [Civil War], and I live, this Indian system shall be reformed!"[24]

The Sand Creek incident in November 1864 comparably stirred official-dom and reinforced doubts about existing policy. Seven hundred volun-teers, commanded by Colonel John Chivington, erstwhile Methodist preacher, destroyed a Cheyenne camp in southeastern Colorado. Before then they had been tracking warriors who had attacked miners, burned ranches, and killed families. Indians in Sand Creek were not responsible for this bloody work. Their chief, Black Kettle, had personal assurance from Major Edward Wynkoop of nearby Fort Lyon that no harm would befall the innocent tribesmen. They had deposited the bulk of their weapons at Lyon in token of good faith. Yet Chivington, ambitious for fame and eager for vengeance, ordered an assault. It began with howitzer fire. Cavalry charges concluded the action. It lacked pretense of restraint. Captain Silas Soule, a participant in the fight, testified: "It was hard to see little children on their knees have their brains beat out by men professing to be civilized." Lieutenant Joseph Crammer, also at Sand Creek, gave this witness: "A squaw ripped open and a child taken from her. Little children shot while begging for their lives"[25]

More than 150 unsuspecting people were killed, even as an American flag, hoisted by Black Kettle beside his tent, flew to indicate friendliness. Cheyenne corpses were mutilated, some looted for body parts. They were displayed by Chivington's men to Denver residents.[26]

Newspaper accounts and findings by three official inquiries shocked audiences. Wisconsin's Senator James Doolittle said that Sand Creek made his blood run cold. California's Senator John Conness condemned "the hand of murder." Charles Sumner called the massacre one of the worse misdeeds in US history. Kit Carson, legendary Indian fighter (against Apaches and Navajos), also damned Chivington.[27]

Only in the Rockies and on the plains did Chivington's action find defenders. Teller labored for years in Congress to vindicate Sand Creek against critics. They stacked one calumny atop another, he argued. He recalled for easterners the history of their ancestors, who in concern for lives and property had eliminated Indian neighbors. Yet his charge of double standard could not reverse the verdict of an 1865 military inves-tigation. It judged that Sand Creek disgraced the army uniform, "which should be the emblem of justice and humanity." General Grant thought Chivington an ordinary murderer. Most professional soldiers agreed.[28]

The years between Sand Creek and Grant's presidency were domi-nated by drama at Appomattox and the turbulence of Reconstruction. The South seethed. Freedmen sought respectable station in a universe of unfriendliness. Andrew Johnson barely escaped removal from office. Simultaneous with this turmoil, western violence escalated as immigrants encroached upon the last Indian enclave. Numerous engagements were fought on the plains from 1865 onward, fueled by Sand Creek and featuring Sioux, Arapaho, Southern Cheyenne. Episodes included the annihilation of Captain William Fetterman's 80-man troop by Oglala Sioux braves in 1866. Red Cloud's Sioux defeated the army in 1868 and forced evacuations of three forts along the Bozeman Trail (which ran from Wyoming to eastern Montana's gold fields). George Custer's 1868 surprise attack at Washita in Indian Territory caught survivors of Sand Creek and killed Black Kettle, stubborn proponent of white–Indian coexistence. General George Crook, meanwhile, conducted campaigns of attrition against Paiutes along the Oregon–California border.

Pacifist groups at this time, such as the Universal Peace Society, and retired abolitionists – Wendell Phillips, Peter Cooper, Lydia Maria Childs, Henry Ward Beecher – welcomed the report by Senator Doolittle's investigating committee on the state of Native America. The report (January 1867) indicated that Indian peoples were dying at astonishing rate from illness, intemperance, inter-tribal fighting, white violence, loss of lands, and lack of game. The report also dealt with frontiersmen whose aggressiveness provoked Indian violence. Of the resulting wars, Doolittle observed: "They are very destructive, not only of the lives of the warriors engaged . . . but of the women and children also, often becoming [campaigns] of extermination." Regrettably, the army did not always play an affirmative role. Frontier garrisons, in the report's view, were badly officered and radiated such vices as prostitution, easy booze, gambling: "Military posts among the Indians have frequently become centers of demoralization and destruction to the Indian tribes, while the blunders and want of discretion of inexperienced officers in command have brought on long and expensive wars."[29]

Doolittle's findings caused Congress to create the Indian Peace Commission in July 1867. It consisted of four army officers and four civilians of moderate bent. The soldiers included a skeptical Sherman. The civilian side included Samuel Tappan, vocal critic of Chivington, and the Commissioner of Indian Affairs, Nathaniel Taylor.[30] The Commission's charge was to halt the west's cascading violence by diplomacy and a program to coax Indians onto reservations. They in theory would be not only safe from white trespass. They would also be provisioned with means to advance education, farming, and Christian precepts. The Commission's aims were partially realized via the treaty of Fort Laramie in 1868 that applied to northern tribes. It was followed by agreements with Indians in Utah and New Mexico territories. But conditions of life on existing reservations belied the chance of much good flowing from these deals. New Mexico's Bosque Redondo stood as case in point. Washington closed this "southwestern Andersonville" in 1868. A fourth of its Apache and Navajo residents had died from exposure or want of medicine, adequate food, and potable water.[31]

Sherman had no confidence in the Commission's ability to win by diplomacy. He went along. He bided his time. He felt sure that Washington views would shift. They would then permit the army to manage the tribes in keeping with the national interest, defined by needs of railroad and civilian protection. He must have been assured too by General Grant's earlier explaining to journalists that the security of western settlers necessitated the destruction of certain tribes. Besides, as the nation's senior soldier, Grant had issued orders that let subordinates focus force on Indian villages and families to ensure compliance by braves. Sherman had no reason to think that Grant as president would embrace misguided idealists.[32]

Reformers of the Wendell Phillips ilk certainly expected little from the cigar chomping, whiskey-swilling soldier. Grant's rough manner and record of unforgiving campaigns against Confederates seemed to bode ill for Indians. True, his oft quoted words uttered at the 1868 Republican convention appealed in an election waged against a backdrop of southern unruliness: "Let us have peace." But this slogan seemed irrelevant to western ears.[33]

Once installed in the White House, Grant confounded Phillips's expectations. He stunned Sherman. The president adopted measures aimed at Indian rescue. In this project, he was not brilliant, original, or attentive. Unsurprisingly, his Indian policy faltered. It became, like other initiatives of his presidency, hostage to ineptitude.[34] Resignations linked to corruption included two by officers with responsibility for Indian welfare: Secretary of the Interior Columbus Delano, Commissioner of Indian Affairs Ely Samuel Parker. Still, Grant was serious, especially at first, about the desirability of easing Indian hardships. To do less, he told Congress in December 1869, would invite condemnation while encouraging civic degeneration: "A system which looks to the extinction of a race is too horrible for a nation to adopt without entailing upon itself the wrath of all Christendom and engendering in the citizen a disregard for human life and the rights of others, dangerous to society."[35] He extolled forbearance in his second inaugural speech (March 1873):

Our superiority of strength and advantages of civilization should make us lenient toward the Indian. The wrong inflicted upon him should be taken into account and the balance placed to his credit. The moral view of the question should be considered and the question asked, Can not the Indian be made a useful and productive member of society by proper teaching and treatment?[36]

The genesis of Grant's Peace Policy lay in his experience as an army officer in the Pacific northwest during the early 1850s. He was galled by instances of civilians bullying local Indians. Municipal governments failed to protect them. Indians, in his opinion, occupied a low rung on the ladder of civilization but nonetheless merited decency. He evidently decided to aid them if possible in the future.[37]

Grant's choosing Parker to head the Bureau of Indian Affairs (BIA) helped shape the Peace Policy. This former brigadier general had served as Grant's aide-de-camp; he was the officer at Appomattox who composed Lee's surrender documents. Parker was not just another army crony, however. He was also a full-blooded Seneca (a chief) and grand sachem of the Iroquois confederation. His selection by Grant signaled the new approach, even as bigots objected to this first appointment of an Indian as BIA director. Parker represented to Grant the hopeful future of Native Americans, entirely at home in the white world and making contribution as patriots. Trained in law and engineering, Parker remained Grant's advisor on Native America until his BIA resignation in 1871.

The decision to consult with Quaker partisans of Indian welfare came from a suggestion by Parker. Grant had been annoyed by their criticism of the army's handling of western tribes. He suspected that sentimentality warped Quaker judgment. Thanks to Parker, a meeting of president and Friends was organized at the White House. Grant liked their idea of replacing grabby agents with religious-minded men, motivated by concern for the uplift of their protégés. He also expressed pleasure at the prospect of Quakers instilling pacifist doctrines among heathens. He told his visitors:

Your advice is good. I accept it. Now give me the names of some Friends for Indian agents and I will appoint them. If you can make Quakers out of the Indians it will take the fight out of them.[38]

Parker was instrumental too in Grant's devising a simple nomenclature. Indians who strayed from their reservations were hostile, by definition legitimate objects of military attention. Indians within reservations were friendly, inappropriate objects of army interest or interference. Thus the War and Interior departments could collaborate gracefully in executing Indian policy. Each knew the physical boundaries of its authority. Parker also tried to ensure that the quality and quantity of goods provided to the reservations were higher than the inferior stuff previously offered at steep prices. Finally, he lobbied for the discontinuance of Washington's making treaties with various tribes. He explained in 1869 that this practice rested on falsehood. It asserted equality between the federal government and tribes when no such thing existed:

The Indian tribes of the United States are not sovereign nations, capable of making treaties, as none of them have an organized government of such inherent strength as would secure a faithful obedience of its peoples in the observance of compacts of this character ... Because treaties have been made with them, generally for the extinguishment of their supposed absolute title to land inhabited by them, or over which they roam, they have become falsely impressed with the notion of national independence. It is time that this idea be dispelled.[39]

Diplomatic charade not only exploited the tribes, Parker contended. It also delayed their integration into wider society, a view shared by Congress. It passed legislation in 1871 that dispensed with Indian treaties in the future, albeit recognizing those already signed. Thus Justice Marshall's concept of "domestic dependent nations" got dismantled in favor of this clarity: Indians were wards of the government, a category half way between foreign aliens and full-fledged citizens.[40]

Other elements of the Peace Policy centered on the primacy of civilian control over Indian affairs, foreshadowed by the 1849 transfer of the BIA from the War Department to the Interior Department. Staffing of key Indian districts (the Central, the Southern) with officials nominated by Friends and approved by Grant signaled this deepening civilian emphasis. Missionaries from other Protestant churches were also assigned to western agencies to teach religion and practical arts: Baptists, Congregationalists, Episcopalians, Lutherans, Methodists, Presbyterians. Rival Catholic missionaries followed close behind. By 1872 more than 70 agencies, encompassing nearly 200,000 Indians, were headed by representatives of a dozen denominations. As for army officers assigned to agencies, they were detached from the military chain of command and answered to civilian authority. Only by invitation of civilian agents could military units enter Indian reservations. In this insulated setting tribal loyalty and communal ways would yield to novel notions: American identity, law, and individual responsibility. Nearly 75 reservations existed at the end of Grant's presidency, not including 28 in Indian Territory.[41]

Congress's establishment of the Board of Indian Commissioners (April 1869) supported Grant's determination to elevate policy above prior levels. The Board hoped to immunize the Indian service against political spoilsmen and expel pilferers who raided reservation-bound funds and supplies. The Board, consisting of Protestants chosen by the president, worked with the Interior Department to ensure fair disbursement of all goods designated for Indian use. Board members served without compensation. They were independent of any formal government structure. Unfortunately, in their advisory role to the Interior Department, they supposed themselves a coequal entity in making decisions on allocations for programs. Confusion and ire over the locus of responsibility resulted.

Despite his frustrations among restless Kiowas and Comanches in Indian Territory (1869–1873), the Quaker agent Lawrie Tatum lauded Grant's Peace Policy: "a great blessing." The religiously inclined General Oliver Otis Howard likewise approved. Bishop Whipple admired Grant's intention and defended it against doubters. He congratulated Grant for his uncommon "kindness."[42] That Grant's policies were yielding benefits was already evident to Parker in late 1869:

The measures to which we are indebted for an improved condition of affairs are the concentration of the Indians upon suitable reservations, and the supplying them the means for engaging in agricultural and mechanical pursuits, and for their education and moral training. As a result, the clouds of ignorance and superstition in which many of this people were so long enveloped have disappeared, and the light of a Christian civilization seems to have dawned upon their moral darkness, and opened a brighter future.[43]

Such testimonials notwithstanding, Grant's Peace Policy did not convince the west. Editorial writers loathed eastern "whelps" and their "humanitarian gabble." Frontier journalists praised Christian missionaries for their evangelizing, but saw nothing practical for them to impart to stone-age dwellers. The whole collection of do-gooders encouraged the "Mogul at Washington" to ignore the murder of white citizens by redskins, incapable of putting vacant lands to agricultural or commercial use.[44] Manifestation of this resentment occurred in April 1871 at Camp Grant in Arizona, a federally sponsored Apache sanctuary. Tucson residents fell upon it. They slaughtered between 85 and 150 people. Thirty Apache children were preserved for servitude.[45]

Not only was Washington's policy unpopular in the region to which it applied. The policy was also undermined by army operations. The wars of the Peace Policy era were bitterly fought. They were waged against Cochise's Apaches, against Modocs in 1872–1873, against tribes on the southern plains in 1874–1875 (Red River War), and against the Sioux and Cheyennes in 1875–1877. This last campaign involved the death of Custer and 250 men of his Seventh Cavalry at the Little Bighorn (June 25, 1876). The costs of these army actions grew. They confirmed critics in their conviction that "conquest by kindness" was inanity, promotion of Indians to civilization preposterous. Only deployment of overwhelming force would drive them from the warpath and keep them on assigned reservations.

The Peace Policy had too little to recommend it to western tribes. Reservations were continuously pressed by cattlemen, settlers, and purveyors of liquor and weapons. Reservations were sometimes entirely overrun, as when in 1875–1876 15,000 gold seekers invaded the Black Hills, sacred ground guaranteed in perpetuity to the Sioux by the Laramie treaty.[46]

Reservations were also subject to reduction by railroads under right of eminent domain. The Union Pacific, Kansas Pacific, the Atchison Topeka, and Santa Fe (plus their branch lines) wrought a revolution. It disrupted the migratory patterns of buffalo and tribes. It transported swarms of white people, among whom came the hunters. Their parties boasted wealthy sportsmen and European aristocrats, including Russia's Grand Duke Alexis, who in 1872 shot with Custer and Buffalo Bill Cody.[47] The exploits of such hunters pushed the buffalo herds to the brink of extinction. They had long sustained the bodies (plus spiritual life) of plains Indians, providing food, clothing, bedding, teepee covering. By 1880 the millions of buffalo that had once roamed, darkening the landscape for miles around, were gone.

Colonel Richard Dodge recounted how in 1873 he followed the trail of hunters over familiar territory: "Where there were myriads of buffalo the year before, there were now myriads of carcasses. The air was foul with sickening stench, and the vast plain, which only twelve months before had teemed with animal life, was a dead, solitary, putrid desert." Dodge pitied the Indians. He assumed they would vanish with the beasts that had nourished them. He published these lines in 1882: "Ten years ago the Plains Indians had an ample supply of food, and could support life comfortably ... Now ... they are reduced to the condition of paupers, without food, shelter, clothing, or any of those necessaries of life which came from the buffalo." He held that the worst blot on the escutcheon of the United States was, next to slavery, the assault on Native America.[48]

Soldiers

Dodge was not alone among officers who possessed feeling for the tribes. Colonel Benjamin Grierson, commanding officer at Fort Sill in 1869–1872, understood that reservations were far from what was promised by the Peace Policy. The erratic delivery of food supplies was a glaring defect; it caused Indians to leave their confined parcels in pursuit of game. Grierson occasionally fed hungry Kiowas and Comanches with army provisions. He otherwise practiced leniency, arousing Sheridan's chagrin and westerners' anger.[49] Another officer, Colonel John Gibbon of the Seventh Infantry (who fought against Nez Perce, Sioux, Cheyenne), voiced these thoughts:

How would *we* feel, how would *we* act if our country were over-run and wrested from us by another race? If our lands were bought with promises to pay which were never fulfilled? If certain other portions of land were guaranteed to us by solemn treaty and these treaties . . . violated as soon as precious metals were found upon the land or for any other reason the other race wanted it? If having been deprived of the food which before was ours for the taking, we had been solemnly assured that in its place we should be supplied by good and wholesome food of other kinds and then our wives and children be left to starve, whether because greedy contractors furnished improper food or none at all perhaps for months, perhaps for years? If our men were debauched . . . our women degraded and our children starved if they did not consent to go to school, and learn, say the Greek Alphabet, and recite verses from the testament of an unknown religion? All these things has the Red Man suffered . . . We need not . . . be surprised at his offering resistance.[50]

Even glory-seeking Custer understood Grierson's impulse and Gibbon's probing questions. He admitted that were he an Indian, he would cast his lot among those of his tribe who defied white dictate; he admired Indian tactics and horsemanship. Generals Pope and Howard, also sensitive to wrongs suffered by Indians, expected that religious instruction and frugal habits would ameliorate – then overcome – Native America's material and spiritual poverty.[51]

General Crook became an exponent of Indian rights. The Boston Indian Citizenship Committee and other philanthropic associations solicited his opinions. After directing difficult campaigns against Geronimo's Apaches in the 1880s, he likened them to the heroes of classical Greece in their resolve to combat oppression. He courted the wrath of Sheridan and President Grover Cleveland by softening Geronimo's unconditional surrender terms in 1886.[52] Crook opposed the deporting of Chiricahua Apaches to Florida (following their surrender to General Nelson Miles). He encouraged Apache self-reliance via jobs and farming–ranching programs. More generally, he condemned the legion of wrongs committed against natives by civilians and military functionaries. "It goes against my conscience," this soldier once said, "to fight Indians when I know that [justice] is on their side and wrong on ours."[53] He supported voting rights for Indians. He held as a matter of conviction that they could be as well integrated into society as any of the immigrants who flooded the United States. He defended various reservation deserters – Poncas, Northern Cheyennes, Bannocks – when they fled hunger and destitution.

General Miles, most renowned of Indian campaigners (against Kiowa, Comanche, Sioux, Apache), championed Chief Joseph. Miles accepted his surrender (October 1877) in northern Montana, just 30 miles from the Canadian line sought by Joseph and his 800 Nez Perce refugees from Oregon's Wallowa Valley. These men, women, and children had trekked 1,700 miles while fending off pursuing cavalry columns under General Howard. As part of the surrender terms, Miles and Howard pledged that Joseph and his people could return to Wallowa (or to Idaho's Lapwai reservation). Sherman rescinded his subordinates' offer. Instead, on his orders, the Nez Perce were sent to Indian Territory, where they suffered grievously. Miles pestered the government for years afterward to let Joseph return to his homeland. A remnant of his group finally was permitted back to the Wallowa area. Not Joseph. He died (1904) on the Coleville reservation in Washington state. Miles thought him a superior soul, "the idol of his tribe."[54] His 1877 surrender speech had combined eloquence with resignation:

I am tired of fighting. Our chiefs are killed ... The old men are all dead ... He who led on the young men is dead. It is cold and we have no blankets. The little children are freezing to death. My people, some of them, have run away to the hills, and have no blankets, no food; no one knows where they are – perhaps freezing to death. I want to have time to look for my children and see how many I can find. Maybe I shall find them among the dead ... I am tired; my heart is sick and sad. From where the sun now stands I will fight no more forever.[55]

Even Sherman was moved. He praised Joseph and his braves for their fortitude.[56] On other occasions, too, Sherman expressed unexpected sympathy. He told his wife in 1868 that the western tribes were languishing. They faced this dilemma: "We kill them if they attempt to hunt and if they keep within the Reservations they starve."[57] Owing to his intervention after inspection, Washington removed Navajo residents from Bosque Redondo. The moody soldier had daydreamed in the Civil War's immediate aftermath of escaping his official burdens (and troubled marriage) by joining the Sioux to wander.[58]

Sheridan too could be sensible about Indian plight. With genuine feeling, he wrote to Sherman (1878) after the Great Sioux war:

Along came the nineteenth-century progress, or whatever it may be called, to disturb [the Indians'] happy condition. The white men crowded on to the grounds of the Indians and made encroachment on [their] rights which no government could stop ... The government made treaties, gave presents, made promises, none of which were honestly fulfilled ... [The Indians] began to see [their] lands wrested from [their] possession, [their] herds of buffalo, which [they] believed the Great Spirit had given them, rapidly diminish, and the elk, deer, and antelope killed for the market, and by the sportsman ... We took away their country and their means of support, broke up their mode of living, their habits of life, introduced diseases and decay among them, and it was for this and against this they made war. Could any one expect less?[59]

Another element of thinking among army officers was their attitude toward local civilians. They needed as much watching as the tribes, Sherman reflected. He and Sheridan scored random acts of settlers' violence against Indians. Miles blamed white greed for the troubles that befell the Nez Perce, who until the 1870s had taken pride in their friendship with the United States (dating to Lewis and Clark).[60] When in June 1874 a Comanche–Cheyenne force attacked Adobe Walls, center for buffalo hunters and whiskey sellers who lived on the edge of legality in Texas's panhandle, General Pope withheld help. He swore that any dispatching of his troops would be for another purpose, to "break up the grogshops and trading establishments rather than protect them." General Alfred Terry in the Dakota department tried, albeit vainly, to eject gold miners from the Black Hills. Intercepted trespassers occasionally brought legal suit against individual soldiers.[61]

Making civilian–army matters worse, senior officers had little affection for those economic refugees who hoped to start afresh in the west as downturns (per the 1873 Panic) and labor unrest roiled the east. Federal soldiers broke the 1877 rail strike. Anarchists in the labor leadership vexed Sherman, as pleased to see them throttled as the Sioux disciplined. The disproportionate number of foreign born troops (Irish, German) and from the lower class, to say nothing of black "buffalo soldiers," meanwhile fed a jaundiced view of military service. The small army (25,000 men in 1874) of enlisted poor and commissioned mediocrities seemed fair target for shrewd entrepreneurs. A recurrent theme among officers was that western businessmen were a kind of predator. They bilked soldiers of paltry pay by overcharging and underserving.[62]

Sentiment among officers for some Indians and against various civilians did not equate with support for the Peace Policy, however. Only a few officers approved it, such as Grierson and Howard. The overwhelming majority ridiculed it. Captain Charles King, who served under Crook against the Sioux, wrote these lines in 1876: "It is in New England ... that the most violent partisans of the peace policy are to be found today. There is method in their cultured mania, for the farther removed the citizen finds himself from the Indian the better he likes him."[63]

Sherman abhorred the Peace Policy. Military strategy for him was premised on the obvious aim, compliance of enemies. Nothing should obscure this goal. He famously pronounced in 1880 that "war is Hell."[64]

This language not only described a stark reality but implied a solution. All possible means should be brought to bear against an adversary – Confederate, Indian, or other – to end hostilities. An enemy's economy and civilian morale were valid targets no less than his armies. War against the South corresponded neatly in this logic with total campaigns against Indians, a notion dignified by Sherman's unswerving confidence: progress and safety in the west were indivisible with military conquest. No place existed for Indians qua Indians in an area designated for space-compressing railroads, bustling cities, and scientific agriculture. Indians, by nature and intellect, were neither suited nor needed by people zealous for improvement. Revolted by these sentiments, Wendell Phillips cursed Sherman for favoring policies of "universal extinction."[65]

The general could not comprehend Phillips's qualms or that of other "namby-pambies." None had bridled at his army's scorching of Georgia or the Carolinas. True, his orders to Sheridan to meet off-reservation tribes with strong force led to the violent deaths of some defenseless Indians. Yet Sherman's "march to the sea" had also inflicted harm on vulnerable civilians. Abolitionists had not protested. Why, Sherman puzzled, should their like get excited when his soldiers enforced federal writ in distant corners of US territory? War eschewed half-measures. After the annihilation of Fetterman and his company, Sherman counseled: "We must act with . . . earnestness against the Sioux, even to their extermination, men, women, and children."[66]

Sheridan also had no doubt about the Peace Policy's deficiencies. Eastern philanthropists infuriated him. They seemed wholly indifferent to agonies endured by people living in the open frontier. He wrote to Sherman in 1870: "I am forced to the alternative of choosing whether I shall regard [the] appeals [of settlers] or allow them to be butchered in order to save myself from the hue and cry of the people who know not the Indians and whose families have not the fear, morning, noon, and night, of being ravished and scalped by them."[67] As for suffering among Indian innocents, it belonged to the category of unintended consequences (collateral damage) experienced by Southern civilians. Sheridan's flinty realism helped exonerate him and his men:

If a village is attacked and women and children killed, the responsibility is not with the soldiers but with the people whose crimes necessitated the attack. During the [Civil War] did any one hesitate to attack a village or town occupied by the enemy because women or children were within its limits? Did we cease to throw shells into Vicksburg or Atlanta because women and children were there?[68]

Sherman and Sheridan encouraged the extirpation of buffalo herds. This action too was akin to Union practice against Southern civilian economy.

Federal troops had wreaked desolation in Virginia's Shenandoah valley so complete that, in Sheridan's phrase, "a crow would be compelled to carry his own rations" over it. By such reasoning one should not get maudlin about Dodge's "putrid desert" dotted with buffalo corpses. Nomadic Indians would be deprived of their "commissary," readier therefore to retire to reservations.[69] The destroying of buffalo herds, in short, was not wanton but a military necessity.

Both generals supported their subordinates against critics when they got incensed over troubling episodes. These included not only the Washita incident. The 1870 obliteration of a Piegan encampment in Montana by two squadrons of cavalry also attained notoriety. Roughly 170 people, weakened already by smallpox, were killed in the fighting begun on Major Eugene Baker's orders. Sherman and Sheridan, moreover, upheld stringency whenever their subordinates were tempted to indulge defeated Indians (per Miles with Nez Perce or Crook with Apaches). "Punishment must follow crime," Sheridan instructed. Indians would grasp the lesson and cherish their reservations more than ever as safe zones.[70]

Army officers rarely questioned the Peace Policy in public fora and did not relish the idea of challenging civilian superiors. Even so, Secretary of the Interior Carl Schurz (1877–1881), eager to preserve elements of the Peace Policy, had to remind Sheridan that his hissing at purported defects was unmannerly. It came parlously close to insubordination.[71]

Unable to assault Indian programs frontally, officers fired discreetly at them. Much fire was concentrated upon the bureaucratic side of the Peace Policy. The divisions of labor between the War Department and the Interior Department's BIA were said to disorder lines of responsibility and baffle the army's chain of command. For years Sherman and Sheridan contended that the BIA should be returned to War Department supervision. They ascribed real and imagined shortcomings to the BIA that cumulatively raised widespread doubt about the wisdom of federal policy. Congressional critics, primarily House Democrats, endorsed the officers' campaign. The War office by these lights had run the BIA just fine in 1824–1849; its return to War jurisdiction would foster needed clarity. Divided authority permitted clever Indians to play departments against one another and jeopardized public security.

War Department control of the BIA would correct the chief flaw of Indian policy, argued the restorationists. A new emphasis on stricture, not pampering, was required. Flatly stated, Indians were more apt to honor treaties if they were enforced by soldiers than by missionaries or BIA men. Sherman testified: "The military authorities of the United States are better qualified to guide the steps of the Indian towards that conclusion which we all desire, self-support and peaceful relations with his neighbors, than the civilian agents."[72] Ordinary soldiers agreed. Captain King wrote acerbically of the BIA and Peace Policy: "The apparent theory of the Bureau is that the soldier is made to be killed, the Indian to be coddled."[73]

Army officers were confident in their ability to deliver and distribute food and farming utensils to reservations. On such matters, the Interior Department and BIA were said to be grossly incompetent. The BIA, advocates of transfer contended, was the institutional guarantor of the Indian ring. This bugaboo of the frontier army amounted to a motley collection: gun runners, liquor merchants, squawmen (unsavory white men married to Indian women), sly contractors, and unscrupulous officials. They never resisted an occasion to sin but lived off the multimillion dollar industry of supplying the reservations.[74]

Criticisms of the BIA sparked resistance. Eastern reformers answered that the army was a murdering force aligned with frontier thugs. The War Department was the worst place imaginable to house the BIA or implement Indian conversion to tranquil society. Transfer, Whipple predicted, would mean gratuitous costs in aboriginal lives and property. Alfred Meacham, another Indian rights advocate, seconded Whipple's points. He editorialized in his journal, *The Council Fire*: "[Transfer] means to make business for the War Department. No well-informed man will assert that it is for *the good of the Indian.*"[75]

Senate Republicans were also unwilling to abandon polices promoted by Grant or by his successor, Rutherford Hayes. They foiled repeated House attempts to effect transfer. The Senate in this cause was inadvertently aided by army actions, as when during deliberations on transfer news reached Washington of the Piegan village tragedy. More than anything, Schurz's efforts in 1877–1878 to improve the Indian service blunted army critiques and brief for transfer. The secretary appointed honest men. He instituted transparency and accountability. He tried to dismantle the spoils system. This reform of a bad system did not cure all problems. Many crept back. But Schurz did startle people by his energy. Sheridan acknowledged that the Indian service was "lifted out of the mire."[76]

Civilization

Tribal restriction to reservations and the end of Indian wars muted debate on the BIA's appropriate departmental site. The main question from the early 1880s onward sprang from what reformers regarded as the next hurdle: erasing Indian personality and redrawing it in the image of white

America. The first superintendent of the Indian Industrial School in Carlisle, Pennsylvania summarized this objective in aphorism: "Kill the Indian, save the man." Federal authority to accomplish this goal encouraged education and moved aggressively on severalty. These institutions would pulverize tribal identity, dissolve reservations, and eradicate the wall separating Indians from white society. They would be affirmed as thoroughly American, henceforth unavailable as curiosities in circus shows or targets of white rascality.[77]

Founded by army Captain Richard Pratt in 1879, with aid from Schurz, the Carlisle school exemplified the ambitions of Indian education.[78] This showcase served as model for similar schools across the United States. The Carlisle motto boomed: "From Savagery into Civilization." Polygamy, wife-beating, superstition, and forms of violent irregularity would be stomped out. They would yield to the sound habits of modernity. Three hundred Indian schools established on such premise existed by 1900. They had combined enrollments of 22,000 students, a hefty percentage of the Native American youth. Congressional spending on Indian education kept this quick pace: $30,000 in 1877, $75,000 in 1880, $992,800 in 1885, more than $1.3 million by 1890.[79]

Carlisle's curriculum emphasized manual subjects useful for students' future employment in farms or factories: carpentry, smithing, masonry. Arithmetic, history as patriotic catechism, English literacy, and Christian precepts complemented this vocational training. Indian modes and costumes were proscribed. Moccasins were discarded as detritus of a primitive past. Students were forbidden from speaking in their native tongues. "I believe in immersing the Indians in our civilization," Pratt told a Baptist convention in 1883, "and when we get them under holding them there until they are thoroughly soaked."[80] The "outing system" at Carlisle placed an Indian child during vacations in the home of a white family. In it the example and language of true civilization could be further absorbed. Were every child placed in such invigorating circumstance, Pratt predicted, "the Indian problem" would wither away.[81]

He recruited students from tribes throughout the west for Carlisle. It rested upon a military regime. Male students donned cadet uniforms, drilled in military formation, and marched to classrooms. Female students wore dresses and studied domestic arts: sewing, cooking, household finance. Roughly 8,000 young men and women from 139 tribes passed through the school before its closing in 1918, including the consummate athlete Jim Thorpe (Sac and Fox). The largest student contingents came from these tribes, each providing 200 or more pupils: Apache, Cherokee, Cheyenne, Chippewa, Oneida, Mohawk, Pueblo, Seneca, Sioux.[82]

Carlisle enjoyed support from devotees of Indian salvation who, beginning in 1883, met annually at Lake Mohonk in upstate New York. Senators George Hoar and Henry Laurens Dawes (both Massachusetts Republicans) were also keen. Yet Pratt and the project of educating Indians had critics. The responsible class produced two noteworthy cases of unvarnished nationalist type: General Sherman, Senator Plumb.

Pratt's absence from military duty entailed by Carlisle annoyed Sherman. As a seasoned officer with combat experience, Pratt ought to serve with his Tenth Cavalry on western assignment, not waste time on quixotic educational experiments. Sherman also opposed his recruiting of other army officers to teach at Carlisle. Against this objection by the nation's senior soldier, Pratt appealed to President Hayes in 1880. Pratt answered that his method of Indian pacification by education was less costly than army operations and far more effective: "I am at this time fighting a greater number of the enemies of civilization than the whole of my regiment put together, and I know further that I am fighting them with a thousand times more hopes of success." His aim differed not at all from that of the War Department whose objective also centered on curbing Indian wars. But as his means held greater promise for a serene western future, he would persevere: "Knowing as I do that I am supremely right, it would be wicked to falter, even though pressure to that end came in threats from the General of the Army."[83]

Support of Carlisle by Hayes and Schurz shielded Pratt against Sherman.[84] This protection, though, did not deter congressmen, particularly not the hearty and back-slapping Senator Plumb. This Ohio-born (1837) Republican had by mulishness survived childhood poverty and smallpox. After college (Kenyon), he had a stint in journalism, founding the *Xenia News*. He afterwards went to Kansas as a Free-State fighter. He then pursued careers in law, cattle, banking, and silver mining. He helped establish pioneer settlements in his adopted state. He served as an officer in the Eleventh Kansas against Confederates. He fought Indians in 1865. Involved in his "whole-souled way" in the business and politics of Kansas, he disliked eastern "twaddle" about supposedly blameless Indians toward whom he bore black antipathy. Their time anyway in the United States had expired, he said. They existed only on white sufferance. They should be placed "out of the way at the proper time." Until then their indolence and occupation of fertile lands prevented immigrants from organizing productive farms or profitable commerce.[85]

Allergic to most types of public spending, Plumb found Carlisle unbearable. Expenditures on Indian education violated public trust, the senator charged. He considered Indian students hopeless and unsusceptible to even the kindest tutelage: "I do not believe that schools like that at

Carlisle ... are calculated to be, in proportion to their cost, of any permanent value to the Indians, nor of value in the settlement of the Indian problem."[86] To impose theories of Americanism upon an unworthy race ignored nature's laws:

You could turn all the Indians that could be educated at [Carlisle] ... for the next fifty years into Pennsylvania and the Indians would starve to death in competition with the people of Pennsylvania. The only thing an Indian is fit for, when it comes to an industrial occupation, is the lower branches of agriculture; something that is in its nature passive, something which requires no perceptible intelligence. He is no more capable of improvement in the sense in which we ordinarily use the term than a wild beast ... When it comes to talk about educating [Indians] and in making them a factor of civilization, that is one of the things which cannot possibly result from anything we can do.[87]

Plumb referred to Pratt and other officers on educational detail as publicity hounds, charlatans, swindlers. They were also cowards who shirked soldierly duties for easy work at extra pay in cushy places – Carlisle or Oregon's Forest Grove School or Virginia's Hampton Institute. These schools deserved closing.[88] Their inmates should be returned whence they came and told to till the earth, "simply putting before the Indian the problem which every white man meets, that he has to labor or die. That is one of those things which we need to apply today [1881], a great deal more than we do, and it would do them much more good than giving them an education [like that] at Carlisle."[89]

Plumb's attacks never discredited Pratt. They did not lose him allies. Well placed ones, such as Dawes, chairman of the Senate Committee on Indian Affairs, gave singular help.

Dawes secured not only funding for Indian education and participated in the affairs of Lake Mohonk as one of its leading lights. He also shepherded through Congress in 1887, with President Cleveland's approval, the nineteenth century's most important legislation concerning Native America: the General Allotment Act (popularly the Dawes Act). Reformers hailed it as Indian liberation, no less momentous than the Magna Carta, Declaration of Independence, or Lincoln's Emancipation Proclamation. Nodding reverentially to Helen Hunt Jackson's 1881 imputation of previous policy, *A Century of Dishonor*, the Mohonk faithful chimed: "Passage of the Dawes bill closes the 'century of dishonor.' "[90]

This Act took aim at the 138 million acres of tribal land under federal custodianship, mostly lying west of the Mississippi and of varying quality (from exhausted earth in arid settings to nutrient rich soils). The Act permitted the president to divide reservations into household allotments of 160 acres. Persons eighteen years old or above would receive an additional 80 acres. Individual children would be allotted 40 acres. Acreage in all cases was doubled if the land in question could support only grazing. Allottees of majority age became US citizens. Provision was also made for Indians who lived off reservations to select land parcels anywhere in the public domain. People who failed to select an allotment within four years of the Act were to have one assigned. Tribes could not elect to live outside of the allotment regime (with exemption for specific ones, including the Five Civilized Tribes in Indian Territory). Residual reservation lands would become available to white settlement. Proceeds of government sale to settlers were to be held in trust for each tribe. Indian allotments could not be alienated by their owners for a period of twenty-five years, according to the original law. After amendment (1891), however, the allotments could be leased or sold to non-Indians if the BIA approved the transaction as serving the owner's interest.[91]

Dawes believed that allotment of lands would accelerate the entry of Native America into society by instilling habits in Indians of thrift, individualism, and enterprise. The Act's compulsory parts served the longterm advantage of Indians by forcing them to adjust to white culture instead of being its perpetual misfits. Indeed, according to Lake Mohonk expertise, in the absence of prodding, tribal economies would remain stagnant. Progress toward civilization would forever stall in social-ism's incompetence. Referring to the Cherokees whose capital in Indian Territory he visited (1885), Dawes lectured that the tribe's economic–social–cultural advance had reached impasse:

They have got as far as they can go, because they own their land in common ... Under that there is no enterprise to make your home any better than that of your neighbors. There is no selfishness, which is at the bottom of civilization. Till this people will consent to give up their lands, and divide them among their citizens so that each can own the land he cultivates, they will not make much more progress.[92]

The reduction of reservations promised additional benefits. It would sever traditional loyalties to autocratic chiefs and ludicrous medicine men. They would be superseded by allegiances to self-reliance, legal codes, and the sanctity of property. Proximity to new white farming neighbors on surplus land would also encourage integration and knowl-edge of good conduct. President Cleveland explained in his 1888 annual message: "Contact with the ways of industrious and successful farmers will, perhaps, add a healthy emulation which will both instruct and stimulate." Finally, the breaking up of large reservations would eliminate from whites the temptation to trespass thereon, which in the sorry past had caused "so many disastrous collisions" (Schurz's words).[93]

Few people opposed the allotment legislation. Practical friends of the Indians, applauded the Indian Rights Association in 1887, knew that

Dawes would fulfill philanthropic hopes dating to Jefferson's promise to uplift Native America and make it a suitable partner in the republic. Developers connected to mining, lumber, and the railroads, as well as settlers, also appreciated the Act. It threw open hitherto inaccessible land. Talk about the desirability of Indian assimilation did not mean much in such context. Nor did jabber about the coziness of having Indian neighbors distract westerners' attention from welcome bonanza.[94]

The most articulate skeptics of allotment were found in what was, by standards of the era, a minority of oddballs. The National Indian Defense Association, led by Dr. Thomas Bland, opposed coerced acculturation. It could not possibly serve Indian well-being, he explained in essays for *The Council Fire*. Indians should be left alone to develop in their own way and shape their own destiny in cultural freedom. Their communal relationships and other values were not devoid of admirable qualities; many were worth preserving or developing further.[95]

Bland's multiculturalist notions surfaced briefly in congressional discussion. House and Senate dissenters doubted whether Indians with their communalist outlook and vague understanding of personal property could comprehend the capitalist economy about to be imposed. The ethnologist Lewis Henry Morgan was cited as authority. He had warned that the result of allotment "would ... be that in a very short time [the Indian] would divest himself of every foot of land and fall into poverty." Aware that allotment experiments in the past had pauperized tribes, some congressmen wondered about the good faith of land reformers.[96] The minority report of the House Committee on Indian Affairs charged in a 1880 debate on severalty:

The real [purpose of this policy] is to get at the Indian lands and open them up to settlement. The provisions for the apparent benefit of the [Indian] are but the pretext to get his lands and occupy them ... If this were done in the name of greed it would be bad enough; but to do it in the name of humanity, and under the cloak of an ardent desire to promote the Indian's welfare by making him like ourselves, whether he will or not, is infinitely worse.[97]

Congress's most unbudging opponent of Dawes's severalty plan was Senator Teller. He called it "fraught with evil."[98] Before his Washington life, he had soldiered as an officer in the Colorado militia. He had helped smooth the path for Colorado statehood in 1876. Western development, especially mines and railroads, was for him an abiding cause. He had been a lawyer admired for encyclopedic knowledge of mining regulations. He had worked as counsel for the Union Pacific. He spent thirty years in Washington in the upper chamber (as Republican and Democrat) beginning in 1876. He interrupted this legislative career to assume the Interior portfolio during Chester Arthur's presidency, 1881–1885.

His overall outlook was unexceptional for a Coloradan of his day. Teller came to identify wholly with the pro-silver chorus. He did not believe in racial equality: "I say that the Caucasian race . . . is superior in mental force, intellectual vigor, and morals to any other branch of the human family."[99] He was testy with criticisms of the way westerners dealt with Indians. He never subjected his fellow Methodist, Chivington, to close scrutiny.

Teller possessed enough of the maverick not to succumb to every prevailing prejudice. Nor did he hate. He objected to the slave South. But he favored a mild Reconstruction after the Civil War. He doubted African capabilities. But he welcomed black emancipation. He entertained more generous ideas about Indians than most whites of his region. The Nez Perce saga compared in his estimation with that of Xenophon and his 10,000 soldiers traipsing through Persia. Of the war fought by Chief Joseph's people, Teller commented: "I believe no set of men ever went to war in the history of war[fare] who had a better cause for war than the Nez Perce Indians."[100] In contrast with Plumb, Teller favored provisions for Indian education; he enhanced its funding while Interior secretary. He visited Carlisle and was friendly with Pratt. Teller enjoyed the confidence of Helen Hunt Jackson. He won the praise of Frederick Douglass, himself a champion of Indian rights.[101]

Teller's skepticism of the allotment idea sprang from knowledge of Indian economies more sophisticated than that of reformers of Dawes's stripe. They would disturb, said Teller. They would create havoc. They would ensure further harm to a damaged people. Better to label severalty "a bill to despoil the Indians of their lands and to make them vagabonds on the face of the earth." They had not asked for severalty. Few understood it.[102] He foretold in Senate chambers:

When thirty or forty years shall have passed and these Indians shall have parted with their title, they will curse the hand that was raised professedly in their defense to secure this kind of legislation and if the people who are clamoring for it understood Indian character, and Indian laws, and Indian morals, and Indian religion, they would not be here clamoring for this at all.[103]

Neither Dawes nor Cleveland was oblivious to the pitfalls of dividing and privatizing the reservations. Were allotment accomplished abruptly or prematurely, Dawes cautioned a Mohonk assembly, before tribes were educated in arcane property law and rudimentary English, they would fall prey to land jumpers and speculators. Protections in the law, though, such as prohibitions on selling allotments before twenty-five years, apparently reassured Dawes, as did his conviction about the need to make Indians into propertied individuals.[104] He subscribed wholly to these words of Merrill Gates, president of Amherst College, when in 1896 he expressed at Lake Mohonk this faith in capital accumulation:

We have, to begin with, the absolute need of awakening in the savage Indian broader desires and ampler wants. To bring him out of savagery into civilization we must make the Indian more intelligently selfish before we can make him unselfishly intelligent. We need to *awaken in him wants*. In his dull savagery he must be touched by the wings of the divine angel of discontent. Then he begins to look forward, to reach out. The desire for property of his own may become an intense educating force. The wish for a home of his own awakens him to new efforts. Discontent with the teepee and the starving rations of the Indian camp in winter is needed to get the Indian out of the blanket and into trousers – and trousers with *a pocket in them, and with a pocket that aches to be filled with dollars!* . . . The truth is, that there can be no strongly developed personality without the teaching of property – material property, and property in thoughts and convictions that are one's own. By acquiring property, man puts forth his personality and lays hold of matter by his own thought and will . . . The Savior's teaching is full of illustrations of the right use of property . . . There is an immense moral training that comes from the use of property.[105]

Andrew Carnegie's *Gospel of Wealth* (1889) contained no clearer statement of Gilded Age devotion to enlightened materialism or its elevating effect.[106] The concerns of Bland or Teller, from such loftiness, seemed mere quibbling. Dawes with Cleveland's help had kept Grant's faith: the United States could create a respectable niche for the land's original occupants. By cajoling and edification, they would be swept into thrilling America.

* * *

Post-Civil War governments sought benefits of pacification by methods short of war, hence the Peace Policy. The small and under-financed army was thinly stretched from occupation in the south (until 1877) to maintaining order in the west: roughly one soldier per 75 square miles in the Departments of Missouri, the Platte and Dakota; one man per 120 square miles in the Texas department.[107] If means were devised for Indians to "take the fight out of them," then costs plus wear and tear on the military could be contained. The army would be preserved for other tasks, such as policing beats in the Caribbean or Central America. Additionally, the army could be liberated from physically grueling, mostly thankless, and frustrating frontier actions.

The Nez Perce chase and bringing Geronimo's handful of renegades to bay proved onerous. Defeats also injured army pride – Fetterman,

Bozeman trail, Custer – and lowered public confidence. Among observers at the time, a consensus arose, supported by historians since: the individual Indian warrior outshone the individual soldier (horsemanship, marksmanship, stamina) and was often better led. The Comanches and Crows fielded some of the world's finest light cavalry.[108] Captain King reported on this prowess: "At full speed the worst horseman among them [the Crow] will dash up hill or down, through torturous and rocky stream beds, every where a goat would go, and he looks upon our boldest rider as a poor specimen."[109]

Mishaps as suffered by the frontier army were not unique in the context of late nineteenth-century great powers. Between the Civil War era and Wounded Knee, British forces faced not only spirited Sepoy rebellion and surrender at Cawnpore (plus murder of prisoners by Nana Sahib). They were also overwhelmed by Zulu warriors at Isandhlwana (1879) and by the Mahdi's Dervishes at Khartoum (1885). Yet the Crown's power in Canada kept a level of order for white subjects and Indians envied by Americans. Critics of Washington's policy looked hopefully to Canada as model of good governance, where fair treatment of indigenous peoples dovetailed with the requirements of domestic peace. This acknowledgment delighted Britons. A few could not help sniping. "We in England," W. T. Franklin told Bland in 1884, "observe the Republic's dealings with the weak and helpless, and I am sorry to say we are compelled to own that our monarchy is greatly superior in true charity and justice to the so-called emblem of freedom and justice – the Republic."[110]

Sheridan denied the applicability of Canadian experience to US conditions. Below the British line a tidal wave of white immigration deluged Indian country and exceeded the ability of any government to control. Indian–white violence was unavoidable, he held. Sparsely populated British Canada experienced little bloodshed in the absence of a large westward-bound population. Lessons could not be drawn by his US army. Indians presented it with a practical problem to security not a topic for moral philosophy.[111]

Late nineteenth-century Indian policy was variant on a question faced by all conquerors: How should they deal with subjugated peoples? The answer as devised by Washington corresponded nicely with its response to European immigration. During 1865–1890 ten million people came to the United States from northwestern Europe: British Isles, Germany, Scandinavia. Another fifteen million followed during the next quarter century from elsewhere: Russia, Austria–Hungary, Italy, Greece, Romania. The national task was to Americanize these foreigners, done in the belief that social–economic coherence required sturdy doses of conformity. The "melting pot" had to produce an English speaking civic responsibility out of hodge-podge. Newcomers had to accept the Constitution as truth. Credible place in this framework could even be found for Catholics and Jews. Admittedly, Asians constituted a special problem, their "indigestibility" expressed in the Chinese Exclusion Act in 1882 and anti-Japanese Gentleman's Agreement in 1907–1908. African Americans in the southeast also posed a perceived difficulty to public safety, hence their fencing-in via Jim Crow laws, supplemented by lynching.[112]

President Grant and successors decided that surviving Native Americans should not be left behind, as Teller–Bland were alleged to prefer. Nor, contra the reservations idea, should they live in continual exclusion or isolation. Neither should they perish violently at the hands of Chivingtons. The goal of Pratt and Dawes was to avert complete disaster in Native America. An honorable place would be established for Indians, irrespective of their unreasoning attachment to traditional ways or unwillingness to embrace US blessings. Enforced integration, Lake Mohonk reasoned, was far better than the fate that befell southern blacks, Asian arrivals, or previous generations of Native Americans.

The allotment and Carlisle solutions, in fact, constituted colossal blunders. The failure was threefold. First, experiments in land ownership and education flunked the standard set by their proponents. Second, as experienced by the people who were to be helped, the innovations miscarried. Third, a latter-day generation of officialdom judged them misconceived. They were abandoned.

Undertakings to make Indians into a type of yeoman farmer via the Dawes Act caused acute distress. It surpassed anything entertained by Sheridan. In his zest to catch Indian raiders in 1874 (Kiowas, Cheyennes, Comanches), he let subordinates in hot pursuit violate prohibitions on army units in reservations. Their residents, in his view, should not feel safe if they disturbed frontier calm, Peace Policy or no. But neither did they deserve to live in pervasive poverty, the main effect of the Dawes Act. Western hunting tribes did not easily adjust to the demands of agricultural life. Cultivation of gardens or fields was typically a woman's role disdained by men. They anyway had other ideas about ownership and were uncertain about the private ideal. Lot, a Spokane chief, once deflected suggestions that his tribe take up land in severalty with these words: "A few might learn to do that kind of farming, but most of our Indians would perish if they tried to get a living on farms of their own. They cannot do it. Set apart a tract big enough for us all and we can cultivate it together."[113] Many allottees never learned to use their parcels to advantage or learned too late. The land base meanwhile that had maintained Indian societies disappeared: leased, sold, squandered.

As Teller predicted, the allotting of land and then issuing of fee patents accelerated the ownership by non-Indians of reservation acreage at bargain rates. By 1891 more than 12 million acres of reservation land – 11.5 percent of all Indian property – had been annexed to the public domain. By turn of the century, 28.5 million acres of Indian land had been stripped away as "surplus." Allotment, when later applied to the Cherokees and other Oklahoma tribes, also yielded untoward results. The Cherokees by mid-twentieth century possessed a minor fraction of the acreage that they had before the Oklahoma land rushes (beginning with the first "Sooner" dash in April 1889). Eventually, 70 percent of all land that resided in Native America at the close of the Indian wars had vanished into white hands. Indian dependence on the federal government for financial aid meanwhile rose steadily. Native Americans were not brought into US society. They were marooned on shrinking poverty patches.[114]

The attempt to bludgeon Indian psyche into something recognizably white also failed. Few versions of the white man's Indian à la Ely Parker appeared. A number of Indians managed to escape the demolition of their identity by mandatory remolding. The Yahi tribesman, Ishi, was case in point, until his capture in 1911 and subsequent tutorials with Berkeley anthropologists.[115] Too often the machinery of assimilation produced a cartoon of white life, once remarked upon by General Howard this way:

In their own native attire the Indians usually appear well. The dress of skins and feathers, however variegated, befits them. But when they put on our clothing and strut about in it their appearance is sometimes comical. A chief in an old shabby uniform, with perhaps a plug hat picked up on the dump pile of a fort, thinks he is pleasing and honoring the white man who in reality is pitying him, or laughing at his senseless vanity.[116]

Depressing too was the continuing recruitment of Native Americans for entertainment in wild west shows. They featured sentimental reenactments of history that trivialized the magnitude of Indian dispossession. Nine years after the Little Bighorn battle, Sitting Bull appeared in Buffalo Bill Cody's show to appreciative audiences. Their pleasure did not lessen his objection to Sioux allotments or prevent his being killed in December 1890 while resisting arrest at Standing Rock Reservation. Neither he nor Howard would have found anything amiss in Edmund Wilson's note to *New Yorker* readers in 1959. Wilson wrote that Native Americans belonged still to a distinctive world as different as a foreign country, despite the 1924 conferring of citizenship: "The Indians do not fit into, and for the most part do not want to fit into, the alien life we have brought here."[117]

Most late nineteenth-century Indians defied in various ways attempts to fold Native America into the United States. Exceptions certainly existed. Geronimo became a Christian, a farmer, a celebrity at the 1904 St. Louis World's Fair. He appeared in Theodore Roosevelt's inaugural parade. But his leadership of Apache resistance defined his career and legend, not his belated acceptance of Euro-American culture. More typical than Geronimo's experience was that maladjustment suffered by Carlisle students. They were subjected to corporal punishment or denied food for lapsing into their tribal tongues. Students were often homesick and attended school despite their parents' wishes. Cases multiplied of parents forced by state authority to surrender their children to Carlisle or other schools, a practice countenanced by Lake Mohonk in 1892: "[When] parents, without good reason, refuse to educate their children, we believe that the government is justified ... in using power to compel attendance. We do not think it desirable to rear another generation of savages."[118] Instances of runaway, despondency, morbidity, and suicide spiraled high. Luther Standing Bear, among the first of Pratt's pupils at Carlisle, recalled: "The change in clothing, housing, food, and confinement combined with lonesomeness was too much, and in three years nearly one half of the [little ones] from the Plains were dead and through with all earthly schools."[119]

Pratt's immersion course also did not render students acceptable to white society. They were still Indians, surely feral below the surface. Nor were returning students readily accepted back into reservation life or well regarded. Graduates, in effect, were stranded in limbo, not at home in the white or Indian worlds, loved in neither. The case of Plenty Horses, a Sioux youth and Carlisle product, illustrated this predicament. He killed Lieutenant Edward Casey on the Pine Ridge Reservation in January 1891 during the Ghost Dance craze. Plenty Horses was acquitted of murder on grounds that he shot Casey in the context of military actions (Wounded Knee). Plenty Horses was innocent of murder, in other words, by virtue of being a combatant; the court judged him a prisoner of war. For his part, however, he had killed to expunge the mark of Carlisle and win back the favor of his tribe.[120] He told the courtroom:

I am an Indian. Five years I attended Carlisle and was educated in the ways of the white man. When I returned to my people, I was an outcast among them. I was no longer an Indian. I was not a white man. I was lonely. I shot the lieutenant so I might make a place for myself among my people. I am now one of them. I shall be hung, and the Indians will bury me as a warrior. They will be proud of me. I am satisfied.[121]

Denied martyrdom, a distraught Plenty Horses returned to Pine Ridge. His wife, Roan Horse, had died along with at least 150 of her people (and 25 US soldiers) at Wounded Knee.

Not until the 1930s did Washington officials begin to overhaul Indian policy with a view to toppling militant assimilation. The revised course rested on the idea that conceptions of life other than Euro-American might have worth. This notion gained ground with the Great War, 1914–1918. This experience persuaded some people that western civilization was wicked and possessed insatiable appetite for violent death. Social worker John Collier shared this disillusionment. He rejected the idea that "the occidental ethos and genius" were "the hope of the world."[122] His enthusiasm for non-western cultures led him to explore those of Native America. He revered the Pueblo society of New Mexico as a "Red Atlantis" that contained secrets of compassion needed by the white order. They should be preserved and taught to the world for the sake of its moral regeneration.[123]

Collier became executive director in 1923 of the newly founded American Indian Defense Association, committed to saving native traditions and undoing the 1887 allotment law. As Commissioner of Indian Affairs during FDR's presidency, he authored an "Indian New Deal." It relied upon new social scientific investigations, notably the Brookings Institution's 1928 Merriam Report. It depicted a Native America scarred by unemployment, weakened by illness, bogged down in gloom. Collier worked for a restoration of communal Indian economy and sociability. He got Congress to pass legislation that checked policies implemented by post-Civil War reformers: the 1934 Indian Reorganization Act. It ended allotment. Millions of acres were returned to the reservations. Prohibitions on native religious observances were lifted. Tribal business corporations were allowed. Political autonomy was increased. Bilingual education programs were adopted to boost Indian literacy and increase the retention rates of children in school.[124] Rollback of Dawes and Pratt had begun.

The BIA made this pledge to Native Americans several decades after the closing of Carlisle: "Never again will we attack your religions, your languages, your rituals, or any of your tribal ways. Never again will we seize your children, nor teach them to be ashamed of who they are."[125]

The American Indian Movement (AIM) was founded eighty years after Wounded Knee to tackle conditions of poor housing, inferior education, and unemployment in Native America. The organization has also worked to improve Indian civil rights while striving to preserve aboriginal customs. Dennis Banks, cofounder of AIM, countered the Dawes–Pratt presumption with rebuttals like this one in 1994:

An eagle is an eagle, still practicing the ways of its ancestors, long since gone. The beaver still makes its home along the streams and creeks of our land. The buffalo still teaches its young and the salmon still travels the thousands of miles to spawn its future generations. If we Native People are to survive as a cultural species, then we must follow the way of our ancestors. We must continue to sing the songs and have ceremonies to welcome each day. Like the eagle and buffalo, we must never abandon our old ways. Those ways have been good to us and they will provide us with direction for our future generations. Like an eagle flying high, we are who we are. Still strong![126]

Relative tolerance of such viewpoint in the twenty-first century measures the conceptual distance traveled by Americans since Grant's presidency. Repudiation of Lake Mohonk mentality arrived too late for Plenty Horses. Yet the new attitude has allowed the United States to maintain a multitude of diverse peoples in its borders – not always gladly, witness attacks on bilingual education, but at least better than before.[127] Cultural empathy may still not be an American strong suit, but the most restrictive reign of conformity belongs to the past.

8   Philippines

Compressed acculturation marked not only post-Civil War Indian policies. It also influenced the exercise of US power beyond New World
confines. The impulse before 1898 had been to Americanize Indians
and foreigners within national borders. The aim thereafter expanded to
Americanize overseas foreigners reachable by US power. President
William McKinley pursued this project in the Philippines: "benevolent
assimilation." It featured ethnocentric zeal comparable to that practiced
upon Native America.

The majority view never doubted the generosity or brilliance of works
accomplished in the Philippines. They served as site where duty consistent with the "white man's burden" could be gallantly discharged.[1] The
archipelago advertised the universality of US institutions. Theodore
Roosevelt said in 1913 with characteristic gusto:

> We established schools everywhere; we built roads; we administered an even-
> handed justice; we did everything possible to encourage agriculture and industry;
> and in constantly increasing measure we employed natives to do their own
> governing ... our whole attention was concentrated upon the welfare of the
> Filipinos themselves, if anything to the neglect of our own interests.[2]

Yet some Americans involved in the Philippines did wonder whether the
islanders had the requisite mental apparatus to improve themselves.
Parliamentary democracy, Protestantism, entrepreneurial energy, English
literacy, and elementary hygiene might forever elude the Filipinos. In this
case, the unfortunates, already handicapped by three centuries of Spanish
misrule, would endure unchanging backwardness. The lowly folk might
salvage what they could in the face of US superiority, exactly like North
American tribes clinging to their shriveling reservations. Still, per the
influential Social Darwin ethic, one need not waste much pity on these
peoples. Biology's laws decreed that weak breeds must always and everywhere yield to the fit. Such appreciation slid easily into modifying
Sheridan's Indian remark: "The only good Filipino is a dead one."
American servicemen in the Philippines referred to the locals as "niggers."[3]

Combat during the Philippine–US war, 1899–1902, produced 20,000 native fatalities. Another 200,000 Filipinos died from military related operations. Scorched earth tactics fostered famine. Internment camps bred virulent diseases. Maltreatment of prisoners and suspect civilians added to the tally. Roughly 120,000 US troops were deployed during these years, at a price of $600 million, to suppress forces led by Emilio Aguinaldo. They caused many more US casualties than had Spanish fire in 1898: 4,200 Americans fell in the Philippines versus 380 killed by Spain.[4]

These costs and prolonged hostilities were inconceivable to US officialdom in April 1898 when Congress declared war on decrepit Spain. McKinley's primary aim was to end violence in Madrid's Cuban colony, only ninety miles from Florida. The Philippines were of marginal interest, not a point of public excitement in spring 1898. Few Americans had heard of them. Fewer still, McKinley included, could locate the islands on a map.[5]

Civilian agony in Cuba, by contrast, had touched the United States for years, where sympathy gravitated toward the insurgency. Its hope to overthrow Spanish rule impressed citizens as consonant with the 1776 revolution. Cuban lobbyists, such as Jose Marti and Evangelina Cosia y Cisneros, embellished this idea while spreading lurid tales of innocent suffering. This bid for independence also made good copy for the dueling newspaper chains, Hearst versus Pulitzer. Their lead stories and headlines blared: remainder of New World's unfinished business with autocratic Europe made urgent by Spanish atrocities against Cubans. Additionally, the case for *Cuba libre* benefited from congressional investigation of island conditions. Senator Redfield Proctor (Republican, Vermont), after touring Cuba in early 1898, reported that the colony was blanketed in cruelty. Its symbol and substance was the *reconcentrado* policy. He dwelt on "the spectacle of a million and half people ... struggling for freedom and deliverance from the worst misgovernment."[6]

Damage to American property, valued at $50 million, plus danger to US nationals in Cuba meanwhile intensified. Escalating violence obliged McKinley in January 1898 to dispatch the battleship *Maine* to Havana to safeguard US interests and citizens. The ship's explosion in mid-February, nearly all hands lost, must have been the work of Spanish deviltry. So said most pundits and Assistant Secretary of the Navy Roosevelt. He excoriated Spain's "dirty treachery."[7] Public indignation rallied to this slogan: "Remember the Maine! To hell with Spain." Adding to the frenzy, careless words by Madrid's envoy in Washington, Enrique Dupuy de Lome, on McKinley's shallowness made their way into public prints. The concurrent crises of *Maine*'s destruction and the diplomat's indiscretion inspirited jingoists, who taught that Spanish enmity ran deep. War on behalf of injured Cuba should commence.

McKinley tried to counter feeling among Americans for armed intervention. Their alarm grew apace with the reality of mounting Cuban casualties: 100,000 dead during 1896–1898. Yet McKinley delayed. He shunned further bloodshed and thought the nation unprepared for war. A Civil War veteran, he stated: "I have been through one war; I have seen the dead piled up, and I do not want to see another."[8] Roosevelt muttered privately that the president was spineless.[9]

McKinley's quest for a diplomatic solution depended on Stewart Woodford, US minister in Madrid. He labored diligently to defuse the crisis.[10] His effort nearly resulted in peaceful settlement, an outcome devoutly sought by the moderate government of Prime Minister Praxedes Mateo Sagasta. Upon assuming power in Madrid (October 1897), he recalled the harsh General Valeriano Weyler from Cuba. Sagasta offered home rule to the island. Complying with the wishes of the queen regent, Maria Cristina, he offered an armistice to the Cuban rebels (April 9–10, 1898). He also signaled a willingness to negotiate the island's independence. These concessions, though, came too late to mollify pro-war agitation in the United States. An offer by Pope Leo XIII to mediate between Madrid and Washington similarly came to naught.[11]

A crescendo mounted of demands for action. Senator Henry Cabot Lodge (Republican, Massachusetts), Proctor, and "yellow press" editors impugned Madrid's diplomacy. McKinley also adjusted his views, a smart tack as midterm elections approached and Democratic hopefuls yapped at his "irresolution." He condemned – April 11, 1898 – Spain's "cruel, barbarous, and uncivilized practices of warfare." They had, he decided, astounded the sensibilities and humane outlook of every American.[12]

The brief conflict (April 21–August 9, 1898) featured US victories on land, despite problems. These included the effect of tropical illnesses on soldiers, resulting in 5,000 deaths. Logistical fumbles in the War Department, headed by lethargic Secretary Russell Alger, and snarls linked to recruiting, concentrating, and transporting the troops created additional mischief. Yet the regular army (25,000), essentially a frontier constabulary, augmented by 200,000 volunteers and state militias, emerged everywhere victorious on Spanish territories: Cuba, Puerto Rico, the Philippines.[13] The better managed navy scored easily against Spain's, as when ships of Admiral William Sampson's Atlantic Squadron met those of Admiral Pascual Cervera y Topete in action off Santiago, Cuba (July 3).

Commodore George Dewey's sinking of Spanish warships in Manila harbor (May 1) led directly to the August capitulation of Spanish troops in the city. They feigned resistance before leaving US forces dominant in the Philippines, which raised questions at the moment of armistice. Should Washington retain Manila? Exert control throughout the islands? If so, to what purpose? Return all or some of them to Madrid? Permit the *insurrectos*, long in opposition to Spanish overlordship, to organize an independent state? The obstacles to realizing this last idea seemed daunting: 7,000 islands spread over 115,000 square miles, populated by 7 million people of diverse ethnicity.

These matters were addressed in the treaty of Paris, signed by Spanish and US emissaries on December 10, 1898.[14] It stipulated the following: Madrid relinquished claims of sovereignty over Cuba and assumed liability for $400 million of Cuban debt. Spain ceded Puerto Rico and Guam (in the Marianas) to the United States. Most significantly, the United States pledged Spain $20 million for title to the Philippines. Senate ratification of treaty provisions on February 6, 1899 – by slenderest margin – made the United States an East Asian power, Manila being 690 miles from Hong Kong.[15]

Asian empire

Ingrained caution made McKinley a hesitant annexationist. As the Philippine war continued, he told a friend that he rued Dewey's staying in Manila after destroying the Spanish ships. Dewey should have sailed away after battle, thus sparing Washington a peck of troubles.[16] McKinley, though, never rejected the idea of retaining the scattered islands.[17] He did think at first of holding only the port of Manila to support US maritime commerce in Asia. Thence he thought to keep the island of Luzon to buttress the US position in Manila. He next added in his mind's eye a few nearby islands; their possession would help consolidate the US grip on Luzon. Finally, he adopted the idea of retaining the whole archipelago as urged by naval officers, Protestant missionaries, traders, and that part of public opinion hungry for glory presumed to reside in imperium.[18] He subsequently orated (autumn 1898), during visits to midwestern and southern cities, on the desirability of keeping the entire archipelago.

His justification ran along several lines. First, return of the islands to Spain would besmirch American honor. The United States had taken them by sure feat of arms. Spanish authorities had forfeited via misrule and military–naval ineptitude. A surrender of spoils would mock the US slain. Second, McKinley rejected transfer of the islands to another power, such as the prowling British, Japanese, French or Germans – the last of whom had expressed unbecoming haste. (Ships of Kaiser Wilhelm's navy had tried to intimidate Dewey's command during its August investment of Manila.) Besides, transfer of the islands to a European empire or Japan, trade rivals of the United States in Asia, would be "bad business" and "discreditable." Third, McKinley reasoned that the Filipinos were unable to govern themselves. They would, left to their own devices, fall victim to varieties of chaos. They would exceed in unpleasantness anything experienced during the Spanish era. Lastly, McKinley, a pious Methodist, persuaded himself that the United States would be acting in tandem with divine purpose by holding fast to the islands. Their wallowing in a farrago of Roman Catholic error, Islamic fanaticism, and native mumbo jumbo need not be a permanent condition. His administration had no honest alternative but "to take them all [islands], and to educate the Filipinos, and uplift and civilize and Christianize them, and by God's grace do the very best ... by them, as our fellow-men for whom Christ also died."[19]

Few of the younger Republican personalities needed coaxing. Whereas McKinley occasionally whispered regret, they celebrated the merits of Asian empire. Indiana's Senator Albert Beveridge (b. 1862) assumed particular prominence by his oratory. He stressed in chambers and elsewhere a number of heady themes: the Philippines were way station to China's "illimitable markets." Other profitable Eastern places would become accessible via the Philippines. The islands were endowed with mineral wealth and agricultural abundance: rice, coffee, sugar, coconuts, hemp, tobacco. Besides, and more important, God had chosen the United States for His purpose of renewing the world. This mission meant, in the case of Filipinos, imparting to them an authentic civilization. Their tumble to perdition luckily broken by Washington's intervention, they could eventually attain self-government with dignity. Before that blessed day, however, the Filipinos must finish a democratic apprenticeship. The US could not evade duty to mighty purpose, Beveridge volunteered: "[God] has made us [Americans] adepts in government that we may administer government among savage ... peoples. Were it not for such a force as this the world would relapse into barbarism and night ... We are trustees of the world's progress, guardians of its righteous peace. The judgment of the Master is upon us."[20]

Roosevelt and Lodge were less prone than McKinley or Beveridge to invoke God's authority to sanction US control in the Philippines. Geopolitical principles, the desirability of naval preparedness per Captain Alfred Mahan, plus a taste for grandeur shaped Roosevelt–Lodge thinking. TR in his 1898 gubernatorial race in New York mentioned welcome duties. Their fulfillment required heavy effort, best antidote to America's creeping indolence and complacency. The country would revive as khaki supplanted frippery, as Americans took responsibility for an enervated people in comprehensive need. Similarly, Lodge advocated a "large policy," necessary to pursue lest the United States fall out of march with the world's leading powers. He believed that with the Philippines in hand, "We hold the other side of the Pacific, and the value to this country is almost beyond imagination."[21] His point was highlighted in 1900, as Philippines-based US troops were rushed to China to join the Allied Expeditionary Force to rescue western missionaries and diplomats from Boxer vengeance.[22]

Apologists also claimed that a military presence in the Philippines betokened US seriousness about Chinese territorial integrity (Open Door policy) and discouraged Europeans and Japanese from carving up the rickety empire.[23] As for the inconvenient principle of self-government, theoretically as applicable to the Philippines as anywhere else, it should not be read literally. It did not apply to unprepared peoples. They required guidance. Children, Native Americans, and Filipinos alike needed supervision. It ought not be suspended until they achieved maturity, chorused Roosevelt and Lodge.[24]

Americans undertook an ambitious program that began with the first civil governor, William Howard Taft. He served in that office during the turbulence of early US occupation. His ostensible aim was to hasten the moment when his Filipino wards, "little brown brothers," could capably tend their own affairs.[25]

This goal entailed establishing a new system of written law, buying and redistributing lands owned by the Spanish friars, staffing primary and manual training schools with hundreds of teachers, eradicating cholera and malaria, and promoting the status of women in the Moslem province of Moro while banning slavery therein. Improvements to transportation–communication infrastructure soon outdid those made by Spanish governors. The building of new roads and train tracks, deepening of river channels and harbors, and erecting of dams and irrigation facilities were meant to shove the islands into modernity.[26]

This enterprise disquieted some Americans. They feared that domestic problems were neglected in preference to resolving difficulties among faraway peoples. Might a modicum of the aid spent on the Filipinos be applied to needy sections of the US population, asked prominent African Americans. Professor Kelly Miller of Howard University wondered in 1902: "If the moral sense of the American people would not leave the distant Filipino to his pitiable fate, but impelled them to reach out a saving hand across the seas and snatch him within the ennobling circle of benevolent assimilation, how much more incumbent is it to elevate the Negro who is within our gates, and is closely associated with our national destiny?" Edward Cooper, editor of the *Colored American*, answered dryly: "Our white friends have a habit of expending their sympathy upon the black man who is farthest off."[27]

This largesse did not seem quite so grand or disinterested from the standpoint of Filipino nationalists. They resented US paternalism, racial typecasting, and noblesse oblige. Filipino lawyers, doctors, and other members of the professional–business classes could not happily resign themselves or their children to small lives of tedium under Washington. Domination by Americans, immodestly confident in their own genius, caused Manuel Quezon to declare: "I would prefer a government run like hell by Filipinos to one run like heaven by Americans."[28]

Aguinaldo and companions viewed the substitution of US rule for Spain as perverted justice. Even so, he never repudiated all things American. Indeed, he admired the United States – at least at first. He was conveyed by US warship from Singapore exile to anti-Spanish action in the Philippines. His fighters cooperated with Dewey's in capturing Manila. Proclaiming himself president of the Philippine Republic in July 1898, he enacted a liberal constitution compatible with US institutions. He sought also to organize a national army along strict lines and account-ability.[29] He hoped, meanwhile, that the United States would guarantee security of the islands against Japanese and European imperialism. Peace with the United States, then, was something to be wished. But it could not be purchased at the price of island liberty. He told his partisans just after the first clash between US and Filipino soldiers (February 1899):

I have tried to avoid, as far as it has been possible for me to do so, armed conflict, in my endeavors to assure our independence by pacific means and to avoid more costly sacrifices. But all my efforts have been useless against the measureless pride of the American Government and of its representatives . . . who have treated me as a rebel because I defend the sacred interests of my country and do not make myself an instrument of their dastardly intentions.[30]

Washington's regard for Aguinaldo dipped with his opposition to occu-pation. He had once enjoyed courtesies from Dewey, who intimated to him that the US had no designs upon the Philippines. Aguinaldo had also won American praise for being a Filipino patriot and stout ally against Spain. But his later opposition seemed synonymous with betrayal and ingratitude. Roosevelt placed Aguinaldo in the same category of infamy as Benedict Arnold.[31]

Factionalism within the nationalist movement cut along class and ideological lines and hampered its war against the United States.

Aguinaldo had presided in 1897 over the arrest, then execution, of his rival: Andres Bonifacio. Two years later members of the president's bodyguard assassinated General Antonio Luna, one-time commander of the nationalist army. Ethnic rivalries, especially ones centered upon the numerous Tagalogs, also damaged the Filipino cause.[32] Still, Aguinaldo's soldiers fought with impressive determination. They switched after defeats in conventional battle to guerrilla tactics earlier proven against Spanish regulars. Aguinaldo's fighters also enjoyed that broad support needed to wage guerrilla warfare. General Arthur MacArthur, senior US soldier in the Philippines during 1900–1901, reported that "almost complete unity of action of the entire native population" sustained Aguinaldo.[33]

The Americans courted Filipino support of their own. They cooperated with such leaders as Trinidad H. Pardo de Tavera and Benito Legarda, founders of the Federalista party (December 1900). It stood for accommodation with US authority and for awhile sought American statehood for the Philippines. The army also made good use of Filipino auxiliaries (5,000 during 1899–1902), who for reasons – personal, political, economic – were not enamored of Aguinaldo or the people around him.[34] A party of Filipino scouts, under the command of General Frederick Funston, captured Aguinaldo in March 1901. Yet the war did not end for another year, despite Aguinaldo's swearing allegiance in April to the United States and urging his troops to halt operations.

A guerrilla surprise in Balangiga on the island of Samar in September 1901 resulted in the slaughter of fifty-eight US soldiers. Their corpses were abused in fiendish ways. Brigadier General Jacob Smith ordered his units in retaliation to make Samar into a "howling wilderness." Boys as young as ten in this instance were said by Smith to be legitimate military targets. His punitive purpose was explicit in this instruction to subordinates: "I want no prisoners. I wish you to kill and burn, the more you kill and burn the better it will please me. I want all persons killed who are capable of bearing arms in actual hostilities against the United States."[35] An orgy ensued of "water cure" torture, summary execution of prisoners, shooting of civilians.[36] Troops destroyed property wholesale. Many plundered.

Soldiers under General Franklin Bell in early 1902 collected the entire civilian population of the province of Batangas in southern Luzon. The people were then incarcerated in camps similar to Weyler's in Cuba. They were meant to deprive forces commanded by Miguel Malvar of assuming civilian cover or receiving protection by local peasants. Bell's men then proceeded to subdue the province. They reduced it to desert. Malvar surrendered in April 1902. President Roosevelt on the fourth of July declared the war over and won.

Thereafter US troops policed the peace. It was marred by periodic violence until 1913. The worst episode occurred in March 1906 at Bud Dajo on the island of Jolo. This so-called battle left 600 Moros dead. Infants, children, and mothers numbered among the fatalities. General Leonard Wood, responsible officer at the time in the Philippines, admitted that pacification entailed roughness: "Work of this kind has its disagreeable side, which is the unavoidable killing of women and children; but it must be done, and disagreeable as it is, there is no way of avoiding it."[37]

Against imperialism

Mark Twain responded sarcastically to Bud Dajo: "I was never so enthusiastically proud of the flag till now!"[38] He had in 1901 accepted a vice presidency of the Anti-Imperialist League; he served in that position until his death in 1910. Founded in Boston in November 1898, the League opened offices throughout the United States. Headquarters were established in Chicago. The League pitied Filipino suffering and criticized US actions: "We denounce the slaughter of the Filipinos as a needless horror." The League also held that reliance upon force and rationalizations of conquest degraded America. The transformation of the Roman republic via empire to unbalanced polity stood as warning. War in the Philippines, in effect, amounted to an assault on republican integrity:

Much as we abhor the war of "criminal aggression" in the Philippines, greatly as we regret that the blood of the Filipinos is on American hands, we more deeply resent the betrayal of American institutions at home. The real firing line is not in the suburbs of Manila. The foe is of our own household. The attempt of 1861 was to divide the country. That of 1899 is to destroy its fundamental principles.[39]

Most people on the League's roster – which numbered more than 30,000 people in the Boston chapter alone – had accepted war against Spain to help Cuba.[40] Twain belonged to this company. Like others in it, he was gratified by passage of the Teller Amendment in 1898 that confirmed US respect for Cuban independence. The withholding of similar guarantees from the Filipinos disappointed him, particularly as he ascribed qualities of greatness to Aguinaldo shared by George Washington and Joan of Arc.[41]

Many League members were high-minded fugitives from the Republican party: mugwumps. They seldom sullied themselves by contact with Washington grime or politicking. They guarded their decency by aloofness from partisan affiliation and strife. Yet the likes of Carl Schurz, E.L. Godkin, Edward Atkinson, Charles Francis Adams,

Thomas Wentworth Higginson, William Endicott, James Burrill Angell, and Moorfield Storey were pushed to act by Pacific events. This confession from Adams could have been uttered by any of them: "I turn green in bed at midnight if I think of the horror of a year's warfare in the Philippines [where] we must slaughter a million or two of foolish Malays in order to give them the comforts of flannel petticoats and electric railways."[42] Nor was Schurz alone when he bewailed the Federalista idea, implying the incorporation by the United States of millions of inscrutable "Asiatics." No more than any other tropical people would Filipinos ever possess the honesty or sobriety to contribute to American life.[43]

Outspoken critics of Philippine policy included the industrialist Andrew Carnegie. He liked the idea of informal commercial empire but not America's becoming another Great Britain. He donated funds to the Anti-Imperialist League; he became one of its vice presidents.[44] Organized workers too had a voice against empire in the person of Samuel Gompers, head of the American Federation of Labor. University presidents in conspicuous opposition were Charles William Eliot (Harvard), David Starr Jordan (Stanford), Henry Wade Rogers (Northwestern). Scholars against the Philippines war could be found at their and other universities: Yale, Princeton, Columbia, Cornell, Chicago, Michigan. The philosopher William James, another vice president of the Anti-Imperialist League, offered this critique in 1899 of US policy: "The issue is perfectly plain ... We are cold-bloodedly, wantonly and abominably destroying the soul of a people who never did us an atom of harm in their lives." The once enlightened American republic had become a "hollow, resounding, corrupting, sophisticating torrent of ... brutal momentum and irrationality."[45]

Sociologist William Graham Sumner despised the US version of white man's burden: "We talk of civilizing lower races, but we have never done it yet."[46] Instead, "we have exterminated them." Expansionism and imperialism were unworthy of a republic. These doctrines had discredited Spain and would stigmatize the United States: "[They] appeal to national vanity and national cupidity ... They are delusions, and ... will lead us to ruin."[47]

Clergymen against the Philippines war included Reverend Charles Parkhurst of New York's Madison Square Presbyterian Church and the city's Episcopal Bishop, Henry Codman Potter. Social reformer Jane Addams lent her name to anti-imperialism. Editorial opinion in the *North American Review*, *Nation*, and *Harper's* castigated the war as did much of the African-American press. This last medium was astonished at the phenomenon of black soldiers doing the white man's filthy work.

The *Reporter* of Helena, Arkansas hoped that black men of conscience would abstain from military service:

Every colored soldier who leaves the United States and goes out to the Philippine Islands to fight the brave men there who are struggling and dying for their country is simply fighting to curse the country with color-phobia, jim-crow cars, disenfranchisement, and lynchers and everything that prejudice can do to blight the manhood of the darker races, and as the Filipinos belong to the darker human variety, [it is] the Negro fighting against himself.[48]

Circumspect Booker T. Washington, agronomist and educator, also questioned whether the United States had much to offer Filipinos. The Supreme Court's separate but equal decision of 1896 (*Plessy v. Ferguson*) indicated not.[49]

Writers against the war counted the philosophically inclined playwright William Vaughn Moody, novelist William Dean Howells, poet Ambrose Bierce, and satirist Finley Peter Dunne.[50] Twain remained the most uncompromising. He claimed that Roosevelt, Funston, and Wood each compounded dementia with criminality. Of the Filipinos, bombarded by Bibles and shells, Twain asked in 1901: "Shall we go on conferring our Civilization upon the peoples that sit in darkness, or shall we give those poor things a rest?"[51] He doubted that their political education would benefit from a people who tolerated Tammany Hall nonsense and left southern blacks to the mercy of white lawlessness (1,450 lynchings during 1887–1900).[52]

Democratic party leaders who attacked the Philippines policy included former president Grover Cleveland and his secretary of state, Richard Olney. Senators Augustus Bacon (Georgia), Edward Carmack (Tennessee), Charles Culberson (Texas), John McLaurin (South Carolina), Thomas MacDonald Patterson (Colorado), and "Pitchfork" Ben Tillman (South Carolina) were impassioned. Instances of Filipino suffering contradicted the proffered benefits of American life. Senator Donelson Caffery (Louisiana) pointed to this irony: "In order to Christianize these savage people we must put the yoke of despotism upon their necks [but] Christianity can not be advanced by force."[53] Additionally, southern Democrats stressed that the Filipinos were intellectually deficient; they could not master the intricacies of self-government. Political missionary work among them would never bear fruit. By a chain of wicked events, however, US citizenship might be conferred upon the islanders. The American polity in that case would collapse under their weight. Better to surrender these souls to a third country than to receive them as voting equals. Missouri's Representative Champ Clark tried to imagine "almond eyed, brown skinned United States Senators" deliberating on legislation: "No matter whether they are fit to govern themselves or not, they are not fit to govern us!"[54]

William Jennings Bryan, presidential candidate in 1900, hoped in the election season to seize upon waxing anti-imperialism. Well handled, it could weaken Republican control over Congress. Bryan this time might occupy the White House – denied him in 1896 – by focusing attention on "the paramount issue": foreign policy gone awry. He said repeatedly: "This nation cannot [stand] half-republic and half-colony."[55] The Democrats' 1900 convention endorsed independence for the Philippines.

The 1900 election did not turn on international affairs. Other matters controlled. Economic recovery during McKinley's first term and the administration's support of tariffs satisfied businessmen. Bryan's harangues against US imperialism, meanwhile, contrasted badly with McKinley's vice presidential running mate, Theodore Roosevelt. He campaigned in his Rough Rider suit and reveled in fresh Filipino defeats. McKinley retained the White House by comfortable margin in the electoral college. Republicans enlarged their majority in both congressional chambers.[56]

Not all members of the GOP, though, supported foreign policy. McKinley from 1898 onward faced criticism by several Republicans, among whom were former president Benjamin Harrison and former Treasury secretary George Boutwell. McKinley's own secretary of state questioned the Spanish war, the ignored and frail John Sherman. He publicly objected to the Philippines affair after resigning his portfolio in April 1898.[57] Maine's imposing Thomas Brackett Reed, speaker of the House of Representatives, opposed both the 1898 showdown with Spain and conquest of the Philippines. He did so not just from antipathy for McKinley, who beat Reed in 1896 for the Republican presidential nomination. He also rejected the theory that stealthy Spaniards had destroyed the *Maine*. He labeled the Philippines the "last colonial curse of Spain." His inability to prevent war in the Caribbean or "theft" in the Pacific caused him to leave national politics in 1899.[58] Senator William Mason (Illinois) exclaimed in 1902 that the cost of fighting Filipinos exceeded any conceivable benefit: "The money we have spent would make a chain of gold that would encircle the world."[59]

Party loyalty and discipline prevented Republican dissenters from launching full-scale mutiny. Only two GOP senators voted against the Paris treaty and its Philippine provisions: George Frisbie Hoar (Massachusetts), Eugene Hale (Maine).

Opponents of Philippine policy were not only outvoted in Congress and in national election. They were also defamed by "large policy" advocates. As with earlier war dissenters – 1812 or 1846 – those of 1899 were said to embolden America's enemy by making him think that

Washington would prematurely end hostilities: fault-finding reinforced the enemy's determination and increased US casualties. Dissenters, irrespective of their intentions, thus provided a type of assistance to the enemy. Funston suggested that critics be tried as traitors, then hanged.[60]

The administration responded hotly when Democrats charged that Filipinos were mistreated by soldiers or that oceanic empire contradicted self-government ideals. Bryan and followers, went the rebuttal, should pay attention to African Americans in Dixie who were denied civil rights, compared to which Filipino frustrations were minor indeed. How ironic, Roosevelt added, was Bryan's censoriousness, when the new president – a month after McKinley's September 1901 assassination – invited Booker T. Washington to dine at the White House. Democratic inconsistency on racial matters led TR to instruct Harvard's Eliot:

To anyone not acquainted with the vagaries of human nature it would seem incredible that the southern Democrats in Congress, who include all the Democratic leaders, should be willing to prate about the doctrines contained in the Declaration of Independence, as applied to brown men in the Philippines, when they themselves owe their political existence, their presence in Congress, their influence in the nation, solely to the fact that they embody a living negation of those doctrines so far as they concern the black man at home.[61]

Roosevelt elsewhere argued that self-government in the Philippines was not canceled. It had been postponed to purchase time, during which the inhabitants could obtain social peace, not merely the outward trappings of liberty. As Frenchmen in Algiers, Britons in Sudan, and Russians in Turkestan had instilled order so Americans promised a sunnier fate for the islanders, a people otherwise lost.[62]

The high percentage of oldsters among anti-war Republicans circa 1900 also caught the attention of policy apologists. Among troublemakers that year, Harrison turned sixty-seven. Boutwell turned eighty-two. Sherman turned seventy-seven (and died). Hoar turned seventy-four. Reed was a relative youth at sixty-one. These seniors had contributed to the Union's preservation, slavery's abolition, and a workable Reconstruction, allowed young Roosevelt (b. 1858). But these "men of a bygone age" had outlived their usefulness. What remained of their gifts seemed irrelevant to life in a new century. TR once disparaged Hoar as senile.[63]

Old men

Roosevelt's crack about Hoar's being dotty was said in pique, not seriously meant. Neither did Roosevelt's words about Hoar as traitor represent the Rough Rider at his best. He did, in fact, acknowledge – privately and publicly – the senator's mental agility.[64] Nevertheless, Hoar exemplified to Roosevelt the psychological infirmities of old age: caution, hyper-sensitivity, aversion to novelty. He warned that these flaws, if absorbed by the nation, would prevent Americans from fulfilling their destiny. Certainly no legislator equaled Hoar in dedication against empire in the Philippines. Hence TR's querulousness.

Hoar at turn of the century was one of Congress's grand men. Colleagues and friends esteemed his scholarly mind; he once served as president of the American Historical Association. They respected his humanitarian viewpoint, nourished by his imbibing of Unitarian precepts. He thought Social Darwinian teaching crude and false. He recommended good-natured tolerance instead.[65] This bespectacled bookworm encouraged mercy toward Indians and supported protections for African Americans. He urged leniency upon Ottoman authorities for their Armenian subjects. He backed social–political claims of women and respected organized labor. He preferred the Boer underdogs to the British empire, "making the best fight since Thermopylae."[66] Self-conscious heir of New England patriots – descended from a signer of the Declaration of Independence, Roger Sherman – Hoar saw himself in a tradition devoted to reform and humane practice. He cast the only senate vote in 1902 against suspension of Chinese immigration; twenty years earlier Nevada residents had burned him in effigy for welcoming Chinese newcomers.[67] He had friendly relations with Jews, Catholics, Irish, and other pariah groups.

Hoar was also a vital force within his beloved Republican party. Its "glory and . . . service to Liberty," he wrote, "are the pride of my life."[68] His heroes were Abraham Lincoln and Charles Sumner. The party stood in Hoar's estimation as the nation's indispensable instrument. It preserved the Union, dismantled slavery, battled bigotry, and upheld sound finance. Fierce partisanship made Hoar uncomfortable in the company of Democrats, whom he discounted for aligning with secession, slavery, and anarchy. He became impatient also with the mugwump heresy. He blamed it for tempting talented young men away from service to the public weal to pursue private satisfactions in oases of comfort.[69] Republican loyalty in 1900 made Hoar campaign for McKinley's reelection despite his disquiet over the administration's imperialist bent. He counted McKinley a person of impeccable character.[70]

Except for the Philippines, Hoar backed the president's foreign policies. He did, at first, view hostilities against Spain with misgiving. But he shed it. "The United States comes to these oppressed people [in Cuba] as a great Deliverer," he avowed.[71] He also overcame doubts to accept

McKinley's case for taking the Hawaiian islands in July 1898. He endorsed this annexation as prudent measure, namely to deny ownership of Hawaii to any naval power that from such vantage could threaten US security along the west coast. But Hoar never discerned any reason for subduing the Philippines. The mania for empire appalled him.[72]

He taught that imperialism was insupportable in US tradition. It existed as counterpoint to the European-based overseas empires. The British model of empire, touted in the 1897 Diamond Jubilee of Queen Victoria's reign, possessed no appeal. Hoar would not depart from what he deemed America's original course; the compass of greatness pointed to justice and well-ordered freedom:

I believe that the highest service the American people can render to mankind and to liberty is to preserve unstained and unchanged the Republic as it came to us from the Fathers. It is by example and not by guns or by bayonets that the great work of America for humanity is to be accomplished ... The danger is that we are to be transformed from a Republic founded on the Declaration of Independence, guided by the counsels of Washington – the hope of the poor, the refuge of the oppressed – into a vulgar, commonplace empire founded upon physical force, controlling subject races and vassal states.[73]

Seizing the Philippines could not be defended by resort to any identifiable US principles. "No nation," he reminded his Senate colleagues, "was ever created good enough to own another."[74] Moreover, the foundational US documents made no provision for the buying or selling of millions of distant men and women, a point not obviated for Hoar by previous land purchases that encompassed alien peoples in Louisiana, northern Mexico, or Alaska. Their numbers were trivial. But $20 million to Spain for title to the Philippines and its inhabitants left him flabbergasted:

Under what doctrine ever heard on the soil of America are peoples – men, women, and children – to be bought and sold like sheep? It is said that the Philippine Islands are already ours by right of conquest ... I deny this alleged right of conquest. Human beings ... are not won as spoils of war or prizes in battle. It may be that such a doctrine finds a place in the ancient and barbarous laws of war. But it has no place under the American Constitution. It has no place where the Declaration of Independence is a living reality.[75]

Hoar told audiences in varied fora to resist the siren call of imperial adventures. Its seductiveness filled town meeting halls and congressional chambers. It beguiled young men. It would, though, undo the United States. It would become an inflated Spain:

The cry that we have outgrown Washington ... that the doctrines of the Declaration of Independence and the Constitution ... are not eternal verities but only the makeshifts of a generation; that they are for little countries and not for large ones ... that the flag stands for trade and for dominion and not for manhood and for self-government; that Washington lived and that Lincoln died only that we might have another Rome or another Spain; that Spain has so revenged herself upon us as that her spirit and ideals have entered into and taken possession of us – these things shall never happen while America is America.[76]

Hoar could not assemble a coalition sufficiently robust to stop ratification of the 1898 treaty. His wariness of mugwumpery in the Anti-Imperialist League hurt; his relations with the League were at best correct. His suspicion of Democrats also damaged the anti-treaty cause. They proved their unreliability to his satisfaction when Bryan in February 1899 suddenly reversed himself and advised Democratic senators to support treaty passage – thus encumbering the government with what he assumed would be an indefensible policy and easy target in the upcoming election. This stunt shocked Hoar. He never forgave the Democrat but accused him of striking the fatal blow to treaty opposition.[77] Unwillingness to embarrass McKinley or complicate Republican chances in the 1900 election additionally undercut Hoar as subversive.

Following the treaty debate, until his death in 1904, he sought to curtail US involvement in the Philippines and reduce the scope of military violence. He hated no less than Twain a war supposedly fought to improve Filipino life. Hoar said of the illogic in 1903:

Governor Taft ... concedes that nothing so far indicates that the existing policy has been good for the United States. It is only the benefit of the people of the Philippine Islands, in saving them from anarchy, or from foreign nations, in establishing schools for them, that vindicates what [the United States has] done so far. What [it has] done so far has been to get some few thousand children actually at school in the whole Philippine dominion. To get this result, [US forces] have certainly slain many times that number of parents.[78]

Hoar also reiterated this standard anti-imperialist theme: history taught that suspension by any republic of moderation abroad corroded the moral–political center. He asserted as a law of political science: "If a strong people try to govern a weak one against its will, the home government will get despotic too. You cannot maintain despotism in Asia and a republic in America. If you try to deprive even a savage or a barbarian of his just rights you can never do it without becoming a savage or a barbarian yourself."[79] This metamorphosis, said he, was evident in army tactics – relocation camps – and outright sadism. He likened the order of General Smith to kill boys aged ten and above to Herod's slaughter of Israel's infant sons.[80]

Hoar pressed for Senate probe of army misbehavior. He got modest satisfaction when an investigation began under auspices of the

206 Dissenting Voices in America's Rise to Power

Philippines standing committee (January–June 1902), chaired by Lodge. Despite Hoar's worry and request for an independently convened investigation free of Lodge's bias, the committee did not whitewash the record. A capable minority went to work. Eugene Hale and four Democrats – Carmack, Culberston, Patterson, Joseph Rawlins (Utah) – grilled administration spokesmen in lengthy hearings. Both Taft and Dewey were subjected to examination. Minority skeptics also interviewed witnesses of their own who testified about episodes that involved soldiers in murder, torture, rape, and larceny. Some such tales made their way into public prints. A few prosecutions resulted. General Smith faced court-martial; he got early retirement. Hoar regretted that more trials failed to materialize. He had hoped too that guilty persons would receive stiffer penalties than were meted out. Yet he took solace in the thought that imperfectly applied justice was better than none: not all miscreants escaped. He tried later via Roosevelt to improve the conditions of captivity for Apolinario Mabini, Aguinaldo's legal–diplomatic advisor incarcerated on Guam. This effort finally led to the prisoner's release. Hoar referred to Guam, designated spot of detention for captured resistance leaders, as a Pacific Bastille. He sought also to check commercial exploitation in the Philippines. He steered legislation through Congress that capped the size of land allotments available to US buyers.[81]

Filipinos respected Hoar. Nationalists relished his statements of admiration for Aguinaldo and Mabini.[82] Conversely critics and much editorial opinion in the United States portrayed Hoar as a Judas who inspired seditious Filipinos to kill Americans.[83] Few servicemen felt anything but anger for the senator. Funston's words against him were so caustic that TR ordered the soldier to cease his fulminating.

Hoar did have one important military ally, however unlikely, in the commanding general of the army, Nelson Miles. He belonged with the senator to that aging cohort unpersuaded by juniors who wanted Pacific provinces. (Miles turned sixty-one in 1900.) Despite slight acquaintance and a gulf of difference – temperamental, educational, vocational – the two men cooperated to bring to public attention the severity of Philippines policy.[84] Indeed, in the absence of Miles's 1902 inspection tour of Guam and interview with Mabini, Hoar might never have learned of his distress. Miles wrote Hoar in November of that year:

I found ... Mabini, a poor, paralytic cripple. He has been unable to walk for six years. Not only his lower limbs, but his lower organs are paralyzed. He is a great sufferer, and I should think he does not weigh more than 90 or 95 pounds. I must confess that the sight of this cripple, who has been deported and is still confined in prison without trial or sentence, did not impress me as creditable to the Great Republic.[85]

This expression of pity came from one of the most exacting soldiers of his era. Not without compassion for adversaries, evinced in leniency toward Chief Joseph, Miles was a tough campaigner. He first won renown as a young Union officer in the Civil War, wherein he saw much action: Antietam, Fredericksburg, Chancellorsville. He was thrice wounded, nearly fatally at Chancellorsville. His bravery in that battle resulted in his receiving the Congressional Medal of Honor.[86] He gained notoriety in the postwar era as the jailer of Jefferson Davis at Fort Monroe, Virginia. Miles at one point had the Confederate president clapped in irons (late May 1865). This action ensured abiding southern hatred of Miles. Davis thought him a "miserable ass."[87]

Miles had no equal in what he proudly termed the "war for civilization along our western frontier."[88] His successes on the Great Plains and in the southwest won him numerous accolades, plus the admiration of men who served under him.[89] Miles's one regret from his years in the west sprang from Wounded Knee. He was the responsible officer at the time, commanding the Division of the Missouri. He had been too removed from the main scene to prevent disaster. But he took strong steps, ultimately blocked, to have the local officer at Wounded Knee cashiered (Colonel James Forsyth). Miles also tried for decades to have Washington pay an indemnity to Sioux survivors of Wounded Knee.[90]

Despite enjoying wide admiration of his valor, Miles never lost his appetite for more recognition. He craved brisker career advancement. He reproved officers who failed to laud adequately his achievements or who, by their own exploits, might eclipse him. Generals Crook and Howard felt the sting of his wounded pride. Miles's ambition so irritated General Sherman that he reprimanded his junior for lusting after promotions. His impatience for preferment equally annoyed civilian superiors. Many thought Miles a warped personality. They disliked his peevishness. They guffawed at his lack of subtlety. They snickered at his infatuation with fancy braid uniforms and ostentatious display of medals. Roosevelt judged Miles wholly pompous.[91] Making matters worse, he made no secret of his disdain for Washington bureaucrats. He spoke endlessly in this vein against the BIA. He later attacked Elihu Root's War Department for trying to reshape the army high command (eliminating the office of Commanding General while creating a new General Staff), which in his view would mix new inefficiencies with existing ones.

Miles by his vanity and carping won more well-placed enemies in Washington than any officer of his day. Yet his enviable military record and retaining the favor of two influential men – his wife's uncles, General Sherman and Senator John Sherman – enabled Miles to reach the loftiest army position in 1895: commanding general. He achieved the army's then most exalted rank in June 1900: lieutenant general.

Miles lacked enthusiasm for the 1898 war. He doubted that Spanish agents were responsible for destroying the *Maine*; they possessed no motive and had every reason to avoid a new crisis.[92] He guessed that an internal accident had caused the ship's explosion (anticipating similar findings of naval inquiry under Admiral Hyman Rickover in 1976). Moreover, Miles disliked the idea of waging a tropical campaign. He worried over the dangers to soldiers posed by exotic diseases and fevers in Cuba. He anyway thought the army too small and unready for hostilities. He tried before their outbreak to check rising war hysteria and hoped for a diplomatic solution.[93] Still, he played his part when war came. He executed a nearly bloodless conquest of Puerto Rico, a feat that entailed his quashing a naval proposal to shell the city of San Juan (sure to have caused many civilian casualties with corresponding levels of postwar bitterness). Earlier he sent Lieutenant Andrew Rowan on his derring-do mission to insurgent General Calixto Garcia to ascertain chances of Cuban–US cooperation.[94]

Miles's knack for creating discord with associates and superiors did not wane during the Spanish war. Miles felt underemployed by McKinley, who did, in fact, try to circumvent the prickly officer in favor of more compliant men. They included General William Shafter. His bungling in Tampa and in Cuban battles provoked the scorn of Miles. Reinforced by his resentment for not getting to head the Cuba expedition, this scorn turned to hatred and public scolding. He also tangled with Secretary Alger about the training of troops, their billeting, and sequence of deployments. Alger accused Miles of insubordination. He countered that Alger's mishandling of the war warranted investigation.[95]

Miles next meddled in two postwar controversies. First, he plunged into the controversy swirling around "embalmed beef." He let loose against its nauseating thousands of troops in the Caribbean and made charges of inexcusable negligence and corruption in Washington. He drew a censure from a military court of inquiry for his diatribe on inedible victuals. McKinley on the basis of this episode, in view of the implied attack upon his own office, considered removing Miles from command.[96]

He next took sides in an unseemly naval dispute. It pitted Commodore Winfield Scott Schley versus Admiral Sampson. It hinged on who deserved most credit for the defeating of Spanish ships off Cuban shores. Miles's pronouncement in favor of Schley drew rebuke from the War Department. It was miffed by the soldier's interference in affairs outside army competence, especially as Miles repudiated a naval court verdict (favoring

Sampson) backed by the White House. It grew weary of Miles. TR let people know: "As regards Miles, I feel that any man who fails to back me up is either a fellow wholly incapable of reasoning or else a man who has never taken the trouble to reason, or, finally, a wrong-headed person."[97]

His relations with Roosevelt were a study in the art of making enemies, confirming Miles's gift for the maladroit. At first dealings between the men showed promise of benefiting both. TR in New York obliged by condemning the unfit beef supplied to his men: "It at once became putrid and smelt so that we had to dispose of it."[98] The general publicly acclaimed Roosevelt's conduct in battle: "He drew his sword among the bravest of the brave on the field of battle."[99] Miles also suggested in private conversations with TR – whose popularity kept rising – that he consider joining a future Republican presidential ticket: Miles to head it, Roosevelt to take the second spot. He demurred. He chuckled with friends at the idea of joining the bothersome soldier with a "Presidential bee in his bonnet."[100]

Yet TR did not hesitate to enlist Miles in his own campaign to obtain the Medal of Honor. TR hungered for this decoration, which he thought himself deserving for daring in the San Juan Hill battle. Miles went along at first. He soon became irked, though, by Roosevelt. Unlike him, war had no glamour for the graying veteran. He held that men should not play at it.[101] Puffed-up amateurs of the TR type were neither needed nor wanted, surely not if they overlooked war's gravity – or deflected attention from Miles. The commanding general concluded that TR was a popinjay. Miles explained in June 1901 at a banquet dinner that TR had not really charged up San Juan Hill. On this matter, Miles had a plausible point, albeit petty. The Rough Riders had taken Kettle Hill, a fortified ridge that flanked San Juan Hill. Roosevelt could not, in any case, bear Miles's pedantry that threatened to tarnish his name:

> This is a good deal like saying that Pickett was not at Gettysburg. In a sense he was not as the charge took place two or three miles from the village of that name. In the same way, the ridge which we ultimately took was sometimes called San Juan and sometimes not. It was a continuation of the ridge to which we commonly gave the name.[102]

To George Lyman, Republican master in Massachusetts, TR exploded: "What a scoundrelly hypocrite the man is!" On another occasion, Roosevelt called Miles a perfect fraud and concocted this smear: "No man of his rank has ever had so purely faked a record."[103]

McKinley was shot just three months after Miles spoke about Roosevelt at San Juan Hill. The general thenceforth had an unforgiving enemy in the White House.

Disagreement between Miles and TR on the Philippines, then, involved not only contrary views on public policy. The dispute constituted a clash between prima donnas. The general could not win. But he did succeed in making Roosevelt's already knotty Pacific project more difficult, a situation which gratified Miles. He calculated that serious charges against Philippine policy would embarrass TR. They might also enhance the chance that the Democratic party – Miles's haven after antagonizing TR – would nominate Miles for president in 1904, a slim prospect given southern enmity but nevertheless chased by him.[104]

No rehearsal of Miles's relations with TR or far-fetched political aims detracts from this point. The army's senior officer earnestly opposed the Philippines war. He thought conquest violated republican principles. He also believed that Americans should concentrate on the intensive development of their continent. Excursions to far-off places of slight utility diverted attention from crucial tasks; clearing Central American jungles pursuant to an isthmian canal or securing the unsettled Philippines were extravagances.[105]

As for the Filipinos, Miles regretted their suffering and he blamed US policy. He wrote after visiting the Philippines in autumn 1902: "I do not think there is today a people so sorely afflicted as the ... millions of inhabitants of this Archipelago. Their country has been devastated by war, and several provinces are now suffering severely as the result of reconcentration."[106] He urged Washington to send food aid (wheat, corn, rice, livestock) to contain the effects of pestilence and famine. Despite the downtrodden condition of the people, he commented favorably upon their industry and courtesy. He also considered them entirely fit for self-rule, having already produced statesmen of excellent caliber. He would have preferred that Washington assist them in establishing the first Asian republic.[107] He admired Mabini and other nationalists whom he met. These men were on a par with the best Americans: "[Mabini] had a benevolent face and an intellectual head, not unlike Abraham Lincoln ... his writings and public documents would compare favorably with those of Thomas Jefferson."[108] Even the maligned Moros produced worthy specimens, thought Miles. He praised Datto Mindi, a Moro luminary, who of his own volition had freed his slaves; he bore the indelibility of a first-rate mind and excellent education.[109]

Concern about stationing troops in hot climes also influenced Miles's view of Philippine policy. Steamy and unhealthful conditions assailed the forces. "The effect of the climate is a most serious detriment to the service," Miles confirmed during his 1902 tour. "The men go there in perfect health and in the prime of manhood, but as a body are seriously affected in the course of ... service. Very few escape ... the majority are debilitated."[110] He worried too lest his army sink into indiscipline or debauchery while fighting elusive guerrillas. He found much fault with local officers. Their recurrent failure was to have allowed, even abetted, a permissive atmosphere. In it atrocities became commonplace. Military necessity had nothing to do with the frequency of water cure, executions, or pummelings. He informed the War Department: "I found that with certain officers the impression prevailed that such acts were justifiable . . . an erroneous and dangerous impression."[111]

He brought charges against some company-grade and field-grade officers that resulted in trials. (They usually resulted in acquittals or light sentences, even for Major Edwin Glenn who had forty-seven prisoners bayoneted.[112]) Miles also ordered senior officers to conform with standards "in accordance with the rules of civilized warfare" and not to permit acts injurious to the army's reputation. "The excuse," he insisted, "that the unusual conditions justify [cruel] measures . . . is without foundation and cannot prevail." They belong, he said, "to a different age and civilization than our own."[113] He called for an investigation of the leveling campaign fought in Batangas.

Even before sailing to the South Pacific, Miles had raised questions with Roosevelt about crimes allegedly committed by soldiers. The number of such acts, as Miles counted, outstripped anything inflicted by the frontier army during its Indian campaigns. Were he given supreme authority in the Philippines, he assured TR, atrocities would cease. Roosevelt objected. He later allowed: "I did not intend to repeat the folly of which our people were sometimes guilty in those days when they petted the hostile Indians." Miles's suggestion that a delegation of Filipinos be permitted to visit Washington to negotiate an end to violence likewise met with TR's rebuff.[114]

Miles originally lodged his criticisms and advice in reports to the War Department, or in meetings at the White House, or in private letters to Hoar. But Miles also wanted to enlarge his audience beyond Washington officialdom. Presumably if he educated the broad public, it would support him in his tussle with TR. That would generate benefits for anti-imperialism and the general's presidential bid. Miles consequently made certain that his ideas got circulated – usually via leaks, at least once by press conference.[115]

Little time passed between the receipt of his Philippine dispatches in the War Department, February 1903, and their appearance in public prints. The *Army and Navy Journal* published his reports in a May volume. The anti-imperial press then eagerly reproduced them.

Roosevelt was incensed by what he viewed as violations of government protocol and confidentiality. He also blasted the essence of Miles's ideas with predictable retort. The anti-imperialists cared nothing for genuine Filipino welfare. It needed a period of US custodianship. Only later would the islanders be ready for independence. TR also harbored no sympathy for Filipino nationalists. He regarded Mabini as inherently destructive.[116]

Miles's giving publicity to army misdeeds drove Roosevelt to new levels of wrath for the irregular soldier. They culminated in this anathema: the general was "a traitor." His Philippine report, Roosevelt gasped to Taft, "was infamous in its baseness and disloyalty, coming from the head of the army and being devoted to slandering that army."[117] Furthermore, the general had demoralized Taft's administration in Manila by meeting with the likes of Mabini and had confused the Filipino mind about Washington's intentions. According to TR, in fact, Miles had always hoped for US defeat in the Philippines. This attitude explained his traducing the army while raising baseless expectation among Filipinos on independence.[118]

Roosevelt contended that the army in the Philippines displayed greater self-restraint than did those detachments under Miles operating at Wounded Knee in 1890. Clearly his caviling about the Philippines was part of a master plan to bring about the government's fall. TR would have gladly fired Miles, but felt restrained as Union and frontier veterans still revered him.[119] Roosevelt believed nevertheless that the officer constituted a menace. Of his unruly conduct, said TR:

If it became at all common among his subordinates, [it] would literally lower our whole army to the level of some South American State where each man is playing for his own hand with utter indifference to the welfare of either the army or the country ... [Miles] has been disloyal to his chief, Secretary Root, and incidentally, of course, to myself and my predecessors; he has been disloyal to the army, therefore disloyal to the country ... he did nothing but intrigue for his own political advancement ... [he] was hoping and praying that the army under him would be beaten and disgraced, so that it might help him to political [office].[120]

TR and Root realized that they would trigger a public fracas by relieving Miles. They chose to avoid it. They instead devised a punishment of applied shabbiness. Roosevelt, for starters, persuaded the French government to drop its plans to award Miles the Legion of Honor.[121]

No doubt TR's order in 1903 that all army officers make a ninety-mile ride on horseback within three days or face retirement had defensible motive: to reduce the number of physically unfit officers in service. An added bonus of this exercise for TR was the chance to humble Miles, then on the eve of his sixty-fourth birthday. But true to form, he failed to cooperate. He ignored the aches of age. He rode the prescribed distance in Oklahoma, from Fort Sill to Fort Reno, in blazing July heat (nine hours, nine mounts). Unfazed by this exertion, he reviewed six infantry companies at Fort Reno, then sped away on horse to El Reno (five miles distance) to take a train north. Editors at the *Army and Navy Journal* saluted his stamina and manly qualities.[122]

When Miles left the army upon reaching the mandatory age of retirement on August 8, 1903 (sixty-four), neither Roosevelt nor Root observed the custom hitherto practiced for decades: publicly acknowledging the nation's senior general upon his completion of service. Roosevelt neither uttered nor wrote a word of thanks for Miles's forty-two years in uniform. Veterans groups criticized the White House's incivility. Pundits marveled. The *New York Times* editorial called the unceremonious treatment "frightful." Roosevelt, though, was unmoved. He only fretted that Miles, "posing as the friend of the soldier," might steal the votes of veterans from the Republican party in 1904. TR told friends that under no circumstances, even those affecting future elections, would he pay tribute to "the most insidious enemy which the army has had during my term of public life." As feeling over discourtesy to Miles simmered, TR growled: "Nothing will hire me to praise him."[123]

Roosevelt crowned Miles's repudiation by filling the army's top position with General Samuel Young, a hardliner on the Philippines, who had participated in combat in northern Luzon. TR touted him as fine fellow, a living retort to Miles's qualms.[124] They had echoed in the general's last order to the army (August 5, 1903):

Every American soldier . . . may by his own conduct exemplify impartial justice to those who have never experienced it, and the results of the highest liberty to those who have been strangers to it, thereby aiding to secure for his country a moral influence not otherwise attainable . . . the Army has confronted enemies representing every stage of human development from the highest civilization yet obtained to savagery and barbarism. It has ever been its duty to observe in war those chivalric and humane principles by which inevitable horrors are so greatly mitigated.[125]

General Young, in contrast with Miles's predilections, never hesitated to embrace or implement stern measures. He urged the concentrating of rural Filipinos in military zones. He favored suspending the laws of war as normally understood – challenging, incidentally, their reaffirmation by the 1899 Hague conference on wartime conventions to which the United States had sent a distinguished delegation.[126] Unsheathed ferocity, Young predicted, would inspire the Filipinos "with a greater fear of the reigning government than they had of the rebels." Obedience to US dictate would be ensured everywhere on the islands.[127] White House acceptance of this concept, concomitant with Miles's retirement, paved the way to Bud Dajo.

* * *

I

Americans in just a century after Jefferson's first inauguration had won a transcontinental domain. Their roving navy made possible the holding of Asian possessions, 85 hundred miles separating Manila from Washington. This achievement constituted one of history's more remarkable creations of political–economic might. Olney boasted to Britain's Lord Salisbury in 1895, during the Venezuelan crisis, that Washington's fiat was law in the Americas: "[The United States] is [sovereign] because, in addition to all other grounds, its infinite resources combined with its isolated position render it master of the situation and practically invulnerable as against any or all other powers."[128] The smashing a few years later of Spanish forces in two hemispheres confirmed the reach and prowess of the US colossus. In this sense, as Lodge perceived in 1899, the war had possessed "world-wide meaning." European power meanwhile began to show signs of wear. TR felt that London's military difficulties in the Boer War (1899–1902) reflected British decadence and augured decline.[129]

New World capacity by 1900 was plain in several indices pegged to wealth and the sinews of military strength. American coal production stood at 244 million tons, Great Britain 228, Germany 149, Austria–Hungary 39, France 33.4, Russia, 16.2, Italy 0.5. Comparative levels in pig-iron also underscored US dynamism. The country produced 14 million tons in 1900, Great Britain 9, Germany 7.5, Russia 2.9, France 2.7, Austria–Hungary 1.5. The United States produced 10 million tons of steel, Germany 6.7, Great Britain 5, France 1.6, Russia 1.5, Austria–Hungary 1.2. The rate of manufacturing production in the United States also slipped past that of Europe. Moreover, the US population of 76 million people surpassed others, except for that of chronically backward Russia at 103. Germany in millions stood at 56, Austria–Hungary 45, France 39, Great Britain 41, Italy 32.[130]

This zooming power had strained national solidarity in the nineteenth century, manifest in regional suspicions that snapped in 1861. Problems related to labor unrest, surging immigration, and urban congestion marked the century's final decades. Volatile economic cycles aggravated matters further as in the 1893 depression. The country, though, kept a semblance of cohesion. Ethnic, racial, religious, and class antipathies did not splinter the country apart. Continent-spanning rail and telegraph lines symbolized and gave substance to national unity. Civil War veterans from both sides – including Confederate Generals Fitzhugh Lee, Joe Wheeler – sealed it when they agreed to fight Spain. Virginia-born Professor Woodrow Wilson savored the war as proof of new patriotism and Union. Roosevelt's secretary of state, John Hay, termed the conflict "splendid."[131]

Other Americans bemoaned empire building circa 1900, even if it eased lingering bitterness from 1861–1865. Hoar's company objected to the country's transformation from republic to ordinary imperium, groaning under garrisons, naval bases, proconsuls, and decrees. Its security–economic concerns traversed thousands of oceanic miles. Millions of Filipinos lived in colonial captivity, barely protected by vague promises of a radiant future. Hoar delivered this indictment in 1903:

We crushed the only republic in Asia. We made war against the only Christian people in the East. We converted a war of glory to a war of shame. We vulgarized the American flag. We introduced perfidy into the practice of war. We inflicted torture on unarmed men to extort confession. We put children to death. We established reconcentrado camps. We devastated provinces. We baffled the aspirations of a people for liberty.[132]

Even worse, he added, Americans had abandoned the courage of their earlier conviction when they embarked in the radical direction of overseas empire; they had discarded the power of example as a component of greatness in international life. Justice and decency generated influence abroad beyond anything ever devised by the grasping nations. The best of US tradition, then, was sacrificed to passing fancy for imperial status. Genuine superiority, he sighed, had been lost in the Philippine sordidness.[133]

II

The origins of Cuban war and US imperialism is an ongoing subject of competing interpretations. They have included explanations tied to psychic crisis, evolving masculine identities, search for markets, desire to partake in the scramble for overseas possessions, and drive for hegemony.[134] Irrespective of the relative merits of these interpretations, three features of US imperialism stand out.

First, it was a piddling affair compared to those enterprises undertaken by French, British, and other governments. American overseas possessions in 1900 were dwarfed by those of Europeans. Between 1870 and turn of the century, the United States had acquired 125,000 square miles abroad, Great Britain 4.7 million square miles, France 3.5, Germany 1.0.[135] The US dalliance with creating an overseas empire did not last deep into the twentieth century. Second, most Americans were eager to avoid showdown with other great powers over imperial prerogatives comparable to the 1898 Anglo-French contest of nerves at Fashoda. Roosevelt concluded in 1907 that the United States should actually liquidate its stake in the Philippines. It would become a strategic liability, probably attracting Japan's naval–political interest.[136] Third, Americans were tentative, in some sense abashed by their imperialism and nervous about the cost of colonial upkeep. Washington never established a colonial office with departmental heads, bureaucratic machinery, or cabinet representation.[137] Even imperial apologists circa 1900 talked about the inevitability of future Filipino self-determination. An informal empire abroad was better suited to American tastes, as in Cuba where Washington retained influence but not direct control via the 1901 Platt Amendment (abrogated in 1934 as part of FDR's Good Neighbor Policy). Nor was the American use of lethal force in imperial context more indiscriminate or unrestrained than others. Belgian inhumanity in the Congo was spectacular, retailed in Joseph Conrad's 1902 *Heart of Darkness*. German troops in South West Africa (Namibia) killed 65,000 seminomadic Herero tribesmen in 1904, "baboons" to their tormentors.[138] Fair to say: protests by Hoar and Miles against extreme measures helped prevent Filipino misery comparable to that visited by Belgians or Germans in captive Africa.

Hoar was an ambivalent dissenter. American culpability was normally beyond what his mind could credit. Taking a position on major policy against party and president also violated his convictions. But Hoar felt ultimately constrained by other obligation, namely to prevent the United States from forsaking first republican tenets. He declared: "However unpleasant may be [my] duty, as Martin Luther said, God help me, I can do no otherwise."[139] Yet from the standpoint of diehard anti-imperialists, Hoar disappointed. His campaigning for McKinley in 1900 seemed equal parts mysterious and hypocritical. Boutwell, by contrast, and no less a GOP man, voted for Byran consistent with anti-imperialism. Hoar was then reviled as traitor, and not only by Funston. Mugwumps and anti-imperialists ridiculed Hoar as fickle or duplicitous.[140]

Neither Funston's frothing nor mugwump snivel bothered Hoar. But possible ejection from the Republican party upset him. He nevertheless carried on until death in 1904 saved him from the ignominy of outright ostracism.

Miles lived for more than two decades after his army retirement. He remained egotistical. He became more petulant. Miles did not waver in his hostility to TR, who considered Miles a pest even after his entering civilian life.[141]

He got his name placed in nomination at the 1904 Democratic convention. But Alton Parker outpaced Miles for the party nod. He also sought a seat in Congress from the Third Congressional District of Massachusetts in 1913 as a Republican. Party chieftains instead selected the politically reliable Calvin Paige to run. Miles meantime involved himself in the antics of the Guardians of Liberty, a collection of anti-Catholic and anti-immigrant bigots whom he naively thought would serve as vehicle for his aspirations. They anointed him their "chief guardian."[142]

Miles did speak sensibly about the needs of national preparedness on the eve of US intervention in World War One. He tendered offers of service to the army in 1917–1918. They were politely rejected by a bemused War Department. His last hurrah occurred in 1925. The elderly soldier went to the aid of embattled General Billy Mitchell in his campaign to alert Congress and the defense establishment to the revolutionary nature of military aviation.

Miles was a bundle of contradictions: military virtues versus character flaws, perspicacity versus obtuseness. Still, his enduring contribution remains unambiguous, namely the vigorous affirmation of right conduct in international life, even in conditions of duress. American participation in the post-World War Two military tribunals at Nuremberg and Tokyo constituted Miles's vindication. The words he issued to the army in the Philippines, November 1902, fit that later moment: "Any orders, circulars, or personal instructions, or any parts thereof, from whatever source, that suggest, inspire, encourage, or permit any acts of cruelty and unwarranted severity be annulled, canceled and rescinded, and such acts are hereby strictly prohibited."[143]

This injunction helped educate the army in the mentality of the Hague outlook. It in turn helped prevent the army from wholesale lapses as disgraced many elements of the German and Japanese armed forces. Miles, in effect, nurtured within the US army a sturdy conscience. It matured in time to join the international prosecution of German and Japanese war crimes.

General Yamashita Tomoyuki numbered among the Axis officers punished in 1946. He was hanged for unpardonable acts committed by his men against civilians in Manila. The US officer who confirmed

Yamashita's death sentence was General Douglas MacArthur. He said in the spirit of Miles:

The soldier, be he friend or foe, is charged with the protection of the weak and unarmed. It is the very essence and reason for his being. When he violates this sacred trust, he not only profanes his entire cult but threatens the very fabric of international society.[144]

While directing forces in the Philippines decades earlier, MacArthur's father had pressed to the limit of what Miles held tolerable. He seemed to officers of the Arthur MacArthur stamp a tiresome creature, who failed to understand the pressures weighing upon men fighting an unconventional war in wretched setting.[145] Miles in actuality honored US soldiers by holding them to meaningful standards. Adherence to them won the army respect in two world wars. Deviation later led to atrocity at My Lai and Haditha and shame at military prisons: Abu Graib, Guantanamo Bay.[146]

Part III

Hazards

9   Armageddon

Brigadier General John J. Pershing disagreed in 1913 with the notion that war had become obsolete, that evolving humanity would shed this vestige of primitivism. Believers in a pacific future pointed to progress made in the two Hague conferences (1899, 1907). Conferees had provided for a permanent court of arbitration. They had adopted rules to reduce suffering caused by war. Planning for a third Hague meeting, scheduled for summer 1915, evidenced steady pace toward a better world. Scholarly writers, meanwhile, notably Britain's Norman Angell in 1909 (*The Great Illusion*), deduced that war had become so unprofitable that it could not again occur on a large scale. The English Marxist historian, H. N. Brailsford, said in March 1914: "The dangers which forced our ancestors into European coalitions and Continental wars have gone never to return."[1] The working class too contributed to the peace momentum when (1907, 1910) the Second International enacted measures to prevent the bourgeoisie from making wars. Against this hopefulness, Pershing told journalists: "Universal peace is as far away as the Millennium ... With different languages, different interests, different traits of character, different instincts and customs, different religions, Universal Peace in the world, even among the leading powers, is impossible."[2] Pershing had earlier in 1913 directed a blistering operation against Moro fighters in the Philippines. His command in June on Jolo island killed more than 500 Moros at Bud Bagsak.[3]

Nothing that happened at Bud Bagsak or elsewhere in the Philippines during his tours (1900–1903, 1907–1908, 1909–1913) prepared Pershing for the Great War's enormity. Prior assignments in Cuba in 1898 and against restive tribes in New Mexico and South Dakota were equally irrelevant to the experience of total war. His pursuit with 6,000 cavalrymen of Pancho Villa (1916–1917) into Mexico was also beside the point in a contest that employed multimillion men armies. When Pershing expressed doubt in 1913 about the dawning of peace, he had in mind ongoing scrapes in the Balkans, colonial suppression of natives, the 1904/05 Russo-Japanese clash, and Germany's wars of unification under

Bismarck that culminated in 1871 with victory over France. All of these recent conflicts, however sharp or bitter for the defeated, were of brief duration. Nothing about them jarred the thought of Pershing or his brother officers. An upheaval that would mangle a generation of youths, provoke butchery in Armenia, batter economies, topple dynasties, shatter empires, sap colonialism, spawn Bolshevism, and unleash furies that contrived fascism defied imagination in 1913.

Three years later the US enrollment of army regulars hovered around 130,000 while land and sea battles devoured men plus machines at Verdun, Jutland, the Somme. In the end, twelve million men died in battle during 1914–1918, "half the seed of Europe" mourned the officer–poet Wilfred Owen.[4] Many more were wounded or otherwise impaired. Widows abounded. The war produced nine million orphans and ten million refugees. These populations were left more susceptible than others to the 1919 killer influenza.[5] This magnitude of destruction dwarfed all previous military experience, by which measure sputtering violence in the Philippines seemed trivial. The Great War substantiated this old pessimism: "With what little wisdom the world is governed."[6]

Diplomacy of neutrality

President Woodrow Wilson hoped at the outset of hostilities in August 1914 to steer America away from European hazards. An admirer of British political institutions, he tended to sympathize privately with London. But he publicly vouched for the wisdom of strict neutrality. He urged his compatriots to act in "the spirit of impartiality and fairness and friendliness to all concerned."[7] Neither the war nor its causes, he professed, need directly involve Americans. Secretary of State William Jennings Bryan in similar vein told the J. P. Morgan Company that granting loans to any belligerent would mar US non-alignment.[8] Concurrent with issuance of these injunctions, Wilson offered to mediate between the British–French–Russian and German–Austrian–Turkish coalitions. He sent his confidant, Colonel Edward House, on peace errands to Europe (1915, 1916). Wilson hoped that a non-punitive deal might be brokered. It should not be burdened by smug victors or sullen losers: "Only a peace between equals can last."[9]

Prudence and a desire to help did not alone shape US neutralism. Wilson wanted to pursue domestic reforms consistent with his *New Freedom*. Distractions abroad could undermine his progressive agenda. It aimed to curb child labor (Keating–Owen Act), establish an eight-hour day for railway workers (Adamson Act), mandate protections for federal employees (Workmen's Compensation Act), crack the trusts (Clayton

Act), buttress farmers (Farm Loan Act), tax inheritances, and tax profits made by munitions manufacturers. The president also upheld liberal immigration when he vetoed a bill in January 1915 that required newcomers to demonstrate literacy.

The US ethnic mix additionally inhibited Wilson from taking sides. Vocal German-American groups were eager that Washington not enlist on London's side.[10] Irish Americans felt similarly, especially after suppression of the 1916 Easter uprising in Dublin. Wilson himself doubted that the United States could simultaneously wage war and maintain internal equilibrium: "It will be easy to excite passion and difficult to allay it."[11]

His packed foreign policy schedule also argued for neutrality. To quell New World disorders, he dispatched troops to Haiti (1915), then to Santo Domingo (1916). Skirmishes between Pershing's soldiers and those of President Carranza in Carrizal (June 1916) suggested that diplomacy had reached an impasse with Mexico. Embroilment south of the border would cancel adventures in Europe.

Neutrality came under pressure as the intensity of European combat increased and its scope widened. British actions against US maritime commerce strained Wilson's forbearance. The Royal Navy intercepted US merchant ships suspected of carrying contraband cargo (broadly defined) to Germany. Cargoes were impounded. Ships were confiscated. Partial restitution might then be paid. This noxious practice caused Wilson to deliver protests to London in December 1914. More followed. Anglo-US problems were further aggravated by London's use of submerged mines. They made no distinction between American or other vessels on North Sea routes to German ports. British interdiction of US mails also hurt. The "Blacklist" in July 1916 irritated too, proscribing trade with US firms that dealt with the Central Powers. Execution that year of Irish nationalists, Sir Roger Casement among them, enraged Hibernian clubs in the United States and Wilson expressed displeasure. Anglo-American relations reached a nadir in 1916.[12]

German behavior also infuriated. Growing numbers of Americans in 1914–1916 viewed it as worse than Britain's transgressions. The invasion of neutral Belgium sparked condemnation. The use of tens of thousands of Frenchmen and Belgians as forced labor in Germany aroused strong feeling. Additionally, Berlin's espionage was resented. The *New York World* published sensational reports in July 1915 about a network of covert German operatives doing mischief in the United States. The murder of Armenians by Germany's Turkish ally was especially shocking. Former president Theodore Roosevelt urged war upon the Ottoman empire as "the only policy that will permanently put a stop to such massacres." Their heinousness surpassed even German misdeeds, he alleged.[13]

American lives and commerce were endangered by Germany's submarine warfare, waged to disrupt Britain's importing of vital goods and to offset the Royal Navy's supremacy. Citizens died when they sailed upon Allied civilian ships torpedoed in Germany's declared "zone of war" around the British Isles: *Falaba* in March 1915, *Arabic* in August 1915, *Sussex* in March 1916. The most notorious case involved the British passenger liner *Lusitania* on May 7, 1915 off Ireland's coast. One hundred and twenty-eight Americans perished along with a thousand other people. The Italian liner *Ancona* carried 27 Americans when an Austrian submarine sank it in November 1915. Depredations on the high seas also included German assaults on US merchant ships bound for Allied ports. Vessels targeted in 1915 included *William P. Frye* (January), *Cushing* (April), *Gulflight* and *Nebraskan* (May), *Leelanaw* (July), *Petrolite* (December).

Ambassador Walter H. Page in London and Republican stalwarts – TR, Senator Henry Cabot Lodge – were adamant in their brief for war against Germany to aid the Anglo-French. The president's advisers also tended to favor the Allies, especially House and Wilson's second secretary of state, Robert Lansing. German behavior not only offended them. These men worried too about the viability of Europe's balance of power, threatened by surging German strength. They held that the North Atlantic community, binding British–French–Canadian–US well-being in an economic–political web, would unravel with German victory. It would jeopardize US primacy in the New World.

Wilson managed to check interventionist advocates, even as they called craven his praise in May 1915 of a nation "being too proud to fight." He drew some of the critics' sting by embracing the preparedness campaign, which created training camps for combat-age men. He approached Congress in December 1915 with requests to expand the size of the army. Legislation in summer 1916 pursuant to increasing the number of warships also enhanced Wilson's position against skeptics. His repeated warnings obliged Berlin in May 1916 to suspend submarine attacks on US shipping. He successfully campaigned that year for reelection with an appealing slogan: "He kept us out of war."

Two exacting tests of Wilson's commitment to neutrality occurred in 1915. The first centered on the Armenian genocide. The applicability of this term is still contested by Turkish apologists. Yet if the word retains analytical usefulness and moral content, it plainly applies to the wholesale devastation that began in April. The second episode, torpedoing of the *Lusitania* in May, instigated an emergency in German–US relations and revealed irresolvable differences between Wilson and Bryan.[14] The secretary resigned to protest a "reckless" policy.

Ambassadorial diplomacy and Armenia

Wilson expected upon taking office in 1913 to concentrate on domestic matters, wherein his political passion lay. He had slight interest in foreign affairs, an indifference that meshed with his disapproval of the traditional line of US ambassadors. He disparaged them as illiberal and unsuited for association with his innovations. Tied to the moneyed class, they had too narrow a vision to understand the collective good. He commented in 1913:

We find that those who have been occupying the legations and embassies have been habituated to a point of view which is very different, indeed, from the point of view of the present administration. They have had the material interests of individuals in the United States very much more in mind than the moral and public considerations which it seems to us ought to control.[15]

This disdain did not translate into recruiting abler diplomats, however. Few of Wilson's represented an advance over the older type. Better men – competent with pertinent experience – refused ambassadorial offers, leaving only the donor class and party faithful. Consequently, by Wilson's own standard, the apparatus through which Washington conducted business abroad continued to atrophy.

He rarely sent ambassadors on consequential business. He thought James Gerard, Tammany Hall contributor, in Berlin an "idiot." Wilson ignored his emissary in St. Petersburg, George Marye, an elderly Californian with the requisite wealth to maintain official residence in Russia. Wilson deemed this Democratic loyalist utterly vacuous. David Francis, Missouri businessman–politician, succeeded Marye to Russia in 1916. Francis proved too befuddled to make sense of Lenin, Trotsky, or Bolshevik ambitions.[16] Wilson's men in Paris (William Sharp), Rome (Thomas Nelson Page), and Madrid (Joseph Willard) followed similar patterns of patronage and scant qualification.[17] An exception to this body of mediocrity was Wilson's choice for London, the lucid and presentable editor–publisher Walter Hines Page. Unfortunately, he made himself objectionable to Wilson during the period of neutrality by arguing nonstop on behalf of the Allies: German conduct, above all against Belgium, assured History's censure. Wilson's confidence in Page had dissolved by late 1915.[18]

Wilson's choice for the Ottoman empire, Henry Morgenthau, had much in common with the president's other ambassadors, despite Jewish faith and German birth (1856). He possessed a fortune – made in law practice, finance, real estate. He had lately been involved in Democratic party activity. The Princeton pedagogue–New Jersey governor impressed Morgenthau as a pragmatic idealist. Their first meeting inspired mutual enthusiasm.[19] Morgenthau subsequently spent time and money on Wilson's 1912 campaign. He chaired the Democrats' election finance committee.

He expected a cabinet post in reward, Commerce or Treasury. These positions instead went to other claimants. The president, however, did want somehow to reward Morgenthau and decided upon an embassy. Wilson offered Constantinople, partly on the assumption that a Jew would be attentive to an empire that contained Jerusalem and coreligionists in Palestine. Other Jews had previously represented the United States in Turkey: Solomon Hirsch, Oscar Straus.

Morgenthau hesitated at first. He suspected that the post had acquired a Jewish designation which implied that Jews should aspire to none other in the foreign arena. Acceptance of Constantinople, then, would be perpetuating of limited choices for publicly oriented Jewish Americans. "I share the feeling of other Jews," he told Wilson, "that it is unwise to confirm that this is the only field for them in diplomatic service."[20] Morgenthau overcame his dissappointment, though, and accepted the Turkish posting. Jewish persons also helped persuade, including the eminent Rabbi Stephen Wise.[21]

Morgenthau's Constantinople assignment spanned twenty-six months, December 1913 to February 1916. Bryan's instructions were unexceptional, premised on the reasonable assumption that little would occur during Morgenthau's tenure. Initially, the envoy regretted nothing. He enjoyed society. The Orient delighted him as something exotic in which to luxuriate. He acted dutifully in 1913–1914 to advance US commercial interests: Standard Oil, Singer Sewing Machine, corporate buyers of Turkish tobacco. He goaded officials in Constantinople – in the name of universal progress – to suppress the "white slave trade." He recommended to his hosts "the gospel of Americanism."[22] He counseled the empire's leaders – Minister of War Enver, Minister of Interior Talaat, Minster of Navy Djemal – on how they might democratize Turkey. He visited the Holy Land. Zionist pioneers and petitioners thronged him. He became friendly with Protestant missionaries who ran educational–medical institutions in Turkey. He admired these people as "advance agents of civilization" in a realm inhabited by rough men and secluded women.[23]

The pleasant routine of diplomatic office ended in the first convulsions of world war. Turkey entered on the German side in October/November 1914. The embassy subsequently cared for the interests of several Allied nations, most importantly Britain, France, Russia. This responsibility added to the embassy's workload, already burdened by alarms connected to US nationals bewildered by wartime events. Morgenthau kept pace. He and his staff proved effective in shielding enemy aliens from Turkish vindictiveness. He took a personal interest in promoting Jewish safety in Palestine, where local authorities were agitated about possible Anglo-Zionist collaboration against the empire. He meanwhile monitored the impact of hostilities on the Ottoman polity. He evaluated the pervasive German influence on Turkey. He evinced compassion for its ragged conscripts and squeezed peasantry.[24]

Unfolding military campaigns focused still more of his attention. They involved the ill-fated Anglo-French landing at Gallipoli plus Russian–Turkish fighting in Armenia. This second theater of operations triggered what Morgenthau in 1918 called "the greatest crime in modern history."[25]

Persecution of Armenians and other Christian minorities (Greeks, Slavs, Syrians) had ample precedent in the waning Ottoman empire. More than 100,000 Armenians were killed in 1894–1896 during the rule of Sultan Abdul Hamid II. William Gladstone dubbed him "the great assassin."[26] In 1909 roughly 20,000 Armenians were killed in or near Adana. Doubt about their loyalty had fueled these rampages. The Armenian situation subsequently improved with the ascendancy of the Committee of Union and Progress: the "Young Turks." Their embracing of modernity meant improved civil rights for non-Muslim subjects, Christians of all denominations, and Jews. This new tolerance, alas, did not withstand the stresses of world war nor militant notions of Turkish identity taught by such theorists as Ziya Gokalp.[27]

Ottoman leaders, among them confirmed atheists like Talaat, called for holy crusade against the British–French–Russian infidels. Secular and religious spokesmen encouraged Muslim subjects in the Allied empires to rise against their Christian masters. This mobilization of Islam unavoidably compromised the status of Christian minorities in Turkey with links to the Allied side, primarily Greeks and Armenians. Cautions by the Athens government and military preparations – augmented by the 1914 purchase of two US warships – helped relax Ottoman pressure upon resident Greeks. Harassment of them in 1914–1918 was crude, but did not end in disaster. "The Greeks," observed Morgenthau, "had a government [wholly] interested in their welfare."[28] Not so the Armenians.

Their homeland straddled the mountainous border zone between czarist Russia and Turkey, antagonists of long standing. Russian agents in 1914 urged Turkish Armenians to join the czar's in a war of liberation against Islam. Some Ottoman Armenians did collaborate with the Russian army that tangled with the Turks from late 1914 onward. Two outstanding nationalists were Karekin Pastermadjian and Shabin Karahissar. They led czarist-organized units of Armenian soldiers against Turkey, thus rekindling Ottoman suspicions and anomosity. The ebb and flow of battle in northeastern Anatolia, in which Russia's troops never achieved a permanent advantage, left Armenia vulnerable. Fighting in spring 1915 between Turkish forces versus Armenian resistors around the ancient city of Van meant death for thousands of local civilians.[29]

Ottoman authorities gave orders on April 24, 1915, coinciding with the arrival of Allied forces on the Gallipoli peninsula, to arrest prominent Armenians in Constantinople and elsewhere: intellectuals, civic leaders, artists, lawyers, doctors. Hundreds of these people were then executed. In the euphemistic language of state reason, "The Ottoman [state] had to take firm measures."[30]

Enver and Talaat also decreed the following. Armenians as an undifferentiated group – irrespective of sex, age, occupation, political allegiance – were to be deported in columns of thousands from the scene of purported treachery to various corners of the empire: Syrian deserts, Aleppo, Damascus. Churches were thereafter desecrated, homes sacked, livestock killed, crops burned. Under the guise of expulsion, officialdom determined to eradicate a twofold nuisance: revolutionaries plotting sedition, a nation that collaborated with Turkey's mortal enemies.

Depopulation of Ottoman Armenia (nearly 2 million inhabitants) was well launched by mid-1915. Morgenthau aptly called the deportations a "death warrant" for an indicted race. Hundreds of thousands of Armenians died, perhaps totaling one and a half million.[31] Many were killed outright by Turkish soldiers or Kurdish raiders. Starvation, thirst, exposure, and disease played their parts. Talaat congratulated himself: "I have accomplished more toward solving the Armenian problem in three months than Abdul Hamid accomplished in thirty years!"[32]

Survivors owed their lives to the occasional kindness of Turkish or Arab rescuers. They gave shelter and varieties of help. Mercy was otherwise scarce. A deportee recollected:

The soldiers would come and give us a bad time. Others from the hills and mountains would come and snatch girls and baggage, or whatever they could. You scream, "Gendarme, gendarme," but there was no help, because they [the soldiers and abductors] were all together in this ... I saw them snatch girls and goods right from the horses or wagons, dragging them by force. I can still picture the whole thing right now ... They had brought some deportees on the cliff. They would tie them, shoot them and throw them in the river ... Sometimes it would be the turn of a pregnant woman. They would look at each other and say, "boy or girl," and pierce her belly with the sword.[33]

Morgenthau's embassy quickly assembled details of these events, despite Turkish efforts to conceal them, dispose of incriminating evidence, or disqualify witnesses.[34] American missionaries sent accounts from Armenian provinces, such as the Reverend Henry Riggs in Harpoot. He also protested the eviction policy to municipal officials. Their rejoinders underscored Armenian betrayal of Turkish trust. Diplomats in the field, meantime, filed reports with Morgenthau, beginning in June 1915 (which persisted even as Ottoman authorities scrambled embassy communications with isolated districts). Leslie Davis, who headed one of thirteen US consulates in Turkey, also hid eighty Armenians in his residence while helping others to escape harm. Missionaries and diplomats of other countries, including Germany, shared corroborating intelligence with Morgenthau. Eye-witnesses, moreover, of diverse backgrounds told him directly of women raped, men shot, children forsaken.[35] "Terrible vengeance is being taken" upon the Armenians, he cabled Washington in July 1915: "Most of the sufferers are innocent and have been loyal to Ottoman Government." He estimated in early November that two-thirds of the Armenians had been displaced or annihilated. The term genocide not yet coined, he spoke of "race murder."[36]

Washington's response disappointed him. He had suggested that Wilson or the secretary of state publicly scold the Turks. Such rebuke could have been supplemented by diplomacy to ease the Armenians' plight via talks with Ottoman authorities or by pressing Berlin to intercede. The Turks should also be prevailed upon to allow delivery of food and medical supplies. Instead the administration, intent upon neutrality, rebuffed Morgenthau (though House toyed with the idea of issuing protests). Complications with a German ally, concurrent with the submarine controversy, might conspire to push America into unwanted war. Thus while the *New York Times* published graphic Armenian tales, while Allied governments warned Constantinople to cease "crimes against humanity," while the State Department amassed data, and while Armenian Americans implored Wilson, he chose not to fuss.[37] He did express misgivings to acquaintances about events. He wrote a brief note to Morgenthau in October 1915, thanking him for his performance of duty, but added: "I have nothing special to write about."[38] Secretary Lansing also lacked ideas concerning Armenia except for the obvious: private Americans everywhere in Turkey should be protected. He thought too, as a matter of courtesy, to notify Turkish officials of the adverse effect expulsions had on US opinion.[39]

Wilson's brand of neutrality toward Turkey enraged TR. Therein, he cried, occurred "atrocities so hideous that it is difficult to name them."[40] They equally disconcerted Morgenthau, but he never berated his Washington superiors. Nor did the diplomat's nerve fail. Morgenthau acted energetically in the absence of adequate instruction. Aware of conventions forbidding an envoy's interfering in the affairs of his assigned country, he anyway confronted Enver and Talaat.[41] The ambassador attacked the idea of collective Armenian guilt. He entreated that women, children, and blameless men should not pay with their lives for the intrigues of individual insurrectionists. He invoked the court of world opinion and cosmopolitan sensibility as sanction against cruelty. He urged a halt to removals plus establishment of affirmative Armenian programs. He offered personally to raise a million dollars to provide transport for imperiled people to America. He sought to convince the German ambassador, Baron Hans von Wangenheim, to pressure Turkey in the direction of leniency. Germany would otherwise be viewed everywhere as an accomplice. "The guilt of these crimes," Morgenthau warned Wangenheim, "will be your inheritance forever."[42]

Morgenthau's hosts thought his unsolicited advice impertinent. The ambassador should not pry into the affairs of a sovereign state that patiently suffered his presence. Besides, his concern about Armenian welfare was misplaced. Turks in tens of thousands had died because of Armenian trickery. The ambassador should not worry over the fate of knaves who made common cause with invaders. Admittedly, some innocents resided among the Armenian victims. But Ottoman officials, improvising in emergency, had no time to separate upright from culpable. Fastidiousness belonged to peacetime. Moreover, Talaat gibed, a self-respecting Jew ought not bother himself over the fate of a rebellious Christian community.[43] And by the way, Talaat suggested at one meeting, Morgenthau should provide a list of Armenians who had policies with US life insurance firms (New York Life Insurance Company, Equitable Life of New York) as the Turkish government was rightful beneficiary of those who had disappeared with their heirs. This request caused Morgenthau to drop diplomatic courtesies. He abruptly broke off the meeting.[44]

Ambassador Wangenheim regarded the Armenians as disloyal "vermin." He did make a perfunctory protest to the Turkish foreign ministry, the chief value being to disassociate his government from odious deeds. He was, though, unwilling to do anything that might demoralize an ally. German soldiers in Turkey concurred. Marshal Liman von Sanders let Morgenthau know that the Armenian affair need not concern Americans. General Bronsart von Schellendorf secretly scorned Morgenthau as a miserable Jew, no better than the wily Armenians.[45]

Constantinople took a toll on him. The intransigence of Enver and Talaat hardened while he became more strident about Armenia. German non-cooperation emphasized his impotence. Wilson's government remained detached. Unsurprisingly, Morgenthau showed signs of nervous strain. His usual ebullience evaporated. His dispirited wife left Turkey in September 1915. Stopping in Sofia on her way home, she told Queen Eleanor of Ottoman cruelties and urged that Bulgaria avoid cooperation with Turkey. The Bulgarian ambassador in Constantinople shortly afterward protested the Armenian persecutions, which led to Talaat's reprimanding Morgenthau for his blathering wife. He finally quit the capital in February 1916: "My failure to stop the destruction of the Armenians had made Turkey for me a place of horror, and I found intolerable my further daily association with men who ... were still reeking with the blood of nearly a million human beings ... I had reached the end of my resources."[46]

While making for Washington, he hoped to stop in Geneva to meet with Colonel House, then conferring with Wilson's ambassador to Austria. But House could not spare extra time. He left Geneva shortly before Morgenthau arrived with breathless Armenian news.[47]

Once back in America, Morgenthau did not waste time. He wrote and lectured to raise awareness of Armenian needs. He dwelt on the desirability of a League of Nations mandate managed by Americans in the interest of Armenians, not to be relinquished until they could assume their affairs in safety. He was subsequently gratified by, and took some credit for, the twelfth of Wilson's Fourteen Points (January 1918). It called for an end to Turkish misrule in Armenia with guarantees: "undoubted security of life and an absolutely unmolested opportunity of autonomous development."[48] Wilson at Paris in 1919 also accepted, subject to Senate approval, US mandate responsibility for Armenia. (The Senate rejected this proposal in June 1920.[49]) Morgenthau meantime helped organize private subsidies and philanthropy for Armenia, a task he had surreptitiously begun while still in Constantinople. He helped form the Armenian Relief Committee. He later sat on the board of trustees of its successor organization, Near East Relief. The Rockefeller Foundation and churches made sizable donations. Almost $20 million made its way to Armenian rescue by 1920. Countless orphans were fed, clothed, housed.[50] Thus Morgenthau's ambassadorial career was not entirely in vain. Washington officials and other people finally came to grasp the dimension of events and made provisions.

Resignation

Morgenthau's struggles in 1915 were waged far from the seat of US government. This inconvenient man could be ignored. His dilemmas and pleading had gone unacknowledged for weeks at a stretch. The country's chief diplomatic officer, by contrast, was not so easily overlooked.

Shambling Bryan lacked the stuff of a first-rate foreign secretary. His evangelical certitude and sanctimoniousness were liabilities, not eased by his incuriosity. His unwillingness to delve deeply into subjects beyond the interests of his rural southern and western constituencies also pinched. He got the diplomatic portfolio by virtue of his standing in the Democratic party, House averred: "a purely political necessity."[51] Page lampooned the failed Democratic presidential candidate – beaten in 1896, 1900, 1908 – as a provincial crank. TR derided him in 1913 as "the most contemptible figure we have ever had as Secretary of State."[52]

Even Wilson had at one time cast aspersions on Bryan's character. He neither expected nor wanted much from the Great Commoner.[53] Additionally, Wilson thought Bryan "strange" and was apprehensive that foreign governments did not respect him.[54] Yet the two men did cooperate in cabinet and were cordial. Wilson, above all, never lost view of Bryan's popularity among Democrats. It endowed him with standing apart from the department he led. All other bureaucratic heads depended on Wilson's gift for their prestige.

Wilson's regard for Bryan never threatened House's connection to the president. He preferred the ingratiating Texan to whom he entrusted sensitive diplomatic tasks, which usurpation upset Bryan. He thought the dignity of his office degraded by Wilson's reliance upon an adviser without portfolio.[55] Vigilant in protecting this coziness, House stealthily undermined anyone who might endanger it, including Bryan. He never gained admittance to the inner circle but flitted on its fringes.[56]

Attachment to the non-violent resolution of international problems made him a near pacifist. He admired the Christian anarchical philosophy of Leo Tolstoy. Bryan abominated war as the "sum of all evils."[57] He believed as an article of faith that Americans with few arms lived securely. "All the European Powers were armed to the teeth," he exclaimed in 1914, "and always maintained that this heavy armament was necessary to protect them from war. Now the fallacy is obvious. We alone live in peace because we are unarmed."[58]

His tenure avoided most missteps that fluster novices. The exception to this record of competence occurred in May 1915 during the *Lusitania* crisis. Bryan inadvertently misled the Austrian ambassador, Constantin Dumba. He misconstrued Bryan's ambiguously phrased statement on feelings in Washington about the ship's destruction. Dumba conveyed to Vienna the erroneous notion that tough-worded protests by Wilson were meant as a sop to domestic opinion but should not be interpreted seriously. This Dumba confusion embarrassed Bryan. It required public explanations by him. They sounded convoluted. Critics twitted Wilson with this evidence of the hayseed's inability.[59]

Unlucky timing undid Bryan, not personal fumbling. He initiated soon after taking office a series of so-called cooling off treaties. Thirty were signed. They provided for arbitration commissions to adjudicate claims between disputing governments. Preparations for war would be suspended for a year. Efforts should be made during this time to resolve peaceably the given controversy. An arbitration commission would make recommendations and submit a fact-finding report. Bryan was hugely proud of these treaties as their implementation could quicken the coming of global peace. James Brown Scott of the Carnegie Peace Foundation pronounced: "[The treaties] constitute the greatest contribution of an official nature made at any time, by any one man."[60] The burst of European violence made hash of his endeavor, even as British, French, and Russian signatories affixed their names to "cooling off" agreements in late summer 1914.

Bryan clung to the hope that waxing popular sympathy for the Allies would not sway Washington against Germany and that by diplomacy the United States could avoid hostilities. Specific German actions did anger him: Belgian invasion, deployment of submarines against neutral shipping, first battlefield use of poison gas (second Ypres, April–May 1915). But he also tracked Allied violations of wartime conventions: unauthorized use of the US flag by British munitions ships, implicitly encouraging civilians to travel on vessels carrying contraband in war zones, confiscating US property on the high seas. He held the Royal Navy's food blockade of Germany to be unconscionable for its indiscrimination and injury to non-combatants. He sought to give these Allied doings public notice equal to that shone upon German offenses. He meant to keep Wilson true to neutrality theology by rhetorically asking: "Why be shocked at the drowning of a few people, if there is to be no objection to starving a nation?"[61]

Bryan decried what he called the British use of human shields: "A ship carrying contraband should not rely upon passengers to protect her from attack – it would be like putting women and children in front of an army."[62] He urged Americans to desist from traveling in neutral or Allied ships through battle zones where German submarines lurked. Such heedlessness by private citizens practically invited Berlin–Washington confrontations. On this point, though, Wilson relied upon an exact reading of international law: neutrals in the conduct of their innocent affairs must be left unmolested. Legitimate naval actions by definition respected the safety of non-combatants and the citizens of non-belligerent states. A submarine commander at minimum had to give fair warning (even if this risked ramming by merchant ships or attack by naval escorts). He had to provide however possible for the safety of crew and passengers. In short, he had to act in conformity with those rules that governed surface raiders. A week after *Lusitania*'s sinking, Wilson reiterated: "We mean to support our citizens in the exercise of their right to travel both on our ships and on belligerent."[63]

The loss of life on *Lusitania* horrified Bryan no less than Wilson. Yet the secretary reflexively looked for mitigating circumstances. He asked whether the ship carried contraband. Quick investigation proved to his satisfaction that *Lusitania* had, indeed, stored *matériel* in its hull warranting German interest. He denounced once again use by Britain of "our citizens to protect her ammunition!"[64]

Bryan endorsed Wilson's condemnation of the torpedoing. However, he also hoped and expected that the president would examine British claims to purity. Bryan advised to this end that neutrality required sending a note to London against the blockade simultaneous with protests to Berlin. Independence of action would be preserved by putting both camps on notice of US intent to guard innocents against all malefactors. He also suggested that Wilson take steps to prevent citizens from booking Atlantic passage on Allied ships.

Wilson did not closely consult Bryan in framing the *Lusitania* notes. The president's first communication to Berlin (May 13) demanded disavowal of the sinking, payment of reparations, and discontinuance of unrestricted submarine warfare.[65] No simultaneous message was transmitted to London on blockade or affronts to US shipping. Bryan glumly went along with this asymmetry. It ignored complexity and reinforced US drift toward the Allies: "I can not bring myself to the belief that it is wise to relinquish the hope of playing the part of a friend to both sides in the role of peace maker."[66]

The German Foreign Ministry delayed answering Wilson. The reply when written, partly influenced by Dumba's garble, emphasized *Lusitania*'s being armed and laden with munitions. This note also pointed to the publicity given by the German embassy in Washington before the ship sailed from New York, namely Americans thinking of taking passage should pause before sailing under the British flag into a declared war zone. Berlin did not apologize or offer indemnity.

Wilson responded with a second note on June 9. It repeated the points of the first, elaborating at length on submarine violence to the principles of humanity.[67] Bryan interpreted the second note – stark in tone – as an instigation of war. Unable to back the president's stand, nursing hurt pride over House, and badly played in the Dumba incident, Bryan resigned. He wrote to Wilson on June 8: "You have prepared for . . . the German Government a note in which I cannot join without violating what I deem to be an obligation to my country . . . the prevention of war."[68] Wilson accepted the resignation with regrets. He worried that he would lose Bryan Democrats needed for reelection in 1916.

Wilson filled the State Department vacancy with a functionary, Robert Lansing, who had served as counselor under Bryan. Lansing's credentials were meager imagination, absence of political standing, deference to authority: the consummate cipher. Wilson became his own secretary of state. He dispensed altogether with State Department machinery in preference for other organized intelligence, instituted by the Inquiry's founding in September 1917.[69]

Released from cabinet constraints, Bryan attacked policies leading to war (even as detractors abused him for deserting Wilson in a delicate moment). He spoke publicly against the preparedness program. He praised Henry Ford's venture in December 1915 via the *Oscar II* peace ship to end hostilities by Christmas. He supported the February 1916 Gore–McLemore resolution in Congress, another stillborn initiative to prevent Americans from traveling on Allied ocean liners.[70] He inveighed against "warmongers" of the TR ilk. He assailed those financiers and "manipulators" of the public mind who "snickered" at Christian pacifism.[71]

Intervention

American neutrality snapped in 1917. Kaiser Wilhelm to break London's strangling blockade of German ports approved in January a resumption of unrestricted submarine warfare near the British Isles (and in the Mediterranean). Neutral ships would henceforth be targeted without reference to their civilian or military function if thought to aid the Allies. Wilson replied by measures barely shy of war. He severed relations with Berlin in early February 1917. Germany's ambassador, Johann von Bernstorff, received his passport, convinced that only by abandoning the submarine stratagem could war with the US be averted.[72] Ambassador Gerard left Berlin on February 10.

Wilson a short time later authorized armed neutrality: equipping civilian ships with guns and naval personnel. German submarines were not deterred, however. They sank the *Housatonic* in February. Five merchant ships went down in March: *Algonquin, City of Memphis, Vigilante, Illinois, Healdton.* Foreign Minister Zimmermann's wayward note meanwhile aggravated anti-German sentiment. Zimmermann hoped, if German–US squabbling culminated in war, to establish a partnership with Mexico and Japan against America. This alliance would stipulate German financial aid to Mexico and assist with recovery of territory lost in 1848: Texas, Arizona, New Mexico.[73]

Rage in Washington over Zimmermann, plus the submarine renewal, pushed Wilson on April 2 to seek a declaration of war. Victory should make the world "safe for democracy," he told Congress. In any case, American patience had been depleted as twenty-five US ships had been targeted by German/Austrian naval forces since 1914. More than 300 citizens had died aboard these or other vessels.[74] War would not restore the losses, but it would vindicate the rights of non-belligerents. Wilson stated sadly: "It is a fearful thing to lead this great peaceful people into war, into the most terrible and disastrous of all wars, civilization itself seeming to be in the balance."[75]

This reluctant interventionist believed that US participation in hostilities would give him broad influence in Europe's peace deliberations.[76] They could inaugurate a new order in which US political ideals – that he held were shared by all "forward-looking men and women" – would be everywhere adopted.[77] Progress would be ensured by establishing an association of peacefully inclined democratic states: "a concert of free peoples." Both congressional chambers approved Wilson's war request after short debate. The Senate voted for action against Germany by 82 to 6, the House by 373 to 50. Not until December did Congress declare war on Austria. The United States did not declare against Turkey (or Bulgaria). But diplomatic relations between Washington and Constantinople were suspended (April 20, 1917).

Recruitment, training, and transport of Pershing's troops took time. Their appearance in large numbers in battle occurred only during the last months of war, late May to November 11, 1918. Yet the doughboys' freshness and inexhaustible numbers lifted sagging Anglo-French morale. Pershing paid this tribute to the veterans of Château-Thierry, Belleau Wood, St. Mihiel, and Meuse-Argonne: "No commander was ever privileged to lead a finer force."[78]

Contra intervention

Wilson's catalogue of German turpitude included Wilhelm's misrule, which supposedly paid no heed to Berlin's subjects. But their "liberation," Wilson assured Congress, would eventuate with "the ultimate peace of the world." Until then they would live ignored by the conceited Kaiser and his circle of overbearing men bent on aggression. They smuggled agents into America to sabotage industry and subvert government, sought Mexican and Japanese confederates to ravage the United

States, and prosecuted war unlawfully by deliberately victimizing innocent citizens of neutral nations.[79] Wilson's litany did not, however, mention Turkey or Armenians, even as he proclaimed America champion of "the rights of mankind."[80]

Only a couple of pro-war congressmen alluded to the ongoing genocide. Senator Henry Myers (Democrat, Montana) spoke of "the unspeakable Turk who is a stench in the nostrils of the Christian nations"; he should be forced from the Holy Land and his remaining Balkan provinces. Senator John Sharp Williams (Democrat, Mississippi) reproached the Turks for "oppressing" Armenia.[81] But neither he nor Myers nor anyone else in Congress suggested that Wilson apply economic–diplomatic pressure on Constantinople. The house of Hohenzollern alone constituted the heart of darkness.

Congressional opponents of war were also mute on the subject of Armenia. They instead followed Bryan on the desirability of neutrality. They amplified upon his theme of a cabal of financiers, newspaper editors, industrialists, and military–naval enthusiasts. These schemers hungered for big profits and more power. Foremost among doves who leveled such charges were two Republican senators, Robert La Follette (Wisconsin) and George Norris (Nebraska).

They identified with the progressive wing of their party in wanting to abolish poverty and privilege. Both men were confident in the ability of ordinary folk to handle the business of self-government. Each senator, in his own way, had worked for years in support of female suffrage, conservation of natural resources, non-partisan civil service, regulation of business conglomerations, organized labor, and hard-pressed farmers. While governor of his state (1901–1906), La Follette had presided over a body of enlightened legislation: the "Wisconsin Idea." It involved direct primary elections, enhanced taxation of corporate wealth, and moderation of railroad rates. These and like programs made Wisconsin a model to American liberals. Civil rights for blacks and Indians also enjoyed La Follette's attention. Norris endorsed him in his 1912 bid for the presidency (before transferring allegiance to TR's Bull Moose campaign). Wilson's *New Freedom* won the respect of La Follette and Norris. They were the only Republican senators to back Wilson's appointment of Louis Brandeis (1916) to the Supreme Court, contra a drove of GOP partisans and anti-Semites.[82]

Insofar as La Follette and Norris followed diplomacy, they opposed a "large policy" orientation. They favored an end of US occupation in the Philippines. They objected to incursions into Mexico.[83] But not until April 1917 did the senators break cleanly with Wilson over an international question. To them the warring Europeans were morally equivalent.

Theirs was a clash of rapacious empires. Neither side had legitimate claim on US attention. Americans ought to adhere to Wilson's original neutral line. They should resist the call of jingoists and profiteers who sought gain with working-class lives while repudiating republican principles.

La Follette and Norris had, from the war's start, wanted to keep Americans off ships plying submarine infested waters. Both midwesterners too had led the campaign against armed neutrality, thereby earning Wilson's rancor: "willful men, representing no opinion but their own."[84] They doubted that public support ran hard for intervention in spring 1917. They called for a national referendum to determine whether the nation should go to war and predicted that voters by a margin of ten to one would indicate peace.[85]

Both senators gave fiery responses on April 4 in chambers to Wilson's war speech. Norris regretted the lending by US banks of hundreds of millions of dollars to the Anglo-French. Repayment of these loans, said he, could be assured only by Allied victory, hence the cooperation of finance captains with Wilson. Norris beat upon his theme: a "great combination of wealth ... has a direct financial interest in our participation in the war." He meant to expose Wall Street and its dissembling publicists:

The enormous amount of money loaned to the allies in this country has been instrumental in bringing about a public sentiment in favor of our country taking a course that would make every bond worth a hundred cents on the dollar and making the payment of every debt certain and sure. Through this instrumentality and also through the instrumentality of others who have not only made millions out of the war in the manufacture of munitions, etc., and who would expect to make millions more if our country can be drawn into the catastrophe, a large number of the great newspapers and news agencies of the country have been ... enlisted in the greatest propaganda that the world has ever known, to manufacture sentiment in favor of war. It is now demanded that the American citizens shall be used as insurance policies to guarantee the safe delivery of munitions of war to belligerent nations. The enormous profits of munitions manufacturers, stockbrokers, and bond dealers must be still further increased by our entrance into the war. This has brought us to the present moment, when Congress, urged by the President and backed by artificial sentiment, is about to declare war and engulf our country in the greatest holocaust that the world has ever known.[86]

Childhood poverty and wartime grief in Ohio colored Norris's class analysis (lean farm times, a brother killed in the Civil War). He skewered tycoons who, he submitted, drove the country toward conflict but in the event would stay safe: "They will be concealed in their palatial offices on Wall Street, sitting behind mahogany desks, covered up with clipped coupons – coupons soiled with the sweat of honest toil, coupons stained with mothers' tears, coupons dyed in the lifeblood of their fellow men."

Over hisses and hoots from Wilson backers, Norris drew this conclusion. The Senate had forfeited its faculties of mind to the mandate of wealth: "I wish we might delay our action until reason could again be enthroned in the brain of man. I feel that we are about to put the dollar sign upon the American flag."[87]

Once commotion on the floor subsided, La Follette spoke. He held forth for more than three hours. He joined Norris in defending in advance of their service those men destined to "rot in the trenches," drawn from the expendable poor.[88] La Follette also challenged Wilson's assumptions as they touched upon German criminality, Allied merit, and the roseate democratic future. With an eye to the record compiled by Germany's Social Democrats, he argued that Berlin did not resemble the despotism sketched by Wilson. In fact, La Follette lectured, solutions to municipal–social–industrial problems were further advanced in Germany than anywhere else. He also reminded his listeners that Britain fell short of democratic standards. A rigidly stratified society stifled the ambition of factory workers and their families. A monarchy and hereditary aristocracy mocked republican ideals. Ireland, Egypt, and India choked under British imperial bulk. Talk of home rule for these lands seldom surfaced in London. The United States by siding with Britain would acquiesce in its imperial pretensions. Even worse, the United States would be implicated in London's food blockade of Germany, "starving to death the old men and women, the children, the sick and the maimed."[89] The best course, La Follette advised, would be to avoid moral compromise. The United States should stay neutral toward a war that benefited a greedy few "wholly indifferent to the awful suffering" borne by "the masses."[90]

Other dissenters echoed the Norris–La Follette critique. Senator Asle Gronna (Republican, North Dakota) condemned the national pride that started the war, then prolonged it. In the House, the only woman in Congress, the just elected Jeannette Rankin (Republican, Montana) bespoke her love of America. Yet she detested the "commercial war." She also distrusted Wilson's high-pitched language and disbelieved Allied propaganda. Additionally, she felt obliged as a woman to take a stand against war as the negation of her sex. She explained years after casting her no ballot: "I felt at the time that the first woman [in Congress] should take the first stand, that the first time the first woman had a chance to say no to war she should say it."[91]

The immediate response in Congress to its antiwar minority signaled stormy times ahead for civility. Senator James Reed (Democrat, Missouri) revived the old vocabulary of betrayal, applied to dissenters from foreign wars since 1812. He said of Norris's speech: "If that be not treason it takes on a character and guise that is so near to treason that the enemies of America will gain from it much consolation."[92] Senator Ollie James (Democrat, Kentucky) insinuated that Norris would not object to placing a picture of the Kaiser on the US flag to complement the dollar sign. Mississippi's Williams also attacked Norris, but saved his main salvos for La Follette: "I heard from him a speech which was pro-German, pretty nearly pro-Goth, and pro-Vandal, which was anti-American President and anti-American Congress, and anti-American people. I heard his eulogy of the German Government."[93] Not even Chancellor Bethmann-Hollweg before the Reichstag would have gone so far to slander Americans or their political institutions, roared Williams. Other lawmakers agreed. Months later, with La Follette still faulting Wilson's war policy, Frank Kellogg (Republican, Minnesota) suggested that the dissenter henceforth refrain from defaming US leaders or helping German efforts. Senator Joseph Robinson (Democrat, Arkansas) concurred in October 1917 with those editorial writers who advised La Follette to abandon his Senate office and take a seat in the Reichstag. Therein he would find people of like mind: "If the Senator from Wisconsin had his will ... liberty would become a memory, honor a tradition, and tyranny the ruling power throughout this world."[94]

As for Rankin, some feminists were anguished. Might her antiwar stance damage their cause as she aligned with a dubious minority? Carrie Chapman Catt, head of the National American Woman Suffrage Association, thought that Rankin had set female suffrage back by decades.[95]

Vilification of dissenters intensified as military involvement deepened in Europe and George Creel's Committee on Public Information spun its stories of Teutonic bloodlust. Even Wilson, against his better angel, lent his prestige to people who condemned nonconformists as traitors or dupes. Passage of the Espionage Act in June 1917 led to the Justice Department's prosecuting 2,000 cases against persons who supposedly disrupted army recruitment or promoted mutiny within the armed services. Socialist and antiwar activist Eugene Debs received a ten-year sentence under the Act for labeling the war a capitalist crime. Justice Department agents in September 1917 ransacked offices of the anti-conscription Industrial Workers of the World (Wobblies). The 1918 Sedition Act further curtailed civil liberties. Academic freedoms were eroded at universities (most memorably at Columbia) where scholars against the war were muzzled or fired. The teaching of German literature and language was viewed askance, as were performances of German music (Bach, Beethoven, Brahms). In the language of Senator William Kenyon (Republican, Iowa): "It is a time for 100 percent Americanism."[96]

Norris and La Follette remained inviting targets in this delirious environment. They were snubbed socially, even on Washington trolley cars where riders vacated the premises after the senators boarded. They were elsewhere jeered as pro-German obstructionists and threatened with bodily harm. They were hanged in effigy. Political cartoonists depicted them receiving the Iron Cross from Wilhem for service to the Fatherland. They were scrutinized by federal agents – to the point of snooping into family origins, partly German in the case of Norris.[97]

A movement led by Kellogg, seconded by TR and William Howard Taft, got under way to expel La Follette from the Senate, where an investigating committee examined his antiwar motivations. He should be arrested in accordance with the Espionage Act, critics proposed. All but two of the 420 professors at La Follette's alma mater, the University of Wisconsin, signed a petition that expressed sorrow over his public utterances to fortify German morale. The Wisconsin legislature judged him guilty of sedition, as did Wilson. He also wondered whether German-American voters in Wisconsin (30 percent of the state total) exercised baleful influence on the senator.[98]

These aspersions rattled Norris and La Follette. Rankin ducked zanier ridicule only because of her newcomer status in Washington and unwillingness of most congressmen to be ungallant toward a lady, however misguided her opinions.[99]

Norris contemplated retiring from public life or joining the Marines in France.[100] La Follette spent more time away from Congress in 1918 than normal (to nurse his ill son, Bobbie). Rankin buried herself in matters related to suffrage and children's welfare. These legislators meanwhile supported most measures before Congress pursuant to winning the war: bond drives; bills for military training, ammunition, equipment; allocations for building ships; aviation appropriations. But at no time were the three lawmakers dissuaded of the wisdom of their original stand. Nor, despite temptations of escape into sundry tasks, did the dissenters lose their critical edge. They invoked the rights of political minorities to voice disagreement in which connection La Follette cited Lincoln/Webster against the Mexican war. He also fired: "More than in times of peace it is necessary that the channels for free public discussion of government policies shall be open and unclogged."[101] He, Norris, and Rankin opposed the Espionage and Sedition Acts, which proved more detrimental to domestic freedom than useful against German infiltration.[102] Norris busied himself with disproving tales concerning German infamy: food products laced with broken glass, American POWs tortured. Rankin tended to the feminist faith that women in power would one day rid all nations of war: "Peace is woman's job."[103]

La Follette was the most defiant. He opposed conscription, unless approved in a national referendum. He worked to protect harassed conscientious objectors. He sought pardon for Debs, who praised him as an honest citizen hounded by lawless officials and "their prostitute press." La Follette tried to prod Congress to define US war aims in preference to those outlined by the "Wilsonian autocracy". He wanted to tax profits of corporations that made military hardware by 80 percent to defray government costs and check "war millionaires." He objected to armed intervention in Russia in 1918, where he imagined Bolsheviks strove on behalf of the martyred proletariat.[104]

La Follette outlasted all attempts to eject him from Congress. He also brought libel suits against besmirchers of his patriotism. He congratulated himself in 1922 with this vindication, in his mind equally applicable to Norris and Rankin: "I would be remembered as one who, in the world's darkest hour, kept a [clear] conscience and stood in the end for the ideals of the American [republic]."[105]

La Follette and Norris savored a bit of retribution soon after the November 1918 armistice. They helped block Senate ratification of Wilson's Versailles treaty, a turnabout for men almost politically extinguished in 1917–1918.

Peace treaty

The Versailles peace treaty of June 1919 was harder than Wilson desired, who had previously spoken on the need to safeguard "all the [world's] peoples."[106] Germany was yoked with blame for the war. Prohibitions on the size of German armed forces were imposed, along with reduction of territory, demilitarization and Allied occupation of the Rhineland, payment of reparations (finally placed at $33 billion), and Berlin was stripped of colonial holdings.[107] Shaped by France's Georges Clemenceau, and supported by Britain's David Lloyd George, these provisions were meant to prevent Germany from again acquiring power to endanger Anglo-French security. Only Wilson's counterbalance in Paris thwarted the Anglo-French leaders from implementing more draconian designs. Even so, moderate-minded Britons and Americans were livid with Wilson for what they perceived as his recreance. John Hobson, John Maynard Keynes, Walter Lippmann, Harold Nicolson, and Thorstein Veblen were among the disillusioned. They called the treaty's guilt clause gratuitous, the reparations onerous, and the League of Nations an attempt to revive Holy Alliance reaction.[108]

Wilson accepted the treaty despite its deficiencies. These could be borne, he occasionally ventured, by the demands of righteousness: "[Versailles] is a very severe settlement with Germany, but there is not anything in it that she did not earn."[109] He anyway trusted that the treaty would be modified over time in a liberal direction. And he placed much faith in the League of Nations, its covenant sewn into the first part of treaty text. He expected that this organization by its deliberations and timely actions would prevent cataclysms on the scale of 1914.[110]

Wilson's conception of a resilient peace lived in article 10 of the League Covenant and implied far-reaching concert against future troublemakers: "The Members of the League undertake to respect and preserve as against external aggression the territorial integrity and existing political independence of all Members of the League."[111] Proponents of the League originally included most leading Anglo-American personalities, such as Taft and London's former foreign minister, Sir Edward Grey. Jane Addams of the Women's Peace Party, plus pacifist and feminist associations in America and Britain, likewise supported institutionalized cooperation among nations.

Before America even entered the Great War, Wilson publicly praised the idea of diplomatically inclined states acting together, an exercise in which Washington should partake. The balance-of-power system ought also to cease, its purported worth thoroughly discredited in 1914; only an association of pooled power could sustain peace.[112] Wilson had delighted audiences when he addressed the League to Enforce Peace along such lines in May 1916. By the time he elaborated upon them to the Senate in January 1917, he had decided to Americanize the internationalist framework. It required this twist to a venerable notion: "The nations should with one accord adopt the doctrine of President Monroe as the doctrine of the world: that no nation should seek to extend its polity over any other nation or people, but that every people should be left free to determine its own polity, its own way of development, unhindered, unthreatened, unafraid, the little along with the great and powerful."[113] Insofar, then, as the world adopted US principles and practices, it could be rescued from the abyss into which it had stumbled.

Wilson assumed that US participation in the League would provide leadership and foster policies harmonious with order. New World involvement *ipso facto* should also reassure pundits who worried that the League would become an engine to uphold an iniquitous settlement.[114]

While Wilson dreamed in 1919 of guiding the nations "into pastures of quietness and peace such as the world never [imagined] before," dissenters got ready.[115] They wanted to rethink the treaty and to qualify, or if need be bar, US membership in the League. Subsequent Senate refusal to ratify Versailles struck Wilson as myopic, consigning unborn generations of Americans to obliterating violence.[116]

Against Versailles

Senator Lodge doubted the efficacy of international institutions to achieve anything, let alone give substance to humanity's ancient wish for lasting peace. A modestly defined league of nations, he conceded in 1915, might in conjunction with other instruments – law, treaties, arbitration – soften the jagged edge of foreign affairs. But his underlying viewpoint was akin to Pershing's realism. Perpetual peace lived in a mythical future. Utopian yearnings ought not divert statesmen from the primacy of force in the interaction of nations, a regrettable but incontrovertible fact of life. The United States must cultivate its own resources to preserve safety. To confuse fond hopes with practical policy was delusion: "We must deal with things as they are."[117] Realization of Wilson's League also seemed inimical to US sovereignty. League interests and policies might not always correspond with those of Americans, but they would as League subjects have to accommodate themselves, perhaps with contributions of naval–military forces and funds. Lodge believed by late November 1918, as Wilson prepared for Paris, that the League idea had become "one very dangerous thing."[118]

Senate debates in 1919–1920 over the Versailles treaty drew heat from the storied Wilson–Lodge antagonism. Both men were de facto heads of their respective political parties, Lodge being not only chairman of the Senate Foreign Relations Committee but also majority leader in the upper house (where Republicans had slight advantage of 49 to 47 Democrats). He wanted the GOP's dignity to be felt – its leaders and experts having been banished from Paris negotiations, and then consulted only perfunctorily by the White House. As leader of the legislative branch, Lodge also wanted to reassert Congress's prerogatives in making foreign policy, eclipsed by Wilson's domineering executive style in wartime. Aggravating matters, both men seldom credited a political adversary with acting in good faith. Philosophically, they were also opposite. Wilson possessed a generous faith in human ability to fashion an improved future. Lodge, by contrast, was impressed by human fallibility and the record of follies perpetrated on behalf of lofty cause. He explained in 1917 with a view to the law of unintended consequences: "I do not wish to plunge blindly forward, misled by phrases and generalities, into undertakings which threaten worse results than the imperfect conditions now existing."[119] As for Washington's international role, he believed that the US experience could not be universalized. America as salutary example of order and lawfulness made sense to him, not global crusading.[120]

Lesser differences played a part too. The Dixie-born president romanticized the gallantry of the Confederacy. He cherished the "Lost Cause."

The Massachusetts patrician sprang from a family that opposed slavery. Of Southern vanquishment, he once testified: "The war was fought to save the Union, but it was slavery which had put the Union in peril. Slavery was a crime against humanity."[121] Even a shared passion for scholarship subtly separated Wilson and Lodge along the methodological lines of their academic disciplines. The latter, a trained historian (Harvard Ph.D.), did not live long enough to see the scientism or abstruseness that captured much American political science in the twentieth century. But Wilson's sweeping commentary, fed by his belief in political science as the "synthesizing discipline," came at the expense of a historian's penchant for specificity.[122] Wilson, once head of the American Political Science Association and a founder of the discipline (Johns Hopkins Ph.D.), simply annoyed Lodge. He leaned toward the particularity of events, theoretical caution, and reluctance to generalize. Of Wilson's League outline, he said: "This is a matter which cannot be determined by ... adherence to a general principle. Everything here depends upon the details."[123]

Lodge's original preference had been for Wilson to present the Senate with two distinct propositions, one to end hostilities with Germany, the other League-centered. The German and League matters, to the senator's mind, were conceptually unrelated; they should be treated according to their separate merits. Melding the two questions invited confusion bound to mask the League's defects and lower public vigilance against fine sounding but dangerous beguilement. But at Wilson's behest, the Senate had to pass verdict on the entire German–League packet as approved in Paris. The German provisions did not bother Lodge. If anything, he sought sterner treatment of the enemy plus a Franco-US arrangement to preempt German resurgence. His chief worry concerned the League.[124]

He and fellow skeptics developed fourteen reservations (amendments) that required incorporation into the treaty. Otherwise these "strong" reservationists, mostly Republicans, would oppose ratification. The proposed improvements as evolved by late 1919 aimed to make membership in the League compatible with national security while reaffirming Congress's part in formulating external policy. Among Lodge's points were these: Only Congress, charged with sole power under the Constitution to declare war or authorize force, could decide whether to deploy US military and naval units in support of League actions via article 10. Only if Congress agreed would the United States accept responsibility for a League of Nations mandate. Only Congress could determine the level of US financial contributions to the League. Only people approved by the Senate would be authorized to represent the United States in League agencies and deliberations. Additional Lodge revisions reserved for Washington exclusive rights to decide questions of US domestic jurisdiction. The United States would brook no League interference in the functioning of the Monroe Doctrine; its interpretation should remain exclusively in Washington's provenance. The United States rejected the treaty's Shantung (Shandong) articles that transferred Germany's concession to Japan instead of returning the territory to China. Congress retained the right to determine the amount of spending on armaments in times of danger irrespective of League decrees that generally applied. Washington would not recognize the authority of any League vote in which a power cast more than one ballot "in the aggregate" by imperial proxies – i.e. Britain operating through Canada, New Zealand, Australia, South Africa.[125]

None of these or other adjustments were treaty killers, not individually or collectively. Yet Lodge hoped through them and lengthy hearings by the Senate Foreign Relations Committee (begun in summer 1919) to peck the treaty apart.[126] This approach contrasted with that of two other Senate groups: the "mild" reservationists, the "irreconcilables." The former, led by Kellogg and Irvine Lenroot (Republican, Wisconsin), sought treaty ratification. Their tinkering and emendations were meant to polish and ensure the treaty's passage. They worked constructively with the president's men, notably the Senate minority leader Gilbert Hitchcock (Democrat, Nebraska).[127]

Lodge's apparent willingness, at least in public, to allow some sort of League dissatisfied Versailles's militant opponents. The "irreconcilables" functioned as allies to the "strong" reservationists, sometimes tacitly, other times explicitly. The "irreconcilables" (known too as "bitterenders") occasionally doubted the steadfastness of Lodge. But they also recognized his indispensability in checking the treaty. The irreconcilables' tactics and temperament constituted the main difference from Lodge. He wanted to educate the popular mind about the treaty's shortcomings, an exercise that required a purchase of time, hence summer hearings to study the Paris results. Against this stratagem, the "irreconcilables" (14 Republicans, 2 Democrats) favored a frontal assault. They had no patience with prolonged debate. They had not a scintilla of confidence in the Versailles procedures: they had made a mash of Europe, fattened the Anglo-French empires, served the ambitions of unscrupulous bankers, and tightened existing bonds on colonized peoples. The League aimed to uphold an indefensible status quo. La Follette declaimed in November 1919:

The little group of men who sat in secret conclave for months at Versailles were not peacemakers. They were war makers. They cut and slashed the map of the old world in violation of the terms of the armistice. They patched up a new map of the old in consummation of the terms of the secret treaties the existence of which they had denied because they feared to expose the sordid aims and purposes for which men were sent to death by the tens of thousands daily. They betrayed China. They locked the chains on the subject peoples of Ireland, Egypt, and India. They partitioned territory and traded off peoples in mockery of that sanctified formula of the 14 points, and made it our Nation's shame. Then, fearing the wrath of outraged peoples, knowing that their new map would be torn to rags and tatters by the conflicting, warring elements which they had bound together in wanton disregard of racial animosities, they make a league of nations to stand guard over the swag![128]

La Follette could not head the "irreconcilable" bloc. His pariah status since April 1917 disqualified him. His statements on German suffering right after the war placed him further beyond respectability.[129] The other two "irreconcilables" unsuited to lead, by virtue of having voted against Wilson's war, were Gronna and Norris. They perforce demurred to the untainted in 1919–1920. Hiram Johnson (Republican, California) played a part, condemning the League as a "gigantic war trust."[130] But principal leadership fell to progressive William Borah (Republican, Idaho), a flamboyant character who had unhesitatingly supported Wilson's war call. He later recanted and watched with trepidation as civil liberties crumbled. He once suggested that the Espionage Act plus conscription equaled Prussian victories over America.[131]

Borah enjoyed cordial relations with Republicans and Democrats alike. His warmth charmed even Wilson, otherwise disinclined to forgive enemies of his League. Borah had nothing of Lodge's vanity or Svengalian slyness. He remained on civil terms with Versailles adherents. Personal decency did not inhibit him from waging a sharp campaign, however: "If the Savior of mankind would revisit the earth and declare for a League ... I would be opposed to it."[132] He stumped midwestern cities (Chicago, Des Moines, St. Louis, Omaha) in September to denounce the League plan. The United States must not take upon itself the protection of Britain's far-flung empire. The United States should not internationalize its manpower and economy or place them at the disposal of foreigners. The United States must not permit Europeans or Japanese to pursue selfish ends in the New World under the aegis of a putative peace-promoting League. Above all, Americans must retain faith in their way of life and not invest in an untested association of states. Nothing about it suggested genuine hopefulness for an unhappy world. Borah's core message was that an unencumbered United States stood as the single reliable bulwark against postwar revolutions and economic turbulence. He asked fellow senators:

How shall we help to bring order out of chaos? Shall we do so by becoming less or more American? Shall we entangle and embarrass the efforts of a powerful and independent people, or shall we leave them in every emergency and in every crisis to do in that particular hour and in that supreme moment what the conscience and wisdom of an untrammeled and liberty-loving people shall decide is wise and just? Or shall we [tie] our deliberations to forces we can not control and leave our people to the mercy of powers which may be wholly at variance with our conception of duty?[133]

Borah answered that cooperation with other nations and lending them aid on a per need basis was sensible. But that did not mean permanent alliance or an end to autonomy.[134] He also let fly that any substitution of League guidance for the wisdom of Congress or the citizenry would destroy republican life and Washington's autonomy:

I do not want this Republic . . . to go into partnership with and to give control of the partnership to those many of whom have no conception of our civilization and no true insight into our destiny. What we want is . . . a free, untrammeled Nation, imbued anew and inspired again with the national spirit; not isolation but simply the unembarrassed and unentangled freedom of a great Nation to determine for itself and in its own way where duty lies and where wisdom calls . . . The moment this Republic comes to any other conclusion it has forfeited its right to live as an independent and self-respecting Republic.[135]

To Wilson the League came as close as any political instrument could to effecting human salvation. His tenacity in trying to secure US membership presaged tragedy. A physically unwell man after his Paris toils, plus emotionally brittle, he ruined what remained of his health in the struggle for treaty ratification.[136] His September 1919 tour of hinterland cities to rally popular support for the League ended in severe stroke. Compromise, never his forte, discretion, and balanced judgment were thereafter nearly impossible for him to muster. The urgings of his wife, Edith Bolling Galt, to find common ground with the reservationists to establish a League were unavailing as was similar counsel from Grey, Bryan, Lansing, Colonel House, Hitchcock, et al. Bereft of close colleagues in 1919–1920, underscored by estrangement from House, the lonesome president blundered forward. He did not recognize gradations of opposition among treaty critics but lumped them together, damning the lot as Anglophobes, German sympathizers, and pro-Bolshevik louts.[137] Wilson loyalists, taking their cues from him, also became shrill. Mississippi's Williams charged that Borah's hostility to the League sprang from a preference for the ways of tooth and claw. Other hyperbole likened a rejection of the treaty to wickedness unsurpassed since Christ's crucifixion.[138]

Wilson ordered Hitchcock and Democrats not to pass any version of the Paris treaty amended by Lodge and company. Consequently, the president's men voted (November 19, 1919) against the treaty with its Lodge revisions. The "irreconcilables," eschewing League membership under any circumstance, joined these Democrats to defeat the Lodge-altered treaty, 55 to 39. The treaty without amendments was then defeated by a "strong" reservationist/"irreconcilable" combination, 53 against to 38 in support. A second vote (March 19, 1920) produced another Democratic/"irreconcilable" coalition, the president still adamant against Lodge's handiwork. This time the pro-Lodge senators won a majority, 49 to 35, but below the two-thirds needed for treaty approval.

Ailing and desperate, Wilson next placed his hopes in the 1920 presidential election (in which he briefly considered running). He portrayed it as a referendum on the League. The balloting, however, resulted in a landslide victory for the GOP's affable Senator Warren G. Harding (Ohio). He outdistanced his Democratic rival, Governor James Cox (Ohio), by 7 million votes. The electoral college count was equally telling: 404 for Harding, 127 for Cox. Harding proved a mediocrity in office, uninterested in Wilson's international project, eager only to return the country to "normalcy." A saturnalia of corruption ensued. It culminated in the Teapot Dome oil scandal. Not until 1921 did the United States officially end hostilities with Germany by signing an accord separate from Versailles.

Lodge gloated over the collapse of Wilson's treaty. He placed all blame on the president. He was, said the senator, unable because of egotism and obstinacy to cooperate with Congress in creating a better world. Lodge charged that the president's personal flaws had conspired to block America's League membership:

He was given the greatest opportunity ever given to any public man in modern times ... Having this opportunity he tried to use it and failed. The failure necessarily equaled the opportunity in magnitude and the failure was complete and was all his own. No one could have destroyed such a vast opportunity except the man to whom it was given, and in this work of destruction unaided and alone Mr. Wilson was entirely successful.[139]

***

The United States emerged from the Great War as an economic giant with corresponding political influence. The country had lost its debtor status to become the world's premier creditor. American soldiers had performed skillfully. They made themselves for a fleeting but critical moment a military power on the European continent. The contrast between US strength and prosperity versus European need was confirmed in the postwar activity of Hoover's American Relief Administration. It distributed food, medicines, and clothing on unprecedented scale, particularly in the famine districts of civil war Russia. Millions of people were saved. This aid gave tangibility to Wilson's words in 1919, "the American spirit" had "made conquest of the world."[140]

Wilson to achieve this "conquest" had led his country into an optional war. Prohibitions on civilian travel through naval war zones would not have blemished national honor or undercut US rights and would have bolstered neutrality. But he rejected the counsel of Bryan, La Follette, Norris, and others. Wilson also willfully ignored the indiscriminate quality of Britain's food blockade (which operated past the date of armistice to fan German resentments). It made no more distinction between combatant and non-combatant, between legitimate target and inappropriate, than German submarines.

Professedly fought to advance world democracy, the war bred intolerance in America, as La Follette and Norris foresaw.[141] The progressive cause that Wilson had earlier pushed got stymied. The rollback of legal protections and due process continued after hostilities to abet an insurgency against civil liberties: "Red Scare," Attorney General Palmer's extremism. Vigilantism and anti-black pogroms nearly unhinged Dixie.[142]

The League of Nations was not the construct of Immanuel Kant or other idealists. It was enmeshed in a design concocted by an implacable Clemenceau, slippery Lloyd George, and maladroit Wilson. Dissenters properly challenged it. The League and treaty might have been usefully modified had Wilson possessed in 1919–1920 enough political acumen to succeed in a brawling republic. His poor health plus Lodge's uncooperative maneuverings dashed ratification.

The basic question for war objectors/treaty critics versus Wilson resided in rival concepts of America's international role. He upheld the idea of US activism whose expansiveness grew naturally from rescuing downtrodden Cubans in 1898 to helping Europe convalesce. The "little Americans," an epithet that amused Borah, wanted stricter boundaries consistent with nationalist and republican traditions: the United States should limit military commitments to New World zones, husband resources, and concentrate on mending social–political ills at home. Ad hoc cooperation with one or more European powers might occasionally do. Entanglement with Versailles would not, nor would a repeat of 1917.

A decade after US intervention, Norris stated: "The result of this great war was a defeat for everybody."[143]

However plausible the dissenters of 1917 or 1919–1920, their objections did not constitute eternal or immutable laws of statesmanship. The vocabulary and mentality right for La Follette's era were wrong for the next. The disastrous turns of international life in the thirties made nonsense of the 1935 Neutrality Act (thrice renewed), passed by a Congress that rued its 1917 decision. Axis aggression made voting against going to war in December 1941 also insupportable, although Rankin did. A member again of the House of Representatives, she opposed action congruent with her 1917 stance: "As a woman I can't go to war, and I refuse to send anyone else." She believed that cunning Britain had a second time inveigled Americans into fighting a futile war.[144]

Rankin's pacific sentiments struck Norris as good in principle, but inapplicable after damages to Hawaii's naval–military installations. He voted for war in December 1941. He did not doubt the imminence of Axis danger in contradistinction to that posed by Germany in 1917:

In 1917 there was no immediate threat of war reaching American soil. In 1941 an act of war was committed by Japan against the United States at Pearl Harbor under the most treacherous ... circumstances, and the following day Germany and Italy issued declarations of war against the American people ... the Axis plan of aggression and conquest in my eyes constituted a direct threat.[145]

Even clear-eyed Norris did not entirely grasp the radical nature of Axis challenge. Exterminations by late 1941 were making Asia and Europe into charnel houses – Armenia redux.

The Ottoman war against Armenians presented a dilemma to US statecraft unconnected with whether to retaliate against Germany in 1917 for its foolhardy submarine policy. Wilson needed prodding on this score, Morgenthau realized. To this end, he risked disavowal by authorities in Washington – distracted by problems centered on Berlin – or expulsion by irate Turks. The latter had the full weight of international custom on their side: a resident diplomat does not ask nosy questions about the domestic affairs of his hosts or interfere.

Violation of this convention in US diplomatic practice has rarely occurred, even in circumstances comparable to those faced by Morgenthau. Ambassador William Dodd, for example, posted to Berlin in 1933–1937, regretted Nazi persecution of German Jews. Incarcerations, loss of livelihoods, confiscation of property, humiliations, and murders not only prefigured the Shoah. They also constituted an ongoing assault on conscience. Dodd felt too constrained to say or do much, however.

He repeatedly reminded supplicants: "I have no authority to approach any German official about such [matters]."[146] George Kennan felt likewise while on the legation staff in Prague in March 1939. He and colleagues chose not to antagonize Czechoslovakia's new German governors by sheltering Jewish acquaintances or other asylum seekers. Nor did he inconvenience the routine of his household by hiding persons hounded by Nazi agents.[147]

Obedience to diplomatic norms in anguished times does not condemn Dodd or Kennan. But it does put in vivid relief the imagination and courage of Morgenthau. He belonged to an outstanding breed (as did Leslie Davis for converting his home into an Armenian haven). It includes Sweden's Raoul Wallenberg. From a legalistic standpoint, he too abused his diplomatic position by aiding thousands of Jews in Nazi-occupied Hungary. Selahattin Ulkumen, Turkey's consul general on Rhodes in 1944, also belongs to the category of diplomat-as-cosmopolitan hero. He protested to the island's German commander against the impending deportation of resident Jews. Ulkumen also granted Turkish exit visas to hunted Jews. Forty-two Jewish families consequently survived. German armed forces later struck back. They bombed his house and fatally wounded his pregnant wife. Ulkumen recalled years afterward: "All I did was carry out my duty as a human being."[148] So too Morgenthau.

Armenian genocide helped ease the way for Germany's later murder of Europe's Jews. Hitler felt that he could succeed in this extermination without arousing much protest. Few public leaders, after all, had gotten excited at the moment of Armenian crisis. Western steps taken to ameliorate Armenian plight came after the slaughter. They anyway did not uphold the independence of a short-lived independent Armenia (1918–1920) or bring justice to most perpetrators of crime.[149] Hitler asked in 1939 while anticipating the destruction of Jews, Poland, and other targets: "Who ... speaks today of the annihilation of the Armenians?"[150]

Franz Werfel published *The Forty Days of Musa Dagh* six years before Hitler raised his cynical question. This historical novel by a German Jew depicted Armenian suffering as "extirpation" of a race. *Forty Days* attracted audiences throughout the Third Reich in 1933. Morgenthau plus various Europeans, especially German missionaries, who tried to slow or stop the killing were sympathetically portrayed. The book also contained subversive teaching. Werfel had his Dr. Johannes Lepsius, a Protestant pastor, say to Enver: "If my government ... behaved unjustly, unlawfully, inhumanely ... to our fellow countrymen of a different race, a different persuasion, I should clear out of Germany at once and go to America."[151] Hitler banned the book.

Just as Werfel's novel was drawing popular attention and Nazi censors, the Armenian poet, Vahan Tekeyan, wrote of his desolated homeland: "Any shock can erase you and no eye will even blink."[152] Menace of oblivion similarly approached European Jewry, though its precariousness seemed less obvious in 1933.

10 Axis

A group of eminent thinkers, Americans plus exiles in the United States, professed faith in November 1940 that the human future held promise of affirmative meaning. The Protestant theologian Reinhold Niebuhr and Nobel laureate Thomas Mann were among those who asserted in manifesto – *The City of Man* – that a transcendent purpose informed human affairs. It would ultimately prevail. It would enthrone mercy with justice. Bigotry, persecutions, and totalitarian audacity would fail. People of goodwill to hasten this end had to act in ecumenical concert:

> A divine intention governs the universe – be it called God or Deity or the Holy Ghost or the Absolute or Logos or even Evolution. The direction of this intention is from matter to life and from life to spirit, from chaos to order, from blind strife and random impulse to conscience and moral law, from darkness to light ... Man's growth or progress or evolution is not backward toward the savagery of the superman or the gleam of the beast of prey, but forward toward the radiance of the angel ... The pursuit of the good, under the inspiration of faith, hope, and charity, must imply resistance to evil, with battle when necessary.[1]

This statement entailed a measure of daring by its authors. They wrote to support an unpopular position in 1940 America: military intervention in the unfolding war.

Apart from advancing a minority view, *The City of Man* contained a second eccentricity. Axis power contradicted the signatories' underlying optimism, evidenced since the mid-1930s as Nazi Germany, fascist Italy, and militaristic Japan rearranged the distribution of power. The new configuration vindicated their opposition to the Versailles status quo and validated their wisdom of partnership, formalized in the Tripartite Pact (September 27, 1940).

Japanese aggressors under its protective cover continued to maul China. They had earlier won (1931–1932) a rich province at China's expense, nominally sovereign Manchukuo, presided over by the pitiable Emperor Pu-Yi. They began an undeclared war against China in summer 1937 to add more territory to imperial holdings. The fighting blighted rural districts. It ruined cities. It bled China and crippled the nation's economy. Tokyo expansionists in 1940 also pushed into French Indochina. They looked covetously even further afield: Burma, Dutch East Indies, Malaya, Philippines.

Axis fortunes in Europe soared too as German diplomacy in 1939 soothed Soviet unease via accommodation, the non-aggression deal with secret protocols. It allowed Hitler's armies to master the continent practically unmolested, from Poland to the English Channel plus Scandinavia. Vaulting German armies humbled France in June 1940. Thereafter air bombardment and threat of invasion put ebbing British power in check.

Interventionist ambassadors

Japanese brutality in China appalled Americans. They honored its Generalissimo Chiang Kai-shek (Jiang Jie-shi), designated by *Time* magazine as man of the year in 1938. They resented Tokyo's vow to expel white nations from Asia per the "Greater Co-Prosperity Sphere." The blitzkrieg in Europe also unsettled Americans. They regretted French defeat. They reproved Vichy compliance.[2] Most hoped for British victory. Even the USSR, Hitler's one-time collaborator and violator of plucky Finland, became an object of favorable attention in summer 1941 when German armies struck.[3]

Yet the majority of citizens, high and low, prayed that Washington had learned the "lessons" of 1917. They taught war's futility. Tendentious scholarship by historians – Harry Barnes, Charles Beard, Sidney Fay, Walter Millis – reinforced pacific preferences. Popular literature echoed them, as in *Merchants of Death* (1934) by Helmuth Englebrecht or Dalton Trumbo's *Johnny Got His Gun* (1939). Congressional investigation led by Senator Gerald Nye (Republican, North Dakota) dignified such sentiments when it delved into the purported deviousness of financiers and weapons manufacturers in 1917. Nye proclaimed them guilty of exerting foul influence on US foreign policy. Congress should spare the country another involvement in European hostilities, hence the Neutrality Acts.[4] They stipulated restrictions on sale of arms and delivery by US ships to warring states, banned maritime travel in combat zones, and disallowed loans to belligerents.

This desire to avoid conflict stemmed not only from revulsion with the Great War. Dismay also shaped isolationism as world institutions crumbled (League of Nations, Kellogg–Briand outlawry of war) and the status quo powers (France, Britain) cringed before Axis swagger. Japanese trespass against China, Mussolini's Abyssinian campaign, German–Italian intervention in Spain's civil war, and Czechoslovakia betrayed at Munich belied Wilson's promise: the exertions of 1917 would end wars, a semblance of decency could take root among nations. Dreary events, combined with economic malaise, ameliorated but not remedied by the New Deal, inclined Americans to shelter behind their Atlantic and Pacific buffers. They could presumably deflect war while Washington and the commercial class revived the stagnant economy. Franklin Roosevelt in 1940 endorsed Congress's latest neutrality act. He also spoke eloquently that year in his reelection bid against sending youths abroad to fight for causes remote to America.[5]

Privately, however, after France fell, FDR sensed that only direct US action against Axis power would defeat it. Otherwise, the balance of power in Europe, so too Asia, would further disintegrate with dire consequences for US safety. He consequently sought to position America against the Axis while shoring up Allied strength. He maneuvered cautiously to this end, lest he solidify against himself the varied objections of skeptics. They ranged from isolationists in his own Democratic party, to socialist Norman Thomas, to congressional partisans such as Senator Robert Taft (Republican, Ohio), to the aviator Charles Lindbergh and the America First Committee.

Roosevelt sent a budget to Congress in January 1940 that included nearly $2 billion for defense spending. He asked for more defense appropriations in the spring with specific reference to increasing aircraft and warship production, the latter to ensure a "two-ocean navy." He established the Office for Emergency Management. He got the War Department to sell surplus arms and munitions to Britain. He organized a joint Canada–US board of defense. He boosted defense solidarity with Latin America. He inaugurated conscription. He embargoed the export of scrap metal to Japan (plus elsewhere). After the November election gave him an unprecedented third presidential term, FDR announced that the United States must become the world's "arsenal of democracy."

These initiatives, albeit welcome, were insufficient to reverse the avalanche of international misfortune, so said two of Roosevelt's abler diplomats: Nelson Johnson in China, William Bullitt in France. Neither the language of these ambassadors nor their philosophical outlook matched that in *The City of Man*. Both men embraced its urgency, however, tangibly greater than that of FDR whom they tried to spur into bolder action.

China

The Second World War commenced not in Europe in 1939 but in China, early July 1937. Sino-Japanese skirmishing at the Marco Polo Bridge, located on the outskirts of Peking (Beijing), triggered vast violence.

Chiang could not launch major offensives, constrained as he was by an ineffectual officer corps, poorly trained soldiers, and inadequate *matériel*. The intrigues of erstwhile communist allies under Mao Tse-tung (Mao Zedong) also distracted him. Still, Chiang hoped by a war of attrition to grind down Japanese esprit and strength. This stratagem relied upon China's bountiful space and population to consume well equipped Imperial armies (eventually more than a million troops). This contest between politically divided China, additionally hobbled by industrial incapacity and technological impoverishment, versus Japanese dynamism resulted in roughly 20 million Chinese fatalities in 1937–1945, the majority civilian.[6]

Chiang's forces forfeited Peking and Shanghai during the first phase of warfare. Japanese units in December 1937 captured the capital, Nanking (Nanjing), on the southern banks of the Yangtze. An orgy ensued of rape and murder – roughly 300,000 Chinese perished in a matter of weeks. Johnson wrote to the State Department: "Never again … will a Japanese be able to hold his head high in pride when the story of Nanking is told."[7] Chiang's westward retreat stopped first at Wuhan, then at the desolate city of Chungking (Chongqing). It remained the capital of unoccupied China for the duration of hostilities. The city withstood Japanese aerial assaults. It suffered varieties of pestilence and privation. The government in Tokyo by autumn 1941, headed by General Tojo Hideki, controlled China's coastal fringe, occupied a third of the country's territory, and policed 40 percent of the population.[8]

Ambassador Johnson and entourage accompanied Chiang's fleeing government on its long trek from Nanking. He installed himself in Chungking, where the dilapidated buildings that served as makeshift embassy and staff housing were as vulnerable as any in the city. His own residence barely escaped destruction by Japanese bombing. Incessant hardships and air raids drained him. "Whatever one may feel about his own safety," Johnson reported, "it is a terrible ordeal just to have to sit helplessly by and watch men, women, and children killed in cold blood by these cowards of the sky who float in safety high in the air dropping their death where they will."[9] He gratefully left for new assignment in Australia in mid-May 1941.[10] He had served by that time for eleven years as head of mission in China, a length of assignment with few rivals in US diplomatic history.[11]

He began his China service in 1907 as a youngster (b. 1887). He translated for the austere US emissary, William Woodville Rockhill.[12] Johnson became fluent in Chinese, although his mastery of reading and writing was less proficient. He also avidly studied Asian affairs and Chinese politics. Gregarious, intellectually engaged, and democratic, he had a genius for friendship. Chinese officials warmed to him as did his associates in the Foreign Service. His early China stints included consul work in Mukden, Harbin, and Chungking plus assessor to the Mixed Court in Shanghai. Rotated back to Washington in 1918, he next served in the State Department's Division of Far Eastern Affairs. He became its head in 1925, by which time he had earned recognition as one of his generation's best Sinologists. Two years later he was named assistant secretary of state with East Asia portfolio. He served in that capacity until returned to China as chief of mission.[13]

Johnson over the years of his Chinese residence became enamored of the country's ancient culture. He also hoped for Chiang's triumph against warlords, communists, and predator powers (primarily Japan, USSR). He thought that China at some point in the future would assume a significant world role. But until then the fragile Chinese state would have to suffer gangsters, domestic and foreign. American governments, he taught, had to bolster as best they could whatever passed for central-ized Chinese authority. By so doing, Washington would preserve its commercial–missionary interests in China and contribute to a viable East Asian balance of power. The latter had overriding importance for Johnson as the best guarantor of America's diplomatic–economic posi-tion and Pacific holdings.[14]

A geopolitical orientation, leavened by attachment to things Chinese, thus stamped Johnson's viewpoint. It placed him in the 1920s–1930s with advocates who wanted to dismantle the system of privilege which foreign-ers had enjoyed for decades: extraterritoriality and external control of Chinese tariffs.[15] Johnson also urged Washington's continued support of agreements adopted by the great powers after the World War to buttress China internationally. This elaboration upon the Open Door concept centered on the Nine Powers treaty of 1922, which pledged the signato-ries – among whom were the United States, Japan, Britain, France – along several lines: to respect Chinese territorial integrity, encourage political independence, promote equal opportunity for every foreign commercial interest, and refrain from unilateral grabbing. The Kellogg–Briand pact of 1928 likewise commanded Johnson's respect; applied to the Far East, the pact would advance the compatible causes of Chinese and Americans.[16]

Incursions by Japan's Kwantung army against China in 1931–1932 broke Johnson's faith in legalism (the Nine Powers agreement and Kellogg–Briand). Its inability to prevent violence became obvious as Tokyo violated treaties to which it was party, then ignored protests by the League of Nations (which Japan abandoned in 1933). Yet even as Far Eastern conditions deteriorated and the balance of power swung against America, Johnson doubted that the United States would act to counter

Japan: economic woes reinforced pacifism to inhibit Washington. Besides, he sensed, even if Americans were inclined, they could do little in China as long as Chiang's government vacillated between outright appeasement and desultory resistance. Consequently, he accepted the so-called Stimson Doctrine that withheld US recognition of Japan's gains in Manchuria as contra the Open Door principle. This disapprobation kept the record straight, Johnson felt, while laying the basis for tough policy should Washington ever rouse itself. Until then, he decided, he would wait with as much grace as possible until events dislodged Washington from inertia and spurred Chiang to greater activity.[17] Japanese power meantime was consolidated in Manchuria and seeped southward through Jehol province, then moved past the Great Wall.

Not until late 1937 did the ambassador's patience wholly desert him.[18] Johnson approved the tenor of Roosevelt's "Quarantine" speech in October: "It is ... a matter of vital interest and concern to the people of the United States that the sanctity of international treaties and the maintenance of international morality be restored."[19] But FDR's failure to give tangible backing to these words made Johnson inwardly break with Washington. To him the administration ignored the obvious: Japan intended to conquer China and drive the United States from East Asia.[20] Sinking of the US gunboat *Panay* during the Nanking battle – plus attacks on three American oil tankers also on the Yangtze – plainly indicated Japan's aims (notwithstanding Tokyo's apology and indemnities for *Panay*). The Nanking atrocities themselves had for Johnson a quality of anti-American and anti-occidental animus: the killing of unarmed people demonstrated to their brethren that dependence upon Western power for security was vanity. They should come to terms with Japan.[21]

Johnson's agitation for firm measures grew steadily. He wrote in December 1937 to Stanley Hornbeck, Secretary of State Cordell Hull's advisor on the Far East: "I yield to no one in my horror of war; I have seen as much of it as I want to see." Yet Johnson added, with realpolitik conviction and in the way of his favorite statesman, Theodore Roosevelt: "We must be prepared to fight if we want to be respected."[22] The ambassador was equally explicit when, six months later, he again addressed Hornbeck:

We will never realize America's heritage as the hope of a war weary world unless we are prepared to stand at Armageddon with the powers of righteousness and the rule of law against the gangsterdom that is raising the banner of might, force and international bad faith. The Democracies of the world are crying out for a leader that can think and speak clearly the language of leadership in the course of law and order. Let him stand forth in America if he is to be found there. He will find plenty of support when he cuts away the confused thinking that is bemusing the minds of people today.[23]

Attempts by Chiang and Mao in 1937–1938 to reconcile differences and forge a unified front heartened Johnson. He read the new cooperation, however ephemeral in fact, as positive proof of China's will to fight Japan.[24] He insisted to Hull – also in an impassioned letter to FDR – that US aid to Chiang would be well employed, neither squandered by misuse nor by Japanese capture. Washington should, therefore, be generous to the Chinese who were fighting not only for themselves but also, in an objective sense, for US aims.[25] Johnson advised Washington to sell hundreds of warplanes to Chiang. It should detail American pilots to train Chinese airmen. It should provide China with loans to purchase Anglo-US weaponry. Additionally, FDR should apply biting economic sanctions on Japan.[26]

These pleas to cooperate with Chungking had an impact in Washington during 1937–1940, though less than Johnson hoped. His advice had not only to overcome congressional reluctance for a showdown with Japan, but had also to block a seductive alternative offered by Joseph Grew, ambassador in Tokyo: the US had no vital interest in China to justify alienating Japan or creating discord. Proper regard for Tokyo, argued Grew, as valued trade partner and an appreciation for the distribution of East Asian power – wherein Japan balanced the USSR – recommended tactfulness, not bluster or creating impediments to Pacific peace.[27]

Perseverance paid off for Johnson in small dividends. Roosevelt quietly accepted the assistance program sought by him (and Hornbeck). The president asserted that Congress's neutrality legislation did not control because Japan had not declared itself at war with China; neither sales of munitions nor aid to Chiang would stand in technical violation of US law.[28] This eligibility resulted in November 1940 with a credit to Chungking of $100 million. Fifty fighter planes were sent (with pledges of more). Roosevelt permitted citizens to volunteer as pilots and instructors in the Chinese air force: Claire Chennault's Flying Tigers.[29] The government also abrogated the 1911 Japan–US commercial treaty and stiffened the language of "moral embargo."

Johnson by the time he left China was disturbed over the level of US assistance since 1937. He thought it derisory: less than $200 million of credits and loans, only $25 million worth of *matériel*. Chiang was also baffled by apparent American stinginess.[30] To Washington, though, the aid question appeared differently and had nothing to do with callousness toward China (an object of sentimental interest to FDR) or indifference to Japan's push for Asian hegemony. The main problem, instead, sprang from the limited ability of the "arsenal of democracy" to satisfy all needs, not only those of China. The British also, and by extension the entire north Atlantic community, inescapably tied to the United States, labored under excruciating pressure. When Johnson left China, Britain had been fighting for a year without a major continental ally against unstoppable Germany.

France

The contrast between China at war with Japan versus France at war with Germany was vivid from US perspective. Japanese armies inflicted immense damage in China. But they did not knock it out of commission. Significant numbers of Japanese soldiers and resources were continuously engaged in China, thereby diverted from efforts against Anglo-American forces. The military balance in East Asia, however precarious for the West (particularly in 1941–1942), never shifted decisively. In Europe, though, the defeat of France in June 1940 demolished the balance of power and left Germany ascendant.

French collapse constituted a near-catastrophe for Anglo-American safety. Yet neither Roosevelt nor Congress was willing at the critical moment to respond briskly. Explanation for this slackness lies partly in the unexpected swiftness of German victories in May–June 1940. They arose from the Third Republic's social–political maladies, the Wehrmacht's tactical superiority, and a paralysis of imagination in the French high command that filtered down the ranks (but not to Brigadier General Charles de Gaulle, commander of the 4th Armored Division).[31] Most Washington analysts had believed the French army would give a good account similar to that of 1914–1918, even in the absence of Germany's fighting an eastern-front war. Few experts guessed that Frenchmen would sue for peace (June 22, 1940) after a campaign of only six weeks or that the British Expeditionary Force would vacate the continent (Dunkirk) amid Paris–London recriminations.

Events might have gone better for France with benefit to Anglo-American security had Bullitt persuaded FDR in 1940 on the wisdom of large measures. Bullitt's failure to persuade had nothing to do with lack of persistence. Indeed, the envoy in 1940 was ardent on the subject of aid for France. The problem, instead, lay in wishful thinking, entrenched in Congress and not dispelled by Roosevelt. European matters would somehow right themselves. Americans need not get militarily excited. Against this imperturbability, as the battle of France became earnest, Bullitt erupted: "I feel certain that if Hitler should be able to conquer France and England he would turn his attention at once to South America and [try to establish] a Nazi government in the United States."[32]

Bullitt's Paris posting (1936–1940) came atop a career studded with adventure, romance, and private tribulation. Scion of Philadelphia aristocrats, he had obtained renown by the time of his French mission, but not the higher offices for which he yearned. He had accepted with alacrity as a young man (b. 1891) an errand to Moscow in 1919 to determine whether an understanding might be negotiated between Bolsheviks and capitalism's wary leaders, hunkered in Paris to reassemble Europe. His work in Russia, however, was disowned by Woodrow Wilson and Lloyd George. Previously a votary of the president, Bullitt then turned fiercely on him. Bullitt testified in Senate hearings against the Versailles treaty and League of Nations. His sweetest revenge took shape in a biography of Wilson that advertised his defects, real and imagined. Bullitt enlisted Sigmund Freud in composing this lopsided account (getting his imprimatur) while at the same time becoming infatuated with psychoanalysis.[33]

Bullitt lived awhile after the World War in France, a country familiar to him since boyhood visits. He socialized with other compatriots of "the lost generation." He befriended Ernest Hemingway and F. Scott Fitzgerald. Bullitt led a quasi-bohemian life. It produced forgettable literary works (pulp).[34] It mixed passion with politics. His marriage to the widow of John Reed, the irrepressible Louise Bryant, ended in her alcoholism and divorce.

Bullitt got another chance at diplomacy in 1933 when FDR became president. He recognized Moscow in the hope that the specter of Soviet–US cooperation would slow Japan's East Asian expansion and have sobering effect on Berlin's Nazis. Roosevelt appointed Bullitt, whom at the time he admired, to be ambassador. He presented his credentials with customary panache at a Kremlin ceremony in December 1933. The exuberance of revolutionary Russia that had captivated him in 1919 had died by the time of his ambassadorship, however. Collectivization, purges, and random terror mocked earlier Bolshevik promises of a radiant future. Bullitt's illusions shattered. Relations between Moscow and Washington meanwhile got stuck in interminable wrangles connected to Soviet debt repayment to US creditors. American unwillingness to collaborate in the containing of Japan and Germany also eroded Stalin's confidence in Washington, a devaluation marked by NKVD intrigues against embassy personnel. Bullitt left Moscow (May 1936) in anti-Soviet pique and morbidly suspicious of all communists.

Paris revitalized him as diplomat. The isolation and apprehension that engulfed him in Moscow melted. He embraced as his own the French capital – sophisticated, effervescent, tolerant. His wit and intelligence endeared him to leading figures in the popular front government: Léon Blum, Edouard Daladier, Paul Reynaud. Bullitt's intimacy with them and other personages led Harold Ickes, FDR's secretary of the Interior, to quip: "Bullitt practically sleeps with the French cabinet."[35] His country retreat in Chantilly exuded elegance. French officials exaggerated his place as Washington insider. Still, they were not deceived by his abiding loyalty to twin causes: Franco-American cooperation, French security.

The main problem, as Bullitt conceived it early in his tenure, was twofold. First, Paris officialdom had to understand that Americans would help those who helped themselves.[36] This attitude meant that US goodwill for France would not in the event of crisis mean intervention on the ground as in 1917. Yet goodwill could take the form of plentiful *matériel* aid, despite obstacles imposed by neutrality legislation. (Bullitt's eagerness to reassure French interlocutors about assistance caused Hull, more than once, to amend the ambassador's overstatements.) Second, French diplomacy should aim at détente with Germany or, better yet, genuine concord. Another Franco-German war, Bullitt predicted, would enfeeble Europe and let the USSR organize the survivors according to Stalinist dictate. Not only would the balance of power disappear, Europe would also sink into a new dark age. To advance Franco-German rapport, he helped oust Washington's uncompromisingly anti-Nazi ambassador in Berlin, William Dodd. With his successor, Hugh Wilson, Bullitt then tried behind the scenes to promote Franco-German reconciliation through Hermann Goering (a necessarily subtle exercise in view of Bullitt's Jewish background on his mother's side). The Munich fiasco ended this approach. Bullitt thenceforth dismissed Franco-German rapprochement as improbable. He expected that France could improve its chances by close cooperation with Britain. And he tried to coax FDR into making commitments to Paris.[37]

The core of commitments, to Bullitt's mind, was warplanes. Fighter planes, bombers, qualified pilots were wanted. He had been impressed by Daladier's avowal after Munich that the conference would have taken a different twist – or not have convened – if France had possessed an air component comparable to the Luttwaffe: "If I had had three or four thousand aircraft, Munich would never have happened."[38] The United States, Bullitt told FDR, should redress this imbalance in European air power with delivery of 10,000 warplanes in 1940. The ambassador otherwise had confidence in the efficacy and élan of French armed force: impenetrable Maginot Line, modern warships, ample armor formations, dedicated servicemen. Still, unless or until France's air power were boosted – a task of production that would strain French industrial capacity – Germany would enjoy overall advantage. Consequently, from Munich onward, he lobbied Washington, virtually in lockstep with Daladier and Reynaud, to devise ways to improve France's air force. Bullitt recommended that FDR, without exactly violating the neutrality laws, authorize the following: American training of French airmen, erection of US sponsored warplane factories in Canada, construction in the United States of planes for French purchase. Roosevelt did not reject these ideas to circumvent neutrality legislation. Indeed, they paralleled his own cash and carry scheme (approved by Congress in November 1939). He subsequently tried to implement them while placating isolationists within Congress – such as Senators J. B. Clark (Democrat, Missouri) and Hiram Johnson (Republican, California) – and military officers like General Henry Arnold of the Army Air Corps, opposed to providing advanced weaponry to any foreign government. Bullitt could nudge FDR so far against such opposition, but not past the point that he judged politically inexpedient in an election season. Alternately amenable and guarded, Roosevelt delayed planes for France in 1939–1940.[39]

Once the battle of France was launched, Bullitt continued to tell FDR that the Third Republic enjoyed high morale. The government and armed forces stood indivisible. The country was bound to fight valiantly. It deserved unstinting help and would put it to effective use.[40]

French entreaties for US aid became frantic once the trend of battle turned. Bullitt alone came forward. He glowed with affection for the French: "I cannot express my admiration for the courage with which the French are meeting one of the most tragic situations in history."[41] He practically demanded the immediate transfer of thousands of US warplanes (which would have depleted existing inventories and taxed production schedules). He asked for prompt sale of World War I era destroyers to France. He requested the dispatch of naval units to the Mediterranean to discourage Mussolini's attacking France or its North African possessions.[42] None of these suggestions was approved in Washington. France succumbed, contrary to what Bullitt had told FDR about its prowess. Swarms of war machines, meanwhile, that Bullitt had led Daladier and Reynaud to believe would arrive from the New World never materialized. The French possessed fewer than 140 assembled US warplanes in May 1940.[43]

The crushing of French resistance horrified the envoy. He could also hardly believe that US power went unused: "It [is] sad that civilization in the world should fall because a great nation with a great President could simply talk."[44]

Perhaps, Bullitt, if he allowed himself introspection, was also chagrined by this thought. His impetuosity and eagerness for Franco-American alliance had caused him, inadvertently, to misinform officials in Paris and Washington about the intention and resolve of the other. These mistaken notions contributed to inflated French trust in American intervention plus US nonchalance in sending aid to a supposedly capable state. In any event, no evidence exists to show that Bullitt ever learned this truth about the Anglo-French air forces: their defeat in the battle of France came from faulty deployment not a dearth of planes whose number matched those of Germany in the main categories. Less than half of France's available fighter planes were used against the German offensive (418 of 900). And Winston Churchill chose not to commit the main body of RAF assets but kept them in reserve as a matter of caution.[45]

Bullitt paced the same room with Daladier when he got news from General Maurice Gamelin that German tanks had broken through Sedan. Later, an emotional diplomat attended mass at Notre Dame, where petitioners prayed for national deliverance. He actually stayed in Paris after the government fled, a decision smacking of heroic stunt – condemned by Roosevelt, Hull, and de Gaulle who thought an ambassador's duty obliged him to remain with his official hosts (e.g., Johnson with Chiang).[46] Bullitt expected by staying in Paris to dampen communist-inspired disorders, which he thought would follow the Third Republic's humiliation. He also took upon himself, in role of informal mayor, to expedite a transfer of municipal authority to the Germans. They entered the city on June 14, 1940.[47]

He hoped upon return to America to join FDR's cabinet, either as secretary of War or of Navy (or better yet as State Department head should Hull leave). But Roosevelt had by then tired of Bullitt, maybe irritated with the confidential tone that he used in missives, surely vexed by his scolding as Washington let France sink. The president, in any case, selected two international-minded Republicans – Henry Stimson for War, Frank Knox for Navy – to fortify bipartisanship in his third term. Bullitt was left to speechify to the public on behalf of preparedness. Increasingly ignored by the White House, he occupied himself after Pearl Harbor with miscellaneous assignments or sulked. He also indulged in some skullduggery, helping to expose the homosexuality of Undersecretary of State Sumner Welles. Bullitt finally joined the Free French. De Gaulle commissioned him a major in 1944.[48]

As for France: it had to adjust in 1940 to becoming a German satellite under Marshal Henri Philippe Pétain, no less an abject figure than Pu-Yi. Pétain's cabinet instituted policies that autumn in conformity with Berlin. They required, among other things, that Jews register with their local authority. Businesses owned or managed by them had to display posters to indicate "Jewish enterprise." Jews were precluded from holding political offices or other positions of public trust. Jacques Doriot of the Parti

Populaire Français bleated: "Down with the Jews." Reinhard Heydrich in planning the details of the "Final Solution" (Wannsee Conference, January 1942) complimented Vichy's reliability: "In occupied and unoccupied France the taking of the Jews for evacuation can in all probability proceed without great difficulties."[49]

Shoah

However ruthless Japan's war against China or arresting Germany's mastery of France, the conquests were part of ancient continuity. Aggrandizing states disrupted the status quo to add space, resources, populations. Forms of German–Japanese exploitation in occupied lands also belonged to long, if bleak, custom. The Athenian comment in Thucydides' chronicle of the Peloponnesian War applied equally to German–Japanese practitioners of realpolitik and their victims: "They that have odds of power exact as much as they can, and the weak yield to such conditions as they can get."[50]

German aims in World War II did not stop at these goals, ordinary in the sense of their being understood and pursued since time immemorial by nations. Germany in 1939–1945 was preeminently radical. Berlin's leaders sought to create a European order that nullified the metaphysical understandings in *The City of Man*, nestled at the core of Western ethical teaching. Hitler ridiculed them as obsolete. They and their iterations, from the Decalogue and Sermon on the Mount to Kant's categorical imperative, did not suit an age dominated by revolutionary race biology. Antiquated and scientifically groundless ideas were antithetical to the reality of racial hierarchy and needs of Aryan rule. The latter mandated not just the reaching of "definite lines," but also the annihilation of "inferior" enemies, above all the loathsome Jews and shiftless Roma. Hitler's ethic led to the "Holocaust Kingdom." Europe should be *Judenrein* for which *Einsatzgruppen* and gas chambers were indispensable. Bureaucratic procedure, industrial technique, railroad infrastructure, and finance were subsequently harnessed to Nazi zeal. The murdered included 1.2 million Jewish children.[51]

Rudolf Hoess, Auschwitz's commandant (May 1940–December 1943), recorded in his memoirs this question from a doomed mother: "One woman approached me as she walked past and, pointing to her four children who were . . . helping the smallest ones over the rough ground, whispered: 'How can you bring yourself to kill such beautiful, darling children?' "[52] No record exists of Hoess's answer, if any. But the authors of *The City of Man* knew wherein the problem lay. Without God, "or Deity or the Holy Ghost or the Absolute or Logos," anything had become possible. Elie Wiesel, an Auschwitz inmate, concluded that men had killed God.[53]

Deception of the victims and secrecy were necessary to Nazi success. Jewish families, for example, were told at the point of embarkation that they were to be resettled for labor in Polish preserves. Once arrived in the death camps, people were ordered to report for showers. Not everyone was deceived at the final moment, however. Hoess recalled after the war: "We endeavored to fool the victims into thinking that they were going through a delousing process. Of course, frequently they realized our true intentions and we sometimes had riots and difficulties due to that fact."[54]

Apart from spontaneous unruliness, organized Jewish resistance in the camps disrupted their smooth functioning. Revolts at Treblinka and Sobibor and the dynamiting of two crematoria at Auschwitz were made against overwhelming odds. The battle by remnants of the Warsaw ghetto (April 1943) marked the first urban uprising in German-conquered Europe.[55]

The scale of murder enterprise complicated its concealment. "Whoever lived in Poland at that time," observed Pope John Paul II in 1994, an avatar of postwar Jewish–Catholic reconciliation, "came into contact with this reality [Shoah]."[56] People living in zones around Auschwitz, Belzec, Chelmno, Majdanek, and other sites could not help knowing, even if they tried. Hoess explained in 1946: "The foul and nauseating stench from the continuous burning of bodies permeated the entire area and all of the people living in the surrounding communities knew that exterminations were going on at Auschwitz."[57]

Brave non-Jews in neighboring locales harbored camp escapees. People elsewhere in Hitler's Europe (including Catholics, Protestants, Marxists) helped smuggle weapons plus food into the ghettos. Rescue operations were mounted, as in Denmark when in October 1943 most of the country's 8,000 Jews were ferried to safety in neutral Sweden. The villagers of Le Chambon hid 5,000 hunted French Jews. As many as 25,000 Jews may have found shelter in Dutch homes. Between 100,000 and 150,000 Jews were saved by ordinary people in terrorized Poland.[58] The Vatican allowed its premises to be used as refuge for Jews (perhaps 1,000) during the German occupation of Rome. The Vatican's Budapest legation sponsored safe houses for Jews in 1944 to confound their Arrow Cross and German pursuers.[59] Even governments allied with Germany became obstacles to the slaughter. Objections by King Boris III resulted in the survival of Bulgaria's 50,000 Jews. Finnish authorities acted to protect a small population of 2,000 Jews. Neither did Benito Mussolini cooperate in the destruction of Italian Jewry nor Admiral Miklos Horthy in Hungary. Only after the German occupation of these two countries (northern Italy in September 1943, Hungary in March 1944) did the roundup, tabulating, and transport of indigenous Jews occur.

Despite Jewish resistance, aid from non-Jews, and non-compliance of Germany's allies, Nazi-dominated Europe was scene to executions for the crime of existence: six million Jews, half a million Roma. This destruction of one-third of world Jewry (per 1939 censuses) by the Third Reich was abetted by non-German accomplices. They included a collaborationist government in Vichy, venal informers, and anti-Semites from the Atlantic shoreline to Ukraine who lusted for the blood and property of their neighbors.[60] In the absence of this cooperation, Germany's genocidal machine would have worked slower, less thoroughly.

Governments and supranational institutions outside the Nazi realm did relatively little to prevent the murders. Papal silence and the reticence of the International Red Cross were cases in point. Pius XII never threatened Catholic persecutors of Jews with excommunication or ordered them to desist. He never urged non-cooperation upon German/Austrian Catholics, who comprised a third of the Reich's population. (Hitler, Heinrich Himmler, Joseph Goebbels, and Hoess were nominally Catholic.) Pius remained mute in October 1943 as SS troops invaded Rome's Jewish quarter. Red Cross inspectors did not demand to examine conditions at Auschwitz or any other such camp.[61] As a result of wartime operations against Germany, Soviet forces did end the assaults on Jewry in eastern Europe. Their discontinuance, though, was never an aim of Joseph Stalin. As for the Anglo-American governments, rescue of European Jewry was, at best, a low priority. Hardly anyone noticed or pretended to care about the Roma.

Before Europe's war began, Nazi persecution of Jews in the Third Reich, exemplified by the 1935 Nuremberg Laws, had created disquiet in America. At Roosevelt's behest an international conference convened at Evian, France (July 1938) to devise means of succoring thousands of German/Austrian Jews fleeing Hitler. FDR also recalled Ambassador Wilson from Berlin for "consultation" after the *Kristallnacht* mayhem (November 9–10, 1938).[62] Alas, neither Wilson's recall nor the Evian meeting bore results. The administration did not cut diplomatic ties with Germany in the late 1930s or, contrary to Jewish-American hopes, impose economic sanctions. Evian resulted in the issuance of tepid pronouncement against anti-Jewish discrimination in the Third Reich. No country, the United States included, then awash with anti-Semitism and anti-alien feeling, eased the plight of German Jewry by relaxing immigration codes.[63] The president did not extend his prestige or support to the Wagner–Rogers bill in Spring 1939. Passage by Congress would have let 20,000 Jewish-German children, under age fourteen, enter the United States without reference to the immigration quota in effect for Germany. The demise of Wagner–Rogers by nibbling amendments and parliamentary dickering comforted Laura Delano, an FDR cousin and wife of the immigration commissioner. She predicted: "Twenty thousand charming children would all too soon grow into twenty thousand ugly adults."[64] Senator Borah, who helped smother the legislation, was told by a P. G. Ingram of Chicago that the last thing needed in the economically strapped United States was a new influx of undesirables, no matter their age. Ingram suggested that Borah examine the benefits of Jewish removal: "America can be made ... a thousand times better by loading all the Jews in the land onto cattle boats for deportation to some point within the antarctic circle ... Why must the gentiles of America be forever exploited, baited, and persecuted by the brutal Jews?"[65] The president, no less, once confidentially stated that American Jews – like Catholics – enjoyed civil rights by "sufferance" of the Protestant majority.[66]

Eleanor Roosevelt told a friend – after Evian, *Kristallnacht*, and the Wagner–Rogers decision – that Jewish attainments probably deserved rollback. The problem with Hitler sprang from his methods, she opined. His goals were understandable: "I realize quite well that there may be a need for curtailing the ascendancy of the Jewish people, but it seems to me it might have been done in a more humane way ..."[67] Unsurprisingly, in view of such sentiment, actions in prewar America on behalf of German Jewry were nugatory or aborted. Only later did the First Lady realize the scope of Nazi malice and Jewish vulnerability, by which time she also despaired of Jewish survival. She wrote in her syndicated column, *My Day*, in August 1943: "I do not know what we can do to save the Jews in Europe ... [but] we will be the sufferers if we let great wrongs occur without exerting ourselves to correct them."[68]

Albeit engaged against Germany as of December 1941, FDR's government did not exert itself much to "correct" these "great wrongs." Initially, Washington officials did not comprehend the extent of Hitler's eradication policy.[69] When in late summer 1943 Jan Karski (Polish Catholic army officer) told Supreme Court Justice Felix Frankfurter (Jewish) of cattle cars crammed with people and of death factories, he responded in disbelief. Neither did Karski convince in his interviews with FDR or Stimson.[70] The legal scholar Raphael Lemkin (Polish Jew), who coined the term genocide, reported frightening tales to FDR and Vice President Henry Wallace. Lemkin advised prompt condemnation. Neither Roosevelt nor Wallace grasped the man's urgency, however. Lemkin should be "patient."[71] The American public was anyway not unduly concerned or brilliantly informed by the press. It chose, the *New York*

Times included, to downplay the annihilation, which tended to blur into other news of wartime suffering. Touchy about his own Jewishness, Walter Lippmann never mentioned the distress of European Jews in his newspaper columns, not even after personal briefing by Karski. Recollection of exaggerated reports of German misbehavior in 1914, meanwhile, inclined readers toward skepticism of grisly stories.[72]

Jewish groups repeatedly expressed alarm about Nazi persecution. They sponsored days of prayer and giant rallies. These included New York's Madison Square Garden demonstration (March 1943), when 75,000 people, Jews and Christians, vowed to "Stop Hitler Now."[73] Five hundred rabbis went to Washington in 1943 to petition FDR and Congress to adopt measures: warning German leaders to halt or face retribution, welcoming refugees, bombing feeder railways to Auschwitz. But disunity among Jewish activists prevented them from speaking with one voice about methods of rescue (witness the bitterness between Rabbi Stephen Wise of the American Jewish Congress versus Peter Bergson of the Emergency Committee to Save the Jewish People of Europe). FDR himself felt constrained in speaking strongly against Germany's homicidal policies, lest rascals – like Representative John Rankin (Democrat, Mississippi) or Father Charles Coughlin – ridiculed the war as one fought only to advance Jewish ends, thereby intensifying anti-Semitic feeling, which had earlier been mobilized to malign the New Deal (the Jew Deal). Roosevelt wondered about, but did not investigate deeply, the possibility of converting the Cameroons or Paraguay into Jewish havens. He spoke glibly of conveying European Jews to Palestine and moving Arab inhabitants out.[74]

State Department officials charged with paving the way for Jewish immigration or organizing rescue wound up subverting their task. Assistant Secretary of State Breckinridge Long, the FBI, and army intelligence thought that German agents might enter America via the Jewish refugee stream. In any case, Long thought, a horde of Jews and other foreigners bode no good for the future of US domestic tranquillity and so strove to slow or thwart their arrival. Compounding matters, the War and Navy departments were unwilling to divert men or *matériel* from fighting Germans to executing risky rescue missions. Rather, as Stimson held (a man not drawn to Jews), the best way to help Hitler's victims was to defeat Germany as quickly as possible. For this purpose no military assets could properly be spared.[75]

Apathy, hoary anti-Semitism (genteel to crude), and concentration on routine military objectives spelt disaster for Jewry. The country best able to help stood aloof. The Anglo-US conference at Bermuda in 1943, overlapping with the Warsaw ghetto uprising, met ostensibly to invent ways to aid Europe's Jews. This meeting produced platitudes while camouflaging the paucity of State Department and Foreign Office initiatives. Bermuda gave further confirmation, were one needed, for Hitler's earlier prediction: the Western powers might complain or preach but at the fateful hour would not move on behalf of deicides and money swindlers. Propaganda Minister Goebbels entered in his diary (December 1942): "At bottom ... I believe both the English and Americans are happy that we are exterminating the Jewish riff-raff."[76]

Niebuhr reviled the Bermuda charade, as did the CIO's president Philip Murray, and a smattering of congressmen. Rabbi Wise called Bermuda an evasion of humanitarian duty.[77] Szmul Zygielbojm, attached to the Polish National Council in London, committed suicide (May 1943) to protest Anglo-American inaction. "I was unable to do anything during my life," he wrote in his last letter, "perhaps by my death I shall contribute to destroying the indifference of those who are able and should act."[78]

Secretary of the Treasury Henry Morgenthau, Jr., was preoccupied by the wartime demands of his portfolio. This preoccupation involved planning for the postwar international economy. His role at the Bretton Woods conference (July 1944) won him deserved praise. He and his aides were pivotal in creating institutions to ensure economic stability: the International Monetary Fund, the Bank for Reconstruction and Development. Not without feeling for European Jewry, Morgenthau nevertheless paid slight attention and grasped nothing of the disaster's scale until late 1943. He qualified before then as indictable for indifference by Zygielbojm's standard.

Morgenthau, son of Woodrow Wilson's ambassador to Constantinople, was not an observant or religiously minded Jew. He felt entirely comfortable in mainstream society. He wanted never to be misidentified with the two million exotic East European Jews – Orthodox, impecunious – who made their way to the United States around the turn of the century and embarrassed their secular cousins of German origin. Heir to privilege (b. 1891), he attended Phillips Exeter Academy and Cornell University (where he compiled mediocre academic records). He enjoyed a lark as "office boy" to his father during his Constantinople tenure, and, upon US intervention in World War One, served as a naval officer. Young Morgenthau thereafter led the life of a gentleman farmer in New York's Dutchess County, where he became obsessively friendly with the local squire, debonair Franklin Roosevelt. Morgenthau lacked his friend's insouciance. He had nothing of FDR's charisma or gift for repartee. Deliberate to the point of graceless, and mentally plodding, Morgenthau's redeeming quality was loyalty to FDR. He, in turn, accepted Morgenthau as an intimate – the only Jew ever personally close to Roosevelt – and rewarded his devotion with handsome positions. As governor of New York (1928–1932), FDR appointed Morgenthau to posts dealing with agriculture and forest/wildlife conservation. President Roosevelt named Morgenthau to head the Farm Credit Administration in 1933, and used him in exploratory talks with Maxim Litvinov on normalization of Soviet–US relations.[79] The president subsequently appointed Morgenthau to the Treasury (November 1934), thus recruiting the second Jew to serve in cabinet. The first had been Theodore Roosevelt's secretary of Commerce and Labor, Oscar Straus.

Morgenthau, as court Jew, avoided overstepping on behalf of his co-religionists in America or abroad. Berlin's anti-Jewish violence nevertheless shook him. He recommended in cautious tone to FDR (1938) that London and Paris be pressed to offer their Guiana colonies as sanctuaries for dispossessed German Jews. Roosevelt's breezy disapproval of this idea did not elicit response from Morgenthau: "It would take the Jews five to fifty years to overcome the fever."[80] Upon war's outbreak in 1939, he became the most outspoken interventionist in FDR's government, and so remained until Stimson joined the cabinet in summer 1940. Still, Morgenthau couched his interventionist arguments only in reference to saving Britain and preserving US security. He did not allow, perhaps not even to himself, that Hitler's anti-Semitism colored his longing to see the Nazis overthrown.

Immersion from December 1941 onward in waging war along the financial front let Morgenthau, for a while, to bear lightly the tug of Jewish misery. But he could not ignore it entirely. Rabbi Wise urged him to take official notice, to use his presumed influence with FDR for humanity's sake. Morgenthau's confidential secretary, Henrietta Klotz (Jewish), also tried to sway her boss in meaningful direction. The example, meantime, of his father's efforts in Turkey for Armenians gnawed at his conscience.[81] The senior Morgenthau's chairmanship of a presidential commission to investigate anti-Jewish violence in post-1918 Poland also haunted the son. Most dramatically, Protestant lawyers on the Treasury staff (Josiah DuBois, John Pehle, Randolph Paul) presented him in autumn 1943 with irrefutable evidence, acquired in fragments, of State Department obstruction: thwarting disbursement of dollars by the World Jewish Congress to spring tens of thousands of French and Romanian Jews from Nazi clutches. Morgenthau consequently called a meeting with Hull and Long. It was a tense confrontation that confirmed him in his sad conclusion: the State Department was guilty of ineptitude, or worse, in its handling of refugee matters. Morgenthau thus became, against his will and slowly, the sole resolute proponent of rescue in

FDR's inner circle. He was prepared to sacrifice cabinet position and friendship with the president for a cause mostly ignored by the responsible class.[82]

The denouement occurred on January 16, 1944 when Morgenthau delivered to FDR a report penned by DuBois: "Acquiescence of this Government in the Murder of the Jews." The paper detailed State Department dereliction:

> One of the greatest crimes in history, the slaughter of the Jewish people in Europe, is continuing unabated.
>
> This Government has for a long time maintained that its policy is to work out programs to save those Jews of Europe who could be saved.
>
> ... certain officials in our State Department, which is charged with carrying out this policy, have been guilty not only of gross procrastination and willful failure to act, but even of willful attempts to prevent action from being taken to rescue Jews from Hitler ...
>
> Unless remedial steps of a drastic nature are taken ... to prevent the complete extermination of the Jews in German controlled Europe [then] this Government will have to share for all time responsibility for this extermination.[83]

Specific State Department officers were censured in the Treasury report, Long particularly. They had not used government machinery at their disposal but employed it to hinder Jewish rescue. They had not cooperated with other organizations trying to mount authentic rescues and had even tried to foil them. State Department people were also upbraided for preventing dissemination of information on Nazi murder policies. Finally, the State Department had tried to hide its guilt by providing misleading explanations to Congress and blunting press inquiry.[84]

Morgenthau told FDR that failure to respond to the report's findings would invite awkwardness. Congressmen fed-up with delay, and preparing legislation (Gillette–Rogers) to organize a rescue commission independent of the State Department, would drive in directions sure to embarrass the White House. Morgenthau intimated that Thomas Dewey and Wendell Willkie, contenders for the GOP presidential nomination in 1944, would reap benefits in New York and elsewhere if voters perceived FDR as obdurate. Alert to the danger of appearing apathetic or callous, FDR mollified Morgenthau via executive order and established the War Refugee Board (WRB) on January 22, 1944.[85] Its compass, though made without specific reference to Jewry, virtually repudiated previous policy. The WRB would do everything possible to "rescue the victims of enemy oppression who are in imminent danger of death and ... afford such victims all possible relief and assistance consistent with the successful prosecution of the war."[86]

The WRB fell under the joint direction of Hull, Stimson, and Morgenthau. Only the Treasury secretary felt deeply committed to it. He had to contend with Stimson's skepticism about the feasibility of rescue and hapless Hull, who was lukewarm to the WRB and whose connection to public events anyway was becoming attenuated as his health failed.[87] Morgenthau got his own man, Pehle, named as executive director of the WRB. With a small staff (not more than thirty), using funds primarily collected from private agencies, and mostly ignored by FDR, Pehle headed a belated campaign to save condemned people. It included the employment of Sweden's Wallenberg in his effort on behalf of Hungarian Jews.[88]

The WRB could eventually claim credit for saving 200,000 Jews and 20,000 additional persons. Morgenthau ultimately got Roosevelt to issue a public statement (March 1944) that referred explicitly to Germany's war on Jewry. The secretary also joined that small body of protestors that urged Anglo-US bombing of Auschwitz and the railroad network that fed it. They were overruled by Stimson's War Department in summer 1944, a judgment upheld by FDR, who worried over the advantages to Nazi propagandists of prisoners killed by Allied bombs. Against the advice of Morgenthau and Pehle – against the fervent wishes of Auschwitz's living dead, including Wiesel and Primo Levi – this reasoning still trumped: "The suggested air operation is impracticable for the reason that it could be executed only by diversion of considerable air support essential to the success of our forces now engaged in decisive operations . . . it is considered that the most effective relief to victims of enemy persecution is the early defeat of the Axis, an undertaking to which we must devote every resource at our disposal."[89] The result, even as synthetic oil refineries in or near Auschwitz were struck by Allied planes (late 1944, early 1945), was that no military actions – from bombing to landing paratroopers – were taken against the camp's gas chambers, crematoria, or Hungarian–Polish railway junctions.[90]

Morgenthau cherished postwar words of gratitude by rescued Jews for his WRB role. Previously content in his secularism, indeed disconcerted by expressions of Jewish piety, the assimilated Morgenthau also converted after 1945 to traditional religiosity and later support of Israel.

Yet he was staggered by the Shoah's dimensions. He derived no pride in a policy that came too late for countless people.[91] Adding to his sorrow, he had to cope with rejection in 1945 of his blueprint for a "pastoralized" Germany, the so-called Morgenthau Plan. Harry Truman, who later fired Morgenthau from Treasury, thought his German scheme "crazy." Stimson reproved it as a Carthaginian peace; a better solution to the postwar German problem would be a tonic of "Christianity and kindness."[92] To such argument, Morgenthau answered that his idea, admittedly rough, would preempt German rearmament and risk of Berlin's starting war again. Implementation of his proposal would also punish the gas-chamber nation: "We didn't ask for this war; we didn't put millions of people through gas chambers ... They (Germans) have asked for it."[93] After briefly accepting the secretary's Germany plan (at the September 1944 Quebec conference), FDR dropped it as too vindictive. He opted for moderation to reintegrate Germany into Europe.

Maybe Morgenthau, given to brooding, ruminated thus in the years after 1945. His idol, Roosevelt, had been too distracted or uninterested to push for a robust Jewish rescue. The president, more than his inglorious State Department, bore responsibility for inadequate response. Only 21,000 Jews gained entry into the United States during the Shoah years, 10 percent of those eligible under tight immigration law. FDR voiced no objection or gave much utterance of cosmopolitan complaint.[94] As commander in chief, he, not the generals or their civilian supervisors, had the power to authorize the bombing of Auschwitz's facilities or related targets. He decided oppositely.

Nuremberg

Morgenthau in the waning months of war said that Berlin's arch-villains should be summarily shot upon Allied capture. He had no taste for any form of judicial evaluation; it might result in penalties less than capital punishment or other versions of clemency. He later thought that the US prosecutor at Nuremberg, meticulous Robert Jackson (Supreme Court justice), would take too lenient a line with the perpetrators of genocide.[95]

Feeling among Allied heads also ran toward swift retribution for German (and Japanese) leaders. Churchill wanted to have the top Germans – six or seven men – executed immediately after their arrest, a view favored by the Lord Chancellor, John Simon. Stalin famously suggested at the Tehran conference in 1943 that 50,000 prominent Germans ought to be shot. Roosevelt casually spoke of punishment centered on eugenics: castrating German men, forcibly breeding the Japanese with peaceful Pacific islanders to produce docile hybrids. He anyway had no objection to quick disposal of Axis chiefs.[96]

Naked revenge did not recommend itself everywhere, however. Stimson and his War Department lieutenant, John McCloy, argued for adoption of court trial and unimpeachable procedures. They would constitute an exercise in justice. They would permit punishment when properly indicated. They would strengthen international law along with ideas of right conduct. A public trial would also advertise Nazi iniquity for all time. This exposure, in turn, would clear the way to purge Nazis in Berlin and return Germany to international society.[97] Stimson persuaded FDR and through him reached the British cabinet. The London Agreement and Charter of August 1945 eventuated with provisions for a military trial of Germany's senior officials.

The presiding judges at Nuremberg came from not only Great Britain and the United States but also France and the USSR. The justices officiated from November 20, 1945 to August 31, 1946 (403 open sessions featuring 113 witnesses). Published records of the trial filled forty-two thick volumes. A German counsel represented each defendant. Verdicts and sentencing were delivered on September 30 and October 1, 1946. Nine of the guilty defendants were hanged in mid-October. Former Attorney General Francis Biddle, who represented the United States on the bench, later recalled: "There was no end to the horrors of testimony."[98]

Several charges were leveled against the defendants, the foremost of which focused on "crimes against peace." Individual responsibility was said to attach to the conspiratorial planning and executing of aggressive war. Men in the dock were also accused of "war crimes." They included mistreating enemy civilians, shooting of prisoners, wanton destruction of property. Finally, the defendants were tried for committing premeditated "crimes against humanity," genocide preeminently but also the enslavement and deportation of peoples.[99]

Findings against the defendants varied. The tribunal pronounced guilt and sentence of death upon Hermann Goering (Luftwaffe chief, designated heir to Hitler), Joachim von Ribbentrop (foreign minister), Field Marshal Wilhelm Keitel (chief of staff of the armed forces), Ernst Kaltenbrunner (head of the Reich Central Security Office), Alfred Rosenberg (minister for Occupied Eastern Territories), Hans Frank (governor of German-occupied Poland), Wilhelm Frick (interior minister), Julius Streicher (publisher of the anti-Semitic *Der Stürmer*), Fritz Sauckel (head of conscript labor organization), Colonel General Alfred Jodl (operations chief of the armed forces), Arthur Seyss-Inquart (commissioner of German-occupied Holland), and Martin Bormann (secretary of the Party Chancery). Goering committed suicide hours before his scheduled execution. Bormann, tried in absentia, evaded capture. How he departed this earth remains unknown. Of the devastation visited upon European Jewry, Hans Frank gulped: "A thousand years will pass and this guilt of Germany will still not be erased."[100]

Three men received verdicts of guilty and sentences of imprisonment for life: Rudolf Hess (deputy Führer until 1941), Walther Funk (Reichsbank president), Grand Admiral Erich Raeder (chief of navy).

Lesser sentences were meted out to these men. Grand Admiral Karl Doenitz (chief of the U-boat fleet, later head of navy and successor to Hitler) got imprisonment for ten years. Baldur von Schirach (head of Hitler Youth) got twenty years. Albert Speer (minister for armaments and war production) also got twenty years. Konstantin von Neurath (foreign minister before Ribbentrop, Protector of Bohemia and Moravia in 1939–1941) received fifteen years. Additionally, the tribunal pronounced five organizations to be criminal: Leadership Corps of the Nazi Party, *Schutzstaffel* (SS), *Sicherheitsdienst* (SD), *Sturmabteilung* (SA), *Geheime Staatspolizei* (Gestapo).

Three defendants were acquitted: Hjalmar Schacht (Reichsbank president before Funk, minister of the economy), Franz von Papen (vice chancellor under Hitler), and Hans Fritzsche (chief of radio propaganda). The Soviet judge, Major General I. T. Nikitchenko, wrote a dissenting opinion. These acquittals were baseless, he contended. Monsters were set free. He asserted that Hess deserved the death penalty. Nikitchenko thought the tribunal also mistaken for not criminalizing two organizations: the Reich Cabinet, and General Staff and High Command of the Armed Forces.[101]

American opinion, on an order of 75 percent of voters polled, approved of the Nuremberg judgments. A majority of editorial writers, lawyers, and clergymen refrained the dominant viewpoint. Truman exclaimed that the trial was one of the "greatest things to come out of [the] war." Justice seemed to have been implicated with law, an ethical leap over the Leipzig trials of 1920 (in which German courts exonerated or lightly penalized the Kaiser's officials for deeds in 1914–1918). Injured civilization, Justice Jackson's locution, had gotten satisfaction this time by dogged pursuit of evildoers.[102] Stimson declared that the judgments constituted a deterrent to future aggression: "A standard has been raised to which Americans, at least, must repair; for it is only as this standard is accepted, supported, and enforced that we can move onward to a world of law and peace."[103] Europeans also praised the trials, including Pius XII. The acquitted von Papen hailed them for having "awakened the conscience of the world."[104]

This endorsement of the trial buoyed subsequent US tribunals at Nuremberg for lesser Nazi fry ("second line"), prosecuted by Brigadier General Telford Taylor. These trials ran in 1946–1949. They centered on German "medical experiments," SS officers in command of concentration camps and labor battalions, confiscation of Jewish property, mistreatment of civilians in southeastern Europe, SS officials involved in mass murders, the exploitation of slave labor by industries (I.G. Farben, Krupp), and offenses against POWs or civilians in multiple

Nazi-controlled zones.[105] The original Nuremberg exercise also added legitimacy to trials held elsewhere in Europe, as in Poland, where Hoess was hanged by authorities in 1947 at Auschwitz. The procedures and principles employed at the primary Nuremberg trial were also adopted with modifications in the Far Eastern International Military Tribunal in Tokyo (May 1946–November 1948). There eleven judges from countries previously at war with Japan investigated the legality of actions taken by twenty-eight military and civilian leaders. These included Tojo Hideki, head of state in 1941–1944, and Hirota Koki, foreign minister during the Nanking massacre. Verdicts of guilt and sentences, from hanging to imprisonment (life to seven years), were produced. No acquittals. Tojo and Hirota were executed in 1948. As with Nuremberg, the judges did not achieve consensus. India's Justice Rabhabinod Pal was fervid in his dissent. He found the defendants innocent on all counts of conspiracy to commit atrocities or wage aggression. He denied that prohibitions on aggressive war had ever been established in international law. He suggested that the United States, by its use of atomic bombs in August 1945 (Hiroshima, Nagasaki), had itself committed the sin of "indiscriminate slaughter."[106]

The Pal critique – that the Tokyo trial was farcical – rang true for a minority of Americans already troubled by the Nuremberg proceedings. The spectrum of complaint ranged widely.[107] Mississippi's Rankin called Nuremberg an instance of "sadistic" Jewish vengeance to embarrass Germany, already writhing from comprehensive privation. Other congressmen, only slightly less astonishing, such as Senator William Langer (Republican, North Dakota) and Representative George Dondero (Republican, Michigan) argued that Nuremberg was guided by left-wingers to serve Soviet ends. The tribunal by its very convening depressed German morale and elevated that of international communism; the judges also indirectly weakened the armed forces of the United States by insisting that a subordinate should, in certain circumstance, disobey orders. General Dwight Eisenhower, incidentally, though not voicing his concern in public, was upset by verdicts against top German military/naval officers. Irrespective of their other faults, he believed, these men had complied with the military code everywhere: unswerving obedience.[108]

Other Americans disliked what they saw as overly determined courtroom dramas. Whatever their theatrical value, said these skeptics – including editorialists in the *Chicago Daily Tribune* and *Fortune* magazine – or educational function, they were incompatible with recognizable law. They amounted to victor's justice; the vanquished were naturally convicted of nefariousness. A couple of Jackson's own colleagues on the

Supreme Court echoed these sentiments. The "pretense" of organizing a court trial for people who inevitably got what they deserved bothered Chief Justice Harlan Stone; executive action would have preempted much trouble and conceptual muddle.[109] Justice William O. Douglas seethed over Jackson's lengthy absence in Nuremberg and resultant heavier load of work borne by the Court staff. Douglas also resented the political ambitions that Jackson harbored: governor of New York, possibly president of the United States. "From a political viewpoint," Douglas once wrote, "it was desirable for him to be our Nuremberg prosecutor, since the Jewish vote is important in many parts of our country."[110] Douglas's most telling criticism was that Hitler's associates should have been tried for murder, but Jackson's emphasis on the alleged criminality of aggressive war posed a problem. It constituted the retroactive application of law; nothing like a precise or universally acknowledged definition of aggressive war had ever existed. The Nuremberg proceedings, in short, were "unprincipled" from the standpoint of Anglo-American legal norms.[111]

Nor did every respectable scholar care for Nuremberg. Niebuhr found fault because it flattered Americans, further deflated the Germans who were trying to recover their moral equilibrium, and trivialized this existential fact. All human beings are sinful creatures, prey to extreme misconduct, entangled in evil. Evidence for these truths, said he, abounded, even in the Anglo-American war record; it revealed susceptibility to temptations of unreflecting hegemonial purpose. The political scientist Hans Morgenthau, a Jewish-German refugee (unrelated to the Treasury secretary), also criticized Nuremberg. It misled the public mind about the clash of power that everywhere and always dominates international politics. Germans in the dock – Japanese too – were no more guilty than other leaders; all tried to improve the security of their countries by the amassing of power. Law, treaties, diplomacy – and Allied military tribunals – were froth on the surface of the global distribution of power. They should not confuse Americans, he lectured, about the reality of political life, leading them to think that Nuremberg could atone for past errors (appeasement) or bring about a safer world by solemnly condemning aggression.[112]

The most highly visible American to dissent from Nuremberg, and who generated greatest controversy, was Senator Taft, a lawyer by training and of strict constitutionalist bent. Admired even by New Dealers for his unblemished integrity, this GOP leader had earned the sobriquet, Mr. Republican. Unsuccessful aspirant to the party's presidential nomination in 1940, he wanted to prepare himself in 1946 for another try. Republican victories that year – especially in congressional elections – would improve the chance that this son of a president (William Howard Taft) would win the White House in 1948.

The senator belonged to that school of thought which disliked overseas ventures as they degraded the country's moral standing and created governmental bloating inimical to civil freedoms. Taft repudiated every move of "American imperialists abroad." They would, if left unsupervised, over-commit the United States. He adhered to this credo: "An unwise and over ambitious foreign policy, and particularly the effort to do more than we are able to do, is the one thing which might in the end destroy our armies and prove a real threat to the liberty of the people of the United States."[113]

This orientation placed Taft against the activist wing of his own party (Wendell Willkie, Thomas Dewey) and in conflict with the internationalism of FDR and Truman. Taft in the first decade of his Senate tenure opposed Lend-Lease, objected to conscription, disparaged Bretton Woods, doubted the United Nations, criticized the Marshall Plan, and rejected NATO. The Nuremberg trials were for him yet another example of US involvement in wayward enterprise, evidenced by the seating of Soviet judges on the court bench. The suspected truth about Katyn forest (thousands of Polish officers killed by NKVD agents), Soviet absorption of the Baltic republics, Stalin's wars in 1939 (Poland, Finland), and Moscow's relentless attack on religion/property/civility disqualified the USSR from playing a Nuremberg role.[114] Soviet offenses, he reasoned, were not different in kind from those committed by Germany: "It is certainly ridiculous for the Russians to sit on a court and condemn men to death for making an aggressive war which was participated in by Mr. Stalin and Mr. Molotov. They marched into Poland with the Germans."[115] Not only did Soviet presence defy the idea of impartial justice evenly applied. Taft also held, in line with Douglas, that the entire Nuremberg exercise contravened Anglo-American jurisprudence.

Taft first expressed concern in February 1946, months before verdicts were read at Nuremberg, to a Republican gathering in Texas. He accused Truman of having accepted the philosophy of force as the dominant element in international life and of slighting the rule of law. Taft charged that the "elaborate procedure" at Nuremberg could not prettify or hide simple revenge. A bogus court trial would cast a pall upon global politics: "At the end of a frightful war, we should view the future with more hope if even our enemies believed that we had treated them justly."[116]

Not until after the verdicts were delivered did Taft give definitive judgment on Nuremberg. The occasion was an October 1946 symposium at Kenyon College: "The Heritage of English Speaking Peoples and

Their Responsibility." He numbered among several speakers, including the British socialist–political theorist Harold Laski. Taft chided FDR's flirtation with the Morgenthau Plan. He attacked denazification in the US zone of German occupation as destructive of Washington's goal of educating Germans in republican virtues. Worst of all, at Nuremberg (and Tokyo), the United States had departed from its own definition of fair treatment of persons and discarded articles in the Constitution against prosecution by *ex post facto* law:

I believe that most Americans view with discomfort the war trials which have just been concluded in Germany and are proceeding in Japan. They violate that fundamental principle of American law that a man cannot be tried under an *ex post facto* statute. The hanging of the eleven men at Nuremberg will be a blot on the American record which we shall long regret.

The trial of the vanquished by the victors cannot be impartial no matter how it is hedged about with the forms of justice. I question whether the hanging of those, who, however despicable, were the leaders of the German people, will ever discourage the making of aggressive war, for no one makes aggressive war unless he expects to win. About this whole judgment there is the spirit of vengeance, and vengeance is seldom justice.

In these trials we have accepted the Russian idea of the purpose of trials, government policy and not justice, having little relation to our Anglo-Saxon heritage. By clothing vengeance in the forms of legal procedure, we may discredit the whole idea of justice in Europe for years to come.[117]

Taft added that he would have preferred permanent exile or life imprisonment for German leaders. But such treatment should have been a matter of Allied policy, not the result of a pre-determined trial in Stalinist fashion. Laski, by contrast, defended Nuremberg and the sentences as appropriate.[118]

Appreciations of Taft's Kenyon stand came from diverse commentators. Herr von Papen told reporters of his agreement with Taft, who would have lived gladly without that particular testimonial. Justice Henry Herman of the Washington State Supreme Court also came to Taft's defense. Young Senator John Kennedy later sided indirectly with Taft in a tribute to him in *Profiles in Courage*, 1955. A dozen years later, conservative scholar Russell Kirk published an apology for Taft as champion of legal principles.[119]

Taft drew a flock of angry critics in 1946. Some contrasted the Nuremberg tribunal – that employed able defense lawyers, three acquittals, gradations of penalty – with the Third Reich's judicial travesties. Hoess and the mother with four children were merely one instance of perversion. A few critics detected whiffs of anti-Semitism about Taft. This suspicion, however, ignored his vigorous condemning of German racism and his 1944 co-sponsorship (with New York's Robert Wagner) of a Senate resolution that urged London to lift restrictions on Jewish emigration to Palestine and ratify a Jewish homeland.[120] (Taft in 1948 was unequivocal in wanting Washington to recognize Israel and assist Holocaust survivors.[121]) Yet the columnist Walter Winchell wondered about his reticence at Kenyon over the documented outrages committed by Nuremberg defendants. Taft's adjective for them – "despicable" – seemed too mild as term of opprobrium. A cartoon in the *CIO News* showed Taft alongside Nuremberg's acquitted defendants over a caption that referred to his Nazi "friends." This scrutiny of Taft got energy from the supercharged political season. The Democratic organization in New York state invited him to explain to voters, especially Jews and Poles, why Nazis deserved mercy or why victims should renounce justice. He was rebuked in Washington by Truman and Democratic Senators Alben Barkley (Kentucky), James Huffman (Ohio), and Scott Lucas (Illinois); they puzzled as "his heart bled" for German criminals. New York's Governor Thomas Dewey and House candidate Jacob Javits were among Republicans who hurriedly distanced themselves from Taft by extolling Nuremberg's inherent fairness.[122]

The tempest caused by Taft's Kenyon speech ended abruptly with the November elections. From them the Republicans emerged with majorities in both congressional houses, the first time since 1928. Taft had done his party no damage. Voters were more concerned with matters close to home (inflation, strikes, abolition of wartime shortages and controls) than with the merit of his Nuremberg quibbles.[123] Misplaced at worst, they hardly seemed reason to punish the GOP or reward the long-reigning Democrats with another lease on legislative power. Taft himself was better regarded than ever after the 1946 elections and had perfect reason to think that his run for the Republican presidential nomination would carry.

His defeat by Dewey for the nomination in 1948, again by Eisenhower in 1952, sealed the ascendancy of the GOP's internationalist wing. Thereafter Taft's version of caution in foreign affairs amounted to rearguard action. He had reproved novelty and the pretension of US power to create law for a disordered world. But to his critics – moved by the success of US arms in two giant theaters of war – this viewpoint belonged to a bygone era, not one in which Americans enjoyed economic–military preponderance and moral authority.

* * *

The redistribution of power to US advantage occasioned by World War II permitted Washington officials not only to deliver law (Nuremberg,

Tokyo). They were also able to tailor to US preference the world's economy (Bretton Woods), political life (United Nations), and security (premised on monopoly of atomic power). No contender existed in 1945/46 to challenge the United States whose territory was unscathed, whose economy boomed, whose confidence publisher Henry Luce captured in slogan: the "American century." Germany and Japan were prostrate. Crumpled cities dotted their landscapes. France lay sullen beneath memory of 1940 defeat and Vichy stain. Great Britain, albeit technically victorious, teetered on bankruptcy. The Red Army's sweep over German forces in 1943–1945 did not cancel the USSR's numbing human and material sacrifice: 27 million people dead, millions left maimed or homeless, cities in shambles, agricultural districts denuded of cultivation.

Roosevelt had postponed as long as possible US entry into this "most merciless of all the wars" (Churchill).[124] Even as swelling Axis strength undermined the plausibility of delay, he sought to defer the inevitable. With purchases of time, the United States could muster trained troops and produce abundant arms. He wagered that Allied power would contain the menace until such time that US force could intervene. American postponement came at the expense of two states riven by internal dissension and unable to mount offensives against Axis foes. China barely survived. France fell. By the time US power finally joined that of the Anglo-Soviet, Germany held most of Europe captive. Japan had advanced its co-prosperity sphere into the Pacific and deeper onto the Asian mainland. Ambassadors Johnson and Bullitt had earlier exerted themselves to energize Washington's policy lest events culminated in irretrievable disaster. It would not only extinguish Chinese and French power, but would reduce future margins of US safety and expose too late the isolationist fallacy.

French debacle in May/June 1940 left Bullitt incredulous over US lethargy as Hitler rearranged Europe's power balance. As for Johnson, he felt vindicated by FDR's overdue firmness: the July 1941 freezing of Japanese assets in the United States and oil embargo. Coming when they did, however, these actions helped ignite the Japanese–US war. It could have been averted, in Johnson's view, had Americans awakened earlier to gathering dangers and defused them.

Absolute catastrophe overtook European Jewry and Roma, supplemented by additional murders on prodigious scale of Poles and Russians. The dilatory US response to genocide had actually been foreshadowed in 1933, when Moscow and Washington negotiated terms of formal recognition. Roosevelt uttered not a word to Stalin's representative, Maxim Litvinov, about the state-induced famine that in the early

1930s killed 6 million peasants in Ukraine and the North Caucasus.[125] American passivity – silence and withholding of help from starving zones – had the virtue of not complicating delicate diplomacy.[126] A decade later the administration was again unresponsive to an ongoing humanitarian crisis until Morgenthau, a person of average talent and allergic to tempting FDR's disfavor, took actions. He shamed the government. He moved it against indolence and State Department bad faith to act, thereby saving the United States from the ignominy of being a purely bystander nation. (The State Department's Policy Planning Staff still minimized the Shoah in 1948, blandly referring to the wartime "mistreatment of Jews in Europe."[127]) New Zealand, Australia, and Canada admitted only token numbers of European Jews during the emergency years. South American governments were likewise unfriendly to Jewish immigration.[128] Churchill's cabinet never authorized anything comparable to the War Refugee Board. London meanwhile sought to jam avenues of Jewish escape from Europe, namely the precarious land and sea routes to Palestine. Foreign Minister Anthony Eden's reason, supported by Stimson and General Marshall, was that more Jewish arrivals would exacerbate the simmering Jewish–Arab feud in Palestine. It might then explode into open warfare, leaving Germany the beneficiary of Arab/Muslim wrath and damaging the Allied hold on Mideastern oil fields.[129]

Nearly 4 million Jews had been killed by the time Roosevelt established his late and little War Refugee Board. Nazi racism, interacting with centuries of Christian contempt for Jewry, fed the gas chambers.[130] Depravity in Nazi guise touched the nadir in so-called medical experiments on Jews and Roma conducted by Dr. Josef Mengele. Japanese experiments on Chinese POWs, prostituting of Korean women, and legendary mistreatment of captured Anglo-US servicemen – of which the 1942 Bataan Death March was an instance – also added to the catalogue of Axis reprehensibility while raising anew questions of theodicy.

Yet Berlin–Tokyo did not possess a monopoly on cruelty. Battlefield atrocities were committed by *both* sides in the Pacific war: spontaneous, gratuitous, atavistic. Hundreds of thousands of German women were raped by Soviet soldiers during the last phase of hostilities and its aftermath, perhaps even as many as 2 million victims (girls to grandmothers).[131] Anglo-American carpet-bombing of Axis cities ignored the norms of warfare, based on principles of proportionality and time-honored discriminations: legitimate versus illegitimate targets, combatant versus non-combatant. Berlin, Cologne, Dresden, Hamburg, Osaka, Yokohama, and Tokyo numbered among the Axis cities broken by incendiaries, super explosives, and fire storms. Only an elastic definition of military necessity justified this destruction.[132] It flouted the Western ethical canon, said the Anglican bishop of Chichester, George Bell. He protested in the House of Lords, February 1944:

I do not forget the Luftwaffe, or its tremendous bombing of Belgrade, Warsaw, Rotterdam, London, Portsmouth, Coventry, Canterbury and many other places ... There is no decent person on the Allied side who is likely to suggest that we should make [Hitler] our pattern or attempt to be competitors in that market ...

The point I want to bring home ... is that it is no longer definite military and industrial objectives which are the aim of the bombers, but the whole town, area by area, is plotted carefully out. The area is singled out and plastered on one night; that area is singled out and plastered on another night; a third, a fourth, a fifth area is similarly singled out and plastered night after night, till, to use the language of the Chief of Bomber Command with regard to Berlin, the heart of Nazi Germany ceases to beat. How can there be discrimination in such matters when civilians, monuments, military objectives and industrial objectives all together form the target?

... Why is there this inability to reckon with moral and spiritual facts? Why is there this forgetfulness of the ideals by which our cause is inspired? How can the War Cabinet fail to see that this progressive devastation of cities is threatening the roots of civilization? ... The sufferings of Europe, brought about by the demoniac cruelty of Hitler ... are not to be healed by the use of power only, power exclusive and unlimited. The Allies stand for something greater than power. The chief name inscribed on our banner is "Law." It is of supreme importance that we who, with our Allies, are the liberators of Europe should so use power that it is always under the control of law.[133]

No ranking Briton or American publicly revealed misgivings during the war on "city busting" equal to Bell's statement. A year after it, as the magnitude of ruin rained on Dresden by Anglo–US bombers (February 13–14, 1945) sank into Allied awareness, Churchill let himself question, before the British Chiefs of Staff, the nature of punitive air raids. The destroying of lives (50,000 dead) and cultural treasure in Dresden also affected Stimson; he later advised that the United States should avoid getting a "reputation of outdoing Hitler in atrocities."[134] Yet the saturation bombings did not abate. They were driven by the logic of total war and Allied aim: unconditional surrender. These imperatives in 1945 – scarcely examined, seemingly automatic – culminated in Hiroshima's and Nagasaki's incineration. It produced endless litters of instant death, lingering infirmity, genetic distortions, and deformities in children later conceived. One woman, who as a schoolgirl in Hiroshima witnessed hideous scenes, subsequently asked: "Those scientists who invented the atomic bomb, what did they think would happen if they dropped it?"[135]

Nobody in Truman's cabinet or in the military objected to the atomic bombs at the time of their contemplated use, though traces of ambivalence appeared. Admiral William Leahy of the Joint Chiefs, a self-proclaimed ordnance expert, was skeptical about any atomic device from an engineering standpoint. He pronounced just days before the Hiroshima attack of August 6: "I do not think it will be as effective as is expected. It sounds like a professor's dream to me!" But not until after the war was won did he label the atomic bomb a repellant weapon, adding that it "was of no material assistance in our war against Japan. The Japanese were already defeated and ready to surrender."[136] Marshall, who had once considered using poisonous gas against Japanese soldiers, predicted that dropping the bomb on civilian concentrations would lead to the heaping of obloquy upon Washington. He did not press this matter, however, when his concern was rebuffed by Stimson.[137] The secretary himself unhesitatingly approved the bomb's use. He afterward gave justifications based on shortening the war and saving lives, Japanese as well as American.[138] He had, though, removed Kyoto from the list of possible targets. Perhaps regret over Dresden influenced him. In any case, he had determined, despite some military grumbling, to spare the city as splendid shrine of Japanese art and culture. Leveling it, he intuited, would embitter the Japanese for years to come, a situation bound to hamper US occupation and postwar diplomacy.[139] As for Truman, he claimed after the war not to have lost a night's sleep over ordering the atomic attacks. But in the anxious days between the Nagasaki bombing (August 9) and Emperor Hirohito's announcement of capitulation (August 15), he expressed qualms about inflicting more atomic death upon non-combatants. Secretary of Commerce Henry Wallace recorded in his diary on August 10 what Truman that day allowed in cabinet: "The thought of wiping out another 100,000 people was too horrible. He didn't like the idea of killing 'all those kids.'"[140]

Other ways of ending the war might have been found short of the atomic bomb (or invasion of Japan).[141] Peace feelers, for one, emanating from the Imperial foreign ministry might have been encouraged or otherwise developed. Or as Stimson and Undersecretary of State Joseph Grew suggested in summer 1945, unconditional surrender policy could have been modified: demands on dismantling the institution of the emperor might have been dropped, thereby strengthening the peace faction in Japan against diehards. Another option, demonstration explosion of the atom bomb on a barren island, might have jolted Tokyo's militarists and led to their surrender, as suggested by a group of Manhattan Project scientists headed by Jerome Franck. Issuance of candid warning to Japan before threatened use of the bomb was an idea favored by

Stimson, Grew, and Secretary of the Navy James Forrestal. Ralph Bard, Forrestal's chief lieutenant at Navy, phrased the case succinctly in June 1945: "Japan should have . . . preliminary warning for some two or three days in advance of [atomic bombing]. The position of the United States as a great humanitarian nation and the fair play attitude of our people generally is responsible . . . for [my] feeling."[142] Truman's decision in the event to withhold precise warning caused the Federal Council of Churches and Niebuhr to condemn (1946) the Hiroshima–Nagasaki bombings as wicked.[143]

The atomic attacks culminated the indignations of 1937–1945: Nanking, slave labor, saturation bombing, and, above all, methodical genocide. The existential problem after Axis vanquishment hinged on whether the miasma of race idolatry and state worship could be dispelled. Could *The City of Man*'s hopefulness be confirmed? The political question was whether reasonable standards of conduct would be salvaged for international life. The Nuremberg and Tokyo tribunals were attempts at reaffirmation. But the flaws attending these trials were legion, many identified by Taft. His rehearsing them at a time when most Americans hailed Nuremberg credits his courage (equal to his lonely condemning in 1942 of Washington's internment of Japanese Americans). Applications of *ex post facto* law, wartime notice by Allied leaders of their intention to punish Axis officials, and Soviet violations of peace treaties (such as making war upon Japan in August 1945 contra the 1941 Moscow–Tokyo neutrality pact) debased Nuremberg from the standpoint of existing positive law. Still, the Taft objection, albeit sound in respects, missed the bigger picture. Summary execution of top Germans or their imprisonment/exile without trial would have denied to the public an early evaluation of the Third Reich and made denazification problematic. By concentrating on individual culprits, the Nuremberg prosecutors also undercut assumptions of collective German guilt. Had they taken root, they would have impeded Germany's return to European society and invited sporadic acts of revenge comparable to those that marred Armenian–Turkish relations for decades after 1915.

A trial of Nazi bigwigs at the International Court of Justice in The Hague would doubtless have been fairer, less open to criticism. Yet the Nuremberg tribunal supported worthy legal innovations congenial to natural law theory and its advocates. None put the point more elegantly than Robert Jackson in his opening statement to the justices at Nuremberg (November 21, 1945):

The real complaining party at your bar is Civilization. In all our countries it is still a struggling and imperfect thing . . . But it points to the dreadful sequence of aggressions and crimes ... it points to the weariness of flesh, the exhaustion of resources, and the destruction of all that was beautiful or useful in so much of the world, and to greater potentialities for destruction in the days to come ... The refuge of the defendants can only be their hope that International Law will lag so far behind the moral sense of mankind that conduct which is crime in the moral sense must be regarded as innocence in law. Civilization asks whether law is so laggard as to be utterly helpless to deal with crimes of this magnitude by criminals of this order of importance.[144]

Jackson did not expect that anything accomplished at Nuremberg would eradicate future war or atrocities. He nonetheless hoped that the precepts and prohibitions upheld there would provide a basis for future advances.[145] In this matter, he, not Taft, was right as governments in the postwar era proposed better standards. In the absence of Nuremberg, and despite the embarrassing Soviet presence, resultant agreements – their vocabulary, their sensibility, their vibrancy – would likely have been denied to the post-Nazi world. Nuremberg ideals were manifest in the UN's 1948 adoption of two breakthroughs: the Universal Declaration of Human Rights, the Convention on the Prevention and Punishment of the Crime of Genocide. Agreements of like spirit have followed. They include the 1949 Geneva Conventions on treatment of prisoners; the International Covenant on Economic, Social, and Cultural Rights; prohibitions on racial discrimination; prohibitions on torture; prohibitions on discrimination against women; protections of the rights of children. Enforcement of these and related norms/laws has been spotty, of course. But the durability of Nuremberg notions, something of their sturdiness, was palpable in late twentieth-century undertakings by the UN International Criminal Tribunals for Yugoslavia and Rwanda and the permanent International Court in The Hague.[146]

11   Containment

Adjustment marked the aftermath of World War II. The war had destroyed the European balance of power and fractured the pillars upon which it rested. Alien armies occupied Germany. Clement Attlee's Labour government edged Britain away from empire, dramatized by India's 1947 independence. France proved immune to resuscitation as a major force, despite Charles de Gaulle's efforts and mannered dignity. This debility in the three states created a vacuum. The two extra-European powers, residing hitherto on the sides, filled the void. They established a new balance of power with distinctive spheres of influence. Therein the Americans and Soviets arranged political–social–economic life according to their respective desiderata. Soviet–US rivalry centered in Europe extended elsewhere. Ideological differences between Washington and Moscow compounded the intensity of Cold War confrontation.

Containment as it evolved during Truman's presidency became the organizing axiom of US foreign policy, so remaining until dissolution of the Cold War order in 1989–1991. The main object was to prevent Stalin, then his successors, from expanding the USSR's territorial–political influence past lines reached by the Red Army in 1945. Zones deemed vital by Washington encompassed not only liberal-industrial Western Europe, but also Japan and Mideastern oil producers. Not all peripheral areas were ignored by post-1945 administrations, evidenced by US actions in Korea and Vietnam. Containment's second objective was to make Soviet power recede from its East European tract, a buffer against intrusion but also antipathetic to Anglo–US interests (economic, security) and sensibility (anticommunism). In places where Stalin's allies had seized power independent of Soviet army intervention, ways were sought to weaken commitments between the Kremlin and its comrades – as in Marshal Tito's Yugoslavia or Mao's China. The communist monolith, seemingly coherent but laced with fissures, might disjoin, yielding centers of Marxist ideology and politics beyond Soviet control.

Varieties of strategy marked containment over the decades.[1] Still, its practitioners did employ three major devices throughout. First, military instruments were meant to keep the USSR in place, exemplified by the founding of NATO and creation of a nuclear–strategic arsenal premised on deterrence. Second, economic–political means were deployed to counter the putative allure of Soviet communism and bolster the economies of partners, per the European Recovery Program (Marshall Plan). Third, covert–psychological programs played a major supplemental role as did propaganda.

Containment in the late 1940s amounted to bellicosity short of open conflict. Leon Trotsky's earlier formula captured the situation: "neither peace nor war." As read by Truman and advisors – Dean Acheson, James Byrnes, Clark Clifford, Averell Harriman, James Forrestal, George Marshall – all evidences indicated Soviet antipathy for the West, born of ambitions to spread Marxist faith, ensure tyranny's survival in Moscow, and shape global affairs. Stalin in February 1946 in a widely broadcast speech, called a declaration of war by Justice Douglas, spoke of inherent incompatibilities between capitalism and socialism. The "contradictions" foretold future showdown.[2] Stalin delayed Red Army withdrawal from northern Iran. He pressed Ankara to revise Soviet–Turkish frontiers in Moscow's favor. He emplaced puppet regimes in 1946–1947 on Poland, Hungary, Bulgaria, Romania. Soviet-inspired Czech communists staged a coup in February 1948 that shifted Prague into Moscow's orbit. Stalin's blockade of Berlin that same year threatened to end Anglo-US access to the city and force it into Soviet submission. The next year Moscow's scientists tested an atomic bomb, thus breaking US monopoly on such weaponry. A triumphant Mao proclaimed in July that Marxist China would henceforth side with the USSR. North Korean armies invaded South Korea less than a year later – with Moscow's approval or under Stalin's direction, so concluded Washington officials. Either way, they believed, the North Korean move signaled Soviet escalation by proxy against the American-led nations. Acquiescence to this latest provocation would have repeated the misguided appeasement of Nazi Germany, said Truman. Aggressors invariably pounded forward in the absence of countervailing firmness.[3] He consequently ordered US armed forces under United Nations aegis to repulse the North Koreans. He tripled defense spending in fiscal 1951 per recommendations of the National Security Council's seminal study, NSC 68.[4]

Against Cold War

Not all pundits or members of the responsible class approved Truman's hardline. Walter Lippmann warned in 1947 that it would fritter away US resources. It could also spark an otherwise avoidable third world war. He labeled containment a "strategic monstrosity." He winced at the Truman Doctrine's hyperbole.[5] Reinhold Niebuhr sounded tocsins against national pride and sanctimony.[6] Senator Taft bemoaned the financial burdens of militarization. Democratic Senators Glen Taylor (Idaho) and Claude Pepper (Florida) admonished Truman for what they perceived as his unilateralism, disregard for diplomacy, and disrespect for civil liberties via the 1947 Loyalty Act (Executive Order 9835).[7]

The most vociferous dissenter was Henry Agard Wallace, who made a run for the presidency on the Progressive ticket in 1948. (Taylor took the vice presidential slot.) Before then this prosperous Iowa farmer and agrarian publicist had occupied foremost position on the Democratic party's left wing along with portfolios: secretary of Agriculture, 1933–1940; FDR's vice president, 1941–1945; secretary of Commerce, 1945–1946. Except for Roosevelt himself, no New Dealer sparked as much controversy as Wallace. Reactionaries reviled him. Liberal votaries esteemed him, his reforms, and his espousal of "progressive capitalism."

Not an easy man for contemporaries to know – devoid of small talk – he remains an enigma for historians. His mental mix combined devotion to empirical science, particularly with application to hybrid crops and animal husbandry, abiding concern with the uplift of destitute people irrespective of race or sex, and spiritual yearning. This last quality animated his religious quest. He began with Protestantism inherited from his parents, Presbyterian and Methodist. He consumed William James's *Varieties of Religious Experience*. He pushed through Theosophy, glanced off Native American practice (rain dance), dabbled in astrology, studied Buddhist renunciation, and doubted Darwin. He flirted with Roman Catholicism, Baha'ism, Hinduism. Wallace landed finally in the liturgically satisfactory and dogmatically relaxed Episcopal fold. It allowed him to nurse pet convictions about the "divine spark" dwelling in all people, to emphasize the essential goodness of humanity – even human perfectibility – over the universality of original sin, and to seek common ground among disparate nations.[8] Critics during the 1930s scoffed at his unconventional religiosity.[9] They called him occult weirdo and levitating mystic, patently unqualified for public office. They relished opportunities, which in clumsy ways he created, to mortify him, by advertising a batch of his purloined correspondence with improbable spiritual mentors: the "Guru letters."[10]

Not oblivious to damage that such ridicule might create, FDR nonetheless appreciated Wallace's tireless efforts at Agriculture to overcome rural poverty: promoting soil conservation, farm supports, food storage. He consequently plucked Wallace, over the protests of Dixiecrats and city bosses, for the vice presidential spot on the 1940 Democratic ticket. He acquitted himself as a hard-hitting campaigner, who equated votes for Willkie with encouragement for Hitler.[11] Wallace served effectively as a wartime vice president. He chaired the Board of Economic Warfare, until squeezed out in a bureaucratic turf battle with Secretary of Commerce Jesse Jones. Wallace conducted a goodwill tour of Latin America to shore up western hemispheric solidarity. He made a goodwill trip in spring 1944 to China and Siberia. (Soviet officials in the latter tricked Wallace into identifying the inhabitants of Magadan, a slave labor center, as happy pioneers on the socialist frontier – an error that later chagrined him.[12]) His vision of the postwar world took FDR's statements as points of reference – Atlantic Charter, Four Freedoms – which he at first embellished. But he soon went further to promote heady themes of his own: Soviet–US cooperation based on sympathetic understanding, reduction of sovereignty in deference to free trade and a United Nations organization (equipped with army and air force), broad substitution everywhere of welfare for warfare, the convergence of capitalist and Marxist societies to ensure human advancement. In the coming reign of the "common man," Wallace promised, every person would enjoy improved standards of nutrition, live unfettered by imperialist powers or avaricious cartels, and enjoy the blessings of science, modern production, and democracy. Americans, Soviets, Britons, Chinese, Germans, Japanese, and other peoples would "learn war no more." Their political-economic fates should instead entwine in unprecedented freedom and equality.[13]

Roosevelt did not check Wallace's roseate depiction of an abundant future, even as snipers like Clare Booth Luce took pot shots at the vice president's "globaloney." FDR seems, in fact, to have valued Wallace's rhetoric as inspiration to a weary public, giving him needed margin to concentrate on the shaky Grand Alliance, negotiate with cunning colleagues (Stalin, Churchill), and preside over immense military–naval machinery. Wallace for his part sought to goad FDR, whom he regarded as an unfocused lightweight, into accepting grander ideas than his mind would have naturally dreamt.[14]

Roosevelt's White House successor had slight regard for Wallace as New Deal warhorse, none as prophet of innovative world order. Truman eventually came to view him as something worse: an amalgam of communist sucker, dissembler, and loony in Stalin's "sabotage front." Nor does Wallace appear to have ever respected Truman, scorning him as Pendergast hack, then usurper.[15] Had FDR not acceded to fixers at the 1944 Democratic convention – over whom he rode roughshod in 1940 – the Iowan would have become president upon his boss's death. Wallace "had no reason to love me or be loyal to me," Truman once coolly observed, but wanted to recover his snatched White House.[16]

Roosevelt had made Wallace secretary of Commerce as consolation for dumping him from the ticket and in recognition of his good-natured campaigning during autumn 1944. From this cabinet perch, Wallace opposed Truman's Soviet policy and then began that insurgency which culminated in his presidential bid. Apart from his grudge against Truman the man, the Commerce secretary thought him the witless tool of Catholic militants, reactionary capitalists, and Pentagon warmongers (Forrestal and General Leslie Groves in Wallace's demonology), themselves seduced by the oozing charm of London Tories eager to enlist Americans in saving British imperialism. Wallace held that no Cold War would have erupted had FDR lived longer.[17]

Wallace tried while still in cabinet to steer Truman in a direction away from colliding with Stalin and maintained that the president should not dispense with FDR's admittedly difficult task: trying to build a solid relationship with Moscow based upon respect. This attitude did not mean, as was Wallace's repeated message in epistles and in cabinet conferences, that one should ignore philosophical or institutional differences with the USSR in economics, politics, or culture.[18] He had himself opposed FDR's recognition of Moscow in 1933, partly because of Stalin's persecution of the kulaks (whose defiance Wallace knew resulted in their deaths).[19] Nor should Soviet leaders think that they could take a cavalier attitude toward US interests, let alone trespass against them with impunity. He also never doubted the ethical–productive superiority of free enterprise over command economies. Yet as Anglo-American collaboration with the Soviet Union had proven in 1941–1945, East and West could undertake joint ventures on behalf of a larger good. The longterm aim should be the blending of contrary economies to produce "one world" – the alternative being a series of escalating threats climaxing in catastrophe.[20] People in the West, then, had to appreciate how the history of Russian wartime sufferings, from Mongol hordes to German armies, colored Moscow's statecraft. It sought buffers plus secure borders as insurance against future invasion while easing the constriction generated by "capitalist encirclement." An acceptable detour on the way to "one world" would be clearly defined spheres of influence. Americans should stay calm while Stalinists cultivated Moscow-oriented regimes in Eastern Europe:

We should recognize that we have no more business in the *political* affairs of eastern Europe than Russia has in the *political* affairs of Latin America, western Europe, and the United States. We may not like what Russia does in eastern Europe. Her type of land reform, industrial expropriation, and suppression of basic liberties offends the great majority of the people of the United States.

But whether we like it or not the Russians will try to socialize their sphere of influence just as we try to democratize our sphere of influence ...

The Russians have no more business in stirring up native communists to political activity in western Europe, Latin America, and the United States than we have interfering in the politics of eastern Europe and Russia ... we have to recognize that the Balkans are closer to Russia than to us – and that Russia cannot permit either England or the United States to dominate the politics of that area.[21]

Wallace rejected Churchill's "iron curtain" speech (March 5, 1946) and called it infamous, contrary to a workable East–West modus vivendi.[22] He had earlier taken a charitable view of Stalin's ideological spouting (February) that had so alarmed Douglas. "We were challenging [Stalin] and his speech was taking up the challenge," Wallace explained.[23] He also proposed to Truman that the administration grant a multibillion dollar loan to Moscow via the Export-Import bank to help repair the war-battered Soviet economy and rejuvenate East–West trade.

The most far-reaching advice from Wallace centered on ways to avoid an atomic arms race, a cause pressed upon him by the Manhattan Project's morally anguished J. Robert Oppenheimer. Wallace originally argued, as did Henry Stimson before leaving government (September 1945), that Washington should reassure Moscow of benign US purpose: American scientists ought to share theories/principal findings with their Soviet counterparts. But the Americans would keep to themselves the technique of bomb making, leaving that riddle for Soviet engineers to solve. In any case, the Kremlin's denizens should be impressed by the gesture, which would not come at cost to the United States. American scientists did not own the knowledge of atomic physics and lacked means to prevent its dissemination; the Soviets before long would have mastered the mysteries, such as they were. Wallace held, therefore, that the potential payoff of scientific collaboration was high, the risks illusory.[24]

He dropped in subsequent iterations the awkward distinction between atomic knowledge and bomb "know-how." He focused instead on the ready accessibility of nations to nuclear science and their production of massively destructive weapons. To avert an arms race, Washington should lobby for international agreements. They could provide for joint pooling of information on atomic energy and its use for peaceful purposes (like the 1946 Acheson–Lilienthal scheme but with fewer conditions). The alternative, Wallace told Truman in July 1946, was a world heaving with doomsday weapons and divided into two antagonistic camps. The Americans had to try to see themselves as other peoples did, then ease their anxiety by open-handedness. The

Soviets, for one, were not suffering from paranoia but had reason for anxiety:

How do American actions since [victory over Japan] appear to other nations? I mean by actions the concrete things like $13 billion for the War and Navy Departments, the Bikini tests of the atomic bomb and continued production of bombs, the plan to arm Latin America with our weapons, production of B-29s and planned production of B-36s, and the effort to secure air bases spread over half the globe from which the other half of the globe can be bombed. I cannot but feel that these actions must make it look to the rest of the world as if we were only paying lip service to peace . . . These facts rather make it appear either (1) that we are preparing ourselves to win the war which we regard as inevitable or (2) that we are trying to build up a predominance of force to intimidate the rest of mankind. How would it look to us if Russia had the atomic bomb and we did not, if Russia had 10,000-mile bombers and air bases within a thousand miles of our coastlines and we did not?[25]

The government, urged Wallace, should negotiate an accord with the Soviets to reduce war dangers and build multilateral relationships. The Americans, by this idea, would entrust nuclear knowledge to agencies of the UN and eliminate the US stockpile of atomic bombs; the Soviets would refrain altogether from developing such things.[26]

Wallace's suggestion to imagine the world from a Soviet perspective did not convince Truman. Neither did he discern merit in abnegating whatever bonus atomic monopoly afforded US diplomacy, even if such advantage proved fleeting. He had absolutely no confidence in the secretary's approach to Soviet affairs. Truman later wrote: "Wallace's dream of appeasement was futile . . . if allowed to materialize, it would be tragic . . . the Russians only understood force."[27]

The president had qualms about firing Wallace, connected to keeping his adherents loyal to the post-New Deal White House: northeastern liberals, farm bloc activists, organized labor, celebrities such as Thomas Mann and Helen Keller.[28] Still, Truman by late summer 1946 realized that emergent containment and Wallace's viewpoint – not always expressed in confidential settings, but also spectacularly at New York's Madison Square Garden on September 12th – were irreconcilable. Pressured by Secretary of State Byrnes, who felt his authority disrupted by Wallace, Truman hastened to do what had become inevitable, firing (September 20) "the most peculiar fellow I ever came in contact with."[29] Truman confided to his wife: "I believe [Wallace] is a real Commy and a dangerous man."[30]

Released from all cabinet obligations, but atop a visible platform as newly appointed editor of the *New Republic* (October 1946), Wallace inveighed against policies that he thought unsound.[31] His fervor was reminiscent of William Jennings Bryan in similar circumstances of war, peace, and presumed presidential delinquency. Wallace ripped into Truman's call for aid ($400 million) to Greece and Turkey in March 1947. The measure would lead to unbridled costs and enervation: "Once American loans are given to the undemocratic governments of Greece and Turkey, every reactionary government and every strutting dictator will be able to hoist the anti-Communist skull and bones, and demand that the American people rush to his aid ... American dollars will be the first demand, then American army officers and technicians, then American GIs."[32] He likewise decried Truman's Loyalty Act for inaugurating a regime of domestic terror:

Our civil liberties are on the point of being lost when a worker can't act politically for fear of losing his job; when a businessman fears to speak his mind or attend a political meeting because of the danger of reprisals in his business life; when government employees and teachers in fear of being branded as communists ... refuse to express any ideas except the most reactionary. The first step toward fascism and war is the destruction of civil liberties.[33]

Wallace opposed peacetime conscription. As Progressive presidential candidate, he called Congress's passage of the Selective Service Act (June 1948) an insult to individual freedom and certain to confirm a thicket of Soviet fears about US purpose.[34] He proposed a program to endow the UN with $10 billion to overcome world poverty while faulting the Marshall Plan ("Martial Plan") for deepening Europe's political–ideological trench.[35] He also blamed the ambassador to Prague, Laurence Steinhardt, and unnamed Czech reactionaries for provoking the communist coup (and mysterious death of Foreign Minister Jan Masaryk); the Soviets were acting defensively, understandably. Wallace additionally interpreted the Berlin blockade as not unreasonable but an opportunity to deal constructively with Moscow on resolving German problems.[36]

Candidate Wallace engaged in a public exchange of letters with Stalin to find an exit from the Cold War impasse. This correspondence emphasized reinvigorated trade, scientific exchanges, and a series of agreements to reduce troop deployments, reintegrate divided Europe, and quicken arms control. Concerning this last point, Wallace wrote in his primer, *Toward World Peace*:

The atom bomb keeps ticking away, saying just one thing: "International morality based on justice or world suicide?" Either a world-wide practical religious approach takes hold of the hearts and minds of us all or we shall experience the incredible folly of World War III.[37]

Not only did Truman rebuff Wallace. Mainstream intellectuals and union leaders got fed up with him in 1948, as he and the Progressive party accepted support from anyone, communists included. The decision to deny none stemmed from his impatience with red-baiting, indulged, he said, by Truman no less than the House Committee on Un-American Activities. Yet to Niebuhr, Hubert Humphrey, John Kenneth Galbraith, Walter Reuther, Walter White, Arthur Schlesinger, Jr., and other movers in devoutly anticommunist liberal circles – embodied by Americans for Democratic Action (ADA) – Wallace had strayed far in dicey direction. They rued his opening the Progressive organization to fellow travelers whose first allegiance Moscow claimed. "Poor Henry is really a prisoner of the Commies," Niebuhr concluded. The Socialist Party's perennial presidential candidate, Norman Thomas, lambasted Wallace for sharing too much of the Progressive agenda with homebred Stalinists. Even his friend from New Deal days, Henry Morgenthau, tore into Wallace.[38]

Anticommunist fundamentalists, meantime, set upon him. Representative William Colmer (Democrat, Mississippi) charged that he slavishly followed the Kremlin's voice.[39] Representative John Rankin, invoking supposed authority in the 1799 Logan Act, urged that Wallace be imprisoned for making anti-American speeches. His jeremiads on class stratification and racial estrangement also caught the attention of J. Edgar Hoover's FBI. Its close scrutiny caused the candidate, in turn, to warn against totalitarian surveillance and an embryonic police state. Appearances in public fora with controversial Paul Robeson and speeches to racially integrated audiences in Dixie stirred uproar plus more derision of the "corn fed mystic." Unbowed by glowering whites or overt intimidation, he kept blasting Jim Crow laws while on southern tour (gaily accompanied by banjo-strumming Pete Seeger): "The unforgivable sin is looking down on other people and other races as inherently inferior."[40]

The electorate in 1948 spurned Wallace. He had expected at one time to poll 5 million votes, to win something in the electoral college – New York, perhaps. In the event, he won a mere 1,157,063 popular votes. Nothing in the electoral college. Strom Thurmond's States' Rights Party fared better, winning 39 electoral votes from Alabama, Mississippi, Louisiana, South Carolina. The defection of Wallace-type liberals and Thurmond-southerners in 1948, the unbinding of FDR's coalition, did not, miraculously, tip the scales for Thomas Dewey. Wallace's *bête noire* squeaked by in memorable upset.[41]

Despite getting clobbered at the polls, Wallace did not go quietly. He hoped to keep the Progressive faith alive, if for no other reason than to make the Democrats less brazen abroad, more humane at home. He surely took solace in Truman's pre-election support of antilynching laws, increases to the minimum wage, universal health care, and desegregation of the military forces – unlikely "concessions" in the absence of leftist thunder. Nevertheless, Wallace continued to criticize after 1948, particularly Truman's external policy. He denounced NATO's establishment in 1949. It constituted, to his mind, another assault on jangled Soviet nerves and damaged the UN ideal.[42]

Wallace's understanding of world affairs altered somewhat in 1949. The stringency of communist rule in Prague bothered him – prefiguring the show trial and execution of Rudolf Slansky in 1952.[43] Soviet bluster over Berlin and Mao's ruthlessness in new China also disturbed Wallace, enough for him to admit, however tentatively, that US diplomacy had traces of reason.

His dissenting career ended on June 25, 1950 as North Korean armies swept over the 38th parallel. He praised Truman's decision to intervene with troops under General Douglas MacArthur. Wallace welcomed the UN's imprimatur. "Undoubtedly the Russians could have prevented the attacks by the North Koreans," he declared in July 1950, "and undoubtedly they could stop the attack any time they wish. I hold no brief for the past actions of the United States or Russia but when my country is at war and the United Nations sanctions that war, I am on the side of my country and the United Nations."[44] He urged in August the use of atomic weapons should matters go awry for Americans in their "just war."[45] That same month he resigned from the Progressive party, after it failed to back Washington's Korean action.

He then fled public affairs in favor of horticultural glories and the contemplative life on his Farvue Farm (Westchester County, New York).[46] Only rarely did Wallace break from his private routine as in 1952, when he published an unexpected article: "Where I Was Wrong." A recantation of his earlier anti-containment position, he informed readers that he had previously not grasped the iniquity of Soviet totalitarianism or foreign policy. The man who would be president was not even certain that his incumbency would have benefited the United States.[47]

Wallace voted for an army general in the 1956 election, Dwight Eisenhower. By so doing, the lapsed dissenter refuted earlier distrust of soldiers, all of whom he had thought unsuited for republican trust, naturally inclined toward imperialist pursuits. He once huffed: "Three cheers for the military! They are so helpful to humanity."[48]

Korea and MacArthur

The campaign to reunite Korea under Pyongyang met with dazzling success in June 1950. While Premier Kim Il Sung professed innocence – victim of "an all-out offensive" waged by the "traitorous Syngman Rhee clique" – his infantry and armor sliced through the South Korean line.[49] Seoul fell to them on June 28. They continued steadily until stalled in September along the southeastern corner: Pusan Perimeter. They would have taken the whole country per Kim's assurances to Stalin, but for the insertion of US soldiers, complemented later by other UN-approved forces (primarily from British Commonwealth countries and Turkey). These rallied what remained of the dispirited South Korean army. They launched a counter-offensive after MacArthur's Inchon surprise on September 15. They recaptured Seoul. They apprehended, killed, or expelled most invaders by October 1.

Emboldened by UN decree, US-led forces then entered North Korean territory to extinguish the communist regime and conquer the divided nation for Seoul.[50] Anxiety in Washington over possible Soviet or Chinese intervention to save Kim and prevent US power from touching Manchurian–Siberian borders had dissipated in the euphoria of hard-won combat. MacArthur's anodyne words for Truman at Wake island (October 15, 1950) on the certainty of complete triumph, without widening the war or drawing Sino-Soviet forces into Korea, also calmed jitters and encouraged officials to discount Chinese warnings. They were meant in earnest, however. They presaged the pouring in of Chinese armies led by Marshal Peng Teh-huai. They routed overextended United Nations forces in November/December. They abandoned Seoul in early January 1951 amid speculation about their evacuating the entire Korean peninsula. Only after absorbing massive Chinese offensives did they recover the shattered capital (March 14). The war then sputtered in deadlock and attrition.

Final casualty tallies included 33,600 Americans killed in combat, 59,000 fatalities among South Korean forces. Estimates of Chinese and North Korean military dead range from between 500,000 to 1.5 million. Casualty figures among civilians (south and north) remain in the unknown millions. American expenditure on the war exceeded $70 billion.[51] Peace parleys did not conclude until after Eisenhower became president in 1953. The armistice of July 27 recognized neither winners nor losers. It ratified with minor territorial change the prewar status quo.[52] This stalemate was far from MacArhur's conception: "There is no substitute for victory."

Few military careers have been as replete with distinction as that enjoyed by MacArthur. He compiled a stellar record as a West Point cadet, class of 1903. After tour in the Philippines, he served as aide-de-camp to President Theodore Roosevelt. MacArthur in the First World War won awards for valor and wound up commanding the 42nd (Rainbow) Division. He served as superintendent of West Point from

1919 to 1922 where he introduced needed reforms. Subsequent promotions and assignments in the Philippines and stateside were capped by President Herbert Hoover's naming him army chief of staff in 1930. His dispersal of the Bonus Marchers in Washington in July 1932 did threaten to sully his name among unemployed veterans, but did not endanger his overall standing. A military advisor to the Philippines Commonwealth in 1935, he accepted appointment in 1936 as its Field Marshal. He retired from active service in December 1937, only to be reactivated on FDR's orders (July 1941) to command US army forces in the Far East. His perseverance during dark moments of 1942 and island-hopping campaigns won him renown. He received the Medal of Honor, promotion to five-star rank, and acceptance of Japanese surrender aboard the *Missouri* in Tokyo Bay. Republican strategists, such as Michigan's Senator Arthur Vandenberg, were so smitten by him that they fantasized about his running for president in 1944 (1948 too), a notion that flattered his pride and fanned his political hankerings.[53] From October 1945 onward MacArthur was the Supreme Commander Allied Powers in Tokyo. He became, in effect, the law of occupied Japan whose first phase bore MacArthur's indelible mark. Simultaneous with this Japanese responsibility, he served as the senior US/UN officer in Korea from summer 1950 to his dismissal, at age seventy-one, from all commands in April 1951.

He possessed unwavering faith in his vocation as man of destiny. He exuded complacency in his knowledge of broad topics: the Asian mind, communism, New Deal deficiencies. He held quasi-philosophical convictions on religion, democracy, and the upward trajectory of history. Denigrating of men whom he regarded as dim, he often offended. Neither Eisenhower nor Marshall overflowed with affection for MacArthur, under whom they had both served and chafed. General Omar Bradley, chairman of the Joint Chiefs of Staff during the Korean war, thought MacArthur a megalomaniac and magnet for sycophants.[54]

He could survive the skepticism of these officers, but not that of his commander-in-chief. MacArthur's ties to Republican congressmen revolted Truman and fed his suspicions of the soldier's White House ambition. Reminiscent of TR on Nelson Miles, Truman thought the general an uncommon egoist, who, by self-appointment, filled the "seat next to God."[55] The former haberdasher once entered in his diary this comment on "Mr. Prima Donna, Brass Hat, Five Star MacArthur":

He's worse than the Cabots and the Lodges – they at least talked with one another before they told God what to do. Mac tells God right off. It is a very great pity we have to have stuffed Shirts like that in key positions. I don't see why in the Hell

Roosevelt didn't order Wainwright home [from Corregidor in 1942] and let MacArthur be a martyr ... We'd have had a real general and fighting man if we had Wainwright and not a play actor and a bunco man such as we have now.[56]

MacArthur at times in his career had been disinclined to follow orders strictly. He had stretched those that annoyed to barely allowable limits. This habit of mind in World War II led to his inappropriate attempt to recruit Churchill and Australia's prime minister, John Curtin, to his cause, namely persuading FDR to allocate more men and *matériel* to the Pacific theater. MacArthur did not always feel obliged to tell the Joint Chiefs, or obtain their approval, of various amphibious operations. Their success and Washington's distance encouraged Pentagon officers to acquiesce, thereby reinforcing his independence of attitude and action. He found ways during his overlordship in Tokyo to duck Truman's directive to visit Washington for consultation; the president fretted, but repressed his impulse to nag or sack.[57]

Cumulative irritations, then, were background to the 1951 Truman–MacArthur affray, albeit not the core question. It flowed from disagreement over policy, and the officer's impertinence that smacked of disobedience.

MacArthur believed that Truman's emphasis on the European power balance and Atlantic security shortchanged US interests in Asia. This approach represented regrettable continuity with FDR's inability to comprehend the area's significance. Pacific Asia would become the world pivot, the region where America's future would be won or lost: "Europe is a dying system. It is worn out and run down." MacArthur also prophesied: "The lands touching the Pacific with their billions of inhabitants will determine the course of history for the next ten thousand years. Stalin ... also knows the Pacific picture and ... is actually looking over his shoulder toward Asia."[58] Rising expectations among Asia's disenfranchised peoples fueled nationalist sentiment and their desire to seize political control from alien masters. Communist connivers were eager to stir this brew of longing and resentment against Western nations. Their only chance for success resided in working with fledgling democratic parties in Asia. This cooperation, said MacArthur, required US economic–military support of local friends comparable to largess bestowed upon Europeans (Marshall Plan, NATO). Europe itself would otherwise be lost as communism in Asia, guided by Moscow and Peking, crept westward to eclipse centers of parliamentary life.[59] The Korean intervention, from his standpoint, gave the United States an unexpected second chance to salvage its Asian standing.[60]

MacArthur pressed his points with deeds and words. They altogether discomfited Washington. Among his misdemeanors, he interfered with its subtle China diplomacy, developed by Secretary of State Acheson (and members of his Policy Planning Staff – George Kennan, John Paton Davies).[61] Seconded by the British, it aimed before Sino-US clashes in Korea to coax the People's Republic away from an exclusive orientation on Moscow, whereby Mao might become an East Asian Tito and China the functional equivalent of Yugoslavia. Achievement of this goal implied Washington's distancing itself from Mao's defeated foes on Taiwan. But MacArthur, neither in sympathy with this idea nor well-versed in it, embraced Chiang's Kuomintang, which presumed still to be China's ruling party. It hoped one day to recover the mainland, lost through ineptness despite years of US help (detailed in the State Department's 1949 *China White Paper*).[62] Acheson held that demise of the Nationalists was inevitable; the United States should not act further on their behalf lest Peking's wrath turn upon Americans and distract it from Moscow's designs on China's northern territory (Sinkiang, Inner Mongolia, Manchuria): "We should not deflect from the Russians to ourselves the righteous anger and hatred of the Chinese people."[63]

MacArthur tacitly cooperated with Republican critics of Truman's China policy. Foremost among them were former president Hoover and Senators William Knowland (California), Styles Bridges (New Hampshire), Joseph McCarthy (Wisconsin), Alexander Wiley (Wisconsin), H. Alexander Smith (New Jersey), and Taft. Before the Korean War, MacArthur in Tokyo had leaked (January 1950) an informational document prepared by the State Department, the gist of which held that Taiwan's fall to Mao would not compromise America's Pacific defense perimeter. Thereupon Knowland, Taft, et al. denounced Truman's stance as irresponsible and repugnant. They also pledged anew to withhold recognition from Mao's regime and do whatever necessary to improve Chiang's viability.[64] Later, MacArthur visited Taiwan (July) to confer with Chiang about island defenses and soothe the Generalissimo's bruised feelings after Truman rejected the Nationalist offer to send troops to South Korea. Without consulting Washington, MacArthur afterward issued a florid statement that expressed his admiration for Chiang. He reciprocated in kind. An impression was thus created of budding Nationalist–US alliance, when none existed and anyway ran against the grain of Truman–Acheson concepts. MacArthur also arranged for three squadrons of air force jets to be transferred to Taiwan, another initiative taken without notifying the Pentagon.[65] The president's interposing of Seventh Fleet ships between Taiwan and China in late June 1950 – to secure the island from amphibious invasion and inhibit Nationalist raids along the coast – meanwhile caused MacArthur to wonder at decisions "to protect the Communist mainland."[66]

He rejected notions of accommodation with Mao's regime as betrayal of an honorable ally. In a communication to the Veterans of Foreign Wars convention, August 27, he touted Taiwan's geo-military importance: "unsinkable aircraft carrier and submarine tender" off the Sino-Soviet shoreline. He also slammed Acheson's State Department, by extension the president too. MacArthur's words were reprinted by the news media. Truman played with the idea of relieving MacArthur for his outburst, for speaking without permission, and withholding advance copy from Washington superiors.[67] His unauthorized words made an impression, even though he tried after the damage – under orders – to withdraw them from circulation:

Nothing could be more fallacious than the threadbare argument by those who advocate appeasement and defeatism in the Pacific that if we defend [Taiwan] we alienate continental Asia. Those who speak thus do not understand the Orient. They do not grant that it is in the pattern of the Oriental psychology to respect and follow aggressive, resolute and dynamic leadership – to quickly turn on a leadership characterized by timidity or vacillation – and they underestimate the Oriental mentality. Nothing in the last five years has so inspired the Far East as the American determination to preserve the bulwarks of our Pacific Ocean strategic position from future encroachment, for few of its peoples fail accurately to appraise the safeguard such determination brings to their free institutions. To pursue any other course would be to turn over the fruits of our Pacific victory to a potential enemy. It would shift any future battle area five thousand miles eastward to the coasts of the American continents ... it would completely expose our friends in the Philippines, our friends in Australia and New Zealand, our friends in Indonesia, our friends in Japan, and other areas, to the lustful thrusts of those who stand for slavery as against liberty, for atheism as against God.[68]

Truman finessed his response by uncharacteristic indirection. He issued orders in December 1950 to *all* high-ranking civilian and military personnel that they had henceforth to obtain State Department clearance before making public statements on foreign policy. These people, moreover, had to exercise care in speaking on sensitive matters.[69] Had MacArthur wanted, he probably could not have made himself comply. He was too much at odds with existing diplomacy and habituated to having his own way. In any case, he had already decided to resist – covertly if possible, openly if necessary – courses of action that he thought would imperil US safety. Truman correctly read this resistance as an attempt to subvert policy made at levels of authority far above MacArthur; he would sabotage the principle of military subordination to civilian authority.[70]

His evolving views on Korea proceeded, at first, in tandem with those of the government. Like it, MacArthur had not felt in the late 1940s that South Korea properly belonged inside the US defense perimeter.[71]

He had no problem in January 1950 when Acheson, in conformance with Joint Chiefs of Staff thinking at the time, traced for the National Press Club's edification a line of geographical security anchored in the Aleutians, Japan, the Ryukyus, and the Philippines. It excluded South Korea, as well as Taiwan.[72] But MacArthur's view of Korea changed as rapidly as Truman's with the June invasion. Flagrant aggression by a communist state should not go unanswered. A Korea under Kim would pose a plain threat to nearby Japan. American credibility as guarantor of Western security also came to the fore, a matter of concern to European members of newly hatched NATO.[73]

Less grave to MacArthur was this worry that shrouded Washington in summer 1950. The North Korean action might be prelude to Moscow-directed aggression elsewhere, perhaps a feint to divert US attention from Soviet assault on Western Europe. Neither did MacArthur care about Truman's felt need to demonstrate on the eve of congressional elections that the administration could act decisively – the "loss of China" aside – against communist marauding. MacArthur, in any case, hailed Truman's decision to fight in Korea. His Inchon feat, his able field commanders, and the Eighth US Army reversed a parlous situation.

Truman tried to capitalize on MacArthur's successes via the meeting at Wake island – political theatrics but not brilliantly orchestrated. MacArthur greeted his commander in chief with a handshake, not a salute, and dressed casually (if not slovenly).[74]

The Truman–MacArthur relationship, fragile at best, imploded under China's intervention and punishment of US/UN armies. Compelled to retreat south and forced to surrender Seoul, MacArthur's men could not return triumphantly "home by Christmas." Their chief gloomily concluded that "a new war" had begun. To win, he told the Pentagon, the government should not restrict his radius of operations. It should, in fact, be expanded in several directions. First, a naval blockade of Chinese ports ought to be imposed to prevent imported *matériel* from making its way to the Korean sector. Second, Chinese military infrastructure in Manchuria that served the Korean campaign should be bombed. Third, Chinese troops involved in the Korean fighting should not enjoy sanctuary north of the Yalu; they should be struck where found by long-range naval bombardment and air sorties. MacArthur did not envision deploying US soldiers to China, but by all other means wanted to cripple its war making capacity.[75] He intimated too the advantage of using atomic weapons, which under certain contingencies Truman and Secretary of Defense Marshall also thought appropriate (a prospect that triggered Attlee's breathless cautions to Washington).[76] Finally, MacArthur hoped that Chiang's 600,000 soldiers would be allowed to land on the mainland opposite Taiwan, supported by US naval and air power. Only by these measures could the US and South Korea prevail – could Asia be saved from despotic "engulfment."[77]

MacArthur's recommendations got nowhere. Truman, Acheson, Marshall, and the Joint Chiefs of Staff wanted to localize the violence. An Asian war along MacArthur's lines would use too many men and their logistics. It would strip bare the US position in Europe, a vulnerability likely to tempt Soviet mischief. Even worse, an expanded Asian war could escalate rapidly into open Soviet–US fighting. It might entail the loss of understaffed NATO forces or surrenders by European allies. America's atomic weapons might have to be used (despite Pentagon concern about their small number and the limited availability of long-range bombers capable of delivering them). Levels of destruction produced in a third world war would surely overshadow those of 1939–1945. As for an amphibious assault by Taiwan's forces, they had proven their ineffectiveness in the Chinese civil war. They would probably get bogged down on the mainland, which then would necessitate risky rescue by the US navy in a version of Dunkirk. Any Taiwan–US venture against People's China would also squash whatever slim chance still existed of exploiting Sino-Soviet tensions to Western advantage. Limited war in Asia, in summary, and a husbanding of resources were the better part of wisdom. The major contest, in Bradley's analysis, involved the USSR, not China:

As long as we keep the conflict within its present scope, we are holding to a minimum the forces we must commit and tie down.

The strategic alternative, enlargement of the war in Korea, to include Red China, would probably delight the Kremlin more than anything else we could do. It would necessarily tie down additional forces, especially our sea power and our air power, while the Soviet Union would not be obliged to put a single man into the conflict.

... Red China is not the powerful nation seeking to dominate the world ... This [MacArthur] strategy would involve us in the wrong war, at the wrong place, at the wrong time, and with the wrong enemy.[78]

MacArthur remained unconvinced. He countered that Soviet leaders would not leap to China's aid with commitments of their own military forces. They were thinly stretched, Germany to Vladivostok, and by no means fully recovered from their war against Hitler. Western Europe, moreover, protected by a quasi US nuclear umbrella, did not elicit Soviet acquisitiveness. "I am no seer to predict," he later said, "whether or not the Soviet aims at ultimately provoking and engaging in a global struggle. I give him infinitely more credit, however, than to believe he would embark upon so reckless and ill-conceived a course."[79] As for China, it could be handled by super applications of conventional fire power.

The dispatch of Chiang's armies to the mainland, if well supported, could also produce results better than pessimists guessed.

The Washington view held, in common with established practice, that MacArthur as officer in charge of ongoing operations should freely offer advice up the chain of command. He could also disagree with decisions made by the cabinet and in the Pentagon, as long as he executed orders.[80] He repeatedly tested this unexceptional understanding, however. For example, contrary to instructions, he had sent US forces (late October 1950) to occupy North Korean districts abutting the nervous Manchurian and Siberian borders. His reason? He wanted to avoid anything that Mao or Stalin might mistake as propitiation. Besides, he maintained, the South Korean army lacked the élan to fulfill this mission. Washington leaders had insufficient resolve at the time to bring MacArthur in line. The aura of infallibility and invincibility that clung to him after Inchon was too great. But after his assurances about Chinese inability proved false, and his forces retreated, he was brought to closer account. Alas too late to avoid political fireworks.

He learned in March 1951 of a State Department *démarche* to draw China and North Korea into ending hostilities per the status quo antebellum. He hastened to scuttle this plan, hoping still to reunite Korea and smash communist armies by reintensified warfare. Without consulting senior officials beforehand, he loosed public taunts against the Chinese side (March 24). He derided its inadequate military supplies, inferior air power, poor communications, and wasteful "human wave tactics." He did offer to meet with Chinese generals to end the effusion of blood. Yet their continued intransigence, MacArthur stated, would end UN/US restraint and justify strikes against scattered Chinese bases. The inevitable result, he added, would be the country's military downfall.[81] The response from Washington was instantaneous: a reminder, tersely worded, of the December directive that forbade making statements without approval.[82] A livid Truman privately decided to fire MacArthur at the next opportunity. It arose on April 5 via the GOP's House minority leader, Joseph Martin (Massachusetts).[83]

Martin publicized non-confidential correspondence that he had recently enjoyed with MacArthur. Therein he recapitulated his criticisms of Truman's international policy, which mistakenly emphasized Europe over Asia:

It seems strangely difficult for some to realize that here in Asia is where the Communist conspirators have elected to make their play for global conquest, and that we have joined the issue thus raised on the battlefield; that here we fight Europe's war with arms while the diplomats there still fight it with words; that if we lose the war to communism in Asia the fall of Europe is inevitable, win it and Europe most probably would avoid war and yet preserve freedom.[84]

MacArthur reiterated his policy ideas to Martin: the desirability of using Nationalist troops against the mainland to lessen Chinese pressure in Korea and the application of "maximum counter-force" to achieve a surrender of all communist forces in the area. "We must win," MacArthur closed. "There is no substitute for victory."[85]

Truman consulted with advisors before doing what he anyway intended.[86] They included his "big four": Acheson, Marshall, Bradley, Harriman. They agreed that MacArthur had overstepped. He had again not cleared a statement bearing on crucial matters. He had undermined the president as spokesman on security policy, baffling public under-standing at home and abroad about US aims and means. MacArthur had challenged the principle of military obedience to civilian authority. By firing him (done on April 11) Truman could also appoint a general not opposed to Washington – or about unilaterally to expand the war – whom he found in the obliging Matthew Ridgway.[87]

MacArthur's recall ignited a firestorm, as Truman expected.[88] Long a darling of the Republican right wing, the general now became a martyr, sacrificed on the altar of defeatism by the priests of Democratic perfidy: "Red" Dean Acheson and his presidential dupe.

MacArthur returned to the United States, the first time in fourteen years, to a hero's welcome. He was visibly gratified as crowds of well-wishers greeted him in Honolulu, San Francisco, Washington, and New York. Millions of citizens celebrated him. Not since the Civil War had any soldier been the object of such veneration. Retired Admiral William Halsey, MacArthur's comrade in the Pacific war, said to his friend (April 14) in a letter: "I am thoroughly aroused by the events that have transpired in the past few days." Halsey wanted MacArthur to redeem the moment and rescue the country from "appeasers" in Washington:

You are beloved ... by millions of good solid American citizens. These same citizens are hoping for some one to lead them out of the depths of despair, uncertainty, and frustrations under which they now labor. Like them, I feel you know more about the Orient and Orientals, than any man in this country. Maybe the crisis we face at home is greater than the present crisis in the Orient. They and I would rally to your banner, if you take on the stupendous task of leading us out of the fog of frustration now surrounding us.[89]

His April 19th address to Congress won MacArthur acclamation as orator, selfless patriot, visionary. "Old soldiers never die, they just fade away," he recited in farewell.[90] Representative Dewey Short (Republican,

Missouri) expressed the feeling of awestruck listeners: "We heard God speak here today, God in the flesh, the voice of God."[91]

Truman and Acheson for their sins were burned in effigy in cities across the country. Telegrams, letters, and petitions swamped Congress and the White House to extol the general. A Gallup poll taken in mid-April indicated that 62 percent of respondents disapproved of Truman's action; fewer than 30 percent supported it. State legislatures (Illinois, Michigan, California, Florida) passed resolutions that backed the warrior and condemned Truman's "capricious" decision.[92] The editors of *Time*, *U.S. News and World Report*, and the *Chicago Tribune* joined the fury; they were despondent over the nation's shame. Brigadier General Julius Klein of the Illinois National Guard was so grating in his defense of MacArthur and disparaging of the White House that Governor Adlai Stevenson fired him.[93]

Republican party spokesmen hoped that Truman would be impeached or Acheson forced to resign. None surpassed the stridency of McCarthy. He had earlier claimed (February 1950) that communists infested the State Department. He now charged: "Truman is the President of this country in name only ... the real President who discharged MacArthur is a rather sinister monster of many heads and many tentacles, a monster conceived in the Kremlin, and then given birth to by Acheson ... and nurtured into Frankenstein proportions by the (Alger) Hiss crowd, who still run the State Department."[94] Jenner similarly claimed that MacArthur's dismissal confirmed evil facts: "This country today is in the hands of a secret inner coterie which is directed by agents of the Soviet Union."[95] Senator Kenneth Wherry (Nebraska) demanded that thinking Americans make a critical evaluation before too late: "Compare the monumental record of General MacArthur with that of his accusers, with their record of moral decay, greed, corruption, and confusion of these weaklings in the Truman administration." The senator vowed that "the pygmies" would not be allowed to "bring down this giant, this tower of strength and deserving idol of the American people."[96] Even Taft, thirsting for the 1952 GOP presidential nomination, used caustic language while lauding anew the soldier; he did not forsake Asian friends or kowtow to foreign and domestic bullies.

Two Senate committees (Foreign Affairs, Armed Services) held joint hearings in early May–late June 1951 to evaluate Asian policy and the Korean crisis. MacArthur was the first witness called to testify. Respectfully treated by all members, Democrats no less than Republicans, he used his time (three days) to explain his recent conduct and chastise Truman's policy. He exonerated himself of miscalculations on Chinese intervention. Aware of growing strains in the Sino-Soviet alliance, he suggested that Stalin would let Korean combat drag on to the last Chinese soldier; but Soviet bombast would not turn to war against the United States. MacArthur rejected as outlandish allegations that he sought a world war. He accused the president of ludicrous indecision in Korea. Limited war for limited ends made no sense but was a euphemism for failure. Morality and meaningful security lay in an adversary's unconditional surrender. Anything less was synonymous with losing: "if the United States doesn't bring the Korean War to a decisive and victorious end, she will have to accept all of the consequences of a disastrous defeat."[97]

Senators competed in delivering panegyrics on MacArthur during the hearings. Many also calumniated the government. Acheson testified before the two committees for eight days of badgering and interrogation. He was disingenuous and evasive, said several members in their published findings. Even worse, they observed: "It would appear from the record, that, under his guidance, the objective of American foreign policy has been primarily to conciliate certain of our associates [read Attlee's Britain] in the United Nations rather than to advance the security of the United States ... the Secretary was unable to defend successfully the postwar policies of the State Department in the Far East."[98] Other witnesses subject to senators' grilling included Marshall, Bradley, General Hoyt Vandenberg (Air Force), General Lawton Collins (Army), Admiral Forrest Sherman (Navy). None of them voiced support of MacArthur. All echoed Truman on the general's misbehavior.

Taft had to say that he no longer trusted Bradley's judgment or that of any politicized officer among the Joint Chiefs of Staff. He acidly added that such men had surrendered professional judgment for the sake of comfort and preferment.[99]

Indignant congressmen lacked the power to reinstate MacArthur to any of his commands and knew that a president – no matter how befuddled – could select or fire senior officers as he saw fit.[100] Gradually public attention shifted elsewhere; interest in the hearings faded noticeably after MacArthur testified. Opinion too began to drift away from him, a tendency reinforced by Ridgway's bloodying of Chinese offensives and recovery of battlefield control. Although US forces were authorized to retaliate if attacked by enemies operating outside of Korea, few people, when pushed, desired a widened war.[101]

No more than Wallace earlier did MacArthur quietly depart the scene in summer 1951. He undertook a national speaking tour to press familiar themes. To the Texas legislature he complained (June): "Oblivious to [history's] lessons, we now practice a new and yet more dangerous form of appeasement – appeasement on the battlefield whereunder we soften our blows, withhold our power, and surrender military advantages, in apparent hope that in some nebulous way by so doing a potential enemy will be coerced to desist from attacking us."[102] Nor did he hesitate to air ideas contrary to Republican tastes, suggesting that he had – as Truman liked to impute – lost touch with US laws and institutions. MacArthur came close to saying at the Massachusetts statehouse (July) that some conditions permitted military officers to override civilian superiors: "I find in existence a new and heretofore unknown and dangerous concept that the members of our armed forces owe primary allegiance or loyalty to those who temporarily exercise the authority of the Executive Branch of the Government rather than to the country and its Constitution which they are sworn to defend."[103]

MacArthur gave the keynote address at the 1952 GOP convention in Chicago. There he again lashed the Democrats' supine Asian policy.[104] Not a serious candidate for presidential nomination, his erstwhile supporters deserted to Taft (luckless again, this time to Ike). Yet MacArthur must have been pleased when GOP figures during their campaign against Stevenson adopted militant language. John Foster Dulles, notably, ridiculed containment as passive and self-abasing. He imagined that "rollback" and "liberation" would topple Stalinism.

MacArthur offered advice (December 1952) to incoming-President Eisenhower on how best to end Korean fighting. Should Mao and Stalin let it last, then overwhelming means should be used to clear communist forces from North Korea: "This could be accomplished through the atomic bombing of enemy military concentrations and installations in North Korea and the sowing of fields of suitable radio-active materials, the by-products of atomic manufacture, to close major lines of enemy supply and communication leading south from the Yalu, with simultaneous amphibious landing on both coasts of North Korea." Mainland China ought to be hit, its ability to wage modern warfare entirely degraded, leading ultimately to regime change. Nationalist forces from Taiwan could contribute much to a successful mission: "This could be accomplished by the destruction of Red China's limited airfields and industrial and supply bases, the cutting of her tenuous supply lines from the Soviet [Union] and the landing of China's Nationalist forces in Manchuria near the mouth of the Yalu, with limited continuing logistical support until such time as the communist government of China has fallen."[105]

Eisenhower politely thanked MacArthur for his suggestions, but did not develop them or again consult their author. He had evidently outlived his usefulness as Asian expert; he retired to chair the Remington Rand Corporation. Bits of his hardline preference did surface in later foreign

policy, however. Eisenhower implicitly threatened to use atomic weapons
in 1953 against Chinese sites if communist negotiators were not forthcoming in the Panmunjon armistice talks.[106]

MacArthur's approach was discernible in other forcefulness.
Eisenhower continued to recognize Chiang in Taiwan as the sole legitimate ruler of China. Washington and Taipei officials signed a security
pact in December 1954. During both Offshore Islands crises (1955,
1958) the administration aided Taiwan, to the point of rattling nuclear
sabers to cow mainland leaders. Financial support of Chiang increased
through the 1950s. Eisenhower and Dulles sustained an economic
embargo against the People's Republic. They steadfastly opposed
Peking's gaining UN admission or place on the Security Council. Not
overthrown per MacArthur's counsel, Mao was nonetheless pressed hard
as pariah – unrecognizable, inadmissible, illegitimate – and obliged to rely
upon an increasingly wary Kremlin.

* * *

Despite obvious differences, Wallace and MacArthur belonged to the
same club: men fired by Truman. They included Harold Ickes
(Interior), Louis Johnson (Defense), Julius Krug (Interior), Howard
McGrath (Justice), Henry Morgenthau (Treasury). Simple criteria determined club membership. Did Truman doubt his subordinate's personal
loyalty or commitment to policy? He made just one exception in applying
these standards: George Marshall. While secretary of state (1947–1949),
he opposed US recognition of Israel in May 1948. Such a move, he
expected, would alienate Arab nations and drive them, along with oil
access, into the Soviet camp. Cheap and plentiful petroleum, tagged to
the recovery of European economies, would then be forfeited. The
Soviets also would win a prize worth manifold political dividends in the
developing world. Marshall became exasperated with Truman's position
and considered resigning. He nearly accused the president to his face (but
not publicly) of jeopardizing the national interest to secure Jewish votes in
the November election. A comparable dig by anyone else would have
meant dismissal and hot words. But Truman retained Marshall, whom he
considered "the greatest living American." His steadying hand was
needed to surmount Cold War obstacles: "I can't afford to lose General
Marshall."[107] Wallace and MacArthur, by contrast, were eminently
expendable, personifying as they did bids to replace Truman plus alternatives to containment.

Truman's containment dilemma involved not only the checking of
Soviet power. The administration had also to create a modicum of

312 Dissenting Voices in America's Rise to Power

consensus in Congress, and in the public, to support Cold War policy. Objections to it by people on Truman's left flank were contained in 1948. That year's election results smothered Wallace's challenge. The ADA, the only other plausible group on Truman's left, split bitterly with Wallace, endorsed the president, and cheered his line against Stalinism. To Niebuhr the notion of trying to establish common ground with the USSR was foolish. Flogging the dead horse of conciliatory thought, he wrote during the Korean war:

Modern communist tyranny is certainly as wrong as the slavery which Lincoln opposed ... The hope that the conflict [between East and West] could be composed if only we could hold a seminar on the relative merits of [communism] and [capitalist] democracy, is, in fact, an expression of sentimental softness in a liberal culture and reveals its inability to comprehend the depth of evil to which individuals and communities may sink, particularly when they try to play the role of God to history.[108]

By the time these words were published, Wallace, though still loathing Truman, had accepted Cold War logic. Wallace became, incidentally, by end of the decade worried over dangers to "free humanity" emanating from China.[109] Not until the Vietnam war did he again examine the tenets of US foreign policy. Unsurprisingly, he blamed Truman for the Southeast Asian mess. "The wrong turning was taken," Wallace opined in 1965, "when I was getting the hell kicked out of me for suggesting that we were taking on more than we could chew." Truman had set the country on a path that led to Vietnam, "which will make the USA bleed from every pore."[110]

During the 1960s some students of Cold War history ("revisionists") revisited and, to varying degree, admired Wallace against Truman. None matched Linus Pauling, twice Nobel laureate (Chemistry, Peace) and social activist. He wrote in 1970 to vindicate Wallace's dissent:

Who can say what the world [would] have been like if Wallace had remained as Vice-President in 1944? ... [There is] the possibility that he could have been successful in averting the cold war. If Wallace had remained as Vice-President in 1944, there might have been no American involvement in a war in Korea, Vietnam, Cambodia, or Laos. The military dictatorships sponsored by the United States in many countries might not have come into existence. Tens of thousands of people who are now political prisoners might have remained free. International treaties might have been made that would have saved the United States and the Soviet Union hundreds of billions of dollars ... we might have a far better world today.[111]

Truman's attempts to contain the center-right did not produce much success. Unlike the left, the right did not splinter, despite tensions below the crust of outward unity. Repugnance for the New Deal and craving for White House control fostered solidarity and unlikely alliances. Prim Taft thus cooperated with boozy McCarthy, encouraged his antics, and joined the cackle about Truman's "selling out" Chiang's China, promoting Mao, and courting aggression in Korea. The cashiering of MacArthur counted as yet another instance in the Democrats' wretched catalogue.

Contra pious maxims at the time, politics did not "stop at the water's edge" during the early Cold War. Rather, they grew fierce. Insults hurled at Truman and Acheson during the partisan row over MacArthur helped lame what remained of Democratic tenure, drove its public support downward (popular approval hovered around 25 percent in 1952), and paralyzed attempts to execute a flexible Far Eastern diplomacy.[112]

Containment of the right, when occasionally achieved, was imposed by GOP figures, as occurred in June 1950. Senator Margaret Chase Smith (Maine) publicly reprimanded McCarthy. She repudiated his method of sowing "fear, bigotry, ignorance, and intolerance."[113] Later, not one Republican on the Senate commission to probe the MacArthur incident suggested that Truman had exceeded Constitutional prerogatives in recalling the officer. None claimed, as hotheads of the McCarthy stripe did, that Truman was traitorous.

Premised on perceived security emergency, containment paradoxically ended US wars by declaration of Congress. Unbeknownst to legislators in 1950, when they suppressed their scruple on war without formal authorization, they inaugurated their abdication of war-making responsibility (a situation guessed at by Taft who reproached Truman for not going to Congress on Korea). This condition remained unaltered for the rest of the twentieth century and beyond. The Korean war as "police action" amounted to verbal legerdemain. It helped concentrate more power in the executive branch at the expense of Congress while making way for subsequent wars by executive fiat: Vietnam, the 1991 Gulf conflict, Afghanistan in 2001, the 2003 invasion of Iraq.[114] Limited wars for the United States, these were total for the weaker participants whose grievances lingered for years.

Containment entailed not only a middle position between the chastisers of Cold War policy, Wallace and MacArthur. Containment also marked a new fact of international life. The United States had chosen a career as European power, manifest in those military forces committed to NATO and resident on the continent for decades after 1945. The same applied to Asia, where the Unites States had arrived as a power to stay – with uniformed personnel and facilities in Japan, Korea, and so forth. Containment, in effect, underscored a global US involvement that wove unsurpassed military power with economic preeminence. This projection of influence – Pax Americana – had no equal in history.

Cold War governments after Truman were prepared to fight a total war if necessary, should deterrence fail. But no responsible person disputed the effect of such mishap. On this subject even MacArthur could be eloquent, as in January 1955 when he abjured war as an antiquated instrument of policy. Warfare, he told a Los Angeles audience of veterans, had become uncontrollable and politically useless:

At the turn of the century, when I entered the Army, the target was one enemy casualty at the end of a rifle or bayonet or sword. Then came the machine gun designed to kill by the dozen. After that, the heavy artillery raining death upon the hundreds. Then the aerial bomb to strike by the thousands – followed by the atom explosion to reach the hundreds of thousands. Now, electronics and other processes of science have raised the destructive potential to encompass millions.

This very triumph of scientific annihilation ... has destroyed the possibility of war being a medium of practical settlement of international differences. The enormous destruction to both sides of closely matched opponents makes it impossible for the winner to translate [victory] into anything but his own disaster.

To this recital on the unfeasibility of modern war MacArthur attached a comment on Asian affairs. It revealed moderation greater than he had previously allowed. His utterance amounted to a retraction of sorts, albeit not as dramatic as Wallace's 1952 contriteness. He gave this belated nod to people in Truman's Washington who had sought to prevent Korea from spreading into wide war. "Whatever betides the ultimate fate of the Far East," he said, "will not be settled by force of arms. We may all be practically annihilated – but war can no longer be the arbiter of survival."[115] As though to emphasize his point, the Atomic Energy Commission reported in February 1955 that the explosion of a single hydrogen bomb – of the type then being tested by Americans and Soviets – would devastate an area of 700 square miles.

12   Dissenters

American foreign policy since the Korean war has operated in an increasingly complex setting. By early twenty-first century, the pretensions of the sovereign state, acknowledging no authority higher than its own political–moral formulas, had been eroded. The abrading elements included public international agencies, of which the United Nations was premier. Regional economic–political blocs were taking hold, most importantly the European Union. Transnational finance capital leapt political borders. It made nonsense of them, so too imperious multinational companies. Pandemic diseases, AIDS above all, and accelerating ecological deterioration highlighted the state's inability to cope and growing obsolescence. The number of distressed or failed states climbed. A global political culture, meanwhile, gained vitality. It featured increasingly robust courts and laws, human rights norms, plus sundry non-governmental organizations committed to good causes. Politicized religion, manifest in Islamic lands but not restricted to them, added yet another complication to international life. Unaffiliated with states and having shadowy allegiance, terrorist groups achieved more notoriety and lethality, as with the New York–Washington attacks of September 11, 2001 (plus Bali, Madrid, London).

But the nation-state, for good or ill, had proven resilient. The Westphalian order that arose in seventeenth-century Europe from the bloodletting of Protestant–Catholic wars still obtained. Roughly 190 entities laid claim in 2000 to the prerogatives of traditional sovereignty, adorned by diplomatic custom, knit by popular loyalties, validated by tangible control over discrete territories. Seen in this context, the United States was essentially one country among others and, like all of them, absorbed in a perpetual contest for security and economic benefit in an unruly environment. As such, the primary interest of the United States also remained the same as before and like every nation's: to survive, if possible to prosper.

Yet the US system of power by 2000 was plainly not an ordinary one. Rather, the country enjoyed superiority over every variety of competition,

whether posed by emergent innovations (the European Union) or produced by rival states of Westphalian type. The absence of any peer,
signified by the term "sole superpower" (or "hyperpower"), was a tribute
to that expansion and consolidation of US strength from the Louisiana
Purchase onward. The United States on entering the new millennium
constituted an empire. Its supremacy eclipsed even the previous Roman
and British amalgams of might. This American colossus spanned a continent, by formal and informal means retained overseas holdings,
embraced a large population (surpassed only by India and China), was
nourished by a thriving economy, and boasted a popular culture whose
brashness aroused the imaginations – sometimes umbrage – of people
elsewhere. Americans maintained their security with military forces rang-
ing from strategic–nuclear to counter-insurgency teams, and deployed
troops, warplanes, and carrier battle groups around the globe. The
United States spent more on its defense budget than the next eight
major powers combined. The last secretary of state in the twentieth
century, Madeleine Albright, enthused that America had become the
indispensable nation. From its writ the entire world supposedly
benefited.[1]

Since Korea

However impressive or singular the United States stood by 2000, the
years after Korea had not been devoid of arguments on the nature or
purpose of American power. They flared throughout the remaining years
of Cold War and beyond. The responsible class yielded dissenters no less
vivid than in previous generations, suitable subject for another book, say
American Superpower and Its Critics. It might broaden the scope of review
to include additions to the national security apparatus – CIA chiefs,
special advisors, recent retirees.

Congressmen

The House and Senate still led as site for dissent, constantly renewing
Congress's reputation for "unfettered debate."[2] Efforts to thwart or alter
policies included those by Senator J. William Fulbright (Democrat,
Arkansas), who broke from party ranks and his president in the mid-
1960s to challenge Washington's Vietnam course. He called it wasteful
and arrogant. He had been preceded in this line by Senators Wayne
Morse (Democrat, Oregon) and Ernest Gruening (Democrat, Alaska).
Other Democratic senators followed, prominently Robert Kennedy
(New York), Eugene McCarthy (Minnesota), George McGovern

(South Dakota). Outspoken Republican critics in the Senate included George Aiken (Vermont), Mark Hatfield (Oregon), and Jacob Javits (New York). Dissenters' revenge was briefly realized in 1973, when Congress passed the War Powers Act to limit future military commitments by presidential discretion.[3]

Against détente in the 1970s, Senator Henry Jackson (Democrat, Washington) warned of Soviet machinations and Moscow's putative bad faith. Neither the Republican administration of Nixon–Kissinger nor later Carter Democrats escaped his criticism, vindicated in the senator's view by the 1979 Soviet invasion of Afghanistan and a US response of heightened vigilance.[4]

Dissent since the end of the Cold War has pulsed with signs of life. The chairman of the Senate Armed Services Committee, Sam Nunn (Democrat, Georgia), questioned the wisdom of suspending economic sanctions against Iraq after Saddam Hussein's invasion of Kuwait. He objected to what he termed a rush to violence in 1991.[5] Before and during the second Iraq war of 2003, Senator Robert Byrd (Democrat, West Virginia) excoriated President George W. Bush for deceiving the public mind into thinking that the 9/11 carnage and Al Qaeda were of one piece with the regime in Baghdad or that it possessed weapons of mass destruction. Byrd equated Bush's preemption doctrine with aggression. He protested in 2004: "Radical, having no basis in existing law, this new foreign policy [of preemption] was dangerous in the extreme ... Our metamorphosis on the world stage from powerful, peaceful giant to swaggering Wild West bully, with little regard for cooperative agreements, sensitivities, or diplomacy in general, means a different kind of world in years to come." He had earlier voted with twenty-two other senators against granting authority to the White House to attack Iraq. Byrd declared: "I do not want history to remember my country as being on the side of evil."[6] Representative John Murtha (Democrat, Pennsylvania), senior member on the House's Defense Appropriations Subcommittee, charged in November 2005 that Bush's war constituted "a flawed policy wrapped in illusion." The second Iraq war also wore thin among some Republicans. The GOP's Senator Chuck Hagel (Nebraska) doubted by summer 2005 that the US and its coalition partners could win. He equated quagmire in Vietnam with stalemate in Iraq; he demanded that an exit strategy be devised, then implemented. Melvin Laird, former member of the House of Representatives and Defense head during Nixon's presidency, also offered sober Iraq–Vietnam comparisons.[7]

As in previous generations, post-Korea congressmen acted not only to restrain presidential initiative. They also tried to push policy in directions otherwise neglected or rejected. The Congressional Black Caucus (CBC) sought during the last decades of the twentieth century to press US diplomacy against white minority rule in Rhodesia – rechristened Zimbabwe in 1980 – and apartheid in South Africa.[8] Representatives Shirley Chisholm (Democrat, New York), Ronald Dellums (Democrat, California), and Barbara Jordan (Democrat, Texas) were particularly vocal CBC proponents of affirmative change in southern Africa.

Military officers

Military dissenters were in evidence too after Korea, albeit none so flamboyant as Miles or MacArthur. Matthew Ridgway in the 1950s, serving as army chief of staff, publicly disputed President Eisenhower's New Look with its slashing of non-nuclear forces and tighter lid on expenditures. Obliged to preside over army reductions, both in personnel and budget share, Ridgway endured agonies of spirit.[9] His criticisms of defense cuts meanwhile led to pronounced unpleasantness before his retirement in 1955.

General Curtis LeMay, air force chief of staff, skirted the fringes of insolence in a manner kindred to MacArthur. During the 1962 Cuban missile crisis, LeMay insinuated in conversations with JFK that Munich-style appeasement was in the offing.[10] LeMay, though, did not try to scuttle the critical decisions once they were made. He accepted the imposition of naval blockade ("quarantine") instead of so-called surgical air strikes or amphibious invasion.

The Marine Corps commandant, General David Shoup, expressed misgiving in the early 1960s about escalating levels of US commitment to South Vietnam. He doubted the feasibility of winning a guerrilla war on behalf of a decrepit Saigon regime. After his retirement (December 1963), he joined other officers – former army Generals Ridgway, James Gavin, Maxwell Taylor – to remonstrate against LBJ's Southeast Asian policy.[11] Their military records and corresponding credibility with the public made an impression. Antiwar activist Dr. Benjamin Spock equated the efficacy of dissent by one general with "the objections of ten professors or ministers."[12]

Serving officers since the Cold War have not fallen in line behind every decision for military solution. General Fred Woerner, who headed the Southern Command, objected in 1989 to the proposed invasion of Panama and apprehension of a trivial thug, Manuel Noriega. Woerner had for years rued the record of military forays against Latin American states. He tried to foster trust between the Yankee behemoth and Latin peoples. He counseled patience to Washington, where he was perceived as a hindrance to resolute action. Secretary of Defense Dick Cheney consequently, and unceremoniously, relieved Woerner of command. His replacement, gung-ho General Maxwell Thurman, then directed the December assaults. The capture of Noriega came at small cost to the United States: twenty-three American soldiers died. Several hundred Panamanians, though, were killed.[13]

Retired chairmen of the Joint Chiefs of Staff (JCS), Admiral William Crowe and General David Jones, both testified in autumn 1990 in Senate hearings on the desirability of diplomatic pressure and continuance of sanctions against Iraq. Their likely success over time would, in Crowe's estimation, avoid war, its attendant sacrifices, and its uncertainties.[14] General Colin Powell, Crowe's successor as JCS chairman, shared the admiral's reservations, but did not push them vigorously.[15] He instead executed the administration's mandate: to drive Iraqi forces from Kuwait.

Of the second war against Iraq, Crowe again protested, along with retired Admiral Stansfield Turner, who had also served as CIA director for Jimmy Carter. Brent Scowcroft, retired lieutenant general and former national security advisor to George H. Bush, hotly condemned the US war/occupation of Iraq. In October 2004, he called it "a failing venture."[16] The bluntest military critic was General Anthony Zinni of the Marines. He had retired from service in 2000 and then served as special envoy to the Middle East (2002–2003). He published this account in 2004, by which time his pronouncements had made him persona non grata in Washington:

In the lead-up to the Iraq war and its later conduct, I saw, at a minimum, true dereliction, negligence, and irresponsibility; at worst, lying, incompetence, and corruption. False rationales presented as a justification; a flawed strategy; lack of planning; the unnecessary alienation of our allies; the underestimation of the task; the unnecessary distraction from real threats; and the unbearable strain dumped on our overstretched military.[17]

Diplomats

Ambassadorial dissenters since Korea include John Kenneth Galbraith. He represented the United States in India (1961–1963) while holding informal portfolio for broader Asia. He watched glumly as hostilities consumed South Vietnam and Washington officials beguiled themselves into thinking that they could fix intractable problems. He believed Ngo Dinh Diem vile and warned against steps that would place Washington in a neo-colonial role or patron of a lost cause. Galbraith expressed this thought in October 1961: "There is nothing that the New Frontier needs less than a new Korea in South Vietnam."[18]

Andrew Young, a veteran of the antiwar movement and once an aide to Martin Luther King, served as Carter's envoy to the United Nations, 1977–1979. Young drew rebukes for his impolitic candor, especially from Republicans such as Senators Robert Dole (Kansas) and Orrin Hatch (Utah). It touched on the racism that he detected in British, Swedish, and Soviet societies. Young also referred favorably to Fidel Castro. To Carter's displeasure, Young volunteered in an interview (July 1978) with a correspondent from Paris's *Le Matin* that political prisoners were moldering in US jails, not unlike the USSR. Nor could Carter and Secretary of State Cyrus Vance comprehend Young's referring in early 1979 to Iran's Ayatollah Khomeini as a possible future saint.[19] These verbal gaffes tarnished the ambassador's reputation. They tested Carter's forbearance. Young was not undone, though, until he violated rules then in place that forbade contact between US officials and members of the Palestine Liberation Organization (PLO). Against existing prohibitions, he spoke (July 1979) with the PLO's representative to the UN, Zehdi Terzi. Upon initial questioning by journalists, Young denied that he had met formally with any PLO representative, although admitting vaguely to a chance encounter. Subsequent revelations of the truth led to Young's forced resignation in August. Protests ensued from incensed African Americans – Coretta Scott King, Vernon Jordan – who praised Young's human rights endeavors and lauded the ambassador for improving US relations with Third World peoples. He wrote years later with evident dyspepsia: "I understood very well the depth of the hatred and bitterness between Jews and Palestinians. But I also understood that they would have to learn to live together as brothers or perish together as fools."[20]

No ambassador since Young has made comparable headlines as dissenter. But the resignation (March 2003) of John Brady Kiesling, political counselor in Embassy Athens, did elicit press comment on the eve of second hostilities against Iraq. He told Secretary of State Powell in public letter: "Our fervent pursuit of war with Iraq is driving us to squander the international legitimacy that has been America's most potent weapon . . . since the days of Woodrow Wilson."[21] A number of retired ambassadors also condemned the 2003 war as hasty or ill-advised. These included Dean McHenry (to the United Nations, 1979–1981), Arthur Hartman (to Moscow, 1981–1987), and Jack Matlock (to Moscow, 1987–1991). In an under-reported but stinging indictment of policy (June 2004), they called for regime change in Washington.[22] At roughly the same time, fifty former diplomats and intelligence chiefs advised Bush to rethink policy toward the Israeli–Palestinian conflict. The president should become an honest broker, the retirees averred. Their call for even-handedness came from concern about diminished US status: "[America's] unqualified support of Sharon's extra-judicial assassinations, Israel's Berlin Wall-like barrier, its harsh military measures in occupied territories, and [US] endorsement of Sharon's unilateral plans are costing our country its creditability, prestige and friends."[23] The retirees, official spokesmen retorted, omitted reference to suicide bombings or other attacks on Israeli civilians. Scowcroft subsequently charged that Bush the younger was "mesmerized" by Sharon, who was himself pure "trouble."[24]

Cabinet officers

Future historians may discover in Powell a foreign secretary who resisted the war clamor in 2003, only to be outmaneuvered by Defense Department chief Donald Rumsfeld, then overawed by a president bent on preemption. If true, future historians will also review Powell's decision to stay in the cabinet, perhaps explicable as an exercise in amelioration or based on the reasonable supposition that events are easier influenced from within the center of power than without.

Such a tale, if true, would complement the one told by Robert McNamara, according to which the Defense boss came to doubt the wisdom of LBJ's Vietnam adventure. In that narrative, he issued cautions – similar in tone and substance to those by Under Secretary of State George Ball – while remaining in the cabinet to avert complete disaster. "We have been too optimistic" about a military solution, McNamara told Johnson in 1965; a diplomatic exit from Vietnam was indicated.[25] "Continuation of our present course of action," the Defense secretary apparently told him two years later, "would be dangerous, costly in lives, and unsatisfactory to the American people."[26] Not until despairing entirely of the war did McNamara relinquish (late 1967) the Defense post. Still, he did not publicly object as US combat operations continued. Loyalty to the government apparently constrained him, as did felt responsibility. He had stayed in the cabinet far longer than did William Jennings Bryan – or, later, Cyrus Vance – in comparably trying circumstances.

Carter's secretary of state opposed in advance the April 1980 military mission to rescue diplomats taken hostage by Iranian students. Vance thought it impetuous. He argued that existing backchannel efforts and the cooperation of allies on sanctions, which he worked assiduously to coordinate, would lead to the hostages' release. Only if the lives of the diplomats were in imminent jeopardy would he approve of military procedure. Otherwise time favored diplomacy. He added that a display of restraint should help calm revolutionary frenzy, but an armed incursion, however limited, would further irritate Iranian grievances. Washington's relations with the Islamic world would plummet too. Moscow stood to gain sizable benefits.

Nobody in the cabinet supported Vance's line. It discounted political damages borne by the government at home and abroad as national humiliation intensified.[27] The secretary saw no alternative to resigning. He so informed Carter before he ordered the rescue attempt: "I could not honorably remain as secretary of state when I so strongly disagreed with a presidential decision."[28] Vance's resignation was broadcast just days after news broke of the aborted mission and desert fiasco – three helicopters disabled by sand, helicopter–cargo plane collision, the death of eight servicemen.[29]

Dissent as vocation

No more than dissenters examined in previous chapters have those of post-Korea sought martyrdom. They have preferred the exercise of power, its accouterments, and prestige. Fulbright confessed as much in 1989: "If I am remembered, I suppose it will be as a dissenter. That was not what I had in mind."[30] The post-Korea dissenters also, like their predecessors, have wanted high standards applied to the world but sympathetic understanding for themselves. Too often the dissenter's agreeable task of applying such measure to other people has been tempered by counterbalances: conformity, intolerance.

Pressures to conform have inhibited defiance. The power of "group think" has demoralized independent thought or meant marginalization. The results for foreign policy, Galbraith once mused, have been calcification of imagination and inability to adjust to original error. The hand of "controlling rigidity" and discipline slapped not only him but also other people living in the shadow of executive power during the post-Korea decades: Vance, Woerner, Young. Earlier sufferers included Bryan, MacArthur, Miles, Trist, Wallace. Equally frustrating, the leverage needed to change policy or overcome inertia has proven elusive, as with Morgenthau senior in Turkey or Bullitt's French mission. Galbraith wrote in 1999:

The man or woman who fully accepts the policy and has belief therein is known as a good soldier ... The administration of foreign policy thus comes very close to the enforcement of belief. Such commitment is never total; some of those involved manage to maintain their independence of thought. But in so doing, they risk being seen as unreliable – in the common State Department expression ... they are not useful. The usual case, however, is acceptance.

[A] consequence is that the requisite belief, once established, cannot easily be changed, perhaps not changed at all. One must be consistent in one's faith. One accepts the policy ... however improbable.[31]

Intolerance as enforcer of conformity has threatened dissenters with swift penalty, obvious during moments of security crisis but also evident in relatively tranquil times. Nor has intolerance, from the dissenting standpoint, become more attenuated with time's passing. Fulbright approvingly quoted this observation from Tocqueville on the dearth of US debate: "I know of no country in which there is so little independence of mind and real freedom of discussion as in America."[32] Since Korea, and by no means confined to the McCarthy hysteria, epithets centered on "traitor" or "quitter" have been flung – against Byrd, Fulbright, Gruening, Hagel, Hatfield, Murtha, and Zinni among others. Critics derided Woerner, a decorated combat soldier in Vietnam, as a "wimp" for his opposing the Panama invasion. At a minimum, he "had gone native," Cheney complained.[33] Thus continued unabated the pillorying of dissenters – their patriotism, motive, and fortitude loudly doubted.

Establishment dissenters have not been defenseless against conformity or vilification. Rather, they have sought to counter that shibboleth about politics ending at the shoreline. In the nineteenth century, Carl Schurz stressed that dissent was obligatory against varieties of error: "Our country, right or wrong. When right, to be kept right; when wrong, to be put right."[34] Blustery TR charged (1918) that passive acceptance of wrong diplomacy constituted moral treason. Senator Vandenberg argued that no doctrine was more pernicious than one that would suffocate foreign policy debates.[35] Taft put the case most forcefully, shortly after Pearl Harbor and Congress's war declaration in December 1941:

There can be no doubt that criticism in time of war is essential to the maintenance of any kind of democratic government ... Too many people desire to suppress criticism simply because they think it will give some comfort to the enemy ... If that comfort makes the enemy feel better for a few moments, they are welcome to it as far as I am concerned, because the maintenance of the right of criticism in the long run will do the country maintaining it a great deal more good that it will do the enemy, and will prevent mistakes which might otherwise occur.[36]

Dissenters have also drawn strength from acting according to conviction about right behavior even at the price of career or good name. Fulbright stood in line with other congressmen – from Frelinghuysen to Giddings to Hoar to Norris and La Follette – when he declared during the Vietnam war that the measure of the nation's "falling short" was "the measure of the patriot's duty of dissent."[37] Similarly, Zinni told midshipmen in 2003 at Annapolis that military subordination to civilian authority did not absolve them as future officers from giving frank advice. It implies proper pride in the discharge of serious duty. The shades of Wool, Scott, Sheridan, Sherman, Miles, and MacArthur must have nodded when Zinni reported:

I have been amazed that men who bravely faced death on the battlefield are later, as senior officers, cowed and unwilling to stand up for what is right or point out what is wrong ... Moral courage is often more difficult than physical courage ... There are ... times when you disagree and you have to speak out, even at the cost of your career. If you're a general, you might have to throw your stars on the table ... I have often been called "outspoken." I am.[38]

Dissenters in the responsible class have also been succored by politically engaged elements in the larger society. Public sentiment bolstered Everett and Webster for Greece. Frelinghuysen needed Jeremiah Evarts to quicken the senator's stance against Cherokee removals. New England's objection during 1812 and 1846 braced the spirit of congressional doves. Soon after voting against the war declaration upon Germany in 1917, Norris received this favor from a George Seibel of Pittsburgh: "Amid a generation of ... poltroons, blood-thirsty wretches and hirelings of foreign governments, you ... are standing up against this unholy and unnecessary war like [a] hero of old."[39]

Establishment dissenters at the same time have heartened popular objection by endowing it with their presumed distinction – Spock on the value of senior military officers. This symbiotic relationship, however, has not always run smoothly. Hoar rapped what he regarded as mugwump self-indulgence, though his stand against the Philippines war would have been lonelier without the fabled grumblers. Radical members of the 1960s antiwar movement did not esteem Fulbright. They thought him overly cautious. He, in turn, recoiled from certain protesters, too raucous for his taste or involved in exotic counterculture. He instructed in 1966:

With due respect for the honesty and patriotism of the student demonstrations, I would offer a word of caution to the young people ... We are, for better or worse, an essentially conservative society; in such a society soft words are likely to carry more weight than harsh words and the most effective dissent is dissent expressed in an orderly, which is to say a conservative manner.

For these reasons such direct action as the burning of draft cards does more to retard than to advance the views of those who take such action ...

Frustrating though it may be to some Americans, it is nonetheless a fact that in America the messages that get through are those that are sent through channels, through the slow, cumbersome institutional channels devised by the founding fathers.[40]

Not only did Fulbright's defense of decorum fail to sway youthful activists. They also disdained the southerner's segregationist preference, which in their view had delayed justice and improvements in Dixie.

Irrespective of whether Fulbright approved, changes occurred to the social composition of the responsible class in the twentieth century. They ultimately helped to replenish dissent and broaden its scope. Jeanette Rankin had based her opposition to US intervention in two world wars on an understanding of the feminist mission: to cure men of the war incubus. Both Morgenthaus brought a sensibility to bear on their respective tasks that had been conditioned by Jewish experience in the gentiles' world. Morgenthau senior stated in May 1915 as Turkey made war upon the Armenians: "Their fate reminds me very much of that of the Jews."[41] So, too, the saga of African-American resistance to white prejudice emboldened the CBC and Young to turn US diplomacy in directions previously untried or taboo.

Yet increased representation within the responsible class along gender, ethnic/race, and religious lines has not produced a fundamental reorientation in foreign affairs, as many proponents of diversity once expected. Rankin would have been dumbfounded by Albright in 1993. Then ambassador to the United Nations, she asked this question of General Powell as the Clinton government examined Bosnia options: "What's the point of having this superb military that you're always talking about if we can't use it?" Powell recorded in his 1995 memoirs: "I thought I would have an aneurysm."[42] A few years later Albright, the first female secretary of state, did get a bombing war against Serbia.

Rankin's confidence in the pacifistic quality of feminism would also have been dented by the careers of these people, each a woman, each a mother, each a wartime leader of her respective country: Indira Gandhi, Golda Meir, Margaret Thatcher. In the early twenty-first century, another woman, National Security Advisor Condoleezza Rice, advocated war against Iraq. Maybe Rankin would have taken such women to task had she lived to see them in power. Or she might have concluded that their actions in office demonstrated that the feminist ethic required considerably more time to sink roots; a handful of women could not by themselves transform the male-freighted politics of national security, national prestige, and competitions of power. Or Rankin might have decided that practical diplomacy is no respecter of feminist idealism but the logic of international reality trumps it, along with all utopian visions.

Other permutations on the diversity theme deserve a word. Notwithstanding the late discovery of her family's religious origins, Albright was the second foreign-born Jewish refugee to become secretary of state, the first having been Henry Kissinger. In neither case was anything like "Jewishness" a determinant of diplomacy. The Harlem-born Powell, son of Jamaican immigrants, became the first black secretary of state. So too his "blackness" did not stamp foreign policy.

Powell's successor, Rice, was born and reared in segregated Alabama. This African-American woman during her January 2005 confirmation hearings was closely questioned by a number of Democratic senators, notably Barbara Boxer (California), dismayed by her part in the Iraqi war. Byrd was also highly critical of Rice as advisor to Bush and for helping to devise the preemption doctrine. Byrd voted against her confirmation. He had been in an earlier incarnation a member of the Ku Klux Klan. This ugly fact did not detract from the merits of his case on Iraq nor was Rice's brief for war enhanced by her having surmounted hurdles of racism. Still, Rice and Byrd must have paused for a moment during the confirmation process to wonder at the twist of fate that cast Rice as defender of policy, the repentant Klansman as dissenter.

Strands of dissent

The impact of establishment dissenters upon policy varied between the Louisiana Purchase and MacArthur's Korean tribulation. Twice they decisively shifted the drift of events: Trist in Mexico, reservationists in the 1919 Versailles/League fight. Dissenters more frequently lost. Such was the case with these: Timothy Pickering and the northeastern Federalists to Jefferson; congressional doves to war declarations (1812, 1846, 1898, 1917, 1941); objectors to Jackson's 1830 removal scheme; opponents to Alaskan purchase; Miles to Theodore Roosevelt; Bryan to Wilson in the *Lusitania* crisis; Bullitt in Paris to isolationism; Taft to Nuremberg reasoning; Wallace and MacArthur to Truman's containment strategy.

Other dissenters landed between the poles of outright victory or plain defeat. Gallatin acted adroitly as negotiator in 1814 to end a losing war against which he had lobbied in vain. Officially sanctioned private philanthropy for Greece was less than what Everett and Webster hoped but did play a role in helping a stricken people. Generals Wool and Scott managed to lessen slightly the suffering of evicted tribes. Later, along an opposite tack, Generals Sherman and Sheridan, miffed at variations on Grant's Peace Policy, managed to undercut most of them. Ambassadors Morgenthau in Turkey and Johnson in China got some satisfaction. Washington gave eventual notice to their reportage and pleas, then offered dollops of aid to victims. The War Refugee Board – despite shortcomings, but better than nothing – owed its existence to Secretary Morgenthau.

Dissenters in the responsible class since Korea can likewise be located along the spectrum of success and failure. Senator Jackson did not enjoy absolute victory in his anti-détente campaign. But it limited public confidence, as Kissinger readily acknowledged, in the White House–Kremlin rapprochement.[43] Dissenters clearly defeated would include Ridgway by Eisenhower; Galbraith and other doves by Vietnam zeal in the early 1960s; Vance by impatience for rescue of diplomats; Woerner in Panama by Bush senior; doubters by executive decisions to conduct both Iraqi wars. The following people may not have been entirely routed but perhaps managed to exert some effect. Historians might eventually determine that McNamara's supposed coolness, then rejection of Vietnam, encouraged LBJ's quest for a diplomatic solution. Young's PLO *démarche*, albeit disavowed in its day, probably did reflect and abet growing pragmatism in Washington on how to deal with the Israeli–Palestinian tragedy. Powell's and Nunn's caution about war against Iraq after the Kuwait invasion might – in future findings of scholars – have helped contain the scope of hostilities in 1991.

The varying effect that dissenters had on policy is only an aspect of their significance. From the standpoint of democratic theory, the role played by dissent as a corrective to false starts or as a check against tyranny is a recurrent and verifiable datum, not just an article of faith. Generous allowance for dissent is the hallmark of a mature republic.[44]

Individual dissenters provide edifying examples of courage and character, enough to cheer the gloomiest moralist. Hoar invoked the authority of GOP tradition (Lincoln, Union, abolition) to justify his defiance on the Philippines. Vance defended his resignation with reference to old-fashioned honor. Zinni proudly proclaimed himself independent-minded – not insubordinate but not bashful either. The long list of such cases even touches upon MacArthur–Truman insofar as the president wanted to fire the general before he could gracefully resign.[45]

Dissenters whose ideas over time have been vindicated in a conceptual sense should gratify metaphysically inclined observers or anyone who seeks solace in taking the long view. Giddings, Frelinghuysen, and Hoar may not have prevailed operationally in the debates of their day. But these men gave testaments of humanity, significant for posterity and rejuvenating America's morale in the wake of failure: brutality to native tribes, black slaves, Mexicans, Filipinos. Rankin during two low moments, when the preponderance of evidence ran against the logic of her position, retained hope in peace and trusted in a better world to come.

From the perspective of political history, the deep weave of dissent in America's rise to power contains distinctive strands, not necessarily running in the same direction but crisscrossing. The four mentioned in this book's introduction, and threading in different ways through chapters, can here be revisited: prophetic, republican, nationalist, cosmopolitan. What they share in common is a mood: pervasive anxiety. It exists at odds with that abundant American optimism which holds the future will always outshine the past, both morally and materially. To anxious dissenters, the United States lived in danger of not fulfilling its promise, of proving too flimsy or unworthy. Thus, held those persons burdened by prophetic anxiety, Americans were wont – unless checked – to discard divine guidance and stray disastrously into iniquity. Republican anxiety has stemmed from those dislocations said to derive from the embrace of empire. Nationalist anxiety has sprung, so its sufferers have evidenced, from concern that the United States lacks the will for power, which alone assures safety in a treacherous world. Cosmopolitan anxiety has been stoked by fear that the United States will forsake humane duties in deference to a pinched political imagination. These points warrant added comment.

The US version of prophetic tradition stemmed from Biblical interpretation and covenant orientation. Contemporary theologians may debate the validity of a doctrine that assumes that God is directly involved in any state's history, dispensing blame or praise, chastisement or reward, according to deeds. Yet for a conspicuous kind of nineteenth-century Protestant believer, and later spiritual descendants, a God of justice was intimately involved in the life of His human creation. Divine retribution for America's deviating from the path of rectitude could be as fearful as any visited upon the ancient Hebrews when they broke pledges to God.

Scriptural based dissenters who stood in awe of a God of righteous wrath could not compromise. They believed in the core of their beings that national disaster – punishment – would follow in the wake of sin, defined as persecution of Native Americans, aggression against Mexico, or territorial grabs to enlarge the slavery zone. Frelinghuysen and Giddings perceived no alternative to stiffening their compatriots against temptations that would place the United States on God's wrong side. Even the unorthodox Henry Wallace held that Americans had to wed the "fundamentals" of Christianity and the prophets' everlasting wisdom to foreign policy. Or else the United States would forfeit its own redemption.[46]

Individuals such as Frelinghuysen and Giddings anticipated, in the language of their faith, the penalty of America's ethical failure, rehearsed by Lincoln in his second inaugural address (March 4, 1865). He lamented but understood, as did they, that God had punished the sin of slavery with the inferno of civil war:

If we shall suppose that American Slavery is one of those offenses which, in the providence of God, must needs come, but which, having continued through His appointed time, He now wills to remove, and that He gives to both North and South, this terrible war, as the woe due those by whom the offense came, shall we discern therein any departure from those divine attributes which the believers in a Living God always ascribe to Him? Fondly do we hope – fervently do we pray – that this mighty scourge of war may speedily pass away. Yet, if God wills that it continue, until all the wealth piled by the bond-man's two hundred and fifty years of unrequited toil shall be sunk, and until every drop of blood drawn with the lash, shall be paid by another drawn with the sword, as was said three thousand years ago, so still it must be said "the judgments of the Lord, are true and righteous altogether."[47]

The republican strand of dissent, compatible with the prophetic (though of secular tint), arose from the material–political–moral costs of national aggrandizement and empire-building. The problem here was not one of betraying allegiance to God but a matter of infidelity to republican ideals or eschewing the virtues of moderation and restraint. In opposition to them, militant assimilation at home and conversion abroad marked the US rise to power. Therein people who resisted suasion or were thought to be of doubtful humanity were brushed aside in the manner of African-American slaves, who counted as three-fifths of a person in the original legal framework. Native Americans, whose essential nature was also unclear to whites, were expelled or confined to reservations. Recalcitrant Filipinos met a severe fate too. Germans, Japanese, Vietnamese, and Iraqis were among those people in later years subject to rescue from their "reversible" misfortune, not being fully realized Americans, and paid a steep price in bombing, invasion, occupation.[48] The Soviets were contained before succumbing to collapse in 1991. Yet costs to the United States have also been high, a band of dissenters has chorused over the decades, agitated by the gallop and sweep of power. Calhoun and Trist opposed the inclusion of people in the US realm whom they thought religiously or racially unsuitable. To other critics, the exhaustion of human and material resources, the compromising of legal norms, and violating of democratic values have nullified benefits derived from expanding might.

Corollary to this outlook has been the idea founded on the power of US example: a well-ordered society with provisions for fairness, distributive justice, and political choice radiates influence abroad sturdier than that produced just by armaments, military interventions, or coercive diplomacy. As such, US greatness is not for Americans to trumpet but for other peoples to acknowledge. Phrased otherwise, walking softy with a big stick did not mean clubbing nations to make them adopt the US brand of *mission civilisatrice*. Reminiscent of Gallatin on the Mexican conflict or Hoar on the Philippines, Fulbright declared at the height of the Vietnam war that America had forsaken its better self by substituting the dross of imperium for genuine purpose:

We have embraced the ideas that are so alien to our experience – the idea that our wisdom is as great as our power, and the idea that our lasting impact on the world can be determined by the way we fight a war rather than by the way we run our country . . .
    The crisis will not soon be resolved, nor can its outcome be predicted. It may culminate, as I hope it will, in a reassertion of the traditional values, in a renewed awareness of the creative power of the American example. Or it may culminate in our becoming an empire of the traditional kind, ordained to rule for a time over an empty system of power and then to fade or fall, leaving, like its predecessors, a legacy of dust.[49]

The nationalist strand of dissent, darting through America's rise to eminence, ran counter to the religiosity of a Frelinghuysen or the emphasis of a Gallatin, Hoar, and Fulbright. Americans had no need to apologize for the exercise of power or for enlarging the US portion of it in a universe unforgiving of diffidence and contemptuous of weakness. Thus taught those men – Sherman to MacArthur to LeMay to Henry Jackson – crabbed by what they saw as inexcusable squeamishness in the face of clear and present danger or obstacles to grandeur. In the words of Nelson Johnson (quoted in chapter 10): "We must be prepared to fight if we want to be respected."[50] Unsentimental realism held that nothing about Washington's possession of power was less wholesome than that of other governments. Failure would concede swaths of the world to peoples eager to capitalize on Peace Policy or League of Nations or varieties of appeasement. Rivals did not feel constrained from shrinking the US realm given the chance, against which Americans should press back for their own safety and honor. The Bush policy of preemption in the 2003 Iraq war suggested that this line of toughness would lengthen into the twenty-first century. Certainly previous proponents of power-centered politics had little to regret by the standard they set for themselves. The United States had gone from strength to strength in the nineteenth and twentieth centuries, despite occasional setbacks.

    In opposition to claims of realpolitik, the cosmopolitan strand of dissent sprang from an assumption not directly of Kantian origin but related to it. The United States has ethical obligations – a version of categorical imperative – that reach beyond its political frontier.[51] Strength, in other words, did not exist solely for itself or as an object of idolatry. Instead, this dissenting sect had a sense, if not fully articulated, that US responsibility in the world entailed duty to humanity. Greeks, Poles, Armenians, and Jews numbered among those peoples said, at one time or another, to deserve rescue. Rarely granted, and too thin for mastering the magnitude of problems, such aid as was offered did demonstrate that "a decent respect to the opinions of mankind" was never a matter of total US indifference.[52]

Such an outlook when combined with a power orientation could produce distorted outcomes, as in the Philippines fighting. But the mixing of humanitarian concern with that of power did not always misfire. Henry Jackson's efforts for Soviet Jews wishing to emigrate and for persecuted people of conscience – the Alexander Solzhenitsyns, the Andrei Sakharovs – placed Cold War hardliners on a higher moral plane than they would have attained had their attention been restricted to counting intercontinental ballistic missiles, assessing qualities of nuclear warheads, and calculating mega-destruction. Carter's human rights policy similarly attempted to implicate justice with manipulations of power.

* * *

Apart from illuminating past contentious episodes, the chronicles of dissent underscore the wages exacted by deviation and the courage needed to persevere against executive authority. The White House has dominated discourse, strutted the panoplies of power, and had most latitude for initiative. Unsurprisingly, dissenters from White House orthodoxy compiled an uneven record in the years from Jefferson to MacArthur. Still, it constituted a legacy of sorts to which post-Korea dissenters have since added.

All dissenters were not equal. Some of those treated in this book commanded attention in their respective eras and wielded, for good or ill, wide influence on events. These people are remembered still by the politically literate public. Others agitated in relative obscurity or shone only briefly, while yet others sank into disrepute. Specific instances of dissent, naturally, varied in trenchancy, both when first expressed and as revealed by time's test.

Strands of dissent evident in the past will extend into the foreseeable future in one guise or another. Few members of the responsible class, or the public generally, share with previous generations belief in a God who, in an immediate or literal sense, judges history or administers justice. But the pertinence of a moral compass that points to true right, and whose misreading invites mishap, still pertains and will doubtless inform dissenters distraught over the promiscuous use of force (or wars of preemption, if there be any so reckless again). The continuing exercise of dread power will also produce dissenters who, as in the past, will warn against delusions of empire, bankruptcy, and degradation of republican ideals. So, too, parties primarily concerned with preserving the national security will have moments to protest – recently against the "Vietnam syndrome," perhaps next against an "Iraq syndrome." Nor will cosmopolitan dissenters be short of cause, although they may be startled by Washington's detachment, evidenced from 1820s Greece to Sudan's Darfur in 2005. Even so, Norris's optimism from 1927 can inspire them:

> In the aggregate of the years, we are going forward. Our people, stupefied by the maddening rush for gold, with sensibilities somewhat dimmed by the cruelties of war, will yet see the light; we will go forward and we will eventually do justice to those who are weak and will practice as a national policy the golden rule.[53]

Mention of Norris leads back via historical/conceptual concatenations to Wilson's diplomacy. They, in turn, point to links between Wilson and post-September 11 foreign policy. Historian John Lewis Gaddis has succinctly identified the connection between Wilson and the younger Bush's international aims: "The United States must now finish the job that Woodrow Wilson started. The world, quite literally, is to be made safe for democracy, even those parts of it, like the Middle East, that have so far resisted that tendency."[54]

Gaddis's observation suggests a question. How might Wilson's original critics have viewed recent attempts to realize neo-Wilsonian goals? Answers to such a question are obviously conjecture. One can, though, imagine roughly the position taken by a La Follette.

He might have said that mention of certain facts of US life does not make one a pessimist or myopic isolationist. Collectively they do not equal decline. But, he would likely argue, they demand a progressive's attention. They require allocation of resources in short supply as billions of dollars are diverted to Iraq, an elective war that has led to "nation building" amid chaos. An underclass composed of millions of people, faltering educational attainments, increasingly rigid class stratification, ballooning federal deficits, and a failed public health system – all confirmed by the social/racial cleavages bared by hurricane Katrina in September 2005 – would have alarmed La Follette. He almost certainly would have cited them as ills allowed to fester while the price of US empire soars and republican currency falls. He would doubtless have regretted that countries previously well-disposed toward America had grown nervous about its exercise of seemingly unrestrained military power – an anxiety intensified by revelations about "renditions" and astonishing interrogations in sequestered detention facilities.

La Follette once addressed such concerns in a meditation on the enmities aroused by imperium. He would surely argue that his words then (1919) have continuing relevance for the US superpower. Its crashing about may yet produce clusters of disaffected states, deplete national wealth, compromise civil protections (the Patriot Act as resuscitated Espionage/Sedition laws), perplex citizens, and stretch finite armed force past good sense:

I do not covet for this country a position in the world which history has shown would make us the object of endless jealousies and hatreds, involve us in perpetual war, and lead to the extinction of our domestic liberty. I, for one, harbor no ambition to see this country start upon the path which has lured other nations to their ruin ... We cannot, without sacrificing this Republic, maintain world dominion for ourselves.[55]

Notes

Introduction

1 See table showing orders of magnitude among the great powers in 1952 in Alastair Buchan, *The End of the Postwar Era: A New Balance of World Power* (London: Weidenfeld and Nicolson, 1974), p. 322, and Paul Kennedy, *The Rise and Fall of the Great Powers: Economic Change and Military Conflict from 1500 to 2000* (New York: Random House, 1987), p. 369.

2 See David Mayers, *Wars and Peace: The Future Americans Envisioned, 1861–1991* (New York: St. Martin's Press, 1998).

3 Robert Jackson, *The Global Covenant: Human Conduct in a World of States* (Oxford: Oxford University Press, 2000), p. 134.

4 Robert Jackson, *Classical and Modern Thought on International Relations: From Anarchy to Cosmopolis* (New York: Palgrave Macmillan, 2005), p. 71. Also see "Politics as a Vocation" in H. H. Gerth and C. Wright Mills, eds., *From Max Weber: Essays in Sociology* (New York: Oxford University Press, 1958), pp. 77–128 and Michael Joseph Smith, *Realist Thought from Weber to Kissinger* (Baton Rouge: Louisiana State University Press, 1986), pp. 45–48.

5 "Perpetual Peace: A Philosophical Sketch" in Hans Reiss, ed., *Kant: Political Writings* (Cambridge: Cambridge University Press, 1991), p. 93.

6 Mayers, *Wars and Peace: The Future Americans Envisioned, 1861–1991*, pp. 2, 125 #4.

7 A. J. P. Taylor, *The Trouble Makers: Dissent over Foreign Policy, 1792–1939* (New York: Penguin Books, 1985), p. 156.

8 Arthur Schlesinger, Jr., *War and the American Presidency* (New York: W. W. Norton and Company, 2004), p. 46.

9 In addition to John Kennedy's *Profiles in Courage* (New York: Harper and Row, 1964) and Taylor's *The Trouble Makers: Dissent over Foreign Policy, 1792–1939*, see Richard Hofstadter's *The American Political Tradition* (New York: Vintage Books, 1957).

10 Andrew Siegel, "Steady Habits under Siege: The Defense of Federalism in Jeffersonian Connecticut" in Doron Ben-Atar and Barbara Oberg, eds., *Federalists Reconsidered* (Charlottesville: University Press of Virginia, 1998), p. 200.

11 Stuart Miller, *Benevolent Assimilation: The American Conquest of the Philippines, 1899–1903* (New Haven: Yale University Press, 1982), p. 1.

12 Minority Report Signing (June 23, 1812), Reel 37, Josiah Quincy Papers, Massachusetts Historical Society.
13 Stanley Weintraub, *MacArthur's War: Korea and the Undoing of an American Hero* (New York: Free Press, 2000), pp. 338, 343.
14 John Winthrop, A Modell of Christian Charity (1630) in Daniel Boorstin, ed., *An American Primer* (Chicago: University of Chicago Press, 1966), p. 22.
15 Notes on the State of Virginia (1782) in Merrill Peterson, ed., *The Portable Thomas Jefferson* (London: Penguin Books, 1986), p. 215.
16 Professor Hans Morgenthau of the University of Chicago was the main popularizer of realpolitik in mid-twentieth-century America. The diplomat–historian George Kennan also helped spread the realist gospel. See David Mayers, *George Kennan and the Dilemmas of U.S. Foreign Policy* (New York: Oxford University Press, 1988), p. 319.
17 Mark Neely, *The Last Best Hope of Earth: Abraham Lincoln and the Promise of America* (Cambridge, Mass.: Harvard University Press, 1993), p. v.
18 See Hedley Bull, *The Anarchical Society: A Study of Order in World Politics* (London: Macmillan Press, 1977), John Rawls, *The Law of Peoples* (Cambridge, Mass.: Harvard University Press, 1999), and Jackson, *The Global Covenant: Human Conduct in a World of States*.
19 See Raymond Aron, *The Imperial Republic: The United States and the World 1945–1973* (Englewood Cliffs, New Jersey: Prentice-Hall, 1974).
20 Remarks on the Policy of the Allies with Respect to France (1793) in Edmund Burke, *Works* (Boston: Charles C. Little and James Brown, 1839), Vol. IV, p. 121.

Chapter One

1 David Weber, *The Spanish Frontier in North America* (New Haven: Yale University Press, 1992), pp. 291–293; Stephen Ambrose, *Undaunted Courage: Meriwether Lewis, Thomas Jefferson, and the Opening of the American West* (New York: Simon and Schuster, 1996), p. 102.
2 Charles de Gaulle declared to French-speaking throngs while visiting Montreal in 1967: "Vive le Quebec libre!" Cited in "Canada's Other French-Speakers Cope," *New York Times* (September 6, 1999), p. A6.
3 Merrill Peterson, *Thomas Jefferson and the New Nation: A Biography* (New York: Oxford University Press, 1970), p. 771.
4 The American population in 1800 totaled 5,308,483 people. Slightly more than a million were black (mostly enslaved) and the rest white with origins primarily in the British Isles. See Barry Turner, ed., *The Statesman's Yearbook, 1998–1999* (New York: St. Martin's Press, 1998), p. 1516.
5 Alexander DeConde, *This Affair of Louisiana* (New York: Charles Scribner's Sons, 1976), p. 180; Samuel Eliot Morison, *Harrison Gray Otis: The Urbane Federalist* (Boston: Houghton Mifflin Company, 1969), p. 269; Robert Tucker and David Hendrickson, *Empire of Liberty: The Statecraft of Thomas Jefferson* (New York: Oxford University Press, 1990), p. 89.
6 Dumas Malone, *Jefferson the President: First Term, 1801–1805* (Boston: Little, Brown and Company, 1970), p. 348.

7 Henry Adams, *History of the United States of America during the Administration of Thomas Jefferson 1801–1805* (New York: Library of America, 1986), pp. 334–335; Frederick Jackson Turner, "The Significance of the Louisiana Purchase" in *Review of Reviews*, May 1903, p. 584; Samuel Flagg Bemis, *John Quincy Adams and the Foundations of American Foreign Policy* (New York: W. W. Norton and Company, 1949), p. 118; Samuel Eliot Morison, *The Oxford History of the American People* (New York: Oxford University Press, 1965), p. 366; William Appleman Williams, ed., *The Shaping of American Diplomacy, 1750–1914* (Chicago: Rand McNally and Company, 1970), p. 44.

8 Gilbert Lycan, *Alexander Hamilton and American Foreign Policy: A Design for Greatness* (Norman: University of Oklahoma Press, 1970), p. 417.

9 Ibid., p. 418.

10 Reference to a "palsied" Federalist party appeared in a letter from Theodore Sedgwick to Rufus King in December 1799. See Winfred Bernhard, *Fisher Ames: Federalist and Statesman, 1758–1808* (Chapel Hill: University of North Carolina Press, 1965), p. 318.

11 Peterson, *Thomas Jefferson and the New Nation*, p. 792; McMaster cited in Robert McCaughey, *Josiah Quincy 1772–1864: The Last Federalist* (Cambridge, Mass.: Harvard University Press, 1974), p. 30; Bemis, *John Quincy Adams and the Foundations of American Foreign Policy*, p. 132; Ambrose, *Undaunted Courage*, p. 102.

12 DeConde, *This Affair of Louisiana*, p. 94; Robert McColley, ed., *Federalists, Republicans, and Foreign Entanglements 1789–1815* (Englewood Cliffs, New Jersey: Prentice-Hall, 1969), pp. 14–17.

13 DeConde, *This Affair of Louisiana*, pp. 95–96.

14 Ibid., pp. 68–69, 82, 84; Lawrence Kaplan, *Thomas Jefferson: Westward the Course of Empire* (Wilmington, Delaware: Scholarly Resources, 1999), pp. 50, 67–68, 126, 131; Gerard Clarfield, *Timothy Pickering and American Diplomacy, 1795–1800* (Columbia, Missouri: University of Missouri Press, 1969), pp. 121–122.

15 Lynn Turner, *William Plumer of New Hampshire, 1759–1850* (Chapel Hill: University of North Carolina Press, 1962), pp. 104–106.

16 Jefferson to Robert Livingston (April 18, 1802) in Merrill Peterson, ed., *The Portable Thomas Jefferson* (Middlesex, England: Penguin Books, 1986), pp. 485–486.

17 Garry Wills, *Negro President: Jefferson and the Slave Power* (Boston: Houghton Mifflin Company, 2003), p. 114.

18 Kaplan, *Thomas Jefferson*, pp. 137–139; Lawrence Kaplan, *Jefferson and France: An Essay on Politics and Political Ideas* (New Haven: Yale University Press, 1967), pp. 8–9; DeConde, *This Affair of Louisiana*, pp. 152, 155, 193–196; Charles Christian, *Black Saga: The African American Experience* (Washington: Counterpoint, 1999), p. 77; Doris Graber, *Public Opinion, the President, and Foreign Policy: Four Case Studies from the Formative Years* (New York: Holt, Rinehart and Winston, Inc., 1968), p. 158.

19 Jefferson to Senator John Breckinridge (August 12, 1803) in Peterson, *The Portable Thomas Jefferson*, p. 497.

20 Wills, *Negro President: Jefferson and the Slave Power*, p. 125.
21 Malone, *Jefferson the President*, p. 348.
22 Ambrose, *Undaunted Courage*, p. 101; DeConde, *This Affair of Louisiana*, p. 178; Hervey Putnam Prentiss, *Timothy Pickering as the Leader of New England Federalism* (New York: Da Capo Press, 1972), p. 14; George Cabot to Rufus King (March, 1804) in Henry Adams, ed., *Documents Relating to New England Federalism, 1801–1815* (Boston: Little, Brown and Company, 1905), pp. 362–364; Ames to Christopher Gore (October 3, 1803) in Seth Ames, ed., *Works of Fisher Ames* (Boston: Little, Brown and Company, 1854), Vol. I, pp. 322–326; Lycan, *Alexander Hamilton and American Foreign Policy*, p. 416.
23 The three-fifths rule in the Constitution allowed five black slaves to count as three whites for purposes of apportioning representation in the House of Representatives.
24 Prentiss, *Timothy Pickering as the Leader of New England Federalism*, p. 7.
25 Turner, *William Plumer of New Hampshire*, p. 103; Ames to Dwight Foster (February 6, 1803) in Ames, *Works of Fisher Ames*, Vol. I, pp. 317–318; Pickering to My Dear Becky (December 8, 1803), Vol. II, Timothy Pickering Papers, Peabody Essex Museum; Gerard Clarfield, *Timothy Pickering and the American Republic* (Pittsburgh: University of Pittsburgh Press, 1980), p. 221; Adams, *New England Federalism*, p. 347.
26 Malone, *Jefferson the President*, pp. 177, 214.
27 Griswold to My Dear Fanny (January 24, 1803) and Griswold to My Dear Fanny (February 7, 1803), Box 3, Roger Griswold Papers, Yale University.
28 Pickering to Rufus King (March 4, 1804), Reel 14, Timothy Pickering Papers, Massachusetts Historical Society; Adams, *Documents Relating to New England Federalism*, p. 351.
29 Everett Brown, ed., *William Plumer's Memorandum of Proceedings in the United States Senate, 1803–1807* (New York: Da Capo Press, 1969), p. 113.
30 Ibid., pp. 124–125.
31 Ibid., pp. 66, 113, 124; Linda Kerber, *Federalists in Dissent: Imagery and Ideology in Jeffersonian America* (Ithaca: Cornell University Press, 1970), p. 43.
32 Brown, *William Plumer's Memorandum*, pp. 111, 114, 116, 118–120, 251.
33 Morison, *Harrison Gray Otis*, p. 270; Turner, *William Plumer of New Hampshire*, p. 139; DeConde, *This Affair of Louisiana*, p. 191.
34 Timothy Pickering to Theodore Lyman, February 11, 1804 in Adams, *Documents Relating to New England Federalism*, pp. 343–346.
35 Kerber, *Federalists in Dissent*, pp. xi, 41–42.
36 Charles Upham, *The Life of Timothy Pickering* (Boston: Little, Brown, and Company, 1873) Vol. IV, p. 79.
37 Ames to Christopher Gore (November 16, 1803) in Ames, *Works of Fisher Ames*, Vol. I, pp. 331–332; DeConde, *This Affair of Louisiana*, pp. 189–190.
38 Brown, *Plumer's Memorandum*, p. 6; DeConde, *This Affair of Louisiana*, pp. 190–191.
39 Ames to Thomas Dwight (October 26, 1803) and Ames to Thomas Dwight (October 31, 1803) in Ames, *Works of Fisher Ames*, Vol. I, pp. 327–331.
40 Gerard Clarfield, *Timothy Pickering and the American Republic*, p. 234.

41 Forrest McDonald, *Alexander Hamilton: A Biography* (New York: W. W. Norton and Company, 1979), p. 319. Also see Pickering to Elizabeth Hamilton (August 1, 1827), Timothy Pickering Papers, Reel 55, Massachusetts Historical Society.

42 Brown, *Plumer's Memorandum*, pp. 439, 458.

43 Clarfield, *Timothy Pickering and American Diplomacy*, p. 212; Clarfield, *Timothy Pickering and the American Republic*, p. 266; Prentiss, *Timothy Pickering as the Leader of New England Federalism*, pp. 5–6, 11; David Hackett Fischer, *The Revolution of American Conservatism: The Federalist Party in the Age of Jeffersonian Democracy* (New York: Harper Torchbooks, 1965), p. 255.

44 Observations Introductory to Reading the Declaration of Independence by Pickering (July 4, 1823), pp. 11–12, Timothy Pickering Papers, Massachusetts Historical Society; Address by Pickering on July 4, 1826, pp. 8, 10, Timothy Pickering Papers, Vol. II, Peabody Essex Museum; Upham, *The Life of Timothy Pickering*, Vol. IV, pp. 470–476.

45 Pickering to My Dear Becky (January 1, 1805), Timothy Pickering Papers, Vol. II, Peabody Essex Museum.

46 David McLean, *Timothy Pickering and the Age of the American Revolution* (New York: Arno Press, 1982), pp. 355–356; Clarfield, *Timothy Pickering and American Diplomacy*, pp. 28–30, 161–162.

47 Henry Cabot Lodge, *Studies in History* (Boston: Houghton Mifflin Company, 1885), pp. 215–216; Clarfield, *Timothy Pickering and the American Republic*, pp. 267–269.

48 Upham, *The Life of Timothy Pickering*, Vol. IV, pp. 54–57.

49 Pickering to My Dear Becky (March 13, 1804), Timothy Pickering Papers, Vol. II, Peabody Essex Museum; Adams, *History of the United States of America during the First Administration of Thomas Jefferson 1801–1805*, p. 409. On the point by Adams, also see Richard Buel, *America on the Brink: How the Political Struggle over the War of 1812 Almost Destroyed the Young Republic* (New York: Palgrave Macmillan, 2005), p. 23.

50 Pickering to Richard Peters (December 24, 1803); Pickering to George Cabot (January 29, 1804); Tapping Reeve to Uriah Tracy (February 7, 1804); Pickering to Theodore Lyman (February 11, 1804) in Adams, *New England Federalism*, pp. 338–346.

51 McColley, *Federalists, Republicans, and Foreign Entanglements 1789–1815*, pp. 108–110; Clarfield, *Timothy Pickering and the American Republic*, p. 228.

52 Bernhard, *Fisher Ames*, pp. 340–342; Robert Ernest, *Rufus King: American Federalist* (Chapel Hill: University of North Carolina Press, 1968), pp. 280–281; George Cabot to Pickering (February 14, 1804), Theodore Lyman to Pickering (February 29, 1804), Alexander Hamilton to Theodore Sedgwick (July 10, 1804) in Adams, *New England Federalism*, pp. 346–350, 365–366.

53 Upham, *The Life of Timothy Pickering*, Vol. IV, p. 112.

54 Prentiss, *Timothy Pickering as the Leader of New England Federalism*, p. 33.

55 DeConde, *This Affair of Louisiana*, pp. 48, 50–51.

56 Jefferson to John Breckinridge (August 12, 1803) in Peterson, *The Portable Thomas Jefferson*, p. 496; Peterson, *Thomas Jefferson and the New Nation*, p. 772.

57 Turner, *William Plumer of New Hampshire*, pp. 150, 345; McColley, *Federalists, Republicans, and Foreign Entanglements*, pp. 116–119; Adams, *History of the United States during the First Administration of Thomas Jefferson 1801–1805*, p. 416.
58 Jefferson Davis, *The Rise and Fall of the Confederate Government* (New York: Thomas Yoseloff, 1958), Vol. I, pp. 55, 72–73, 76.
59 Napoleon Bonaparte on the Sale of Louisiana (1803) in Thomas Paterson, ed., *Major Problems in American Foreign Policy*, Vol. I (Lexington, Mass.: D. C. Heath and Company, 1989), pp. 111–112; David Mayers, *Wars and Peace: The Future Americans Envisioned, 1861–1991* (New York: St. Martin's Press, 1998), pp. 5–8.
60 Morison, *Harrison Gray Otis*, pp. 272–274.
61 DeConde, *This Affair of Louisiana*, pp. 212, 252.
62 Anthony Wallace, *Jefferson and the Indians: The Tragic Fate of the First Americans* (Cambridge, Mass.: Harvard University Press, 1999), p. 338; Robert Remini, *Andrew Jackson and His Indian Wars* (New York: Viking, 2001), p. 115.
63 Kaplan, *Thomas Jefferson*, p. 83; Christian, *Black Saga*, p. 83.
64 Andrew Siegel, "Steady Habits under Siege: The Defense of Federalism in Jeffersonian Connecticut" in Doron Ben-Atar and Barbara Oberg, eds., *Federalists Reconsidered* (Charlottesville: University Press of Virginia, 1998), pp. 217–218.
65 See No. 10 in *The Federalist* (New York: Modern Library, 1937), pp. 53–62; Second Inaugural Address (March 4, 1805) in Peterson, *The Portable Thomas Jefferson*, pp. 317–318.
66 Buel, *America on the Brink: How the Political Struggle over the War of 1812 Almost Destroyed the Young Republic*, p. 243.
67 Kerber, *Federalists in Dissent*, pp. 50, 64; Clarfield, *Timothy Pickering and the American Republic*, p. 264; Pickering to My Dear Becky (July 19, 1780), Reel 53, Timothy Pickering Papers, Massachusetts Historical Society.
68 A. J. P. Taylor, *The Trouble Makers: Dissent over Foreign Policy 1792–1939* (London: Penguin Books, 1957), p. 13; Bernhard, *Fisher Ames*, p. 321.
69 Pickering to My Dear Becky (March 6, 1804), Timothy Pickering Papers, Vol. II, Peabody Essex Museum.
70 Robert Remini, *The Life of Andrew Jackson* (London: Penguin Books, 1988), pp. 180–181.

Chapter Two

1 Entry of December 3, 1812 in Charles Francis Adams, ed., *The Diary of John Quincy Adams 1794–1845* (Philadelphia: J. B. Lippincott and Co., 1874), Vol. II, p. 424.
2 Jefferson to Thomas Leiper (June 12, 1815) in Paul Leicester Ford, ed., *The Works of Thomas Jefferson* (New York: G. P. Putnam's Sons, 1905), Vol. XI, p. 475.
3 Victor Weybright, *Spangled Banner: The Story of Francis Scott Key* (New York: Farrar and Rinehart, Inc., 1935), p. 57.

4 J. C. A. Stagg, *Mr. Madison's War: Politics, Diplomacy, and Warfare in the Early American Republic, 1783–1830* (Princeton: Princeton University Press, 1983), p. 501 #3; E. James Ferguson, ed., *Selected Writings of Albert Gallatin* (Indianapolis: Bobbs-Merrill Company, 1967), p. 282.

5 Samuel Eliot Morison, *The Oxford History of the American People* (New York: Oxford University Press, 1965), p. 383; Walter LaFeber, *The American Age: U.S. Foreign Policy at Home and Abroad* (New York: W. W. Norton and Company, 1994), Vol. I, p. 63.

6 "Universal Peace" from *The National Gazette* (February 2, 1792) in Gaillard Hunt, ed., *The Writings of James Madison* (New York: G. P. Putnam's Sons, 1906), Vol. VI, pp. 88–91.

7 Special Message to Congress (June 1, 1812) in Gaillard Hunt, ed., *The Writings of James Madison* (New York: G. P. Putnam's Sons, 1908), Vol. VIII, p. 192; Henry Adams, *The First Administration of James Madison 1809–1813* (New York: Antiquarian Press, 1962), Vol. II, pp. 222–223.

8 Doris Graber, *Public Opinion, the President, and Foreign Policy: Four Case Studies from the Formative Years* (New York: Holt, Rinehart and Winston, Inc., 1968), p. 203.

9 Richard Buel, *America on the Brink: How the Political Struggle over the War of 1812 Almost Destroyed the Young Republic* (New York: Palgrave Macmillan, 2005), p. 36.

10 Christopher Gore to Rufus King (December 8, 1808) in Charles King, *The Life and Correspondence of Rufus King* (New York: G. P. Putnam's Sons, 1898), pp. 110–112.

11 Graber, *Public Opinion, the President, and Foreign Policy: Four Case Studies from the Formative Years*, p. 203.

12 Stagg, *Mr. Madison's War*, p. 99.

13 L. B. Kuppenheimer, *Albert Gallatin's Vision of Democratic Stability: An Interpretive Profile* (Westport, Conn.: Praeger, 1996), p. 81; Graber, *Public Opinion, the President, and Foreign Policy: Four Case Studies from the Formative Years*, pp. 204–205; Stephen Knott, *Secret and Sanctioned: Covert Operations and the American Presidency* (New York: Oxford University Press, 1996), p. 101.

14 From the Inhabitants of Knox County, Indiana Territory (July 31, 1811) and From the Inhabitants of St. Clair County, Illinois Territory (September 6, 1811) in J. C. A. Stagg et al., eds., *The Papers of James Madison: Presidential Series* (Charlottesville: University Press of Virginia, 1996), Vol. III, pp. 397–399, 446–447; Willard Sterne Randall and Nancy Nahra, *Forgotten Americans: Footnote Figures Who Changed American History* (Reading, Mass.: Perseus Books, 1998), p. 131; Jefferson to John Adams (April 20, 1812) in Ford, *The Works of Thomas Jefferson*, Vol. XI, p. 238; Reginald Horsman, *Expansion and American Indian Policy, 1783–1812* (East Lansing: Michigan State University Press, 1967), p. 167.

15 Graber, *Public Opinion, the President, and Foreign Policy: Four Case Studies from the Formative Years*, pp. 204–205; Raymond Walters, *Albert Gallatin: Jeffersonian Financier and Diplomat* (New York: Macmillan Company, 1957), p. 250; Stagg, *Mr. Madison's War*, p. 105; James Monroe to Gallatin (June 1, 1812) in Henry

Adams, ed., *The Writings of Albert Gallatin* (New York: Antiquarian Press, 1960), Vol. I, pp. 520–521.

16 Clifford Egan, *Neither Peace Nor War: Franco-American Relations, 1803–1812* (Baton Rouge: Louisiana State University Press, 1983), p. xv; Samuel Eliot Morison, Frederick Merk, and Frank Freidel, *Dissent in Three American Wars* (Cambridge, Mass.: Harvard University Press, 1970), p. 3; Patrick White, *A Nation on Trial: America and the War of 1812* (New York: John Wiely and Sons, 1965), p. 122; Adams, *The First Administration of James Madison 1809–1813*, Vol. II, p. 122; Stagg, *Mr. Madison's War*, pp. 111–115; George Roger Taylor, ed., *The War of 1812: Past Justifications and Present Interpretations* (Westport, Conn.: Greenwood Press, 1974), pp. 15–17.

17 Walters, *Albert Gallatin*, p. 248; Stagg, *Mr. Madison's War*, pp. 39–40, 44, 46–47, 94; Julius Pratt, *Expansionists of 1812* (Gloucester, Mass.: Peter Smith), 1967), p. 51.

18 Jefferson to General Thaddeus Kosciusko (June 28, 1812); Jefferson to William Duane (August 4, 1812); Jefferson to the Marquis de Lafayette (February 14, 1815) in Ford, *The Works of Thomas Jefferson*, Vol. XI, pp. 258–262, 264–267, 454–464; Thomas Jefferson to Gallatin (March 19, 1815) in Adams, *The Writings of Albert Gallatin*, Vol. I, pp. 647–648; Adams, *The First Administration of James Madison 1809–1813*, Vol. II, p. 212; Reginald Stuart, *United States Expansionism and British North America, 1775–1871* (Chapel Hill: University of North Carolina Press, 1988), pp. 54–55; Morison, Merk, Freidel, *Dissent in Three American Wars*, p. 4.

19 See George Ingraham's "The Story of Laura Secord Revisited," *Ontario History*, 1965, #57; Mary Agnes FitzGibbon, *A Veteran of 1812: The Life of James FitzGibbon* (Toronto: William Briggs, 1894), pp. 81–85.

20 H. William Brands, *The United States in the World: A History of American Foreign Policy* (Boston: Houghton Mifflin Company, 1994), Vol., I, p. 94.

21 Richard Rush to Gallatin (August 4, 1813), Reel 8, Albert Gallatin Papers, New-York Historical Society.

22 Francis Paul Prucha, *The Great Father: The United States Government and the American Indians* (Lincoln: University of Nebraska Press, 1984), pp. 76–80; Randall and Nahra, *Forgotten Americans*, p. 133.

23 John K. Mahon, *The War of 1812* (New York: Da Capo Press, 1972), p. 221; Edmund Quincy, *Life of Josiah Quincy of Massachusetts* (Boston: Fields, Osgood, and Co., 1869), p. 359.

24 Robert Remini, *Daniel Webster: The Man and His Time* (New York: W. W. Norton and Company, 1997), pp. 122–123; Jefferson to James Monroe (January 1, 1815) in Ford, *The Works of Thomas Jefferson*, Vol. XI, p. 442.

25 King to Christopher Gore (September 9, 1812) in Rufus King Papers, New-York Historical Society; King to Christopher Gore (August 30, 1814) in King, *The Life and Correspondence of Rufus King*, pp. 410–411.

26 Irving Bartlett, *Daniel Webster* (New York: W. W. Norton and Company, 1978), p. 61; King to Jeremiah Mason (September 2, 1814) in Rufus King Papers, New-York Historical Society.

27 Mahon, *The War of 1812*, p. 314.

28 Jefferson to James Monroe (October 16, 1814) in Ford, *The Works of Thomas Jefferson*, Vol. XI, pp. 436–438.
29 Stagg, *Mr. Madison's War*, p. 3; Mahon, *The War of 1812*, pp. 14, 17, 144, 335.
30 Knott, *Secret and Sanctioned*, p. 105; Charles Christian, *Black Saga: The African American Experience* (Washington: Civitas, 1999), pp. 84–86.
31 Stagg, *Mr. Madison's War*, p. 506.
32 Bradford Perkins, *Prologue to War: England and the United States 1805–1812* (Berkeley: University of California Press, 1961), p. 267; Stagg, *The Papers of James Madison*, Vol. III, p. xxxii; Graber, *Public Opinion, the President, and Foreign Policy: Four Case Studies from the Formative Years*, p. 209; Robert Ernest, *Rufus King: American Federalist* (Chapel Hill: University of North Carolina Press, 1968), p. 327.
33 Gallatin eventually headed two US diplomatic missions: Paris (February 1815–May 1823) and London (May 1826–October 1827).
34 William Edward Buckely, *The Hartford Convention* (New Haven: Yale University Press, 1934), p. 5.
35 See for the Hartford Convention: James Banner, *To the Hartford Convention: The Federalists and the Origins of Party Politics in Massachusetts, 1789–1815* (New York: Alfred Knopf, 1970); Buckley, *The Hartford Convention*; Samuel Eliot Morison, *Harrison Gray Otis: The Urbane Federalist 1765–1848* (Boston: Houghton Mifflin Company, 1967), Theodore Dwight, *History of the Hartford Convention* (New York: N. and J. White, 1833).
36 Irving Brant, *James Madison: Commander in Chief 1812–1836* (Indianapolis: Bobbs-Merrill Company, 1961), p. 360; Madison to Thomas Jefferson (August 17, 1812) and Madison to Wilson Cary Nicholas (November 26, 1814) in Hunt, *The Writings of James Madison*, Vol. VIII, pp. 210–213, pp. 318–320.
37 Jefferson to Thomas Leiper (June 12, 1815) in Ford, *The Works of Thomas Jefferson*, Vol. XI, p. 475; Mahon, *The War of 1812*, pp. 256, 385–386; Stagg, *Mr. Madison's War*, pp. 510–512; Richard Rush, *Memoranda of a Residence at the Court of London* (Philadelphia: Key and Biddle, 1833), p. 162.
38 Webster to Charles March (June 6, 1813) in Charles Wiltse, ed., *The Papers of Daniel Webster: Correspondence, 1798–1824* (Hanover, New Hampshire: University Press of New England, 1974), Vol. I, pp. 146–147.
39 Count Gallatin, ed., *The Diary of James Gallatin, 1813–1827* (New York: Charles Scribner's Sons, 1920), pp. 5, 50.
40 Entry of August 15, 1823 in Charles Francis Adams, *The Diary of John Quincy Adams*, (Philadelphia: J. B. Lippincott and Co., 1875), Vol. VI, p. 173; Albert Gallatin to Quincy (December 9, 1830), Reel 44, Josiah Quincy Papers, Massachusetts Historical Society.
41 Leonard White, *The Jeffersonians: A Study in Administrative History, 1801–1829* (New York: Macmillan Company, 1951), pp. 484–485.
42 Henry Cabot Lodge, *Studies in History* (Boston: Houghton Mifflin Company, 1885), p. 280.
43 Gallatin to Thomas Jefferson (October 21, 1807) in Ferguson, *Selected Writings of Albert Gallatin*, pp. 293–296; Stagg, *Mr. Madison's War*, pp. 79–80; Garry

Wills, *Negro President: Jefferson and the Slave Power* (Boston: Houghton Mifflin Company, 2003), p. 164.

44 Walters, *Albert Gallatin: Jeffersonian Financier and Diplomat*, pp. 245–247; Perkins, *Prologue to War: England and the United States 1805–1812*, p. 363; Stagg, *Mr. Madison's War*, p. 90.

45 Gallatin to Thomas Jefferson (March 10, 1812) in Adams, *The Writings of Albert Gallatin*, Vol. I, p. 517.

46 Gallatin to Thomas Jefferson (December 18, 1812) ibid., pp. 530–531.

47 Gallatin's Suggestion for Campaigns of 1812 (n.d.), Reel 8; Gallatin's Notes on General Staff of U.S. Army (n.d.), Reel 8; John Armstong to Gallatin, (October 4, 1812), Reel 8, Albert Gallatin Papers, New-York Historical Society; Walters, *Albert Gallatin: Jeffersonian Financier and Diplomat*, pp. 252–253, 257–258.

48 The British delegates were Lord Gambier (vice-admiral), Henry Goulburn (under-secretary in the Colonial Office), and William Adams (admiralty lawyer).

49 Mahon, *The War of 1812*, pp. 378–379.

50 Ferguson, *Selected Writings of Albert Gallatin*, p. 343; Henry Adams, *The Life of Albert Gallatin* (New York: Peter Smith, 1943), p. 546.

51 Ralph Ketcham, *James Madison: A Biography*, (New York: Macmillan Company, 1971), p. 454; Irving Brant, *James Madison: Commander in Chief 1812–1836*, pp. 158–159; Norman Risjord, *The Old Republicans: Southern Conservatism in the Age of Jefferson* (New York: Columbia University Press, 1965), pp. 4, 134, 162–163; Robert Dawidoff, *The Education of John Randolph* (New York: W. W. Norton and Company, 1979), p. 11.

52 Adams, *The First Administration of James Madison 1809–1813*, Vol. II, p. 211.

53 Hugh Garland, *The Life of John Randolph of Roanoke* (New York: D. Appleton and Company, 1850), Vol. I, pp. 291, 294–295.

54 William Cabell Bruce, *John Randolph of Roanoke 1773–1833* (New York: G. P. Putnam's Sons, 1922), Vol. I, p. 406.

55 Garland, *The Life of John Randolph of Roanoke*, Vol. I, pp. 290, 292–293.

56 Ibid., pp. 296–297.

57 Ibid., pp. 295–296.

58 Ketcham, *James Madison: A Biography*, pp. 526–527; Henry Adams, *John Randolph* (Boston: Houghton, Mifflin and Company, 1883), p. 248.

59 Randolph loved his nephews as though they were his sons. He never married. He was almost certainly without sex, the result of a mysterious illness in his youth. See Dawidoff, *The Education of John Randolph*, p. 25.

60 Randolph to a New England Senator (December 15, 1814) in Russell Kirk, *John Randolph of Roanoke: A Study in American Politics with Selected Speeches and Letters* (Chicago: Henry Regnery Company, 1964), p. 209.

61 See Volume of Letters to Josiah Quincy (1812–1826), John Randolph Papers, Library of Congress; Edmund Quincy, *Life of Josiah Quincy of Massachusetts*, p. 94.

62 "The good cause" appears in Quincy to Fisher Ames (1806, n.d.), Reel 36, Josiah Quincy Papers, Massachusetts Historical Society.

63 Robert McCaughey, *Josiah Quincy: The Last Federalist* (Cambridge, Mass.: Harvard University Press, 1974), pp. 30–32, 34, 68; Buel, *America on the*

Brink: How the Political Struggle over the War of 1812 Almost Destroyed the Young Republic, p. 113.

64 Quincy, *Life of Josiah Quincy of Massachusetts*, pp. 214, 357–358; Speech on the Invasion of Canada (January 5, 1813) in Edmund Quincy, ed., *Speeches Delivered in the Congress of the United States by Josiah Quincy* (Boston: Little, Brown and Company, 1874), p. 412.

65 Dawidoff, *The Education of John Randolph*, pp. 50–53; Linda Kerber, *Federalists in Dissent: Imagery and Ideology in Jeffersonian America* (Ithaca: Cornell University Press, 1970), pp. 60–61; Quincy, *Life of Josiah Quincy of Massachusetts*, p. 535.

66 "Invasion of Canada" in Quincy, *Speeches Delivered in the Congress of the United States by Josiah Quincy*, p. 357; Quincy, *Life of Josiah Quincy of Massachusetts*, pp. 281, 286., 292.

67 Invasion of Canada in Quincy, *Speeches Delivered in the Congress of the United States by Josiah Quincy*, p. 374.

68 "On the Pay of Non-Commissioned Officers" (January 5, 1813) ibid., p. 279.

69 McCaughey, *Josiah Quincy: The Last Federalist*, pp. 71, 74; Gerald Clarfield, *Timothy Pickering and the American Republic* (Pittsburgh: University of Pittsburgh Press, 1980), pp. 249–250; Buckley, *The Hartford Convention*, p. 4; Harry Coles, *The War of 1812* (Chicago: University of Chicago Press, 1967), pp. 18–19; Roger Brown, *The Republic in Peril: 1812* (New York: W. W. Norton and Company, 1971), p. 167.

70 McCaughey, *Josiah Quincy: The Last Federalist*, pp. 78–79.

71 William Cabell Bruce, *John Randolph of Roanoke 1773–1833*, Vol. II, p. 38; Merrill Peterson, *The Great Triumvirate: Webster, Clay, and Calhoun* (New York: Oxford University Press, 1987), p. 41.

72 Robert Remini, *Daniel Webster: The Man and His Time* (New York: W. W. Norton and Company, 1997), pp. 99–100; Rockingham Memorial (August 5, 1812) in Charles Wiltse, ed., *The Papers of Daniel Webster: Speeches and Formal Writings* (Hanover, New Hampshire: University Press of New England, 1986), Vol. I, p. 6.

73 Maurice Baxter, *One and Inseparable: Daniel Webster and the Union* (Cambridge, Mass.: Harvard University Press, 1984), p. 35; Remini, *Daniel Webster: The Man and His Time*, pp. 101–102, 104–105; Ernest, *Rufus King: American Federalist*, pp. 407–408.

74 Webster to Charles March (June 24, 1813) and Richard Stockton to Webster (July 23, 1813) in Charles Wiltse, ed., *The Papers of Daniel Webster: Correspondence*, Vol. I, pp. 152–153, 156–157; Remini, *Daniel Webster: The Man and His Time*, pp. 108–110; Baxter, *One and Inseparable: Daniel Webster and the Union*, p. 42; Ketcham, *James Madison: A Biography*, pp. 560–561.

75 See The Conscription Bill (December 9, 1814) in Wiltse, *The Papers of Daniel Webster: Speeches and Formal Writings*, Vol. I, pp. 19–31.

76 Morison, *Harrison Gray Otis: The Urbane Federalist*, p. 370; Remini, *Daniel Webster: The Man and His Time*, pp. 123–124; Irving Bartlett, *Daniel Webster* (New York: W. W. Norton and Company, 1978), p. 64; Notice of Portsmouth Committee of Defense (September 10, 1814) and Webster to Ezekiel Webster

(November 29, 1814 and January 9, 1815) in Wiltse, *The Papers of Daniel Webster: Correspondence*, Vol. I, pp. 169–170, 177–180.

77 King to Christopher Gore (September 1813), Rufus King Papers, New-York Historical Society.

78 Gallatin to Matthew Lyon (May 7, 1816) in Adams, *Writings of Albert Gallatin*, pp. 700–701; Gallatin, *The Diary of James Gallatin*, p. 45; Quincy, *Life of Josiah Quincy of Massachusetts*, pp. 372–373; James Madison to Quincy (February 18, 1830), Reel 44, Josiah Quincy Papers, Massachusetts Historical Society.

79 David Mayers, *The Ambassadors and America's Soviet Policy* (New York: Oxford University Press, 1995), p. 22.

80 Jefferson to the Marquis de Lafayette (February 14, 1815) in Ford, *The Works of Thomas Jefferson*, Vol. XI, p. 454; Morison, *Harrison Gray Otis: The Urbane Federalist*, p. 395.

81 Madison to S. Spring (September 6, 1812) in Hunt, *The Writings of James Madison*, Vol. VIII, pp. 214–215; Remini, *Daniel Webster: The Man and His Time*, p. 122; Baxter, *One and Inseparable: Daniel Webster and the Union*, p. 44; Peterson, *The Great Triumvirate: Webster, Clay, and Calhoun*, p. 39; McCaughey, *Josiah Quincy: The Last Federalist*, p. 79.

82 Timothy Pickering to Gouverneur Morris (October 21, 1814) in Henry Adams, ed., *Documents Relating to New England Federalism* (Boston: Little, Brown, and Company, 1905), pp. 400–402; King to Christopher Gore (September 19, 1812), Rufus King Papers, New-York Historical Society; Brown, *The Republic in Peril: 1812*, pp. 173–174.

83 Edmund Burke, *Reflections on the Revolution in France* (Cambridge: Hackett, 1987), p. 27.

Chapter Three

1 Monroe had recommended (March 8, 1822) the recognition of Argentina (Rio de La Plata), Colombia, Chile, Peru, and Mexico.

2 Deno Geanakoplos, "The Diaspora Greeks: The Genesis of Modern Greek National Consciousness" in Nikiforos Diamandouros et al., eds., *Hellenism and the First Greek War of Liberation (1821–1830): Continuity and Change* (Thessaloniki: Institute for Balkan Studies, 1976), p. 59; Adam Zamoyski, *Holy Madness: Romantics, Patriots and Revolutionaries 1776–1871* (New York: Viking, 2000), p. 123.

3 M. S. Anderson, *The Eastern Question 1774–1923* (London: Macmillan, 1966), p. 51; Douglas Dakin, *The Unification of Greece 1770–1923* (New York: St. Martin's Press, 1972), pp. 20–23.

4 William St. Clair, *That Greece Might Still Be Free* (London: Oxford University Press, 1972), p. 1.

5 Nikos Kazantzakis, *Report to Greco* (London: Faber and Faber, 1965), p. 108.

6 Douglas Dakin, *British and American Philhellenes during the War of Greek Independence, 1821–1833* (Thessaloniki: Institute for Balkan Studies, 1955) p. 6; Edward Everett, "Coray's Aristotle," *North American Review* (October 1823), p. 420.

7 Lloyd Kramer, *Lafayette in Two Worlds: Public Cultures and Personal Identities in an Age of Revolutions* (Chapel Hill: University of North Carolina Press, 1996), p. 103.

8 Ibid., p. 105.

9 Entry of February 9, 1829 in Laura Richards, ed., *Letters and Journals of Samuel Gridley Howe: The Greek Revolution* (Boston: Dana Estes and Company, 1906), p. 333.

10 Eli Smith, Notes on Greece during a journey in that country in 1829, ABC: 17.3, Vol. 1, American Board of Commissioners for Foreign Missions, Harvard University; St. Clair, *That Greece Might Still Be Free*, pp. 198, 356.

11 James Field, *America and the Mediterranean World 1776–1882* (Princeton: Princeton University Press, 1969), p. 127; Harold Spender, *Byron and Greece* (London: John Murray, 1924), p. 11; C. M. Woodhouse, *The Philhellenes* (Rutherford: Fairleigh Dickinson University Press, 1969), p. 15; Douglas Dakin, *The Greek Struggle for Independence 1821–1833* (Berkeley: University of California Press, 1973), p. 120.

12 Lord Byron, "Don Juan: Canto III" in G. B. Harrison, ed., *Major British Writers* (New York: Harcourt, Brace and World, Inc., 1959) Vol. II, p. 231.

13 Henry Mayer, *All On Fire: William Lloyd Garrison and the Abolition of Slavery* (New York: St. Martin's Press, 1998), p. 36; Stephen Larrabee, *Hellas Observed: The American Experience of Greece 1775–1865* (New York: New York University Press, 1957), pp. 30, 99, 145–146; St. Clair, *That Greece Might Still Be Free*, pp. 177, 337; Paul Pappas, *The United States and the Greek War of Independence, 1821–1828* (New York: Columbia University Press, 1985), p. 29; Paul Revere Frothingham, *Edward Everett: Orator and Statesman* (Boston: Houghton Mifflin Company, 1925), pp. 37–38; Paul Varg, *Edward Everett: The Intellectual in the Turmoil of Politics* (Selinsgrove: Susquehanna University Press, 1992), pp. 17, 20; Richards, *Letters and Journals of Samuel Gridley Howe: The Greek Revolution*, p. 21; Laura Richards, *Samuel Gridley Howe* (New York: D. Appleton-Century Club, 1935), pp. 9, 25; Harold Schwartz, *Samuel Gridley Howe: Social Reformer 1801–1876* (Cambridge, Mass.: Harvard University Press, 1956), pp. 18, 24, 28.

14 Zamoyski, *Holy Madness: Romantics, Patriots and Revolutionaries 1776–1871*, p. 238; Field, *America and the Mediterranean World 1776–1882*, pp. 121, 123; Pappas, *The United States and the Greek War for Independence, 1821–1828*, pp. 28, 32–33, 35, 41, 43; Larrabee, *Hellas Observed: The American Experience of Greece 1775–1865*, pp. 55, 152; Edward Mead Earle, "American Interest in the Greek Cause, 1821–1827," *American Historical Review* (1927), Vol. 33, p. 44; Dexter Perkins, *The Monroe Doctrine, 1823–1826* (Cambridge, Mass.: Harvard University Press, 1927), p. 40.

15 *Annals of the Congress of the United States* (Washington: Gales and Seaton, 1856), Eighteenth Congress, First Session, Senate, Vol. I, p. 80; Pappas, *The United States and the Greek War for Independence, 1821–1828*, pp. 43, 63; Larrabee, *Hellas Observed: The American Experience of Greece 1775–1865*, pp. 55, 67–68.

16 Entry of May 10, 1824 in Charles Francis Adams, ed., *The Diary of John Quincy Adams 1795–1848* (Philadelphia: J. B. Lippincott and Co., 1875), Vol. VI, p. 324.

17 Ernest May, *The Making of the Monroe Doctrine* (Cambridge, Mass.: Harvard University Press, 1975), p. 234. Also see Samuel Raphalides's "United States Policy toward the Greek War of Independence" (New School for Social Research: unpublished Ph.D. dissertation, 1974), pp. 155–157, #9.

18 Carl Schurz, *Life of Henry Clay* (Boston: Houghton Mifflin Company, 1887), Vol. I, p. 210.

19 Norman Graebner, "Northern Diplomacy and European Neutrality" in David Donald, ed., *Why the North Won the Civil War* (Baton Rouge: Louisiana State University Press, 1960), p. 73; Samuel Flagg Bemis, *John Quincy Adams and the Foundations of American Foreign Policy* (New York: W. W. Norton and Company, 1949), p. 64; Raphalides, "United States Policy toward the Greek War of Independence," pp. 4, 6. Also see Adams to Hugh Nelson (April 28, 1823) in Worthington Chauncey Ford, ed., *Writings of John Quincy Adams* (New York: Macmillan Company, 1917), Vol. VII, pp. 370–371.

20 John Quincy Adams, *An Address Delivered at the Request of the Committee of Arrangements for Celebrating the Anniversary of Independence at the City of Washington on the Fourth of July 1821* (Cambridge, Mass.: Hilliard and Metcalf, 1821), pp. 3, 31, 34.

21 Entry of December 2, 1823 in Adams, *Memoirs of John Quincy Adams*, Vol. VI, p. 224.

22 Pappas, *The United States and the Greek War for Independence, 1821–1828*, pp. 47, 97; Seventh Annual Message (December 2, 1823) in Stanislaus Murray Hamilton, ed., *The Writings of James Monroe* (New York: G. P. Putnam's Sons, 1902), Vol. VI, p. 340; Dexter Perkins, "The Monroe Doctrine" in Daniel Boorstin, ed., *An American Primer* (Chicago: University of Chicago Press, 1966), p. 259.

23 Seventh Annual Message (December 2, 1823) in Hamilton, *The Writings of James Monroe*, Vol. VI, p. 339.

24 Entries of August 15 and November 21, 1823 in Adams, *Memoirs of John Quincy Adams*, Vol. VI, pp. 173, 194.

25 See the following in Reel 12, Albert Gallatin Papers, New-York Historical Society: Marquis de Lafayette to Gallatin (August 6, 1821); N. Piccolo and C. Polychroniades to Gallatin (August 16, 1821); Gallatin to N. Piccolo and C. Polychroniades (August 17, 1821); Marquis de Lafayette to Gallatin (July 5, 1822); Alexandros Mavrocordatos to Gallatin (June 21, 1823); Marquis de Lafayette to Gallatin (October 13, 1823). Also see Pappas, *The United States and Greek War for Independence, 1821–1828*, pp. 28, 59 and Raphalides, "United States Policy toward the Greek War of Independence," pp. 133–134.

26 Entry of November 24, 1823 in Adams, *Memoirs of John Quincy Adams*, Vol. VI, pp. 198–199.

27 J. H. Powell, *Richard Rush: Republican Diplomat 1780–1859* (Philadelphia: University of Pennsylvania Press, 1942), pp. 151–152.

28 Adams to Robert Walsh (July 21, 1821) and Adams to Edward Everett (January 31, 1822) in Ford, *Writings of John Quincy Adams*, Vol. VII, pp. 127, 197.
29 Pappas, *The United States and the Greek War for Independence, 1821–1828*, p. 50; Raphalides, "United States Policy toward the Greek War of Independence," pp. 54–64; Madison to James Monroe (October 30, 1823) in Gaillard Hunt, ed., *The Writings of James Madison* (New York: G. P. Putnam's Sons, 1910) Vol. IX, pp. 157–160.
30 Field, *America and the Mediterranean World 1776–1882*, pp. 124–125; entry of November 26, 1823 in Adams, *Memoirs of John Quincy Adams*, Vol. VI, p. 204.
31 Harry Ammon, *James Monroe: The Quest for National Identity* (Charlottesville: University Press of Virginia, 1990), p. 510; May, *The Making of the Monroe Doctrine*, pp. 214–217; Entries of November 21 and 22, 1823 in Adams, *Memoirs of John Quincy Adams*, Vol. VI, pp. 195–198.
32 Eighth Annual Message (December 7, 1824) in Hamilton, *The Writings of James Monroe*, Vol. VII, p. 43.
33 See Charles Wiltse, ed., *The Papers of Daniel Webster: Speeches and Formal Writings* (Hanover: University Press of New England, 1986), Vol. I, p. 84.
34 Irving Bartlett, *Daniel Webster* (New York: W. W. Norton and Company, 1978), pp. 102, 260; Merrill Peterson, *The Great Triumvirate: Webster, Clay, and Calhoun* (New York: Oxford University Press, 1987), p. 77; Robert Remini, *Daniel Webster: The Man and His Time* (New York: W. W. Norton and Company, 1997), pp. 217–219; *Annals of the Congress of the United States*, Eighteenth Congress, First Session, House, Vol. I, pp. 1127–1132; Edward Everett, ed. *The Works of Daniel Webster* (Boston: Little, Brown and Company, 1854), Vol. I pp. lxxv–lxxvi; Jeremiah Mason to Webster (February 1, 1824) and Webster to Joseph Hopkinson (March 17, 1824) in Charles Wiltse, ed., *The Papers of Daniel Webster: Correspondence* (Hanover: University Press of New England, 1974), Vol. I, pp. 351–352, 355; Rufus King to Charles King, January 19, 1824, Rufus King Papers, New-York Historical Society.
35 Webster's letters to Edward Everett (November 16, 1823 and December 5, 1823 and December 6, 1823) in Wiltse, *The Papers of Daniel Webster: Correspondence*, Vol. I, pp. 332–333, 338–339; Daniel Webster to Everett (November 1823), Reel 2, Edward Everett Papers, Massachusetts Historical Society; Maurice Baxter, *One and Inseparable: Daniel Webster and the Union* (Cambridge, Mass.: Harvard University Press, 1984), p. 104; Remini, *Daniel Webster: The Man and His Time*, pp. 210, 214 #16; Bartlett, *Daniel Webster*, p. 101.
36 Samuel Breck's resolution of December 22, 1823 in *Annals of the Congress of the United States*, Eighteenth Congress, First Session, House, Vol. I, p. 849; entries of January 2, 1824 and January 27, 1824 in Adams, *Memoirs of John Quincy Adams*, Vol. VI, p. 227; Joel Poinsett to Webster, [1823?] in Wiltse, *The Papers of Daniel Webster: Correspondence*, Vol. I, p. 344; Baxter, *One and Inseparable: Daniel Webster and the Union*, pp. 100–102; Arthur Whitaker, *The United States and the Independence of Latin America, 1800–1830* (Baltimore: Johns Hopkins University Press, 1941), pp. 540–541.

37 *Annals of the Congress of the United States*, Eighteenth Congress, First Session, House, Vol. II, Appendix, pp. 2923–2928; Webster to Edward Everett (January 2, 1824) in Wiltse, *The Papers of Daniel Webster: Correspondence*, Vol. I, pp. 344–345; Baxter, *One and Inseparable: Daniel Webster and the Union*, p. 100; May, *The Making of the Monroe Doctrine*, pp. 234–235.

38 J. Fred Rippy, *Joel R. Poinsett, Versatile American* (New York: Greenwood Press, 1968), pp. 80–82; Webster to Jeremiah Mason (February 15, 1824) in Wiltse, *The Papers of Daniel Webster: Correspondence*, Vol. I, pp. 353–355.

39 "The Revolution in Greece" (January 19, 1824) in Wiltse, *The Papers of Daniel Webster: Speeches and Formal Writings*, Vol. I, p. 85.

40 Ibid.

41 *Annals of the Congress of the United States*, Eighteenth Congress, First Session, House, Vol. I, pp. 1150–1155, 1177–1178; Bartlett, *Daniel Webster*, p. 102; Charles Christian, *Black Saga: The African American Experience* (Washington: Counterpoint, 1999), p. 93; "On the Greek Revolution" (January 20 1824) in Henry Clay, *Life and Speeches* (New York: Greeley and McElrath, 1843), Vol. I, p. 185; Ichabod Bartlett to Clay (January 29, 1824), Reel 1, Henry Clay Papers, Library of Congress.

42 Supporting Recognition of Greek Independence (January 22, 1824) in Amelia Williams and Eugene Barker, eds., *The Writings of Sam Houston 1813–1863* (Austin: Pemberton Press, 1970), Vol. I, p. 21; Llerena Friend, *Sam Houston: The Great Designer* (Austin: University of Texas Press. 1954), p. 10.

43 *Annals of the Congress of the United States*, Eighteenth Congress, First Session, House, Vol. I, pp. 1115–1126, 1139–1150, 1155–1158; May, *The Making of the Monroe Doctrine*, p. 236.

44 *Annals of the Congress of the United States*, Eighteenth Congress, First Session, House, Vol. I, pp. 1150–1155, 1158–1160, 1182–1190, 1203–1213. On the distribution of Greeks in the Ottoman empire, see Dakin: *The Unification of Greece 1770–1923*, pp. 1–2. Roughly 2 million lived in the area later encompassed by modern Greece, with 1.8 million in Asia Minor and 300,000 in Constantinople and environs.

45 King to Charles King (January 30, 1824), Rufus King Papers, New-York Historical Society.

46 *Statesman* of April 10, 1824 cited in Raphalides, *United States Policy Toward the Greek War of Independence*, p. 123.

47 Remini, *Daniel Webster: The Man and His Time*, p. 219; Peterson, *The Great Triumvirate: Webster, Clay, and Calhoun*, p. 109; "The Bunker Hill Monument" (June 17, 1825) in Everett, *The Works of Daniel Webster*, Vol. II, p. 59.

48 Entry of November 10, 1824 in Adams, *Memoirs of John Quincy Adams*, Vol. VI, p. 429; Pappas, *The United States and the Greek War for Independence, 1821–1828*, pp. 53–54.

49 Entry of February 13, 1820 in Allan Nevins, ed., *The Diary of John Quincy Adams 1794–1845* (New York: Frederick Ungar Publishing Co., 1969), pp. 226–227; Garry Wills, *Lincoln at Gettysburg: The Words that Remade America* (New York: Simon and Schuster, 1992), pp. 34, 45; Varg, *Edward Everett: The Intellectual in the Turmoil of Politics*, p. 9; Thomas Jefferson to Everett (October 15, 1824), Reel 2, Edward Everett Papers, Massachusetts Historical Society.

50 Frothingham, *Edward Everett: Orator and Statesman*, p. 36.
51 Field, *America and the Mediterranean World 1776–1783*, pp. 121–122.
52 Everett, "Coray's Aristotle," pp. 415–416.
53 Ibid., p. 419; Wiltse, *The Papers of Daniel Webster: Correspondence*, Vol. I, p. 336, #3; Frothingham, *Edward Everett: Orator and Statesman*, p. 77.
54 Webster's letters to Edward Everett (November 28 and December 21, 1823) in Wiltse, *The Papers of Daniel Webster: Correspondence*, Vol. I, pp. 335–336, 342.
55 Larrabee, *Hellas Observed: The American Experience of Greece, 1775–1865*, pp. 150–151; Pappas, *The United States and the Greek War for Independence, 1821–1828*, pp. 117, 165 #1; *Debates of Congress, from 1789 to 1856* (New York: D. Appleton and Company, 1858), Vol. IX, pp. 363–364.
56 *Debates of Congress, from 1789 to 1856*, Vol. IX, pp. 364–366.
57 Charles Carroll to Everett (February 26, 1827), Reel 2, Edward Everett Papers, Massachusetts Historical Society.
58 Alexandros Mavrokordatos's letters to Everett (December 11, 1824 and May 12, September 16, and October 15, 1827), Reel 2, Everett to Alexandros Mavrokordatos (n.d.), Reel 25, Edward Everett Papers, Massachusetts Historical Society.
59 Everett to Samuel Gridely Howe (September 5, 1825), ibid.
60 Everett to J. P. Miller (September 5, 1825) and Everett to George Jarvis (September 6, 1825) and Everett to Matthew Carey (January?, 1827), Reel 25, Everett to Gentlemen of the Executive Committee for the Relief of the Greeks (February 4, 1827), Reel 2, Edward Everett Papers, Massachusetts Historical Society; Larrabee, *Hellas Observed: The American Experience of Greece 1775–1865*, p. 149; St. Clair, *That Greece Might Still Be Free*, pp. 339, 343; Schwartz, *Samuel Gridely Howe: Social Reformer 1801–1876*, pp. 21, 29.
61 *Debates of Congress, from 1789 to 1856*, Vol. IX, p. 365; Alexandros Contostavlos's letters to Everett (August 20, 1826 and September 6, 1826), Reel 2, Edward Everett Papers, Massachusetts Historical Society; Pappas, *The United States and the Greek War for Independence, 1821–1828*, pp. 95–115.
62 Pappas, *The United States and the Greek War for Independence, 1821–1828*, p. vii.
63 See Angelo Repousis, "The Cause of the Greeks: Philadelphia and the Greek War for Independence, 1821–1828," *Pennsylvania Magazine of History and Biography* (October 1999).
64 Entry of May 27, 1825 in Count Gallatin, ed., *The Diary of James Gallatin 1813–1827* (New York: Charles Scribner's Sons, 1920), pp. 253–254; Marquis de Lafayette to Gallatin (December 9, 1825), Reel 13, Albert Gallatin Papers, New-York Historical Society; Gilbert Chinard, ed., *When Lafayette Came to America: An Account from the Dubois Martin Papers in the Maryland Historical Society* (Easton, Penn.: The American Friends of Lafayette, 1948), p. 1; James Nolan, *Lafayette in America Day by Day* (Baltimore: Johns Hopkins University Press, 1934), p. 289.

65 Everett to General Lafayette (December 6, 1826), Reel 25, Edward Everett Papers, Massachusetts Historical Society.
66 Entry of May 28, 1824 in Adams, *Memoirs of John Quincy Adams*, Vol. VI, pp. 364–367; Larrabee, *Hellas Observed: The American Experience of Greece 1775–1865*, pp. 73–74; Pappas, *The United States and the Greek War for Independence, 1821–1828*, pp. 84–91; Everett to the President of the United States (September 29, 1826), Reel 25, Edward Everett Papers, Massachusetts Historical Society.
67 Entry of August 15, 1823, Adams, *Memoirs of John Quincy Adams*, Vol. VI, p. 172.
68 Larrabee, *Hellas Observed: The American Experience of Greece 1775–1865*, p. 169.
69 Leland James Gordon, *American Relations with Turkey 1830–1930: An Economic Interpretation* (Philadelphia: University of Pennsylvania Press, 1932), pp. 8–12.
70 Dakin, *The Unification of Greece 1770–1923*, p. 54.
71 Dr. William Thornton to Gallatin (October 29, 1827), Reel 15, Albert Gallatin Papers, New-York Historical Society.
72 Field, *America and the Mediterranean World 1772–1882*, pp. 132, 254; *Principal Officers of the Department of State and United States Chiefs of Mission, 1778–1988* (Washington: United States Department of State, 1988), p. 54.
73 Gordon, *American Relations with Turkey 1830–1930: An Economic Interpretation*, pp. 41–47; Field, *America and the Mediterranean World 1772–1882*, pp. 133, 167, 170.
74 Graham Stuart, *Latin America and the United States* (New York: D. Appleton-Century Company, 1943), p. 49.
75 Bolivar cited in "On Top of the World?" *Boston Globe* (August 20, 2000), p. F1.
76 Remini, *Daniel Webster: The Man and His Time*, pp. 698–705.
77 On the sources of Western political imagination see Maria Todorova's *Imagining the Balkans* (New York: Oxford University Press, 1997).
78 Everett, "Coray's Aristotle," p. 417.
79 Acacius to Webster (July 1825) in Wiltse, *The Papers of Daniel Webster: Correspondence*, Vol. II, p. 66.

Chapter Four

1 See Michael Walzer's *Arguing About War* (New Haven: Yale University Press, 2004), p. 81.
2 "Indians get Apology from U.S. Agency," *Boston Globe* (September 9, 2000), p. A11.
3 "An Apology and a Milestone at Indian Bureau," *New York Times* (September 9, 2000), p. A7.
4 Robert Remini, *Andrew Jackson and His Indian Wars* (New York: Viking, 2001), p. 115; James Fenimore Cooper, *The Last of the Mohicans* (New York: Simon and Schuster, 1957), p. 420.

5 Indian Removal Act (May 28, 1830) in Francis Paul Prucha, ed., *Documents of United States Indian Policy* (Lincoln: University of Nebraska Press, 1990), pp. 52–53.

6 Ronald Satz, *American Indian Policy in the Jacksonian Era* (Lincoln: University of Nebraska Press, 1975), p. 97; Robert Remini, *The Legacy of Andrew Jackson: Essays on Democracy, Indian Removal, and Slavery* (Baton Rouge: Louisiana State University Press, 1988), p. 81; Remini, *Andrew Jackson and His Indian Wars*, p. 238.

7 Michael Paul Rogin, *Fathers and Children: Andrew Jackson and the Subjugation of the American Indian* (New York: Alfred A. Knopf, 1975), p. 206; Remini, *Andrew Jackson and His Indian Wars*, p. 277.

8 Angie Debo, *A History of the Indians of the United States* (Norman: University of Oklahoma Press, 1970), p. 110; Satz, *American Indian Policy in the Jacksonian Era*, pp. 107, 114.

9 Thomas Pangle and Peter Ahrensdorf, *Justice Among Nations: On the Moral Basis of Power and Peace* (Lawrence: University Press of Kansas, 1999), p. 88.

10 Ralph Waldo Emerson's letter to Martin Van Buren in Louis Filler and Allen Guttmann, eds., *The Removal of the Cherokee Nation: Manifest Destiny or National Dishonor?* (Lexington, Mass.: D. C. Heath and Company, 1962), p. 94.

11 Frances Trollope, *Domestic Manners of the Americans* (London: George Routledge and Sons, 1927), p. 186.

12 Alexis de Tocqueville, *Democracy in America* (New York: Harper and Row, 1966), pp. 298–299, 312.

13 James Fenimore Cooper, *Notions of the Americans* (New York: Frederick Ungar Publishing Co., 1963), Vol. II, p. 286.

14 Second Annual Message of President Andrew Jackson (December 6, 1830) in James Richardson, ed., *A Compilation of the Messages and Papers of the Presidents: 1789–1897* (New York: Bureau of National Literature, 1897), Vol. III, p. 1082.

15 Remini, *Andrew Jackson and His Indian Wars*, p. 215.

16 First Annual Message of President Andrew Jackson (December 8, 1829) in Richardson, *A Compilation of the Messages and Papers of the Presidents: 1789–1897*, Vol. II, p. 456; Jackson to Captain James Gadsden, October 12, 1829 in John Spencer Bassett, ed., *Correspondence of Andrew Jackson* (Washington: Carnegie Institution of Washington, 1929), Vol. IV, p. 81.

17 Remini, *The Legacy of Andrew Jackson: Essays on Democracy, Indian Removal, and Slavery*, p. 47; Anthony Wallace, *The Long, Bitter Trail: Andrew Jackson and the Indians* (New York: Hill and Wang, 1993), p. 7.

18 John Milligan, "Slave Rebelliousness and the Florida Maroon," *Prologue: The Journal of the National Archives* (Spring 1974), pp. 4–18; John Mahon, *History of the Second Seminole War* (Gainesville: University of Florida Press, 1967), p. 23; Remini, *Andrew Jackson and His Indian Wars*, p. 131.

19 The Jefferson quotation is from William McLoughlin, *Cherokee Renascence in the New Republic* (Princeton: Princeton University Press, 1986), p. 33. Also see Stephen Ambrose, *Undaunted Courage: Meriwether Lewis, Thomas Jefferson,*

and the Opening of the American West (New York: Simon and Schuster, 1996), p. 333; Anthony Wallace, *Jefferson and the Indians: The Tragic Fate of the First Americans* (Cambridge, Mass.: Harvard University Press, 1999), p. 20; Wallace, *The Long, Bitter Trail: Andrew Jackson and the Indians*, pp. 38–39; Theda Perdue and Michael Green, eds., *The Cherokee Removal: A Brief History with Documents* (Boston: Bedford Books of St. Martin's, 1995), pp. 24–25.

20 Wallace, *Jefferson and the Indians: The Tragic Fate of the First Americans*, p. 336; Wallace, *The Long, Bitter Trail: Andrew Jackson and the Indians*, p. 56.

21 Second Annual Message (December 6, 1830) in Ronald Shaw, ed., *Andrew Jackson 1767–1845: Chronology–Documents–Bibliographical Aids* (Dobbs Ferry, New York: Oceana Publications, 1969), p. 33.

22 Farewell Address of Andrew Jackson (March 4, 1837) in Richardson, *A Compilation of the Messages and Papers of the Presidents: 1789–1897*, Vol. II, p. 541; Remini, *Andrew Jackson and His Indian Wars*, pp. 113, 180.

23 Willard Carl Klunder, *Lewis Cass and the Politics of Moderation* (Kent, Ohio: Kent State University Press, 1996), pp. 70–71.

24 Lewis Cass, "Removal of the Indians," *North American Review* (January 1830), pp. 62–121.

25 Geoffrey Ward, *The West* (Boston: Little, Brown and Company, 1996), pp. 81–82.

26 Satz, *American Indian Policy in the Jacksonian Era*, pp. 14–15.

27 *Debates of Congress from 1789 to 1856* (New York: D. Appleton and Company, 1860), Vol. XI, pp. 96–105.

28 Wilson Lumpkin's speech before Congress on May 17, 1830 in Filler and Guttmann, *The Removal of the Cherokee Nation: Manifest Destiny or National Dishonor?*, p. 31.

29 *Debates of Congress from 1789 to 1856*, Vol. X, pp. 532–535.

30 Francis Paul Prucha, ed., *Cherokee Removal: The William Penn Essays and Other Writings by Jeremiah Evarts* (Knoxville: University of Tennessee Press, 1981), p. 16; Satz, *American Indian Policy in the Jacksonian Era*, pp. 24, 43.

31 Guide to Papers of the American Board of Commissioners for Foreign Missions, p. 1, Houghton Library, Harvard University.

32 Perdue and Green, *The Cherokee Removal: A Brief History with Documents*, p. 18; Satz, *American Indian Removal in the Jacksonian Era*, pp. 13, 17.

33 Prucha, *Cherokee Removal: The William Penn Essays and Other Writings by Jeremiah Evarts*, pp. 30–31.

34 Ibid., p. 211.

35 Talbot Chambers, *Memoir of the Life and Character of Hon. Theo. Frelinghuysen* (New York: Harper and Brothers Publishers, 1863), p. 138.

36 Frelinghuysen to Dorothea Dix (February 27, 1845), Dorothea Dix Papers, Houghton Library, Harvard University.

37 Chambers, *Memoir of the Life and Character of Hon. Theo. Frelinghuysen*, p. 223; Robert Eells, *Forgotten Saint: The Life of Theodore Frelinghuysen – A Case Study of Christian Leadership* (Lanham, Maryland: University Press of America, 1987), pp. xiii, 62.

38 Eells, *Forgotten Saint: The Life of Theodore Frelinghuysen – A Case Study of Christian Leadership*, p. 47.

39 Henry Mayer, *All On Fire: William Lloyd Garrison and the Abolition of Slavery* (New York: St. Martin's Press, 1998), p. 138; Chambers, *Memoir of the Life and Character of Hon. Theo. Frelinghuysen*, p. 64.

40 Speech of the Hon. Theodore Frelinghuysen (April 7–9, 1830) in Jeremiah Evarts, ed., *Speeches on the Passage of the Bill for the Removal of the Indians Delivered in the Congress of the United States, April and May, 1830* (Boston: Perkins and Marvin, 1830), pp. 3, 5, 8–9, 24, 29.

41 Ibid., pp. 7–8, 27, 29.

42 The Substance of the Speech of the Hon. Edward Everett (May 19, 1830) ibid., pp. 278, 286, 293, 298.

43 A Sketch of the Remarks of the Hon. David Crockett (May 19, 1830) ibid., pp. 251–253; David Crockett, *Life of David Crockett* (New York: Perkins Book Company, 1903), p. 160; Mark Derr, *The Frontiersman: The Real Life and the Many Legends of Davy Crockett* (New York: William Morrow and Company, 1993), pp. 172–176; James Shackford, *David Crockett: The Man and the Legend* (Chapel Hill: University of North Carolina Press, 1956), p. 117.

44 Remini, *The Legacy of Andrew Jackson: Essays on Democracy, Indian Removal, and Slavery*, p. 80; Satz, *American Indian Policy in the Jacksonian Era*, p. 106.

45 W. A. Croffut, ed., *Fifty Years in Camp and Field: Diary of Major General Ethan Allen Hitchcock* (New York: G. P. Putnam's Sons, 1909), p. 77.

46 Wallace, *Jefferson and the Indians: The Tragic Fate of the First Americans*, p. 335; Wallace, *The Long, Bitter Trail: Andrew Jackson and the Indians*, pp. 100–101; Frank Laumer, *Dade's Last Command* (Gainesville: University Press of Florida, 1995), p. 215; John Mahon, *History of the Second Seminole War 1835–1842*, pp. 241, 325–326; Francis Paul Prucha, *The Great Father: The United States Government and the American Indians* (Lincoln: University of Nebraska Press, 1984), Vol. I, p. 233.

47 Mahon, *History of the Second Seminole War 1835–1842*, pp. 108–113; Paul Francis Prucha, *The Sword of the Republic: The United States Army on the Frontier 1783–1846* (New York: Macmillan Company, 1969), pp. 268–275.

48 George Julian, *The Life of Joshua R. Giddings* (Chicago: A. C. McClurg and Company, 1892), p. 95.

49 Ibid., p. 98; entry of February 6, 1845 in Charles Francis Adams, ed., *Memoirs of John Quincy Adams* (Philadelphia: J. B. Lippincott and Company, 1874–7), Vol. XII, pp. 162–163.

50 Joshua Giddings, *The Exiles of Florida: or, The Crimes Committed by our Government against the Maroons, Who Fled from South Carolina and Other Slave States, Seeking Protection under Spanish Laws* (Columbus: Follett, Foster and Company, 1858), p. v; James Brewster Stewart, *Joshua R. Giddings and the Tactics of Radical Politics* (Cleveland: Press of Case Western Reserve University, 1970), p. 268.

51 Mahon, *History of the Second Seminole War 1835–1842*, pp. 266–267; Entry of March 9, 1840 in Charles Francis Adams, *Memoirs of John Quincy Adams*, Vol. X, p. 233.

52 *Debates of Congress, from 1789 to 1856*, Vol. XIV, p. 35.
53 Mahon, *The Second Seminole War 1835–1842*, p. 270.
54 Croffut, *Fifty Years in Camp and Field: Diary of Major General Ethan Allen Hitchcock*, pp. 122, 127–129; Timothy Johnson, *Winfield Scott: The Quest for Military Glory* (Lawrence: University Press of Kansas, 1998), pp. 121, 125–126; Winfield Scott, *Memoirs* (New York: Sheldon and Company, 1864), Vol. I, p. 264; Prucha, *The Sword of the Republic: The United States Army on the Frontier 1783–1846*, pp. 289–290; Wallace, *The Long, Bitter Trail: Andrew Jackson and the Indians*, pp. 99–100.
55 Boudinot changed the name of his newspaper in 1829 to *Cherokee Phoenix and Indians' Advocate*.
56 Theda Perdue, ed., *Cherokee Editor: The Writings of Elias Boudinot* (Knoxville: University of Tennessee Press, 1983), p. vii; Samuel Carter, *Cherokee Sunset: A Nation Betrayed* (Garden City: Doubleday and Company, 1976), p. 52; Perdue and Green, *The Cherokee Removal: A Brief History with Documents*, p. 44.
    "These Indians have assuredly displayed as much natural genius as the European peoples in their greatest undertakings," Tocqueville wrote. See his *Democracy in America*, p. 307.
57 Stanley Hoig, *The Cherokees and Their Chiefs: In the Wake of Empire* (Fayetteville: University of Arkansas Press, 1998), pp. 126, 163.
58 The Substance of the Speech of Hon. Edward Everett (May 19, 1830) in Evarts, *Speeches on the Passage of the Bill for the Removal of the Indians*, p. 276.
59 See, for example, Resolution by Missionaries in Jack Frederick Kilpatrick and Anna Gritts Kilpatrick, eds., *New Echota Letters: Contributions of Samuel A. Worcester to the Cherokee Phoenix* (Dallas: Southern Methodist University, 1968), pp. 82–92.
60 Speech of the Hon. Theodore Frelinghuysen in Evarts, *Speeches on the Passage of the Bill for the Removal of the Indians*, p. 23; Debo, *A History of the Indians of the United States*, pp. 104–105; Colonel Robert Love to Jackson (November 17, 1831) and Jackson to Colonel Robert Love (December 10, 1831) in Bassett, *Correspondence of Andrew Jackson*, Vol. IV, pp. 376–377, 382; Perdue and Green, *The Cherokee Removal: A Brief History with Documents*, pp. 19, 62; Perdue, *Cherokee Editor: The Writings of Elias Boudinot*, pp. 21–23; Charles Royce, *The Cherokee Nation of Indians* (Chicago: Aldine Publishing Company, 1975), pp. 132–133.
61 See, for examples, "Committee and Council of the Cherokee Nation in General Council Convened to the People of the U.S." in *Cherokee Phoenix and Indians' Advocate* (July 24, 1830); "Memorial of the Cherokee Nation" in *Niles's Weekly Register* (August 21, 1830); Dale Van Every, *Disinherited: The Lost Birthright of the American Indian* (New York: William Morrow and Company, 1966), p. 13.
62 Ross to David Crockett (January 13, 1831) in Gary Moulton, ed., *The Papers of Chief John Ross, 1807–1839* (Norman: University of Oklahoma Press, 1985), Vol. I, p. 210.

63 Richard Peters, ed., *Report of Cases Signed and Adjudicated in the Supreme Court of the United States: January Term, 1832* (Philadelphia: Thomas Cowperthwaite and Company, 1845), Vol. V, pp. 15–20.

64 Worcester vs. the State of Georgia in Filler and Guttmann, *The Removal of the Cherokee Nation: Manifest Destiny or National Dishonor?*, p. 69.

65 Joan Gilbert, *The Trail of Tears across Missouri* (Columbia: University of Missouri Press, 1996), p. 22; Perdue, *Cherokee Editor: The Writings of Elias Boudinot*, p. 160; McLoughlin, *Cherokee Renascence in the New Republic*, p. 448.

66 Webster to Hiram Ketchum (May 12, 1838) in Charles Wiltse, ed., *The Papers of Daniel Webster: Correspondence, 1835–1839* (Hanover: University Press of New England, 1980), Vol. IV, p. 298; Robert Remini, *Henry Clay: Statesman for the Union* (New York: W. W. Norton and Company, 1991), pp. 371, 478, 489; "On Our Relations with the Cherokees" (February 4, 1835) in Daniel Mallory, ed., *The Life and Speeches of the Hon. Henry Clay* (New York: Van Amringe and Bixby, 1844), Vol. II, p. 208; Remini, *Andrew Jackson and His Indian Wars*, p. 222.

67 *Debates of Congress from 1789 to 1856*, Vol. XII, pp. 656–657.

68 Hoig, *The Cherokees and Their Chiefs: In the Wake of Empire*, pp. 164, 175.

69 Carter, *Cherokee Sunset: A Nation Betrayed*, pp. 234, 296 #18.

70 Royce, *The Cherokee Nation of Indians*, p. 164.

71 Wilson Lumpkin, *The Removal of the Cherokees from Georgia 1827–1841* (New York: Augustus M. Kelley Publishers, 1971), Vol. II, pp. 67–70, 318.

72 Gilbert, *The Trail of Tears across the Missouri*, pp. 34, 45, 50–51; William McLoughlin, *Champions of the Cherokees: Evan and John B. Jones* (Princeton: Princeton University Press, 1990), p. 139.

73 Harwood Hinton, "The Military Career of John Ellis Wool, 1812–1863" (University of Wisconsin, unpublished Ph.D. dissertation, 1960), p. 65.

74 Ibid., p. 51; Robert Utley, *Frontiersmen in Blue: The United States Army and the Indian, 1848–1865* (New York: Macmillan Company, 1967), p. 178.

75 Defense of Brigadier General Wool in *American State Papers: Military Affairs* (Washington: Gales and Seaton, 1861), Vol. VII, pp. 567–571; Ross to Joel Poinsett (May 4, 1837) in Moulton, *The Papers of Chief John Ross, 1807–1839*, Vol. I, p. 489–490; Ross to John Spencer (June 28, 1842) and Ross to Pierce Butler (November 18, 1843) in Gary Moulton, ed., *The Papers of Chief John Ross, 1840–1866* (Norman: University of Oklahoma Press, 1985), Vol. II, pp. 136–137, 187–188.

76 Thurman Wilkins, *Cherokee Tragedy: The Story of the Ridge Family and the Decimation of a People* (New York: Macmillan Company, 1970), p. 304; Carter, *Cherokee Sunset: A Nation Betrayed*, p. 200; Hinton, "The Military Career of John Ellis Wool, 1812–1863," pp. 114, 119.

77 James Corn, "Conscience or Duty: General John E. Wool's Dilemmas with Cherokee Removal," *Journal of Cherokee Studies* (Winter 1978), p. 36.

78 To the Senate and House of Representatives (February 22, 1837) in Moulton, *The Papers of Chief John Ross, 1807–1839*, Vol. I, pp. 470–474.

79 Hinton, "The Military Career of John Ellis Wool, 1812–1863," p. 91.

80 Wool to Mrs. Nathaniel Warren (November 21, 1836), John Wool Papers, Library of Congress; John Ehle, *Trail of Tears: The Rise and Fall of the Cherokee Nation* (New York: Doubleday, 1988), pp. 308–310.
81 Lumpkin, *The Removal of the Cherokee Indians from Georgia 1827–1841*, Vol. II, p. 306.
82 Defense of Brigadier General Wool in *American State Papers: Military Affairs*, Vol. VII, p. 571.
83 Ibid.
84 Ibid.
85 Ross to Lewis Ross, April 5, 1838 in Moulton, *The Papers of Chief John Ross 1807–1839*, Vol. I, pp. 622–624.
86 Winfield Scott, *Memoirs* (New York: Sheldon and Company, 1864), Vol. I, pp. 320–321.
87 Ibid., pp. 317–320, 326–329. A good example of Scott's seeking of preferment is in his letter to "Gentlemen" of October 25, 1841, Winfield Scott Papers, Library of Congress.
88 Gilbert, *The Trail of Tears across the Missouri*, p. 33.
89 Ross to a Gentleman of Philadelphia (May 6, 1837) in Moulton, *The Papers of Chief John Ross 1807–1839*, Vol. I, p. 495.
90 Satz, *American Indian Policy in the Jacksonian Era*, pp. 42–43; Debo, *A History of the Indians of the United States*, p. 108.
91 Robert Remini, *The Life of Andrew Jackson* (New York: Penguin Books, 1990), p. 215; Remini, *The Legacy of Andrew Jackson: Essays on Democracy, Indian Removal, and Slavery*, p. 80; Remini, *Andrew Jackson and His Indian Wars*, pp. 271, 281.
92 Wallace, *The Long, Bitter Trail: Andrew Jackson and the Indians*, p. viii.
93 From Garrison's "To the Hon. Theodore Frelinghuysen, on Reading His Eloquent Speech in Defense of Indian Rights" in Chambers, *Memoir of the Life and Character of Hon. Theo. Frelinghuysen*, pp. 70–71.
94 The Substance of the Speech of the Hon. Edward Everett (May 19, 1830) in Evarts, *Speeches on the Passage of the Bill for the Removal of the Indians*, pp. 278–279.
95 Royce, *The Cherokee Nation of Nations*, p. 165; Remini, *The Legacy of Andrew Jackson: Essays on Democracy, Indian Removal, and Slavery*, p. 81.
96 Hinton, "The Military Career of John Ellis Wool, 1812–1863," p. 173.

Chapter Five

1 David Pletcher, *The Diplomacy of Annexation: Texas, Oregon, and the Mexican War* (Columbia: University of Missouri Press, 1973), p. 185.
2 David Weber, *The Mexican Frontier, 1821–1846: The American Southwest Under Mexico* (Albuquerque: University of New Mexico Press, 1982), p. xv.
3 Walt Whitman cited in Ramon Eduardo Ruiz, ed., *The Mexican War: Was It Manifest Destiny?* (New York: Holt, Rinehart and Winston, 1963), p. 8.
4 Walter McDougall, *Promised Land, Crusader State: The American Encounter with the World Since 1776* (Boston: Houghton Mifflin Company, 1997), p. 93; K. Jack Bauer, *The Mexican War 1846–1848* (Lincoln: University of Nebraska

Press, 1974), p. viii; Polk's Fourth Annual Message (December 5, 1848) in James Richardson, ed. *Messages and Papers of the Presidents* (New York: Bureau of National Literature, Inc., 1897), Vol. V, p. 2479.

5 Octavio Paz, *The Labyrinth of Solitude: Life and Thought in Mexico* (New York: Grove Press, Inc., 1961), p. 124.

6 Ann Fears Crawford, ed., *The Eagle: The Autobiography of Santa Anna* (Austin: Pemberton Press, 1967), pp. 88, 115; Richard Griswold del Castillo, *The Treaty of Guadalupe Hidalgo* (Norman: University of Oklahoma Press, 1990), p. xii; Cecil Robinson, ed., *The View from Chapultepec: Mexican Writers on the Mexican–American War* (Tucson: University of Arizona Press, 1989), p. ix.

7 Lars Schoultz, *Beneath the United States: A History of U.S. Policy Toward Latin America* (Cambridge, Mass.: Harvard University Press, 1998), p. 14.

8 Gene Brack, *Mexico Views Manifest Destiny, 1821–1846: An Essay on the Origins of the Mexican War* (Albuquerque: University of New Mexico Press, 1975), pp. 53–54.

9 Weber, *The Mexican Frontier, 1821–1846: The American Southwest under Mexico*, pp. 275–276.

10 Charles and Mary Beard, *Basic History of the United States* (Garden City: Doubleday and Company, 1960), p. 186; McDougall, *Promised Land, Crusader State: The American Encounter with the World since 1776*, p. 90.

11 Akira Iriye, *From Nationalism to Internationalism: U.S. Foreign Policy to 1914* (London: Routledge and Kegan Paul, 1977), p. 33.

12 Robinson, *The View from Chapultepec: Mexican Writers on the Mexican–American War*, pp. xxiv, 195; Homer Camp Chaney, "The Mexican–United States War as Seen by Mexican Intellectuals, 1846–1956" (Stanford University: unpublished Ph.D. dissertation, 1959), p. 2; Brack, *Mexico Views Manifest Destiny, 1821–1846: An Essay on the Origins of the Mexican War*, pp. 11, 170.

13 Calhoun to Anna Maria Calhoun Clemson (December 27, 1846) in Clyde Wilson and Shirley Cook, eds., *The Papers of John C. Calhoun* (Columbia: University of South Carolina Press, 1998), Vol. XXIV, p. 42–44.

14 Chaney, "The Mexican–United States War as Seen by Mexican Intellectuals, 1846–1956," pp. 12–15; Robinson, *The View from Chapultepec: Mexican Writers on the Mexican–American War*, p. xxviii.

15 Weber, *The Mexican Frontier, 1821–1846: The American Southwest under Mexico*, p. 274.

16 Polk to the Senate and House of Representatives (May 11, 1846) in Richardson, *Messages and Papers of the Presidents*, Vol. V, p. 2292.

17 *Congressional Globe: Appendix, First Session of the Twenty-Ninth Congress* (Washington: Blair and Rives, 1846), p. 646.

18 Ibid., p. 792.

19 John Eisenhower, *So Far from God: The U.S. War with Mexico 1846–1848* (New York: Random House, 1989), pp. xviii, xxv; Anders Stephanson, *Manifest Destiny: American Expansionism and the Empire of Right* (New York: Hill and Wang, 1995), p. 37; Bauer, *The Mexican War 1846–1848*, pp. xix, 374, 395; Norman Saul, *Distant Friends: The United States and Russia, 1763–1867* (Lawrence: University Press of Kansas, 1991), p. 173.

20 Bernard DeVoto, *The Year of Decision 1846* (Boston: Little, Brown and Company, 1943), p. 278; Winfield Scott, *Memoirs* (New York: Sheldon and Company, 1864), Vol. II, pp. 392–396; Otis Singletary, *The Mexican War* (Chicago: University of Chicago Press, 1960), pp. 144–147; Sam Haynes, *James K. Polk and the Expansionist Impulse* (New York: Longman, 1997), pp. 152–153, 174.

21 John Fuller, *Movement for the Acquisition of All Mexico 1846–1848* (Baltimore: Johns Hopkins University Press, 1936), pp. 49, 79; Bauer, *The Mexican War, 1846–1848*, p. 368.

22 McDougall, *Promised Land, Crusader State: The American Encounter with the World Since 1776*, p. 95.

23 Haynes, *James K. Polk and the Expansionist Impulse*, p. 168.

24 Samuel Eliot Morison, *The Oxford History of the American People* (New York: Oxford University Press, 1965), pp. 561–562; Bauer, *The Mexican War 1846–1848*, p. 364.

25 Resistance to Civil Government in William Rossi, ed., *Henry David Thoreau: Walden and Resistance to Civil Government* (New York: W. W. Norton and Company, 1992), p. 229.

26 John Schroeder, *Mr. Polk's War: American Opposition and Dissent, 1846–1848* (Madison: University of Wisconsin Press, 1973), p. 105; Henry Mayer, *All on Fire: William Lloyd Garrison and the Abolition of Slavery* (New York: St. Martin's Press, 1998), pp. 360–361; Theodore Parker, *Sermon of War* (Boston: Charles C. Little and James Brown, 1846), p. 41.

27 Abiel Abbot Livermore, *The War with Mexico Reviewed* (Boston: American Peace Society, 1850), p. 14; Schroeder, *Mr. Polk's War: American Opposition and Dissent, 1846–1848*, pp. 94–95. Also see Loring Moody's 1847 study, *Facts for the People: Showing the Relations of the United States Government to Slavery* (Freeport, New York: Books for Libraries Press, 1971).

28 Thomas Wortham, ed., *James Russell Lowell's The Biglow Papers* (DeKalb: Northern Illinois University Press, 1977), p. 53.

29 Seba Smith, *My Thirty Years Out of the Senate by Major Jack Downing* (New York: Derby and Jackson, 1860), p. 281.

30 Ibid., pp. 283–284; Milton Rickels and Patricia Rickels, *Seba Smith* (Boston: Twayne Publishers, 1977), pp. 125–127.

31 U.S. Grant, *Personal Memoirs* (Lincoln: University of Nebraska Press, 1996), Vol. I, p. 37; Robert Ryal Miller, *Shamrock and Sword: The Saint Patrick's Battalion in the U.S.–Mexican War* (Norman: University of Oklahoma Press, 1989), pp. 111–112; Eisenhower, *So Far from God: The U.S. War with Mexico 1846–1848*, p. xvii; Sister Blanche Marie McEniry, *American Catholics in the War with Mexico* (Washington: Catholic University of America, 1937), pp. 73–98.

32 Ernest McPherson Lander, *Reluctant Imperialists: Calhoun, the South Carolinians, and the Mexican War* (Baton Rouge: Louisiana State University Press, 1980), pp. 23, 67; Robert Johannsen, *To the Halls of the Montezumas: The Mexican War in the American Imagination* (New York: Oxford University Press, 1985), pp. 294–295; J. Fred Rippy, *Joel Poinsett, Versatile American* (New York: Greenwood Press, 1968), pp. 226–230.

33 Michael Hunt, *Ideology and U.S. Foreign Policy* (New Haven: Yale University Press, 1987), p. 34; Reginal Horsman, *Race and Manifest Destiny: The Origins of American Racial Anglo-Saxonism* (Cambridge, Mass.: Harvard University Press, 1981), pp. 269–270.

34 Peace with Mexico in E. James Ferguson, ed., *Selected Writings of Albert Gallatin* (Indianapolis: Bobbs-Merrill Company, 1967), p. 486.

35 Frederick Merk, *Manifest Destiny and Mission in American History: A Reinterpretation* (New York: Alfred A. Knopf, 1963), p. 185; Polk's Second Annual Message (December 8, 1846) in Richardson, *Messages and Papers of the President*, Vol. V, p. 2323; Justin Smith, *The War with Mexico* (New York: Macmillan Company, 1919), Vol. II, pp. 280–281.

36 Entry of January 5, 1847 in Milo Milton Quaife, ed., *The Diary of James K. Polk* (Chicago: A. C. McClurg and Company, 1910), Vol. II, p. 308.

37 Schroeder, *Mr. Polk's War: American Opposition and Dissent, 1846–1848*, p. 57; Charles Wiltse, ed., *The Papers of Daniel Webster: Correspondence* (Hanover: University Press of New England, 1984), Vol. VI, p. 209; Haynes, *James K. Polk and the Expansionist Impulse*, p. 155; Leonard Richards, *The Life and Times of Congressman John Quincy Adams* (New York: Oxford University Press, 1986), p. 173.

38 David Donald, *Lincoln* (New York: Simon and Schuster, 1995), pp. 123–124, 126.

39 Spot Resolutions in the U.S. House of Representatives (December 22, 1847) and Speech in the U.S. House of Representatives on the War with Mexico (January 12, 1848) in Don Fehrenbacher, ed., *Abraham Lincoln: Speeches and Writings 1832–1858* (New York: Library of America, 1989), pp. 158–159, 161–171.

40 Pleasant Stovall, *Robert Toombs: Statesman, Speaker, Soldier, Sage* (New York: Cassell Publishing Company, 1892), pp. 53, 59–60.

41 Schroeder, *Mr. Polk's War: American Opposition and Dissent, 1846–1848*, p. 28.

42 "The Mexican War" (March 1, 1847) and "Objects of the Mexican War" (March 23, 1848) in Charles Wiltse, ed., *The Papers of Daniel Webster: Speeches and Formal Writings, 1832–1852* (Hanover: University Press of New England, 1988), pp. 435–445, 447–476; entry of March 3, 1848 in Quaife, *The Diary of James K. Polk*, Vol. III, pp. 370–371.

43 For John Quincy Adams's testament of friendship with Giddings, see Samuel Flagg Bemis, *John Quincy Adams and the Union* (New York: Alfred A. Knopf, 1970), p. 423.

44 Samuel Eliot Morison, Frederick Merk, and Frank Freidel, *Dissent in Three American Wars* (Cambridge, Mass.: Harvard University Press, 1970), pp. 42; Stephanson, *Manifest Destiny: American Expansionism and the Empire of Right*, p. 34; Richards, *The Life and Times of Congressman John Quincy Adams*, pp. 182, 188, 190.

45 James Brewer Stewart, *Joshua R. Giddings and the Tactics of Radical Politics* (Cleveland: Press of Case Western Reserve University, 1970), pp. 73–74; Alfred Aldrich to Calhoun (September 21, 1847) in Wilson and Cook, *The*

Papers of John C. Calhoun, Vol. XXIV, p. 568; Smith, *The War with Mexico,* Vol. II, p. 496, #24.

46 Stewart, *Joshua R. Giddings and the Tactics of Radical Politics,* pp. 40–41, 94; Thomas Hietala, *Manifest Design: Anxious Aggrandizement in Late Jacksonian America* (Ithaca: Cornell University Press, 1985), pp. 38–39; David Donald, *Charles Sumner and the Coming of the Civil War* (New York: Alfred A. Knopf, 1967), p. 162; Schroeder, *Mr. Polk's War: American Opposition and Dissent, 1846–1848,* p. 30.

47 "The Mexican War" (May 12, 1846) in Joshua Giddings, *Speeches in Congress* (New York: Negro Universities Press, 1968), p. 177.

48 Ibid., p. 178.

49 "The President's Annual Message" (December 15, 1846) in Giddings, *Speeches in Congress,* p. 265.

50 Ibid.; George Julian, *The Life of Joshua Giddings* (Chicago: A. C. McClurg and Company, 1892), p. 195.

51 "The Wilmot Proviso" (February 13, 1847) in Giddings, *Speeches in Congress,* p. 202; Stewart, *Joshua R. Giddings and the Tactics of Radical Politics,* p. 131.

52 Stewart, *Joshua R. Giddings and the Tactics of Radical Politics,* pp. 125, 134, 147, 167–168.

53 "Mexican War" (July 14, 1846) in Giddings, *Speeches in Congress,* pp. 250–264; Mayer, *All on Fire: William Lloyd Garrison and the Abolition of Slavery,* p. 361.

54 Ruiz, *The Mexican War: Was it Manifest Destiny?,* pp. 1–7; Eisenhower, *So Far from God: The U.S. War with Mexico 1846–1848,* pp. vx, 374; Friedrich Engels's "Democratic Pan-Slavism" "February 15, 1849" in David Fernbach, ed., *Karl Marx: The Revolutions of 1848* (New York: Vintage Books, 1974), pp. 229–230; Calhoun to Thomas Clemson (June 15, 1847) in Wilson and Cook, *The Papers of John C. Calhoun,* Vol. XXIV, p. 398.

55 Irving Bartlett, *John C. Calhoun: A Biography* (New York: W. W. Norton and Company, 1993), p. 336. On the warlike character of the United States, see p. 244 of First Speech on the Bill for an Additional Military Force (July 16, 1848) in Wilson and Cook, *The Papers of John C. Calhoun,* Vol. XXV, p. 235.

56 Hietala, *Manifest Design: Anxious Aggrandizement in Late Jacksonian America,* p. 243; Lander, *Reluctant Imperialists: Calhoun, the South Carolinians, and the Mexican War,* p. 32; Bartlett, *John C. Calhoun: A Biography,* p. 340.

57 Calhoun to Joseph Lesesne (July 19, 1847) in Wilson and Cook, *The Papers of John C. Calhoun,* Vol. XXIV, pp. 462–464.

58 Ibid.

59 Speech on the War with Mexico (January 4, 1848) ibid., Vol. XXV, p. 54.

60 Ibid.

61 Ibid.; Speech on the War with Mexico (February 9, 1847) in Wilson and Cook, *The Papers of John C. Calhoun,* Vol. XXIV, p. 115.

62 Lander, *Reluctant Imperialists: Calhoun, the South Carolinians, and the Mexican War,* p. 160; Calhoun to Anna Maria Calhoun Clemson (December 27, 1846) in Wilson and Cook, *The Papers of John C. Calhoun,* Vol. XXIV, pp. 42–44; entry of December 19, 1846 in Quaife, *The Diary of James K. Polk,* Vol. II, pp. 281–284.

63 Speech on the War with Mexico (February 9, 1847) in Wilson and Cook, *The Papers of John C. Calhoun*, Vol. XXIV, p. 115.

64 Entry of December 24, 1846 in Quaife, *The Diary of James K. Polk*, Vol. II, pp. 292–293; John Niven, *John C. Calhoun and the Price of Union: A Biography* (Baton Rouge: Louisiana State University Press, 1988), p. 304.

65 Arthur Schlesinger, *War and the American Presidency* (New York: W. W. Norton and Company, 2004), p. 77.

66 *Congressional Globe: The First Session of the Thirtieth Congress*, Part I, p. 123.

67 Robert Arthur Brent, "Nicholas Philip Trist: Biography of a Disobedient Diplomat" (University of Virginia: unpublished Ph.D. dissertation, 1950), p. 19; Smith, *The War with Mexico*, Vol. II, pp. 127–128.

68 Brent, "Nicholas Philip Trist: Biography of a Disobedient Diplomat," pp. 79, 85.

69 Jesse Reeves, *American Diplomacy under Tyler and Polk* (Gloucester, Mass.: Peter Smith, 1967), pp. 31–32, 312.

70 Brent, "Nicholas Philip Trist: Biography of a Disobedient Diplomat," p. 119; Thomas Fleming, "Nicholas Trist: The Disobedient Diplomat" in Susan Ware, ed., *Forgotten Heroes* (New York: Free Press, 1998), p. 78; Anna Kasten Nelson, *Secret Agents: President Polk and the Search for Peace with Mexico* (New York: Garland Publishing, 1988), p. 7; George Lockhart Rives, *The United States and Mexico 1821–1848* (New York: Charles Scribner's Sons, 1913) Vol. II, p. 425.

71 Entry of April 10, 1848 in Quaife, *The Diary of James K. Polk*, Vol. II, p. 465.

72 Norman Graebner, *Empire on the Pacific: A Study in American Continental Expansion* (Santa Barbara: ABC-Clio, Inc., 1983), pp. 192–194; Pletcher, *The Diplomacy of Annexation: Texas, Oregon, and the Mexican War*, pp. 499–501, 504; Eisenhower, *So Far from God: The U.S. War with Mexico 1846–1848*, pp. 290–291, 298–299; Reeves, *American Diplomacy under Tyler and Polk*, p. 311.

73 Entry of April 13, 1847 in Quaife, *The Diary of James K. Polk*, Vol. II, p. 471; James Buchanan to Nicholas Trist (April 15, 1847) in William Manning, ed. *Diplomatic Correspondence of the United States: Inter-American Affairs 1831–1860* (Washington: Carnegie Endowment for International Peace, 1937), Vol. VIII, p. 201.

74 Graebner, *Empire on the Pacific: A Study in American Continental Expansion*, pp. 195–196; Merk, *Manifest Destiny and Mission in American History: A Reinterpretation*, p. 114.

75 Brent, "Nicholas Philip Trist: Biography of a Disobedient Diplomat," p. 157; Winfield Scott, *Memoirs* (New York: Sheldon and Company, Publishers, 1864), Vol. II, p. 579; Nicholas Trist to James Buchanan (July 23, 1847) in Manning, *Diplomatic Correspondence of the United States: Inter-American Affairs 1831–1860*, Vol. VIII, pp. 915–916; entry of January 24, 1848 in Quaife, *The Diary of James K. Polk*, Vol. III, pp. 311–313.

76 Nicholas Trist to James Buchanan (June 13 and September 27, 1847) in Manning, *Diplomatic Correspondence of the United States: Inter-American Affairs 1831–1860*, Vol. VIII, pp. 908–914, 953–956; J. Fred Rippy, *Rivalry*

of the United States and Great Britain over Latin America, 1808–1830 (New York: Octagon Books, 1972), pp. 247–248; Pletcher, *The Diplomacy of Annexation: Texas, Oregon, and the Mexican War*, pp. 502–504; Haynes, *James K. Polk and the Expansionist Impulse*, p. 95; Bauer, *The Mexican War 1846–1848*, pp. 284–286; Castillo, *The Treaty of Guadalupe Hidalgo: A Legacy of Conflict*, pp. 27–29; Oakah Jones, *Santa Anna* (New York: Twayne Publishers, 1968), pp. 114–115; A. Brooke Caruso, *The Mexican Spy Company: United States Covert Operations in Mexico, 1845–1848* (Jefferson, North Carolina: McFarland and Company, 1991), pp. 155–156.

77 James Buchanan to Nicholas Trist (December 21, 1847) in Manning, *Diplomatic Correspondence of the United States: Inter-American Affairs 1831–1860*, Vol. VIII, pp. 218–219.

78 Entry of October 4, 1847 in Quaife, *The Diary of James K. Polk*, Vol. III, p. 185.

79 James Buchanan to Nicholas Trist (October 6 and October 25, 1847) in Manning, *Diplomatic Correspondence of the United States: Inter-American Affairs 1831–1860*, Vol. VIII, pp. 214–218.

80 Nicholas Trist to James Buchanan (December 6, 1847) ibid., p. 984.

81 Nicholas Trist to James Buchanan (October 25, 1847) ibid., p. 958.

82 Schoultz, *Beneath the United States: A History of U.S. Policy Toward Latin America*, p. 34.

83 Treaty of Guadalupe Hidalgo in Charles Bevans, ed., *Treaties and Other International Agreements of the United States of America* (Washington: Department of State, 1937), Vol. IX, pp. 791–806; Weber, *The Mexican Frontier, 1821–1846: The American Southwest under Mexico*, p. 274.

84 Entry of January 15, 1848 in Quaife, *The Diary of James K. Polk*, Vol. III, p. 300.

85 Entries of February 19 and 21, 1848 ibid., pp. 344, 347.

86 *Congressional Globe: The First Session of the Thirtieth Congress*, Part I, p. 501.

87 Bauer, *The Mexican War 1846–1848*, p. 399.

88 Castillo, *The Treaty of Guadalupe Hidalgo: A Legacy of Conflict*, p. 53.

89 Frederick Tolles, "Henry David Thoreau" in Daniel Boorstin, ed., *An American Primer* (Chicago: University of Chicago Press, 1966), pp. 338–340.

90 Petitions to Congress by Trist (and his friends) for compensation are in Reels 10 and 11 of the Nicholas P. Trist Papers in the Library of Congress. He petitioned frequently and at length during the 1850s and 1860s.

91 Scott, *Memoirs*, Vol. II, p. 580.

92 Fleming, "Nicholas Trist: The Disobedient Diplomat" in Ware, *Forgotten Heroes*, p. 84; Merk, *Manifest Destiny and Mission in American History: A Reinterpretation*, p. 184, #6; Brent, "Nicholas Philip Trist: Biography of a Disobedient Diplomat," pp. 238, 243–246, 248.

93 Donald, *Lincoln*, pp. 128, 133, 140, 226; Fourth Lincoln–Douglas Debate (September 18, 1858) in Fehrenbacher, *Abraham Lincoln: Speeches and Writings 1832–1858*, pp. 636; entry of April 6, 1847 in Quaife, *The Diary of James K. Polk*, Vol. II, pp. 457–459; Niven, *John C. Calhoun and the Price of Union*, p. 309; Charles Wiltse, *John C. Calhoun: Sectionalist, 1840–1850* (New York: Russell and Russell, 1968), p. 319.

94 Robinson, *The View from Chapultepec: Mexican Writers on the Mexican–American War*, p. 2; Rives, *The United States and Mexico 1821–1848*, Vol. II, p. 647; Castillo, *The Treaty of Guadalupe Hidalgo: A Legacy of Conflict*, pp. 49–51.

95 Scott, *Memoirs*, Vol. II, pp. 581–582.

96 Calhoun to Anna Maria Calhoun Clemson (December 27, 1846); Calhoun to Sarah Mytton Maury (February 18, 1847); Speech in Reply to Thomas H. Benton on the Mexican War (February 24, 1847) in Wilson and Cook, *The Papers of John C. Calhoun*, Vol. XXIV, pp. 42–44, 164–165, 195–210.

97 Schoultz, *Beneath the United States: A History of U.S. Policy Toward Latin America*, p. 38; John Lewis Gaddis, *Surprise, Security, and the American Experience* (Cambridge, Mass.: Harvard University Press, 2004), pp. 32–33; Garry Wills, *Negro President: Jefferson and the Slave Power* (Boston: Houghton Mifflin Company, 2003), p. 225.

98 Richards, *The Life and Times of Congressman John Quincy Adams*, p. 186.

99 David Mayers, *George Kennan and the Dilemmas of U.S. Foreign Policy* (New York: Oxford University Press, 1988), p. 263.

Chapter Six

 1 See Gideon Welles, *Lincoln and Seward* (Freeport, New York: Books for Libraries Press, 1969), p. 7.

 2 Some Thoughts for the President's Consideration (April 1, 1861), Reel 188, William Henry Seward Papers, Library of Congress.

 3 Welles, *Lincoln and Seward*, p. vi.

 4 Some Thoughts for the President's Consideration (April 1, 1861), Reel 188, William Henry Seward Papers, Library of Congress.

 5 Norman Ferris, *Desperate Diplomacy: William H. Seward's Foreign Policy, 1861* (Knoxville: University of Tennessee Press, 1976), p. 6; Frederic Bancroft, *William H. Seward* (New York: Harper and Brothers Publishers, 1900), Vol. II, pp. 134–135.

 6 D. P. Crook, *The North, the South, and the Powers 1861–1865* (New York: John Wiley and Sons, 1974), p. 61.

 7 Albert Woldman, *Lincoln and the Russians* (Cleveland: World Publishing Company, 1952), p. 93.

 8 James McPherson, *Ordeal By Fire: The Civil War and Reconstruction* (New York: Alfred A. Knopf, 1982), p. 215.

 9 Disraeli Looks into the Future (1863) in Belle Becker Sideman and Lillian Friedman, eds., *Europe Looks at the Civil War* (New York: Orion Press, 1960), p. 233.

10 John Hawgood, "The Civil War and Central Europe," in Harold Hyman, ed., *Heard Round the World: The Impact Abroad of the Civil War* (New York: Alfred A. Knopf, 1969), p. 147.

11 For France's nineteenth-century imperial ambitions, see "Grand Design for the Americas" in Alfred Jackson Hanna and Kathryn Abbey Hanna, *Napoleon III and Mexico* (Chapel Hill: University of North Carolina Press, 1971), p. xv

and Jack Autrey Dabbs, *The French Army in Mexico 1861–1867* (The Hague: Mouton and Company, 1963), p. 15.

12 James McPherson, *Ordeal by Fire: The Civil War and Reconstruction*, pp. 217–218.

13 Robin Winks, *Canada and the United States: The Civil War Years* (Baltimore: Johns Hopkins University Press, 1960), pp. x, 378; Eugene Berwanger, *The British Foreign Service and the American Civil War* (Lexington: University Press of Kentucky, 1994), p. 32.

14 Crook, *The North, the South, and the Powers 1861–1865*, p. 224.

15 Richard Cobden to Charles Sumner (February 13, 1863) in Sideman and Friedman, *Europe Looks at the Civil War*, p. 220.

16 Norman Saul, *Distant Friends: The United States and Russia, 1763–1867* (Lawrence: University Press of Kansas, 1991), p. 326.

17 David Mayers, *The Ambassadors and America's Soviet Policy* (New York: Oxford University Press, 1995), pp. 39–43.

18 Thornton Kirkland Lothrop, *William Henry Seward* (Boston: Houghton Mifflin Company, 1899), pp. 108–111; Ronald Jensen, *The Alaska Purchase and Russian–American Relations* (Seattle: University of Washington Press, 1975), p. 26; Burton Hendrick, *Lincoln's War Cabinet* (Gloucester, Mass.: Peter Smith, 1965), p. 250; Lincoln to Joshua Speed (August 24, 1855) in Don Fehrenbacher, ed., *Abraham Lincoln: Speeches and Writings 1832–1858* (New York: Library of America, 1989), pp. 360–363; Woldman, *Lincoln and the Russians*, pp. 3–13.

19 Joseph Wieczerzak, *A Polish Chapter in Civil War America: The Effects of the January Insurrection on American Opinion and Diplomacy* (New York: Twayne Publishers, 1967), p. 38.

20 Lincoln to George Robertson (August 15, 1855) in Fehrenbacher, *Abraham Lincoln: Speeches and Writings 1832–1858*, pp. 359–360.

21 David Mayers, *Wars and Peace: The Future Americans Envisioned, 1861–1991* (New York: St. Martin's Press, 1998), p. 9.

22 Jefferson Davis, *The Rise and Fall of the Confederate Government* (New York: Thomas Yoseloff, 1958), Vol. II, pp. 376–379; Saul, *Distant Friends: The United States and Russia, 1763–1867*, pp. 334–335; Proposals Will Be Made to Russia (October 1862) in Sideman and Friedman, *Europe Looks at the Civil War*, pp. 184–185; Norman Graebner, "Northern Diplomacy and European Neutrality" in David Donald, ed., *Why the North Won the Civil War* (Baton Rouge: Louisiana State University Press, 1960), p. 64.

23 European governments did permit Confederate commissioners to present their case. Yet none of them won recognition of Confederate independence – not John Mason in London, not John Slidell in Paris, not Pierre Rost in Madrid, not Dudley Mann in Belgium.

24 Saul, *Distant Friends: The United States and Russia, 1763–1867*, pp. 343, 354.

25 R. F. Leslie, *Reform and Insurrection in Russian Poland 1856–1865* (Westport, Conn.: Greenwood Press, 1969), pp. 175–176, 182; John Kutolowski, *The West and Poland: Essays on Governmental and Public Responses to the Polish Nationality Movement, 1861–1864* (New York: Columbia University Press, 2000), p. 295.

26 Thomas Bailey, *America Faces Russia: Russian–American Relations from Early Times to Our Day* (Gloucester, Mass.: Peter Smith, 1964), p. 84.

27 Entry of December 13, 1863 in Donald Cole and John McDonough, eds., *Benjamin Brown French: Witness to the Young Republic: A Yankee's Journal, 1828–1870* (Hanover: University Press of New England, 1989), p. 441.

28 Bailey, *America Faces Russia: Russian–American Relations from Early Times to Our Day*, pp. 84–86; Saul, *Distant Friends: The United States and Russia, 1763–1867*, pp. 353–354; Woldman, *Lincoln and the Russians*, pp. 148–149.

29 Wieczerzak, *A Polish Chapter in Civil War America: The Effects of the January Insurrection on American Opinion and Diplomacy*, p. 247 #1; John Stoessinger, *Nations in Darkness: China, Russia, and America* (New York: Random House, 1978), p. 106.

30 Saul, *Distant Friends: The United States and Russia, 1763–1867*, p. 322; Woldman, *Lincoln and the Russians*, pp. 41, 47; A Russian Diplomat Reports in 1861 in Sideman and Friedman, *Europe Looks at the Civil War*, p. 40.

31 A Russian Diplomat Reports in 1863 in Sideman and Friedman, *Europe Looks at the Civil War*, p. 244.

32 Saul, *Distant Friends: The United States and Russia, 1763–1867*, p. 338; Wieczerzak, *A Polish Chapter in Civil War America: The Effects of the January Insurrection on American Opinion and Diplomacy*, pp. 188, 249 #25; Dean Mahin, *One War at a Time: The International Dimensions of the American Civil War* (Washington: Brassey's, 1999), p. 193; Miecislaus Haiman, *Polish Past in America 1608–1865* (Chicago: Polish Roman Catholic Union, 1939), p. 148.

33 Harold Blinn, "Seward and the Polish Rebellion of 1863," *American Historical Review* (July 1940), pp. 829–830.

34 Ibid., p. 832; Seward to Dayton (May 11, 1863) in *Papers Relating to Foreign Affairs* (Washington: Government Printing Office, 1864), Part I, pp. 667–668; Gorchakov to Seward (May 22, 1863) in *Papers Relating to Foreign Affairs* (Washington: Government Printing Office, 1864), Part II, pp. 796–797; Glyndon Van Deusen, *William Henry Seward* (New York: Oxford University Press, 1967), pp. 538–539.

35 David Smiley, *Lion of White Hall: The Life of Cassius M. Clay* (Madison: University of Wisconsin Press, 1962), pp. 198–199; Saul, *Distant Friends: The United States and Russia, 1763–1867*, pp. 318–319, 339; Wieczerzak, *A Polish Chapter in Civil War America: The Effects of the January Insurrection on American Opinion and Diplomacy*, pp. 39, 83, 106–107, 109, 191–196.

36 Saul, *Distant Friends: The United States and Russia, 1763–1867*, pp. 370–377; Mayers, *The Ambassadors and America's Soviet Policy*, pp. 37, 43–44; Hans Rogger, "Russia and the Civil War" in Hyman, *Heard Round the World: The Impact Abroad of the Civil War*, pp. 237–239; Bailey, *America Faces Russia: Russian–American Relations from Early Times to Our Day*, pp. 96–99.

37 Nikolai Sivachev and Nikolai Yakovlev, *Russia and the United States* (Chicago: University of Chicago Press, 1979), p. 13.

38 Jensen, *The Alaska Purchase and Russian–American Relations*, pp. 9–22, 96–97; Saul, *Distant Friends: The United States and Russia, 1763–1867*, pp. 385–396; Bailey, *America Faces Russia: Russian–American Relations from Early Times to Our Day*, pp. 101–102, 104; Edward Richardson, *Cassius Marcellus Clay:*

Firebrand of Freedom (Lexington: University Press of Kentucky, 1976), p. 95; Van Deusen, *William Henry Seward*, pp. 539–540, 544.

39 "The Cession of Russian America to the United States" (April 9, 1867) in Charles Sumner, *Complete Works* (New York: Negro Universities Press, 1969), Vol. XV, p. 43.

40 R. F. Leslie, *The History of Poland since 1863* (Cambridge: Cambridge University Press, 1980), pp. 5, 39; R. F. Leslie, *Reform and Resurrection in Russian Poland 1861–1865* (Westport, Conn.: Greenwood Press, 1969), pp. 196, 202; Brian Porter, *When Nationalism Began to Hate: Imagining Modern Politics in Nineteenth-Century Poland* (New York: Oxford University Press, 2000), p. 43; Wieczerzak, *A Polish Chapter in Civil War America: The Effects of the January Insurrection on American Opinion and Diplomacy*, p. 44, 62–63, 85, 149, 160; Nicholas Riasanovsky, *A History of Russia* (New York: Oxford University Press, 1984), pp. 378–380.

41 Entry in notebook (September 8, 1831) in E. L. Voynich, ed., *Frédéric Chopin's Letters* (New York: Dover Publications, 1988), p. 148.

42 Address of the Central Polish Committee (April 29, 1863) in Wieczerzak, *A Polish Chapter in Civil War America: The Effects of the January Insurrection on American Opinion and Diplomacy*, p. 212.

43 Address of the Polish Committee to the Land of the Free and the Home of the Brave (December 1, 1863) ibid., p. 216.

44 Stephen Engle, *Yankee Dutchman: The Life of Franz Sigel* (Fayetteville: University of Arkansas Press, 1993), p. 18; Rogger, "Russia and the Civil War," in Hyman, *Heard Round the World: The Impact Abroad of the Civil War*, p. 239; Wieczerzak, *A Polish Chapter in Civil War America: The Effects of the January Insurrection on American Opinion and Diplomacy*, p. 134; Franz Sigel to Charles Sumner (March 19, 1869), Charles Sumner Papers, Harvard University.

45 LeRoy Fischer, *Lincoln's Gadfly, Adam Gurowski* (Norman: University of Oklahoma Press, 1964), pp. 26–27, 41, 84–85, 203–204.

46 Henry Adams, *The Education of Henry Adams* (New York: Library of America, 1983), p. 748.

47 Berwanger, *The British Foreign Service and the American Civil War*, p. 35; Ferris, *Desperate Diplomacy: William H. Seward's Foreign Policy, 1861*, p. 62.

48 Seward to Dayton (April 24, 1863) in *Papers Relating to Foreign Affairs*, Part I, pp. 662–663.

49 "Our Foreign Relations" (September 10, 1863) in Charles Sumner, *Complete Works* (New York: Negro Universities Press, 1969), Vol. X, pp. 71, 85, 144; Sumner to John Bright (October 6, 1863) in Beverly Wilson Palmer, ed., *The Selected Letters of Charles Sumner* (Boston: Northeastern University Press 1990), Vol. II, pp. 197–198.

50 Jay Monaghan, *Diplomat in Carpet Slippers: Abraham Lincoln Deals with Foreign Affairs* (Indianapolis: Bobbs-Merrill Company, 1945), p. 344; Wieczerzak, *A Polish Chapter in Civil War America: The Effects of the January Insurrection on American Opinion and Diplomacy*, pp. 243 #25, 253 #88.

51 Statistics on the number of native people living in Alaska in the late nineteenth century are unreliable. The 1880 census revealed that fewer than 500 whites

lived in the territory. See Robert Utley, *The Indian Frontier of the American West 1846–1890* (Albuquerque: University of New Mexico Press, 1984), p. 267.

52 David Donald, *Charles Sumner and the Rights of Man* (New York: Alfred A. Knopf, 1970), p. 306; Sumner to John Bright (April 16, 1867) in Palmer, *The Selected Letters of Charles Sumner*, Vol. II, pp. 392–393; Paul Holbo, *Tarnished Expansion: The Alaska Scandal, the Press, and Congress, 1867–1871* (Knoxville: University of Tennessee Press, 1983), p. 9; Van Deusen, *William Henry Seward*, p. 543.

53 Donald, *Charles Sumner and the Rights of Man*, pp. 304–310; Palmer, *The Selected Letters of Charles Sumner*, p. 452.

54 The Cession of Russian America to the United States (April 9, 1867) in Sumner, *Complete Works*, Vol. XV, p. 52.

55 William Parker, *The Life and Public Services of Justin Smith Morrill* (Boston: Houghton Mifflin Company, 1924), pp. 208–209, 215; Charles Jellison, *Fessenden of Maine: Civil War Senator* (Syracuse: Syracuse University Press, 1962), p. 219; Albert Castel, *The Presidency of Andrew Johnson* (Lawrence: Regents Press of Kansas, 1979), p. 121; Jensen, *The Alaska Purchase and Russian–American Relations*, pp. 84–85.

56 Gaillard Hunt, *Israel, Elihu and Cadwallader Washburn: A Chapter in American Biography* (New York: Macmillan Company, 1925), pp. 366–367; Walter LaFeber, *The American Age: U.S. Foreign Policy at Home and Abroad* (New York: W. W. Norton and Company, 1994), Vol. I, p. 167.

57 Norman Saul, *Concord and Conflict: The United States and Russia, 1867–1914* (Lawrence: University Press of Kansas, 1996), pp. 5–6; Richard Welch, "American Public Opinion and the Purchase of Russian America" in Stephen Haycox and Mary Childers Mangusso, eds., *An Alaska Anthology: Interpreting the Past* (Seattle: University of Washington Press, 1996), p. 102; Holbo, *Tarnished Expansion: The Alaska Scandal, the Press, and Congress, 1867–1871*, pp. 12–13; Van Deusen, *William Henry Seward*, p. 546; Castel, *The Presidency of Andrew Johnson*, p. 204.

58 Chester Hearn, *When the Devil Came Down to Dixie: Ben Butler in New Orleans* (Baton Rouge: Louisiana State University Press, 1997), pp. 6, 228, 237–238; General Benjamin Butler, *Private and Official Correspondence during the Period of the Civil War* (Norwood, Mass.: Plimpton Press, 1917), Vol. V, p. 721; Howard Nash, *Stormy Petrel: The Life and Times of General Benjamin F. Butler 1818–1893*, (Rutherford, New Jersey: Fairleigh Dickinson University Press, 1969), pp. 231, 260.

59 Richard West, *Lincoln's Scapegoat General: A Life of Benjamin F. Butler 1818–1893* (Boston: Houghton Mifflin Company, 1965), p. 348.

60 Benjamin Butler, *Butler's Book* (Boston: A. M. Thayer and Co., 1892), p. 966; Robert Werlich, *Beast Butler: The Incredible Career of Major General Benjamin Franklin Butler* (Washington: Quaker Press, 1962), p. 138.

61 *Congressional Globe: Second Session of the Fortieth Congress* (Washington: Office of the Congressional Globe, 1868), pp. 1874–1875.

62 Hunt, *Israel, Elihu and Cadwallader Washburn: A Chapter in American Biography*, p. 67; Jensen, *The Alaska Purchase and Russian–American Relations*, pp. 114–115.

63 Holbo, *Tarnished Expansion: The Alaska Scandal, the Press, and Congress, 1867–1871*, pp. 104–109; Saul, *Concord and Conflict: The United States and Russia, 1867–1914*, p. 10; Fawn Brodie, *Thaddeus Stevens: Scourge of the South* (New York: W. W. Norton and Company, 1959), pp. 358–359; Hans Trefousse, *Thaddeus Stevens: Nineteenth-Century Egalitarian* (Chapel Hill: University of North Carolina Press, 1997), pp. 213–214; Van Deusen, *William Henry Seward*, pp. 545, 547–548; Jensen, *The Alaska Purchase and Russian–American Relations*, pp. 109, 128–132; Victor Farrar, *The Annexation of Russian America to the United States* (Washington: W. F. Roberts Company, 1937), pp. 100–103.

64 Jensen, *The Alaska Purchase and Russian–American Relations*, p. 132.

65 William H. Seward on Alaska (1869) in Thomas Paterson, ed., *Major Problems in American Foreign Policy* (Lexington, Mass.: D. C. Heath and Company, 1989), Vol. I, p. 340.

66 McPherson, *Ordeal By Fire: The Civil War and Reconstruction*, p. 488.

67 Kutolowski, *The West and Poland: Essays on Governmental and Public Responses to the Polish National Movement, 1861–1864*, p. 298.

68 "The Polish Refugees in Switzerland to the Great Nation the Republic of the United States" in Sideman and Friedman, *Europe Looks at the Civil War*, p. 296.

69 LaFeber, *The American Age: U.S. Foreign Policy at Home and Abroad*, Vol. I, p. 159.

70 "Naboth's Vineyard" (December 21, 1870) in Sumner, *Complete Works*, Vol. XVIII, p. 297; Walter LaFeber, *The New Empire: An Interpretation of American Expansion 1860–1898* (Ithaca: Cornell University Press, 1963), p. 39.

71 Eric Foner, *Reconstruction: America's Unfinished Revolution 1863–1877* (New York: Harper and Row, 1988), p. 496.

72 See "Naboth's Vineyard" (December 21, 1870) in Sumner, *Complete Works*, Vol. XVIII, p. 297.

73 See George Kennan (elder), *Siberia and the Exile System* (Chicago: University of Chicago Press, 1958), 2 vols.; Frederick Travis, *George Kennan and the American–Russian Relationship, 1865–1924* (Athens, Ohio: Ohio University Press, 1989); Saul, *Concord and Conflict: The United States and Russia, 1867–1914*, pp. 286, 396.

74 Saul, *Distant Friends: The United States and Russia, 1763–1867*, p. 348; Mayers, *The Ambassadors and America's Soviet Policy*, p. 60.

Chapter Seven

1 Robert Wooster, *The Military and United States Indian Policy 1865–1903* (New Haven: Yale University Press, 1988), pp. 33–34.

2 Robert Utley, *The Indian Frontier of the American West 1846–1890* (Albuquerque: University of New Mexico Press, 1984), p. 12.

3 Russell Thornton, *American Indian Holocaust and Survival: A Population History Since 1492* (Norman: University of Oklahoma Press, 1987), p. 160.

4 Josiah Royce, *California: From the Conquest in 1846 to the Second Vigilance Committee in San Francisco* (Santa Barbara: Peregrine Publishers, 1970), p. 286.

5 Estimates vary on the size of the pre-European native population in areas later incorporated as Canada and the United States. The subject is extremely controversial. The number of pre-contact natives peoples in Canada/USA is variously estimated, between two million and eighteen million people. See Thornton, *American Indian Holocaust and Survival: A Population History Since 1492* and the following: Theodore Taylor, *The Bureau of Indian Affairs* (Boulder, Colorado: Westview Press, 1984), p. 14; Barry Turner, ed., *The Statesman's Yearbook, 1998–1999* (New York: St. Martin's Press, 1998), pp. 1516–1517; Leonard Carlson, *Indians, Bureaucrats, and Land: The Dawes Act and the Decline of Indian Farming* (Westport, Conn.: Greenwood Press, 1981), p. 187; Frederick Jackson Turner, "The Significance of the Frontier in American History," *Proceedings of the Forty-first Annual Meeting of the State Historical Society of Wisconsin*, 1894.

6 Stanley Vestal, *Warpath and Council Fire: The Plains Indians' Struggle for Survival in War and in Diplomacy* (New York: Random House, 1948), p. 309; Cochise, "I Am Alone" (1866) in Peter Nabokov, ed., *Native American Testimony: A Chronicle of Indian–White Relations from Prophecy to the Present, 1492–1992* (New York: Viking, 1991), p. 176.

7 Francis Paul Prucha, *The Great Father: The United States Government and the American Indians* (Lincoln: University of Nebraska Press, 1984), Vol. I, p. 491.

8 See Wallace Farnham, "The Weakened Spring of Government: A Study in Nineteenth-Century American History," *American Historical Review* (April 1963); Francis Paul Prucha, *American Indian Policy in Crisis: Christian Reformers and the Indian, 1865–1900* (Norman: University of Oklahoma Press, 1976), pp. 30–31, 326; Loring Benson Priest, *Uncle Sam's Stepchildren: The Reformation of United States Indian Policy, 1865–1887* (New York: Octagon Books, 1969), p. 183.

9 See the following by Prucha: *The Great Father: The United States Government and the American Indians*, Vol. II, pp. 624–625 and *Indian Policy in the United States: Historical Essays* (Lincoln: University of Nebraska Press, 1981), pp. 27–28.

10 Inaugural Address (March 4, 1869) in John Simon, ed., *The Papers of Ulysses S. Grant* (Carbondale, Illinois: Southern Illinois University Press, 1995), Vol. XIX, p. 139.

11 Prucha, *American Indian Policy in Crisis: Christian Reformers and the Indian, 1865–1900*, p. 30.

12 Robert Utley, *Frontier Regulars: The United States Army and the Indian 1861–1891* (New York: Macmillan Company, 1973), p. 410; Lee Kennett, *Sherman: A Soldier's Life* (New York: HarperCollins Publishers, 2001), p. 294.

13 Priest, *Uncle Sam's Stepchildren: The Reformation of United States Indian Policy, 1865–1887*, p. 148.

14 Prucha, *American Indian Policy in Crisis: Christian Reformers and the Indian, 1865–1900*, p. 403.

15 Elmer Ellis, *Henry Moore Teller: Defender of the West* (Caldwell, Idaho: Caxton Printers, 1941), p. 48; Robert Mardock, *The Reformers and the American Indian* (Columbia: University of Missouri Press, 1971), p. 22.

16 Bruce Johansen, *Shapers of the Great Debate on Native Americans: Land, Spirit, and Power* (Westport, Conn.: Greenwood Press, 2000), p. 195.
17 Paul Hutton, *Phil Sheridan and His Army* (Lincoln: University of Nebraska Press, 1985), p. 117.
18 Henry Fritz, *The Movement for Indian Assimilation, 1860–1890* (Philadelphia: University of Pennsylvania Press, 1963), p. 115; Robert Winston Mardock, *The Reformers and the American Indian*, p. 87.
19 Sheridan denied making the "dead Indian" remark. Captain Charles Nordstrom of the Tenth Cavalry claimed that Sheridan said in January 1869 to Toch-a-way of the Comanches: "The only good Indians I ever saw were dead." See Bruce Hampton, *Children of Grace: The Nez Perce War of 1877* (New York: Henry Holt and Company, 1994), p. 186; Hutton, *Phil Sheridan and His Army*, p. 180; Philip Weeks, *Farewell, My Nation: The American Indian and the United States in the Nineteenth Century* (Wheeling, Illinois: Harlan Davidson, Inc., 2001), p. 159.
20 Sophie Bost to Ami and Timothee (September 14, 1862) in Ralph Bowen, ed., *A Frontier Family in Minnesota: Letters of Theodore and Sophie Bost 1851–1920* (Minneapolis: University of Minnesota Press, 1981), pp. 217–218.
21 David Nichols, *Lincoln and the Indians: Civil War Policy and Politics* (Columbia: University of Missouri Press, 1978), p. 79; James Wilson, *The Earth Shall Weep: A History of Native America* (New York: Grove Press, 1998), p. 270; Oliver O. Howard, *My Life and Experiences among Our Hostile Indians* (New York: Da Capo Press, 1972), p. 109.
22 Theodore Bost to Dearest Ami (September 13, 1862) and Theodore Bost to Dear Parents (November 21, 1862) in Bowen, *A Frontier Family in Minnesota: Letters of Theodore and Sophie Bost 1851–1920*, pp. 216–217, 220–222.
23 Weeks, *Farewell, My Nation: The American Indian and the United States in the Nineteenth Century*, pp. 104–111; Robert Utley, *The Indian Frontier of the American West 1846–1890*, pp. 78–81.
24 Henry Benjamin Whipple, *Lights and Shadows of a Long Episcopate* (New York: Macmillan Company, 1899), pp. 127, 137.
25 Howard, *My Life and Experiences among Our Hostile Indians*, p. 488–489; "Senator, a Native American, seeks memorial to massacre," *Boston Globe* (September 15, 2000), p. A9; "1864 massacre of tribe getting recognized," *Boston Globe* (November 13, 2000), p. A2.
26 See the account by Stanley Hoig, *The Sand Creek Massacre* (Norman: University of Oklahoma Press, 1961).
27 Nichols, *Lincoln and the Indians: Civil War Policy and Politics*, pp. 171, 173; Vestal, *Warpath and Council Fire: The Plains Indians' Struggle for Survival in War and in Diplomacy*, pp. 74–75.
28 Ellis, *Henry Moore Teller: Defender of the West*, p. 109; Weeks, *Farewell, My Nation: The American Indian and the United States in the Nineteenth Century*, p. 118; Geoffrey Ward, *The West* (Boston: Little, Brown and Company, 1996), p. 204.
29 Report of the Doolittle Committee (January 26, 1867) in Francis Paul Prucha, ed., *Documents of United States Indian Policy* (Lincoln: University of Nebraska Press, 1990), pp. 102–105.

30 Robert Athearn, *William Tecumseh Sherman and the Settlement of the West* (Norman: University of Oklahoma Press, 1956), p. 172.

31 Anne Makepeace, *Edward S. Curtis: Coming to Light* (Washington: National Geographic, 2001), pp. 52–53.

32 Utley, *The Indian Frontier of the American West 1846–1890*, p. 125; Wooster, *The Military and United States Indian Policy 1865–1903*, p. 132; Kennett, *Sherman: A Soldier's Life*, p. 297; General William Sherman to Senator John Sherman (September 23, 1868) in Rachel Sherman Thorndike, ed., *The Sherman Letters: Correspondence Between General Sherman and Senator Sherman from 1837–1891* (New York: Da Capo Press, 1969), pp. 321–322.

33 Mardock, *The Reformers and the American Indian*, p. 49.

34 Utley, *The Indian Frontier of the American West 1846–1890*, p. 151.

35 First Annual Message (December 6, 1869) in Philip Moran, ed., *Ulysses S. Grant 1822–1885: Chronology–Documents–Bibliographical Aids* (Dobbs Ferry, New York: Oceana Publications, 1968), p. 25.

36 Second Inaugural Address (March 4, 1873) ibid., p. 68.

37 Mardock, *The Reformers and the American Indian*, pp. 52–53; U. S. Grant, *Personal Memoirs* (Lincoln: University of Nebraska Press, 1996), pp. 122–124; William McFeely, *Grant: A Biography* (New York: W. W. Norton and Company, 1981), pp. 306, 317.

38 Lawrie Tatum, *Our Red Brothers and the Peace Policy of President Ulysses S. Grant* (Lincoln: University of Nebraska Press, 1970), pp. 17–18.

39 Henry Waltmann, "Ely Samuel Parker 1869–1871," in Robert Kvasnicka and Herman Viola, eds., *The Commissioners of Indian Affairs, 1824–1977* (Lincoln: University of Nebraska Press, 1979), pp. 123–133.

40 Wilson, *The Earth Shall Weep: A History of Native America*, pp. 278–279.

41 Prucha, *The Great Father: The United States Government and the American Indians*, Vol. I, pp. 562–563; Mardock, *The Reformers and the American Indian*, pp. 82, 168.

42 Tatum, *Our Red Brothers and the Peace Policy of President Ulysses S. Grant*, p. 1; Howard, *My Life and Experiences among Our Hostile Indians*, pp. 120–122; Mardock, *The Reformers and the American Indian*, p. 139.

43 Prucha, *Indian Policy in the United States: Historical Essays*, pp. 38–39.

44 Richard Ellis, *General Pope and U.S. Indian Policy* (Albuquerque: University of New Mexico Press, 1970), p. 135.

45 Utley, *Frontier Regulars: The United States Army and the Indian 1866–1891*, pp. 192–193.

46 Theodore Taylor, *American Indian Policy* (Mt. Airy, Maryland: Lomond Publications, 1983), pp. 52–53.

47 Norman Saul, *Concord and Conflict: The United States and Russia, 1867–1914* (Lawrence: University Press of Kansas, 1996), pp. 65–66.

48 Richard Dodge, *Our Wild Indians: Thirty-three Years' Personal Experience among the Red Men of the Great West* (Freeport, New York: Books for Libraries Press, 1970), pp. 295–296, 639–640.

49 Hutton, *Phil Sheridan and His Army*, pp. 227, 230, 234.

50 Colonel John Gibbon, "Our Indian Question," *Journal of the Military Service Institution* (1881), Vol. II, pp. 108–109.
51 Hutton, *Phil Sheridan and His Army*, p. 145; Vestal, *Warpath and Council Fire: The Plains Indians' Struggle for Survival in War and Diplomacy 1851–1891*, p. xi.
52 George Crook, *Autobiography* (Norman: University of Oklahoma Press, 1946), pp. 263–265, 269; Tatum, *Our Red Brothers and the Peace Policy of President Ulysses S. Grant*, p. 15.
53 Hutton, *Phil Sheridan and His Army*, pp. 128–129; Utley, *Frontier Regulars: The United States Army and the Indian 1866–1891*, p. 309.
54 Peter DeMontravel, *A Hero to His Fighting Men: Nelson A. Miles, 1839–1925* (Kent, Ohio: Kent State University Press, 1998), pp. 108, 120; Nelson Miles, *Personal Recollections and Observations* (Chicago: Werner Company, 1896), p. 280; Nelson Miles, *Serving the Republic* (New York: Harper and Brothers Publishing, 1911), p. 181; Utley, *Frontier Regulars: The United States Army and the American Indian 1866–1891*, p. 316.
55 Chief Joseph, "I Want To Look For My Children" (October 5, 1877) in Nabokov, *Native American Testimony: A Chronicle of Indian–White Relations from Prophecy to the Present, 1492–1992*, pp. 180–181.
56 Hampton, *Children of Grace: The Nez Perce War of 1877*, p. 311.
57 Hutton, *Phil Sheridan and His Army*, p. 34.
58 Kennett, *Sherman: A Soldier's Life*, pp. 290–291, 295, 298–299; Stanley Hirshon, *The White Tecumseh: A Biography of General William T. Sherman* (New York: John Wiley and Sons, 1997), p. 336.
59 Report of Lieutenant General Sheridan to General of the Army (October 25, 1878), Reel 86, Papers of Philip Sheridan, Library of Congress.
60 General William Sherman to Senator John Sherman (October 31, 1866) in Thorndike, *The Sherman Letters: Correspondence between General Sherman and Senator Sherman from 1837 to 1891*, pp. 279–282; Robert Utley, *Indian, Soldier, and Settler: Experiences in the Struggle for the American West* (St. Louis: Jefferson National Expansion Historical Association, 1979), p. 43; Hutton, *Phil Sheridan and His Army*, p. 10; DeMontravel, *A Hero to His Fighting Men: Nelson A. Miles, 1839–1925*, p. 108.
61 Brian Pohanka, ed., *Nelson A. Miles: A Documentary Biography of His Military Career* (Glendale, California: Arthur H. Clark Company, 1985), p. 127; Hutton, *Phil Sheridan and His Army*, pp. 245–246; Ellis, *General Pope and U.S. Indian Policy*, p. 183; Peter Cozzens, *General John Pope: A Life for the Nation* (Urbana: University of Illinois Press, 2000), pp. 313–314; Wooster, *The Military and United States Indian Policy 1865–1903*, pp. 106, 161.
62 Michael Fellman, *Citizen Sherman: A Life of William Tecumseh Sherman* (New York: Random House, 1995), pp. 294–295; Utley, *Indian, Soldier, and Settler: Experiences in the Struggle for the American West*, p. 42.
63 Charles King, *Campaigning with Crook* (Norman: University of Oklahoma Press, 1964), p. 39.
64 Athearn, *William Tecumseh Sherman and the Settlement of the West*, p. 236.
65 Fellman, *Citizen Sherman: A Life of William Tecumseh Sherman*, p. 275.
66 Ibid., p. 264, Whipple, *Lights and Shadows of a Long Episcopate*, pp. 311–312.
67 Hutton, *Phil Sheridan and His Army*, pp. 184, 186.

68 Ibid., p. 185.

69 Kennett, *Sherman: A Soldier's Life*, pp. 297, 299; Richard O'Connor, *Sheridan the Inevitable* (Indianapolis: Bobbs-Merrill Company, 1953), p. 326; Weeks, *Farewell, My Nation: The American Indian and the United States in the Nineteenth Century*, p. 131; Cozzens, *General John Pope: A Life for the Nation*, p. 314.

70 Hutton, *Phil Sheridan and His Army*, pp. 16, 69, 98; DeMontravel, *A Hero to His Fighting Men: Nelson A. Miles, 1839–1925*, p. 128; Fritz, *The Movement for Indian Assimilation, 1860–1890*, p. 126; Cozzens, *General Pope: A Life for the Nation*, pp. 302–303; O'Connor, *Sheridan the Inevitable*, pp. 299, 328.

71 Hutton, *Phil Sheridan and His Army*, p. 339.

72 Dodge, *Our Wild Indians: Thirty-three Years' Personal Experience among the Red Men of the Great West*, p. xxxviii.

73 King, *Campaigning with Crook*, p. 136.

74 Prucha, *The Great Father: The United States Government and the American Indians*, Vol. I, p. 586; Gibbon, "Our Indian Question," p. 119. The October 25, 1878 Report of Lieutenant General Sheridan to General of the Army contains tart reference to "wretched mismanagement." Reel 86, Papers of Philip Sheridan, Library of Congress.

75 Mardock, *The Reformers and the American Indian*, p. 169; Prucha, *The Great Father: The United States Government and the American Indians*, Vol. I, p. 557.

76 Hans Trefousse, *Carl Schurz: A Biography* (New York: Fordham University Press, 1998), pp. 242–243; Weeks, *Farewell, My Nation: The American Indian and the United States in the Nineteenth Century*, p. 210.

77 Delos Sacket Otis, *The Dawes Act and the Allotment of Indian Lands* (Norman: University of Oklahoma Press, 1973), p. 72.

78 Pratt retired from the army in 1903 with the rank of brigadier general.

79 Wilson, *The Earth Shall Weep: A History of Native America*, p. 316; Weeks, *Farewell, My Nation: The American Indian and the United States in the Nineteenth Century*, p. 234.

80 Richard Henry Pratt, *Battlefield and Classroom: Four Decades with the American Indian, 1867–1904* (New Haven: Yale University Press, 1964), p. 335.

81 Ibid., p. 259.

82 Ibid., pp. 312–314.

83 Ibid., p. 251.

84 See Schurz to My Dear Sir (December 18, 1880) in *Congressional Record*, Forty-Sixth Congress, Third Session (Washington: n.p.), Vol. XI, p. 818.

85 William Connelley, *The Life of Preston B. Plumb 1837–1891* (Chicago: Browne and Howell Company, 1916), pp. 243, 270, 290; Ellis, *Henry Moore Teller: Defender of the West*, p. 109.

86 *Congressional Record*, Forty-Sixth Congress, Third Session, Vol. XI, p. 818.

87 Connelley, *The Life of Preston B. Plumb 1837–1891*, pp. 241–242.

88 Ibid., pp. 288–290.

89 *Congressional Record*, Forty-Sixth Congress, Third Session, Vol. XI, p. 820.

90 Otis, *The Dawes Act and the Allotment of Indian Lands*, pp. 6, 57; Prucha, *Indian Policy in the United States: Historical Essays*, p. 40. Also see Helen Hunt Jackson, *A Century of Dishonor* (New York: Harper and Row, 1965).

91 See texts of Dawes Act of 1887 and Act of 1891 in Otis, *The Dawes Act and the Allotment of Indian Lands*, pp. 177–188; Hampton, *Children of Grace: The Nez Perce War of 1877*, p. 373, #49; Carlson, *Indians, Bureaucrats, and Land: The Dawes Act and the Decline of Indian Farming*, pp. 3, 10.

92 Wilson, *The Earth Shall Weep: A History of Native America*, p. 300.

93 Carlson, *Indians, Bureaucrats, and Land: The Dawes Act and the Decline of Indian Farming*, pp. 3, 10; Otis, *The Dawes Act and the Allotment of Indian Lands*, p. 67; Prucha, *American Indian Policy in Crisis: Christian Reformers and the Indian, 1865–1900*, p. 243.

94 Siobhan Senier, *Voices of American Indian Assimilation and Resistance* (Norman: University of Oklahoma Press, 2001), pp. 5, 42; Prucha, *American Indian Policy in Crisis: Christian Reformers and the Indian, 1865–1900*, p. 227.

95 Priest, *Uncle Sam's Stepchildren: The Reformation of United States Indian Policy, 1865–1887*, p. 197; Mardock, *The Reformers and the American Indian*, p. 221; Weeks, *Farewell, My Nation: The American Indian and the United States in the Nineteenth Century*, p. 227; Prucha, *American Indian Policy in Crisis: Christian Reformers and the Indian, 1865–1900*, p. 196.

96 Otis, *The Dawes Act and the Allotment of Indian Lands*, pp. 50–53; Johansen, *Shapers of the Great Debate on Native Americans: Land, Spirit, and Power*, p. 187.

97 Johansen, *Shapers of the Great Debate on Native Americans: Land, Spirit, and Power*, p. 187.

98 *Congressional Record*, Forty-Sixth Congress, Third Session, Vol. XI, p. 934.

99 Ellis, *Henry Moore Teller: Defender of the West*, p. 124.

100 Ibid., p. 102.

101 Ibid., pp. 143–144, 169; Pratt, *Battlefield and Classroom: Four Decades with the American Indian, 1867–1904*, pp. 277–278.

102 Otis, *The Dawes Act and the Allotment of Indian Lands*, p. 44; *Congressional Record*, Forty-Sixth Congress, Third Session, Vol. XI, p. 934.

103 *Congressional Record*, Forty-Sixth Congress, Third Session, Vol. XI, p. 783.

104 Fritz, *The Movement for Indian Assimilation, 1860–1890*, p. 213; Prucha, *American Indian Policy in Crisis: Christian Reformers and the Indian, 1865–1900*, pp. 248–250.

105 Otis, *The Dawes Act and the Allotment of Indian Lands*, pp. 152–153.

106 See Andrew Carnegie, *The Gospel of Wealth* (New York: Carnegie Corporation of New York, 2001), p. 13.

107 Hutton, *Phil Sheridan and His Army*, p. 332.

108 Utley, *Frontier Regulars: The United States Army and the Indian 1866–1891*, p. 6; Utley, *The Indian Frontier of the American West 1846–1890*, p. 19.

109 King, *Campaigning with Crook*, p. 62.

110 Priest, *Uncle Sam's Stepchildren: The Reformation of United States Indian Policy, 1865–1887*, pp. 169, 228 #12.

111 Report of Lieutenant General Sheridan to General of the Army (October 25, 1878), Reel 86, Papers of Philip Sheridan, Library of Congress.

112 Charles Christian, *Black Saga The African American Experience* (Washington: Civitas, 1999), p. 262.

113 Quotation from Howard, *My Life and Experiences among Our Hostile Indians*, pp. 439–440. See Weeks, *Farewell, My Nation: The American Indian and the United States in the Nineteenth Century*, p. 172; Hutton, *Phil Sheridan and His Army*, p. 248; Prucha, *Indian Policy in the United States: Historical Essays*, p. 43.

114 Weeks, *Farewell, My Nation: The American Indian and the United States in the Nineteenth Century*, p. 230; Wilson, *The Earth Shall Weep: A History of Native America*, pp. 304, 308, 328–329; Prucha, *The Great Father: The United States Government and the American Indians*, Vol. II, p. 671.

115 Theodora Kroeber, *Ishi in Two Worlds: A Biography of the Last Wild Indian in North America* (Berkeley: University of California Press, 1969), p. 117.

116 Howard, *My Life and Experiences among Our Hostile Indians*, p. 266.

117 Edmund Wilson, *Apologies to the Iroquois* (New York: Vintage Books, 1959), pp. 55, 275.

118 Prucha, *The Great Father: The United States Government and the American Indians*, Vol. II, p. 707.

119 Wilson, *The Earth Shall Weep: A History of Native America*, p. 315.

120 Pratt, *Battlefield and Classroom: Four Decades with the American Indian, 1867–1904*, p. xvi.

121 Johansen, *Shapers of the Great Debate on Native Americans: Land, Spirit and Power*, pp. 200–201.

122 Kenneth Philip, *John Collier's Crusade for Indian Reform, 1920–1954* (Tucson: University of Arizona Press, 1977), pp. 1, 23.

123 Ibid., p. 24; Lawrence Kelly, *The Assault on Assimilation: John Collier and the Origins of Indian Policy Reform* (Albuquerque: University of New Mexico Press, 1983), p. xiii.

124 Carlson, *Indians, Bureaucrats, and Land: The Dawes Act and the Decline of Indian Farming*, pp. 16–17; Philip, *John Collier's Crusade for Indian Reform 1920–1954*, pp. 212–213; Kenneth Philip, "John Collier 1933–1945" in Kvasnicka and Viola, *The Commissioners of Indian Affairs, 1824–1977*, pp. 276–277.

125 http://www.ustrek.org/odyssey/semester1/010601/010601irenecarlisle.html.

126 Dennis Banks's Foreword in Duane Champagne, *Native America: Portrait of the Peoples* (Detroit: Visible Ink Press, 1994), p. xiv.

127 George Steiner, *Errata: An Examined Life* (New Haven: Yale University Press, 1998), pp. 89–90.

Chapter Eight

1 H. Wayne Morgan, ed., *Making Peace with Spain: The Diary of Whitelaw Reid* (Austin: University of Texas Press, 1965), p. 13; Frederick Funston, *Memories of Two Wars: Cuban and Philippine Experiences* (New York: Charles Scribner's Sons, 1911), p. vii. The connection in the American mind between Native America and the Filipinos was captured in a *San Francisco Bulletin* editorial, under this title: "The Character and Customs of the Warlike Filipinos" (April 1899). It explained: "The United States is not entirely inexperienced in the

handling of native tribes ... and it is to be hoped that the lessons which we have learned in dealing with North American Indians may bear fruit in deciding as to what is best for our oceanic possessions." Cited in Anne Paulet, "Racing the Filipinos: The Question of Filipino Identity and U.S. Policy at the Turn of the Twentieth Century," SHAFR Conference, Austin, Texas, June 2004, p. 12.

2 Theodore Roosevelt, *An Autobiography* (New York: Da Capo Press, 1985), p. 544.

3 Stuart Creighton Miller, *Benevolent Assimilation: The American Conquest of the Philippines, 1899–1903* (New Haven: Yale University Press, 1982), p. 180.

4 Stanley Karnow, *In Our Image: America's Empire in the Philippines* (New York: Random House, 1989), p. 194; Walter LaFeber, *The American Age: United States Foreign Policy at Home and Abroad to 1920* (New York: W. W. Norton and Company, 1994), pp. 215–216.

5 Julius Pratt, *Expansionists of 1898: The Acquisition of Hawaii and the Spanish Islands* (Chicago: Quadrangle Books, 1964), p. 326.

6 Redfield Proctor on Spain's Reconcentrado Policy (March 17, 1898) in Dennis Merrill and Thomas Paterson, eds., *Major Problems in American Foreign Relations* (Boston: Houghton Mifflin Company, 2000), Vol. I, p. 352.

7 Roosevelt to B. H. Diblee (February 16, 1898) in Elting Morison, ed., *The Letters of Theodore Roosevelt* (Cambridge, Mass.: Harvard University Press, 1951), Vol. I, p. 775.

8 Gerald Linderman, *The Mirror of War: American Society and the Spanish–American War* (Ann Arbor: University of Michigan Press, 1974), p. 29.

9 Paxton Hibben, *The Peerless Leader: William Jennings Bryan* (New York: Farrar and Rinehart, 1929), p. 212.

10 John Offner, *An Unwanted War: The Diplomacy of the United States and Spain Over Cuba, 1895–1898* (Chapel Hill: University of North Carolina Press, 1992), p. 56.

11 Charles Campbell, *The Transformation of American Foreign Relations 1865–1900* (New York: Harper and Row, 1976), pp. 263–264.

12 McKinley's speech to Congress (April 11, 1898) in Harry Sievers, ed., *William McKinley 1843–1901: Chronology, Documents, Bibliographical Aids* (Dobbs Ferry, New York: Oceana Publications, 1970), p. 47.

13 Graham Cosmas's Introduction in *Correspondence Relating to the War with Spain* (Washington: Center of Military History, 1993), Vol. I, p. 1; Warren Zimmermann, *First Great Triumph: How Five Americans Made Their Country a World Power* (New York: Farrar, Straus and Giroux, 2002), p. 276.

14 See text of treaty in Henry Cabot Lodge, *The War with Spain* (New York: Harper and Brothers Publishers, 1899), pp. 267–276.

15 Senate votes exceeded by one the two-thirds majority needed to approve the treaty: 57 to ratify, 27 opposed.

16 Karnow, *In Our Image: America's Empire in the Philippines*, p. 106.

17 LaFaber, *The American Age: U.S. Foreign Policy at Home and Abroad to 1920*, p. 213.

18 Richard Welch, *Response to Imperialism: The United States and the Philippine–American War, 1899–1902* (Chapel Hill: University of North Carolina Press,

1979), p. 10; Walter McDougall, *Promised Land, Crusader State: The American Encounter with the World Since 1776* (Boston: Houghton Mifflin Company, 1997), pp. 112–113.

19 McKinley's Remarks to Methodist Delegation (November 21, 1899) in Daniel Schirmer and Stephen Shalom, eds., *The Philippines Reader: A History of Colonialism, Neocolonialism, Dictatorship, and Resistance* (Boston: South End Press, 1987), pp. 22–23.

20 *Congressional Record*, Fifty-Sixth Congress, First Session (Washington: Government Printing Office, 1900), Vol. XXXIII, pp. 704–712.

21 E. Berkeley Tompkins, *Anti-Imperialism in the United States: The Great Debate, 1890–1920* (Philadelphia: University of Pennsylvania Press, 1970), p. 5; Richard Welch, *George Frisbie Hoar and the Half-Breed Republicans* (Cambridge, Mass.: Harvard University Press, 1971), p. 261; Karnow, *In Our Image: America's Empire in the Philippines*, p. 109.

22 "Remember Pekin!" Leaflet of the Republican Club of Massachusetts in Schirmer and Shalom, *The Philippines Reader: A History of Colonialism, Neocolonialism, Dictatorship, and Resistance*, pp. 32–33.

23 Miller, *Benevolent Assimilation: The American Conquest of the Philippines, 1899–1903*, p. 135.

24 Howard Beale, *Theodore Roosevelt and the Rise of America to World Power* (New York: Collier Books, 1962), pp. 77–78.

25 Glenn May, *Social Engineering in the Philippines: The Aims, Execution, and Impact of American Colonial Policy, 1900–1913* (Westport, Conn.: Greenwood Press, 1980), p. 17.

26 Joseph Sears, *The Career of Leonard Wood* (New York: D. Appleton and Company, 1919), p. 194; John Holme, *The Life of Leonard Wood* (Garden City: Doubleday, Page and Company, 1920), pp. 149–151; Karnow, *In Our Image: America's Empire in the Philippines*, p. 197; Bonifacio Salamanca, *The Filipino Reaction to American Rule 1901–1913* (New Haven: Shoe String Press, 1968), pp. 19–20.

27 William Gatewood, *Black Americans and the White Man's Burden 1898–1903* (Urbana: University of Illinois Press, 1975), p. 324.

28 Karnow, *In Our Image: America's Empire in the Philippines*, p. 16.

29 Aguinaldo's statement of January 16, 1899 to "brother Filipinos" and "military officers." Emilio Aguinaldo Papers, Library of Congress.

30 President Emilio Aguinaldo to the Philippine People, February 5, 1899 in Schirmer and Shalom, *The Philippines Reader: A History of Colonialism, Neocolonialism, Dictatorship, and Resistance*, pp. 20–21.

31 Brian McAllister Linn, *The U.S. Army and Counterinsurgency in the Philippine War, 1899–1902* (Chapel Hill: University of North Carolina Press, 1989), p. 7; Beale, *Theodore Roosevelt and the Rise of America to World Power*, p. 79.

32 John Morgan Gates, *Schoolbooks and Krags: The United States Army in the Philippines, 1898–1902* (Westport, Conn.: Greenwood Press, 1973), pp. 273–274, 276.

33 Daniel Schirmer, *Republic or Empire: American Resistance to the Philippine War* (Cambridge, Mass.: Schenkman Publishing Company, 1972), p. 225.

34 Miller, *Benevolent Assimilation: The American Conquest of the Philippines, 1898–1903*, p. 269.

35 Zimmermann, *First Great Triumph: How Five Americans Made Their Country a World Power*, p. 408.

36 Quantities of water were forced down the victim's throat in the "water cure." The subsequent swelling made normal breathing impossible. A soldier would kick the victim's stomach or jump on it to expel the water. A number of people died from this treatment.

37 Andrew Bacevich, *Diplomat in Khaki: Major General Frank Ross McCoy and American Foreign Policy, 1898–1949* (Lawrence: University Press of Kansas, 1989), pp. 38–39.

38 Comments on the Moro Massacre (March 12 and 14, 1906) in Jim Zwick, ed., *Mark Twain's Weapons of Satire: Anti-Imperialist Writings of the Philippine–American War* (Syracuse: Syracuse University Press, 1992), p. 173.

39 Platform of the American Anti-Imperialist League, October 18, 1899 in Henry Steele Commager, ed., *Documents of American History* (New York: Appleton-Century-Crofts, 1968), Vol. II, pp. 11–12.

40 Campbell, *The Transformation of American Foreign Relations 1865–1900*, p. 304.

41 Zwick, *Mark Twain's Weapons of Satire: Anti-Imperialist Writings of the Philippine–American War*, p. xxxii.

42 Beale, *Theodore Roosevelt and the Rise of America to World Power*, pp. 71–72, #5.

43 Karnow, *In Our Image: America's Empire in the Philippines*, p. 110; Robert Beisner, *Twelve against Empire: The Anti-Imperialists 1898–1900* (New York: McGraw-Hill Book Company, 1968), pp. 23–24.

44 Beisner, *Twelve against Empire: The Anti-Imperialists, 1898–1900*, p. 174.

45 William James, Letter to *Boston Evening Transcript*, March 1, 1899 in Schirmer and Shalom, *The Philippines Reader: A History of Colonialism, Neocolonialism, Dictatorship, and Resistance*, pp. 27–29.

46 David Healy, *U.S. Expansionism: The Imperialist Urge in the 1890s* (Madison: University of Wisconsin Press, 1970), p. 238.

47 William Graham Sumner, The Conquest of the United States by Spain, 1898 in Robert Goldwin and Harry Clor, eds., *Readings in American Foreign Policy* (New York: Oxford University Press, 1971), p. 108.

48 "May Negroes Who Volunteer Get Ball-Stung," *Reporter* (February 1, 1900) in George Marks, *The Black Press Views American Imperialism, 1898–1900* (New York: Arno Press, 1971), p. 167.

49 Healy, *U.S. Expansionism: The Imperialist Urge in the 1890s*, pp. 240–241.

50 See Peter Dunne's brilliant *Mr. Dooley in the Hearts of His Countrymen* (Boston: Small, Maynard and Company, 1899).

51 To the Person Sitting in Darkness (February 1901) in Zwick, *Mark Twain's Weapons of Satire: Anti-Imperialist Writings of the Philippine–American War*, p. 24.

52 Ibid., p. xxxi; Charles Christian, *Black Saga: The African American Experience* (Washington: Counterpoint, 1999), pp. 281, 283–284, 286, 289.

53 Pratt, *Expansionists of 1898: The Acquisition of Hawaii and the Spanish Islands*, p. 351.

54 Miller, *Benevolent Assimilation: The American Conquest of the Philippines, 1899–1903*, p. 26.
55 Paolo Coletta, *William Jennings Bryan: Political Evangelist 1860–1908* (Lincoln: University of Nebraska Press, 1964), p. 233.
56 McKinley won 7,219,000 popular votes versus 6,358,000 for Bryan. The electoral college gave 292 votes to McKinley versus 155 for Bryan.
57 Theodore Burton, *John Sherman* (Boston: Houghton Mifflin Company, 1906), p. 416.
58 William Robinson, *Thomas B. Reed: Parliamentarian* (New York: Dodd, Mead and Company, 1930), pp. 359–360, 379; Samuel McCall, *Thomas B. Reed* (Boston: Houghton Mifflin Company, 1914), p. 237.
59 Senator William Mason, Civil Government of the Philippine Islands (June 2, 1902) in Goldwin and Clor, *Readings in American Foreign Policy*, p. 102.
60 Also see *Congressional Record*, Fifty-Sixth Congress, First Session, Vol. XXXIII, pp. 704–712 for stern remarks by Senator Beveridge on dissidents.
61 Roosevelt to Charles William Eliot, April 4, 1904 in Morison, *The Letters of Theodore Roosevelt*, Vol. IV, p. 767.
62 Beale, *Theodore Roosevelt and the Rise of America to World Power*, pp. 77–78.
63 Roosevelt to Henry Cabot Lodge, February 7, 1899 in Morison, *The Letters of Theodore Roosevelt*, Vol. II, p. 935; Miller, *Benevolent Assimilation: The American Conquest of the Philippines, 1899–1903*, p. 117.
64 Roosevelt to William Howard Taft (December 26, 1902) ibid., Vol. III, pp. 398–399.
65 Welch, *George Frisbie Hoar and the Half-Breed Republicans*, p. 314; George Hoar, *Autobiography of Seventy Years* (New York: Charles Scribner's Sons, 1903), Vol. II, p. 320.
66 Frederick Gillett, *George Frisbie Hoar* (Boston: Houghton Mifflin Company, 1934), p. 269.
67 Welch, *George Frisbie Hoar and the Half-Breed Republicans*, p. 193, #39.
68 Hoar, *Autobiography of Seventy Years*, Vol. II, p. 324.
69 Moorfield Storey and Edward Emerson, *Ebenezer Rockwood Hoar: A Memoir* (Boston: Houghton Mifflin Company, 1911), pp. 268–269.
70 Hoar, *Autobiography of Seventy Years*, Vol. II, p. 317; Speech at Twentieth Century Club (December 20, 1901), pp. 7–8, Box 106, George Hoar Papers, Massachusetts Historical Society.
71 Speech at Mechanics Hall in Worcester, Massachusetts (November 1, 1898), p. 5, Box 106, George Hoar Papers, Massachusetts Historical Society.
72 Hoar, *Autobiography of Seventy Years*, Vol. II, p. 307.
73 Speech at Mechanics Hall (November 1, 1898), p. 6.
   Although Hoar emphasized the tensions between US republicanism and empire, he was, like most American anti-imperialists, well-versed in the ideas and experiences of empire critics in Europe, especially those in Britain. Hoar read in Senate chambers this testimony of Lord Elgin (Victor Alexander Bruce), viceroy of India during 1894–1899. Hoar was especially alarmed by Elgin's words on the dehumanization of relations between colonists and

colonized: "It is a terrible business . . . this living among inferior races. I have seldom from man or woman since I came to the East heard a sentence which was reconcilable with the hypothesis that Christianity had ever come into the world. Detestation, contempt, ferocity, vengeance, whether Chinamen or Indians be the object. One moves among them with perfect indifference, treating them not as dogs, because in that case one would whistle to them and pat them, but as machines with which one can have no communion or sympathy. When the passions of fear and hatred are engrafted on this indifference, the result is frightful – an absolute callousness as to the sufferings of the objects of these passions, which must be witnessed to be understood and believed." Quoted by Hoar in his Speech on Philippines, May 1903, p. 10.

74 *Congressional Record*, Fifty-Fifth Congress, Third Session (Washington: Government Printing Office, 1899), p. 501.

75 Speech at Mechanics Hall, p. 7.

76 Ibid., p. 15.

77 Preparation for Speeches, Campaign 1900, Box 106, George Hoar Papers, Massachusetts Historical Society.

78 Speech on Philippines (May 1903), ibid., p. 2.

79 Ibid., p. 4.

80 Ibid., p. 8.

81 Roosevelt's letters to Hoar (December 12, 1902, January 12, 17, 1903) in Morison, *The Letters of Theodore Roosevelt*, Vol. III, pp. 394–395, 403–404, 405–406; Beisner, *Twelve against Empire: The Anti-Imperialists 1898–1900*, p. 162; Zimmermann, *First Great Triumph: How Five Americans Made Their Country a World Power*, p. 392.

82 Hoar, *Autobiography of Seventy Years*, Vol. II, pp. 324–325.

83 "Did Senator Hoar Cause the Philippine Rebellion?" (July 27, 1900) in Philip Foner and Richard Winchester, eds., *The Anti-Imperialist Reader: A Documentary History of Anti-Imperialism in the United States* (New York: Holmes and Meier Publishers, 1984), Vol. I, p. 413; Zwick, *Mark Twain's Weapons of Satire: Anti-Imperialist Writings of the Philippine–American War*, p. xl.

84 Schirmer, *Republic or Empire: American Resistance to the Philippine War*, p. 237. On the differences between Hoar and Miles: the former was a Harvard graduate, a lawyer, a contemplative. Miles did not attend college. He knew only soldiering. He could be thoughtful but above all prized action. The extant letters of Hoar to Miles are few. They suggest mutual respect but nothing of intimacy. See Hoar's letters to Miles (November 6, 1890 and April 14, 1902), Box 2, Nelson Miles Papers, Library of Congress.

85 Nelson Miles to Hoar (November 27, 1902), Box 8, George Hoar Papers, Massachusetts Historical Society.

86 Brian Pohanka, ed., *Nelson A. Miles: A Documentary Biography of His Military Career 1861–1903* (Glendale, Calif.: Arthur H. Clark Company, 1985), p. 27.

87 Ibid., p. 67; Robert Wooster, *Nelson A. Miles and the Twilight of the Frontier Army* (Lincoln: University of Nebraska Press, 1993), p. 236.

88 Nelson Miles, *Personal Recollections and Observations* (Chicago: Werner Company, 1896), p. 51.
89 Joseph Hamblen Sears, *The Career of Leonard Wood* (New York: D. Appleton and Company, 1919), p. 31.
90 Pohanka, *Nelson A. Miles: A Documentary Biography of His Military Career 1861–1903*, p. 189.
91 Edmund Morris, *The Rise of Theodore Roosevelt* (New York: Coward, McCann and Geohegan, 1979), p. 611.
92 Nelson Miles, *Serving the Republic* (New York: Harper and Brothers Publishers, 1911), p. 269.
93 Miles to Secretary of War (April 18, 1898) in *Correspondence Relating to the War with Spain*, Vol. I, pp. 8–9; Peter DeMontravel, *A Hero to His Fighting Men: Nelson A. Miles, 1839–1925* (Kent, Ohio: Kent State University Press, 1998), p. 357; Virginia Johnson, *The Unregimented General: A Biography of Nelson A. Miles* (Boston: Houghton Mifflin Company, 1962), p. 315.
94 David Trask, *The War with Spain in 1898* (New York: Macmillan Company, 1981), p. 174; Johnson, *The Unregimented General: A Biography of Nelson A. Miles*, p. 339.
95 John Dobson, *Reticent Expansion: The Foreign Policy of William McKinley*, (Pittsburgh: Duquesne University Press, 1988), p. 76; Wooster, *Nelson A. Miles and the Twilight of the Frontier Army*, p. 220; Johnson, *The Unregimented General: A Biography of Nelson A. Miles*, p. 343.
96 Johnson, *The Unregimented General: A Biography of Nelson A. Miles*, p. 350.
97 Lewis Gould, *The Presidency of Theodore Roosevelt* (Lawrence: University Press of Kansas, 1991), p. 48; Roosevelt to Robert Wilson Patterson (December 21, 1901) and Roosevelt to James Brander Matthews (December 31, 1901) in Morison, *The Letters of Theodore Roosevelt*, Vol. III, pp. 210–211, 213–214.
98 Roosevelt to Nelson Miles (January 9, 1899) in Morison, *The Letters of Theodore Roosevelt*, Vol. II, pp. 903–904.
99 Wooster, *Nelson A. Miles and the Twilight of the Frontier Army*, p. 233.
100 Roosevelt to Henry Cabot Lodge (August 10, 1899) in Morison, *The Letters of Theodore Roosevelt*, Vol. II, pp. 1047–1049.
101 Roosevelt to Henry Cabot Lodge (December 6, 1898) ibid., p. 892; Richard Hofstadter, *The American Political Tradition* (New York: Vintage Books, 1957), p. 212; Miles, *Serving the Republic*, p. 313; DeMontravel, *A Hero to His Fighting Men: Nelson A. Miles, 1839–1925*, p. 357.
102 DeMontravel, *A Hero to His Fighting Men: Nelson A. Miles, 1839–1925*, p. 332; Pohanka, *Nelson A. Miles: A Documentary Biography of His Military Career 1861–1903*, p. 230; Roosevelt to George Hinckley Lyman (June 18, 1901) in Morison, *The Letters of Theodore Roosevelt*, Vol. III, pp. 95–96.
103 Wooster, *Nelson A. Miles and the Twilight of the Frontier Army*, p. 239; Roosevelt to George Hinckley Lyman (June 22, 1901) and Roosevelt to Hermann Henry Kohlsaat (March 24, 1902) in Morison, *The Letters of Theodore Roosevelt*, Vol. III, pp. 98–99, 248.
104 Miller, *Benevolent Assimilation: The American Conquest of the Philippines, 1899–1903*, p. 257.

105 Wooster, *Nelson A. Miles and the Twilight of the Frontier Army*, pp. 250–251, 253.
106 Nelson Miles, *The Philippines* (Boston: Anti-Imperialist League, 1909) p. 6.
107 Miles, *Serving the Republic*, pp. 305, 308.
108 Ibid., p. 307.
109 Miles, *The Philippines*, p. 3.
110 Ibid., p. 4.
111 Ibid., p. 7.
112 Zimmermann, *First Great Triumph: How Five Americans Made Their Country a World Power*, p. 409.
113 Miles, *The Philippines*, pp. 7–8.
114 Roosevelt to Elihu Root (February 18, 1902) in Morison, *The Letters of Theodore Roosevelt*, Vol. III, pp. 232–233.
115 Miller, *Benevolent Assimilation: The American Conquest of the Philippines, 1899–1903*, p. 258.
116 Roosevelt to George Hoar (June 16, 1902 and January 12, 1903) in Morison, *The Letters of Theodore Roosevelt*, Vol. III, pp. 276–277, 403–404.
117 Roosevelt to William Howard Taft (September 3, 1903) ibid., p. 585.
118 Roosevelt to Elihu Root (March 7, 1902), Roosevelt to George Hoar (December 23, 1902), Roosevelt to Oswald Garrison Villard (March 31, 1903), and Roosevelt to Elihu Root (October 3, 1903) in ibid., pp. 240–242, 394–395, 460, 610–613; Roosevelt to Charles William Eliot (April 4, 1904) in Morison, *The Letters of Theodore Roosevelt*, Vol. IV, pp. 767–770.
119 Roosevelt to Elihu Root (March 19, 1902), Roosevelt to Hermann Henry Kohlsaat (June 10, 1902), and Roosevelt to John Hay (July 22, 1902) in Morison, *The Letters of Theodore Roosevelt*, Vol. III, pp. 244–247, 271, 300–301.
120 Roosevelt to George Brinton McClean Harvey (January 22, 1904) ibid., p. 702.
121 Zimmermann, *First Great Triumph: How Five Americans Made Their Country a World Power*, p. 409.
122 DeMontravel, *A Hero to His Fighting Men: Nelson A. Miles, 1839–1925*, p. 353.
123 Ibid., pp. 353–356; Gould, *The Presidency of Theodore Roosevelt*, pp. 122–123; Wooster, *Nelson A. Miles and the Twilight of the Frontier Army*, p. 248; Roosevelt to Lemuel Clarke Davis (August 20, 1903) and Roosevelt to Henry Cabot Lodge (September, 3, 1903) in Morison, *The Letters of Theodore Roosevelt*, Vol. III, pp. 567, 585–588.
124 Roosevelt to Anna Roosevelt Cowles (June 19, 1901) in Morison, *The Letters of Theodore Roosevelt*, Vol. III, p. 96.
125 Miles, *Serving the Republic*, pp. 310–311.
126 The educator–diplomat Andrew Dickson White led the US delegation at the 1899 Hague meetings.
127 Miller, *Benevolent Assimilation: The American Conquest of the Philippines, 1899–1903*, p. 260; Gates, *Schoolbooks and Krags: The United States Army in*

the Philippines, 1898–1902, pp. 190, 283; Dorothy Jones, *Toward a Just World: The Critical Years in the Search for International Justice* (Chicago: University of Chicago Press, 2002), pp. 4–9.

128 Richard Olney Responds to the Venezuela Crisis (July 20, 1895) in Merrill and Paterson, *Major Problems in American Foreign Relations,* Vol. I, pp. 318–320.

129 Henry Cabot Lodge, *The War with Spain,* Preface; William Tilchin, *Theodore Roosevelt and the British Empire: A Study in Presidential Statecraft* (New York: St. Martin's Press, 1997), p. 27.

130 Barry Turner, ed., *The Statesman's Yearbook, 1998–1999* (New York: St. Martin's Press, 1998), p. 1517; A. J. P. Taylor, *The Struggle for Mastery in Europe 1848–1918* (New York: Oxford University Press, 1971), pp. xxv, xxix–xxxi.

131 David Mayers, *Wars and Peace: The Future Americans Envisioned, 1861–1991* (New York: St. Martin's Press, 1998), p. 25.

132 Hoar, Speech on Philippines, May 1903, p. 10.

133 Ibid., p. 9.

134 See the following: Richard Hofstadter, "Manifest Destiny and the Philippines" in Daniel Aaron, ed., *America in Crisis: Fourteen Crucial Episodes in American History* (New York: Alfred A. Knopf, 1952); Walter LaFeber, "That Splendid Little War in Historical Perspective" in *Texas Quarterly,* 11 (1968); Ernest May, *Imperial Democracy: The Emergence of America as a Great Power* (New York: Harcourt, Brace, and World, 1961) and *American Imperialism: A Speculative Essay* (New York: Atheneum, 1968); Louis Perez, *Cuba and the United States: Ties of Singular Intimacy* (Athens, Georgia: University of Georgia Press, 1990); Kristin Hoganson, *Fighting for American Manhood: How Gender Politics Provoked the Spanish–American and Philippine–American Wars* (New Haven: Yale University Press, 1998).

135 LaFeber, *The American Age: U.S. Foreign Policy at Home and Abroad,* Vol. I, p. 226.

136 Richard Hofstadter, *The Paranoid Style in American Politics and Other Essays* (New York: Alfred A. Knopf, 1965), p. 187; Karnow, *In Our Image: America's Empire in the Philippines,* p. 80.

137 Samuel Eliot Morison, *The Oxford History of the American People* (New York: Oxford University Press, 1965), p. 806; George Kennan, *American Diplomacy 1900–1950* (Chicago: University of Chicago Press, 1951), p. 19.

138 "A Namibian People Mark 1904 Genocide," *Boston Globe* (August 15, 2004), p. A7.

139 *Congressional Record,* Fifty-Fifth Congress, Third Session, Vol. XXXIII, p. 494.

140 Welch, *George Frisbie Hoar and the Half-Breed Republicans,* pp. 268–270.

141 Roosevelt to Leonard Wood (September 12, 1902) in Morison, *The Letters of Theodore Roosevelt,* Vol. III, pp. 597–598.

142 Wooster, *Nelson A. Miles and the Twilight of the Frontier Army,* pp. 255–256.

143 Miles, *The Philippines,* p. 8.

144 Cited in Telford Taylor, *Nuremberg and Vietnam: An American Tragedy* (New York: Bantam Books, 1971), front page.

145 DeMontravel, *A Hero to His Fighting Men: Nelson A. Miles, 1839–1925*, pp. 347–352.
146 Andrew Bacevich, *The New American Militarism: How Americans Are Seduced by War* (New York: Oxford University Press, 2005), p. 66. The erosion of Hague/Geneva principles in Washington from September 2001 to August 2004 is documented in Karen Greenberg and Joshua Dratel, eds., *The Torture Papers: The Road to Abu Ghraib* (New York: Cambridge University Press, 2005).

Chapter Nine

1 A. J. P. Taylor, *The Trouble Makers: Dissent over Foreign Policy 1792–1939* (London: Penguin Books, 1985), p. 122.
2 Donald Smythe, *Guerrilla Warrior: The Early Life of John J. Pershing* (New York: Charles Scribner's Sons, 1973), p. 182.
3 Ibid., p. 200.
4 "The Parable of the Old Man and the Young" in C. Day Lewis, ed., *The Collected Poems of Wilfred Owen* (New York: New Directions, 1965), p. 42.
5 I. C. B. Dear and M. R. D. Foot, eds., *The Oxford Companion to World War II* (Oxford: Oxford University Press, 1995), p. xv; Brian Bond, *War and Society in Europe, 1870–1970* (New York: Oxford University Press, 1986), p. 100.
6 *Quantula sapientia mundus regitur.* Variations on this phrase come from Sweden's Count Oxenstierna in his oft quoted letter to his son in 1648, and from Pope Julius III. See also J. William Fulbright with Seth Tillman, *The Price of Empire* (New York: Pantheon Books, 1989), p. ix.
7 Wilson's Message to the Senate, August 19, 1914 in Henry Steele Commager, ed., *Documents of American History* (New York: Appleton-Century-Crofts, 1968), Vol. II, pp. 96–97.
8 Paolo Coletta, *William Jennings Bryan* (Lincoln: University of Nebraska Press, 1969), Vol. II, p. 264.
9 Address to the Senate (January 22, 1917) in Arthur Link, ed., *The Papers of Woodrow Wilson* (Princeton: Princeton University Press, series), Vol. XL, p. 536.
10 John Hedler, president of the German Army Veterans of the USA, to Bryan (June 10, 1915), Box 30, William Jennings Bryan Papers, Library of Congress.
11 Wilson's Message to the Senate (August 19, 1914) in Commager, *Documents of American History*, Vol. II, pp. 96–97; Walter LaFeber, *The American Age: United States Foreign Policy at Home and Abroad* (New York: W. W. Norton and Company, 1994), Vol. I, p. 285; David Mayers, *Wars and Peace: The Future Americans Envisioned 1861–1991* (New York: St. Martin's Press, 1998), p. 43.
12 John Milton Cooper, *The Warrior and the Priest: Woodrow Wilson and Theodore Roosevelt* (Cambridge, Mass.: Harvard University Press, 1983), p. 295; Ernest May, *The World War and American Isolation 1914–1917* (Cambridge, Mass.: Harvard University Press, 1959), p. 338.
13 Roosevelt to Cleveland Dodge (May 11, 1918), Roosevelt to Paul Shimmon (July 10, 1918), Roosevelt to Lioubomir Michailovitch (July 11, 1918), and Roosevelt to James Gallivan (August 22, 1918) in Elting Morison, ed., *The*

Letters of Theodore Roosevelt (Cambridge, Mass.: Harvard University Press, 1954), Vol. VIII, pp. 1316–1318, 1348–1351, 1363–1366.

14 Correspondence between Bryan and Wilson during 1913–1915 is in Box 59, William Jennings Bryan Papers, Library of Congress.

15 Arthur Link, *Wilson the Diplomatist: A Look at His Major Foreign Policies* (Baltimore: Johns Hopkins University Press, 1957), pp. 24–25.

16 Ibid., p. 26; David Mayers, *The Ambassadors and America's Soviet Policy* (New York: Oxford University Press, 1995), pp. 4, 70.

17 Gregory, *The Origins of American Intervention in the First World War*, p. 24.

18 Burton Hendrick, ed., *The Life and Letters of Walter H. Page* (Garden City: Doubleday, Page and Company, 1925), Vol. I, p. 346; William Bain, "Walter Hines Page" in Cathal Nolan, ed., *Notable U.S. Ambassadors Since 1775* (Westport, Conn.: Greenwood Press, 1997), p. 282; Robert Lansing, *War Memoirs* (Indianapolis: Bobbs-Merrill Company, 1935), p. 15.

19 Henry Morgenthau, *All in a Life-Time* (Garden City: Doubleday, Page and Company, 1922), p. 132.

20 Henry Morgenthau III, *Mostly Morgenthaus: A Family History* (New York: Ticknor and Fields, 1991), p. 103.

21 Melvin Urofsky, *A Voice that Spoke for Justice: The Life and Times of Stephen S. Wise* (Albany: State University of New York Press, 1982), pp. 113–114.

22 On white slave trade see Morgenthau to Secretary of State (March 24, 1925) and Morgenthau to Claude Montefiore (May 12, 1915) in Box 473, Henry Morgenthau (senior) Papers, Franklin D. Roosevelt Library; Morgenthau, *All in a Life-Time*, pp. 198–202, 204.

23 Henry Morgenthau, *Ambassador Morgenthau's Story* (Garden City: Doubleday, Page and Company, 1918), p. 236; Morgenthau, *All in a Life-Time*, pp. 176, 194–195.

24 Morgenthau, *Ambassador Morgenthau's Story*, p. 66.

25 Ibid., Preface.

26 Ibid., p. 289.

27 Donald Miller and Lorna Touryan Miller, *Survivors: An Oral History of the Armenian Genocide* (Berkeley: University of California Press, 1993), p. 39.

28 Morgenthau, *Ambassador Morgenthau's Story*, p. 325.

29 Ibid., p. 299.

30 Samantha Power, *A Problem from Hell: America and the Age of Genocide* (New York: Basis Books, 2002), p. 2; Esat Uras, *The Armenians in History and the Armenian Question* (Istanbul: Documentary Publications, 1988), p. 885.

31 Morgenthau, *Ambassador Morgenthau's Story*, p. 309; Margaret Macmillan, *Paris 1919: Six Months that Changed the World* (New York: Random House, 2002), p. 378; Miller and Miller, *Survivors: An Oral History of the Armenian Genocide*, p. 44.

32 Morgenthau, *Ambassador Morgenthau's Story*, p. 342.

33 Miller and Miller, *Survivors: An Oral History of the Armenian Genocide*, pp. 88–89.

34 Morgenthau to Secretary of State (May 25, 1915) in Box 473, Henry Morgenthau (senior) Papers, Franklin D. Roosevelt Library; Morgenthau, *Ambassador Morgenthau's Story*, p. 327.

35 Henry Riggs, *Days of Tragedy in Armenia: Personal Experiences in Harpoot 1915–1917* (Ann Arbor: Gomidas Institute, 1997), p. 140; Susan Blair, ed., *The Slaughterhouse Province: An American Diplomat's Report on the Armenian Genocide, 1915–1917* (New Rochelle: Aristide D. Carantzas, 1989), p. 8; Morgenthau, *Ambassador Morgenthau's Story*, pp. 303, 318–322, 327–328.

36 Morgenthau to Secretary of State (July 10, 1915), *Foreign Relations of the United States 1915, Supplement: The World War* (Washington: Government Printing Office, 1929), pp. 982–984; Morgenthau to Secretary of State (November 4, 1915), *Foreign Relations of the United States: The Lansing Papers, 1914–1920* (Washington: Government Printing Office, 1939), Vol. I, pp. 762–766; Power, *A Problem from Hell: America and the Age of Genocide*, p. 6.

37 Morgenthau to Secretary of State (August 11, 1915) in Box 473, Henry Morgenthau (senior) Papers, Franklin D. Roosevelt Library; Power, *A Problem from Hell: America and the Age of Genocide*, pp. 5, 10; Morgenthau, *Mostly Morgenthaus: A Family History*, p. 170; Edward Mandell House to Wilson (October 1, 1915) and Haigazoun Hohannes Topakyan to Wilson (October 22, 1915) in Link, *The Papers of Woodrow Wilson*, Vol. XXXV, pp. 3, 104–105.

38 Wilson to Haigazoun Hohannes Topakyan (October 28, 1915), Wilson to Henry Morgenthau (October, 28, 1915), William Nesbitt Chambers to Wilson (December 10, 1915), and Wilson to William Nesbitt Chambers (December 13, 1915) in Link, *The Papers of Woodrow Wilson*, Vol. XXXV, pp. 119, 337, 349.

39 Robert Lansing to Henry Morgenthau (July 16, 1915) and Lansing to Morgenthau (October 4, 1915) in *Foreign Relations of the United States 1915 Supplement: The World War*, pp. 984, 988–989.

40 Theodore Roosevelt, *Fear God and Take Your Own Part* (New York: George H. Doran Company, 1916), p. 381.

41 Morgenthau, *All in a Life-Time*, p. 199; Roger Smith, "The Armenian Genocide: Memory, Politics and the Future" in Richard Hovannisian, ed., *The Armenian Genocide: History, Politics, Ethics* (New York: St. Martin's Press, 1992), p. 10; Rouben Paul Adalian "American Diplomatic Correspondence in the Age of Mass Murder: The Armenian Genocide in the U.S. Archives" in Jay Winter, ed., *America and the Armenian Genocide of 1915* (Cambridge: Cambridge University Press, 2003), pp. 149–150, 152.

42 Power, *A Problem from Hell: America and the Age of Genocide*, p. 12; Morgenthau, *Ambassador Morgenthau's Story*, p. 381.

43 Morgenthau, *Ambassador Morgenthau's Story*, pp. 333–334; Morgenthau to Secretary of State (July 10, 1915) in *Foreign Relations of the United States 1915 Supplement: The World War*, pp. 982–984.

44 Morgenthau, *Ambassador Morgenthau's Story*, pp. 328, 339, 364; Morgenthau, *Mostly Morgenthaus: A Family History*, p. 169.

45 Vahakn Dadrian, *German Responsibility in the Armenian Genocide: A Review of the Historical Evidence of German Complicity* (Watertown, Mass.: Blue Crane Books, 1997), pp. 120–121, 143; Morgenthau, *Ambassador Morgenthau's Story*, pp. 374, 378; Ambassador Bernstorff to Secretary of State (October 8, 1915) in *Foreign Relations of the United States 1915 Supplement: The World*

War, pp. 989–990; David Fromkin, *A Peace to End All Peace: Creating the Modern Middle East 1914–1922* (New York: Henry Holt and Company, 1989), pp. 211–213.

46 Morgenthau, *Ambassador Morgenthau's Story*, pp. 339–342, 385; Henry Morgenthau to Wilson, March 23, 1916 in Link, *The Papers of Woodrow Wilson*, Vol. XXXVI, pp. 356–357.

47 House to Gordon Auchincloss (February 4, 1915) in Charles Seymour, *The Intimate Papers of Colonel House* (Boston: Houghton Mifflin Company, 1926), p. 160.

48 Fourteen Points (January 8, 1918) in Daniel Boorstin, ed., *An American Primer* (Chicago: University of Chicago Press, 1966), pp. 773–779.

49 Lloyd Ambrosius, *Woodrow Wilson and the American Diplomatic Tradition: The Treaty Fight in Perspective* (Cambridge: Cambridge University Press, 1987), p. 258.

50 Morgenthau to James Barton (November 4, 1915) in Box 474, Henry Morgenthau (senior) Papers, Franklin D. Roosevelt Library; Mandates or War in Morgenthau, *All in a Life-Time*, pp. 423–437; Power, *A Problem from Hell: America and the Age of Genocide*, p. 11; Miller and Miller, *Survivors: An Oral History of the Armenian Genocide*, p. 120; James Barton, *Story of Near East Relief* (New York: Macmillan Company, 1930), pp. 4–6, 47, 430.

51 Cooper, *The Warrior and the Priest: Woodrow Wilson and Theodore Roosevelt*, p. 230.

52 Ross Gregory, *Walter Hines Page: Ambassador to the Court of St. James* (Lexington: University Press of Kentucky, 1970), pp. 101–103; Burton Hendrick, *The Life and Letters of Walter Page* (Garden City: Doubleday, Page and Company, 1925), Vol. II, pp. 27, 190; Cooper, *The Warrior and the Priest: Woodrow Wilson and Theodore Roosevelt*, pp. 271–272.

53 William Jennings Bryan and Mary Baird Bryan, *The Memoirs of William Jennings Bryan* (Chicago: John C. Winston Company 1925), p. 332; Ross Gregory, *The Origins of American Intervention in the First World War* (New York: W. W. Norton and Company, 1971), p. 19; Patrick Devlin, *Too Proud to Fight: Woodrow Wilson's Neutrality* (New York: Oxford University Press, 1975), p. 70; Sigmund Freud and William C. Bullitt, *Thomas Woodrow Wilson: A Psychological Study* (Boston: Houghton Mifflin Company, 1966), p. 153.

54 Wilson to Edith Bolling Galt (June 8, 1915) in Link, *The Papers of Woodrow Wilson*, Vol. XXXIII, pp. 366–367; Bryan and Bryan, *The Memoirs of William Jennings Bryan*, p. 350; Gregory, *The Origins of American Intervention in the First World War*, p. 20.

55 Kendrick Clements, *William Jennings Bryan: Missionary Isolationist* (Knoxville: University of Tennessee Press, 1982), p. 106; Coletta, *William Jennings Bryan*, Vol. II, pp. 340, 356.

56 Cooper, *The Warrior and the Priest: Woodrow Wilson and Theodore Roosevelt*, pp. 245, 267.

57 Charles DeBenedetti, *The Peace Reform in American History* (Bloomington: Indiana University Press, 1980), p. 70; David Anderson, *William Jennings Bryan* (Boston: Twayne Publishing, 1981), pp. 160, 214.

Bryan was not an absolute pacifist. He served as colonel in a Nebraska
unit during the 1898 Spanish war. He was prepared to enlist after Congress
declared war in 1917. See Coletta, *William Jennings Bryan*, Vol. III, p. 57.
58 Count Johann von Bernstorff, *My Three Years in America* (New York: Charles
Scribner's Sons, 1920), p. 68.
59 Bryan and Bryan, *The Memoirs of William Jennings Bryan*, pp. 377–382;
Clements, *William Jennings Bryan: Missionary Isolationist*, p. 109; Coletta,
William Jennings Bryan, Vol. II, pp. 325–326; Bernstorff, *My Three Years in
America*, pp. 155–156.
60 Bryan and Bryan, *The Memoirs of William Jennings Bryan*, pp. 374–375,
383.
61 Richard Hofstadter, *The American Political Tradition* (New York: Vintage
Books, 1957), p. 202; Bryan and Bryan, *The Memoirs of William Jennings
Bryan*, pp. 396–397.
62 William Jennings Bryan to Wilson (May 9, 1915) in Link, *The Papers of
Woodrow Wilson*, Vol. XXXIII, pp. 134–135.
63 Bryan and Bryan, *The Memoirs of William Jennings Bryan*, p. 403.
64 Ibid., p. 421. Bryan wrote to My dear Bennett (September 30, 1917): "I first
learned of the ammunition two or three days after the sinking of the
Lusitania." Box B80, Robert La Follette Papers, Library of Congress.
65 First Lusitania Note (May 13, 1915) in Commager, *Documents of American
History*, Vol. II, pp. 102–105.
66 William Jennings Bryan to Wilson (May 12, 1915) in Link, *The Papers of
Woodrow Wilson*, Vol. XXXIII, pp. 165–167.
67 Clements, *William Jennings Bryan: Missionary Isolationist*, pp. 110–111.
68 Bryan and Bryan, *The Memoirs of William Jennings Bryan*, pp. 404, 406–408.
69 See Lawrence Gelfand, *The Inquiry: American Preparations for Peace,
1917–1919* (New Haven: Yale University Press, 1963).
70 John Whiteclay Chambers, ed., *The Eagle and the Dove: The American Peace
Movement and United States Foreign Policy 1900–1922* (Syracuse: Syracuse
University Press, 1991), pp. 67–69.
71 Coletta, *William Jennings Bryan*, Vol., II, p. 343; Anderson, *William Jennings
Bryan*, pp. 176–177; Clements, *William Jennings Bryan: Missionary Isolationist*,
p. 115.
72 Bernstorff, *My Three Years in America*, p. 380.
73 Zimmermann Note, released March 1, 1917, Commager, *Documents of
American History*, Vol. II, p. 128.
74 *Congressional Record, First Session of the Sixty-Fifth Congress* (Washington:
Government Printing Office, 1917), Vol. LV, p. 240; *Congressional
Record, First Session of the Sixty-Fifth Congress: Appendix and Index to
Parts 1–8*, (Washington: Government Printing Office, 1917), Vol. LV,
p. 7891.
75 Address to a Joint Session of Congress (April 2, 1917) in Link, *The Papers of
Woodrow Wilson*, Vol. XLI, p. 519.
76 Thomas Knock, *To End All Wars: Woodrow Wilson and the Quest for New World
Order* (New York: Oxford University Press, 1992), p. 118.

77 Address to the Senate (January 22, 1917) in Link, *The Papers of Woodrow Wilson*, Vol. XL, p. 539.
78 John J. Pershing, *My Experiences in the World War* (New York: Frederick A. Stokes Company, 1931), Vol. I, p. xvi.
79 Address to a Joint Session of Congress (April 2, 1917) in Link, *The Papers of Woodrow Wilson*, Vol. XLI, p. 519.
80 Ibid., p. 525.
81 *Congressional Record: First Session of the Sixty-Fifth Congress*, Vol. LV, pp. 223, 238.
82 Robert Maxwell, ed., *La Follette* (Englewood Cliffs, New Jersey: Prentice-Hall, 1969), p. 5; David Thelen, *Robert M. La Follette and the Insurgent Spirit* (Boston: Little, Brown and Company, 1976), p. 125; Norman Zucker, *George W. Norris: Gentle Knight of American Democracy* (Urbana: University of Illinois Press, 1966), p. 1; Alfred Lief, *Democracy's Norris: The Biography of a Lonely Crusader* (New York: Stackpole Sons, 1939), p. 179.
83 Nancy Unger, *Fighting Bob La Follette: The Righteous Reformer* (Chapel Hill: University of North Carolina Press, 2000), p. 236; Richard Lowitt, *George W. Norris: The Persistence of a Progressive 1913–1933* (Urbana: University of Illinois Press, 1971), p. 44.
84 Unger, *Fighting Bob La Follette: The Righteous Reformer*, p. 246; Edward Doan, *The La Follettes and the Wisconsin Idea* (New York: Rinehart and Company, 1947), p. 85.
85 *Congressional Record, First Session of the Sixty-Fifth Congress*, Vol. LV, pp. 212, 228.
86 Ibid., p. 213.
87 Ibid., p. 215; Lief, *Democracy's Norris: The Biography of a Lonely Crusader*, p. 201.
88 *Congressional Record, First Session of the Sixty-Fifth Congress*, Vol. LV, pp. 226, 228.
89 Ibid., p. 227.
90 Ibid., p. 228.
91 Ibid., p. 220; Ronald Schaffer, "Jeannette Rankin, Progressive–Isolationist" (Princeton University: Ph.D. dissertation, 1959), pp. 62, 83–84; Hannah Josephson, *Jeannette Rankin: First Lady in Congress* (Indianapolis: Bobbs-Merrill Company, 1974), p. 76.
92 *Congressional Record, First Session of the Sixty-Fifth Congress*, Vol. LV, p. 215.
93 Ibid., p. 235.
94 *Congressional Record, First Session of the Sixty-Fifth Congress: Appendix and Index to Parts 1–8*, Vol. LV, p. 7890.
95 Josephson, *Jeannette Rankin: First Lady in Congress*, p. 77.
96 Mayers, *Wars and Peace: The Future Americans Envisioned 1861–1991* pp. 46–47; Woodrow Wilson to Max Eastman (September 18, 1917) in Chambers, *The Eagle and the Dove: The American Peace Movement and United States Foreign Policy 1900–1922*, p. 125; *Congressional Record, First Session of the Sixty-Fifth Congress*, Vol. LV, p. 219.
97 George Norris, *Fighting Liberal: The Autobiography of George W. Norris* (New York: Macmillan Company, 1945), p. 199.

98 John Kennedy, *Profiles in Courage* (New York: Harper and Row Publishers, 1964), p. 175; Unger, *Fighting Bob La Follette: The Righteous Reformer*, pp. 250, 255–259; Norris, *The Autobiography of George W. Norris*, pp. 199, 201.

99 See Representative Richard Austin (Tennessee), Remarks (January 19, 1918), Reel 3, Jeannette Rankin Papers, Schlesinger Library, Harvard University.

100 Lowitt, *George W. Norris: The Persistence of a Progressive 1913–1933*, p. 93.

101 Notes for Freedom of Speech in Wartime (n.d.), pp. 4–5, Box 231, Robert La Follette Papers, Library of Congress; People Retain Right to Control Government (October 6, 1917) in Ellen Torelle, ed., *The Political Philosophy of Robert M. La Follette* (Madison: Robert M. La Follette Co., 1920), p. 237.

102 Josephson, *Jeannette Rankin: First Lady in Congress*, pp. 84–86.

103 Peace and the Disarmament Conference (n.d.), p. 4, Reel 3, Jeannette Rankin Papers, Schlesinger Library, Harvard University.

104 Eugene Debs to Robert La Follette (October 15, 1917), Box B80, Robert La Follette Papers, Library of Congress; "What is to be done with conscientious objectors serving terms in our military prisons?" (n.d.), Box B209, Robert La Follette Papers, Library of Congress; Thelen, *Robert M. La Follette and the Insurgent Spirit*, pp. 148–152.

105 Unger, *Fighting Bob La Follette: The Righteous Reformer*, pp. 2, 253.

106 Wilson's Fourteen Points (January 8, 1918) in J. A. S. Grenville, ed., *The Major International Treaties 1914–1973* (London: Methuen and Company, 1974), pp. 57–58.

107 Treaty of Versailles (June 28, 1919) ibid., pp. 59–71. See essays on reparations and conflicting interpretations of them in William Keylor, ed., *The Legacy of the Great War: Peacemaking, 1919* (Boston: Houghton Mifflin Company, 1998), pp. 119–167. The victors expected that about half of the $33 billion would be paid.

108 Mayers, *Wars and Peace: The Future Americans Envisioned 1861–1991*, pp. 49–50.

109 An Address in the City Auditorium in Pueblo, Colorado, (September 25, 1919) in Link, *Papers of Woodrow Wilson*, Vol. LXIII, p. 501.

110 See the words of one League backer and Wilson partisan, Senator Robert Owen (Democrat, Oklahoma), in *Congressional Record: First Session of the Sixty-Sixth Congress* (Washington: Government Printing Office, 1919), Vol. LVIII–Part 9, p. 8784.

111 Treaty of Peace between the Allied and Associated Powers and Germany (June 28, 1919) in Grenville, *The Major International Treaties 1914–1972*, p. 60.

112 Address to the Senate (January 22, 1917) in Link, *The Papers of Woodrow Wilson*, Vol. XL, p. 535.

113 Ibid., p. 539.

114 Taylor, *The Trouble Makers: Dissent over Foreign Policy 1792–1939*, p. 160.

115 Knock, *To End All Wars: Woodrow Wilson and the Quest for a New World Order*, p. 275.

116 An Address in the Denver Auditorium (September 25, 1919) in Link, *The Papers of Woodrow Wilson*, Vol. LXIII, p. 494.

117 Speech of February 18, 1917 in Henry Cabot Lodge, *The Senate and the League of Nations* (New York: Charles Scribner's Sons, 1925), p. 274.

118 Lodge to Roosevelt (November 26, 1918) in *Selections from the Correspondence of Theodore Roosevelt and Henry Cabot Lodge, 1884–1918* (New York: Charles Scribner's Sons, 1925), Vol. II, pp. 546–548.

119 William Widenor, *Henry Cabot Lodge and the Search for an American Foreign Policy* (Berkeley: University of California Press, 1980), pp. 352–353; Speech of February 18, 1917 in Lodge, *The Senate and the League of Nations*, p. 295.

120 Widenor, *Henry Cabot Lodge and the Search for an American Foreign Policy*, p. 326.

121 Henry Cabot Lodge, *Early Memories* (New York: Charles Scribner's Sons, 1925), p. 133.

122 David Ricci, *The Tragedy of Political Science: Politics, Scholarship, and Democracy* (New Haven: Yale University Press, 1984), p. 213.

123 Speech of February 18, 1917 in Lodge, *The Senate and the League of Nations*, p. 287.

124 John Garraty, *Henry Cabot Lodge: A Biography* (New York: Alfred A. Knopf, 1968), pp. 360, 371–372; Widenor, *Henry Cabot Lodge and the Search for an American Foreign Policy*, pp. 331–332.

125 *Congressional Record: First Session of the Sixty-Fifth Congress*, Vol. LVIII, Part 9, pp. 8777–8778. Regarding the Monroe Doctrine, Wilson did arrange for its explicit recognition in the League Covenant – a fact that Lodge chose to ignore.

126 Widenor, *Henry Cabot Lodge and the Search for an American Foreign Policy*, p. 308.

127 See Herbert Margulies, *The Mild Reservationists and the League of Nations Controversy in the Senate* (Columbia: University of Missouri Press, 1989).

128 "The War Makers of Versailles" (November 13, 1919) in Torelle, *The Political Philosophy of Robert M. La Follette*, p. 251.

129 "The Terms of the Peace Treaty" (November 18, 1919) ibid., p. 268.

130 Claudius Johnson, *Borah of Idaho* (New York: Longmans, Green and Company, 1936), p. 236.

131 Marian McKenna, *Borah* (Ann Arbor: University of Michigan Press, 1961), pp. 143, 145, 154, 167.

132 Ibid., p. 153; Johnson, *Borah of Idaho*, p. 233.

133 *Congressional Record: Third Session of the Sixty-Fifth Congress* (Washington: Government Printing Office, 1919), Vol. LVII, p. 3915.

134 Ibid.

135 Ibid. Also see Borah to Frank Dunshee (June 22, 1921), Box 87, William Borah Papers, Library of Congress.

136 For an assessment of Wilson's medical condition in 1919 see Bert Park's "Wilson's Neuralgic Illness during the Summer of 1919" in Link, *The Papers of Woodrow Wilson*, Vol. LXII, pp. 628–638.

137 Ambrosius, *Woodrow Wilson and the American Diplomatic Tradition: The Treaty Fight in Perspective*, p. 177.

138 Johnson, *Borah of Idaho*, pp. 226, 245.

139 Lodge, *The Senate and the League of Nations*, p. 226.

140 An Address in Convention Hall in Kansas City (September 6, 1919) in Link, *The Papers of Woodrow Wilson*, Vol. LXIII, p. 74.

141 Andrew Bacevich, *The New American Militarism: How Americans Are Seduced by War* (New York: Oxford University Press, 2005), p. 14.

142 Mayers, *Wars and Peace: The Future Americans Envisioned 1861–1991*, pp. 55–56.

143 Norris to Henry Luckey (April 13, 1937), Box 46, George Norris Papers, Library of Congress.

144 Josephson, *Jeannette Rankin: First Lady in Congress*, p. 162; Jeannette Rankin 1974 interview, pp. 9, 145–147, 214, Suffragists Oral History Project, University of California at Berkeley.

145 Norris, *Fighting Liberal: The Autobiography of George W. Norris*, p. 190.

146 William Dodd, Jr. and Martha Dodd, eds., *Ambassador Dodd's Diary 1933–1938* (New York: Harcourt, Brace and Company, 1941), p. 39. Also see pp. 5, 9, 20, 134, 249.

147 George Kennan, *Memoirs 1925–1950* (Boston: Little, Brown and Company, 1967), p. 98; Personal Notes (March 21, 1939) in George Kennan, *From Prague after Munich: Diplomatic Papers 1938–1940* (Princeton: Princeton University Press, 1968), pp. 85–86.

148 "Turkish Diplomat saved Jews of Rhodes" in *Globe and Mail* (Toronto), June 10, 2003, p. R5.

149 Erik Goldstein, *The First World War Peace Settlements, 1919–1925* (London: Longman, 2002), p. 51.

Lodge cooperated after the war with people such as Morgenthau to lessen Armenian suffering. The senator also served on the executive committee of the American Committee for the Independence of Armenia. Correspondence related to his postwar Armenian concern is preserved on Reel 80, Henry Cabot Lodge Papers, Massachusetts Historical Society. On Armenian gratitude for Wilson's (tardy) help, see Garo Pasdermadjian to Norman Davis, December 9, 1918 in Link, *The Papers of Woodrow Wilson*, Vol. LXVI, pp. 507–508.

150 Vigen Guroian, "The Politics and Morality of Genocide" in Hovannisian, *The Armenian Genocide: History, Politics, Ethics*, p. 312.

151 Franz Werfel, *The Forty Days of Musa Dagh* (New York: The Modern Library, 1934), p. 136; Lionel Steiman, *Franz Werfel: The Faith of an Exile* (Waterloo, Ontario: Wilfrid Laurier University Press, 1985), p. 82.

152 Vahan Tekeyan, "The Country of Dust" in Carolyn Forche, ed., *Against Forgetting: Twentieth-Century Poetry of Witness* (New York: W. W. Norton and Company, 1993), p. 62.

Chapter Ten

1 Herbert Agar et al., *The City of Man: A Declaration on World Democracy* (New York: Viking Press, 1941), pp. 47–48.

2 Despite disapproval of Vichy, FDR's government maintained relations with it until November 1942. London, by contrast, had no dealings with Vichy.

Anglo-Vichy relations broke in early July 1940 in the wake of Royal Navy actions against French warships at Mers-el-Kebir in Algeria. Vichy French forces attacked the British at Gibraltar in retaliation for the Algerian assault.

3 Mark Lincoln Chadwin, *The Warhawks: American Interventionists before Pearl Harbor* (New York: W. W. Norton and Company, 1970), p. 3.

4 Robert Dallek, *Franklin D. Roosevelt and American Foreign Policy, 1932–1945* (Oxford: Oxford University Press, 1979), pp. 85, 285.

5 David Mayers, *Wars and Peace: The Future Americans Envisioned 1861–1991* (New York: St. Martin's Press, 1998), p. 65.

6 I. C. B. Dear and M. R. D. Foot, eds., *The Oxford Companion to World War II* (Oxford: Oxford University Press, 1995), pp. 233, 290.

7 Johnson to Stanley Hornbeck (January 14, 1938) in Box 66, Nelson Johnson Papers, Library of Congress.
Scholarship on Japanese behavior in Nanking includes these books: Joshua Fogel, ed., *The Nanjing Massacre in History and Historiography* (Berkeley: University of California Press, 2000) and Timothy Brook, ed., *Documents on the Rape of Nanking* (Ann Arbor: University of Michigan Press, 1999). Also see Iris Chang, *The Rape of Nanking: The Forgotten Holocaust of World War II* (New York: Basic Books, 1997). The quality of Japanese writing has varied. Tanaka Masaaki's *What Really Happened in Nanking: The Refutation of a Common Myth* (Tokyo: Sekai Shuppan, Inc., 2000) is dreadful. Mahahiro Yamamoto's *Nanking: Anatomy of an Atrocity* (Westport: Praeger, 2000) is solid.

8 Robert Schulzinger, *American Diplomacy in the Twentieth Century* (New York: Oxford University Press, 1990), p. 179.

9 Johnson to Wilbur Carr, (n.d., 1939), Box 36, Nelson Johnson Papers, Library of Congress. Also see Johnson to Stanley Hornbeck (June 18, 1940), Box 66, Nelson Johnson Papers, Library of Congress.

10 Russell Buhite, *Nelson T. Johnson and American Policy Toward China 1925–1941* (East Lansing: Michigan State University Press, 1968), pp. 144–146; Waldo Heinrichs, *American Ambassador: Joseph C. Grew and the Development of the United States Diplomatic Tradition* (New York: Oxford University Press, 1986), p. 288.

11 Johnson served first as minister, then as ambassador. His appointment as minister lasted from 1930 to 1935. He became ambassador in 1935, when the US mission in China was upgraded from legation to embassy.

12 Nelson Johnson Oral History, p. 82, Columbia University.

13 Buhite, *Nelson T. Johnson and American Policy Toward China 1925–1941*, pp. 1–2, 6–8, 14, 151; Richard Burns and Edward Bennett, eds. *Diplomats in Crisis: United States–Chinese–Japanese Relations, 1919–1941* (Santa Barbara: ABC-Clio Press, 1974), pp. 9–10; Alan Wood, "Nelson Trusler Johnson" in Cathal Nolan, ed., *Notable U.S. Ambassadors Since 1775* (Westport, Conn.: Greenwood Press, 1997), p. 201; Arthur Waldron, ed., *How the Peace Was Lost: The 1935 Memorandum: Developments Affecting American Policy in the Far East Prepared for the State Department by John Van Antwerp MacMurray* (Stanford: Hoover Institution, 1992), pp. 114–115.

14 Heinrichs, *American Ambassador: Joseph C. Grew and the Development of the United States Diplomatic Tradition*, p. 270.

15 Extraterritoriality meant that foreign governments had the right to charge, punish, or exonerate in their own courts those nationals accused of crimes against Chinese citizens. The US and British governments suspended their extraterritoriality privilege in 1943.

16 Buhite, *Nelson T. Johnson and American Policy Toward China 1925–1941*, pp. 55, 64; Burns and Bennett, *Diplomats in Crisis: United States–Chinese–Japanese Relations, 1919–1941*, p. 4.

17 James Thomson, *While China Faced West: American Reformers in Nationalist China, 1928–1937* (Cambridge, Mass.: Harvard University Press, 1969), p. 30; Heinrichs, *American Ambassador: Joseph C. Grew and the Development of the United States Diplomatic Tradition*, p. 219; Paul Schroeder, *The Axis Alliance and Japanese–American Relations 1941* (Ithaca: Cornell University Press, 1958), p. 5; Buhite, *Nelson T. Johnson and American Policy Toward China, 1925–1941*, pp. 10–11, 68, 71, 77, 86–87.

18 Johnson to Joseph Grew (November 10, 1937), Box 33, Nelson Johnson Papers, Library of Congress.

19 Franklin Roosevelt, Quarantine Address (October 5, 1937) in Daniel Boorstin, ed., *An American Primer* (Chicago: University of Chicago Press, 1966), p. 850.

20 Nelson Johnson Oral History, pp. 667–668, Columbia University; Nelson Johnson to Secretary of State (December 21, 1937) in *Foreign Relations of the United States 1937: The Far East* (Washington: Government Printing Office, 1954), Vol. III, p. 826; Dorothy Borg, *The United States and the Far Eastern Crisis of 1933–1938* (Cambridge, Mass.: Harvard University Press, 1964), p. 454; Michael Schaller, *The U.S. Crusade in China, 1938–1945* (New York: Columbia University Press, 1979), p. 18.

21 Nelson Johnson to Secretary of State (January 11, 1938) in *Foreign Relations of the United States 1938: The Far East*, Vol. III, p. 13.

22 Buhite, *Nelson T. Johnson and American Policy Toward China 1925–1941*, p. 135.

23 Ibid., p. 137.

24 Johnson felt that Japanese severity would ultimately undermine Tokyo's conquest and governance of China. See Johnson to Secretary of State Cordell Hull (May 27, 1938), Box 34, Nelson Johnson Papers, Library of Congress. Here is a vivid excerpt.

Thus far ... the Japanese have betrayed one fundamental lack, which I believe renders impossible the success of the mission upon which they have fixed their ambitions. The Japanese soldiery, apparently with the connivance of the younger and older officers, have shown themselves undisciplined and willful in their dealings with the civilian population with which they have come in contact. Widespread shootings of civilians, shootings of soldiers who have surrendered or been captured, attacks upon women, systematic looting of property: these activities have become so widespread that they may almost be said to be characteristic of the Japanese soldier. I receive reports of this kind of terrorism from all parts of the areas now occupied by the Japanese military, including indiscriminate bombing and machine gunning of open and defenseless cities. It is this lack of self-control, this utter disregard for the civilian

population of the country which they wish ultimately to exploit politically and
commercially, that leaves in my mind considerable doubt as to the eventual
ability of the Japanese to make the conquest of China ... Pure terrorism and
maltreatment of civilians such as this can, I believe, result only in so arousing
the hatred of the Chinese people that the Japanese will never be able to
overcome it. It may result in establishing a kind of slave-master psychology
under which the master will fear, hate and despise his slave, and the slave will
fear, hate and despise his master. Wherever the Japanese hand may weaken it
may be certain that the slave will turn and treat him as cruelly as he himself has
been treated.

25 Buhite, *Nelson T. Johnson and American Policy Toward China 1925–1941*,
    pp. 126–127, 140; John Boyle, *China and Japan at War 1937–1945: The
    Politics of Collaboration* (Stanford: Stanford University Press, 1972), p. 301;
    Thomson, *While China Faced West: American Reformers in Nationalist China,
    1928–1937*, p. 33; Paul Varg, *The Closing of the Door: Sino-American Relations
    1936–1946* (East Lansing: Michigan State University Press, 1973), p. 14.
26 Youli Sun, *China and the Origins of the Pacific War, 1931–1941* (New York:
    St. Martin's Press, 1993), p. 145; Buhite, *Nelson T. Johnson and American
    Policy Toward China 1925–1941*, p. 138.
27 Burns and Bennett, *Diplomats in Crisis: United States–Chinese–Japanese
    Relations, 1919–1941*, pp. xv–xvi; Edward Bennett, "Joseph Clark Grew" in
    Nolan, *Notable U.S. Ambassadors Since 1775*, p. 128.
28 Wayne Cole, *Roosevelt and the Isolationists 1932–1945* (Lincoln: University of
    Nebraska Press, 1983), p. 241.
29 Boyle, *China and Japan at War 1937–1945: The Politics of Collaboration*, p. 304.
30 William Langer and S. Everett Gleason, *The Undeclared War 1940–1941* (New
    York: Harper and Brothers Publishers, 1953), pp. 296–297, 490–491; Nelson
    Johnson to Secretary of State, (November 3, 1939) in *Foreign Relations of the
    United States 1938: The Far East*, Vol. III, pp. 363–366.
31 William Keylor, "France and the Illusion of American Support, 1919–1949"
    in Joel Blatt, ed., *The French Defeat of 1940: Reassessments* (Providence:
    Berghahn, 1998), pp. 207–208.
32 William Bullitt to Secretary of State (May 18, 1940) in *Foreign Relations of the
    United States 1940: General* (Washington: Government Printing Office, 1959),
    Vol. I, p. 230.
33 See Sigmund Freud and William Bullitt, *Thomas Woodrow Wilson: A
    Psychological Study* (Boston: Houghton Mifflin Company, 1966).
34 Orville Bullitt, ed., *For the President: Personal and Secret: Correspondence
    Between Franklin D. Roosevelt and William C. Bullitt* (Boston: Houghton
    Mifflin Company, 1972), p. 169; William Brownell and Richard Billings, *So
    Close to Greatness: A Biography of William C. Bullitt* (New York: Macmillan
    Company, 1987), p. xi.
35 Brownell and Billings, *So Close to Greatness: A Biography of William C. Bullitt*,
    p. 191.
36 Arnold Offner, *American Appeasement: United States Foreign Policy and
    Germany, 1933–1938* (New York: W.W. Norton and Company, 1976),
    pp. 175–176.

37 Brownell and Billings, *So Close to Greatness: A Biography of William C. Bullitt*, pp. 206–209, 223; Bullitt to Mr. President (November 8, 1936) in Bullitt, *For the President: Personal and Secret: Correspondence Between Franklin D. Roosevelt and William C. Bullitt*, p. 181.
38 Brownell and Billings, *So Close to Greatness: A Biography of William C. Bullitt*, p. 223.
39 Ibid., p. 230; William Bullitt to FDR (December 11, 1939) in Box 31, President's Secretary's File, Franklin D. Roosevelt Library; Cole, *Roosevelt and the Isolationists 1932–1945*, p. 288.
40 Mario Rossi, *Roosevelt and the French* (Westport: Praeger, 1993), p. 38. See for US attitude and policy toward France, John Haight, *American Aid to France, 1938–1940* (New York: Athenaeum, 1970).
41 William Bullitt to Secretary of State (June 10, 1940) in *Foreign Relations of the United States 1940: General*, Vol. I, p. 245.
42 William Bullitt to Secretary of State (May 31, 1940) in Box 31, President's Secretary's File, Franklin D. Roosevelt Library.
43 Secretary of State to Bullitt (May 14, 1940), Bullitt to Secretary of State (May 14, 1940), Bullitt to Secretary of State (May 15, 1940), Secretary of State to Bullitt (May 16, 1940) in *Foreign Relations of the United States 1940: General*, Vol. I, pp. 219–220, 222–224; Keylor, "France and the Illusion of American Support, 1919–1940" in Blatt, *The French Defeat of 1940: Reassessments*, p. 242.
44 Bullitt to Secretary of State (May 28, 1940) in *Foreign Relations of the United States 1940: General*, Vol. I, p. 237.
45 Bullitt, *For the President: Personal and Secret: Correspondence Between Franklin D. Roosevelt and William C. Bullitt*, pp. x–xi, 409, 420–424; Horne, *To Lose a Battle: France 1940*, p. 573; Keylor, "France and the Illusion of American Support, 1919–1940" in Blatt, *The French Defeat of 1940: Reassessments*, p. 242.
46 FDR to William Bullitt (June 9, 1940) (not sent) in Box 31, President's Secretary's File, Franklin D. Roosevelt Library; Alistair Horne, *To Lose a Battle: France 1940*, p. 477; Charles de Gaulle, *The Complete War Memoirs* (New York: Carroll and Graf Publishers, 1998), p. 61; Cordell Hull, *The Memoirs* (New York: Macmillan Company, 1948), Vol. I, p. 789–791.
47 The French government in early September 1914 began moving ministerial offices to Bordeaux, lest the German offensive at the Marne succeed, followed by Paris's capture. But the US ambassador, Myron Herrick, stayed on. His gesture of confidence in French arms was appreciated by Parisians. It became part of Franco-American diplomatic lore and influenced Bullitt's decision to remain in Paris in 1940.
48 William Bullitt to FDR (September 8, 1939) and Bullitt to FDR (November 1, 1939) in Box 31, President's Secretary's File, Franklin D. Roosevelt Library; Beatrice Farnsworth, *William C. Bullitt and the Soviet Union* (Bloomington: Indiana University Press, 1967), pp. 171–172, 176; Chadwin, *The Warhawks: American Interventionists before Pearl Harbor*, p. 79; Bullitt, *For the President: Personal and Secret: Correspondence Between Franklin D. Roosevelt and William C. Bullitt*, pp. xi, 498.

49 Chargé in France to Secretary of State (August 15, 1940), Chargé in France to Secretary of State (October 4, 1940), Chargé in France to Secretary of State (October 18, 1940) in *Foreign Relations of the United States 1940: General and Europe* (Washington: Government Printing Office, 1957), Vol. II, pp. pp. 565–568; Minutes of the Wannsee Conference, (January 20, 1942) in John Heineman, ed., *Readings in European History: A Collection of Primary Sources 1789 to the Present* (Dubuque: Kendall/Hunt Publishing Company, 1979), p. 519.

50 Richard Schlatter, ed., *Hobbes's Thucydides* (New Brunswick: Rutgers University Press, 1975), p. 379.

51 Samantha Power, *A Problem from Hell: America and the Age of Genocide* (New York: Basic Books, 2002), p. 23; Emil Fackenheim, *The Jewish Return into History: Reflections in the Age of Auschwitz and a New Jerusalem* (New York: Schocken Books, 1978), pp. 45, 108.

52 Rudolf Hoess, *Commandant of Auschwitz: The Autobiography of Rudolf Hoess* (Cleveland: World Publishing Company, 1959), p. 165.

53 Elie Wiesel, *Night* (New York: Avon Books, 1969), pp. 75–76.

54 Affidavit of Rudolf Hoess (April 5, 1946) in Heineman, *Readings in European History: A Collection of Primary Sources 1789 to the Present*, p. 534.

55 Yuri Suhl, ed., *They Fought Back: The Story of the Jewish Resistance in Nazi Europe* (New York: Schocken Books, 1967), p. 92; Gerhard Weinberg, *A World at Arms: A Global History of World War II* (Cambridge: Cambridge University Press, 1994), p. 528.

56 John Paul II, *The Threshold of Hope* (New York: Alfred A. Knopf, 1994), p. 97.

57 Affidavit of Rudolf Hoess (April 5, 1946) in Heineman, *Readings in European History: A Collection of Primary Sources 1789 to the Present*, p. 535.

58 Jonathan Glover, *Humanity: A Moral History of the Twentieth Century* (New Haven: Yale University Press, 2000), pp. 385–387; Gay Block and Malka Drucker, *Rescuers: Portraits of Moral Courage in the Holocaust* (New York: Holmes and Meier Publishers, 1992), p. 113; Simon Sebag Montefiore, "A Great Betrayal," *The New York Review of Books* (July 13, 2004), p. 15.

59 John Lukacs, "The Siege of Budapest," *The New York Review of Books* (April 7, 2005), p. 36.

60 See, for example, Jan Gross's *Neighbors: The Destruction of the Jewish Community in Jedwabne, Poland* (London: Penguin, 2001).

61 Monty Penkower, *The Jews Were Expendable: Free World Diplomacy and the Holocaust* (Urbana: University of Illinois Press, 1983), pp. 215, 225.

62 Henry Feingold, "Courage First and Intelligence Second: The American Jewish Secular Elite, Roosevelt, and the Failure to Rescue" in Verne Newton, ed., *FDR and the Holocaust* (New York: St. Martin's Press, 1996), p. 77.

63 Arthur Schlesinger, Jr., "Did FDR Betray the Jews? Or Did He Do More Than Anyone Else to Save Them?" ibid., p. 160.

64 Saul Friedman, *No Haven for the Oppressed: United States Policy Toward Jewish Refugees, 1938–1945* (Detroit: Wayne State University Press, 1973), pp. 91–103; Richard Breitman and Alan Kraut, *American Refugee Policy and European Jewry, 1933–1945* (Bloomington: Indiana University Press, 1987), p. 74.

65 P. G. Ingram, Jr., to Senator Borah (December 11, 1938), Box 767, William Borah Papers, Library of Congress.

66 Michael Beschloss, *The Conquerors: Roosevelt, Truman and the Destruction of Hitler's Germany, 1941–1945* (New York: Simon and Schuster, 2002), p. 51.

67 Rochelle Chadakoff, ed., *Eleanor Roosevelt's My Day* (New York: Pharos Books, 1989), p. 141.

68 Ibid., pp. 270–271, 303.

69 Martin Gilbert, *Auschwitz and the Allies* (New York: Holt, Rinehart and Winston, 1981), p. 13.

70 Power, *A Problem from Hell: America and the Age of Genocide*, p. 34; Kai Bird, *The Chairman: John J. McCloy: The Making of the American Establishment* (New York: Simon and Schuster, 1992), pp. 205–206; Beschloss, *The Conquerors: Roosevelt, Truman and the Destruction of Hitler's Germany, 1941–1945*, p. 40; E. Thomas Wood and Stanislas Jankowski, *Karski: How One Man Tried to Stop the Holocaust* (New York: John Wiley and Sons, 1994), pp. 188, 196–201; Breitman and Kraut, *American Refugee Policy and European Jewry, 1933–1945*, pp. 245–246.

71 Power, *A Problem from Hell: America and the Age of Genocide*, pp. 27–28.

72 Ibid., p. 36; Bird, *The Chairman: John J. McCloy: The Making of the American Establishment*, pp. 205–206; David Wyman, *The Abandonment of the Jews: America and the Holocaust 1941–1945* (New York: New Press, 1998), p. 320; David Wyman and Rafael Medoff, *A Race against Death: Peter Bergson, America, and the Holocaust* (New York: New Press, 2002), p. 75. On the reticence of the *New York Times*, see Laurel Leff's *Buried by the Times: The Holocaust and America's Most Important Newspaper* (Cambridge: Cambridge University Press, 2005).

73 Penkower, *The Jews Were Expendable: Free World Diplomacy and the Holocaust*, pp. 105–106.

74 John Morton Blum, *From the Morgenthau Diaries: Years of War 1941–1945* (Boston: Houghton Mifflin Company, 1967), pp. 207–208.

75 Bird, *The Chairman: John J. McCloy: The Making of the American Establishment*, p. 213; Beschloss, *The Conquerors: Roosevelt, Truman and the Destruction of Hitler's Germany, 1941–1945*, p. 88; Joseph Bendersky, *The Jewish Threat: Anti-Semitic Politics of the U.S. Army* (New York: Basic Books, 2000), pp. 289, 314, 337; Feingold, "Courage First and Intelligence Second: The American Jewish Secular Elite, Roosevelt, and the Failure to Rescue" in Newton, *FDR and the Holocaust*, p. 76.

76 Penkower, *The Jews Were Expendable: Free World Diplomacy and the Holocaust*, p. 95.

77 Wyman, *The Abandonment of the Jews: America and the Holocaust 1941–1945*, p. 121; Melvin Urofsky, *A Voice that Spoke for Justice: The Life and Times of Stephen S. Wise* (Albany: State University of New York Press, 1982), pp. 329, 331.

78 Power, *A Problem from Hell: America and the Age of Genocide*, p. 37; Penkower, *The Jews Were Expendable: Free World Diplomacy and the Holocaust*, p. 113.

79 Henry Morgenthau III, *Mostly Morgenthaus: A Family History* (New York: Ticknor and Fields, 1991), pp. 270–271.

80 Blum, *From the Morgenthau Diaries: Years of War 1941–1945*, p. 207.

81 John Morton Blum, *Roosevelt and Morgenthau* (Boston: Houghton Mifflin Company, 1972), p. 8.
82 Urofsky, *A Voice that Spoke for Justice: The Life and Times of Stephen S. Wise*, p. 330; Beschloss, *The Conquerors: Roosevelt, Truman and the Destruction of Hitler's Germany, 1941–1945*, p. 55.
83 Report to the Secretary on the Acquiescence of this Government in the Murder of the Jews (January 13, 1944) in Wyman and Medoff, *Race against Death: Peter Bergson, America, and the Holocaust*, pp. 187–188.
84 Ibid., p. 188.
85 Ibid., pp. 47–49.
86 Executive Order 9417 (January 22, 1944) ibid., p. 217; Yehuda Bauer, *American Jewry and the Holocaust: The American Jewish Joint Distribution Committee, 1939–1945* (Detroit: Wayne State University Press, 1981), pp. 401–402; Penkower, *The Jews Were Expendable: Free World Diplomacy and the Holocaust*, p. 141.
87 Wyman and Medoff, *A Race against Death: Peter Bergson, America and the Holocaust*, p. 163.
88 Morgenthau admired Wallenberg and followed the tale of his mysterious disappearance in Soviet-occupied Budapest. See Raoul Wallenberg file in Box 811 of Henry Morgenthau (junior) Papers, Franklin D. Roosevelt Library.
89 Breitman and Kraut, *American Refugee Policy and European Jewry, 1933–1945*, p. 220; Beschloss, *The Conquerors: Roosevelt, Truman, and the Destruction of Hitler's Germany, 1941–1945*, pp. 59, 66–67; Primo Levi, *Survival in Auschwitz* (New York: Summit, 1986), p. 118; Wiesel, *Night*, pp. 71–72.
90 Rafael Medoff, "Why the Allies Refused to Bomb Auschwitz: A Reply to William J. Vanden Heuvel," *Passport* (August 2003), pp. 5, 7.
91 Blum, *From the Morgenthau Diaries: Years of War 1941–1945*, pp. 222–223.
92 See Henry Morgenthau, Jr., *Germany Is Our Problem* (New York: Harper and Brothers Publishers, 1945); Truman to Jonathan Daniels (February 26, 1950) in Monte Poen, ed. *Strictly Personal and Confidential: The Letters Harry Truman Never Sent* (Boston: Little, Brown and Company, 1982), p. 76; Henry Stimson and McGeorge Bundy, *On Active Service in Peace and War* (New York: Harper Brothers Publishing, 1948), p. 569; Beschloss, *The Conquerors: Roosevelt, Truman and the Destruction of Hitler's Germany, 1941–1945*, pp. 105, 237.
93 Blum, *From the Morgenthau Diaries: Years of War 1941–1945*, p. 355.
94 Michael Marrus, "Bystanders to the Holocaust" in Newton, *FDR and the Holocaust*, p. 153.
95 Blum, *From the Morgenthau Diaries: Years of War 1941–1945*, pp. 397, 640.
96 Michael Schaller, *The American Occupation of Japan: The Origins of the Cold War in Asia* (New York: Oxford University Press, 1985), p. 4; Joseph Persico, *Nuremberg: Infamy on Trial* (New York: Penguin Books, 1994), p. xi; William Bosch, *Judgment on Nuremberg: American Attitudes Toward the Major German War-Crime Trials* (Chapel Hill: University of North Carolina Press, 1970), pp. 23, 26, 35; Eugene Gerhart, *America's Advocate: Robert H. Jackson* (Indianapolis: Bobbs-Merrill Company, 1958), p. 446; Beschloss, *The*

Conquerors: Roosevelt, Truman and the Destruction of Hitler's Germany, 1941–1945, p. 145; Bird, *The Chairman: John J. McCoy: The Making of the American Establishment*, p. 258.

97 Stimson and Bundy, *On Active Service in Peace and War*, p. 384.
98 Francis Biddle, *In Brief Authority* (Garden City: Doubleday and Company, 1962), p. 432.
99 Robert Jackson, *The Case against the Nazi War Criminals: Opening Statement for the United States and Other Documents* (New York: Alfred A. Knopf, 1946), pp. 100–101.
100 Office of United States Chief Counsel for Prosecution of Axis Criminality, *Nazi Conspiracy and Aggression: Opinion and Judgment* (Washington: United States Government Printing Office, 1947), p. 78.
101 Ibid., pp. 166–188.
102 Bosch, *Judgment on Nuremberg: American Attitudes Toward the Major German War-Crime Trials*, pp. 6–7, 28, 96, 103, 109; Jackson, *The Case against the Nazi War Criminals: Opening Statement for the United States of America and Other Documents*, p. 90; Gerhart, *America's Advocate: Robert H. Jackson*, p. 435.
103 Stimson and Bundy, *On Active Service in Peace and War*, p. 591.
104 Gerhart, *America's Advocate: Robert H. Jackson*, p. 439.
105 Dear and Foot, *The Oxford Companion to World War II*, p. 828.
106 John Dower, *War without Mercy: Race and Power in the Pacific War* (New York: Pantheon Books, 1986), pp. 37–38; John Dower, *Embracing Defeat: Japan in the Wake of World War II* (New York: W. W. Norton and Company, 1999), pp. 459, 464, 473–474.
107 Winston Churchill thought in 1948 that the prosecution of Tojo was "stupid" as Americans needed the cooperation of Japanese leaders. Moreover, as James Forrestal recorded in his diary: "No ruler of a country can control the actions of his troops. On the same theory, both Roosevelt and (Churchill) would have been executed if the Allies had lost the war." Entry of November 12, 1948 in Walter Millis, ed., *The Forrestal Diaries* (New York: Viking Press, 1951), p. 524.
108 Bosch, *Judgment on Nuremberg: American Attitudes Toward the Major German War-Crime Trials*, pp. 82–85, 171–172.
109 Ibid., p. 133.
110 William O. Douglas, *The Court Years 1939–1975* (New York: Random House, 1980), p. 28.
111 Ibid., p. 29; Douglas to Keith Thompson (June 25, 1975) in Melvin Urofsky, ed., *The Douglas Letters: Selections from the Private Papers of Justice William O. Douglas* (Bethesda: Adler and Adler Publishers, 1987), p. 161.
112 Bosch, *Judgment on Nuremberg: American Attitudes Toward the Major German War-Crime Trials*, pp. 122–123, 155.
113 *Congressional Record: Proceedings and Debates of the 79th Congress, Second Session, Appendix* (Washington: United States Government Printing Office, 1946), Vol. XCII, Part 9, p. A1052; Robert Taft, *A Foreign Policy for Americans* (Garden City: Doubleday and Company, 1951), p. 101.

114 Montefiore, "A Great Betrayal," *The New York Review of Books*, p. 14.
115 Taft to Judge Henry Herman, November 1, 1946 in Clarence Wunderlin, ed. *The Papers of Robert A. Taft* (Kent, Ohio: Kent State University Press, 2003), Vol. III, p. 223.
116 *Congressional Record: Proceedings and Debates of the 79th Congress, Second Session, Appendix*, Vol. XCII, Part 9, p. A1052.
117 Justice and Liberty for the Individual (October 5, 1946) in Wunderlin, *The Papers of Robert A. Taft*, Vol. III, p. 200.
118 Taft to Mr. Westbrook Pegler (October 14, 1946) ibid., p. 215 and in Box 877, Robert Taft Papers, Library of Congress; Persico, *Nuremberg: Infamy on Trial*, p. 438.
119 John Kennedy, *Profiles in Courage* (New York: Harper and Row, 1964), pp. 185–197; Russell Kirk and James McClellan, *The Political Principles of Robert A. Taft* (New York: Fleet Press Corporation, 1967), pp. 100, 102–103.
120 Speech at Dinner of the American Palestine Committee (March 9, 1944) in Wunderlin, *The Papers of Robert A. Taft*, Vol. II, pp. 531–534.
121 Statement on Recognition of Israel (October 26, 1948) ibid., Vol. III, pp. 468–469.
122 Kennedy, *Profiles in Courage*, pp. 193–195; Kirk and McClellan, *The Political Principles of Robert A. Taft*, p. 101; James Patterson, *Mr. Republican: A Biography of Robert A. Taft* (Boston: Hougton Mifflin Company, 1972), pp. 327–329; Bosch, *Judgment on Nuremberg: American Attitudes Toward the Major German War-Crime Trials*, pp. 77–79.
123 William White, *The Taft Story* (New York: Harper Brothers Publishing, 1954), pp. 55–56; Melvyn Leffler, *A Preponderance of Power: National Security, the Truman Administration, and the Cold War* (Stanford: Stanford University Press, 1992), p. 140.
124 Winston Churchill, *Their Finest Hour* (Boston: Houghton Mifflin Company, 1949), p. 3.
125 David Mayers, *The Ambassadors and America's Soviet Policy* (New York: Oxford University Press, 1995), p. 104.
126 Senator George Norris in 1933 did favor Washington's recognition of Moscow and was apparently unconcerned about the kulaks. Norris to Mrs. E. B. Hardeman, Box 41, George Norris Papers, Library of Congress.
127 PPS/21, The Problem of Palestine (February 11, 1948) in Anna Kasten Nelson, ed., *The State Department Policy Planning Staff Papers 1948* (New York: Garland Publishing, 1983), Vol. II, p. 81.
128 Morgenthau, *Mostly Morgenthaus: A Family History*, p. 332.
129 Taft to Secretary of War Henry Stimson (September 12, 1944), Box 734, Robert Taft Papers, Library of Congress; Arthur Krock, "Reliance on Marshall: General's Testimony on Palestine Issue Shows Congressional Confidence in Him," *New York Times* (March 8, 1944); Wyman, *The Abandonment of the Jews: America and the Holocaust 1941–1945*, pp. 96–99, 239.
130 See Catholic theologian Hans Kung's *On Being A Christian* (New York: Pocket Books, 1978), p. 169. Kung wrote: "After Auschwitz there can be no more excuses. Christendom cannot avoid a clear admission of its guilt."

131 Norman Naimark, *The Russians in Germany: A History of the Soviet Zone of Occupation 1945–1949* (Cambridge, Mass.: Harvard University Press, 1995), pp. 132–133.

132 Ian Buruma estimates that 600,000 Germans "burned, or choked, or boiled to death" in Allied bombing raids. See his "The Destruction of Germany," *The New York Review of Books* (October 21, 2004), p. 8.

133 Bishop George Bell, "Obliteration is not a justifiable act of war" in Brian MacArthur, ed., *The Penguin Book of Twentieth-Century Speeches* (London: Penguin Books, 1999), pp. 223–227.

134 Beschloss, *The Conquerors: Roosevelt, Truman and the Destruction of Hitler's Germany, 1941–1945*, p. 190; Barton Bernstein, "Understanding the Atomic Bomb and Japanese Surrender: Missed Opportunities, Little-Known Near Disasters, and Modern Memory," in Michael Hogan, ed., *Hiroshima in History and Memory* (Cambridge: Cambridge University Press, 1996), p. 77.

135 Glover, *Humanity: A Moral History of the Twentieth Century*, p. 99. Also see the account by Takashi Nagai, a medical doctor living in Nagasaki when the atomic bomb was dropped: *The Bells of Nagasaki* (Tokyo: Kodansha International, 1984).

136 William Leahy, *I Was There* (New York: McGraw-Hill Book Company, 1950), pp. 431, 441.

137 Bernstein, "Understanding the Atomic Bomb and the Japanese Surrender: Missed Opportunities, Little-Known Near Disasters, and Modern Memory" in Hogan, *Hiroshima in History and Memory*, pp. 78–79.

138 See Henry Stimson, "The Decision to Use the Atomic Bomb," *Harper's Magazine* (February 1947).

139 Forrest Pogue, *George C. Marshall: Statesman 1945–1959* (New York: Viking Press, 1987), pp. 18–19; Stimson and Bundy, *On Active Service in Peace and War*, p. 625; Martin Sherwin, *A World Destroyed: The Atomic Bomb and the Grand Alliance* (New York: Vintage Books, 1977), pp. 230–231.

140 Bernstein, "Understanding the Atomic Bomb and the Japanese Surrender: Missed Opportunities, Little-Known Near Disasters, and Modern Memory" in Hogan, *Hiroshima in History and Memory*, p. 73.

141 Estimates by military planners during summer 1945 on the number of US casualties in an invasion of Japan is a hotly debated topic. See Michael Kort's "Casualty Projections for the Invasion of Japan, Phantom Estimates, and the Math of Barton Bernstein," *Passport* (December 2003) and Baton Bernstein's "Marshall, Leahy, and Casualty Issues – A Reply to Kort's Flawed Critique," *Passport* (August 2004). Also see letters to the editor by Robert James Maddox and Michael Kort in the December 2004 volume of *Passport*, pp. 55–57.

142 Ralph Bard's Dissent (June 28, 1945) in Sherwin, *A World Destroyed: The Atomic Bomb and the Grand Alliance*, p. 307.

143 Robert Newman, "Hiroshima and the Trashing of Henry Stimson," *The New England Quarterly* (March 1998), p. 7. Also see Newman's *Enola Gay and the Court of History* (New York: Peter Lang, 2004).

144 Jackson, *The Case against the Nazi War Criminals: Opening Statement for the United States and Other Documents*, p. 90.

145 Ibid., pp. 90–91; Telford Taylor, *The Anatomy of the Nuremberg Trials* (New York: Alfred A. Knopf, 1992), p. 636.
146 Samantha Power, "The Lesson of Hannah Arendt," *The New York Review of Books* (April 29, 2004), p. 36. For texts of the universal human rights declaration and genocide convention, see Ian Brownlie, ed. *Basic Documents on Human Rights* (Oxford: Clarendon Press, 1971), pp. 106–112, 116–120.

Chapter Eleven

1 See Wilson Miscamble, *George F. Kennan and the Making of American Foreign Policy* (Princeton: Princeton University Press, 1992) and John Lewis Gaddis, *Strategies of Containment: A Critical Appraisal of Postwar American National Security Policy* (New York: Oxford University Press, 1982).
2 Michael Sherry, *In the Shadow of War: The United States Since the 1930s* (New Haven: Yale University Press, 1995), p. 126.
3 Harry Truman, *Memoirs: Years of Hope and Trial* (Garden City: Doubleday and Company, 1956), p. 337.
4 James Chace, *Acheson: The Secretary of State Who Created the American World* (New York: Simon and Schuster, 1998), p. 286; Ernest May, ed., *American Cold War Strategy: Interpreting NSC 68* (Boston: Bedford/St. Martin's, 1992), p. 15.
5 David Mayers, *George Kennan and the Dilemmas of U.S. Foreign Policy* (New York: Oxford University Press), p. 114; Ronald Steel, *Walter Lippmann and the American Century* (Boston: Little, Brown and Company, 1980), pp. 438–439, 578. Also see Walter Lippmann's *The Cold War: A Study in U.S. Foreign Policy* (New York: Harper Brothers Publishing, 1947).
6 Reinhold Niebuhr, *The Irony of American History* (New York: Charles Scribner's Sons, 1952), pp. 138, 172–174.
7 See Thomas Paterson, "The Dissent of Senator Claude Pepper," William Pratt, "Senator Glen H. Taylor: Questioning American Unilateralism," and Henry Berger, "Senator Robert A. Taft Dissents from Military Escalation" in Thomas Paterson, ed., *Cold War Critics: Alternatives to American Foreign Policy in the Truman Years* (Chicago: Quadrangle Books, 1971), pp. 114–204.
8 Henry Wallace Oral History, pp. 49, 52, Columbia University; Graham White and John Maze, *Henry A. Wallace: His Search for a New World Order* (Chapel Hill: University of North Carolina Press, 1995), pp. 8, 29; Mark Kleinman, *A World of Hope, a World of Fear: Henry A. Wallace, Reinhold Niebuhr, and American Liberalism* (Columbus: Ohio State University Press, 2000), pp. 14–15; John Morton Blum, ed. *The Price of Vision: The Diary of Henry A. Wallace 1942–1946* (Boston: Houghton Mifflin Company, 1973), pp. 13–15.
9 The Holocaust did shake Wallace's optimistic view of human nature. See Wallace to Herman Neaderland (August 16, 1946), Reel 42, Henry Wallace Papers, Library of Congress.
10 Dwight Macdonald, *Henry Wallace: The Man and the Myth* (New York: Garland Publishing, 1979), pp. 116–127; Norman Markowitz, *The Rise and Fall of the People's Century: Henry A. Wallace and American Liberalism, 1941–1948* (New

York: Free Press, 1973), pp. 333–341; White and Maze, *Henry A. Wallace: His Search for a New World Order*, pp. 64, 143.

11 Richard Walton, *Henry Wallace, Harry Truman, and the Cold War* (New York: Viking Press, 1976), p. 4; Torbjorn Sirevag, *The Eclipse of the New Deal and the Fall of Vice-President Wallace, 1944* (New York: Garland Publishing, 1985), p. 546; White and Maze, *Henry A. Wallace: His Search for a New World Order*, p. 141.

12 Henry Wallace, *Soviet Asia Mission* (New York: Reynal and Hitchcock, 1946), p. 34; James Chace, "The Presidency of Henry Wallace" in Robert Cowley, ed., *What If? Eminent Historians Imagine what Might Have Been* (New York: Berkley Books, 2001), p. 390; Edward Schapsmeier and Frederick Schapsmeier, *Prophet in Politics: Henry A. Wallace and the War Years, 1940–1965* (Ames: Iowa State University Press, 1970), p. 91.

13 The Price of Free World Victory (May 8, 1942) in Blum, *The Price of Vision: The Diary of Henry A. Wallace 1942–1946*, pp. 635–640.

14 Henry Wallace Oral History, p. 4954, Columbia University; White and Maze, *Henry A. Wallace: His Search for a New World Order*, pp. 107, 124, 146.

15 Harry Truman, *Memoirs: Year of Decisions* (Garden City: Doubleday and Company, 1955), pp. 558, 560; Clark Clifford, *Counsel to the President: A Memoir* (New York: Random House, 1991), p. 120; Arnold Offner, *Another Such Victory: President Truman and the Cold War, 1945–1953* (Stanford: Stanford University Press, 2002), p. 202; White and Maze, *Henry A. Wallace: His Search for a New World Order*, pp. 206, 239; John Culver and John Hyde, *American Dreamer: The Life and Times of Henry A. Wallace* (New York: W. W. Norton and Company, 2000), p. 425.

16 Truman to Jonathan Daniels (February 26, 1950) in Monte Poen, ed., *Strictly Personal and Confidential: The Letters Harry Truman Never Mailed* (Boston: Little, Brown and Company, 1982), p. 77. Also see Truman to Bess (September 15, 1946) in Robert Ferrell, ed., *Dear Bess: The Letters from Harry to Bess Truman, 1910–1959* (New York: W. W. Norton and Company, 1983), p. 537.

17 Henry Wallace Oral History, p. 5191, Columbia University; White and Maze, *Henry A. Wallace: His Search for a New World Order*, p. 257; Henry Wallace, *Toward World Peace* (New York: Reynal and Hitchcock, 1948), p. 18.

18 See, for example, Wallace to Truman (July 23, 1946) in Blum, *The Price of Vision: The Diary of Henry A. Wallace 1942–1946*, pp. 589–601 or Wallace to Truman (March 14, 1946) in Truman, *Memoirs: Year of Decisions*, pp. 555–556.

19 White and Maze, *Henry A. Wallace: His Search for a New World Order*, p. 119; Walton, *Henry Wallace, Harry Truman, and the Cold War*, p. 6; Markowitz, *The Rise and Fall of the People's Century: Henry A. Wallace and American Liberalism 1941–1948*, p. 164; Wallace, *Toward World Peace*, p. 50.

20 The Way to Peace (September 12, 1946) in Blum, *The Price of Vision: The Diary of Henry A. Wallace 1942–1946*, p. 664.

21 Ibid., pp. 665–666.

22 Hugh De Santis, *The Diplomacy of Silence: The American Foreign Service, the Soviet Union, and Cold War, 1933–1947* (Chicago: University of Chicago

Press, 1980), p. 173; Gregg Herken, *The Winning Weapon: The Atomic Bomb in the Cold War 1945–1950* (New York: Vintage Books, 1982), p. 144; Markowitz, *The Rise and Fall of the People's Century: Henry A. Wallace and American Liberalism, 1941–1948*, p. 179; Fraser Harbutt, *The Iron Curtain: Churchill, America, and the Origins of the Cold War* (New York: Oxford University Press, 1986), p. 199.

23 Entry of February 12, 1946 in Blum, *The Price of Vision: The Diary of Henry A. Wallace 1942–1946*, p. 547.

24 Entry of September 21, 1945 and Wallace to Truman (September 24, 1945) ibid., pp. 482–487; Stimson Memos on A-Bomb Control in Barton Bernstein and Allen Matusow, eds., *The Truman Administration: A Documentary History* (New York: Harper Colophon Books, 1966), pp. 219–224.

25 Wallace to Truman (July 23, 1946) in Blum, *The Price of Vision: The Diary of Henry A. Wallace 1942–1946*, pp. 591, 597.

26 Ibid., p. 594.

27 Truman, *Memoirs: Years of Trial and Hope*, p. 185.

28 Wallace to Thomas Mann (November 21, 1946), Reel 42, Henry Wallace Papers, Library of Congress.

29 Robert Messer, *The End of an Alliance: James F. Byrnes, Roosevelt, Truman, and the Origins of the Cold War* (Chapel Hill: University of North Carolina Press, 1982), p. 206; James Byrnes, *Speaking Frankly* (New York: Harper and Brothers Publishers, 1947), pp. 239–243; Truman to Mama and Mary (September 20, 1946) in Truman, *Memoirs: Year of Decisions*, p. 560.

30 Truman to Bess (September 20, 1946) in Ferrell, *Dear Bess: The Letters from Harry to Bess Truman, 1910–1959*, p. 539.

31 Wallace to Employees of the Department of Commerce (September 20, 1946), Reel 42, Henry Wallace Papers, Library of Congress.

32 White and Maze, *Henry A. Wallace: His Search for a New World Order*, p. 246.

33 Wallace, *Toward World Peace*, pp. 111–112.

34 Ibid., pp. 85–86.

35 Walter McDougall, *Promised Land, Crusader State: The American Encounter with the World Since 1776* (Boston: Houghton Mifflin Company, 1997), p. 164.

36 Kleinman, *A World of Hope, a World of Fear: Henry A. Wallace, Reinhold Niebuhr, and American Liberalism*, pp. 292–293.

37 Wallace, *Toward World Peace*, pp. 117–118.

38 Richard Fox, *Reinhold Niebuhr: A Biography* (New York: Pantheon Books, 1985), p. 236; Fraser Harbutt, *The Cold War Era* (Oxford: Blackwell Publishers, 2002), p. 56; Henry Wallace Oral History, pp. 5081–5082, Columbia University; Schapsmeier and Schapsmeier, *Prophet in Politics: Henry A. Wallace and the War Years, 1940–1965*, pp. 189–190; Jeffrey Madrick, "A Mind of His Own," *The New York Review of Books* (May 26, 2005), p. 16.

39 Southern Response to Civil-Rights Speech, Remarks by Representative William Colmer (April 8, 1948) in Bernstein and Matusow, *The Truman Administration: A Documentary History*, p. 109.

40 Henry Wallace Oral History, p. 5181, Columbia University; "Corn-fed Mystic" is the title of chapter 6 in Macdonald's *Henry Wallace: The Man and*

the Myth; White and Maze, *Henry A. Wallace: His Search for a New World Order*, pp. 249, 279.

41 Robert Donovan, *Tumultuous Years: The Presidency of Harry S. Truman 1949–1953* (New York: W. W. Norton and Company, 1982), p. 15.

42 J. Samuel Walker, *Henry A. Wallace and American Foreign Policy* (Westport, Conn.: Greenwood Press, 1976), pp. 206–207; Karl Schmidt, *Henry A. Wallace: Quixotic Crusade 1948* (Syracuse: Syracuse University Press, 1960), pp. 280–281; Wallace's Attack on NATO (March 27, 1949) in Bernstein and Matusow, *The Truman Administration: A Documentary History*, pp. 279–280.

43 Henry Wallace Oral History, p. 5137, Columbia University.

44 White and Maze, *Henry A. Wallace: His Search for a New World Order*, p. 289.

45 Ibid., p. 290; Henry Wallace Oral History, p. 5097, Columbia University.

46 Henry Wallace Oral History, p. 5197, Columbia University.

47 Kleinman, *A World of Hope, a World of Fear: Henry A. Wallace, Reinhold Niebuhr, and American Liberalism*, pp. 289–290, 292. See Henry Wallace, "Where I Was Wrong," *This Week Magazine* (September 7, 1952).

48 Entry of August 14, 1946 in Blum, *The Price of Vision: The Diary of Henry A. Wallace 1942–1946*, p. 610. Also see pp. 36–37 ibid.

49 Every Effort for Victory in the War (June 26, 1950) in Kim Il Sung, *Selected Works* (Pyongyang: Foreign Languages Publishing House, 1971), pp. 287, 289.

50 Melvyn Leffler, *A Preponderance of Power: National Security, the Truman Administration, and the Cold War* (Stanford: Stanford University Press, 1992), p. 378.

51 Offner, *Another Such Victory: President Truman and the Cold War, 1945–1953*, p. 422.

52 See Roger Dingman, "Atomic Diplomacy During the Korean War," and Rosemary Foot, "Nuclear Coercion and the Ending of the Korean War," both in *International Security*, Winter 1988/89.

53 Arthur Vandenberg, Jr., ed., *The Private Papers of Senator Vandenberg* (Boston: Houghton Mifflin Company, 1952), pp. 75–89.

54 Omar Bradley and Clay Blair, *A General's Life* (New York: Simon and Schuster, 1983), pp. 523–524.

55 Truman to John O'Rourke (November 28, 1952) in Poen, *Strictly Personal and Confidential: The Letters Harry Truman Never Sent*, p. 55.

56 Robert Ferrell, ed., *Off the Record: The Private Papers of Harry S. Truman* (New York: Harper and Row, 1980), p. 47; Bradley and Blair, *A General's Life*, p. 541.

57 D. Clayton James, *Refighting the Last War: Command and Crisis in Korea 1950–1953* (New York: Free Press, 1993), p. 207.

58 Entry of November 17, 1944 in Walter Millis, ed., *The Forrestal Diaries* (New York: Viking Press, 1951), p. 18; John Spanier, *The Truman–MacArthur Controversy and the Korean War* (New York: W. W. Norton and Company, 1965), p. 67.

59 John Lewis Gaddis, "The Strategic Perspective: The Rise and Fall of the Defensive Perimeter Concept, 1947–1951" in Dorothy Borg and Waldo Heinrichs, eds., *Uncertain Years: Chinese–American Relations, 1947–1950* (New York: Columbia University Press, 1980), p. 113, #150.

60 Secretary of State to Certain Diplomatic Offices (August 26, 1950) in *Foreign Relations of the United States 1950: East Asia and the Pacific* (Washington: Government Printing Office, 1976), Vol. VI, p. 453.

61 Mayers, *George Kennan and the Dilemmas of US Foreign Policy*, pp. 170–180.

62 See Acheson's Letter of Transmittal in Lyman Van Slyke, ed., *The China White Paper* (Stanford: Stanford University Press, 1967), Vol. I, p. xvi.

63 Dean Acheson, *Present at the Creation* (New York: W. W. Norton and Company, 1969), p. 356.

64 Spanier, *The Truman–MacArthur Controversy and the Korean War*, pp. 57–58.

65 David Mayers, *Cracking the Monolith: U.S. Policy against the Sino-Soviet Alliance, 1949–1955* (Baton Rouge: Louisiana State University Press, 1986), p. 84.

66 Spanier, *The Truman–MacArthur Controversy and the Korean War*, p. 73.

67 Alonzo Hamby, *Man of the People: A Life of Harry S. Truman* (New York: Oxford University Press, 1995), p. 543; James, *Refighting the Last War: Command and Crisis in Korea 1950–1953*, p. 205; Bernard Brodie, *War and Politics* (New York: Macmillan Company, 1973), p. 82.

68 Secretary of State to Certain Diplomatic Offices (August 26, 1950) in *Foreign Relations of the United States: East Asia and the Pacific*, Vol. VI, p. 453.

69 James, *Refighting the Last War: Command and Crisis in Korea 1950–1953*, p. 204.

70 Truman, *Memoirs: Years of Trial and Hope*, p. 442.

71 Allen Whiting, *China Crosses the Yalu: The Decision to Enter the Korean War* (Stanford: Stanford University Press, 1960), p. 39; Robert Simmons, *The Strained Alliance: Peking, Pyongyang, Moscow and the Politics of the Korean Civil War* (New York: Free Press, 1975), p. 111; Mayers, *Cracking the Monolith: U.S. Policy against the Sino-Soviet Alliance, 1949–1955*, p. 42; Spanier, *The Truman–MacArthur Controversy and the Korean War*, p. 17.

72 MacArthur actually preceded Acheson (March 1949) in publicly placing Korea outside of the US defense perimeter.

73 Truman's explicit reasons for Korean intervention are summarized in *Memoirs: Years of Trial and Hope*, pp. 339–340.

74 Ibid., p. 364; Hamby, *Man of the People: A Life of Harry S. Truman*, p. 543; Memorandum (November 25, 1950) in Ferrell, *Off the Record: The Private Papers of Harry S. Truman*, p. 200.

75 Douglas MacArthur, *Reminiscences* (New York: McGraw-Hill Book Company, 1964), p. 389; James, *Refighting the Last War: Command and Crisis in Korea 1950–1953*, p. 197.

76 Stanley Weintraub, *MacArthur's War: Korea and the Undoing of an American Hero* (New York: Free Press, 2000), p. 262; Leffler, *A Preponderance of Power: National Security, the Truman Administration, and the Cold War*, pp. 399, 406; Forrest Pogue, *George C. Marshall: Statesman 1945–1959* (New York: Viking Press, 1987), p. 488.

77 Courtney Whitney, *MacArthur: His Rendezvous with History* (New York: Alfred A. Knopf, 1956), p. 433; Spanier, *The Truman–MacArthur Controversy and the Korean War*, pp. 140, 198.

78 Testimony of General of the Army Omar N. Bradley (May 15, 1952) in *Military Situation in the Far East: Hearings Before the Committee on Armed*

Services and the Committee on Foreign Relations, United States Senate, Eighty-Second Congress, First Session (Washington: Government Printing office, 1951), Vol. II, pp. 731–732 (hereafter *Military Situation in the Far East*).

79 "Diplomatic Appeasement but Sows the Seed of Future Conflict" (June 13, 1951) in Vorin Whan, ed., *A Soldier Speaks: Public Papers and Speeches of General of the Army Douglas MacArthur* (New York: Frederick A. Praeger, 1965), p. 265.

80 Testimony of Secretary of Defense George C. Marshall (May 7, 1951) in *Military Situation in the Far East*, Vol. I, p. 325.

81 Statement of General MacArthur (March 24, 1951) ibid., Vol. V, p. 3542.

82 Message from Joint Chiefs to General MacArthur (March 24, 1951) ibid., p. 3542.

83 James, *Refighting the Last War: Command and Crisis in Korea 1950–1953*, p. 209; Pogue, *George C. Marshall: Statesman 1945–1959*, p. 481; Weintraub, *MacArthur's War: Korea and the Undoing of an American Hero*, p. 325.

84 Letters exchanged by Honorable Joseph W. Martin, Jr., and General MacArthur (March 1951) in *Military Situation in the Far East*, Vol. V, p. 3544.

85 Ibid.

86 Diary entry of April 6, 1951 in Ferrell, *Off the Record: The Private Papers of Harry S. Truman*, p. 211.

87 Weintraub, *MacArthur's War: Korea and the Undoing of an American Hero*, pp. 332.

88 Truman, *Memoirs: Years of Trial and Hope*, pp. 446–447; James, *Refighting the Last War: Command and Crisis in Korea 1950–1953*, p. 211.

89 William Halsey to MacArthur, p. 1 (April 14, 1951), Douglas MacArthur Papers, Library of Congress.

90 "Old Soldiers Never Die" (April 19, 1951) in Whan, *A Soldier Speaks: Public Papers and Speeches of General of the Army Douglas MacArthur*, p. 232.

91 Hamby, *Man of the People: A Life of Harry S. Truman*, p. 562.

92 Lawrence Wittner, ed., *MacArthur* (Englewood Cliffs, New Jersey: Prentice-Hall, 1971), p. 102; Arthur Schlesinger, *War and the American Presidency* (New York: W. W. Norton and Company, 2004), p. 111; Spanier, *The Truman–MacArthur Controversy and the Korean War*, pp. 211–212.

93 Secret Letter of Tribute from Admiral Halsey to General MacArthur Revealed for the First-Time (Julius Klein), April 1964, Douglas MacArthur Papers, Library of Congress.

94 Senator Joseph McCarthy in Wittner, *MacArthur*, p. 103.

95 Senator William Jenner ibid., 106.

96 Senator Kenneth Wherry ibid., p. 107.

97 *Military Situation in the Far East*, Vol. I, p. 55.

98 Ibid., Vol. V, p. 3575.

99 Spanier, *The Truman–MacArthur Controversy and the Korean War*, p. 272.

100 *Military Situation in the Far East*, Vol. V, p. 3577.

101 Leffler, *A Preponderance of Power: National Security, the Truman Administration, and the Cold War*, p. 406; Offner, *Another Such Victory: President Truman and the Cold War, 1945–1953*, p. 421.

102 "Diplomatic Appeasement but Sows the Seed of Future Conflict" (June 13, 1951) in Whan, *A Soldier Speaks: Public Papers and Speeches of General of the Army Douglas MacArthur*, p. 264.

103 Spanier, *The Truman–MacArthur Controversy and the Korean War*, p. 235.

104 Rosemary Foot, *The Wrong War: American Policy and the Dimensions of the Korean Conflict, 1950–1953* (Ithaca: Cornell University Press, 1985), p. 192.

105 Weintraub, *MacArthur's War: Korea and the Undoing of an American Hero*, pp. 263–264; Memorandum on Ending the Korean War in MacArthur, *Reminiscences*, p. 411.

106 D. Clayton James, *The Years of MacArthur: Triumph and Disaster 1945–1964* (Boston: Houghton Mifflin Company, 1985), p. 655.

107 PPS/19, Position of the United States with Respect to Palestine (January 20, 1948) in Anna Kasten Nelson, ed., *The State Department Policy Planning Staff Papers 1948* (New York: Garland Publishing, 1983), Vol. II, pp. 39–40; Pogue, *George C. Marshall: Statesman 1945–1959*, pp. 371, 373; Clifford, *Counsel to the President: A Memoir*, pp. 3, 13–15; Hamby, *Man of the People: A Life of Harry S. Truman*, pp. 414–416.

108 Niebuhr, *The Irony of American History*, pp. 172–173.

109 Markowitz, *The Rise and Fall of the People's Century: Henry A. Wallace and American Liberalism, 1941–1948*, p. 304.

110 White and Maze, *Henry A. Wallace: His Search for a New World Order*, pp. 310–312.

111 Foreword by Linus Pauling in Schapsmeier and Schapsmeier, *Prophet in Politics: Henry A. Wallace and the War Years, 1940–1965*, p. x.

112 Schlesinger, *War and the American Presidency*, p. 80.

113 Patricia Ward Wallace, *Politics of Conscience: A Biography of Margaret Chase Smith* (Westport, Conn.: Praeger, 1995) p. 106. Also see Patricia Schmidt's *Margaret Chase Smith: Beyond Convention* (Orono: University of Maine Press, 1996), pp. 214–218 and Janann Sherman, *No Place for a Woman: A Life of Margaret Chase Smith* (New Brunswick: Rutgers University Press, 2000), pp. 109–111.

114 Schlesinger, *War and the American Presidency*, pp. 14, 53.

115 "War Is No Longer a Medium of Practical Settlement of International Differences" (January 26, 1955) in Whan, *A Soldier Speaks: Public Papers and Speeches of General of the Army Douglas MacArthur*, pp. 314, 320.

Chapter Twelve

1 Joseph Nye, *The Paradox of American Power: Why the World's Only Superpower Can't Go It Alone* (New York: Oxford University Press, 2002), pp. 1, 36–38, 70–71, 142, 174 #2; Andrew Bacevich, *American Empire: The Realities and Consequences of U.S. Diplomacy* (Cambridge, Mass.: Harvard University Press, 2002), pp. 126, 138, 241; Michael Ignatieff, "The Burden," *New York Times Magazine* (January 5, 2003), p. 22.

2 Robert Johnson, *Ernest Gruening and the American Dissenting Tradition* (Cambridge, Mass.: Harvard University Press, 1998), p. 3.

3 Henry Kissinger, *Years of Upheaval* (Boston: Little, Brown and Company, 1982), p. 510.
4 Robert Kaufman, *Henry M. Jackson: A Life in Politics* (Seattle: University of Washington Press, 2000), pp. 3, 5, 280–281, 299.
5 Bob Woodward, *The Commanders* (New York: Simon and Schuster, 1991), pp. 36, 337, 342.
6 Robert Byrd, *Losing America: Confronting a Reckless and Arrogant Presidency* (New York: W. W. Norton and Company, 2004), pp. 137, 176, 235.
7 See US NEWS.COM for June 27, 2005 and CNN.COM for August 19, 200; www.house.gov/murtha "Important Speech on the War in Iraq"; Melvin Laird, "Iraq: Learning the Lessons of Vietnam," *Foreign Affairs*, November/ December 2005.
8 LaVerne McCain Gill, *African American Women in Congress: Forming and Transforming History* (New Brunswick: Rutgers University Press, 1997), pp. 3, 34, 133.
9 Matthew Ridgway, *Soldier: The Memoirs of Matthew B. Ridgway* (New York: Harper Brothers Publishing, 1956), p. 293; Chester Pach and Elmo Richardson, *The Presidency of Dwight D. Eisenhower* (Lawrence: University Press of Kansas, 1991), p. 81.
10 Ernest May and Philip Zelikow, eds., *The Kennedy Tapes: Inside the White House During the Cuban Missile Crisis* (Cambridge, Mass.: Harvard University Press, 1997), pp. 178, 182, 699.
11 Robert Buzzanco, *Masters of War: Military Dissent and Politics in the Vietnam Era* (Cambridge: Cambridge University Press, 1996), pp. 9, 134–135, 145–146, 342–343.
12 Ibid., p. 344.
13 Bob Woodward, *The Commanders*, pp. 83, 89, 96–98, 104; Bacevich, *American Empire: The Realities and Consequences of U.S. Diplomacy*, pp. 69–70.
14 Woodward, *The Commanders*, pp. 331–332.
15 Ibid., p. 38; Andrew Bacevich, *The New American Militarism: How Americans Are Seduced by War* (New York: Oxford University Press, 2005), pp. 49–50.
16 Arthur Schlesinger, Jr., "The Making of a Mess," *The New York Review of Books* (September 23, 2004), p. 42; "Scowcroft Calls War Failing Venture," *Boston Globe* (October 12, 2004), p. A4.
17 Tom Clancy with Tony Zinni and Tony Koltz, *Battle Ready* (New York: G. P. Putnam's Sons, 2004), pp. 426–427.
18 David Mayers, "JFK's Ambassadors and the Cold War," *Diplomacy and Statecraft* (November 2000), pp. 194–195. Also see Jeffrey Madrick, "A Mind of His Own," *The New York Review of Books* (May 26, 2005), p. 17.
19 Andrew DeRoche, *Andrew Young: Civil Rights Ambassador* (Wilmington: Scholarly Resources, 2003), pp. 77, 83, 98, 102–103, 106.
20 Ibid., pp. 111–113; Gaddis Smith, *Morality, Reason, and Power: American Diplomacy in the Carter Years* (New York: Hill and Wang, 1986), p. 168; Jimmy Carter, *Keeping Faith: Memoirs of a President* (Toronto: Bantam Books, 1982), p. 491; Andrew Young, *An Easy Burden: The Civil Rights Movement and the Transformation of America* (New York: HarperCollins, 1996), p. 418.

21 John Brady Kiesling, "Iraq: A Letter of Resignation," *The New York Review of Books* (April 10, 2003), p. 91.
22 Schlesinger, "The Making of a Mess," p. 42.
23 See US diplomats' letter to George W. Bush, *The New York Review of Books* (November 18, 2004).
24 "Scowcroft Calls War Failing Venture," *Boston Globe* (October 17, 2004), p. A4.
25 Robert McNamara, *Argument Without End: In Search of Answers to the Vietnam Tragedy* (New York: Public Affairs, 1999), p. 316.
26 Clark Clifford with Richard Holbrooke, *Counsel to the President: A Memoir* (New York: Random House, 1991), pp. 456–458; Robert McNamara with Brian VanDeMark, *In Retrospect: The Tragedy and Lessons of Vietnam* (New York: Random House, 1995), p. 307.
27 Cyrus Vance, *Hard Choices: Critical Years in America's Foreign Policy* (New York: Simon and Schuster, 1983), pp. 410–413; Carter, *Keeping Faith: Memoirs of a President*, p. 513.
28 Vance, *Hard Choices: Critical Years in America's Foreign Policy*, p. 410.
29 Smith, *Morality, Reason, and Power: American Diplomacy in the Carter Years*, pp. 204–205.
30 J. William Fulbright, *The Price of Empire* (New York: Pantheon Books, 1989), p. vii.
31 John Kenneth Galbraith, *Name-Dropping: From FDR On* (Boston: Houghton Mifflin Company, 1999), pp. 160–161.
32 Fulbright, *The Price of Power*, p. ix.
33 Woodward, *The Commanders*, pp. 83, 93; Brian Urquhart, "The Good General," *The New York Review of Books* (September 23, 2004), p. 30 #2; Clancy, *Battle Ready*, p. 427; Johnson, *Ernest Gruening and the American Dissenting Tradition*, pp. 243, 274–275, 277; Byrd, *Losing America: Confronting a Reckless and Arrogant Presidency*, p. 256.
34 Arthur Schlesinger, *War and the American Presidency* (New York: W. W. Norton and Company, 2004), p. 82.
35 John Spanier, *The Truman–MacArthur Controversy and the Korean War* (New York: W. W. Norton and Company, 1965), p. 44.
36 Ibid., pp. 73–74.
37 J. William Fulbright, *The Arrogance of Power* (New York: Random House, 1966), p. 22.
38 Clancy, *Battle Ready*, pp. 425–426.
39 George Seibel to Norris (April 4, 1917), Box 47, George Norris Papers, Library of Congress.
40 Fulbright, *The Arrogance of Power*, pp. 38–40.
41 Morgenthau to My dear folks, p. 7 (May 17, 1915), Box 474, Henry Morgenthau (senior) Papers, Franklin D. Roosevelt Library.
42 Colin Powell, *My American Journey* (New York: Random House, 1995), p. 576.
43 Kissinger, *Years of Upheaval*, pp. 984–985; Jussi Hanhimaki, *The Flawed Architect: Henry Kissinger and American Foreign Policy* (New York: Oxford University Press, 2004), p. 368.

44 Schlesinger, *War and the American Presidency*, p. 67.
45 Stanley Weintraub, *MacArthur's War: Korea and the Undoing of an American Hero* (New York: Free Press, 2000), p. 338.
46 Henry Wallace Oral History, p. 5175, Columbia University.
47 Abraham Lincoln, Second Inaugural Address (March 4, 1865) in Daniel Boorstin, ed., *An American Primer* (Chicago: University of Chicago Press, 1966), p. 424.
48 Bill Keller, "Does not Play Well with Others," *New York Times Book Review* (June 22, 2003), p. 9.
49 J. William Fulbright, "The American Example," Robert Goldwin and Harry Clor, eds., *Readings in American Foreign Policy* (New York: Oxford University Press, 1971), pp. 696–697.
50 Russell Buhite, *Nelson T. Johnson and American Policy Toward China 1925–1941* (East Lansing: Michigan State University Press, 1968), p. 135.
51 See Stanley Hoffmann, *Duties Beyond Border: On the Limits and Possibilities of Ethical International Politics* (Syracuse: Syracuse University Press, 1981).
52 Declaration of Independence (July 4, 1776) in Boorstin, *An American Primer*, p. 68.
53 Norris to John Maher (April 12, 1927), Box 46, George Norris Papers, Library of Congress.
54 John Lewis Gaddis, *Surprise, Security, and the American Experience* (Cambridge, Mass.: Harvard University Press, 2004), p. 90. Bacevich makes a similar point about the Wilson–Bush connection in *The New American Militarism: How Americans Are Seduced by War*, pp. 12–13.
55 Ellen Torelle, ed., *The Political Philosophy of Robert M. La Follette as Revealed in His Speeches and Writings* (Madison: Robert M. La Follette Company, 1920), p. 263.

Bibliography

Manuscript collections

Aguinaldo, Emilio, 1869–1964. Library of Congress (Washington, D.C.)
American Board of Commissioners for Foreign Missions. Houghton Library, Harvard University (Cambridge, Massachusetts)
Borah, William, 1865–1940. Library of Congress
Bryan, William Jennings, 1860–1925. Library of Congress
Bullitt, William, 1891–1967. Library of Congress; President's Secretary's File, Franklin D. Roosevelt Library (Hyde Park, New York)
Butler, Benjamin, 1818–1893. Library of Congress
Calhoun, John C., 1782–1850. Library of Congress
Clay, Henry, 1775–1852. Library of Congress
Dix, Dorthea, 1802–1887. Houghton Library, Harvard University
Everett, Edward, 1794–1865. Library of Congress; Massachusetts Historical Society (Boston, Massachusetts)
Fessenden, William Pitt, 1806–1869. Library of Congress
Gallatin, Albert, 1761–1849. New-York Historical Society (New York, New York)
General Records of the Department of State (Record Group 59) in the National Archives – New England Region: Despatches from US Ministers to Mexico, 1823–1906, M97; Records of the Department of State, Communications from Special Agents, 1794–1906, M37 (Waltham, Massachusetts)
Giddings, Joshua Reed, 1795–1864. Library of Congress
Griswold, Roger, 1762–1812. Yale University (New Haven, Connecticut)
Hillhouse, James, 1754–1832. Yale University
Hoar, George Frisbie, 1826–1904. Massachusetts Historical Society
Jesup, Thomas, 1788–1860. Library of Congress
Johnson, Nelson Trusler, 1887–1954. Library of Congress; Oral History Collection at Columbia University (New York, New York)
King, Rufus, 1775–1827. New-York Historical Society
La Follette, Robert, 1855–1925. Library of Congress
Livingston, Edward, 1764–1836. Library of Congress
Lodge, Henry Cabot, 1850–1924. Massachusetts Historical Society
MacArthur, Douglas, 1880–1964. Library of Congress
Miles, Nelson, 1839–1925. Library of Congress
Morgenthau (senior), Henry, 1856–1946. Franklin D. Roosevelt Library; Library of Congress

Morgenthau (junior), Henry, 1891–1967. Franklin D. Roosevelt Library; Library of Congress
Norris, George, 1861–1944. Library of Congress
Pickering, Timothy, 1745–1829. Massachusetts Historical Society; Peabody Essex Museum (Salem, Massachusetts)
Quincy, Josiah, 1772–1864. Massachusetts Historical Society
Randolph, John, 1773–1833. Library of Congress
Rankin, Jeannette, 1880–1973. Schlesinger Library, Harvard University; Suffragists Oral History Project, University of California (Berkeley, California)
Scott, Winfield, 1786–1866. Library of Congress
Seward, William Henry, 1801–1872. Library of Congress
Sheridan, Philip, 1831–1888. Library of Congress
Sherman, William Tecumseh, 1820–1891. Library of Congress
Sigel, Franz, 1824–1902. New-York Historical Society
Sumner, Charles, 1811–1874. Houghton Library, Harvard University; Library of Congress
Taft, Robert A., 1889–1953. Library of Congress
Trist, Nicholas P., 1800–1874. Library of Congress
Wallace, Henry, 1888–1965. Library of Congress; Oral History Collection at Columbia University
Wool, John Ellis, 1784–1869. Library of Congress

Published government documents

American State Papers: Military Affairs (Washington: Gales and Seaton, 1861), Vol. VII
Annals of the Congress of the United States (Washington: Gales and Seaton, series)
Bernstein, Barton and Allen Matusow, eds. *The Truman Administration: A Documentary History* (New York: Harper Colophon Books, 1966)
Bevans, Charles, ed. *Treaties and Other International Agreements of the United States of America* (Washington: Department of State, 1937), Vol. IX
Blair, Susan, ed. *The Slaughterhouse Province: An American Diplomat's Report on the Armenian Genocide, 1915–1917* (New Rochelle, New York: Aristide D. Caratzas Publisher, 1989)
Boorstin, Daniel, ed. *An American Primer* (Chicago: University of Chicago Press, 1966)
Brownlie, Ian, ed. *Basic Documents on Human Rights* (Oxford: Clarendon Press, 1971)
Bryce, Viscount James. *The Treatment of the Armenians in the Ottoman Empire 1915–1916* (Beirut: G. Doniguian and Sons, 1972)
Commager, Henry Steele, ed. *Documents of American History* (New York: Appleton-Century-Crofts, 1968), 2 vols.
Congressional Globe (Washington: Blair and Rives, series)
Congressional Record (Washington: Government Printing Office, series)
Correspondence Relating to the War with Spain (Washington: Center of Military History United States Army, 1993), 2 vols.
Daniels, Robert, ed. *A Documentary History of Communism* (New York: Vintage Books, 1950), 2 vols.

Debates of Congress, from 1789 to 1856 (New York: D. Appleton and Company, series)

Etzold, Thomas and John Lewis Gaddis, eds. *Containment: Documents on American Policy and Strategy, 1945–1950* (New York: Columbia University Press, 1978)

Evarts, Jeremiah, ed. *Speeches on the Passage of the Bill for the Removal of the Indians, Delivered in the Congress of the United States, April and May, 1830* (Boston: Perkins and Marvin, 1830)

Foreign Relations of the United States (Washington: Government Printing Office, series)

Greenberg, Karen and Joshua Dratel, eds. *The Torture Papers: The Road to Abu Ghraib* (New York: Cambridge University Press, 2005)

Grenville, J. A. S., ed. *The Major International Treaties 1914–1973* (London: Methuen and Company, 1974)

Jackson, Robert. *The Case against the Nazi War Criminals: Opening Statement for the United States of America and Other Documents* (New York: Alfred A. Knopf, 1946)

Jensen, Kenneth, ed. *Origins of the Cold War: The Novikov, Kennan, and Roberts Long Telegrams of 1946* (Washington: United States Institute of Peace, 1991)

Kennan, George. *From Prague after Munich: Diplomatic Papers 1938–1940* (Princeton: Princeton University Press, 1968)

Manning, William, ed. *Diplomatic Correspondence of the United States: Inter-American Affairs, 1831–1860* (Washington: Carnegie Endowment for International Peace, 1937), Vols. VIII, IX

Miles, Nelson. *The Philippines: Reports* (Boston: Anti-Imperialist League, 1909, Reprinted from *Army and Navy Journal*, May 2, 1903)

Military Situation in the Far East. Hearings Before the Committee on Armed Services and the Committee on Foreign Relations, United States Senate. 82nd Congress, 1st Session (Washington: Government Printing Office, 1951), 5 vols.

Miller, Hunter, ed. *Treaties and Other International Acts of the United States of America* (Washington: United States Government Printing Office, 1931)

Nelson, Anna, ed. *The State Department Policy Planning Staff Papers* (New York: Garland Publishing, 1983), 3 vols.

Office of United States Chief of Counsel for Prosecution of Axis Criminality. *Nazi Conspiracy and Aggression: Opinion and Judgment* (Washington: Government Printing Office, 1947)

Papers Relating to Foreign Affairs (Washington: Government Printing Office, series)

Principal Officers of the Department of State and United States Chiefs of Mission, 1778–1988 (Washington: United States Department of State, 1988)

Richardson, James, ed. *A Compilation of the Messages and Papers of the Presidents: 1789–1897* (New York: Bureau of National Literature, 1897), 10 vols.

Sarafian, Ara, ed. *United States Official Documents on the Armenian Genocide* (Watertown, Mass.: Armenian Review, 1995)

Van Slyke, Lyman, ed. *The China White Paper* (Stanford: Stanford University Press), 2 vols.

Waldron, Arthur, ed. *How the Peace was Lost: The 1935 Memorandum: Developments Affecting American Policy in the Far East Prepared for the State Department by John Van Antwerp MacMurray* (Stanford: Hoover Institution Press, 1992)

Autobiographies, diaries, edited collections, letters, memoirs, speeches

Acheson, Dean. *Present at the Creation: My Years in the State Department* (New York: W. W. Norton and Sons, 1969)

Adams, Charles Francis, ed. *Memoirs of John Quincy Adams* (Philadelphia: J. B. Lippincott and Co., 1874–1877), 12 vols.

Adams, Henry, ed. *Documents Relating to New England Federalism, 1800–1815* (Boston: Little, Brown and Company, 1905)

Adams, Henry, ed. *The Writings of Albert Gallatin* (New York: Antiquarian Press, 1960), 3 vols.

Adams, John Quincy. *An Address Delivered at the Request of the Committee of Arrangements for Celebrating the Anniversary of Independence at the City of Washington on the Fourth of July* (Cambridge, Mass.: Hilliard and Metcalf, 1821)

Ames, Seth, ed. *Works of Fisher Ames with a Selection from His Speeches and Correspondence* (Boston: Little, Brown and Company, 1854), 2 vols.

Bassett, John Spencer, ed. *Correspondence of Andrew Jackson* (Washington: Carnegie Institution, 1929, 1931), Vols. IV, V

Benton, Thomas Hart. *Thirty Years' View; or, History of the Working of the American Government for Thirty Years, from 1820–1850* (New York: D. Appleton and Company, 1856), 2 vols.

Bernstorff, Count Johann. *My Three Years in America* (New York: Charles Scribner's Sons, 1920)

Biddle, Francis. *In Brief Authority* (Garden City: Doubleday and Company, 1962)

Blum, John Morton. *From the Morgenthau Diaries: Years of War 1941–1945* (Boston: Houghton Mifflin Company, 1967)

Blum, John Morton, ed. *The Price of Vision: The Diary of Henry A. Wallace 1942–1946* (Boston: Houghton Mifflin Company, 1973)

Bowen, Ralph, ed. *A Frontier Family in Minnesota: Letters of Theodore and Sophie Bost 1851–1920* (Minneapolis: University of Minnesota Press, 1981)

Brown, Everett, ed. *William Plumer's Memorandum of Proceedings in the United States Senate 1803–1807* (New York: Da Capo Press, 1969)

Bryan, William Jennings and Mary Baird Bryan. *The Memoirs of William Jennings Bryan* (Chicago: John C. Winston Company, 1925)

Bullitt, Orville, ed. *For the President: Personal and Secret: Correspondence Between Franklin D. Roosevelt and William C. Bullitt* (Boston: Houghton Mifflin Company, 1972)

Butler, Benjamin. *Autobiography and Personal Reminiscences* (Boston: A. M. Thayer and Company, 1892)

Butler, Benjamin. *Private and Official Correspondence* (Norwood, Mass.: Plimpton Press, 1917), Vol. V

Bradley, Omar and Clay Blair. *A General's Life* (New York: Simon and Schuster, 1983)

Byrnes, James. *Frankly Speaking* (New York: Harper Brothers Publishing, 1947)

Byrnes, James. *All in One Lifetime* (New York: Harper and Row, 1958)

Carter, Jimmy. *Keeping Faith: Memoirs of a President* (Toronto: Bantam Books, 1982)

Chambers, Talbot. *Memoir of the Life and Character of the Late Honorable Theodore Frelinghuysen* (New York: Harper and Brothers, 1863)

Clay, Henry. *Life and Speeches* (New York: Greeley and McElrath, 1843), 2 vols.

Clifford, Clark. *Counsel to the President: A Memoir* (New York: Random House, 1991)

Cole, Donald and John McDonough, eds. *Benjamin Brown French, Witness to the Young Republic: A Yankee's Journal, 1828–1870* (Hanover: University Press of New England, 1989)

Cralle, Richard, ed. *Speeches of John C. Calhoun* (New York: D. Appleton and Company, 1888), Vol. IV

Crawford, Ann Fears, ed. *The Eagle: The Autobiography of Santa Anna* (Austin: Pemberton Press, 1967)

Crockett, David. *Life of David Crockett* (New York: Perkins Book Company, 1903)

Crockett, Davy. *Own Story* (New York: Citadel Press, 1955)

Croffut, W. A., ed. *Fifty Years in Camp and Field: Diary of Major General Ethan Allen Hitchcock* (New York: G. P. Putnam's Sons, 1909)

Crook, General George. *Autobiography* (Norman: University of Oklahoma Press, 1946)

Dana, Richard Henry. *An Address Upon the Life and Services of Edward Everett* (Cambridge, Mass.: Sever and Francis, 1865)

De Gaulle, Charles. *The Complete War Memoirs* (New York: Carroll and Graff Publishers, 1998)

Dodd, William, Jr. and Martha Dodd, eds. *Ambassador Dodd's Diary 1933–1938* (New York: Harcourt, Brace and Company, 1941)

Dodge, Richard. *Our Wild Indians: Thirty-Three Years' Personal Experience among the Red Men of the Great West* (Freeport, New York: Books for Libraries Press, 1970)

Doenecke, Justus, ed. *The Diplomacy of Frustration: The Manchurian Crisis of 1931–1933 as Revealed in the Papers of Stanley K. Hornbeck* (Stanford: Hoover Institution Press, 1981)

Douglas, William. *The Court Years 1939–1975* (New York: Random House, 1980)

Eisenhower, Dwight. *Crusade in Europe* (Garden City: Doubleday and Company, 1948)

Eisenhower, Dwight. *Mandate for Change* (Garden City: Doubleday and Company, 1963)

Everett, Edward, ed. *The Works of Daniel Webster* (Boston: Little, Brown and Company, 1854), 2 vols.

Everett, Edward. *Orations and Speeches on Various Occasions* (Boston: Little, Brown and Company, 1883), 3 vols.

Fehrenbacher, Don, ed. *Abraham Lincoln: Speeches and Writings 1832–1858* (New York: Library of America, 1989)

Ferguson, E. James, ed. *Selected Writings of Albert Gallatin* (Indianapolis: Bobbs-Merrill Company, 1967)

Ferrell, Robert, ed. *Dear Bess: The Letters from Harry Truman to Bess Truman, 1910–1959* (New York: W. W. Norton and Company, 1983)

Ferrell, Robert, ed. *Off the Record: The Private Papers of Harry S. Truman* (New York: Harper and Row, 1980)

Ford, Paul Leicester, ed. *The Works of Thomas Jefferson* (New York: G. P. Putnam's Sons, 1905), Vol. XI

Ford, Worthington Chauncey, ed. *Writings of John Quincy Adams* (New York: Macmillan Company, 1917), Vol. VII

Funston, Frederick. *Memories of Two Wars: Cuban and Philippine Experiences* (New York: Charles Scribner's Sons, 1911)

Gallatin, Count, ed. *The Diary of James Gallatin, 1813–1827* (New York: Charles Scribner's Sons, 1920)

Giddings, Joshua. *Speeches in Congress* (New York: Negro Universities Press, 1968)

Grant, U. S. *Personal Memoirs* (Lincoln: University of Nebraska Press, 1969), 2 vols.

Grew, Joseph. *Ten Years in Japan* (New York: Simon and Schuster, 1944)

Grew, Joseph. *Turbulent Era: A Diplomatic Record of Forty Years* (London: Hammond and Company, 1953), 2 vols.

Hamilton, Stanislaus Murray, ed. *The Writings of James Monroe* (New York: G. P. Putnam's Sons, 1902), Vols. VI and VII

Harriman, W. Averell and Elie Abel. *Special Envoy to Churchill and Stalin 1941–1946* (New York: Random House, 1975)

Hemphill, W. Edwin, ed. *The Papers of John C. Calhoun* (Columbia: University of South Carolina Press, 1975), Vol. VIII

Hendrick, Burton. *The Life and Letters of Walter H. Page* (Garden City: Doubleday, Page and Company, 1925), 3 vols.

Hoar, George Frisbie. *Autobiography of Seventy Years* (New York: Charles Scribner's Sons, 1903), 2 vols.

Hoess, Rudolf. *Commandant of Auschwitz* (Cleveland: World Publishing Company, 1959)

Howard, Oliver. *My Life and Experiences among Our Hostile Indians* (New York: Da Capo Press, 1972)

Hull, Cordell, *Memoirs* (New York: Macmillan Company, 1948), 2 vols.

Hunt, Gaillard, ed. *The Writings of James Madison* (New York: G. P. Putnam's Sons, 1906–1910), Vols. VI, VIII, and IX

Hunt, Louise Livingston. *Memoir of Mrs. Edward Livingston with Letters Hitherto Unpublished* (New York: Harper and Brothers, 1886)

Israel, Fred, ed. *The War Diary of Breckinridge Long: Selections from the Years 1939–1944* (Lincoln: University of Nebraska Press, 1966)

Karski, Jan. *Story of a Secret State* (New York: Popular Library, 1944)

Kennan, George. *Memoirs 1925–1950* (Boston: Little, Brown and Company, 1967)

Kiesling, John Brady. "Iraq: A Letter of Resignation," *The New York Review of Books*, April 10, 2003

Kim Il Sung. *Selected Works* (Pyongyang: Foreign Languages Publishing House, 1971), Vol. I

King, Charles. *Campaigning with Crook* (Norman: University of Oklahoma Press, 1964)

King, Charles, ed. *The Life and Correspondence of Rufus King Comprising His Letters, Private and Official, His Public Documents and His Speeches* (New York: G. P. Putnam's Sons, 1898), Vol. V

Kirk, Russell. *John Randolph of Roanoke: A Study in American Politics with Selected Speeches and Letters* (Chicago: Henry Regnery Company, 1964)

Kissinger, Henry. *Years of Upheaval* (Boston: Little, Brown and Company, 1986)

La Follette, Robert. *A Personal Narrative of Political Experiences* (Madison: University of Wisconsin Press, 1960)

Lansing, Robert. *War Memoirs* (Indianapolis: Bobbs-Merrill Company, 1935)

Leahy, William. *I Was There* (New York: McGraw-Hill Book Company, 1950)

Link, Arthur, ed. *The Papers of Woodrow Wilson* (Princeton: Princeton University Press, series)

Lodge, Henry Cabot. *Early Memories* (New York: Charles Scribner's Sons, 1925)

MacArthur, Brian, ed. *The Penguin Book of Twentieth-Century Speeches* (London: Penguin Books, 1999)

MacArthur, Douglas. *Reminiscences* (New York: McGraw-Hill Book Company, 1964)

Mallory, Daniel, ed. *The Life and Speeches of the Hon. Henry Clay* (New York: Van Amringe and Bixby, 1844), 2 vols.

McNamara, Robert with Brian VanDeMark. *In Retrospect: The Tragedy and Lessons of Vietnam* (New York: Random House, 1995)

Miles, Nelson. *Personal Recollections and Observations* (Chicago: Werner Company, 1896)

Miles, Nelson. *Serving the Republic* (New York: Harper Brothers Publishing, 1911)

Millis, Walter, ed. *The Forrestal Diaries* (New York: Viking Press, 1951)

Morgan, H. Wayne, ed. *Making Peace With Spain: The Diary of Whitelaw Reid September–December, 1898* (Austin: University of Texas Press, 1965)

Morgenthau, Henry. *All in a Life-Time* (Garden City: Doubleday, Page, and Company, 1922)

Morgenthau, Henry. *Ambassador Morgenthau's Story* (Garden City: Doubleday, Page and Company, 1918)

Morison, Elting, ed. *The Letters of Theodore Roosevelt* (Cambridge, Mass.: Harvard University Press, 1951–1954), 8 vols.

Moser, Harold et al., eds. *The Papers of Andrew Jackson* (Knoxville: University of Tennessee Press, 1994, 1996), Vols. IV, V

Moulton, Gary, ed. *The Papers of Chief John Ross* (Norman: University of Oklahoma Press, 1985), 2 vols.

Nevins, Allan, ed. *The Diary of John Quincy Adams 1794–1845* (New York: Frederick Ungar Publishing Co., 1969)

Norris, George. *Fighting Liberal: The Autobiography of George W. Norris* (New York: Macmillan Company, 1945)

Palmer, Beverly Wilson, ed. *The Selected Letters of Charles Sumner* (Boston: Northeastern University Press, 1990), Vol. II

Parker, Theodore. *Sermon of War* (Boston: Charles C. Little and James Brown, 1846)

Perdue, Theda, ed. *"Cherokee Editor"*: *The Writings of Elias Boudinot* (Knoxville: University of Tennessee Press, 1983)

Perdue, Theda and Michael Green, eds. *The Cherokee Removal: A Brief History with Documents* (New York: St. Martin's Press, 1995)

Pershing, John. *My Experiences in the World War* (New York: Frederick A. Stokes Company, 1931), 2 vols.

Peterson, Merrill, ed. *The Portable Thomas Jefferson* (London: Penguin Books, 1986)

Pickering, Timothy. *Observations Introductory to Reading the Declaration of Independence* (Salem, Mass.: Warwick Palfray, 1823)

Pierce, Edward. *Memoir and Letters of Charles Sumner* (Boston: Roberts Brothers, 1878), 3 vols.

Poen, Monte, ed. *Strictly Personal and Confidential: The Letters Harry Truman Never Sent* (Boston: Little, Brown and Company, 1982)

Powell, Colin. *My American Journey* (New York: Random House, 1995)

Pratt, Richard Henry. *Battlefield and Classroom: Four Decades with the American Indian, 1867–1904* (New Haven: Yale University Press, 1964)

Prucha, Francis Paul, ed. *Cherokee Removal: The William Penn Essays and Other Writings by Jeremiah Evarts* (Knoxville: University of Tennessee Press, 1981)

Prucha, Francis Paul, ed. *Documents of United States Indian Policy* (Lincoln: University of Nebraska Press, 1990)

Quaife, Milo Milton, ed. *The Diary of James K. Polk* (Chicago: A.C. McClurg and Co., 1910), 4 vols.

Quincy, Edmund, ed. *Congressional Speeches of Josiah Quincy, 1805–1813* (Boston: Little, Brown and Company, 1874)

Richards, Laura, ed. *Letters and Journals of Samuel Gridley Howe: The Greek Revolution* (Boston: Dana Estes and Company, 1906)

Ridgway, Matthew. *Soldier: The Memoirs of Matthew B. Ridgway* (New York: Harper Brothers Publishing, 1956)

Roosevelt, Theodore. *An Autobiography* (New York: Da Capo Press, 1985)

Rush, Richard. *Memoranda of a Residence at the Court of London* (Philadelphia: Key and Biddle, 1833)

Scott, Winfield. *Memoirs* (New York: Sheldon and Company, 1864), 2 vols.

Selections from the Correspondence of Theodore Roosevelt and Henry Cabot Lodge 1884–1918 (New York: Charles Scribner's Sons, 1924), 2 vols.

Seymour, Charles, ed. *The Intimate Papers of Colonel House* (Boston: Houghton Mifflin Company, 1926)

Simon, John, ed. *The Papers of Ulysses S. Grant* (Carbondale, Illinois: Southern Illinois University Press, 1995), Vol. XIX

Stagg, J. C. A., et al., eds. *The Papers of James Madison: Presidential Series* (Charlottesville: University Press of Virginia, 1996), Vol. III

Steiner, George. *Errata: An Examined Life* (New Haven: Yale University Press, 1998)

Stimson, Henry and McGeorge Bundy. *On Active Service in Peace and War* (New York: Harper Brothers Publishing, 1948)

Stoddard, William. *Inside the White House in War Times* (New York: Charles L. Webster and Company, 1890)

Sumner, Charles. *Complete Works* (New York: Negro Universities Press, 1969), Vols. IX, X, XV, XVIII

Thorndike, Rachel Sherman, ed. *The Sherman Letters: Correspondence Between General Sherman and Senator Sherman from 1837–1891* (New York: Da Capo Press, 1969)

Torelle, Ellen, ed. *The Political Philosophy of Robert M. La Follette as Revealed in His Speeches and Writings* (Madison: Robert M. La Follette Company, 1920)

Truman, Harry. *Memoirs: Year of Decisions* (Garden City: Doubleday and Company, 1955)

Truman, Harry. *Memoirs: Years of Trial and Hope* (Garden City: Doubleday and Company, 1956)

Urofsky, Melvin. *The Douglas Letters: Selections from the Private Papers of Justice William O. Douglas* (Bethesda: Adler and Adler, 1987)

Vance, Cyrus. *Hard Choices: Critical Years in America's Foreign Policy* (New York: Simon and Schuster, 1983)

Vandenberg, Arthur, ed. *The Private Papers of Senator Vandenberg* (Boston: Houghton Mifflin Company, 1952)

Voynich, E.L., ed. *Frederic Chopin's Letters* (New York: Dover Publications, 1988)

Whan, Vorin, ed. *A Soldier Speaks: Public Papers and Speeches of General of the Army Douglas MacArthur* (New York: Frederick A Praeger, 1965)

Whipple, Henry Benjamin. *Light and Shadows of a Long Episcopate* (New York: Macmillan Company, 1899)

Wiesel, Elie. *Night* (New York: Avon Books, 1969)

Williams, Amelia and Eugene Barker, eds. *The Writings of Sam Houston 1813–1863* (Austin: Pemberton Press, 1970), 8 vols.

Wilson, Clyde and Shrirley Cook, eds. *The Papers of John C. Calhoun* (Columbia: University of Press of South Carolina, series)

Wilson, Edith Bolling. *My Memoir* (Indianapolis: Bobbs-Merrill Company, 1939)

Wiltse, Charles, ed. *The Papers of Daniel Webster: Correspondence* (Hanover, New Hampshire: University Press of New England, series)

Wiltse, Charles, ed. *The Papers of Daniel Webster: Speeches and Formal Writings* (Hanover, New Hampshire: University Press of New England, series)

Wise, Stephen. *Challenging Years* (New York: G. P. Putnam's Sons, 1949)

Wunderlin, Clarence, ed. *The Papers of Robert A. Taft* (Kent: Kent State University Press, 1997–2003), 3 Vols.

Index